Praise for G. E. Kidder Smith

"The ultimate in architectural guidebooks—an encyclopedic undertaking of unprecedented magnitude that is the first publication of its kind to treat comprehensively the building heritage of the entire country. In successfully bridging the gap between layman and specialist, the author achieves a balanced treatment that is all too often unrealized in architectural guidebooks." —Bryant F. Tolles, Jr., *Antiques*

* * *

"*Source Book* offers more than 550 of Mr. Smith's photographs, as well as his intelligent, informative prose. Mr. Smith includes, too, references to relevant books and architecture journals.... The *Source Book* is full of information—everything from celebrating unsung buildings ... to worthwhile advice on how to see things.... *Source Book* combines beautiful prose and stunning photographs." —Tom Sullivan, *Washington Times*

* * *

"Beautifully laid out and eloquently written.... Overall the material is wide-ranging, resulting in a great pictorial account of American culture." —Clare Melhuish, *Building Design*

* * *

"Smith is not just an expert in this large field. He is an ebullient guide and a lively writer. His purpose—to engage Americans in an active appreciation of their architecture—is gloriously realized." —*The Booklist*

* * *

"The mere compilation of so much information is a feat in itself. But the grace, wit, and erudition with which it is presented make this an invaluable companion on the road or at the desk." —Carter Wiseman, *New York*

Source Book of American Architecture

Source Book of American Architecture
500 Notable Buildings from the 10th Century to the Present

G. E. Kidder Smith, FAIA

Princeton Architectural Press, New York

Published by
Princeton Architectural Press
37 East 7th Street
New York, New York 10003

For a free catalog of books, call 1.800.722.6657
Visit our web site at www.papress.com.

All photographs by G. E. Kidder Smith except the following:
Page 4, ©Bill Timmerman, courtesy The Neurosciences
Institute
Page 5L, ©Solange Fabião
Page 5R, Christophe Valtin, ©Milwaukee Art Museum
Page 306, ©Hedrich Blessing Photographers
Page 322, ©Mark Citret
Page 371, ©Cincinnati Historical Society
Page 601, ©Dan Forer
Page 614, ©Barbara Karant, Karant & Associates
Page 679, ©Franklyn Rollins

Library of Congress Cataloging-in-Publication Data
Smith, G. E. Kidder (George Everard Kidder), 1913–
    Source book of American architecture : 500 notable
  buildings from the 10th century to the present / G. E.
  Kidder Smith.
       p. cm.
    Updated ed. of: The architecture of the United States.
  1st ed. 1981.
    Includes bibliographical references and index.
    ISBN 1-56898-024-8 (cloth : alk. paper). —
  ISBN 156898-025-6 (pbk. : alk. paper)
    1. Architecture—United States—Guidebooks.
  I. Smith, G. E. Kidder (George Everard Kidder), 1913–
  Architecture of the United States. II. Title.
  NA705.S578 1996
  720'.973—dc20   95-49186

Editor's Note
Though every attempt has been made to include accurate
visitor information to the sites in this book, we recom-
mend the reader call ahead to confirm this information
when planning a trip.

CONTENTS

AUTHOR'S NOTE

The architecture of the United States ranges from the work of Native Americans molding primitive shelter with few tools, to the ultimate in technology, the USA-developed skyscraper, which changed the cities of the world forever. The buildings in this book seek to trace our oft-confused, occasionally sparkling, architectural evolution of some thousand years. It is not a history of our architecture but a log book of the stepping stones in the evolution of our shelter. Many splendid structures do not appear, while conversely the inclusion of a few may be unexpected. However, having personally tracked down and photographed almost two thousand distinguished structures in all fifty states, I think the five hundred discussed here are representative of their always-ambitious times.

The first half of the book begins with a brief survey of our Native American inheritance, then traces early New England and Virginia highlights, expanding through the decades with a succession of influences and fashions from Europe. (Spain, of course, had established an early settlement in Florida in 1565, but this was a military outpost, not a community.)

The second half of the book inaugurates the twentieth century, carrying new hope—as, of course, does the imminent twenty-first. Yet the architecture of the earlier part of this century—in spite of the "liberation of steel"—was still timid, the architects and their clients long continuing to drape their skyscrapers with vestiges of Rome and to model their churches on the Gothic of eight hundred years ago.

In the 1930s, however, a forward-looking, dedicated group of American architects became impressed by the new, indeed revolutionary, work evolving in Europe. They realized that our encrusted, largely Classic-inspired buildings were anachronistic and unsuited to meeting twentieth-century needs. Eventually—especially after World War II—what is broadly if imprecisely known as Modern architecture began to flourish. Elementary in its early endeavors, this approach of generating buildings from their needs—not stuffing them behind symmetrical facades—became the lesson of the day. Since then there have been many variations on a theme—sullied at times by the look-at-me school—but the future is very promising. It is hoped that some of the buildings in this book will spark interest in this future—while reminding us of much splendid work from our past.

It will be noted that the descriptions of almost all of the post-1900 buildings carry the initials and date of the architectural magazine where they were published for ease in further research. The magazines are abbreviated as follows:

A	Architecture (AIA)
A+A	Arts + Architecture
AD	Architectural Design
A+BN	Architecture & Building News
AF	Architectural Forum
AJ	Architect's Journal
AP	Architecture Plus
AR	Architectural Record
ARev	Architectural Review
F	Forum (ex-Architectural Forum)
Int	Interiors
JAIA	AIA Journal
LA	Landscape Architecture
NWA	Northwest Architecture
PA	Progressive Architecture
PP	Pencil Points
SAHJ	Society of Architectural Historians Journal
W	Western Architect

ACKNOWLEDGEMENTS

This book is a lineal descendant of my three-volume *The Architecture of the United States*, co-published by the Museum of Modern Art and Anchor Press of Doubleday in 1981. The present volume is a thorough update of the earlier ones and is limited to 500 buildings, half pre-1900, half twentieth century.

Both the earlier volumes and this one could not have been written without the generous and continued support of the Graham Foundation for Advanced Studies in the Fine Arts. Its former director, the late, charismatic John Entenza, started me off on the first books, neither of us dreaming that they would occupy eight years and require 135,000 miles of driving. (The map below shows routes taken—at least once—gathering material.) He was succeeded by the quietly brilliant Carter H. Manny, Jr., FAIA. In addition to the deeply appreciated initial grant from the Graham Foundation and their follow-up on this one, the National Endowment for the Arts, the Ford Foundation, and the Museum of Modern Art gave financial support at critical times, which enabled me to complete the early field research.

Each building described herein was assessed on the spot, and each text reviewed by the building's owner. I thank them all for their time, especially the New York City Landmarks Preservation Commission and the Chicago Architecture Foundation, who checked several sites in their respective cities.

My talented wife Dorothea helped with the descriptions of each building—plus the driving to find them. Patricia Edwards Clyne masterfully edited and typed every page while Nancy Kranz of MoMA organized the production of the earlier edition. Bless 'em all. Kevin Lippert, the genius of Princeton Architectural Press, bravely took on the book; the eagle-eyed Clare Jacobson, aided by Caroline Green and Sarah Lappin—and an incredible computer—knowingly put it all together.

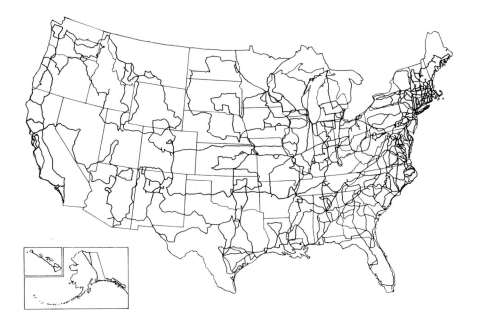

FOREWORD

Paul Goldberger

Five hundred buildings—an arbitrary number, almost too pat, and yet they tell a story. Actually they tell one very large story and five hundred smaller ones, and all of them are important. The striking thing about this book is how much it is a narrative, in spite of itself—not a narrative with much of a plot, more a free-form story out of Donald Barthelme, bits and pieces that do not at first appear to have a structure but that cohere mysteriously, so that by the time you are somewhere in the middle a pattern has begun to emerge.

What is the pattern here? Not of a single stream of history, that is for sure. Looking at these five hundred buildings together makes clear that at no point in the development of American architecture has there ever been a complete sense of agreement about what constituted the building art. Pluralism runs deep in the American grain. So does the picturesque. So does bombast. So do replication and historical allusion, and so does daring, dazzling innovation. It is the pattern of no pattern, in a sense—and yet it is not so simple as that, either. A love of technology, a love of exhibitionism, a reveling in the sensuous aspects of architecture—these are the things we see throughout these pages, and that unite the disparate works that G. E. Kidder Smith documents. These qualities join in a peculiarly American way, and together they loosen the tightness of an early-eighteenth-century Congregationalist church as they warm the harshness of a late-nineteenth-century factory and soften the hard edges of a twentieth-century skyscraper. It is the love of building that comes through here. If these five hundred buildings are truly the five hundred best buildings in the United States (and they are close enough to being so), then American architecture as characterized by Kidder Smith is full of joy. It is not frivolous, but it is not puritanical, either. It takes pleasure in giving pleasure.

I think this is not so much Kidder Smith's personal slant as it is objective fact that he has helped reveal to us. Everything looks a little bit different refracted through the lens of time, of course, and however much American architecture may always have been somewhat looser than its European precedents, more dependent on visual pleasure, we cannot deny that a great deal of it, particularly in the Colonial period, was tight and rigid. Yet Kidder Smith shows us that American architecture as a whole was less tight and doctrinaire than we may have thought, that it has often been deeply sensuous, and that it has almost always tried to express the particulars of place. I am struck by the extent to which almost all of the buildings here are visually appealing, and also by the extent to which certain buildings that I have not, until now, considered among the more notable achievements of American architecture grow in stature when they are placed within Kidder Smith's pantheon. Not the least of the accomplishments of this book is that it convinces you to take certain buildings seriously. You don't have to rank Marina City in Chicago with Rockefeller Center in New York—Kidder Smith certainly does not present them as equals—to nonetheless be able to agree with him that it belongs here.

Kidder Smith set out in *Source Book of American Architecture* to tell the story of American architecture through its masterworks, which in lesser hands would be a dangerous game—in architecture, if not in art or literature, masterpieces often do not tell us as much about the world as more ordinary works do. Yet Kidder Smith manages, partly by his judicious selection and partly by his perceptive text, to pull this off, and to present us not with five hundred disconnected short entries, but with an epic. While it is possible to open this book anywhere and read one or two or ten entries at whim and have them make perfect sense—every one of these five hundred buildings is the subject of an essay that is a clear, self-assured, and exquisite piece of prose in its own right—when you begin with the Pueblos of New Mexico and go on to the Colonial buildings of the seventeenth century in Virginia and Connecticut, and on from there to the churches and plantations and mansions of the eighteenth century, and then to the government buildings and villas and hotels of the nineteenth century and finally, at last, to everything in the twentieth century, from Louis Sullivan to Frank Lloyd Wright to Bertram Grosvenor Goodhue to Cass Gilbert to Eliel Saarinen to Louis I. Kahn and Paul Rudolph and Robert Venturi, you discover that you really have traversed the American continent and its history. You thought you were paging through a sequence of buildings, but Kidder Smith has made you do something more, and it inspires awe. The cavalcade of images and text here is almost cinematic; the buildings come rapid fire one after the other, and you do not know whether to be amazed first at the range of the author or the range of his subject. Both, in the end, are stunning: the scope of American architecture itself, and the breadth of Kidder Smith's investigations of it.

Smith's research contained here is mainly derived from a still-larger project, *The Architecture of the United States*, his three-volume work published in 1981. *Source Book* is a condensation of the earlier work, with a few new buildings added. But it seems, by being tightened, to have gained energy; the somewhat leisurely air of a textbook that marked the original work is absent here, and a sense of urgency, even passion, seems to have taken its place. I say that even though Kidder Smith's tone is as dignified in this book as it was in the earlier volumes. But in the form of a single volume his attitude toward the architecture he is writing about somehow seems more engaging, more connected.

Here is Kidder Smith on Eero Saarinen's Ezra Stiles and Morse Colleges at Yale, of 1962: "Unlike Renaissance buildings, whose facades can be grasped from a one-point perspective, Ezra Stiles and Morse Colleges demand that the viewer move about them to realize their progression of spaces. They do not proclaim their existence, they unfurl it." And here, back almost a century, on Henry Hobson Richardson's Ames Memorial Library, of 1879: "H. H. Richardson combined three elements at North Easton: one, his subsequently famous, almost Dantesque arched opening (here used by him for the first time); two, an offset tower that serves as a vertical agglutinator; and three, an extended horizontal wing with a row of clustered windows. Generated by requirements of the plan, these elements have been put together to form a sim-

Tod Williams and Billie Tsien's Neurosciences Institute, La Jolla, California

ple but skillful hillside composition. Even more important, the building works well inside." And one more snippet, this one back another century, on the Virginia State Capitol of 1792 by Thomas Jefferson, the building which, Kidder Smith writes, "introduced Classical architecture to the budding nation. The country never recovered.... Jefferson was the first architect anywhere to fit a major workaday building into a Classically derived temple form—though not without difficulties."

This is architectural writing of the highest order. It is knowing of history, it is brilliantly balanced between purely formal, aesthetic issues and practical ones, and it is self-assured at no cost to its amiability. Not since Nikolaus Pevsner, I think, has an architectural historian described complex architectural form with this degree of clarity. Kidder Smith came of age with the modernists, and he devoted much of the earlier portion of his career to documenting the architecture of the twentieth century around the world, but what seems most remarkable about him now, I think, was his ability to transcend ideology and to see and love great architecture where he found it.

Source Book of American Architecture has no agenda other than quality. For a scholar born in 1913, Kidder Smith looked at the architecture of the 1980s and early 1990s with a remarkably open mind. And while there is little to be gained by second guessing his historical choices within this book, it is tempting to ponder what he might have included had he lived to the onset of the new century: Tod Williams and Billie Tsien's Neurosciences Institute in La Jolla, Frank Gehry's Schnabel House in Los Angeles, James Stewart Polshek's Rose Center at the American Museum of Natural History, Philip Johnson's "monsta" gatehouse at his Glass House estate, Rafael Moneo's Museum of Fine Arts in Houston, Steven Holl's Chapel of St. Ignatius in Seattle. And, soon enough, Santiago Calatrava's Milwaukee Art Museum, Tadao Ando's Museum of Modern Art in Fort Worth, and Kohn Pedersen Fox's Baruch College in New York, all under construction in 2000, and likely to be equally worthy. The architectural prospect at the beginning of the twenty-first century is a rich one, and it is diminished by the thought that we will not have Kidder Smith to take note of its highest achievements.

left: Steven Holl's Chapel of St. Ignatius, Seattle, Washington
right: Santiago Calatrava's Milwaukee Art Museum, Milwaukee, Wisconsin

THE IDEA OF THE AMERICAN BUILDING

Michael J. Lewis

What is the American building? It is Protestantism given space and materials and turned into architecture. Change any one of these ingredients and the building changes instantly, as a simple look at Holland or Mexico will show. The American building is that familiar place where we practice and fulfill the ritual transactions of our lives; here we may live or work, study or trade, find comfort or be laid in our coffin—the American building cannot help but be like us. It is the American himself, naivete bundled with generosity, the idealistic in service of the materialistic, a thing perpetually divided between the communal and the individual, yearning always for the former but choosing by ancient instinct the latter. It has all the virtues and vices of the Protestant Reformation: the mercantile stance, the distrust of the sensual, and the capacity to make redemptive myths out of everything. And, like the American, it elbows for itself a large parcel of open space. In the end it is the ultimate nonconformist, the self-sufficient loner resting at a wary but amiable distance from its fellows.

This essay introduces G. E. Kidder Smith's remarkable and eclectic catalogue of American buildings. It proposes several motifs that run through his book, touching lofty skyscrapers and stately Georgian piles alike. These themes, of course, are only some strands of the comprehensive fabric of American architecture, and the thoughtful reader who has seen some of this country or who has thought about it will discover others.

Through all these themes, inevitably—perhaps tragically—land is the one theme that embraces all the others. Upon his first visit to the United States, no foreigner, no matter how well informed, fails to be struck by America's profligate relationship to the land. Since its beginnings, American architecture has always been stamped by the extravagant and deliberate use of space. In no other Western country is the proportion of unbuilt to built land so high; nowhere else does the idea of land itself play so central a role, especially in houses. The characteristic image of the American house, even if drawn by a city-dwelling child, requires open space on all four sides. Fewer than four is unacceptable: better four cramped slivers of yard than two generous yards at the cost of having a party wall. Every American suburban house has in it the idea of Jefferson's ideal villa—Monticello perched on its mountaintop above Charlottesville—even if the villa is a 1947-vintage Cape Cod replica and the mountaintop merely a street in Levittown.

From Levittown's Cape Cod imagery to aluminum Georgian pediments that crest the doors of mobile homes, our enduring domestic symbols are invariably Colonial, which is less of an anachronism than it seems. Colonial architecture evokes the image of the first settler and the claiming of land, unlike the infill house, which defers to the character of an existing and stable community. American suburbs still tend to be Colonial in the broadest sense: new settlements, based on a process of radical land clearing and rapid development, with no need to heed what was there.

The most characteristic domestic form, however, remains the New England saltbox, which was already recognizable in its basic outlines in the 1670s. This was among the first of many American building types that originated in the progressive and incremental variations of an existing type in response to local conditions, and not from conscious invention. Originally the form was something of an improvisation: a shed-roof addition to an existing two-story, central-chimney house extended the gable downward to the rear to encompass a pair of additional rooms. This served to differentiate the formal street front, generally oriented to the south, from the now sheltered northern exposure, within which the kitchen functions huddled. As this irregular but quite sensible addition spread, it soon began to look normal and resolved, and soon new houses were planned from the beginning with the unequal roof form.

But if the New England winter found its ideal solution to in the form of the saltbox, the summer posed another problem entirely. The central dilemma was to devise a structure that suited both winter and summer; in much of the United States, a house had to be able to huddle like a shivering man in February, but stretch out like an overheated sunbather in July. The solution was a house that in its core was a cosy, compact volume but that opened up to nature in an attached wooden porch of generous dimensions and multiple breezy outlooks (fig. 1).

fig. 1

The porch is one of those cultural achievements, like the Italian piazza or the Finnish sauna, that is inseparable from a certain national character of life. A conscious adaptation to the climate, it is also an unconscious adaptation to America's social or moral climate. It reinterpreted the stoa of Greece in characteristically private American terms—not as a communal or civic meeting space, but a transitional zone at once public and private. Here the American individual presented himself to public view at the front of his private dwelling, addressing the pedestrian in conversation. This architectural expression of openness and hospitality has no close counterpart in Europe, and certainly not in the more private architecture of England. At their climax, in the late nineteenth century, these wraparound verandas might embrace a full three sides of a house, like the endless tiered decks of a Victorian resort hotel. But their heyday has passed and since the 1940s they have been amputated in large numbers as the automobile and television have together eliminated the citizen-pedestrian. There is no more tragic sign of the atrophying of public life in this country.

Nature is not absent from European architecture, which knows a rustic mode and has its share of grottoes, hermitages, and picturesque parks. But in the European tradition, nature is the cultivated landscape of antiquity rather than the primal one of North America; it is the tilled nature of Nicolas Poussin and Gellée Claude, not the convulsive geology of Jean Louis Rodolphe Agassiz and Charles Lyell. Europe, haunted for centuries by the memory of Rome, measured its buildings not against the land but against the dream architecture of antiquity, and remained ever pessimistic about matching it. Giovanni Battista Piranesi's fantasies were tinged by a sense of inferiority to Rome, even as he trumped its scale. Long after Europe embraced Romanticism and its cult of the natural, and came to understand Edmund Burke's doctrine of the sublime, it lagged in applying these lessons to architecture. It is true that the English writer John Ruskin proposed buildings whose sculptural power might evoke the Alps. But it is also true that H. H. Richardson first realized such structures in the rock cliffs he raised in the heart of Chicago, and in Pittsburgh with his Allegheny County Courthouse (although his stratified geologic language was rather more like that of the Dakotas than the Alps). In more recent decades, Frank Lloyd Wright stands out for his quixotic attempt to embrace the machine and nature simultaneously, from the conch-like spiral ramp of the Guggenheim Museum to the moraine-like scatter of concrete at Fallingwater.

The most direct consequence of this profligacy with the land is that the American building typically reads as a detached object in space. Even in the city the skyscraper is no mannerly herd animal, shoulder to shoulder with buildings of similar height, materials, and expression; instead it rises in solitude. The tower pulls back from all sides to form a separate episode of personality, as lonely and distinct as the New England saltbox house on its bleak and snowy

fig. 2

fig. 3

fig. 4

slope. Raymond Hood's blazing Radiator Building beveled its corners inward to suggest an independent tower, while Skidmore, Owings & Merrill placed the shaft of their Lever Building in an urban plaza invented for that purpose. At all costs, the building must read as an autonomous individual rather than as part of a continuous front, even at the cost of unbuilt urban land. The American city is not a collection of equal buildings arranged in ordered tiers, but rather a collection of competing and rambunctious individuals, engaged in the rude business of shouting one another down. Oddly enough, an eerie premonition of this skyscraper war came to Erastus Salisbury Field, painting in isolation near Amherst, in 1867. In that year he began his *Historical Monument of the American Republic*, a reverie about the founding of the nation that prophesied a height war still another generation in the future and even Minneapolis-like skywalks that were a full century away (*fig. 2*).

But for all the irregularity of Field's fevered vision of America, the plan of the American city is insistently and rigidly ordered. These twin factors—schematic order in two dimensions and riotous disorder in three—are reflexes of the same understanding of space. The American relationship to the land is quite unlike the English one, what has recently been called "the Tory view of landscape."[1] Proximity to existing things, which counts for so much in the conservative English appreciation of the landscape, counts for practically nothing here. Instead the American sense of space, in which space itself is parceled off in the neutral coordinates of an uninflected grid, is fundamentally Cartesian. From the design of Philadelphia in 1682 (*fig. 3*) to the great gridding of the Midwest and West in the nineteenth century, the gridiron remains the standard American form of the city, even on the Monopoly board (*fig. 4*). With its Cartesian space, identical lots, numbered streets, and with no sweeping Baroque diagonals converging at some central place of power, this is the ideal city of the Protestant Reformation, embracing the ideal geometry of the Renaissance and eliminating the spatial dynamics of Catholic urbanism.

It is a peculiar habit of American thought to freight the commercial with spiritual meaning. The prim grid might function as a symbol of ideal order. New Haven, for example, as John Archer has shown, was paced off in regular quadrants to reproduce the actual dimensions of the camps of the Israelites in the wilderness, identifying it as a New Jerusalem. And pietist communities from the Moravians and Ephrata Cloisterers to the Harmonists and Shakers used rectilinearity as a sacred planning tool, conflating righteousness with the right angle. But between this heavenly geometry and the plot plan of the real-estate speculator there is precious little difference. Charles Dickens noted this irony during his American trip and celebrated it in his *Martin Chuzzlewit*, where the one-eyed huckster Zephaniah Scadder ruled off a miasmic swamp into a gridded new "Eden." Not every grid, as Dickens noted, is religious or even egalitarian—and even the Monopoly board is only egalitarian at the beginning of play. For little houses give way to big hotels, and typically, as is ever the case in the American city, once they are replaced by bigger buildings, they are swept away for good, leaving no memory of what was there.

The American traveller in Europe is frequently startled to discover the extent to which Continental manners are based on collective thinking. But Continental buildings likewise tend toward collective values, architectural manners that are corsetted by ancient consensus and policed by municipal authority. Height lines conform, materials and style respect the examples of neighbors, and even the plan must defer to precedent and zoning. The odd European who violated this protocol of the collective, such as Adolf Loos, who proposed an unconventional building on the Michaelerplatz in Vienna, faced official meddling and public ridicule. (Loos seemed to have learned his architectural manners during his years in wild Chicago.) By these European standards, every American building is an unruly loner. This is that second tough fiber in the genetic makeup of the American building: the conception of the building as an individual thing, and not an element of a communal order. In particular, commercial architecture has always shown the greatest impulse to differentiate and define. For much of the nineteenth and twentieth centuries, America's most striking buildings were not civic structures, which as often as not were timid, cringing essays in Classicism—some of America's least distinguished architecture. Instead they were mighty urban banks, company offices, and department stores—the great sprawl of capitalism expressed in architecture. At heart, America remains a commercial society and as a consequence has given the world consistently successful commercial architects. Nowhere else were overstatement, self-aggrandizement, and jaunty confidence projected with more vitality and more cheek. The best of these are invariably gone, and are missing from this book. The more startling a building was in its day, the more likely it was to shock a later generation, who reached for architecture's great blue pencil, the wrecking ball. Such was the fate of Frank Furness, America's most ardent Victorian imaginer. Furness gave Philadelphia an even dozen banks in the 1870s and 1880s, each more startling than the last, and often arrayed across the street from one another as if in combat, which they were. These often terrifying buildings, Gothic behemoths suspended on Gothic columns and arches, were made to celebrate the savings institution they housed—advertising jingles executed in terra-cotta and colored granite. But every advertising jingle wears and grates by repetition, and virtually all of these banks are now gone.

Furness's architectural hitting streak stood unmatched until Raymond Hood's spectacular run of New York skyscrapers in the 1920s. Hood's designs also depended on vivid architectural imagery, brilliant color, and a sense of architectural physiognomy played so broadly that it touched on caricature. Buildings such as the Chicago Tribune Tower and the Radiator Building—that gleaming architectural radiator rendered in black and gold—embody titanic commercial forces and energies at their most primal. These works, and their ilk from the 1920s, represent the last moment when American architecture was largely free of theory, and when architects subordinated their judgement to strongly individualistic clients, whose yardstick for success was neither theoretical nor academic, but rather vigorous in expression and lucidity of commercial content.[2]

In the 1980s, commercial architecture once again enjoyed a brief season of prestige as it had not enjoyed since the 1920s. Its celebrated apostles, including Helmut Jahn and Michael Graves, entered the stage blithely, but also rather nervously, cribbing their best ideas from tried and true models such as the Chrysler Building. The apologetic posture is telling, for since the Depression architects have never felt fully confident in producing unabashedly loud commercial architecture. A death blow was dealt by the Depression, and the model of architectural practice that was imported from Europe in its wake was itself fundamentally incapable of comprehending the demands of a commercial society. As a result the modern architect seems unable to desist from parodying the very product he is selling. Only rarely, as in Helmut Jahn's unbuilt Trump Tower, does anything approach the swagger of the Empire State Building. Then again, swaggering in our culture is less likely to be performed by architecture, and more often by the intangible coin of celebrity and media attention. Perhaps these assets are less easily seized in court.

If the brashness of the American building is the brashness of vitality and energy, it is also touched with a certain poignant insecurity. Many a swagger conceals a shudder, and many an aggressive American building shows the deportment of the nervous bumpkin squeezed into an ill-fitting tuxedo, the same discomfort, the same nervous overstatement. This is the legacy of a society with an open class structure where it is the privilege of each individual to shape his own fortune and status. Being negotiable and elastic, American social status has always required a certain number of rhetorical devices and status marks to prop it up. And from an early age, architecture was enlisted in this mission, communicating success and wealth, good taste and good breeding. Unfortunately these pairs of qualities were generally inversely related. This book records some of the wilder examples, such as Samuel Sloan's fantasia on a Persian theme for the planter Haller Nutt at Natchez, Mississippi; E. T. Potter's rollicking belly laugh of a house at Hartford, Connecticut for Mark Twain; and that gingerbread epiphany at Eureka, California, the Samuel and Joseph C. Newson's Carson Mansion.

All these examples are Victorian, for in that overheated epoch of social change the natural connection between the personality of the owner and his house was pushed to white-hot intensity. Nowhere was this observed more keenly than in Andrew Jackson Downing's *The Architecture of Country Houses* (1850), which understood that the house was the public calling card of the family. For them, the villa "should above all things, manifest individuality. It should say something of the character of the family within—as much as possible of their life and history, their tastes and associations, should mould and fashion themselves upon its walls."[3] Downing's was no rarefied treatise on the French or German model, no exercise in abstract system-building. Nor did he begin with a prescribed set of historical forms. Instead he was the first to show how the architect must address the nature of American life itself, in all its restless, quivering nature. His was the first classic of American architectural literature and he was soon followed by a host of imitators, including Samuel Sloan, Calvert Vaux, George E. Woodward, A. J. Bicknell, Palliser & Company, and, in our century, Gustav Stickley. In their pattern books, all historical styles were marshalled out to stand for nuances of achievement, personality or wealth. This indiscriminate shoplifting of the past was the peculiar privilege of the American architect, who saw himself as the inheritor of the legacy of the old world, and who regarded architectural history as Thomas Cole did in *The Architect's Dream* (fig. 5), his tribute to his friend Ithiel Town—as a Sears Catalogue of possibilities. When Sears itself began to offer pattern book houses in the early twentieth century, the circle closed.

fig. 5

America is hardly unique in tarting up architecture in the service of social representation, and the hand of individualism and commercialism rests on many a European building. But in Europe, these forces were resisted by a web of restraining factors, among them the cautioning influence of architectural academies, the snob appeal of official patronage, the aesthetic control of municipal authorities, and the brake of vernacular tradition. In America, however, these restraints were absent;

it was all spur and no bridle. No formal schools of architecture existed before the 1860s, and even in the present municipal authorities have rarely been able to exercise any aesthetic restriction whatsoever. The occasional expectoration of public disapproval (for example, the ridicule given a crass "folly") often expressed as much envy as outraged taste, which rather tended to blunt the effect of criticism.

In short, a cauldron of fierce social energies and an indulgent attitude toward their expression emerged: such is the mental atmosphere under which American architecture blossomed. Even so, these forces would have exhausted themselves swiftly if not allowed to pour themselves out upon a material that was equally flexible, permissive, and capable of limitless expression. Without wood (and without the lessons taught by wood) American architecture would have tended to remain a provincial, rather conventional variant of northern European architecture.

The American reliance on wood as the primary material of construction is the legacy of the seventeenth century, when the continent was still largely covered by the world's largest surviving temperate forest. All along the coast, the first line of Colonial buildings was built with the felled timbers of this forest: oaks, pines, hemlocks, and chestnuts, marvelously dense woods, superbly impervious to insects and rot. Where the forest melted away, the houses rose. A retreating line of trees was fashioned into houses—first saltboxes, then Greek temples, the Gothic cottages, and then, on the West coast, into bungalows. But if it was a permanent loss, at least it was a trade, and left a gain in the form of a sturdy, honest house. Unfortunately, much subsequent development has claimed these houses and given precious little in return.

The earliest wood buildings were the mighty houses of colonial New England, which were raised on a joined oak frame and built in accordance with the rules of the English joiner. The near medieval Fairbanks House in Dedham, Massachusetts (1636) is perhaps the most ancient of all. Adaptations were swiftly made to climate and to new social circumstances, but the great expressive potential of wood was first realized in the van of the Industrial Revolution. In the mid-nineteenth century, the industrialization of the building process led to the balloon frame, which supplanted the heavy joined frame. Mill-sawn boards replaced the riven clapboards and heavy frame while factory-milled nails replaced the old mortise and tenon joint (fig. 6).

Other building processes were changed or created by the Industrial Revolution. In 1849 James Bogardus patented designs for an all-iron building, while Robert Mook designed a concrete house in Port Chester, New York. But in this lengthening pageant of new materials, the lessons of wood lingered with the American builder. Iron and concrete were used rather freely, but always in terms of the liberating example of wood. Above all, wood is a material of planarity and suggests that buildings are arrangements of folded planes, boxes with the thinnest of walls that define an internal volume. Even when realized in three dimensions, there is a brittle thinness—a sense that architecture is only an affair of outlines and contours, but not of solids. Even in a wildly elaborate and decorative structure, one often finds a certain schematic quality. Such is the mentality of the carpenter, the tendency to conceive of each elevation of the building as a two-dimensional object. This carpenter's mentality stamps much of American architecture, even buildings of brick or steel, and it separates American architecture absolutely and sharply from those countries, such as Italy and France, where architecture was conceived historically in masonry and has always remained a much more plastic affair. A keen ob-

fig. 6

fig. 7

server such as Charles Dickens was taken aback when he encountered this difference, and in his classic *American Notes* he grasped for words to describe it, speaking of "sharp outlines," "razor-like edges," and the "clean cardboard colonnades" of New England.[4]

Even the cast-iron front was itself a thin planar object, like wood, whose form could be varied as cheaply and as infinitely as any advertising billboard, which in fact it was. And like the wood front, its Neo-Romanesque or Neo-Gothic or Neo-Egyptian facade could be cast without any particular structural relationship to the building behind it. The cost of this is an architecture that is, in historical and physical terms, only inches deep (*fig. 7*). Here was the beginning of the great divorce of construction and expression, the beginning of those "sheds" and "billboards" that Robert Venturi sees as so essential to the spirit of American architecture.

In the twentieth century, American architects were innoculated with the ideas of European Modernism. They continued to embrace new materials and methods, but now with a theoretical self-concsciousness. Modern materials were not to be used as cheap and durable substitutes for traditional materials; instead their use was to be governed by certain absolute and rather deterministic principles. Most potent of these was the Modernist doctrine of the machine, with its great imperative of standardization, the law that pushed irresistibly to the replication of interchangable parts. The architectural corollary of this was also standardization, but of a higher order: for example, the doctrine that housing must be designed in serried rows of identical units. Nothing could be further from the mood of American architects who, when exposed to modern materials and rational modes of buildings, regularly used them as instruments of individual expression. Even Frank Lloyd Wright, that champion of new building processes, constantly fondled in his imagination the union of the machine with individuality of expression. His American System-Built houses of 1913–15 were based on an ingenious system of prefabricated concrete elements that could be assembled into houses of dramatically different character, thereby achieving the Victorian goal of variety through the modern technique of standardization.

But through it all, a certain schematic flatness has survived in the American conception of the building. In earlier times, this was due as much to available architectural source material as it was to the use of wood. Throughout the eighteenth century architectural inspiration came from Italy, as filtered through those English pattern books, such as James Gibbs's *A Book of Architecture* (1728) and Colin Campbell's *Vitruvius Britannicus* (1716–25), that were the mainstay of architectural practice. In Newport, Rhode Island, Peter Harrison, one of America's first professional architects, regularly plundered these sources, emulating the distant and monumental stone architecture of the Italian Renaissance. But neither he nor his contemporaries knew their Italian models first hand, only imagining them through the two-dimensional plates of their reference books. In the execution of their versions, these classical prototypes were shrunk in scale, and often simplified and flattened out (as they were pre-flattened in the pattern book engravings). Moldings and cornices projected rather shallowly; the plastic conception of the original turned into a planar affair.

Thomas Jefferson's University of Virginia (1817–25) betrays this same schematic quality. Often called America's finest man-made object, it is a surpassing achievement, a vista of infinite nature at one end with an architectural embodiment of rational order, in the form of his Pantheon of a library, at the other. The subtlety of its landscaping and brilliant siting are precisely what one would expect from a man with an intimate relationship to the land, one that was marinated in economic, political, and religious associations. But for all of his intellectual strengths, Jefferson was at heart an American with little experience or sensitivity for plastic expression. When he came to draft his buildings, he reverted to his standard graph paper, that wonderfully rational drafting aid, allowing the convenient extraction of dimensions and volumes (fig. 8). How far apart this is—at the risk of seeming ridiculous—from the world of Michelangelo, who might build a full-scale wood mock-up of a cornice and hoist it aloft in order to gauge its sculptural qualities under conditions of light and shadow. Contrast this with

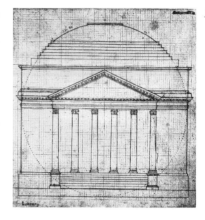

fig. 8

Jefferson's intellectual working method, and his cherished graphs: Jefferson the Platonist fussing with the Classical proportions and Jefferson the frugal planter counting cubic masses of brick. Seldom were American idealism and pragmatism wed so successfully, or seamlessly.

But idealism and pragmatism, though opposites, do not embrace the whole spectrum of human possibilities. There is a whole lobe of the human heart that American architecture does not address, and this is where an honest evaluation of the American building must end.

* * *

American architecture, like American food, shuns the sensual. Rarely have explicitly sensual values—say the play of light and shadow over walls or the sheer physical delight in materials—played a great role in American architecture. The one era of sensual indulgence in American art, the aesthetic movement of the 1880s and 1890s, is the lonely exception to this broad pattern. Louis I. Kahn's late works are another anomaly. American buildings, like American white bread, processed cheeses, and the modern tomato, provide us the shape of the thing, and the color of the thing, but seldom the tart, tang, or zest of the thing. In each instance there persists a certain puritanical disinterest in things sensual that has its origins in, but has lost its moorings from, seventeenth-century puritan theology with its suspicion of the plastic arts, and its outright hostility to the sensual art of Catholic Europe. Even today, the American will characteristically sacrifice sensual delight to the utilitarian or the pragmatic. (Just to reverse the terms and sound them out shows how ingrained these concepts are in us.) Few, if any, arguments in America are settled by an appeal to the aesthetic or the sensual; some are settled by appeals to morality, many more by appeals to efficiency or economy. The great wave of street widening and tree felling that occurred since World War II, and that permanently affected the look of every American city, occurred with virtually no murmur of aesthetic indignation, although it is one of the single greatest changes to the physical character of America in this century. Even environmental lobbying here is successful on utilitarian grounds—health and so forth—rather than aesthetic ones.

Architectural criticism flits from topic to topic but in the end always comes to rest on the formal. Litigation and efficiency, those great shapers of architecture, do not get as much credit as the formal impulse. The most successfully sculptural architecture of this century, the chiseled and modeled skyscrapers of the 1920s, were not the product of a general aesthetic movement. Rather they were the direct consequence of New York's celebrated zoning restrictions of 1916, the famous setback laws. Here the developer's impulse to maximize the volume

fig. 9

of his building met a series of restrictions aimed at reducing its mass systematically at higher levels. The contours resulting from these prescribed setbacks, where cupidity collided with legislation, created a new language of chiseled and angular forms, the characteristic expression of Art Deco America (*fig. 9*). But the germinating idea, the controlling impulse, was based on commercial and civic forces. Perhaps no other major building type in world history was less the product of architects, and more that of lawyers, developers, and politicians.

There is present in American architecture a curious disembodied quality, a powerful utilitarian impulse that exists side by side with the ideal and that often threatens to overpower it. No country was so quick to make buildings that were utilitarian intellectual exercises, cerebral creations rather than historical artifacts. The influential plan of John Haviland's Eastern State Penitentiary in Philadelphia (begun in 1822), America's first widely exported building type, is virtually a mathematical diagram of its function: the central hub with the observation and service core guards the radiating wings with cells and private exercise yards. Here was a utilitarian map of circulation and observation made without reference to historical typology (*fig. 10*).

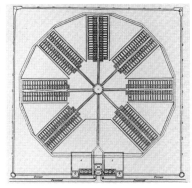

fig. 10

Just as radically utilitarian was Orson Squire Fowler, that nearly demented phrenologist who likewise pursued an abstract diagrammatic architecture, following to an unsound conclusion a sound mathematical principle. This was the rule that the interior area of a polygon increases in proportion as it approaches a circle, which Fowler took as a command to build houses in the forms of octagons. Utilitarian rationality, nearing the point of lunacy, was intensely fashionable in the early 1850s in an America where efficiency counted for much and where the inhibitions against new forms were so weak. There is hardly a New England community without an octagonal house—and scarcely one with two.

Such is that characteristic American willingness to entertain Rube Goldberg schemes, the same impulse that marvels at gadgets for expanding hanger space in clothes closets, or multipurpose Vegematics. At its best, this impulse made American houses the world's best heated, best insulated, and best plumbed, already by the middle of the nineteenth century. At its worst, this impulse led to coldly mechanistic houses, like Buckminster Fuller's Dymaxion House, or to the modern double-wide modular home.

In the past, this utilitarian component was held in rigid check by a ligature of interlocking factors, including the general use of historical source matter, craft standards in the building trades, a strong social compact, and an agrarian relationship to the land, even if a generation or two removed. These checks have in recent decades been loosened. While the lines of continuity traced in this essay connect the seventeenth to the mid-twentieth century, many have been broken. The naive idealism that is so apparent in much of America's historical architecture is conspicuously missing in buildings of the past three decades, starved on the innutritious spiritual diet of this century. Other lines of continuity have been preserved, but have pushed themselves to extremes, like an overrank garden. The planar thinness of American buildings has pushed itself almost to the point of dissolution. American wood is now the flimsy and porous material of rapid-growth commercial species, sitting as lightly on the land as any American building ever did, with little promise of permanence. And the most heralded architectural debates of the last three decades—that between Modernists, Postmodernists, and Deconstructionists—has been essentially a rather barren debate over the proper surface cladding of utilitarian sheds, which in their fundamental construction have not changed appreciably.

During this same time there has occurred a shift in the public attitude toward architecture. At one time new American buildings were intensely popular, and closely followed by a public that understood the conventions and rules that dictated their form. If these buildings were crudely commercial or civic, they needed no intellectual program to be appreciated. But the anti-intellectual tradition that has always underpinned American art and architecture has been overturned since World War II. America's schools of architecture embraced Modernism in the 1930s, and in recent years many have turned to critical literary theory and deconstruction. The intellectualizing of American architecture in now complete, Jacques Derrida in the outermost suburbs and Michel Foucault in the mini-mall. Still, a society that remains at heart solidly anti-intellectual looks on uncomprehendingly at most recent buildings. Few are celebrated now except by the adept professional celebrators in the press and in the academies.

*   *   *

G. E. Kidder Smith's *Source Book of American Architecture* is a personal selection of great American buildings. It does not inventory losses, the toll of which is ponderous, but even so it makes clear that there is a vast architectural legacy in this country. As any personal selection of buildings should, it has all the quirks and idiosyncrasies of one man. It is not the negotiated and filtered product of compromise. It is the current fashion (and probably a passing fashion) to quibble over such lists, and over anyone's authority to compile a canon. But it is a splendid compendium, and like Nikolaus Pevsner's *The Buildings of England* it is filled with generosity of spirit, robust wit, and vigor of expression—qualities that resound in the buildings it extols. It is as close to a canon as anything I have seen. Some might want to add H. H. Richardson's Ames Gate Lodge—but at the cost of a Sullivan bank? Read the book, remembering that architecture is a spatial art, and requires spatial experience. Read it, savor the prose, and then go to the buildings.

And what of the future of American architecture? The American building is a living thing, with organic powers of recuperation and regeneration, and with that capacity of all living things to change infinitely while remaining fundamentally the same. But it is also unlike living things in two cardinal ways. On the one hand, it preserves the embodied memory of itself at almost every earlier stage of its existence, as this great Domesday Book of Kidder Smith shows. And on the other hand, it is not an independent organism that follows its own laws of growth and renewal, but a dependent thing, nourished and sustained by American society. It can survive anything, assimilate anything, except a demoralization of that society. It cannot regenerate itself from within itself, no more than an empty seashell can—this is the reason for that odd hollow ring heard in so much of the architectural debate of recent years.

Notes

1 Nigel Everett, *The Tory View of Landscape* (New Haven: Yale University Press, 1993).
2 For a contemporary overview of the vivid commercial architecture of this period, see the reprint of *Masterpieces of American Architecture*, with essays by George E. Thomas and Michael J. Lewis (New York: Princeton Architectural Press, 1992).
3 A. J. Downing, *The Architecture of Country Houses* (New York: Appleton, 1850), 262.
4 Charles Dickens, *American Notes* (1842). See for instance the section on Worcester, Massachusetts in chapter five.

Illustrations

1 A. J. Downing, from *The Architecture of Country Houses* (New York: Appleton, 1850).
2 Erastus Salisbury Field, *Historical Monument of the American Republic*, 1876 (Museum of Fine Arts, Springfield, Massachusetts, The Morgan Wesson Memorial Collection).
3 Thomas Holme, plan of Philadelphia, 1682 (courtesy Library Company of Philadelphia).
4 Monopoly board (Parker Brothers).
5 Thomas Cole, *The Architect's Dream*, 1840 (Toledo Museum of Art, Gift of Florence Scott Libbey).
6 Edward Shaw, frontispiece from *The Modern Architect* (Boston, 1854).
7 James Bogardus, design from *Cast Iron Buildings: Their Construction and Advantages* (New York, 1856).
8 Thomas Jefferson, elevation and section, University of Virginia Library, c. 1820 (Thomas Jefferson Papers, Special Collections Department, University of Virginia Library).
9 Hugh Ferriss, *Study for Maximum Mass Permitted by the 1916 New York Zoning Law*, 1922 (from Hugh Ferriss, *The Metropolis of Tomorrow*, New York: Ives Washburn, 1929; reprint, Princeton: Princeton Architectural Press, 1986).
10 John Haviland, Eastern State Penitentiary, 1822ff. From George W. Smith, *A View and Description of the Eastern State Penitentiary of Pennsylvania* (Philadelphia, 1830).

PUEBLO BONITO (A.D. 919–1067)
NM 57
Chaco Canyon National Monument, New Mexico

Pueblo Bonito represents the meridian of Native American architectural achievement in what is now the United States. The Yucatan of the Mayas and Machu Picchu of the Incas far outstripped North American work in both scope and technical know-how, but this long-deserted settlement in the Chaco Canyon is nevertheless prodigious. And though its ruins may not be as visually dramatic as those at Mesa Verde National Park, Colorado (see page 23), the architectural sophistication of Pueblo Bonito is far superior to that of the cliffside adaptations of the Colorado Anasazi. Moreover, Pueblo Bonito was not erected for religious rituals, but was an active four- to five-story town of approximately six hundred rooms spread over 3 acres/1.2 hectares. Until the development of the American housing complexes of recent years it was indeed the largest megastructure on these shores.

Bonito was planned in a *D* shape with its high, almost windowless, arced back confronting the cliffs behind. Its contiguous tiers of southerly facing apartments step down in curved terraces to focus, almost like a stadium, on a central plaza, the whole closed by a wall of buildings across the straight side near the Chaco Wash. In front of the rooms are thirty-two clan kivas and two great kivas, the larger 52 feet/16 meters in diameter. Almost all of the cliff settlements, except the smallest, had kivas or ceremonial subterranean chambers, which evolved from early pit houses, were rounded in shape, and were reached only by a ladder via a small

hatch in their roof. They occupied important spots in front of the apartments, each kiva (a Hopi word) being a form of "clan" headquarters and council chamber. Measuring 10–15 feet/3–4.6 meters in diameter, the kivas were approximately 6 feet/1.8 meters tall with a half-dozen masonry "piers" on the periphery providing the vertical structure. On these rested layers of logs, each course angled to the one below until the roof structure was complete; on this mud was packed to seal the roof, which also served as "paving" for the courtyard. In the floor near the center was a fire pit, and, as there was only a small opening for ladder access and smoke exit, a clever ventilation shaft fed fresh air to the bottom of the kiva, with a small wall of sandstone placed so as to block direct draft from the fire itself. A tiny hole in the floor, called a "sipapu," formed the symbolic entrance for the gods of the underworld. In addition to council and religious uses, the kivas doubled as work spaces.

Not only was there a "town plan" for Pueblo Bonito (and other settlements of the Chaco), but construction techniques here were very advanced. The high curved wall that enfolds much of the complex is an outstanding example of stonework of any era. This perimeter enclosure, measuring approximately 800 feet/244 meters long, is faced on both sides with beautifully dressed and fitted small stones, while rubble fills the center—an advanced veneer technique common in ancient Greek and Roman architecture. Wide foundations were laid, with walls properly narrowing toward the top, and doorways were often placed in line, reflecting a considered in the room arrangement. The stonework of the short domestic divisions can only be described as elegant. It should be pointed out that not all masonry was so exact; earlier sections were of crude stone.

Pueblo Bonito was neither the earliest nor the only settlement in the canyon. It was, indeed, one of a system of satellite communities. Humans had been dwelling and farming, instead of nomadic hunting, along the Chaco River at least since the sixth century A.D. (hunters since, perhaps, 7000 B.C.), and dozens of sizable communities were strung along its course. Many of their ruins are visitable today. Remote sensing techniques have outlined an extensive network of uniform, straight roads connecting each pueblo with resource areas beyond the canyon's escarpment. Bonito was the largest and architecturally the most sophisticated of Native American settlements in North America in its overall concept and its level of execution. The settlement was largely abandoned around A.D. 1130–1180, probably in part due to a prolonged drought; increased population, which led to land exhaustion, may also have been partly to blame. But what a monument the people left!

Check in first at the Visitors Center for a self-guiding pamphlet and to see the small museum and its reconstruction of the pueblo. A number of sites will merit a visit, with the Great Kiva at Casa Rinconada (opposite Pueblo Bonito) rating especially high. Built around A.D. 1150, this restored (1933–35) but now unroofed kiva is, at 63.5 feet/19.3 meters in diameter and a maximum height of 12.1 feet/3.7 meters, one of the largest in the country. It is characterized by excellent stonework, which was originally plastered and probably painted. Precise orientation can be seen in the four holes that once held its roof posts: they align with the cardinal points. It is probable that Casa Rinconada (Corner House), unlike most kivas, was an isolated place "of public assembly" (Gordon Vivian and Paul Reiter, *The Great Kivas*, School of American Research, 1965).

Note: The road into Chaco Canyon National Monument can charitably be described as poor: in wet weather it is virtually impassable for a two-wheel-drive vehicle. No tourist facilities exist except for rest rooms and a campground.

From the north, take NM 44 to San Juan County Road to NM 57 south; from the south, take Navajo 9 to NM 57 north. Sites open daily sunrise–sunset. Visitors Center open daily 8:00 A.M.–5:00 P.M. (Memorial Day–Labor Day open daily 8:00 A.M.–6:00 P.M.). Closed Christmas and New Year's Day. Admission is $4 per vehicle. Camping fees are $8 per site per night. From Memorial Day to Labor Day, ranger-guided walks given daily. For more information call (505) 786–7014.

WHITE HOUSE (1066–1275)
Canyon de Chelly National Monument
Chinle, Arizona

White House, located at the base of an extraordinary canyon—a red sandstone Permian slash at times 1,000 feet/305 meters deep—is, like other cliff-dwellings throughout the Four Corners area (Colorado, New Mexico, Arizona, and Utah), far more of nature than of man. But it represents, as do the others, such a logical, functional, and handsome fusion of home beseeching cliff that it offers rewards to all interested in the earliest surviving vernacular of the United States. Its precipitous location did not encroach upon the fertile river-watered land below and also provided reasonable defense. (These factors also prompted the development of Italian hill towns in the Middle Ages.) Nature, of course, furnished much of the shelter, as well as a beauty that will excite anyone spirited enough to hike down and back the 500-foot/ 152-meter drop to the canyon's broad base via a good but strenuous trail. (River-bottom Jeep trips—plus accommodations—are available from Thunderbird Lodge.) But even if one does not go to the canyon base, the automobile trip along the rim, especially with binoculars, is enlightening.

The ruin consists of two sections: a lower part against the base of the cliff and an upper one from which the name is derived. ("White House" comes from the still-surviving white clay plastering of the central room.) Neither section is accessible. The higher part is magnificently perched 40 feet/12 meters above the canyon floor—like the nest of a huge bird—with approximately eleven partially intact rooms notched into the protecting cliffside. Ladders gave access from the roofs of the lower buildings, which once rose three and four floors but which have been reduced by river and weather to ruined hulks today. (Unusually high water in 1930 created severe damage.)

In 1931 the entire area, which covers 130 square miles/337 square kilometers and which also includes Canyon del Muerto, was dedicated as the Canyon de Chelly National Monument. The region was occupied by the prehistoric Pueblo Anasazi culture beginning around A.D. 200, but abandoned at the end of the thirteenth century because of, among other causes, the disastrous drought that seared the entire Four Corners area for more than a generation. (Some two thousand known Anasazi sites are left in the monument area.) Around 1700 the Navajo—the largest of the Native American groups—migrated to the canyon, and today it is their traditional home. Note their hogans scattered along the flat and fertile riverbed. These slightly domed, roughly circular houses are virtually unique to Navajo culture. Hogans are related to the shelters of the Navajo's Athapascan cousins in northwest Canada, but their design changed from bark covering to hide to packed earth and sticks as the early migratory hunters and gatherers moved to and settled in the southwest United States, arriving around 1400–1500. The hogans' basically circular plan, however, remained though the older more conical form evolved into the low "dome" seen here. Religious symbolism affected the design of these shelters: their entryways faced eastward so that they would catch "the first blessing" of the sun. "Even Navajos with modern houses may have hogans for religious rites" (*The World of the American Indian*, National Geographic Society, 1974).

Located 6.5 miles/10 kilometers east of Chinle. Canyon de Chelly National Monument open daily 8:00 A.M.–5:00 P.M. Closed Christmas and New Year's Day. The site can be reached by foot (no charge), by truck tour through the Thunderbird Lodge (prices vary), or by horse tour (prices vary). Visitors owning four-wheel drive vehicles can hire a Navajo guide ($10 per hour, minimum 3 hours). For more information call the Canyon de Chelly Visitors Center at (602) 674–5500.

AZTEC RUINS NATIONAL MONUMENT (1111–15/mid-13th century)
Ruins Road
Aztec, New Mexico

Erroneously called "Aztecs" by early Europeans, the builders of this substantial settlement—whose precise dates were determined using dendrochronology—were the Pueblo (that is, "village") Indians. Their ancestors moved into this San Juan River area about two thousand years ago, and toward the end of the eighth century A.D. began to develop the connected flat-roofed communities the Spaniards called "pueblos." (Some historians think that the Pueblos were driven from Mexico by the Aztecs.) Besides providing us today with an intriguing ruin in the northwest corner of the state, the complex is important in both urban and architectural terms. First, this was a geometrically planned community, built in the shape of a rectangle approximately 278 x 360 feet/85 x 110 meters in size, focused on the circular Great Kiva. Aztec Ruins, moreover, comprises a megastructure, an interconnected block of about five hundred cellular dwelling and storage units. These housed some 450 people in two- and three-story "apartments," each roughly 10 x 12 feet/3 x 3.6 meters in size. On the base level across the back, the pueblo is as much as six rooms deep, and four to five along the sides. The windowless inner rooms were used for storing food during the winter months, for personal possessions, and for work spaces and burial chambers. Finally, like Pueblo Bonito in Chaco Canyon (see page 18) but unlike New Mexico's score of other pueblos, this pueblo is constructed totally of dry sandstone, not adobe. Its workmanship, considering that the cutting and dressing tools were themselves of stone, is astonishing. Note the alternation of wide and narrow bands. The quarries, incidentally, lie 1 mile/1.6 kilometers away.

Aztec Ruins is also distinguished by its Great Kiva (there are twenty-nine smaller ones) that projects half above ground and that has been carefully reconstructed (1934) on the foundations of the original (see Pueblo Bonito—page 18—for an extensive description of the kiva). This startling room—which was probably used by the whole community—should by all means be seen, for it is one of the few extant or restored examples of monumental interior space of early Native American building. Measuring 48.3 feet/14.7 meters in inner diameter, its center section is upheld by four piers made of alternating layers of log sections and stones, with beams across them and other logs on top radiating to the periphery. Surrounding the central section, which is set 8 feet/2.4 meters below grade, are fourteen small chambers (their function is unknown) with two doors each, a small one to the central area and one to the outside. (These latter were sealed during one of the alterations.) An altar, or fire pit, stands opposite the entrance with two mysterious, rectangular pits, or "vaults," on either side. These are held by some to be sudatories, or sweat baths, while others consider them foot drums when covered with hides or wooden planks. A circular stone bench rings the whole.

This splendid kiva and town were abandoned around 1150, not very long after completion, presumably because of lack of rainfall and/or changes in the Chacoan economic and social system. However, the pueblo was reoccupied and in part remodeled by others around 1215. These inhabitants, who displayed cultural traits of the Mesa Verdean people, remodeled many rooms and modified the kiva to suit their needs, only to abandon the site permanently during the great drought of 1276–99—the period of the High Gothic in Europe.

Located .7 mile/1.1 kilometers north of US 550. Memorial Day–Labor Day open daily 8:00 A.M.–6:00 P.M. The rest of the year open daily 8:00 A.M.–5:00 P.M. Closed Thanksgiving, Christmas, and New Year's Day. Admission is $2 per person, free for children under 17. For more information call (505) 334–6174.

CLIFF DWELLINGS (c. 1200–1300)
Mesa Verde National Park, Colorado

For utmost symbiosis between architecture and landscape, man and nature, one need proceed no further than the Mesa Verde cliff dwellings. Circular troglodytic holes in the ground serve as efficient shelter in Tunisia (Matmata), and square ones in China (primarily in Honan Province), but one will find more "architecture," more of the creative act of placing stone on stone, in the hundreds of cliff dwellings along the precipitous bluffs of this southwest corner of Colorado. The settlements—the largest and most numerous of their kind in the country—were established by the ancestors of today's Pueblos.

The mesa itself, rising 1,300–2,000 feet/396–610 meters above the plains (8,572 feet/ 2,613 meters maximum above sea level), offered some natural defense through its height and thus its top has been occupied and its soil cultivated (with beans, squash, and corn) since approximately A.D. 600. Until the mid-eighth century these early people—the "Modified Basket Makers" (A.D. 450–750)—lived atop the mesa in pit houses (that is, half in the ground), then in individual mud and stone dwellings. In the mid-eighth century the Native Americans adopted pole, wattle, and mud to build south-facing arcs of rectangular, attached "row hous-es," the resulting pueblos ("villages") giving them the name Pueblos. By the year 1000 stone began to replace wooden posts: such construction later developed into complexes as long as 50 feet/15 meters and three stories high. Around 1200 the inhabitants moved off the mesas to shelters under the cliff overhangs. It is not known precisely why they moved, for no evidence

of unusual violence has been discovered. Defense against their own people during clan disputes has been suggested, along with overpopulation and environmental factors such as depletion of soil minerals. In any case many moved into the large alcoves, almost caves, that had been created from water and frost acting on the soft sandstone cliffsides. Hundreds of cliff dwellings—five hundred is a frequently used figure (with a maximum of perhaps fifteen hundred rooms)—were then built along the cliff faces of the area. Some were tiny affairs seemingly glued to the canyon wall and obviously capable of holding only one agile family's possessions; others were virtually of village size. The majority of the population, which some authorities believe amounted to about seven hundred people in the 1200s, lived in the many small cliff dwellings, not the few large ones.

One of the largest of the Mesa Verde cliff dwellings is the Cliff Palace, which measures 325 feet/99 meters long, has a maximum depth of approximately 100 feet/30 meters, and accommodated 250 to 400 souls at its peak, with some 200 rooms and 23 kivas. (The 110 steps down and the climb up can be strenuous for some at 7,000 feet/2,134 meters altitude.) Spruce Tree House (near the museum), at 216 x 89 feet/66 x 27 meters, is better preserved and easier of access; it has 114 rooms and 8 kivas. All of them are architecturally ingenious, well-ordered assemblages in a tightly compacted space, in which every square foot was put to use: "a delirium of man-made geometry" (Vincent Scully, *Pueblo*, Viking Press, 1975). As the Pueblos lacked all but the simplest tools, the cliffsides themselves were rarely touched, and the buildings were adapted to the natural morphology of the setting (except for leveling the floor). Some of the "apartments" are four levels high, each entered by a narrow (16–25-inch/41–64-centimeter) rectangular or *T*-shaped door. Almost all exhibit capable masonry work, with the interiors plastered and occasionally decorated. Several stout logs form the ceiling and roof joists, with smaller logs laid upon them at right angles, then branches and adobe added for finish. A single window, often no more than a peephole, admitted a bit of light and air; the doors were closed at night by a sandstone slab. Most units had a small fireplace.

Even more capable work, especially in masonry, can be seen in the nearby Sun Temple, a ceremonial structure superbly situated on a point of Chapin Mesa. This now forms a symmetrical roofless maze whose walls, 8–11 feet/2.4–3.4 meters high and 3 feet/.9 meter thick, describe a *D*-shaped form 121 x 64 feet/37 x 19 meters. Possibly begun around 1270, it was never finished. Except for the reinforcement of the top of the walls no contemporary work has been needed to preserve this tantalizing and mysterious ruin.

The Four Corners area (Colorado, New Mexico, Arizona, and Utah) suffered a severe drought from 1276–99—dates established by dendrochronology. It is thought that this, plus soil loss, forced emigration southward. Cliff Palace lay unknown to the white man until it was discovered by two cowboys in December of 1888. (Several very small cliff dwellings had been discovered in Mancos Canyon in 1874 and 1875.) In 1906 the area—which had been heavily pilfered over the years—was made a National Park; shortly thereafter measures were taken to excavate the sites and stabilize the weakened remains to make them safe for visitors.

In addition to the Mesa Verde cliff dwellings built by the sedentary Pueblos, there are other cliff dwellings in the Four Corners region, notably White House at the Canyon de Chelly National Monument in Chinle, Arizona (see page 20), and the Montezuma Castle National Monument in the central part of that state. All are well worth seeing; the breathtaking views en route to Mesa Verde alone merit the trip.

Park entrance is located 10 miles/16 kilometers east of Cortez. The park is open year round; admission is $5 per vehicle. Far View Visitors Center located 21.5 miles/35 kilometers south of US 160 and is open Memorial Day–Labor Day, daily 8:00 A.M.–5:00 P.M. Tours of Cliff Palace available in summer; tours of Spruce Tree House available in winter. Tickets can be purchased at the Visitors Center. For more information call (303) 529–4475.

TAOS PUEBLO (pre-16th century)
North Pueblo Road
Taos, New Mexico

Wheeler Peak, New Mexico's highest mountain (13,161 feet/4,011 meters), forms the back-drop, a grove of cottonwood rustles nearby, and a mountain stream meanders through—it is no wonder that this spot has been continuously settled for over a millennium. And, further, it is no wonder that its Tiwa-speaking Pueblos, like the ancient Greeks siting their temples, have treated the land religiously; places like Blue Lake in the hills are indeed sacred. Some seven hundred years ago at the beginning of the so-called Pueblo 4 Period (c. 1275–1598), the ances-tors of the present inhabitants, who had long since mastered basic agriculture, moved into the Taos region and commenced building their famous communal houses of adobe, simple pro-totypes of which trace back to, perhaps, the eighth and ninth centuries. The "apartment" com-plexes we observe today are probably little changed from those seen and described (as "pueb-los" or villages) by the first Spanish explorers under Francisco Vásquez de Coronado in 1540. Some experts, John P. Harrington among them, believe that the very word "Taos" is "proba-bly a Spanish variation of the native name 'Tua,' meaning house, houses, or village" (as quoted

by Stanley A. Stubbs in his *Bird's-Eye View of the Pueblos*, University of Oklahoma Press, 1950). The present buildings were largely constructed and slightly relocated around 1700 following the Pueblo Rebellion of 1680–92 and the fire of 1694. Because of their extent and height (up to five stories) they are unique in the Western Hemisphere for adobe construction. (Abroad, one finds more daring in the pisé "skyscrapers" and fortified towns in the Hadhramaut of Yemen and in the Dadés Valley of Morocco, but in these arid spots rain is almost nonexistent. In New Mexico, rain—and snow—must be contended with seasonally.) The word "adobe," incidentally, can be traced back to Egyptian hieroglyphics via Coptic, Arabic, and Spanish versions. This sun-dried brick construction was introduced to the Spaniards by the Moors; its origin extends to Neolithic times.

The plan of the Taos Pueblo, officially San Gerónimo de Taos, is puzzling; an open square with a stream divides the town into north and south houses. Each covers roughly the same area but the north units (to the left of the church) favor one- to five-story construction, while the others are primarily one to two stories. The irregular plaza in the center was for ceremonial and propitiatory (mostly rain) dances. But whichever side of the Rio Pueblo (which flows from Blue Lake) one lived on, egalitarianism of living quarters seemed in order for the approximately one thousand inhabitants. There is democracy in the shelter here without hierarchical distinction even for the governor (annually elected) and the cacique, or high priest (a lifetime appointment). This egalitarianism and its accompanying passivity at one time tempted incursions by nomadic Apaches, Comanches, and Utes, who lived largely on pillage. To protect themselves from raids the Taoseños erected a wall in the mid-eighteenth century around their pueblo, to which, in times of danger, the neighboring Spanish were invited. Land was communally held, while the farmland and the dwellings could be individually or clan owned, but generally under informal community control. The ancient mission of San Gerónimo, 1706, stands in ruins in the northwest corner of the pueblo, shelled into oblivion by American troops in 1847.

It is the extraordinary cellular living units at Taos that most excite the visitor; the piling of cube on cube evokes the splendor of abstract geometry and produces a scale buildup that echoes the surrounding hills. Here is a unique measure of ancient American vernacular: "the greatest aboriginal communal dwelling in the United States" (Earle R. Forrest, *Missions and Pueblos of the Old Southwest*, Rio Grande Press, 1929, reprinted 1965). Moreover, the near solidity of the adobe walls gains emphasis from the contrast with the tenuous wooden outrigging of the shelters in front and by the ladders used to reach the upper terraces. The opensided frameworks are used for drying and to help protect the domical ovens where daily and ritual bread were baked. Most of the wall openings—the doors and large windows seen today—date from the last half of the nineteenth century, when depredations ceased and glass became available. Previously, walls had been nearly solid, except for smoke holes, accessed only by hatches in the roof in kiva fashion.

Detailed inspection of the pueblo reveals a certain unkemptness, particularly following rain or snow, and the whole is finer than the parts, but this whole is so strangely *encantada* (especially in the late afternoon) that the Taos Pueblo will intrigue most observers. Fortunately, 48,000 acres/19,425 hectares of land, seized by the United States Government in 1906, was returned to the Taos in 1970. Thus they are once more in possession of their sacred preserve. Along with the earlier but ruined Pueblo Bonito (see page 18) and the largely ruined cliff dwellings at Mesa Verde (see page 23)—all tribally related—architecture in the United States obviously began with Pueblo culture.

Located 2.6 miles/4.2 kilometers north of downtown Taos. Open daily 8:00 A.M.–5:00 P.M. during the summer, 9:00 A.M.–4:00 P.M. during the winter. Closed for six weeks in spring; call for dates. Admission is $5 per car plus $1 per person. There is also a fee for photographing or sketching. Tours available in summer. For more information call (505) 758–1028.

PU'UHONUA O HONAUNAU NATIONAL HISTORICAL PARK, PLACE OF REFUGE
(16th–17th century/1966–69)
Honaunau, Hawaii, Hawaii

"The cities which you give to the Levites shall be the six cities of refuge, where you shall per-mit the manslayer to flee" (Numbers 35:6, Revised Standard Version). Although the ancient Hawaiian cities of refuge obviously differ in detail from those frequently mentioned in the Old Testament, the concept for both was similar. As stern vengeance, and often death, was visited on all who broke the complex system of sacred Island *kapus* or taboos (*tabu* itself is a Tongan word), these sanctuaries (*pu-uhonuas*) served an essential societal need. Those seeking safety within their sacred confines—often women, children, and old men in times of bitter inter-necine war—found sanctuary and/or absolution from their misdeeds, the latter sometimes rendered by the resident priests in a matter of hours, after suitable prayers. So important was this haven concept in early Hawaii that "cities" of refuge, sometimes just a designated cave, were found on all islands. The most impressive one remaining is this partially restored exam-ple on Honaunau Bay in the Pu'uhonua O Honaunau National Historical Park, not far south of the spot where Captain Cook met his untimely death.

In 1819 King Liholiho (Kamehameha II, who reigned 1819–24) overthrew the *kapu* pro-scriptions—which extended to the type of food women could eat, let alone forbidding them to eat with men—and destroyed most of the existing *heieus*, or temples, a startling act of aposta-sy which undoubtedly facilitated the introduction of Christianity by the missionaries who arrived (providentially?) the following year. However, this Place of Refuge was spared, only to be razed in 1829. It occupies the end of a small peninsula, and is defined on one side by an angled wall approximately 1,000 feet/305 meters long, 10 feet/3 meters high, and 17 feet/5.2 meters thick, and on the other sides by the sea. The ambitious wall, which dates from around 1550, is constructed of rough blocks of lava, some weighing 4–6 tons/3.6–5.4 metric tons laid

without mortar. (The lava came from the 13,677-foot/4,169-meter Mauna Loa, the world's largest active volcano, which lies about 22 miles/35 kilo-meters east of Pu'uhonua O Honaunau. Its most recent ma-jor eruption occurred in 1950 with its lava flowing nearby to the sea; in much earlier blow-outs the lava covered the site.) A large platform that once formed the base of a temple, and that also dates from the mid-six-teenth century, stands within the enclosure near the site of an earlier *heieu*—and was probably built with its stones. The high-light of the compound is the third temple, the Hale-o-Keawe, which served as the Royal Mausoleum. This tent-shaped, thatched structure, built originally around 1650, was meticulously reconstructed by National Park Service experts in 1966–69, aided by sketches made by early European visitors. The temple's sacred ground is protected by a stout fence of sharpened pales, with perhaps more effective protection afforded by the fearsome collection of *akua ki'i* (literally "god images"), here wooden pole-figures representing the gods buried within, some twenty-three deified kings and chiefs. (Are these pole-figures distant cousins of the totem poles of the natives of the northwest continental United States?)

A few hundred yards to the north and near the shore stand six thatched shelters, one left purposefully unfinished to graphically show the complexity of the seemingly simple Polynesian "grass" construction. In sum, Pu'uhonua O Honaunau Historical Park offers an enlightening display of traditional Hawaiian culture. The Park Service has also designed a first-rate orientation building near the entrance.

Located on HI 16, south of HI 11, 21 miles/34 kilometers south of Kailua. Park open daily 6:00 A.M.–12:00 midnight, Visitors Center open daily 7:30 A.M.–5:30 P.M. Admission is $2 per person or $4 per vehicle, free for seniors and for children 16 and under. Orientation talks given at 10:00, 10:30, and 11:00 A.M. and 2:30 and 3:30 P.M. Group tours can be arranged for a $25 fee. For more information call (808) 328–2288.

ST. AUGUSTINE RESTORATION AREA (1565–1821/1960–)
St. George Street
St. Augustine, Florida

St. Augustine is the oldest European settlement in what eventually became the United States. It was, it must be kept in mind, primarily a Spanish military outpost or, as it has been called, "a small poor garrison town" for almost two hundred years. It never approached a fully rounded agricultural or trading colony like the English established from Savannah, Georgia, to Machias, Maine. (Spain had to look after and support almost two hundred other bases and settlements in the New World in the sixteenth century. St. Augustine was their northernmost base on the continent, the eleventh attempted in Florida, and the only one to survive through the years.) Intended to discourage southward excursions by the French and English, as mentioned in the description of the Castillo de San Marcos (see page 42), this Florida community was thus largely inhabited by military men and their families, not by plantation owners or city burghers. The greatest resulting architectural achievement was the superb Castillo, the adjacent village forming a picturesque if uneven background. Since it was a lonely outpost for so long, little grandezza was called for, while destruction by fires, both of the enemy and accidental (the last in 1914), have left but a slender residue of earlier days. There is no building, other than the fort, that survived James Moore's burning of the town in 1702, virtually all construction until that time being of wood and thatch. After that fire masonry became mandatory, with most structures of coquina or "tabby" concrete.

The early town naturally reflected the Spanish urban pattern and lifestyle, particularly of those settlements along the Mediterranean and in the West Indies. Streets were narrow to provide shade and create cool drafts. All dwellings lined the street; in fact their walls defined it. Most were built with fenced or walled, sometimes grassless, patios where much living and work took place, and where the well, the precious vegetable garden, fruit trees, and chickens were safe. An open, south-oriented porch or loggia faced onto the patio, providing a covered open-air work area and shielding the rooms behind from direct sun. The yard and porch also led to the entry to the house; almost no dwellings—as opposed to inns or shops—had a door onto the street. (Compare the somewhat similar Charleston "single house"—see page 134—with front door opening onto a verandah, thence a fenced garden. There is some thought that

Britishers from Charleston, during their occupation of St. Augustine, may have influenced the town's development of second-floor running piazzas.) Few windows appeared in north walls and those facing west were small. Chimneys and fireplaces were infrequent; heat was supplied by charcoal braziers, and cooking via a hearth or in the oft-detached kitchen with only a roof smoke-hole. The modest (and most numerous) early houses were earth-floored, generally one-storied, and sometimes flat-roofed. Two-storied examples—not numerous in the First Spanish Period (1565–1763)—had covered balconies on the street side and pitched roofs more often than not. During the British tenure of 1763–83, when the English took possession of Florida, many fireplaces and chimneys were added to existing houses, direct "front" doors cut, and glazed windows with outside shutters installed (previously shutters had been inside and little glass had been used). These innovations modified subsequent building, but relatively little permanent new construction was undertaken during those twenty years. The Second Spanish Period (1783–1821, when St. Augustine reverted to Spain)—a time of unrest for Spain in Europe (primarily because of Napoleon)—produced only a few new buildings, notably the church now known as the Cathedral of St. Augustine (1793–97), which was designed by the royal engineer. (It was fully restored for the town's 400th anniversary.)

The citizens of St. Augustine began to recognize the importance of this slightly unkempt treasure as early as 1936, but it was not until 1959 that the Historic St. Augustine Preservation Board was set up, and it was 1962 when the non-profit St. Augustine Restoration, Inc. was established (though research and land acquisition had commenced earlier). With the nation's quickened interest in its extraordinary architectural inheritance, work has gathered speed. Now the highly appealing and revelatory St. George Street area, hard by the old City Gate and near the Castillo, is progressing handsomely. These few blocks re-create much of the atmosphere of the town's four major phases, though emphasis is on that of two hundred and more years ago. (The first three periods have been mentioned, the fourth began in 1821 with American occupation.)

Some thirty buildings have been restored or reconstructed with, it is hoped, more to come. Unfortunately the fire of 1702, which destroyed most of the town, also incinerated many civic records that had been stored in the Cathedral. Thus little cold documentation other than foundations and several informative maps exist to aid restoration. The work has been carried out, however, with as much authenticity as modern archeological research permits. The reconstructed dwellings range from the extremely simple Gomez House of wood, virtually a shack, and the almost equally primitive Gallegos House of tabby, both typical of the late First Spanish Period of 1565–1763, to the far more elegant eighteenth-century Ribera House directly across the street. This last is a two-story building of stuccoed coquina (once surrounded by an elaborate garden) that bears witness to the wealth of its early owner. As one progresses from the City Gate southward along St. George Street, other buildings of interest (plus a bit of commercialism) reward the stroller, particularly the often-altered Arrivas House (eighteenth–nineteenth century). With more funding from the state, this area, which was laid out forty-two years before Jamestown and fifty-five before the landing at Plymouth Rock, could be one of our greatest historic streets; it almost is now.

Located at the north end of St. George Street. Most buildings open 9:00 A.M.–5:00 P.M. daily; closed Christmas Day. The Spanish Quarter Museum, a collection of restored eighteenth-century historic houses, is open daily 9:00 A.M.–5:00 P.M.; admission prices are $5 for adults, $2.50 for students ages 6–18, $10 for a family pass (2 adults and all children). For more information call (904) 825-6830. The Museum of St. Augustine is open daily 10:00 A.M.–4:00 P.M.; admission prices are $2 for adults, $1 for students ages 6–18. For more information call (904) 825-5033.

Note: The Historic St. Augustine Preservation Board published a well-illustrated guidebook (1971) to the area, while the St. Augustine Historical Society brought out an extremely thorough book by Albert Manucy entitled *The Houses of St. Augustine* (1962), which the specialist will want to obtain.

A fascinating insight into the original (that is, Native American) settlements in Florida and along the south Atlantic coast is given in *The New World: First Pictures of America*, edited by Stefan Lorant (Duell, Sloan & Pearce, 1946). Jacques Le Moyne de Morgues sailed with René de Laudonniere in 1564 in an attempt to set up French Huguenot colonies in Florida with extensions to the north. Though Laudonniere was routed by the Spanish the following year (with help from a hurricane), Le Moyne, a skilled surveyor and artist, was able to make a number of excellent drawings showing the palisaded villages, granaries, and houses (generally circular and domical) that the French encountered among the natives. Some twenty years later John White, an English artist, made a series of illuminating watercolors of the Huguenot settlement (also short-lived—1585–90) in Virginia. The illustrations of both these men were vividly engraved by Theodore de Bry (1528–98), a talented Flemish artist, as shown in the above-mentioned book. White subsequently (1577) went on to join Frobisher and to delineate "the first European pictures of the Eskimo"—Samuel Eliot Morison (*The Great Explorers*, Oxford University Press, 1978).

JAMESTOWN SETTLEMENT RE-CREATION (1607–14/1957)
Colonial Parkway
Jamestown, Virginia

The beginnings of England's presence in the New World—John Donne's "suburb of the Old"—were established here in 1607, when three improbably small vessels (reproduced at wharfside) tethered their bows to the trees and America's first "permanent" English colony came into being. Twelve years later the colony was to organize English America's first representative assembly. The establishment of Jamestown—on an up-river site to avoid attack by the Spanish—proved to be rough going for its 104 men and boys, too many of whom were city gentry who hesitated to get their hands dirty. Moreover the area had problems with water supply and with, at times, hostile Native Americans. During the severe winter of 1609–10, by which time the first colonists of this commercial, not governmental, expedition had been augmented by three subsequent "supplies," some 150 out of a population of 500 had died, and by that spring an additional 125 had fled. But reinforcements in May of 1610 gave physical and spiritual infusion. The introduction of successful tobacco cultivation (by crossing sweet seed from Venezuela with bitter local varieties) provided a cash crop. Subsequently John Rolfe's marriage to Pocahontas (1614) effected peace with the Native Americans (at least until the uprising of 1622) and matters took a turn for the better. When a group of young "maides" arrived in 1620—the settlement had been a largely masculine semimilitary outpost earlier—the seeds for a permanent colony were planted. Jamestown became the capital of an "empire" that extended "from sea to sea " via James I's expanded Charter of 1609. Most of New England, with its later Pilgrim colonies, was, of course, Northern Virginia (38° to 45° parallel north).

To celebrate the 350th anniversary of the founding of the town, the original palisaded fort, 420 feet/128 meters on the river side, 300 feet/91 meters on the other two, was reconstructed as closely as archeological research and contemporary descriptions permitted (but on a site near to, not on top of, the original town). What we see today is thus an off-site reproduction, but it was carried out with great care, and the results give us a good impression of this early architecture. The more than a dozen buildings reflect post-medieval English prototypes, modified by available materials. A sturdy, squared oak and pine frame (most revealingly expressed in the storehouse interior) constitutes the structure, with walls of mud-daubed wattle and roof of thatch. Well worth a look—and don't forget to inspect the transportation.

Located 10.8 miles/16.4 kilometers southwest of Jamestown. Open daily 9:00 A.M.–5:00 P.M. Closed Christmas and New Year's Day. Admission is $9.00 for adults, $4.25 for children ages 6–12, free for children under 6. For more information call (804) 229–1607.

PALACE OF THE GOVERNORS
(1610–12)
The Plaza
Santa Fe, New Mexico

Santa Fe, founded in 1607, is the second oldest continuously inhabited city in the United States. (St. Augustine, Florida—see page 28—was established in 1565; Jamestown, Virginia—see page 31—was settled in 1607 but abandoned late in the seventeenth century.) At 6,990 feet/2,131 meters above sea level Santa Fe is also the highest state capital. Spaniards from Mexico City, with Don Pedro de Peralta as governor, founded the city, which in 1610 was officially named La Villa Real de la Santa Fe de San Francisco de Asís. They immediately commenced construction of a large presidio or military compound—Casas Reales—containing "Palace," barracks, chapel (possibly later), administrative offices, and services. The presidio's overall measurements were approximately 400 x 800 feet/122 x 244 meters. The Palace itself measures 240 x 36 feet/73 x 11 meters. (In the late 1860s it was shortened a bit for a road program.) The rooms on the front of its stretched rectangular plan overlook the historic plaza; those on the rear open onto an enclosed patio. The presidio of which the building originally formed one part has long since vanished. The one-story facade did not initially have the sheltering *portales*, and it is not known precisely when this peristyle was added. Several eighteenth-century maps indicate, roughly, an arcade, but the only definite knowledge starts with the Mexican period (1821). It is likely that the first building looked somewhat like today's Old Spanish Governor's Palace of 1749 in San Antonio, Texas.

During and after the Pueblo Revolt of 1680 all of the Casas Reales was heavily damaged and the Spanish forced to flee southward. In 1693 the town was retaken and the buildings repaired. In 1909 the ancient structure was given to the Museum of New Mexico—itself created that year—and major (and questionable) repairs undertaken (1911–13). Since then a thorough, long-term restoration has taken place under the museum's auspices and the splendid result today shows the Palace in its evolution from Colonial structure through its Victorian period.

Although there is little architectural distinction in the Palace of the Governors, as an index of very early Spanish-Pueblo building it gives valuable insight into the conditions of some 380 years ago. And it is, of course, our "oldest surviving non-Indian building" (Hugh Morrison, *Early American Architecture*, Oxford University Press, 1952). Its construction traditions go back, perhaps, to a thousand years, adobe—earth—being the basic wall material. The Pueblos had applied adobe in layers until the Spanish showed them the more efficient brick form. Vigas—tree trunks that could be handled by two men—formed roof beams. As is obvious, these often project beyond the eaves. The adobe-viga tradition became so strong that in Santa Fe today there are architectural ordinances to maintain such traditional building appearances.

Be certain to see the other parts of the Museum of New Mexico (adjacent to the Palace). Incidentally, the museum allows Native Americans only (mostly Pueblos) to sell their handmade jewelry and other artifacts in the arcade of the Palace.

Open daily 10:00 A.M.–5:00 P.M.; closed Mondays in January and February. Closed for holidays. Admission is $4 for adults, free for children 16 and under.

PLIMOTH PLANTATION RE-CREATION (1627/1957–76)
137 Warren Avenue
Plymouth, Massachusetts

No archeological foundations or historic graphic material existed for this re-creation of the first Pilgrim settlement (as was the case, for instance, at Williamsburg, Virginia—see page 54—and New Bern, North Carolina—see page 106); there were, however, copious and invaluable inventories. And, as has since been proved, research for the first buildings in the village is now outdated. As the administration puts it,

> In historical accuracy, the most recently constructed dwellings at Plimoth Plantation have a considerable advantage over earlier attempts due to new research. This research, done by Richard Candee and Cary Carson, among others, combined with archaeological information gathered by Dr. James Deetz, has revealed that the most probable design for the houses of 1627 would have been the "posthole" style of construction. This construction uses a frame of heavy oak timbers with sunken corner posts and studs between them that support a wattle-and-daub cladding on the walls, a chimney of the same material, and a heavy reed thatch roof. The clay daub walls are protected from New England weather by an outer layer of riven cedar clapboards fastened to the studs. Other village structures such as the fort, with its thick sawn boards, display other techniques. This village is a living example of seventeenth-century rural life with animal houses, pens and gardens inhabited by animals, and costumed individuals who take on the identities of the original settlers.

With regard to Plymouth Rock (at Water Street in the town), the Colonies' first Thanksgiving was not given here in 1621, as claimed, but in Berkeley Plantation on the James River in the Old Dominion in 1619, where "the day of our ship's arrival . . . shall be yearly and perpetually kept as a day of Thanksgiving." To quote the *Virginia State Guide* (Oxford University Press, 1964), "Virginia narrowly escaped an invasion of the Pilgrim Fathers. . . . Thrown off their course, the Pilgrims set foot on a rock off the coast of northern Virginia." The guide errs somewhat in that the destination was northern Virginia, then near the mouth of the Hudson River: actually the Pilgrims set foot in the New England Grant. To conclude matters, it was not until

1789 that the first national day of Thanksgiving was inaugurated. President Washington proclaimed the day "not in response to the bounties of the harvest but in gratitude for the establishment of the Constitution of the United States" (*Plimoth Plantation Bulletin*). However, not until Lincoln's time—1863—was the last Thursday of November properly set aside.

Located off MA 3 via Plimoth Plantation Highway 3 miles/4.8 kilometers south of Plymouth. April–November open daily 9:00 A.M.–5:00 P.M. Closed December–March. Admission to Plimoth Plantation is $15 for adults, $9 for children ages 6–12. Admission to Mayflower II is $5.75 for adults, $3.75 for children ages 6–12. A combined admission ticket is $18.50 for adults, $11 for children ages 6–12. All tours are self-guided. For more information call (508) 746-1622.

SAN ESTÉVAN (1629–42)
NM 23
Ácoma, New Mexico

The acropolis of Ácoma, verily a city on a hill, is the most dramatically situated pueblo in the country. Surveying a terrain of petrified desolation, its height and steep escarpments have offered protection, hence encouraged settlement, for perhaps two millennia, making it probably the oldest continuously inhabited town in the United States (a distinction that the now crumbling and semiabandoned Oraibi pueblo disputes). (Many dwellings have been partially abandoned as inhabitants have moved to farms on the plain and return mainly for summer or for festivals.) Today, it is readily accessible to motorists via good gravel roads, including one to the top, and it welcomes visitors graciously. (However, be certain to get permission—for a fee—to take photographs or videos or to sketch.)

Ácoma's soilless sandstone mesa, roughly 70 acres/28 hectares in extent, rises some 357 feet/109 meters above the plains and 7,000 feet/2,134 meters above sea level; it is appropriately called "The Sky City." The village's natural defenses are strengthened on the north side by a near-solid lineup of contiguous houses of one to three stories in height that stretch approximately 770 feet/235 meters near the edge of the bluff. These are (or were originally) windowless on the side facing out. Two other rows of stone and adobe cellular dwellings, in roughly parallel lines but more casually dispersed, made up the rest of the urban pattern until 1629. Then the Spanish, who had taken over the village in 1640, built on its south edge the

first church, San Estévan, setting up an antipodal contrast of buildings for conqueror and conquered on opposite sides of an invisible line. The Spaniards did not want their building to impinge upon the village. There is, however, a lack of spatial organization, or even proper plazas for ritual dancing, in the basic layout of Ácoma. In addition to the three lanes of houses there are seven rectangular kivas for the men. All material for building, from adobe and stone to the great beams for the church, had to be lugged to the top via precipitous paths, as the mesa itself offers only bare rock, defense, and views to its inhabitants.

As the Native Americans had few tools to dress stone, and lacked the skill (and the wood for formwork) to construct arches and vaults, the churches of the region were thick-walled, narrow, flat-roofed buildings with few side windows (and these, as at Ácoma, changed occasionally), and sometimes a high transverse transept window illuminating the sanctuary. The Native Americans' building procedures were simple: adobe for walls, and trunks, branches, and packed earth for roofs. Arches and domes were never used in early New Mexico or by Native Americans anywhere except with bent reeds. (Compare the much later vaulted churches in Texas and California.)

San Estévan typifies these building characteristics, and, with its front "yard," its raised cemetery, and its attached convento for resident Franciscan friars, it attains a rough grandeur on the outside and offers a regional treat within. Its nave is long (126 feet/38 meters) and narrow (31 feet/9.4 meters) and without transept, but with a pronounced taper at the chancel, culminating in a painted reredos. As the vigas, here undressed trunks some 37 feet/11 meters long, had to be hauled from forests 20–30 miles/32–48 kilometers away, a restricted nave width was inevitable. These beams were placed atop the stone and adobe walls—how such weights were lifted is not precisely known—and given added bearing by outsized corbels, often fancifully painted. The wooden beams used for the altar were also brought from faraway forests, and for religious reasons were not to touch the ground—"a sacrilege" (Mary Katrine Sedgwick, *Ácoma: The Sky City*, Harvard University Press, 1927). The walls themselves are of great thickness (up to 7.8 feet/2.4 meters), tapering at the top. The building's plan was inevitable; San Estévan had the same ancestry and reflected the same rationale as village churches in Mexico, whose tradition was carried by the padres up the Rio Grande to find expression in New Mexican examples. (New Mexico was so called in the sixteenth century; after Florida it bears the oldest state name.)

San Estévan underwent repairs and small changes through the generations (two windows in the apse were at one time put in and then subsequently walled up), but for much of the last hundred years it has needed more attention than it has received. Undoubtedly parts of the first church (1629) are incorporated in the one we see today, for beams and stone brought to place with such travail were not likely to be thrown away. The Pueblo Revolt of 1680–92, during which many churches and Spanish buildings were ransacked and incinerated, seemingly left it largely in peace. In 1924 the Committee for the Preservation and Restoration of New Mexican Mission Churches undertook major repairs, including a hidden concrete roof. Restoration has been very active of late. One of the great chapters of Native American life and Spanish religious influence, Ácoma is, of course, a National Historic Landmark. (George Kubler in his admirable book *The Religious Architecture of New Mexico*, 1940, reprinted by Rio Grande Press in 1962, offers expert background on all the Hispanic churches in the state. Also recommended is *The Missions of New Mexico*, 1776, Francesco Atanasio Dominguez, translated by Adams and Chavez, University of New Mexico Press, 1956.)

Located 13 miles/21 kilometers southwest of I-40 at Casa Blanca exit, via NM 23. Open daily April–October 8:00 A.M.–7:00 P.M., November–March 8:00 A.M.–4:30 P.M. Closed for some Native American holidays (including July 10–13 and the first weekend in October). Admission is $6 for adults, $5 for senior citizens, $4 for children ages 6–17, free for children under 6. One-hour guided walking tours given daily. For more information call (800) 747-0181.

ST. LUKE'S CHURCH (c. 1632–65)
14477 Benn's Church Boulevard (VA 10)
Smithfield, Virginia

St. Luke's Church proclaims itself to be "The Nation's Oldest Standing Church" and most historians are inclined to agree. The National Register of Historic Places gives its date as 1632. But even if we use the date of 1682 (favored by only a few), St. Luke's is the oldest church in the United States of Gothic derivation that has come down to us essentially as built. Moreover, at nearby Jamestown stands the tower of a brick church constructed there in 1639–47, so it would certainly seem probable that St. Luke's was completed around the early–middle seventeenth century. When speaking of the age of the nation's churches, it is illuminating to read Hugh Morrison in his admirable *Early American Architecture* (Oxford University Press, 1952), who writes, "By 1626 43 churches had been built" by the Spanish in New Mexico. However, none of these survive as constructed, with the probable exception of parts of San Estévan at Ácoma, 1629–42 (see page 34).

The square, almost Norman tower of St. Luke's, the stepped Flemish gables, the round-headed windows with two lancets, the buttresses, the startling interior with its timber trusswork and tie beams and its rood screen—all these elements when put together suggest a medieval south English parish church. There is a primitiveness about it, but the results are ingenuous.

In the late seventeenth century the church was modernized on the interior by plastering over the medieval ceiling and, outside, by adding a story and the quoins to the tower. After disestablishment it languished, in 1821 it was reactivated, in the early middle of the nineteenth century it was semiabandoned, and in 1887 a storm severely injured the roof, causing it to be replaced. In 1953–57, the church was declared a National Shrine. Following the discovery of crumbling foundations and lower walls, and after four years of research, it was meticulously restored to its conjectural original condition. This was based on contemporary English precedent, with the strange exception of the late-nineteenth-century stained glass instead of clear diamond panes, which the first church undoubtedly had. The church is a primitive but illuminating building. As Professor William B. O'Neal points out in his *Architecture in Virginia* (Virginia Museum, 1968), "St. Luke's is the only *original* Gothic building to have survived in the nation."

Located 4 miles/6.4 kilometers southeast of Smithfield, near southwest end of James River Bridge. Open Tuesday–Saturday 9:30 A.M.–4:00 P.M., Sunday 1:00–4:00 P.M. Closed on Mondays, holidays, and the month of January. All visits are guided; free tours given daily. For more information call (804) 357-3367.

HENRY WHITFIELD HOUSE (1639)
248 Old Whitfield Street at Stonehouse Lane
Guilford, Connecticut

The oldest remaining house in Connecticut and the oldest stone house still standing in New England, this ancient dwelling suggests England's Cotswolds, though most of Master Henry Whitfield's Puritan group were from Surrey and Kent (south and southeast of London). Stone was surprisingly little used in rocky New England, for wood was cheaper, easier to work, and offered better insulation. Also, lime for mortar was scarce. Though what we see today represents less than a third of the original Whitfield House, the dwelling remains a fascinating example of seventeenth-century housing. It was built to serve not only as a home but also as a fort. The outer walls range in thickness from 18 to nearly 30 inches (46–76 centimeters), with most of the ground floor taken up by the great hall, some 33 feet/10 meters long and 15 feet/4.6 meters wide. An unusual overhead hinged partition added in the 1930s—which was also used to cut the cross draft set up between opposing fireplaces—can be lowered to divide this lengthy room. Although the south fireplace was not added until 1868, the wall and giant chimney at the north end, whose fireplace occupies almost the full width of the room, are nearly all original, as are about half of the facade and part of the east wall. Most of the rest is restored.

Adjoining as an ell to the main room is the hall or parlor chamber and the stair hall, while above are chambers and a garret. The whole is topped by a roof sharply pitched at an angle of sixty degrees. Additions and changes, including stucco-covered walls from an early date, were made to the house by its various owners through subsequent centuries. Fires demolished parts of the house at least twice but it was always rebuilt—most recently under private ownership in 1868. The state of Connecticut acquired the Whitfield dwelling in 1900. An architect of the time, Norman Isham, prepared the building for use as a museum, removing the second floor to make a large exhibit hall, but it was not until the 1930s that the late J. Frederick Kelly,

a leading expert in old New England architecture, completed (1937), with a minimum of conjecture, the restoration we now see. The furnishings, some English and some American, cover a time span of well over one hundred years. A fine herb garden adjacent to the house shows plants that were in common use in the seventeenth and eighteenth centuries.

1 February–14 December open Wednesday–Sunday 10:00 A.M.–4:30 P.M. 15 December–31 January open by appointment only. Closed Good Friday, Thanksgiving, Christmas, and New Year's Day. Admission is $3 for adults and $1.50 for children ages 6–17 and senior citizens. A brief introductory talk is given upon arrival. Guided tours can be arranged by calling (203) 453–2457.

SAUGUS IRON WORKS NATIONAL HISTORIC SITE
(1646/1948–54)
244 Central Street
Saugus, Massachusetts

This reconstruction of the earliest ironworks in the American colonies, generously financed by the American Iron and Steel Institute, stands high on the list of historic re-creations of industrial beginnings. (An earlier ironworks at Falling Creek, Virginia, was ready to begin operations in 1622 but the workers were killed by Native Americans and the project abandoned.) Restored by Henry Charles Dean, buttressed with technical consultants, and utilizing archeological thoroughness, the ironworks at Saugus gives an illuminating insight into the earliest industrial groundwork of this country. Though the ironworks itself lasted only some twenty years—high production costs, low capital, and lack of skilled labor occasioned its downfall—the foundation of the future nation's iron and steel industry was established here. Six years of patient research and informed conjecture were needed for the complicated technological facets of this reconstruction, as excavations revealed only limited traces of the original. Today, with wheels wheeling and forges forging in simulated operation, the results are fascinating.

In addition to the technological restoration, the nearby Iron Works House (earlier known as the Appleton-Taylor-Mansfield House) is itself very worthy of a visit. It has been standing on the same spot since around 1680 and was continually occupied until 1915. Radically altered through the years, it was restored by Wallace Nutting beginning in 1915. The ironworks and house are now under the aegis of the National Park Service.

May–October open daily 9:00 A.M.–5:00 P.M., November–April open daily 9:00 A.M.–4:00 P.M. Closed Thanksgiving, Christmas, and New Year's Day. Admission is free. During May–October one-hour tours are given daily at 9:45 A.M., 11:15 A.M. 2:15 P.M., and 3:45 P.M. For more information call (617) 233–0050.

OLD HOUSE (1649)
Cases Lane
Cutchogue, Long Island, New York

Eastern Long Island, puzzlingly, did not develop in the Colonial period as did much of New England. With good harbors at Greenport and Sag Harbor, excellent soil, and a sea-moderated climate, it is surprising that greater advantage was not taken of these natural blessings. A number of settlers from the New Haven Colony (of which Cutchogue was a part) and from Connecticut (which absorbed the former in 1665) came over, but their influx, seemingly, was never great. The oldest dwelling that they left, probably the oldest still standing in New York State, is this venerable number: one of the States' major examples of English-inspired domestic building. The facade of Old House, also known as the Horton-Wickham-Landon-Case House, is attended by a rakish quality that stems from its slight cant to the windward (largely fixed in 1990 when the foundation was repaired). The small wave of its shingled roof and eaves (reflected in the curved door lintel), the untethered character of its clapboards (no framing by corner boards), plus a doll's-house window over the front door epitomize a wood skin pierced by openings. A massive, paneled chimney of English inspiration and three-division, diamond-paned windows complete the exterior scene. (Two original triple casements were found in the north wall.) Sea grass and clay were used for insulation. About one hundred years ago barn doors and large windows were cut in its 40-foot/12-meter side (it is 20.5 feet/6.2 meters deep) and it was used as a barn until 1939. At that time the Case family sold the property to the Independent Congregational Church and Society of Cutchogue with the express provision that the house be given to the people of the town. The village itself paid none of the costs. The house, with its bundled chimneys, was then completely restored and refurnished to commemorate the town's tricentennial in 1940. Reputedly built in 1649 in Southold, 5 miles/8 kilometers to the northeast, it was moved to this site in 1659 as the wedding present of the then owner to his daughter.

Located one block south of NY 25. June and September open Saturday–Sunday 2:00–5:00 P.M. July and August open Saturday–Monday 2:00–5:00 P.M. Visits can be arranged in May–October by calling (516) 734–7122. Admission is $1.50 for adults, 50¢ for children under 12. Informal tours are available.

JOHN WHIPPLE HOUSE (c. 1655/c. 1670/c. 1700)
1 South Village Green
Ipswich, Massachusetts

In the John Whipple House we find a good evolutionary example of the "growing" house so often seen in early New England. However, the Whipple House is also unusual in that all the stages of its expansion took place within a forty-five year period, which is much shorter than the standard. Initially the dwelling started life as a two-and-one-half-story box with one room per floor covered then as now by a steeply pitched roof in the post-medieval English tradition. Some years later (c. 1670), a slightly larger section was added to make four rooms; a lean-to ell at the rear followed around 1700. Considering its very early date, its two main rooms are unusually spacious, its hall (also known as the "great room") outstanding. Note, however, that the enormous summer beam, which longitudinally bisects the older part, is supported by cross bracing above the end windows instead of having its weight transferred directly to the ground by an upright post; this ingenious solution allowed for a centrally placed window. Note also that there is no overhang across the front of the house—resulting in a close-cropping—but two at the east gable end.

In the mid-1720s the house was made Georgian, which included cutting off the facade gables, replacing the casement windows with double-hung sash windows, and adding plaster ceilings. The house (then in deplorable shape) was purchased by the Ipswich Historical Society in 1898, restored on its original site and opened to the public the next year. In 1927 it was moved from the center of town across the river to the present location, and in 1953–54 it was again restored. The garden was designed c. 1950–57 by Arthur A. Shurcliff (of Williamsburg fame), who decided on its placement and layout, and Ann Leighton, who chose the plantings based on extensive research (including a 1683 inventory of the Whipple House, which lists its garden "products" then on the shelf). She planted only the typical flowers and herbs raised domestically in the seventeenth century when gardens were basically for function (remedies, seasoning, and dyes), not looks. The house is discussed in detail in Abott L. Cummings's book *The Framed Houses of Massachusetts Bay, 1625–1725* (Harvard University Press, 1979).

Open May to mid-October, Wednesday–Saturday 10:00 A.M.–4:00 P.M., Sunday 1:00–4:00 P.M. Admission is $5 for adults, $2 for children ages 6–12; the admission ticket also includes entry to the nearby Federal-style John Heard House. All visits are guided; tours given every hour on the hour. For more information call (508) 356–2811.

BACON'S CASTLE (c. 1656)
Route VA 10
Surry, Virginia

The almost legendary Bacon's Castle is now fortunately open to the public for at least part of the year. *Preservation News* (of the National Trust) terms the castle "the sole surviving high Jacobean manor house in America" (January 1974), so it is doubly welcome that it can be seen. The Jacobean was an elusive period of English (hence early Colonial) architecture, emerging largely during the reign of James I (1603–25) but picking up the thread of development begun under his predecessor, the redoubtable Elizabeth I. Under James, it moved away from the transitional Tudor style toward greater employment of newly fashionable Renaissance motifs, especially in details. It never fully established itself, however. What it lacked in finesse it sought to assert in bravura. There are awkward moments in the Jacobean—even the use of the Greek *Jakobōs* (James) seems odd—but it made for a spirited scene in domestic building.

At Bacon's Castle (actually built by a man named Arthur Allen) the two boldly curvilinear gable ends, recalling Flemish work, are topped by three square semidetached chimney flues set on the diagonal and rising with Tudor-Jacobean conviction. Note the unusual cross plan of the house with gabled "porches," a typical medieval feature.

In 1856 the dwelling was substantially expanded to the east by uncongenial additions. Partial restoration took place in 1939–41, but by that time the house had lost much of its original medievalism (the casement windows, for example). Also gone is the original roof, which some believe was of stone tiles, as one of them has been discovered. The interior has been altered but the superb paneling installed around 1740 fortunately remains. Note, also, the two original fireplaces with their heavy wood beams finished with a chamfer and "lambs tongue."

Nathaniel Bacon (1647–76), incidentally, organized the first armed rebellion against British authority (the tyranny of Governor William Berkeley) ninety-nine years before the battles of Lexington and Concord. His troops' use of Allen's house in 1676 gave it its subsequent sobriquet. Bacon died during the campaign (of either malaria or poison) but his actions were influential in initiating an "American" consciousness.

Bacon's Castle and 40 acres/16 hectares of land were purchased in 1973 by the Association for the Preservation of Virginia Antiquities. As Professor William H. Pierson, Jr., put it, "Bacon's Castle is a milestone in the history of the Virginia Colony" (*American Buildings and Their Architects*, Doubleday, 1970).

Located off VA 10 just northeast of Surry on VA 617. April–October open Tuesday–Saturday 10:00 A.M.–4:00 P.M., Sunday 12:00 noon–4:00 P.M. November and March open Saturday 10:00 A.M.–4:00 P.M., Sunday 12:00 noon–4:00 P.M. Admission is $5 for adults, $4 for senior citizens, $3 for students, $2 for children ages 6–18. 40-minute tours of the house and 90-minute tours of the house and grounds are available. For more information call (804) 357-5976.

CASTILLO DE SAN MARCOS (1672–95/1738–62)
1 Castillo Drive East (US 1) at the Mantanzas River
St. Augustine, Florida

The Spanish, who were the first Europeans to settle permanently in what came to be the United States, made several determined but futile efforts to set up shop on the New World's mainland before finally establishing a base at St. Augustine in 1565. (Spain was well organized in the West Indies by the early decades of the sixteenth century, having built a fort and town— Isabela, now in the Dominican Republic—following Christopher Columbus's second voyage in 1494.) Juan Ponce de León, who had settled in Puerto Rico (1508), landed in Florida with colonists and cattle near present-day Charlotte Harbor (1521) but Native Americans soon drove him back. In 1526 Spain took five hundred men, women, children, slaves, and animals to Winyah Bay near Georgetown, South Carolina, but they, too, because of Native Americans,

disease, and bad winter, were forced to return to their West Indian base. The Spanish, alarmed by the French Fort Caroline (1564) at the mouth of the St. John's River (near today's Jacksonville), wanted a fortified settlement in Florida to prevent further European incursions. The struggle for bases in Florida was initially between the Spanish and French, but the English burned St. Augustine in 1586, and then continued to move southward down the coast. To counter this movement, the Spanish ordered the construction of an impregnable stone fort (previous ones of wood were of short life and little value). Work began in 1672 and it lasted for many arduous years.

Massive, businesslike, yet strangely elegant, the Castillo de San Marcos (at one time called "Fort Marion") stands as the finest and oldest example of military architecture in the United States. The star-shaped Castillo was designed by Ignacio Daza; it was probably inspired by the principles for bastioned fortifications worked out by Francesco de Marchi (1490–1574) and modified by Italo-Spanish and Dutch examples—with perhaps additional influence from Sébastien de Vauban, whose first *Mémoire* appeared in 1669. It was as successful as it is handsome, never having been taken in battle—though bitterly besieged—and was used as recently as the Spanish-American War to house disciplinary cases.

The fort, which is constructed of coquina, the local shell-based marine stone, was built on the edge of Matanzas Bay around a square courtyard with four-sided, spearlike bastions projecting diagonally at each corner. A 40-foot-/12-meter-wide moat surrounds the whole. The thickness of the scarp, or outer wall, ranges from 13 feet/4 meters at base to nearly 5 feet/1.5 meters at the top of the parapet, which is approximately 30 feet/9.1 meters above the moat. (Until the 1738–40 strengthening, the walls were only 20 feet/6.1 meters high.) To provide sustenance against siege, wells were dug in the courtyard and several of the fort's twenty rooms were used for storing food. The garrison and the people of the village were to rely on these on several desperate occasions.

Modernization of the fort was carried out in three stages: 1738–40, when the previously wooden gun deck, or terreplein, on the east side was replaced by arched masonry walls that could withstand bombardment; 1752–56, when the other three sides were vaulted; and 1762, when the ravelin (a triangular outwork) in front of the gate was enlarged. The fort was made a national monument in 1924, and today, thanks to the National Park Service, is in grand shape. One of the world's great forts, it is among the chief secular inheritances of the Spanish occupation in the United States.

Open daily 8:30 A.M.–5:30 P.M. (last ticket sold at 4:45 P.M.). Closed Christmas. Admission is $2 for adults, free for children 16 and under if accompanied by an adult.

OLD TRINITY CHURCH (c. 1675)
1718 Taylor's Island Road
Cambridge, Maryland

This gem of a small church (38 x 20 feet/12 x 6 meters nave) is set amid an ancient cemetery and along the water that served as a highway for most of the early congregations. One of the oldest churches in the country in continuous active use, it is one of the finest buildings open to the public on Maryland's Eastern Shore. The exterior, though possessed of a certain quaint-ness, carries little architectural distinction, being primarily a simple rectangle with steeply gabled roof. A small semicircular apse (note the neat wood shingle pattern) stirs up this geom-etry, while the burnt headers of the brick add a touch of interest, but the framing and mullions of all windows, while authentic, are weighty. The interior, however, is a pure delight, with a towering, bare wood pulpit in the midst of the congregation on the left wall, surrounded by unpainted box pews. A delicate brass chandelier hangs over the aisle, a fine complement to the wood, to the square bricks of the floor (mostly original), and to the white plastered walls. The church suffered grievously in the 1850s when it was "modernized in the Gothic style," but from 1953 to 1960 it was meticulously restored to its seventeenth-century condition through the generosity of the late Colonel and Mrs. Edgar W. Garbisch, who formerly lived nearby. The restoration's architectural consultant was Louis Osman of London.

Located .9 mile/1.4 kilometers west of Church Creek, off MD 16, 6.3 miles/10 kilometers southwest of Cambridge (take US 50 to Cambridge, then take route 16W for 8 miles). Open Saturday 10:00 A.M.–4:00 P.M. and Sunday 1:00–4:00 P.M. May–October also open Monday, Wednesday, and Friday 10:00 A.M.–4:00 P.M. All other times open by appointment with the rectory at (410) 228–3583. Admission is free, but a donation is suggested. Guided tours available.

OLD MARYLAND STATE HOUSE (1676/1934)
MD 5
St. Mary's City, Maryland

Maryland, under the famous Calvert family, was established as a colony at St. Mary's City in 1634, when some hundred and fifty weary souls stepped ashore from the Ark and the Dove. They had left England in November and did not reach their destination until March. St. Mary's thus became the capital of the new colony and remained such until the government was moved to the more accessible Annapolis in 1695. Isolated geographically near the end of the peninsula where the Potomac enters Chesapeake Bay, and bypassed politically when it lost the seat of power, St. Mary's City entered into a long period of amiable desuetude. When Maryland celebrated its tricentennial in 1934 one of the most laudable acts associated with this birthday was the reconstruction of the statehouse. The original Jacobean building (1676) had been razed in 1829, and its locally made bricks were used to construct Trinity Church. The present reconstruction (1934), therefore, sits near, not on, the spot on which the first structure arose, but it is precisely of its dimensions (measured from the existing foundations) and appearance (known from early documents). Much of the hardware was copied from appropriate prototypes in Annapolis. The two-story result, of modified Greek cross plan and slightly medieval exterior, forms one of the handful of distinguished buildings of the colonies that survived (or, as here, derived from) the seventeenth century. The large ground-floor assembly hall (some 45 x 30 feet/14 x 9 meters) dominates the interior. (It served as a chapel when the capital was moved.) The top floor holds a replica of the former council chamber and a room that was probably originally a waiting room. With hospitable Native Americans, rich soil, and—thanks to Lord Baltimore (Cecilius Calvert)—unprecedented religious freedom (as long as it was Christian—the good Lord was probably also motivated by a desire for more colonists), Maryland was—and is—a favored land, and the well-laid-out city of St. Mary's a picturesque palimpsest of its beginning. Plans are under way to continue preservation and restoration, including a reconstructed Dove.

The Old State House is part of the Historic St. Mary's City Museum. The museum is open 25 March–the last weekend in November, Wednesday–Sunday 10:00 A.M.–5:00 P.M. Admission is $6.50 for adults, $6 for senior citizens and students, $3.25 for children ages 6–12. Group tours can be scheduled by calling (301) 862–0990.

ADAM THOROUGHGOOD HOUSE (c. 1680)
1636 Parish Road
Norfolk, Virginia

On a creek of Lynnhaven Bay, and only a short distance from the Chesapeake, stands one of the oldest brick houses in the United States. It is one of the oldest of any material. (Compare the much-added-to wood-frame Fairbanks House, c. 1637, at Dedham, Massachusetts; St. Augustine's oldest house obviously dates from post-1702 when the British sacked and burned the town.) The Thoroughgood House is a minuscule, medieval affair, one and one-half stories high, girdled by two T-shaped chimneys. The one at right (south) is set on the outside of the wall and marked by four belt courses, the second of which wraps around the house at its eaves to define the upper floor level. The chimney at left lies within the wall to warm the house better (this is the north end). (Compare the great central chimneys of New England.) Brick set in English bond encloses the two sides and the wall facing the river, but the front wall is of the more exacting Flemish bond. The texture is rich, the sharp slope of the gabled roof, now covered with fireproof tiles but of oak shingles originally, medieval, and the whole picturesque. Note the low door and the high-set windows. This dwelling represents a distinct advance over the earlier ones built in the colonies.

There are only two rooms on each floor, with a "hall" (living room/kitchen) and parlor downstairs; a passage and stair were added in 1745 at the time the bedrooms were converted from the original loft area. In 1957 the house was purchased by the city of Norfolk and completely restored; the facade was returned to two windows from three, the late dormers were removed, and the window sash was changed from double-hung to casement. (The largest casements found in the seventeenth century measure only 1 x 2 feet/.3 x .6 meter.)

The Thoroughgood House has been thoughtfully furnished in the late-seventeenth-/early-eighteenth-century fashion, while its garden, with excellent box hedging, has been put back in fine if hypothetical condition. There is little stylistic importance to the Thoroughgood House—it is not high fashion—but it is very useful in showing the survival, with only small adaptations, of English medieval traditions in the earliest American colony.

Take I-64 to Northampton Boulevard, right on Pleasure House Road, then left on Thoroughgood Drive to Parish Road, 8 miles/13 kilometers east of Norfolk. January–March open Tuesday–Saturday 8:00 A.M.–5:00 P.M.; April–December open Tuesday–Saturday 10:00 A.M.–5:00 P.M. and Sunday 12:00 noon–5:00 P.M. Closed New Year's Day, Independence Day, Thanksgiving, and Christmas. Admission is $2 for adults, $1 for senior citizens and children ages 6–18, free for military personnel. A thirty-minute guided tour is included with admission.

VAN CORTLANDT MANOR (c. 1680/1750–1815)
South Riverside Avenue
Croton-on-Hudson, New York

The early Dutch settlements along the Hudson River, which the Lowlanders craftily established as far as Albany, provided that lovely region's earliest and most picturesque domestic types. (Henry Hudson anchored in the river in 1609, while Fort Nassau was built in 1614.) However, the Treaty of Westminster in 1674 gave New Netherland to the English, creating an Anglo-Dutch cultural influence, and a century later, when the lower Hudson became a battleground during the American Revolution, the fighting destroyed and injured much, including the Van Cortlandt Manor.

The earliest part of the house (c. 1680) with 3-foot-/.9-meter-thick sandstone walls probably stems from a pre-Van Cortlandt trading post at the confluence of the Hudson and Croton rivers. Beginning in the 1740s Pierre Van Cortlandt and his wife added a second floor and other improvements and the house was made a permanent home instead of a hunting lodge and trade station. The porch wrapping three sides dates from the same mid-eighteenth-century period. During the Revolution the family had to flee Tory attacks, and when able to return after the war they found the house ill served and in immediate need of attention. Much of the finer work that we see today (the paneling in the main rooms, for instance) dates from this period. The house remained in the family for 200 years (until 1945), and through the generations changes and additions were made, and so although there is not purity in the Van Cortlandt Manor, there is unusual continuity—and appeal. The house, much original furniture, outbuildings, and gardens were purchased through the generosity of John D. Rockefeller, Jr. in 1953, and all has been put back (1953–59) into shape of the 1750–1815 period. Be sure to see the grounds, the restored ferry house, and the reconstructed tenant house.

Located .3 mile/.5 kilometer off NY 9A. April–December open Wednesday–Monday 10:30 A.M.–4:30 P.M. Closed Thanksgiving and Christmas. Admission is $7 for adults, $6 for senior citizens, $4 for children ages 6–17, free for children under 6. Tours given every half hour. For more information call (914) 271–8981.

OLD SHIP MEETING HOUSE (1681–1755)
90 Main Street
Hingham, Massachusetts

As the only surviving relic of the squarish, clapboarded meeting houses of the late seventeenth century, Old Ship ranks high in importance historically and esthetically. It is, moreover, the oldest wooden church in the United States and claims to be the oldest in continuous use. (The seating plan of its 1681 dedication still survives.) The exterior takes advantage of its hillock location, with diamond-paned windows on its broad sides (the top sashes meet the eaves), a hip roof with gently upcurved ridges, and a railed platform at the roof summit, with a belfry spire that carries the sweep of the ridges heavenward. Yet it is the interior that is most fascinating, an interior far more "Gothic" than its clapboarded sides suggest.

Squarish in plan and surrounded by balconies on three sides, the inner space rises to a magnificent framework of three oak trusses and knee braces that uphold the roof with a display of Gothic wood engineering that gave the meeting house its name: inverted, the upper part would resemble the ribs of a ship. This medieval structure—the most efficient means then of spanning such an ambitious width—defines its space to create a memorable interior. The original meeting house, now demarked by the columns upholding the balconies and roof trusses, measured 45 x 55 feet/14 x 17 meters and was entered from the southwest. In 1729–31 the church was extended 14 feet/4.3 meters to the northeast, and in 1755 an equal distance to the southwest, making it 55 x 73 feet/17 x 22 meters overall. This, of necessity, involved a new roof extending above and beyond the old, creating thus a dead "attic" between old roof and new. In 1930 the church was completely restored (by Edgar T. P. Walker of Smith & Walker), and a dropped ceiling was taken out so that the interior structure now stands revealed as it was three hundred years ago. (The low ceiling had been installed only fifty years after completion to reduce the frigid air volume in a stoveless room, particularly with the new lateral expansion.) The restoration left the expansions and pulpit—dating from the mid-eighteenth century—as is.

One hundred years after its completion (1780), the town's civic gatherings were moved elsewhere, and the meeting house became completely religious. In 1791, the parishioners, feeling that their church was old-fashioned compared to the new style of Christopher Wren, voted to tear down the building, a vote that happily was countermanded a year later. They did vote, however, to add the 10 x 10 foot/3 x 3 meter vestibule in front, which is now in use. One of the nation's boldest early buildings.

July–August open daily 12:00 noon–4:00 P.M. September–June open by appointment only; call (617) 749–1679 to arrange a visit. Free 15-minute tours are available.

PARSON CAPEN HOUSE (1683)
1 Howlett Street
Topsfield, Massachusetts

Built in the medieval fashion of its day, and nestled on a low ridge with an enormous ash tree in front and oaks and maples on the side, this picturesque house numbers high among the slender remains of seventeenth-century wooden architecture. (Its precise date of erection, 8 July 1683, is carved on one of the beams.) The unencumbered directness, even purity, of its basic shape is authoritative. Note that its framed overhang projects the second floor 16 inches/41 centimeters over the lower along the front and, at the gable ends, the third floor over the second. Animating what would otherwise have been a simple box form—and visually tying the house to the ground by emphasizing horizontality—these overhangs also demonstrate the skilled heavy carpentry that came to the northern colonies from southeast England. The carved pendants under these overhangs—which also mark the framing of the rooms astride the chimney—are noteworthy. The enclosing clapboards, or "weatherboards" as the English call them, were well known in the mother country, particularly in Kent and Essex.

In plan the ground floor is divided into two slightly unequal rooms that abut a large central chimney fancifully paneled in Tudor fashion. A sizable parlor—as demanded by a parson's duties—occupies the left-hand end while a hall that is kitchen and family room takes up the right. (A reproduction of the kitchen with its 8.3-foot/2.5-meter-wide fireplace was for many years in the American Wing of the Metropolitan Museum of Art.) Bedrooms, reached by the original narrow stairs, occupy the second and third floors; a basement runs beneath. The interior was restored (in 1913–14, by George Francis Dow) to its original (if somewhat theoretical) Puritan condition. Of necessity, much woodwork and all shingles and clapboarding are new. A small museum annex extends at rear. The house is currently owned by the Topsfield Historical Society.

Located at the northeast edge of common. Open mid-June through mid-September, Monday, Friday, Sunday 1:00–4:30 P.M. Also open for tea Wednesday 1:00–4:30 P.M. Open other times by appointment; call (508) 887-3998. Guided tour available. No admission fee, but a donation is requested.

PHILIPSBURG MANOR, UPPER MILLS (c. 1683/1720–50)
381 North Broadway
North Tarrytown, New York

Philipsburg Manor was once part of the enormous holdings of Frederick Philipse (1626–1702), a Dutch carpenter-immigrant turned miller, burgher, and entrepreneur. It was preserved and restored by John D. Rockefeller, Jr., who purchased the 20-acre/8-hectare site in 1940 on hearing of its probable subdivision. The plain but sturdy manor house, begun around 1683, had been added to and tampered with through two centuries. However, its central stone core remained basically intact, and after meticulous study it has been taken back (1943) to its authentic mid-eighteenth century condition. A 1750 inventory listing the contents of all rooms facilitated refurnishing. The second-floor kitchen/dining room is of particular interest. The gristmill, small wharf, and dam had disappeared long before, but archeological excavations uncovered the original foundations, so that general outlines are precise though aboveground appearances are somewhat hypothetical. Even the beams in the reconstruction of the mill were hand-hewn and the nails handmade. Be sure, incidentally, to see the interior of the gristmill; its heavy timbers and wooden gears are fascinating. The dam itself is of oak with stone infilling. The millpond and its birds complete a pastoral scene. Reputedly a century ago there were around fifty thousand operating water mills in the United States. Though relatively few are left today, interest in alternative energy may soon increase their number; Philipsburg Manor offers a fine model.

Located on US 9 at the north edge of North Tarrytown. Open March–December, Wednesday–Monday 10:00 A.M.–5:00 P.M. Closed Thanksgiving and Christmas. Admission is $7 for adults, $6 for senior citizens, $4 for children ages 6–17, free for children under 6. Half-hour tours given every half hour. For more information call (914) 631–3992.

ELEAZER ARNOLD HOUSE (c. 1687/mid–eighteenth century)
487 Great Road (RI 123)
Lincoln, Rhode Island

An obvious primitiveness characterizes the two-and-one-half-story, four-room Arnold house.
A herculean, solid fieldstone wall (original), fairing into a splendid chimney at top, steadies
one entire end of the structure and anchors it against northwest winds. The rest of the
house—called a "stone-ender" in Rhode Island—appends this wall, clutching it for stability
and barely attaining such. Narrow, unpainted clapboards, tiny diamond-paned casements, and
a studded front door (all restored), with the long lean-to of an ell at the rear, mark the exteri-
or, indicating the widened four-room plan of the mid-eighteenth century (the brick chimney
was added at the same time). The interior, some of it original, reveals the medievalism of its
early Colonial day; its substantial summer beam bisects the hall/kitchen in typical fashion,
while unpainted boarding (all new) lines the walls. In 1918 the dwelling was acquired by the
Society for the Preservation of New England Antiquities. In 1952, it was restored (some
authorities believe this restoration questionable in parts); the greatest changes took the exteri-
or back to its seventeenth-century appearance and replaced rotted timbers within. A lack of
funds, presumably, prevented restoration of the gable that once graced the front, and whose
original valley framing beams are still in place

Located west of intersection with RI 126 (3 miles/4.8 kilometers northwest of Pawtucket). Open by appointment only; call the
SPNEA at (617) 227–3956 to arrange a tour. The cost is $2 for adults, $1 for children 5–12, $1.50 for senior citizens, free for
SPNEA members.

JEAN HASBROUCK MEMORIAL HOUSE (1692–1712)
Huguenot Street at North Front Street
New Paltz, New York

Interspersed along Huguenot Street above the Wallkill and Hudson rivers is a group of sur-prisingly unaltered houses built at the end of the seventeenth and early in the eighteenth cen-turies by French Protestant refugees. Highlighted by the Hasbrouck House (1692 beginning, 1712 major part) at the end of the street (a museum-house that has been open to the public since 1899), the collection comprises a vignette from a too-little-known period of early American architecture. Even the street—"the oldest street in America with its original hous-es"—was designated a National Historic Landmark in 1960.

Architecturally the houses show a northern French-Rhinelander-Dutch influence (many Huguenots spent some years in Germany and the Netherlands before fleeing to the New World) with local limestone walls, steep medieval roof, and (often) wood gable ends. The hous-es are directly and simply expressed, but at times, as in the Bevier House, sport an almost fey fenestration. The interiors are structurally impressive, particularly the roof trusses framing the attic where grain was stored, and where enormous hand-hewn beams are revealed. Be sure to notice, also, the unusual open-hearth fireplaces.

Take exit 18 on NY Thruway, west on NY 299/Main Street. Open the Wednesday after Memorial Day until the end of September, Wednesday–Sunday 9:30 A.M.–4:00 P.M. Closed Labor Day. All visits are guided. Tours of one house are $2.75 per person. 1 1/2-hour tours (two houses and the church) cost $3.50 per person. 2 1/2-hour tours are given at 9:30 and 1:30; the cost is $7 for adults, $6 for senior citizens, $3 for children ages 7–11. All tours begin at Deyo Hall. For more information call the Huguenot Historical Society at (914) 255–1660 (office) or (914) 255–1889 (tours).

SAN JOSÉ DE LA LAGUNA (1699–1706)
Exit 114 on I-40
Laguna, New Mexico

San José's exterior massing recalls the softly molded, white-stuccoed architecture of the Mediterranean, while its interior is spiced by energetic wall decorations. The mission and its small church (105 feet/32 meters long by 22 feet/6.7 meters wide) rank high in our inheritance of Spanish-Native American architecture. Note the integration of the twin bells on its planar facade—typical of its Balearic precursors. Though of the same standard plan as, say, the larger San Estévan at nearby Ácoma (see page 34), the Laguna mission is more intimately scaled in its siting and architecture, and, having been reasonably cared for in this century, is also in finer condition. A simple walled courtyard with a few trees,

the priest's house to the left, and a small baptistry to the right with an inner door to the nave of the church form an introduction to the mission.

The church itself is constructed of rough stone covered by whitewashed plaster worn by the elements to a tactile smoothness. The long, darkish interior, with three windows on the south wall plus a smaller one over the entry, reaches a climax at the chancel with its beautiful retablo (1804–05, restored by E. Boyd in 1950). The splayed side walls adjacent to the reredos were at one time also decorated, mostly with scrolls, but they have since been whitewashed out. The ceiling over the chancel is also ornamented. The lower walls of the nave are convoluted with boldly primitive paintings, rich in symbolic colors and designs to represent the elements affecting crop growth. They were probably added some fifty years after the dedication of the church itself. The ceiling of the nave is spanned by the usual vigas, here debarked tree trunks on simple corbels, covered with brightly painted herringboned branches. Father Antonio de Miranda supposedly designed the church and supervised its construction. The mission was in a badly deteriorated condition in the middle of the last century but was eventually stabilized. A new roof was added in 1923 by the Committee for the Preservation and Restoration of New Mexican Mission Churches. In the 1930s and 1940s further restoration was carried out under the supervision of the Franciscan order.

Located on a hillock at the west edge of Laguna. Open Monday–Friday 9:00 A.M.–3:00 P.M. Sunday services held at 10:00 A.M. Tours can be scheduled by calling (505) 552–9330.

COLONIAL WILLIAMSBURG RESTORATION (1699–1780/1927–)
Williamsburg, Virginia

Sir Francis Nicholson, town planner
Perry, Shaw & Hepburn, initial architect of restoration (1927–34)
Colonial Williamsburg Foundation (1935–)

For three quarters of the eighteenth century, Williamsburg epitomized Colonial building in America. Today it is the world's greatest open-air museum of architecture. No other English settlement, either in the South or North, approached the urbane sophistication, the civic unity, and the comeliness achieved here on the high land between the James and the York rivers. (The capital of Virginia was moved here in 1699 to get away from the malarial coast at Jamestown; it was transferred to Richmond in 1780 during the Revolution, where, of course, it remained.) It is beyond the scope of this book to comment more than briefly on the individual buildings and gardens—excellent guides may be had at the site—but let it be clearly stated that any architect, urbanist, or landscape architect can profit enormously from a visit, while the nonprofessional will be immensely rewarded.

The plan of Williamsburg is no casual string of public buildings and houses, but an organized, dynamic play of axis and cross-axis that has immense vitality. The town's essential lesson is not so much one of a carefully restored, beautifully landscaped collection of picturesque, historic buildings as it is of spaces. There are pulsating axial and lateral spaces, building spaces respecting each other, building spaces working with garden spaces, the two together delimiting the street spaces. This climaxes on Duke of Gloucester Street (see photo below), where trees, bricks, and weatherboard are intertwined in an extended urban partnership.

The town, as mentioned, did not simply accrete randomly; it employed one of the first major "composed" plans—not a repetitive unfocused grid—of the colonies. It was based on a Baroque-derived urban layout with the two ends of its spinal avenue, Duke of Gloucester Street (99 feet/30 meters wide), nailed down by an existing college (Wren Building) and the new Capitol, .75 mile/1.2 kilometers away. A cross axis of major importance, composed of a broad green, 210 x 825 feet/64 x 251 meters, with the Governor's Palace facing it, tapped onto this main thoroughfare. With the key foci established, the lesser streets developed from this brilliantly off-center *T* shape. The core in many respects anticipated Pierre-Charles L'Enfant's *T* plan for Washington by ninety-three years.

Though there were ground rules for the placement of houses on their half-acre lots—rules that included mandatory fences against grazing animals—the resulting townscape is not regi-

mented. Sir Francis Nicholson (1655–1728), a too little-known but apparently extraordinary governor, or lieutenant governor, of six American colonies from Nova Scotia to South Carolina, was responsible for the urban plan of the new capital. A few years earlier he also planned Annapolis, a far less successful effort that dimly reflects both Christopher Wren's never-built plan for London and the palace layout at Versailles (Nicholson was familiar with each). For the town of Williamsburg, with a planned population of 2,000, he could scarcely have done better. Alexander Spotswood, governor from 1710–22, made subsequent modifications.

All of the Williamsburg structures are, as would be expected, basically Colonial Georgian with a hint of the slightly earlier Queen Anne, plus an inevitable sea change. Elegance in architecture in the colonies can be said to have begun here. Peripherally, none of the buildings even anticipate the domestic "white pillars" of Greek Revival/Southern Colonial, which first appeared across the front of Mount Vernon (see page 94) at the very end of the eighteenth century.

The concept for restoring this notable town began in 1927 (the "dream" was nurtured twenty years earlier). It was then that the Reverend William Archer Rutherford Goodwin, rector of Bruton Parish Church, persuaded John D. Rockefeller, Jr., that if he would restore the town's splendid but run-down buildings, and reconstruct those whose foundations lay only a few inches beneath their feet, a cultural richness of the greatest magnitude would evolve. Rockefeller, who had visited Williamsburg the previous year to attend the dedication of Phi Beta Kappa Hall (the society was founded at William and Mary in 1776), magnanimously agreed, and preliminary work began shortly thereafter. Seven years later the major buildings were opened. Perry, Shaw & Hepburn and their distinguished consultants were admirably successful in their formidable task of restoring and rebuilding—for the first time in the United States—a whole historic city. Following the completion of the original program for the restoration of the major buildings in 1934, Colonial Williamsburg set up its own architectural office to carry out the remaining work. The nation will be eternally grateful to Rockefeller. It is probably correct to say that the work he made possible here has been the single greatest factor, conscious or not, in our present and future concern for saving the great buildings of our past. Today, after an expenditure of prodigious sums of money and sixty years of work, important restoration and reconstruction still remain to be studied and executed, and the work continues.

The famous Wren Building of William and Mary College, the colonies' second oldest college and their oldest surviving academic building, was still standing in the 1920s, as was Bruton Parish Church. The only major structures that required total rebuilding were the Capitol (opened in 1934), the Palace (1934), and Raleigh Tavern (1932). Altogether 88 buildings have been completely restored, while 413 minor buildings and many simple outbuildings have been built afresh, generally on their early foundations, guided by drawings, inventories, wills, and, of course, excavations. To accomplish this, 454 buildings of the last hundred or so years were removed from the 130-acre/53-hectare historic core.

Some quarrel that the resulting Williamsburg "style" has blighted American architecture by encouraging so many copies of its houses, much as the 1893 World's Columbian Exposition in Chicago congealed the building of its time in a Neo-Classical mold. But considering the state of architecture in the 1930s and '40s, such an accusation does not seem as stultifying now as it once did. Moreover the restoration sparked a keen interest in architectural preservation all across the country. However one assesses Williamsburg (and there are those who say it is "sanitized") there are urban lessons for tomorrow that can readily be gleaned from this restoration of the past. Its architecture gives us an illuminating insight into eighteenth-century English influence on the buildings of Virginia—England's earliest, largest, and (for a time) most populous possession in the New World. It is, thus, not to be missed.

The major buildings deserve brief comment. The Wren Building (see photo left)—designated as such in 1928—initially housed the entire William and Mary College and provided, as mentioned, the flagship building by which the new town was anchored. (The site, where a scattering of buildings stood in 1699, had been established as early as 1633 as Middle Plantation, with a palisade at the west against attack by Native Americans.) First built from 1695–98, the college suffered several fires (1705, 1859, and 1862), which consumed the interior, but the external walls are almost all original, although the building was several times altered. As Professor Marcus Whiffen brings out in his encyclopedic *The Public Buildings of Williamsburg* (Colonial Williamsburg, 1958), the attribution of Christopher Wren as the architect is based solely, thus somewhat strangely, on a book written in 1724 by the Reverend Hugh Jones, a mathematics professor at William and Mary, a man who should certainly have known. Jones wrote in *The Present State of Virginia* (London) that "The Building is beautiful and commodious, being first modeled by Sir *Christopher Wren* [Jones' italics]," immediately adding that it was "adapted to the Nature of the Country by the Gentlemen there," and, after the fire of 1705, "altered and adorned by the ingenious Direction of Governor Spotswood." As it stands, the facade lacks the mastery of proportion we would expect from Wren, particularly in the central pedimented bay (too narrow for the building's length, with arched entry too wide for its bay). For this we can probably thank Alexander Spotswood. (A wide, triple-arched pedimented bay graced the building from the 1865 "rebuilding" to the present restoration.) The Hall, projecting at the rear northward, was part of the original L-shaped building and survived the fires mentioned. The Chapel, at the rear to the south, was not added until 1729–32: the college was initially intended to form a complete rectangle. In front of the academic grouping at south stands The Brafferton, built, as the plaque proclaims, "as an Indian School in 1723." The near-identical President's House (1732–33) stands opposite on the north side of the College Yard. Accidentally burned in 1781, it was restored in 1786 with funds from the French Government.

The Bruton Parish Church seen today is the third for the community; the first, whose precise site and date are unknown, was probably built shortly after 1633, when, as mentioned, the area was settled. It was superseded by the second, which dates from 1681–83, and lasted until the college was established and the capital moved here (1699). Then in 1711, hard by the second church, the present larger edifice, designed by Alexander Spotswood, was started; it was completed in 1715. A 22-foot/6.7-meter expansion, to make the chancel length equal that of the nave, was effected in 1752. In plan the church is symmetrical about both nave and wings, with a square tower and bell steeple (of little elegance) added in 1769. The interior, several times altered, does not match several of its contemporary Virginia churches for brio, being low of ceiling, but the exterior forms a highly useful nodal point, an urban fulcrum, at the intersection of Duke of Gloucester Street and the Palace Green. George B. Tatum points out in *The*

Arts in America—Colonial Period (Scribner's, 1966) that the church "must be counted one of the earliest American examples of the use of the Georgian style by the Church of England."

The Governor's Palace (1706–20) (see photo below) is no arbitrary reconstruction. It is built on the precise excavated foundations of the old building, with a measured plan by Thomas Jefferson—who lived in it for six months while governor of Virginia—filling in the details. The reconstruction of the exterior massing and window treatment was enormously facilitated by a sharp one-point perspective engraving found in the Bodleian Library at Oxford. (This engraving, invaluable to the reconstruction, contains views of four other major buildings at Williamsburg.) Extensive inventories and descriptions helped with the interior and its furnishings. It is a five-bay Georgian mansion (note that the bays vary symmetrically in width), almost square in plan, with two dependencies at right angles in front, the whole wrapped in a double-curved brick wall entered by a well-scaled gate. The dormered roof rises steeply to a balustraded deck flanked by paneled chimneys and topped by a high cupola. Some historians think that Dutch Palladianism was a source of inspiration. A ballroom was added at the north side in 1751, and other subsequent repairs were carried out from 1767–70, possibly to enable the building to meet the challenge of Tryon Palace in New Bern, North Carolina (see page 106). Be certain to see the richly pedimented exterior of the ballroom, which shows the florid later development of the Georgian style. The gardens, too, should not be missed. The palace was burned in 1781 while being used as a hospital for the wounded from nearby Yorktown.

The Capitol (see photo on following page), which forms the climax of Duke of Gloucester Street, was begun in 1701 and finished four years later (but occupied before completion). Two and one-half stories high, it is *H*-shaped in plan (compare the Stratford Hall Plantation, page 65), with two identical wings, round-ended on the south, coupled by a nexus of the same height with an open ground floor piazza framed by three archways. Like the Governor's

Palace, it is built on the foundations of the original building, its exterior restoration greatly helped by the aforementioned Bodleian plate. To avoid the danger of fire there was originally no heating, hence no chimneys—and no candles or smoking—until 1723. Ironically, twenty-four years later, the building burned almost to the ground. The second capitol, on the foundations of the first but differing somewhat in appearance, was commenced in 1747 and completed in 1753. (This, too, burned, in 1832.) It is the restoration of the first capitol which we see today, well proportioned outside, comely within. Incidentally, the double-hung windows in the Capitol represent one of the first such uses in the colonies. (The Venetian blinds are also authentic to the period.)

The houses of the Williamsburg Restoration, the vast majority of which are of wood sheathed in weatherboard, merit careful attention, as do their gardens. Like the major buildings, some have been restored, others totally reconstructed, but all were done meticulously. Two of the finest examples face each other across the green near the Governor's Palace: the wooden Brush-Everard House (1717–19, with later additions), and the imposing, brick Wythe House (1752–54). Both are owned by Colonial Williamsburg and are open to the public. (For detailed guidance consult the *Official Guidebook and Map*, and William B. O'Neal's excellent *Architecture in Virginia*, published by the Virginia State Museum [1968]. For more serious research see Marcus Whiffen's *The Public Buildings of Williamsburg* [1958] and *The Eighteenth-Century Houses of Williamsburg* [1960], both published by Colonial Williamsburg and both very knowledgeable.)

Open daily 9:00 A.M.–5:00 P.M. (hours vary seasonally). A one-day admission pass (does not include museum admission) is $25 for adults, $15 for children ages 6–12. A one-year pass (which includes museum admission) is $30 for adults, $18 for children. Various tours offered daily. For more information call (800) HIS-TORY.

ST. JAMES EPISCOPAL CHURCH (c. 1713–19)
Snake Road
Goose Creek, South Carolina

Though difficult to find, this venerable church in a primitive country setting is well worth the expedition. With its pink stuccoed brick walls, white quoins and woodwork, and jerkin-head roof the exterior is highly unusual among early (or even late) colonial churches. (It should be mentioned that 1708 and 1711 have also been given as dates for its construction.) Note the elaborate, large-scaled door whose pediment depicts a pelican nourishing her young with blood from her breast, the emblem of the Society for the Propagation of the Gospel. The interior is dominated by an extraordinarily elaborate chancel; its sanctuary wall, or reredos, is vigorously molded in stucco and brightly painted. (Note the hatchment of the Izard family on the balcony wall.) The pulpit with its freestanding axial position and prominent sounding board almost speaks by itself; it completely eclipses the altar. The entry end of the church, in contrast, is naively simple.

St. James Episcopal Church was founded and built by Francis LeJau (1665–1717), a Huguenot who fled his native France to safety in England where he eventually became a canon of St. Paul's Cathedral in London. He was sent to South Carolina by the Society for the Propagation of the Gospel in large part "to cater to the desire of the French population." He lies buried near the altar. Many of the early settlers of Charleston and its environs were Englishmen from the Bahamas and Barbados; the "Goose Creek Men" were, supposedly, mostly Barbadians, with some Huguenots. There is, thus, a touch of West Indies background in this pastel-colored, stuccoed masonry church. The church was spared destruction during the American Revolution because the coat of arms of George I was still behind the pulpit, then lapsed into disuse for much of the nineteenth century. The earthquake of 1886 caused grave damage. Makeshift repairs were made from time to time, but not until 1955–60 was a complete restoration and a strengthening of the foundations carried out. The building was repainted in 1973.

Located 15 miles/24 kilometers north of Charleston via US 52 or 78; just north of branching of 52 and 78 turn east .6 mile/ 1 kilometer on Goose Creek Road, then .4 mile/.6 kilometer south at first fork (Snake Road). The church is currently undergoing restoration. Open by appointment only; call (803) 722–1462 to arrange a free tour.

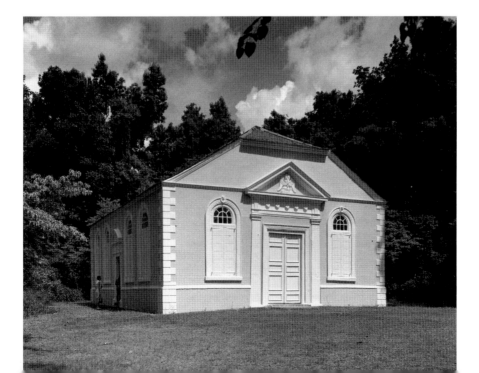

MACPHEADRIS-WARNER HOUSE (1718–23)
150 Daniel Street at Chapel
Portsmouth, New Hampshire

The Macpheadris-Warner House is considered by many to be one of the finest early-eighteenth-century brick dwellings left in New England. With its thick Flemish-bond walls it would be distinguished early Georgian anywhere. (It should be remembered that brick, not wood, was the favored building material at this time throughout the South.) The roof originally had a double gable with two ridges and no dormers. The valley formed by the gables filled with snow and ice in winter, and thus the roof was redesigned as now seen to prevent structural rotting. The anachronistic cupola, however, is original. The Chapel Street end of the house (at left) is crowded by two large chimneys; the opposite end uses only one because the fireplaces are conjoined at the inside corners. Attention to detail can be seen in the segmental pediment over the front door, a shape that is softly echoed by the relieving arches over the windows on the lower floor and the alternate dormers on the roof. (The pedimented door and dormers seem to have been added c. 1760.)

Notable features of the interior include the fascinating, semiprimitive murals of the stairway (restored in 1988), the large size of the rooms (the parlor measures 19.5 feet/6 meters across) and their pine paneling, the marbleizing of the dining room walls, the furnishings (few original), and the portraits: an impressive assembly. In 1931 the dwelling was purchased from the descendants of Jonathan Warner by the Warner House Association so that it could be maintained and opened to the public. Some restoration, particularly in the kitchen, was carried out by Norman Isham and William Perry, and proper refurnishing begun. The fence along Daniel Street was designed in 1953 by Mr. Perry (who did much work at Williamsburg).

Early June–October 31, open Tuesday–Saturday 10:00 A.M.–4:00 P.M., Sunday 1:00 P.M.–4:00 P.M. March 15–early June, open by appointment; call (603) 436–5909. Admission is $4 for adults, $2 for children. Guided tours available.

STANLEY-WHITMAN HOUSE (c. 1720)
37 High Street
Farmington, Connecticut

Weathered oak clapboarding (restored and now protected by a stain), diamond-pane triple windows, massive central chimney, and projecting "framed overhang" with heavy pendants are all hallmarks of one of the best-preserved early eighteenth-century houses in the United States. This quality carries over to the inside, particularly in the hall to the right and the bedrooms above. Roof changes made at the time of a later addition to the house create a straight line from ridge to eaves and thus give the house its saltbox shape. (A fireproof wing was added to the rear during the late nineteenth century to accommodate additional items of local interest.) The plan of the house embraces its central chimney with two rooms per floor each with sizable (and original) fireplace. A tiny staircase (restored) against the chimney gives access to the upper level. Although the "purity" of the house is somewhat compromised by its additions—compare the Parson Capen House in Topsfield, Massachusetts (see page 49), for example—the main body of the Stanley-Whitman remains one of the classics of its type. The framed overhangs that are so prominent in both front and gables of the house—as in the Capen as well—stem from the medieval tradition. Some believe overhangs arose because houses were taxed on the amount of ground they covered; others trace them to cramped town lots. (By comparison, many English windows were walled up from 1696 to 1851 because of the tax levied on them. And, of course, François Mansart's [1598–1666] Mansard roof not only provided more under-roof space, it also avoided the tax per floor on French buildings.) The building was restored by J. Frederick Kelly in 1934–35, and a second restoration was completed in 1988, which returned most of the rooms to their original condition. The horticulturist visiting the Stanley-Whitman House will want to see the herb and flower gardens at the rear.

May–October open Wednesday–Sunday 12:00 noon–4:00 P.M., March, April, November, and December open Sunday 12:00 noon–4:00 P.M. All other times by appointment only. Admission fees are $3 for adults, $2 for children 6–18 and senior citizens. There is an orientation exhibit. To schedule visits or tours call (203) 677–9222.

GRAEME PARK MANSION—KEITH HOUSE (1721–22/1739–55)
859 County Line Road
Horsham, Pennsylvania

The Graeme Park Mansion (also known as the Keith House), with its duck pond, trees, fences, and well-tended lawn, is the center of a complete early-eighteenth-century country gentleman's estate. The exterior of the house is casually dressed fieldstone, with prominent mortar joints and a lack of finesse in its details. The interior was totally renovated in 1739–55 by Dr. Thomas Graeme, the son-in-law of the original owner, Sir William Keith. Richly paneled partitions and large fireplaces are found in the three ground-floor rooms, which are unusually laid out in that there is no central hall.

The nearby barn should be noted, especially the juxtaposition of its massive stone ends with the wooden southern projection, which provides an open-air sheltered work space. Notice, too, the neatly turned white-washed pillars and, on the north side, the ramp to the upper floor. Part of the barn's lower floor has been converted to a visitors center and administrative quarters for the Commonwealth of Pennsylvania, which acquired the property in 1958.

Located .9 mile/1.4 kilometers west of US 611, 3.2 miles/5.1 kilometers north of Horsham. Open Wednesday–Friday 10:00 A.M.–4:00 P.M., Saturday 9:00 A.M.–5:00 P.M., Sunday 1:00 P.M.–5:00 P.M. Closed Veterans Day, Thanksgiving, Christmas, and New Year's Day. There is an admission fee. All visits are guided; 45-minute tours given regularly until one hour prior to closing. For more information call (215) 343–0965.

CHRIST CHURCH—OLD NORTH (1723–24)
193 Salem Street at Hull
Boston, Massachusetts

When the non-Puritan churchgoers of Boston outgrew the first King's Chapel—which was their earliest Anglican parish—and sought to build a second church, they turned to Christopher Wren and James Gibbs for inspiration. Christ Church was the result. It shows the typical English, *U*-shaped, long-aisle interior with balconies, but one tempered by New England simplicity and marked by a primitiveness of detail. Note, incidentally, the cheerful quantity of daylight compared to that in most Boston churches of any period. The building measures 51 feet/15 meters wide by 70 feet/21 meters long. In the approved Church of England manner, Old North's pulpit stands at left—not at center, as in the Puritan tradition—its height enabling those in the balconies and the high box pews to see the minister (and vice versa). The pew boxes were tall to ward off drafts and square in plan so that the occupants could share the foot warmers they brought with them in winter (the church was not heated). The brass chandeliers, which are still used during some services, were made in England; the organ is a 1992 restoration of the 1759 original.

Christ Church today suffers from being closely hemmed in by a packed neighborhood, but the well-tended Washington Garden at its side does let it breathe a bit. It was from this church's superior steeple (190 feet/58 meters high) that Robert Newman hung the celebrated lanterns for Paul Revere. The wooden steeple was several times damaged by gales, and in 1954 was totally destroyed by hurricane. Charles R. Strickland restored it to the original design the following year. The church, probably, and the steeple unquestionably, were designed by William Price, a local draftsman who reputedly had studied Wren's churches when in London. However, the extensive parish records reveal no known architect. Thomas Tippin and Thomas Bennett were the master builders.

Open daily 9:00 A.M.–5:00 P.M. Closed on Thanksgiving. Sunday services held at 9:00 A.M., 11:00 A.M., and 4:00 P.M. No admission fee, but a donation is requested. A short talk on the building is available to all visitors.

TRINITY CHURCH (1725–26)
Queen Anne Square between Spring and Thames streets
Newport, Rhode Island

Richard Munday, architect

Richard Munday designed Trinity Church, or, as has been said, "made a copy in wood of Boston's Old North" (Hugh Morrison, *Early American Architecture*, Oxford University Press, 1952). While the interior is unmistakably derived from London precedents, the outside is sheathed in beaded white clapboards, its wide sides given a lilt by the double row of roundheaded windows. This is accentuated by the scale relation of the narrow clapboarding and the "thirty over twenty-four" panes of the windows. The exterior is also marked by a first-rate steeple (spire and cupola inspired by Old North) with what was supposedly the first church bell to ring in New England. (The steeple has recently been restored.) An open square—dedicated by Queen Elizabeth II in 1976—sets off the whole. The interior was based, as mentioned, on the just-completed interior of Christ Church (that is, Old North—see page 63), but Trinity is longer than the former, having been sliced in half, and had two additional bays, totaling 30 feet/9 meters, added in 1762. (Note the unusual superimposed square columns upholding gallery and vaulted ceiling in each building.) Trinity has otherwise been little touched through the subsequent years even to the extent that real candles are set in the chandeliers that hang down the aisle. This aisle aligns with the prominent wineglass pulpit, whose axial location—and superb sounding board—almost completely blankets the altar: almost unheard of in an Anglican church. The interior is colorful, with white walls and ceiling, light green woodwork, and seasonal vestments.

Open 10:00 A.M.–4:00 P.M. in summer and 10:00 A.M.–1:00 P.M. in winter. Closed for holidays. Admission is free, although a donation is suggested. Tours are available during the summer and on Sunday year round. For more information call (401) 846-0660.

STRATFORD HALL PLANTATION (c. 1725–30)
VA 214
Stratford, Virginia

The visual pleasures of Stratford lie both in its ground-hugging mansion, probing the four points of the compass, and in its collection of dependencies and outbuildings. Stratford, like the Shirley Plantation (see page 67), resembles no other Virginia plantation house. Its *H*-shaped plan derives from Italian books (Serlio) and English publications, and was possibly influenced by the *H*-shaped Capitol at Williamsburg (see page 54).

In any case the house exhibits a remarkable interacting geometry with two symmetrical wings with squared ends jutting out from either side of a recessed central block—thus giving two exposures to each room. The piano nobile is elevated one-half story by its raised basement. Note that the brick size of the lower part differs from that above the water table, though both are laid in Flemish bond. The lower brickwork with its glazed headers is picked up again in the chimneys. Above, topping the intersections of the uniform hipped ridges, erupt two enormous clusters of Vanbrughian chimneys comprised of four interlocking but independent flues. A balustraded lookout couches in each. Flanking the house near the corners stand four dependencies, arranged with Palladian symmetry, the two on the approach side (kitchen at east, clerks' quarters and servants' hall on west) placed at right angles to the overseer's office and gardener's house, which stand on the river side.

The heavily balustraded flights of stairs, one on either side of the central hall block, vanish—that is, narrow sharply from 13 to 5 feet/4 to 1.5 meters—as each ascends to a simple, brick-pedimented door. This creates a visually dominant perspective effect, in spite of the fact that they are sandwiched between the challenging projections of the wings. It must be added that current research reveals that the late Fiske Kimball, who was in charge of a major stage of the restoration, made arbitrary decisions for the splayed stairs (south flight 1935, north 1940) for which there was no archeological evidence. There is, indeed, no documentation that the north stairs existed. These stairs lead onto the great hall with the major rooms disposed in identical rectangular wings on either side, thus producing the *H* plan. The hall (28.5 x 28.7 feet/8.69 x 8.74 meters), with its inverted tray ceiling, handsome painted paneling, and brass chandelier, forms one of the country's impressive entrances. During the first two generations of occupancy by the family of Robert E. Lee, the lower floor, served only by a small interior stair, functioned as a service, storage, and utility area.

Fortunes waned with time, and changes were made (all outside stairs were removed or pushed around, and most interiors, except the hall, altered). In 1929 the Robert E. Lee Memorial Association purchased the house and grounds and undertook its masterful restoration, a process that began in 1933 (initially, as mentioned, under the direction of Fiske Kimball) and that still continues. The rehabilitating and refurnishing of the house cover the eighty-four-year occupancy of the Lee family, c. 1738–1822. No architect has been discovered.

Located 42 miles/68 kilometers east of Fredericksburg on VA 3 to Lerty, then 2 miles/3.2 kilometers northeast on va 214. Open daily 9:00 A.M.–4:30 P.M. Closed Thanksgiving, Christmas, and New Year's Day. Admission is $7 for adults, $6 for senior citizens and the military, $3 for children ages 6–18, free for children under 6. All visits are guided. For more information call (804) 493-8038.

CHRIST CHURCH (1727–44/1754)
2nd and Market streets
Philadelphia, Pennsylvania

Dr. John Kearsley, probable architect

Christ Church represented the most accomplished and urbane development of religious architecture in the colonies at the time of its completion in 1744 (tower and steeple 1754). Its basic design comes straight from London; James Gibbs's St. Martin-in-the-Fields (1721–26) is most frequently mentioned as its inspiration, although its interior, especially, is tamer. Christ Church's red brick walls, projecting chancel, and parapet with balustrade and urn show by their articulation the full development of Georgian architecture. This finds its climax in the 209-foot-/64-meter-high wooden steeple resting easily upon its brick base. (Note the carved heads on this tower.) The richness of the exterior is reflected within by the chancel with its enormous Palladian window—which the church claims is the first of its size in America—and by the ornate entablature. The Tuscan columns with impost blocks that parade down the nave are virtually a Gibbs trademark. From these columns spring arches that carry the elliptical ceiling. In 1954 the Victorian-era stained glass in the great window behind the altar was replaced with clear glass to restore the window to its original style. Six of the downstairs stained-glass windows underwent similar treatment in 1985.

As the founding Anglican church (1695) in Pennsylvania—the colony of Quakers—Christ Church's first building was probably made of wood; in 1727 work was begun on the building we see today. Dr. John Kearsley, a physician, vestryman, and amateur architect who was born (c. 1684) and educated in England, is generally credited with the church's design. The church prospered greatly and was by the mid-eighteenth century the most fashionable in Philadelphia. It was here also in 1789 that the Protestant Episcopal Church in the United States was born, severing ties with the Church of England. Though interior changes were made during the last century, the building stands basically as designed, a significant landmark in Colonial architectural heritage. Seven signers of the Declaration of Independence are buried in its churchyard and nearby graveyard (Arch Street at 5th).

Open Monday–Saturday 9:00 A.M.–5:00 P.M., Sunday 1:00–5:00 P.M. Services held Wednesday at 12:00 noon, Sunday at 9:00 and 11:00 A.M. Closed Thanksgiving, Christmas Eve, Christmas Day, New Year's Eve, New Year's Day. Also closed Monday and Tuesday during January and February. Tours are available; reservations encouraged. For more information call (215) 922–1695.

SHIRLEY PLANTATION (c. 1730/1831)
501 Shirley Plantation Road
Charles City, Virginia

Shirley Plantation stands on property established as a plantation just six years after the founding of Jamestown. Tall and precisely square, with extraordinary outbuildings, this Queen Anne manor has a unique personality among the Virginia river houses; "it alone is of the old monumental style" (Thomas Tileston Waterman, *The Mansions of Virginia*, University of North Carolina Press, 1945). While the house, as Waterman and Hugh Morrison (*Early American Architecture*, Oxford University Press, 1952) both show, stems from the designs of Andrea Palladio, with its two-tiered porticos, the relation of house to dependencies is unique. These outbuildings frame an ingratiating courtyard on the land side of the dwelling. A carefully composed grouping with a brace of two-story gabled houses facing each other—the one at right (north) originally for kitchen, that at left (south) for laundry—occupy the lawn on the land side of the mansion. Beyond lie two one-and-one-half-story warehouses whose L shapes close the composition of the five buildings. These dependencies date from the mid-1700s.

The main house (c. 1730) is of three stories with a steep mansard roof and overly prominent dormers sheltering the third floor. The porticos of Shirley, which are highly similar to those on several South Carolina houses of the period (compare Drayton Hall in Charleston, page 74), were added in 1831 (as recent archeological research has brought out). The plan of the house is unusual in that there is no central hall, but a "hall room" in the northeast corner with a remarkable "flying" stair of walnut and pine, three stories high. Note the details of the underside of the steps and the balustrade. The extensive interior paneling and the carving of fireplace mantels, overmantels, transoms, and cornices are very fine examples of eighteenth-century craftsmanship. Because the plantation has been continuously inhabited—even during the Civil War when nearby Richmond was in flames—the house is remarkably well preserved. Shirley is still a working plantation.

Located west off VA 5, turnoff 19 miles/31 kilometers southeast of Richmond. Open daily 9:00 A.M.–5:00 P.M. Closed Christmas. There is an admission fee; call for rates. Free tours of the house given daily. Self-guided tours of the grounds are also available. For more information call (800) 232–1613.

WESTOVER (c. 1730–34)
7000 Westover Road
Charles City, Virginia

Westover is one of the preeminent houses in this country; however the visitor must keep in mind that what is seen today is only partially as originally built. For the house (like Carter's Grove Plantation, see page 80) has been transformed from a central dwelling with separate flanking dependencies into one extended mansion with three previously detached units connected to it. The house stands close to the James River, with gigantic tulip poplars in front, planted almost two hundred years ago, to shade the building from the sun yet not obstruct the view. Called "the most famous Georgian house in America" (Hugh Morrison), its central block is, indeed, superb. Its distinguished south door with an elaborate scroll pediment is one of the most copied in the country (it, in turn, was largely copied from *Palladio Londinensis* of 1734: the Portland stone enframement itself came from London). William Byrd II, who commissioned Westover and undoubtedly had a hand in its design, possessed a superb architectural library.

Note that the entablature of the door aligns with the pink-painted brick stringcourse to bind the entry to the whole facade. On either side are three segmental brick window frames with arched window heads to match their slight curve; generally such wood framing and glass of the era were rectangular. These windows are repeated on the second floor, and as they rise they diminish slightly in pane size, lending a highly unusual refinement to the facade. Here stands perfection of proportion with a nicety of detail unmatched in the early Georgian architecture of the colonies. Moreover the north (that is, land) facade is almost equally rewarding, for though the doorway—from the same *Palladio Londinensis*—is not as exuberant, it displays equally fine workmanship. In front of this side of the house are wrought-iron gates that were made in England and, it is thought, installed around 1711, before the main house itself was commenced. These gates well merit detailed inspection. The gardens themselves were planted in about 1900.

It would be agreeable if this paean could continue in describing the remainder of the house, but it cannot because of the insensitivity of the hyphens that were put in (1901–05) to connect the house with the two dependencies. (The west dependency was built in the late seventeenth century.) Not only are they weak in design themselves, the hyphens extend the same ridge as the dependencies, thus slurring their junctures. In addition, the east dependency, which had been destroyed in the Civil War, was rebuilt with a gambrel roof so that there is gable, hip, and gambrel along one roof line. (Compare the much more accomplished result in joining together three units at Carter's Grove.) But concentrate on the exterior of the mansion proper and enjoy one of the greatest achievements of American domestic architecture. If possible, arrive during Garden Week, usually toward the end of April, when the interior is also open to the public. The design of the stair and the stunning marble mantel in the drawing room (from James Gibbs's *Book of Architecture*, London, 1728) are particularly recommended.

Located south off VA 5, turnoff 22 miles/35 kilometers southeast of Richmond. Grounds and garden open 9:00 A.M.–6:00 P.M. daily. Admission is $2 for adults, 50¢ for children under 16, free for children under 6. During Garden Week the house interior is also open to the public; admission prices are higher. Tours of the house can be scheduled by calling (804) 829-2882; the cost is $7.50 per person.

MISSION CONCEPCIÓN (1731–55)
807 Mission Road
San Antonio, Texas

Mission Nuestra Señora de la Purísima Concepción de Acuña, alas, no longer ranks among the architectural elite of a legacy of missions that the Spanish founded from Tejas ("friends") to California in the seventeenth and eighteenth centuries. It is, however, well worth a visit. Its large compound, which once housed 247 Native Americans, is gone and the facade of the church (1740–55), though intact, has faded to monochrome; it has also always been marked by a lack of cohesion, and harried by its geometrically determined pediment. Its cruciform interior is today simple to the point of plainness; even the contemporary main altar lacks verve (the transept altars are original). This blandness was not always so, as examination of the baptistery and belfry will suggest, even though their surfaces (but not structure) have largely disintegrated. The vestiges of former frescoes remaining inside recall that at one time both interior and facade were alive with geometric color. In 1824, following complete secularization (it had been partially secularized in 1793), the church was abandoned for thirty-one years, during which period it suffered defacement and partial destruction of the living quarters. But the church itself, 89 feet/27 meters long by 22.5 feet/6.8 meters wide, fortunately remained structurally intact, and claims to be the oldest unrestored church structure in the United States. The church was rededicated in 1887 and has been in active service since. Its strength resides in the 45-inch-/1.1-meter-thick walls constructed of dressed stone on both faces with small stones and some adobe between. The north and east walls were also made windowless against possible attack. Shortly after World War II, the United States Government marked the kitchen of the mission an official fallout shelter. The remaining fragments of the wall and ceiling paintings in the library room of the *convento* (missionaries' quarters) were recently restored to their original vibrancy.

Located near intersection I-10 with US 281. Part of San Antonio Missions National Historical Park. Open daily 9:00 A.M.–6:00 P.M. in summer, 9:00 A.M.–5:00 P.M. in winter. Closed Christmas and New Year's Day. Tours can be scheduled by calling (210) 229–5701.

CHRIST CHURCH (c. 1732)
Routes 646 and 709
Irvington, Virginia

Christ Church rises behind a well-tailored brick wall (restored) with a perfection that makes it a strong contender for the most handsome church exterior in the United States. Its slightly off-set arms, 68 feet/21 meters on a side, are topped by four hipped roofs with an unexpected slight upturn at the eaves, while its three entries are cut precisely into the respective arms of the plan. Understated elegance can be seen from the compact overall proportions down to details such as the rubbed brick-on-brick of the entries with Portland stone caps and bases. This masonry was probably not equaled in the colonies. Note that the main doorway is marked by a delicate segmental pediment, while those over the two transept doors are triangular with unusual oval windows above. The prominently keystoned windows are roundheaded to reflect the main entry. The 3-foot-/.9-meter-thick brick walls, set in Flemish bond, are of three colors to give subtle variety.

Within there is such an abundance of natural light that the two windows in the chancel (east) wall do not produce a glare. The four arms of the church are simply but neatly vaulted in white plaster. (Though the east-west and north-south measurements are identical, the north-south transept is 4 feet/1.2 meters off center, which gives the west arm of the church extra length.) A narrow stringcourse, aligned with the springing of the roundheaded windows and threading the windows visually together, runs throughout the interior. The Ten Commandments stand forth boldly above the altar, attesting to the importance of the Word in the Protestant church and providing a form of prayer book for those who did not possess one. The three-decker pulpit stands at a corner of the transept in the midst of the congregation. The original pews, high-backed to ward off drafts, are of natural-finish pine, while virtually all of the other wood, including paneling, is walnut, its dark color playing against the white of walls and ceiling.

Funds for the church, which occupies the site of an earlier fane (c. 1669), were provided by the famous Robert "King" Carter, and Carter graves can be seen in the chancel and outside. Because of its semi-remote location, and the fact that it was owned by the Carter family until 1961, the church was fortunately spared injury following disestablishment and the Civil War. Only minor restoration has been necessary. A slate roof was added in the 1890s, and a general overhaul, including the brick girdling wall mentioned, was undertaken in 1965–66 under the direction of Professor Frederick D. Nichols. Strangely, the architect is unknown. It is one of the greatest, or as Alan Gowans writes, "It may still claim to be the finest single piece of pure eighteenth-century classical architectural design in America" (*King Carter's Church*, University of Victoria, Maltwood Museum, 1969).

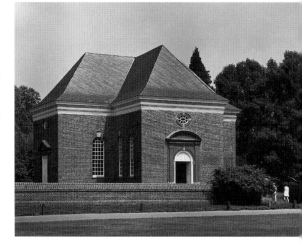

Located 3.6 miles/5.8 kilometers southwest of Kilmarnock via VA 3, 222, 646, and 709. Open daily 9:00 A.M.–5:00 P.M. Closed Christmas. Sunday services held in summer at 8:00 A.M. Free tours available April–November Monday–Friday 10:00 A.M.–4:00 P.M., Saturday 1:00–4:00 P.M., Sunday 2:00–5:00 P.M. Tours can also be scheduled by calling (804) 438–6855.

INDEPENDENCE HALL (1732–56)
5000 Chestnut Street between 5th and 6th streets
Philadelphia, Pennsylvania

Edmund Woolley and Andrew Hamilton, architects

Independence Hall is so emotionally intertwined with the origin of the United States that we often neglect its architecture. It is—in parts (chiefly its tower and interior)—architecturally superb. The brick tower, it should be mentioned, was not even started until 1750, and the first wooden steeple was so poorly built that it had to be removed in 1781. This was rebuilt with major alterations (made more elaborate with clocks and oak wreaths) by William Strickland in 1828—perhaps the earliest Colonial restoration. Without tower and steeple, the Old State House, to use its original name, would be a competent but dullish building. The tower, almost exactly as wide as each flank, and the treed square on the south side save all. From the north (Chestnut Street side) the building is horizontally prominent; from the south it seems vertical. Its park on the south, which was once enclosed by a 7-foot-/2.1-meter-high brick wall, provides a respectful bosky setting for this Palladian-descended group. (The same distinction cannot be claimed for the mall to the north, which has been cleared of earlier buildings and landscaped.) On either side of the Old State House and connected to it by triple open (originally solid) arcades are two curiously scaled office wings (1736), which were built and rebuilt (once by Robert Mills) until the final restoration of 1898. Standing as separate entities on either side of these wings are Congress Hall (the former County Court House) to the west (1787–89) and Old City Hall—the temporary United States Supreme Court (1791–1800)—to the east (1789–91). Their exteriors are basically as originally built; their interior arrangements were altered on several occasions but have now been restored.

The interior of Independence Hall is splendid both in scale and in the detailing of its woodwork. It is divided by a central hall into two equal (but unequal-appearing) rooms. One of these accommodates the supreme court of the province (arched and open to the hall) and the other, to the east, the Pennsylvania Assembly (behind a door), where the Declaration of Independence was signed. Both number among the United States' great early chambers. The second floor, reached by an impressive stair tower, is dominated by a long gallery. Edmund Woolley, a master carpenter, designed the building aided by Andrew Hamilton, a talented lawyer and amateur architect. After neglect following the removal of the state capital to Lancaster in 1799, then a slight sprucing up for the centennial in 1876, the group comprised of Independence Hall, Congress Hall, the Old City Hall, and the square was restored early in this century. In 1951 the buildings came under the watchful protection of the National Park Service.

Open daily 9:00 A.M.–5:00 P.M. (July–August until 8:00 P.M.) All visits are guided; free tours are given every 15 minutes. For more information call (215) 597–8974.

SQUARES OF SAVANNAH (1733–1855)
Savannah, Georgia

James Edward Oglethorpe, planner

James Edward Oglethorpe (1696–1785) was a military man and a humanist, and it can be legitimately argued that the plan he laid out for his new settlement in Georgia combined his career with his concern for mankind. His military experiences ranged from successfully fighting the Turks at Belgrade (1717) to chasing the Spanish from the seas around the colonies (1742). His humanism, as expressed in his concern for prison reform and for "the oppressed Protestant on the continent," was directly responsible for his asking George II if he could set up a colony for these lonely and troubled souls in the New World. This request was granted (primarily as a foil to the northward-looking Spaniards long established in Florida), and in February 1733 the last—and the largest—of the thirteen English colonies was established some 18 miles/29 kilometers up what came to be known as the Savannah River (named, or rather misnamed, for the character of the countryside: a savannah is treeless).

The humanitarian castrum that Oglethorpe immediately began to set up for some 114 colonists (including many debtors)—and that he had determined in principle in England—

was based on a military layout—but military with a difference. Historians disagree as to the inspiration for Oglethorpe's plan—with theories ranging from the plan of Peking, to Palmanova (a marvelous star-shaped city of 1593 in Italy's Veneto—which must have influenced Sébastien le Prestre de Vauban), to London's squares, and to *The Villas of the Ancients Illustrated*, a book that Oglethorpe possessed and that was authored by an architect-friend. In any case the plan that evolved for Savannah was not a rigid gridiron, stereotyped by the Roman city of Timgad, but a town plan based on a series of "wards," precisely dimensioned, with each focused on its own open square. The wards were composed of "tythings" (lots) lined two rows across the north side and two across the south, each row containing ten lots 60 x 90 feet/ 18.3 x 27.4 meters—forty altogether. On these sat identical houses 16 x 22 feet/4.9 x 6.7 meters. Separating the north and south bands of dwellings in each ward was a broad space for community buildings with the center left open as a square. A net of streets, which varied in width from 75 to 37.5 to 22.5 feet/23 to 11.4 to 6.9 meters, subdivided the whole. Such wards created a far more gracious layout for living than an unrelieved grid, yet lacked nothing in military ordination. The central open space of each ward also enabled the outlying settlers and their animals to move into the palisaded town and occupy the squares in case of danger. (Each family had, in addition to its lot, a 5-acre/2-hectare garden plot in the outlying town common, with a 44-acre/18-hectare farm beyond.) Oglethorpe himself is said to have laid out the first four of

his famous wards before returning to England (1743). His module, wondrously, was repeated as the town extended, until 1855, when available common land ran out. Savannah then boasted twenty-four squares, none, it should be added, identical. Mere open spaces—at times with a well and puzzlingly few trees in the earliest days of the settlement—this network of piazze eventually flowered into a series of planted parks, resulting in a unique urban entity. Proper fencing and planting, it might be noted, did not appear until the prosperity that followed the War of 1812.

Virtually all of the world's cities have squares, but none other uses them as patterned cadences to orchestrate the streets. Savannah, however, produced "a plan so exalted that it remains as one of the finest diagrams for city organization and growth in existence" (Edmund N. Bacon, *Design of Cities*, Viking Press, 1967). The scale of these outdoor rooms is human; the local automobile is tolerated, but through traffic is routed on wide avenues. Each square is different not only in planting but in statuary, each square's name and its sculpture recalling a long-deceased hero or statesman. Bull Street—William Bull was an Oglethorpe aide—is one of the most rewarding to stroll along, but meander about. Would that later American cities had employed such pulsations of squares, street layout, and street variations. Instead we often entrust our urban patterns to our water commissioners. Savannah's great contribution, it should be emphasized, lies more in urban planning than in distinctive architecture. In this latter regard Savannah did not produce a domestic response equal to the felicity of the houses of Charleston (see page 134), though both deal with similar site conditions.

Inquire at the Savannah Visitors Center, 305 Martin Luther King Jr. Boulevard, telephone (912) 944–0455, for useful maps and data (open daily 8:30 A.M.–5:00 P.M.). It is housed in the 1860–76 Central of Georgia Railroad Station, accurately restored by Gunn and Meyerhoff in 1975. For a thorough review of each square and the buildings on it see *Historic Savannah* (Historic Savannah Foundation, 1979).

DRAYTON HALL (1738–42)
3380 Ashley River Road
Charleston, South Carolina

Drayton Hall, according to the late Henry Francis du Pont, founder of the Winterthur Museum, is "the greatest house in America." Of the three superb Ashley River plantations open to the public, this is the only one whose plantation house dates from the eighteenth century. (The houses of nearby Magnolia Gardens and Middleton Place were burned by Federal troops.) It is remarkably unchanged from the day it was built except for the disappearance of its two dependencies or flankers, which were built fifteen years after the main house. No plumbing will be found within Drayton's rooms, no electric wires chase through its walls. Even the paint in the great hall is only the second coat. Legend has it that the house was saved from destruction in the Civil War by being used as a smallpox hospital.

Designed roughly at the same time as the great James River houses (and a century before the Louisiana and Mississippi plantations), the entries are a great hall in front and a stair hall on the river side, each superbly paneled. *Antiques* (April 1970) calls the latter "the finest in America." Many of the rooms in the house are fully paneled with rich fireplaces, in general designed after handbooks. The mansion had been slightly vandalized but is now being preserved. Drayton Hall was acquired by the National Trust for Historic Preservation in 1974 and opened to the public in 1978.

Located 9 miles/14 kilometers northwest of city. March–October open daily 10:00 A.M.–4:00 P.M., November–February open daily 10:00 A.M.–3:00 P.M. Closed Thanksgiving, Christmas, and New Year's Day. Admission is $7 for adults, $4 for children and students, free for children 5 and under. Free tours are given every hour on the hour. For more information call (803) 766–0188.

OLD COLONY HOUSE (1739–43/c. 1841–45)
Washington Square
Newport, Rhode Island

Richard Munday, architect

The Old Colony House, or the Old State House, was once the capitol of Rhode Island, the second oldest capitol in the United States (after Philadelphia's Independence Hall, see page 71). For a time it was the largest—and certainly the most ambitious—building in Rhode Island. The location prominently terminates the head of Washington Square with Peter Harrison's Brick Market (see page 100) at the west end. The facade, which shows Dutch influence, displays what might be termed a rustic originality as it sprouts a strange pediment, its truncated triangular shape recalling the gable ends of the building, the whole topped by a balustraded flat deck with octagonal cupola. Every door and window (and even the clock) have received lavish attention, with sandstone quoins emphasizing their shapes in the red brick walls (the building exhibits the city's first major use of brick). Competing with the pediment is the combined entry and balcony, which, with the profusion of other elements, produces a facade of some agitation. However, the one-room main floor, measuring 40 x 80 feet/12 x 24 meters and with a central row of six square Doric columns, makes a substantial meeting hall. As the noted historian Antoinette Downing has written concerning this second floor: "The Senate Chamber, enlarged one bay in 1841, has fine floor-to-ceiling bolection paneling dating from 1740. The Assembly Room, which took its form c. 1841–45, has excellent mid-nineteenth century paneling, coffered ceiling and furnishings. The room was designed by Russell Warren, who was responsible for the Providence Arcade." The Old Colony House was used as a hospital during the Revolution but it was restored in 1785. In 1917 Norman M. Isham carried out a second restoration, in the process opening up the ground floor, which had been partitioned through the years. The whole building is now in excellent condition.

The interior is closed to the public.

FANEUIL HALL (1740–42; 1805–06)
John L. Smibert and Charles Bulfinch, architects

QUINCY MARKET (1824–26)
Alexander Parris, architect

FANEUIL HALL MARKETPLACE (1978)
Benjamin Thompson & Associates, architects of rehabilitation

Dock Square between North and South Market streets
Boston, Massachusetts

"Fan'l" Hall and its market had for years formed a spontaneous browsing and shopping spot for Bostonians and visitors alike, and the building's brilliant restoration for the bicentennial made this area even more enticing. The group is located just east of the government center (Boston City Hall, see page 494) and extends to the Fitzgerald Expressway, which cruelly slashes through the edge of the city. Recently, the city legislature has shown wisdom in recognizing and rehabilitating the surrounding architecture to the advantage of today and tomorrow. There is a vitality in this ancient section of town that in no small part stems from the stimulating variety of its buildings and the intriguing, often unexpected spaces between them.

Faneuil Hall itself was designed by the Edinburgh-born John L. Smibert, the fashionable painter (one of the earliest) of American notables, who this once applied himself to architecture. The accomplished result burned in 1761, leaving only the outer walls, but work was immediately commenced on its rebuilding, a task finished two years later. In 1805 Charles Bulfinch effected a vast enlargement of the hall by increasing the gable end from three bays to seven, adding a third story, and enclosing the previously open ground-floor market. (It should be added that the Bulfinch hall was completely rebuilt of fireproof materials in 1898–99.) With the new interior height Bulfinch created a taller and more handsome assembly room. From the exterior the Bulfinch edition, although copying Smibert's structure for the two lower floors, is less elegant than its prototype (to judge from an old engraving): the three-by-nine-bay original simply could not expand with grace to seven-by-nine plus a fifty percent increase of height. Lumpiness results.

The Greek Revival Quincy Market was designed by Alexander Parris, a Maine-born (1780–1852) architect who did much work in Boston. With Doric porticos clamped on each end and a low domed block rising at the center (dome added in the 1880s), the Quincy Market struggles to maintain cohesiveness over its 535-foot/163-meter length and 52-foot/16-meter width. However, its design and its granite construction—one of its initial backers was a granite contractor—command respect after over one hundred and seventy years of strenuous usage. (The one-piece column shafts were the largest then quarried in the United States.)

The sparkling restoration, really more a recycling than a restoration, by Benjamin Thompson & Associates took the formerly run-down area, jammed with automobiles and lined with often untenanted buildings (the markets having moved to new suburban quarters), and transformed it into a tree-lined pedestrian mall bordered by a series of bright and attractive restaurants and shops. The central backbone market (Quincy) expands laterally via glazed and awninged enclosures that in summer open onto the mall as sidewalk cafes. Numerous benches under the locust trees extend the munching possibilities and add to the informal "do-it-yourselfness" and jollity that characterize the whole development night and day. (Note the multiple twenty-watt lamp standards; also the graphics). Pushcarts—Thompson-designed—and occasional entertainers contribute to the scene.

On the Quincy Market interior the architects and developer were careful to maintain the market heritage and to establish "non-arty" specialty shops and restaurants, generally ethnic (almost all family-owned), without supermarket domination. They also kept Parris's central colonnade to maintain the bazaar atmosphere and ensure circulation ease, established strict rules for signs, and opened up the floor under the restored dome. Tempting sights and redolent smells contribute no small part to the atmosphere. The two flanking buildings are primarily devoted to shops (clothing, jewelry, luggage), with several upper-bracket restaurants and office floors above.

Significantly, the architects not only wanted to make the three-block enclave alive and festive, and, of course, commercially viable, they also sought to create a pedestrian isthmus, the whole acting as an active link between the government center to the west, the new skyscraper development on several sides, and the residential waterfront sector then being rapidly developed—much of it by rehabilitating old docks—to the east. The area shows enlightened urbanism and a marvelous use of the old. The Rouse Company of Columbia, Maryland was its wise and sympathetic developer, while the Boston Redevelopment Authority had a contributory hand in both planning and financing, with preservationists eagerly backing the project. As Ben Thompson has said, "Bringing people and vitality back into the city.... That's what Quincy Market is all about." A glorious urban metamorphosis.

Most buildings open Monday–Saturday 10:00 A.M.–9:00 P.M., Sunday 12:00 noon–5:00 P.M. For more information call (617) 523–1300. PA 9/71, PA 1/75, AR 12/77, JAIA 5/78, Int 1/79, JAIA 6/81

EPHRATA CLOISTER (1740–46)
632 West Main Street
Ephrata, Pennsylvania

The Ephrata Cloister is one of the country's major architectural groups of the eighteenth century and, reputedly, the earliest Protestant monastery in the United States. Fortunately some of its major buildings, which date from the 1740s, survive and have been carefully restored to give a revealing index of Palatinate-inspired architecture. They reflect the northwest German homeland of Georg Konrad Beissel, who founded Ephrata in 1732 as a religious, primarily celibate community for the German Seventh-Day Baptist Church. The society prospered and ran a successful farm, tannery, and several mills; it also founded a noted choral school and established one of the finest printing presses in the fledgling colonies. The most compelling single building is the three-story Saron, or Sisters' House (1743), with steeply pitched roof, shed dormers (instead of gabled ones), vertically lapped shakes, and tiny windows. The attached Saal, or chapel (1741), stands at a right angle, creating a fine medieval, almost Hanseatic, group. Note the projecting framing beams of the Saal capped against the weather.

The interiors, meticulously restored, reflect the frugal life of the community. In what might be called architectural masochism, the halls are lengthy and narrow to suggest the only path to heaven, the doorways are low to encourage humility by requiring constant stooping, and the wooden beds were made too short to allow indulgent rest. The Sisters' House and most of the smaller buildings are of wood (several have vanished), but the Almonry, where not only alms were distributed to the poor but where bread was baked and grain stored, is of local stone. The Saal is of half-timbering and stone. Celibacy, factionalism, and the changing socioeconomic pattern of America's development occasioned the demise of the communal society, and in 1814 it was incorporated into the German Seventh-Day Baptist Church, which used the buildings until 1934. The Pennsylvania Historical and Museum Commission acquired the site in 1941 and restored the surviving buildings.

Open Monday–Saturday 9:00 A.M.–5:00 P.M., Sunday 12:00 noon–5:00 P.M. Closed for holidays. Admission is $5 for adults, $4 for senior citizens, $3 for children ages 6–17. Tours given daily 10:00 A.M.–4:00 P.M. on the hour. For more information call (717) 733–6600.

CARTER'S GROVE PLANTATION (1740–55/1927–28)
8797 Pocahontas Trail
Williamsburg, Virginia

Though the exterior of Carter's Grove has been substantially altered by additions, the house remains one of the nation's most distinguished Georgian examples, while the interior is of the greatest splendor. The kitchen dependency (to the east) is the oldest part of the house; its back section probably dates from 1740. The mansion previously consisted of a two-story central block, hip-roofed and without dormers, 72 feet/22 meters long, and separated by 24.5 feet/7.5

meters from flanking gable-roofed, story-and-a-half dependencies 40 feet/12 meters long. (The dependencies antedate the main house.) It was set in standard plantation pattern, which was derived from the usual English prototypes. Then in 1927–28 carefully designed hyphens were put in to connect the three detached buildings, while rows of dormers were installed on the main roof, which was then raised 11 feet/3.4 meters to accommodate new rooms on the third floor. The entire operation (plus the addition of slate roofing and removal of an old porch) was skillfully carried out, and the house is more impressive as a 201-foot-/61-meter-long, ground-loving mansion than as three individual buildings—as a look at old photographs will confirm. Carter's Grove is very similar to the earlier Westover in Charles City, Virginia (see

page 68), which has also been altered by the addition of hyphens. However the more recent hyphens at Carter's Grove are far superior, as is its elegant massing. The terraced gardens—called "falling gardens" in the eighteenth century—which originally stepped down to the James River, have been reconstructed.

On the interior, the mansion reaches its impressive peak. Its axially aligned entry salon and stair hall have no peer in this country—"the finest room in all Georgian architecture" (Hugh Morrison)—while its parade of other chambers is not far behind. Both entry and hall are paneled in locally cut heart pine, which was painted when the house was built, while stairs and balusters are of walnut. The tread nosings are secured with nails concealed behind inlays in the form of stars and hearts, and the carving of the consoles at the end of each tread is noteworthy. (The stairs from the second to third floor date from the 1927–28 changes.) The hall is vibrant, its space pulling one up the stair while the lateral halls attract one through the front rooms. The interior has recently been reinterpreted to reflect the period of the 1930s through the '50s. The long corridor seen today through and beyond the two riverfront rooms did not exist, of course, before the hyphens were added and the previous windows made into doors.

The conjoined halls, with the suave elliptical arch separating them, are reputedly the work of Richard Bayliss, who came from England to do the woodwork. David Minitree, a local brickmason, was the contractor/builder, while Richard Taliaferro, some authorities believe, may have had a hand in the mansion's overall design. Whoever the progenitor, and whatever we may feel about the changes carried through, the house unquestionably is one of the country's greatest. Upon the death of the owner, the property was purchased in 1963 by the Sealantic Fund and opened to the public the following year. Late in 1969 the Rockefeller-supported fund gave the house to the nearby Colonial Williamsburg Foundation, which wisely doubled the acreage to preserve the estate from intrusion.

Located southwest off US 60, turn off 6.2 miles/10 kilometers southeast of Williamsburg. Run by the Colonial Williamsburg Foundation. Open Tuesday–Sunday 9:00 A.M.–5:00 P.M. Closed from the end of December until the second week in March. Admission is $17 for adults, $10 for children ages 6–12. The Colonial Williamsburg one-year pass ($30 for adults, $18 for children) also allows admission to Carter's Grove. Self-guided tours available. For more information call (804) 229–1000, ext. 2973.

CHARLESTON GARDENS (1741–1920s)
Charleston, South Carolina

Middleton Place, Magnolia Plantation and Gardens, and Cypress Gardens, two on the same road northwest of Charleston and the third nearby, are, in season, among the greatest gardens to be seen. Even in late summer, they will stir the soul, but from February to April, when first the camellias and then the azaleas are in bloom, these plantations will leave the beholder stunned by nature's poetry in plants, trees, lawns, and waters.

MIDDLETON PLACE (1741–51)
Ashley River Road
Charleston, South Carolina

Middleton Place was begun in 1741, and is the country's oldest landscaped garden still in existence. Its 65 acres/26 hectares were formally organized, with enormous parterres stepping down to the Ashley River. Several pools, including the 664-foot/202-meter reflection pool, are appropriately situated. The whole is carefully related to the mansion. It reputedly took one hundred men ten years to lay it out.

The gardens boast uncountable camellias—introduced to Middleton in 1786 by André Michaux, a French botanist: only one of the four original plants are still alive. Azaleas and other flowers abound, while the enormous live oaks, veiled with Spanish moss, add a mysterious dreamlike quality to the landscape. After years of almost total neglect the parterres and gardens were restored primarily through the efforts of the J. J. Pringle Smiths—Mr. Smith was a Middleton descendant—earlier in this century. The Garden Club of America, in celebrating the two hundredth anniversary of Middleton, called it "the most important garden in America."

Unfortunately the main house and the north flanker were destroyed in 1865 during the Civil War; only the battered south wing remains. This "gentlemen's guest wing" was repaired in 1870 by Williams Middleton and adorned with what Hugh Morrison termed "anachronis-

tic Flemish gables" (*Early American Architecture*, Oxford University Press, 1952). The ends indeed resemble the Jacobean influence evident at Bacon's Castle (see page 41) in Surry, Virginia, built c. 1656. The interior, opened to the public in 1975, is well worth seeing, being furnished with many original Middleton furnishings. The stable yards are nearby. The property is administered by the non-profit Middleton Place Foundation.

Located 14 miles/22.5 kilometers northwest of downtown Charleston, on SC 61. Open daily 9:00 A.M.–5:00 P.M. Admission is $12 for adults, $11 for senior citizens and military personnel, $6 for children ages 6–12. Half-hour tours are available Monday 1:30–4:30 P.M., Tuesday–Sunday 10:00 A.M.–4:30 P.M.; the cost is $6 per person. For more information, call (803) 556–6020. Lunch is served in the restaurant (open daily 11:00 A.M.–3:00 P.M.). PA 5/86

While in the vicinity, be sure to see the Middleton Inn (located on Ashley River Road, telephone [803] 556–0500), which opened to the public in 1986. Designed by Clark & Menefee Architects, this imaginative fifty-five-room hotel made predominantly of wood, stucco-covered brick, and concrete is just one-quarter mile from Middleton Gardens. A main lodge plus three smaller buildings of guest rooms with floor-to-ceiling glass windows overlook the Ashley River.

MAGNOLIA PLANTATION AND GARDENS (1830–50s)
Ashley River Road
Charleston, South Carolina

Magnolia Gardens has an ancient horticultural history; the house on the site dates from 1672, and the Flowerdale French formal garden—which remains today—was formed in 1680. The present English formal garden was added in the late 1700s, and a major period of growth and planning occurred in the 1830s. As at Middleton, the original house was wantonly destroyed during the Civil War. The house standing today was moved to this site after the war; it dates from the pre-Revolutionary period. However, the gardens sustained fairly limited damage and were opened to the public in 1870 to provide income for the family. There are, among other flowers, some five hundred varieties of camellias. The layout is more romantic than Middleton, with a number of lakes, including several lined with bald cypress with their typical "knees"; their waters have been made almost black from the tannic acid of these roots. Altogether a dream, or, as John Galsworthy said, "the most beautiful garden in the world."

Located 12 miles/19 kilometers northwest of downtown Charleston, on SC 61. March–November open daily 8:00 A.M.–5:30 P.M. December–February open daily 8:30 A.M.–4:30 P.M. Admission to the grounds and gardens is $9 for adults, $7 for teens, $4 for children ages 6–12, free for children under 6. Admission to the house is $5 per person, free for children under 6. A 45-minute nature-train tour of the plantation is available at a cost of $3 for adults, $2 for teens, $1 for children ages 6–12, free for children under 6. For more information call (803) 571–1266.

CYPRESS GARDENS (1920s)
3030 Cypress Gardens Road
Moncks Corner, South Carolina

The *Taxodium distichum* buff will find at Cypress Gardens a satisfying quota (160 acres/65 hectares) of this wonderful tree, which is best seen by rowboat. (The lake was originally used as a freshwater impoundment for cultivating rice.) The gardens, laid out in the 1920s and amplified by azaleas and other flowers, were generously given to the City of Charleston in 1963.

Located approximately 24 miles/39 kilometers north of Charleston, 4 miles/6.4 kilometers east of US 52. Open daily 9:00 A.M.–5:00 P.M. Closed Thanksgiving, Christmas, and New Year's Day. March–April admission is $6 for adults, $5 for senior citizens, $2 for children ages 6–16. May–February admission is $5 for adults, $4 for senior citizens, $2 for children. For more information call (803) 553–0515.

HUNTER HOUSE (c. 1748)
54 Washington Street at Elm
Newport, Rhode Island

As one of the finest examples of the Colonial period in the country, the Hunter House merits a visit. The house faces Narragansett Bay so that its original owner, the merchant Jonathan Nichols, could watch his ships enter the harbor, a body of water that has seen a busier and tidier past. The dwelling experienced declining fortunes, then serious alterations, beginning in the latter part of the nineteenth century. It served as a convalescent home and later sheltered the Sisters of St. Joseph. Originally the most elaborate entry was on the waterfront side but this disappeared at the time a porch was added (c. 1872). When recently discovered in a nearby rectory the door was retrieved and placed on the front of the house because the water approach is now unimportant (a duplicate was made for the rectory). The beaded clapboards establish a neutrality that emphasizes the garlanded, broken pediment of the entry, one of the period's most regal doorways. But it is within that the chief richness lies. On each of the two main floors there are four rooms, all small in size though the central halls are spacious. The rooms on both floors at the northeast corner (right on entering), with their fireplaces verged on each side by shell cupboards, and with pilasters that fill and turn the corners, are noteworthy, but the wainscoted halls and the other rooms are outstanding. All has been beautifully restored (1949) and refurnished by the Preservation Society of Newport County, a dedicated group organized in 1945. (See Antoinette F. Downing and Vincent J. Scully, Jr.'s admirable *The Architectural Heritage of Newport, Rhode Island*, Harvard University Press, 1952; Clarkson N. Potter, Jr., 1967, for the historic background.)

May–October open daily 10:00 A.M.–5:00 P.M. April open Saturday–Sunday 10:00 A.M.–5:00 P.M. Admission is $6.50 for adults, $3 for children 6–11. Tours available. For more information call (401) 847-1000.

REDWOOD LIBRARY (1748–50)
50 Bellevue Avenue (between Old Beach Road and Redwood Street)
Newport, Rhode Island

Peter Harrison, architect

Palladio's S. Giorgio Maggiore (1560) in Venice was the double-pedimented great-grandfather of the Redwood Library, but its direct parentage, as Fiske Kimball first pointed out, was Edward Hoppus's *Andrea Palladio's Architecture, in Four Books* of 1736. The skillful, British-born and educated Peter Harrison, though a sea captain and merchant by trade and later a Royal Customs Collector, was a knowledgeable architectural amateur who had the Hoppus book in his library, along with works on Inigo Jones and Lord Burlington. For the Redwood Library Harrison mulled the possibility of combining several vocabularies—at that time architecture in America was still largely a vocabulary art—and came up with this accomplished, if derivative, result possibly in association with his brother Joseph. It vaunts, moreover, one of the earliest portico and temple facades in the colonies following the much larger one on the second St. Philip's (1710–23) in Charleston, a church that Harrison had visited. (Harrison also used a portico in his later King's Chapel in Boston—see page 86.) The Classic Revival expression of the library is given greater similarity to its European prototypes by its precise imitation in wood of ashlar construction, with paint sanded to resemble stone. Some feel that Harrison's use of the Classical was the forerunner of Thomas Jefferson's.

A transverse wing by George Snell with octagonal cupola was added to the library in 1858; a larger wing, designed by George C. Mason, was added at the rear in 1875; four other additions were made in this century. Thus when viewed from the side—and only from the side—there is an accretive and even awkward quality to the building. The facade, however, is sophisticated. The interior, in spite of the additions, is surprisingly homogeneous, lofty and dignified. In addition to its rare books—almost half the original collection survives—the library has an important assemblage of eighteenth- and nineteenth-century portraits, including one of Abraham Redwood, for whom the library is named. Note the garden's eighteenth-century octagonal gazebo, which formerly graced the Redwood country house; it is attributed to Harrison.

Open Monday–Saturday 9:30 A.M.–5:30 P.M. Closed for holidays. Group tours can be scheduled; a donation of $50 per group is suggested. For more information call (401) 847–0292.

KING'S CHAPEL (1749–54/1785–87)
58 Tremont Street at School Street
Boston, Massachusetts

Peter Harrison, architect

The truncated exterior of King's Chapel—with 4-foot-/1.2-meter-thick dark granite walls (the first in the colonies of stone) and a highly serious portico—is not inviting. Plans for a towering steeple had to be abandoned when funds ran out, and even the construction of the wood Ionic portico came later (1785–87, but to Harrison's design). But within one finds a lustrous, ambitious nave aglow with chandelier, cream-colored walls, ornate coupled Corinthian columns and entablature, vaulted galleries, a fine canopied pulpit (pulpit 1717, canopy later), and red-damask-lined box pews. A lack of architectural coordination characterizes the chancel, but the nave, which set out to be the most splendid in the colonies, wears well. Some historians consider it the finest Georgian church interior in the United States.

The original parish was established in 1686 as the first Church of England parish in the Massachusetts Colony, and the earliest building was of wood. (The Puritans held organized religion solely in their control until that time.) In the mid-eighteenth century Peter Harrison designed the present structure, influenced by James Gibbs's work in London. The new church was built around the old, which was then thrown out through the windows of the new stone building. The cemetery alongside gives a good contrast to the crowded site around the building. The American Revolution caused, understandably, a period of crisis for the Church of England, and King's Chapel was briefly closed during that war, to open in 1782 as the first Unitarian church in the United States.

June–August open Monday–Saturday 9:30 A.M.–4:00 P.M.; April, May, and September open Monday, Friday, and Saturday 10:00 A.M.–4:00 P.M.; October–March open Saturday 10:00 A.M.–4:00 P.M. Admission is free, although a $1 donation is suggested. Tours can be arranged by calling (617) 227–2155; there is a fee of $5 per person.

PARLANGE (c. 1750)
False River
New Roads, Louisiana

Parlange was built only thirty-two years after New Orleans was founded (1718), so it gives us an informative index of early domestic architecture in Louisiana. (This finds a climax eighty to a hundred years later in the great Mississippi River plantations.) Parlange's architecture is an excellent example of the French-influenced raised cottage style or early Louisiana type. Moreover it has been lived in continuously, *mirabile dictu*, by descendants of the same family for eight generations. The house is built of stuccoed brick on the ground floor for the usual protection against water and dampness (there was no stone in the Delta region for the stone-trained French builders), and the circular columns that help support the gallery that surrounds and "protects" the house are also of brick. (Their original, wedge-shaped formwork still exists.) The upper part of the house was constructed of cypress and moss packed together with clay and stuccoed, a technique known as *bousillage*, literally "bungled" or "botched."

Although some changes have taken place over the years—the front stairs were probably inside the gallery originally, the roof at the rear was extended in the middle of the last century, and the formal garden in front has disappeared—Parlange provides as nostalgic a picture as is to be had of an unfortunately vanishing species of French culture in the United States. Note the unusually steep, French-influenced hip roof—its height precisely equals that of the two floors—and the two dovecotes in front. The interior reveals some fine detailing (note, for instance, the fanlights over the windows). For years only minimum upkeep could be made, but after World War I the family was able to spruce the building up somewhat. The interior and exterior were fully restored in the mid-1980s under the direction of a member of the Parlange family.

Located 8 miles/13 kilometers north off US 190 on LA 1 or LA 78; or on LA 1, 6 miles/9.7 kilometers south of New Roads. Open daily 9:00 A.M.–5:00 P.M. All visits are guided; tours are $7 per person. All visits must be scheduled in advance by calling (504) 638–8410.

AQUIA CHURCH (1751–57)
2938 Jefferson Davis Highway
Stafford, Virginia

Almost hidden atop a knoll, Aquia Church (pronounced *ak-quiah*) stands peacefully surrounded by a graveyard and a vast variety of trees. The muffled sounds of traffic seem eons away. The building was constructed of red brick with prominent, locally quarried, Aquia Creek sandstone quoins, echoed strongly around the doors. (This stone was also used for the United States Capitol and the White House.) A certain quaintness characterizes the exterior but the interior is marked by a lively cheeriness. The church grows from a Greek-cross plan (like that of Christ Church in Irvington, Virginia, see page 70), its all-white plastered and painted interior producing a welcoming atmosphere. The interior is also thought to be a near copy of a parish church in Overwharton, Staffordshire, England, whence came many of the region's early settlers.

There are two dominant elements within that attract attention: the pedimented panel on the sanctuary wall and the three-tiered pulpit known as a "triple decker" at right. The pediment is sharply detailed in white-painted wood with the Ten Commandments, the Apostles' Creed, and the Lord's Prayer in four arched black panels impressively installed above the altar table.

(In most seventeenth- and many early-eighteenth-century churches in England and the colonies these works were built into the architecture because of the scarcity of books. This ordinance stemmed from the 1604 Hampton Court Conference that stated, among other requirements, that "the furniture of a church must include the Ten Commandments on the east wall, with other chosen sentences." Faith, prayer, and law—the Apostles' Creed, the Lord's Prayer, and the Ten Commandments—were commonly used.) The pulpit at Aquia, unlike many of the period, is spatially related to the sanctuary by its angled projection and its triple desks, seasonally vested, creating thus good three-dimensional activity. The balusters in the pulpit stairs and in the sanctuary railing are painted white and topped by dark walnut rails. The square box pews are low and white with the same dark rails seen in the chancel. The organ and choir are in the gallery over the west door. Natural light floods the interior via its double row of windows, the top one roundheaded to emphasize from the outside that only one floor exists within (as at Pohick Church in Lorton, Virginia, see page 109); the whole feeling of space is admirable. (Inigo Jones's Banqueting Hall in London probably inspired the window arrangement.) Though no longer used, note the well-branched chandeliers.

A few years after its completion the church interior burned (1754), but it was rebuilt three years later by the same "undertaker," that is, builder/contractor, a gentleman with the lugubrious name of Mourning Richards, who did the work for 110,900 pounds/50,000 kilograms of tobacco. Though repaired through the years, fortunately no major changes were made. Its upkeep has been noteworthy due to a generous endowment given the church in 1873. James Wren (little or no relation to Christopher) was, some feel, the architect, but this is by no means certain.

Located just east of Aquia exit of I-95 and US 1, 3 miles/4.8 kilometers north of Stafford Aquia Church. The church is open for services on Sunday morning. Visits during the week by appointment only: contact (703) 659–4007.

ST. MICHAEL'S EPISCOPAL CHURCH (1752–61)
14 St. Michael's Alley
Charleston, South Carolina

Samuel Cardy, probable architect

St. Michael's, its neighbor St. Philip's (see page 190), and Philadelphia's Christ Church (see page 66), were three of the colonies' great churches of the mid-eighteenth century. All three derive from English prototypes with inspiration primarily from the architecture of Christopher Wren and James Gibbs. The tower of the steeple of St. Michael's rises in line with the entry wall of the church à la Gibbs, unlike churches by Wren who "attached" towers outside the fabric. The design of the lovely, much-copied, triple-stage, octagonal steeple on a square base hints of Wren's St. Bride, Fleet Street, London (1680), whose slender 227-foot-/69-meter-high steeple has four octagonal stages on a square tower. The designer of the well-knit St. Michael's is not positively known, though the church believes that Samuel Cardy is the likeliest candidate. This conclusion is seconded by Gene Waddell, former director of the South Carolina Historical Society. Cardy is also mentioned by HABS (Historic American Buildings Survey) as probably being responsible for the design, while almost all agree that Cardy undertook construction and supervision of the church. The attribution by some to Peter Harrison of Rhode Island is thus very insubstantial.

St. Michael's is rightly admired for its monumental Roman Doric portico (the present one was rebuilt after the earthquake of 1886), and this was long considered the first of its great size to grace any church in the colonies. (The first English church with a freestanding portico with giant columns was probably London's St. George's, Hanover Square [1712–24] by John James.) However, the argument can be well advanced—and, it is thought, sustained—that the triple porticos at the west end of nearby St. Philip's, built in 1723, though destroyed by fire in 1835, were almost exactly rebuilt (except for degree of projection) in 1835–38, making them the first by almost thirty years. As St. Michael's former historiographer put it, "It is clear that the architect for St. Michael's intended to copy St. Philip's in the way of porticoes and out-do St. Philip's in the way of the tower." (Which he certainly did.) The columns and walls of St. Michael's are of brick stuccoed and painted white, with the tower rising, as mentioned, flush with the front wall, directly behind the portico. (The steeple's high arcade level offers a fine panorama of the city.)

The interior—changed only a bit through the years (1772, 1905)—is daringly trussed from wall to wall, without intermediate supports. (The interior of Nicholas Hawksmoor's St. Allege, Greenwich, England [1712–14] has been mentioned as inspiration and is similarly spanned.) The nave, which measures 70 feet/21 meters long by 51 feet/16 meters wide, tends to be restless, contrasting the white plaster of ceiling and walls with the heavy cedar of the galleries, which encroach upon the nave with their low broadness upheld by one-story supporting columns. Highlighting the insistence of this dark wood is the freestanding, octagonal pulpit, the massive cap of which rises above the gallery on the side. Behind this stands the chancel,

renovated and re-stenciled in 1905, and resplendent in almost Byzantine glory. The Victorian glass of the Palladian chancel window (by Lewis Comfort Tiffany, 1893), like that on the side aisle, is anachronistic to the eighteenth-century spirit of the church. (Such glass gives the same infelicitous effect in several Greek Revival churches and a Greek Revival synagogue also in Charleston.)

A major renovation was completed in 1993, restoring much of the church to its original appearance. The organ, some pipes of which are original, stands in the case initially made for it in 1768 by Johann Snetzler and imported from London. The eight bells in the steeple were also from London (1764), sent back for repairs during the Revolution and again to be recast following their destruction during the Civil War. Be sure to see the adjacent cemetery with delicate wrought-iron gate (1838) by J. A. W. Justi.

Open Monday–Friday 9:00 A.M.–4:45 P.M., Saturday 9:00 A.M.–12:00 noon. Sunday services held at 8:00 and 10:30 A.M. 10-minute tours given after Sunday 10:30 service. For more information call (803) 723–0603.

NASSAU HALL (1754–56; 1855)
Princeton University
Nassau Street at Witherspoon
Princeton, New Jersey

Robert Smith and William Shippen, architects

When Nassau Hall (named for William of Orange and Nassau, who later became William III of England) was finished in 1756 it was the largest academic building in the colonies—and contained the entire facilities of the college. Shelled and injured in the Revolutionary War, it has served such various nonacademic functions as a barracks and, for a brief time, as the capitol of the fledgling United States. The building was designed primarily by Robert Smith, who, fresh from his native Scotland, was working in Philadelphia. Nassau Hall was his first independent commission; Dr. William Shippen was his associate. The building displays a dignified, straightforward facade highlighted only by its projected entry, or pavilion, and pediment. It is simply built of local stone, a material more informal than the hall's Georgian symmetry would normally suggest but one that creates a sympathetic ambiance. Following a fire in 1804 it was repaired by Benjamin Latrobe. The cupola was remodeled (and overly enlarged) in 1855 when the building was rebuilt (John Notman, architect) after another serious fire destroyed much of the interior. Two of the original three front doors were also then removed. The faculty room, which was formerly the chapel, projects at right angles to the building at the rear; it possesses a particularly handsome interior. Nassau Hall was, for its time and the experience of its designer, a surprisingly competent and original building. It exerted considerable influence on New England college building in the late eighteenth century from Harvard (Hollis Hall, 1763), to Brown (University Hall, 1771), to Dartmouth (Dartmouth Hall, 1791).

Open to the public Monday–Friday 9:00 A.M.–5:00 P.M. The interior and exterior of Nassau Hall are part of a free campus tour given by the Orange Key Guide Service. Tours given Monday–Saturday at 10:00 A.M., 11:00 A.M., 1:30 P.M., and 3:30 P.M., Sunday at 1:30 and 3:30 P.M. No tours given on major holidays or during winter or spring recesses. For more information call (609) 258–3603.

TROXELL-STECKEL HOUSE (1755–56)
4229 Reliance Street
Egypt, Pennsylvania

The Troxell-Steckel House and the barn facing it are prime examples of the rural vernacular of eastern Pennsylvania of two hundred years ago. Although most of the region's settlers came from western Germany and Switzerland, hence were more accustomed to constructing with half-timbering and brick than with stone, the limestone ledge that runs just below the soil of the eastern part of Pennsylvania proved an irresistible material. It is this lovely stone—sometimes naively employed (with few arches or corbels)—the direct geometry of its use, and its frequent conjunction with red-painted wood that make this area the home of some of the finest autochthonous farm buildings in the country. The steep roof of the house, its half-timbered interior walls, and its oversized fireplaces suggest medieval German influences in its design. Recently, new shakes have been put on the roof and on the pent roof that marks the top of the ground floor (and helps protect its windows), while the interior has been completely redone. The property was acquired by the Lehigh County Historical Society (1942) and restored by them (1943), with John K. Heyl, architect. It is one of the few farm groups in the Pennsylvania Dutch country accessible to the public. (The "Dutch" misnomer arose either from a garbled "Deutsch" or from the fact that most of the German immigrants to Pennsylvania in the eighteenth century left for the New World from the port of Rotterdam.) The stone lower floor of the barn, the vibrant red paint on the upper wooden section, and the *Hexenfoos* decoration—here indicating propitiation for rain—are typical of the region. (*Hexe* means "witch" or "sorceress" in German.) House and barn are now a most welcome museum.

Located 6 miles/9.6 kilometers north of Allentown on PA 145, left on PA 329. June–September open Saturday–Sunday 1:00–4:00 P.M. Closed for holidays. June–October guided tours are available Saturday–Sunday 1:00–4:00 P.M. For more information call (610) 435-4664. The barn buff will find other examples in the area, though they are not open to the public. PA 143 and PA 662 provide reasonable hunting for examples that can be seen (only) from the road.

GUNSTON HALL (1755–59)
10709 Gunston Road
Mason Neck, Virginia

William Buckland, interiors and woodwork

The exterior of this small but ambitious house, which measures 60 x 40 feet/18 x 12 meters, will not startle the observer. The interior, however, never descends to a level less than handsome, and in the Palladian drawing room achieves the sumptuous. Moreover, the box gardens behind the house are worth the trip themselves.

It is said that George Mason, author of the Virginia Declaration of Rights, had started building Gunston Hall, and had the exterior walls up when he realized that he needed a master joiner to complete the dwelling properly. As his brother Thomson was then finishing his study of law in England, George asked him to find a skilled man there to work as an inden-

tured servant to finish the house. William Buckland, who had just completed his lengthy apprenticeship in the Joiners' Guild, was chosen—happily for the future development of architecture in the colonies—and came to Virginia as an indentured servant, like many before him. Gunston Hall was his first independent work in a career that reached its climax in the famous Hammond-Harwood House (1774–80) in Annapolis, Maryland (see page 116). It is astonishing that Buckland, then in his early twenties, could produce such knowledgeable design and detail as the interior of Gunston, but his innate cleverness and his access to the usual books turned out a rich result.

The drawing room, as mentioned, is the climax of the house, but the dining room, the so-called "Chinese room," was more innovative in that it was one of the first Oriental-influenced examples in the colonies, at a time when the style was coming into high fashion in England (influenced by the China tea trade). (It is the only chinoiserie woodwork scheme to survive from the colonial era.) The central hall, like many in the South, was often used in hot weather as a parlor, as its doors could be opened at both ends, thus forming an enclosed dogtrot, so to speak. The master bedroom was, as usual at that time, on the ground floor, with the children's rooms in the half story above—though room usage then was more flexible than today.

Gunston suffered after the Civil War—its kitchen dependency was replaced by an awkward addition, and its other outbuildings demolished, while its famous garden was largely ignored. Louis Hertie, the last private owner, purchased the house in 1912 and made many improvements; in 1932 he generously willed the estate to the Commonwealth of Virginia. Since then it has been fully restored, while the superb grounds and garden have been put back in impeccable shape under the expertise of the Garden Club of Virginia. Gunston Hall was opened to the public in 1952 under the direction of the National Society of the Colonial Dames of America. A second major renovation was begun in 1982.

In 1974 facilities for visitors were notably expanded by the Ann Mason Building, with Philip Ives as architect. Avoiding specious references to Gunston Hall itself (which stands some hundred yards away), or to the adjacent "Colonial" office block (1957), Ives took the brick and slate used in the eighteenth-century house and built a complex that is both architecturally comfortable with its neighbors and strictly of its time, appropriately scaled and with well-canted roof lines. (Note also the freedom displayed by the outsized panes of glass.) The facilities include reception, exhibition space and museum, gift shop, and a 200-seat auditorium with kitchen adjacent, and extensive parking on two sides.

Located 4 miles/6.4 kilometers east of US 1 on VA 242 (near Lorton). Open 9:30 A.M.–5:00 P.M. daily. Grounds open until 6:00 P.M. Closed on Thanksgiving, Christmas, and New Year's Day. Admission is $5 for adults, $4 for senior citizens, $1.50 for children ages 6–17. Free tours given every half-hour. For more information call (703) 550–9220.

MOUNT VERNON (1757–58/1777–84/1787)
Mount Vernon, Virginia

Ann Pamela Cunningham has not as yet appeared on a United States postage stamp. She should. For this energetic South Carolinian woman not only alerted the women that saved Mount Vernon from disintegration in the 1850s, she and her cohorts saw to it that funds were raised to purchase (1858) and restore the house and grounds. (Unbelievably, the U.S. Government and the Commonwealth of Virginia had each refused to buy the house and property, when, through the decline of its farming potential, the estate was offered for sale.) During the Civil War they personally kept off troops of both sides. This great mansion was preserved, and America was made dramatically conscious of its significant architectural heritage and the need to preserve it. (George Washington's headquarters in Newburgh, New York, built in 1750, had been rescued from demolition in 1850, but this is a small structure.)

In a way it can be said that Thomas Jefferson's Monticello (see page 110) and Washington's Mount Vernon, violently dissimilar though they appear, share several key characteristics: they are both Palladian in plan (with semidetached dependencies in the case of Mount Vernon) and

they both took a great many years to build and rebuild, each starting life with a small initial core that was expanded enormously. Moreover, both buildings freely deployed "textbook" details in doors and windows.

The additions to Washington's dwelling were so substantial and often so poorly coordinated in architectural terms that a price was paid: that price can be seen on the entrance side (only), where we are left with a less than satisfactory facade. A pediment (1778), seemingly tacked on as an afterthought, tries valiantly to pull this flat front together, while the irregular window spacing, instead of lending liveliness, merely looks amateurish. The second-story windows at the northeast end are fake (to disguise the high-ceilinged banquet room that fills this end of the house). Let us say that the rest of the exterior compensates. At the northeast end, a broken-pediment Palladian window—taken direct from Batty Langley's *Treasury of Designs* of 1740—embellishes the end, while along this inspired southeast front we find the country's first two-story, full-width, squared column portico, a feature that is as functional as it is beautiful, as it ties the house to its natural setting.

This "piazza" pioneered a unique architectural development we now imprecisely call "southern Colonial" (even though it took place after the Revolution). Domestic porticos were not previously unknown. Scores of houses—from Andrea Palladio's Villa Capra (possibly the first), to Colin Campbell's Mereworth Castle and Lord Burlington's Chiswick in England—had Palladian-inspired porticos adorning their fronts (and often sides and backs). But these were abutments, so to speak—a focal point on the facade. Washington made his airy, princely porch the facade itself, its ample depth (14 feet/4.3 meters) shielding the southeast wall from summer sun by day, while enabling the upper rooms to keep their bedroom windows open day and night, even in heavy rain. As a place to sit in the late afternoon, with its glorious panoramic view of the Potomac River, this porch was Washington's open-air living room and entertainment center for much of the year. Like an urban arcade it served as a spatial intermedium between architecture and landscape, tying both together in mutual harmony. It was probably Washington's "ignorance" of "correct" architecture—abetted by his natural desire for an outdoor "room"—that prompted its creation.

The first Mount Vernon—ironically named for a British admiral under whom Washington's half-brother Lawrence had served—was a one-and-one-half-story, smallish dwelling (erected mid-1730s). In 1754 George acquired the title to the house, and in 1757–58, in anticipation of his marriage to Martha Dandridge Custis (1759), enlarged the house by the addition of a full second floor, and expanded it laterally by dependencies (which were later replaced). The original farmhouse and its new height form the central part of Mount Vernon today; a hall with two rooms on either side (of slightly unequal size) and chimneys at the ends was incorporated into the final building. The exterior of the house was sheathed with wood beveled in imitation of stone and painted with a sand-finished paint—a Kentish and New England technique not previously used in the South. The popularity of the Washingtons—they were rarely without guests—and the attendant need for larger entertainment space prompted George to make the final expansions to the house, which were carried out from 1777–84, largely during the General's absence. Two additions were made to the central core, one at northeast (23 feet/7 meters) forming a multipurpose dining room, and one at southwest (22 feet/6.7 meters) providing for a study, another flight of stairs, and a pantry on the ground floor, with General Washington's room above. The present dependencies and their connecting colonnades were also constructed at this time, as was the famous piazza. The cupola dates from 1787.

The interiors of Mount Vernon, while not as elaborate as those of some of the James River plantations, are suitably rich; the delicate Adamesque plaster work in the ceiling of the dining room is noteworthy. But the main impact of Mount Vernon does not derive just from the house itself, or even its wonderful portico, but from the house, its situation, its outbuildings, and its extensive gardens (which should by all means be seen). All have been woven together to create a complex that provides one of the highlights of late-eighteenth-century American architecture.

The Mount Vernon Ladies' Association gives Washington complete credit for the design of what we see today. As a surveyor he was, of course, familiar with drafting instruments (a set of which is preserved in the house) and he had the usual English architectural books. Mount Vernon's house and grounds form one of our masterpieces—and not just because they sheltered our first president. The nation will be forever grateful to Ann Cunningham.

Located at end of George Washington Memorial Parkway, 14 miles/23 kilometers south of Washington, D.C. November–February open daily 9:00 A.M.–4:00 P.M.; April–August open daily 8:00 A.M.–5:00 P.M.; March, September, and October open daily 9:00 A.M.–5:00 P.M. Admission is $7 for adults, $6 for senior citizens, and $3 for children ages 6–11. There is a self-guided tour; guides are also available to answer questions.

TOURO SYNAGOGUE (1759–63)
85 Touro Street at Division Street
Newport, Rhode Island

Peter Harrison, architect

Congregation Jeshuat Israel's Sephardic forebears had been attracted to Rhode Island by Roger Williams's espousal in the 1640s of religious tolerance—that startling concept in the early colonies. They built in Newport what is now the oldest synagogue in North America. Peter Harrison, convenient and talented, and with his Redwood Library (see page 85) just up the street, was chosen as its architect. The synagogue's beige exterior, highlighted by a small portico, stands calmly on its open site, its unusual angle to the street arising from the necessity to have the ark face east.

After the reticence of the outside the closely packed architectural activity of the interior hits one with surprising force: it is one of the most accomplished rooms in the American colonies. Slightly longer than it is wide (approximately 40 x 30 feet/12 x 9 meters), the temple's modest size is impacted on three sides by the balconies for the women and by the prominent bema and sanctuary that occupy much of the central floor space. The men of the original congregation sat only on wainscot benches along the sides under the balconies, not in the center. The galleries are supported by twelve columns—Ionic below, Corinthian above—which, of course, recall the twelve tribes of Israel. Columns, balustrade, and entablature are precisely detailed, the balusters around the bema and sanctuary repeating those defining the balconies. Most of these architectural elements, including the basic inner form, were freely adopted from English books, with many details inspired by James Gibbs, but they were incorporated with an innate feeling for both space and detail. Some authorities believe that Bevis Marks, the Spanish and Portuguese synagogue (1701) on Hencage Lane in London—the oldest in England and a building that Harrison had almost undoubtedly seen—was influential in the Newport building, particularly for its interior. The Sephardic synagogue in Amsterdam is also seen by some as a model for this structure.

The synagogue experienced difficult days after the Revolution (as did Newport itself), and almost all of the congregation dispersed to New York; for much of the nineteenth century the synagogue was closed. If it had not been for the thoughtful generosity of the sons of the first rabbi, Isaac Touro, who left funds in their wills for the preservation of the synagogue, and for their sister who saw that those funds were put to proper use—hence giving this structure the popular name it now carries—the building would have vanished. Today, fortunately, it stands in excellent shape, and is in use for services by an active congregation.

In summer, open Sunday–Friday 10:00 A.M.–4:00 P.M. In winter, open Sunday–Friday 1:00–3:00 P.M. All visits are guided; free half-hour tours are given. For more information call (401) 847-4794.

WENTWORTH-GARDNER HOUSE (1760)
50 Mechanic Street
Portsmouth, New Hampshire

Peter Harrison, architect

Locally held to be one of the most nearly perfect examples of Georgian architecture in America, this riverfront house was once owned by New York's Metropolitan Museum of Art. Recent evidence suggests that Peter Harrison was the house's architect and Michael Whidden the master builder. Its ocher facade sports a flat, pine, "blocked front"—that is, wide boards cut in imitation of stone—a lapidary presumption accentuated by the white painted quoins. Clapboards sheathe the other three sides. The plan measures 46.8 x 36.6 feet/14.2 x 11 meters. The magnificent Baroque entry, the neatly pedimented shutterless lower windows, and the hip roof with dormers create a quietly positive presence. The original garden extension to the river has been severed by the road. The interior is notable for its exuberant late Georgian carving—done by local artisans—and for its scenic wallpaper, particularly the hand-painted paper in the dining room. The spacious upstairs hall reels with a parade of pilasters, architrave, frieze, cornice, and cove ceiling. The kitchen should also be seen, for, among other items, its 6.5-foot-/2-meter-wide chimney. The four rooms of the first floor, each with fireplace, some with original English tiles, are directly mirrored above. The whole house was beautifully restored some years ago by a former owner, Wallace Nutting, who removed non-original clapboards from the front and even discovered its lovely stair in another house. It has been well furnished and was opened to the public in 1940.

Open mid-June through mid-October Tuesday–Sunday 1:00–4:00 P.M. Closed July 4 and Labor Day. Admission is $4 for adults, $2 for children over 12. Half-hour tours are available. For more information call (603) 436–4406 (June to October only).

LADY PEPPERRELL HOUSE (1760/1923)
24 Pepperrell Road
Kittery Point, Maine

The Lady Pepperrell House, overlooking the Piscataqua River, stands in somewhat lonely grandeur outside the town of Kittery Point. It attains a highly patrician quality through its central pedimented pavilion boldly delineated by two-story Ionic pilasters. The richness of these pilasters is reemphasized by the simplicity of the sides of the house and the dormer-less roof. (An open porch added by John Mead Howells in 1923 stands at the left end.) Though this Georgian mansion is built entirely of wood, the smooth siding of the pavilion and the quoins at the corners both imitate stone, as was often the fashion of the day. The Lady Pepperrell House was given to the Society for the Preservation of New England Antiquities in 1942, the house donated by Mrs. Lovell Hodge, the contents by Hodge and Catharine Parry. The fireplaces, mantels, and woodwork are outstanding. "This truly elegant house may be counted as one of the very finest Colonial mansions ever built in Maine." (*Maine Forms of American Architecture*, Deborah Thompson, ed., Downeast Magazine, 1976. This book is a highly recommended survey of Maine's notable buildings.)

Located on ME 103, 2 miles/3.2 kilometers west of Kittery Point and 4 miles/6.4 kilometers from Portsmouth, New Hampshire. Privately owned since 1985. The interior is not open to the public.

MOFFATT-LADD HOUSE (1760–63)
154 Market Street
Portsmouth, New Hampshire

Though it was built only three years after the Wentworth-Gardner House, the Moffatt-Ladd House expresses on the exterior far more New England than England with its foursquare, commanding bulk surmounted by a balustraded captain's walk. Records show that it was built under the supervision of Michael Whidden. The house's box form hints of the Federal Style, which reached its zenith years later in the famous town houses of Charles Bulfinch and Samuel McIntire. Moffatt-Ladd establishes a unity with its setting, which is masterminded by the picket fence angling to the front door and by the extensive garden to the rear. The house enjoys a splendid sweep of the Piscataqua River in front—its captain's walk was an active one. The most distinctive features of the facade—one of the first in the town to have three stories— are the line of theatrically pedimented second-floor windows and the subdued portico with flanking windows at entry level. The top-floor windows abut and almost disappear into the cornice. A spacious and elaborate stair-hall, instead of being a routine central divider of the house, occupies the northeast corner, a location more of English than Colonial derivation. Paneling, cornice, and stair are outstanding. In the yellow bed chamber, the unique wallpaper border depicting hunting scenes (taken from copper prints) should be noted, as should the French wallpaper in the hall (1815–20) and the detailing and carving throughout the house. Be certain to see the garden and the separate Counting House (1831–32, off Market Street). The Colonial Dames of America in the State of New Hampshire owns the house, having acquired it from the heirs in 1912.

June 15–October 15 open Monday–Saturday 11:00 A.M.–5:00 P.M., Sunday 2:00–5:00 P.M. Open by appointment the rest of the year. Admission is $4 for adults, $1 for children ages 7–12. All visits are guided; 45-minute tours are given every half-hour. For more information call (603) 436-8221.

BRICK MARKET (1762–72)
Washington Square at Thames Street
Newport, Rhode Island

Peter Harrison, architect

For this market Peter Harrison adopted the design of Somerset House by Inigo Jones and John Webb published in *Vitruvius Britannicus*, volume I (1715–25). (See Carl Bridenbaugh, *Peter Harrison, First American Architect*, University of North Carolina Press, 1949.) Instead of a five-bay frontal design, the Newport version is a three-by-seven-bay freestanding building 33 x 66 feet/10 x 20 meters in size. Thus Harrison, in this, his last major work, as in his first (the Redwood Library—see page 85), was heavily dependent upon his phenomenal collection of architectural books, a not unreasonable possession for an architectural dilettante. The Brick Market, though built for the transaction of goods—its ground floor was originally open in the approved market fashion, while its upper two stories contained offices—was remodeled as a theater in 1793, then from 1853 to 1900 used as the city hall. The exterior was restored (1928) and the interior rebuilt (1930), as the plaque outside proclaims, under Norman M. Isham through the generosity of John Nicholas Brown. The building is owned by the city of Newport. In 1988 it was restored, and in 1993 the Newport Historical Society took over the structure to house the Museum of Newport History.

January–March open Tuesday–Saturday 11:00 A.M.–4:00 P.M., Sunday 1:00–4:00 P.M. April–December open Monday, Wednesday–Saturday 10:00 A.M.–5:00 P.M., Sunday 1:00–5:00 P.M. Closed New Year's Day, Thanksgiving, and Christmas. Admission is $5 for adults, $4 for senior citizens, $3 for children ages 6–13, and $13 per family. Guided tours are available. For more information call (401) 846-0813.

MOUNT CLARE (c. 1763/1906)
1500 Washington Boulevard at Monroe Street (US 1)
Carroll Park
Baltimore, Maryland

Mount Clare—Baltimore's only remaining pre-Revolutionary mansion—does not fall into the routine pattern of Georgian tidewater plantation houses. On the north side it projects an unusual central bay with open portico below and enclosed room above emblazoned with a large Palladian window, and, on the river front, it carries four two-story, two-toned brick pilasters. (The awkward lunette on the river pediment dates from c. 1785.) The original wings and hyphens on either side of the house disappeared well over a century ago, and it was not until 1906 that they were handsomely replaced as we see them today. The interior, much of it in plaster in imitation of wood, still possesses many of the early furnishings. It also contains a magnificent collection of eighteenth-century china, silver, and crystal.

In 1890 the city acquired the property and its extensive grounds (for use as a park). Since 1916 Mount Clare has been under the custody of the National Society of the Colonial Dames of America in the State of Maryland, and is maintained jointly by them with the Baltimore Department of Parks and Recreation.

Open Tuesday–Friday 11:00 A.M.–4:00 P.M., Saturday–Sunday 1:00–4:00 P.M. Closed in January and for major holidays. Admission is $5 for adults, $3 for students, senior citizens, and groups, $1 for children under 12. 45-minute tours given on the hour. For additional information, call (410) 837-3262.

CLIVEDEN (1763–67/1776)
6401 Germantown Avenue (US 422)
Philadelphia, Pennsylvania

William Peters, architect

Withdrawn behind a walled lot and surrounded by magnificent trees (especially the tulip trees), Cliveden set a patrician stage as the summer home of Chief Justice Benjamin Chew (1722–1810). Its design, once believed to be the justice's, is now attributed to his legal colleague William Peters—aided by the various books available, notably those on Palladio's works and on eighteenth-century British patterns—the whole put together by a local master carpenter and a skilled mason/contractor, John Hesser. The estate consists of the main dwelling with two setback dependencies used for a kitchen and a laundry. The kitchen (at left) is attached to the house by a curved colonnade, which was added in 1776. Cliveden's dressed stone facade (the sides and rear are stuccoed), with slightly projecting pedimented entry bay, and rich cornice bear resemblance to Mount Pleasant (in Fairmount Park), a few miles away and a few years earlier. But in plan Cliveden uses a luxurious lateral hall with stairs set dramatically behind four rich Doric columns instead of the more usual central hallway. With its 12-foot/3.6-meter height this hall forms an imposing entry. (A similar T-shaped entry can be seen at Carter's Grove Plantation in Virginia, see page 80.) On either side of the hall are reception rooms, of which the drawing room is the finest (note detail of door and fireplace). The furnishings are almost all from the Chew family, and add greatly to the quality of the interior—and to its livable atmosphere. The furnishings were given by members of the Chew family, whose forebears had occupied the house for over two hundred years.

Cliveden played a major role in the Battle of Germantown (1777), when some 3,000 men under Washington tried to move back into Philadelphia but were repulsed by 120 British soldiers holed up in the house. That the mansion survived the bombardment—scars still abound—is miraculous; it also speaks well of Hesser. The house's purity, however, was compromised in 1867–68 when additions were made at the rear and atop the colonnade to the kitchen.

The dwelling, contents, and 6 acres/2.4 hectares of land were acquired by the National Trust for Historic Preservation in 1972. It is one of the trust's finest properties.

April–December open Thursday–Sunday 12:00 noon–4:00 P.M. The rest of the year open by appointment only; call (215) 848-1777. Admission is $6 for adults, $4 for students. One-hour guided tours are available.

ST. PAUL'S CHAPEL (1764–66/1767–68/1794)
209–211 Broadway
New York, New York

Church architecture in the thirteen colonies underwent an evolution of liturgical mores paralleling that of the mother country. The earliest churches in Virginia and New England were small-windowed, medieval affairs (see St. Luke's Church, Smithville, Virginia, page 36 and Old Ship Meeting House, Hingham, Massachusetts, page 48). Then with the "new" English fashions of Christopher Wren (1632–1723) and James Gibbs (1682–1754), who opened up their churches to snatch scarce sunlight, most churches along the eastern seaboard—as opposed to their contemporaries in the Spanish Southwest—welcomed the sun as far as their building techniques allowed. (The anti-Establishment New England meeting houses—one of the colonies' few architectural contributions—also were awash with light from numerous windows.) Yet since Independence, and largely as a result of the Gothic Revival in the early part of the nineteenth century, churches have tended to avoid luminosity as out of character, hence disquieting.

St. Paul's Chapel, which is the only surviving Colonial church in Manhattan, epitomizes the bright, large-windowed, Gibbs-inspired church. Because New York is ten degrees latitude south of London's gloomier weather, the building takes on an added atmosphere of cheer plus an almost Baroque exuberance. The influence of Gibbs's St. Martin-in-the-Fields can be clearly seen here on Broadway. The spirit of light is carried through to the colors of the interior, which range from pinkish walls, to blue-green vaulted ceiling, to white-and-gold-touched pulpit. Note, too, the *Glory* above the altar, carved by Pierre L'Enfant of Washington, D.C. fame. Sparkle is accented by Waterford chandeliers, five down the central aisle with others in the galleries. Here is a setting for a religion of joy: the interior might well be the most genial around. Thomas McBean is said to be the architect, although there is no evidence to support this. St. Paul's has been little altered since the portico on Broadway was added (1767–68, the church's

previous entry faced the Hudson River and today's Church Street) and the tower shortly thereafter (1794, by James C. Lawrence).

For the antithetical experience in a church nave walk a few blocks south on Broadway to Richard Upjohn's Trinity Church (see page 202). We have in these two a summation of the difference between the Georgian and the Gothic Revival. St. Paul's Chapel, incidentally, is a member of Trinity parish.

Located between Fulton and Vesey streets. Open Monday–Friday 9:00 A.M.–3:00 P.M., Sunday 7:00 A.M.–3:00 P.M. Closed Saturdays and holidays. Free tours can be arranged by calling (212) 602–0872.

POWEL HOUSE (1765–69)
244 South 3rd Street
Philadelphia, Pennsylvania

Charles Stedman, architect

Rescued—like the entire area of Society Hill—from the slum pall that began to creep upon this once desirable section of Philadelphia after people of means moved away from the nearby river, the Powel House stands as eloquent witness to an architectural salvation. It also holds historical significance, as it was the home of Samuel Powel, the first mayor of Philadelphia after the colonies won their independence, and his wife Elizabeth Willing Powel. Though the main dwelling is only 31 feet/9.4 meters wide by 46 feet/14 meters deep, a long back building holding a kitchen and apartment is attached to the rear, with a period garden adjoining. The dark red brick of the chaste exterior is enlivened by the white-painted woodwork of its shutters and by the light marble keystones above each window plus the usual stringcourse.

It is within the house that lavishness takes over. Paneling from two of its finest rooms was purchased by and removed to the Philadelphia Museum of Art and the Metropolitan Museum in New York—at the time acts of kindness. The two major rooms of the second floor—the front ballroom and the back drawing room—are elegant achievements both in overall harmony and refinement of detail. The front room, which extends the width of the house, is unusual in that its walls are wainscoted all the way up to the finely carved cornice that encircles the chamber. A delicately ornamented ceiling tops all. Charles Stedman was the designer (and first owner) of the Powel House but the English architectural "text" books of the day were obviously of importance for the decoration. When deterioration set in at the end of the nineteenth century, the house was used as a horsehair factory as well as a mattress factory; finally when threatened in 1930 with almost immediate destruction it was saved by the Herculean efforts of Frances Anne Wister, who later formed the Philadelphia Society for the Preservation of Landmarks in order to preserve select historic structures in the area. (The society also maintains the nearby Hill-Physick House [1786] at 321 South 4th Street, and Grumblethorpe [1744] at 5267 Germantown Avenue.) In 1994 one bedroom was completely restored; restoration work on the rest of the interior is slowly progressing. In spite of the uses and misuses of the Powel House through the years, the mansion stands as one of the handsomest Georgian dwellings in the city.

Open Tuesday–Saturday 10:00 A.M.–4:00 P.M. Closed in January and on Easter, Thanksgiving, and Christmas. Admission is $3 for adults, $2 for senior citizens, $1 for children. Various tours available. Tours can also be scheduled by calling (215) 627–0364.

CHOWAN COUNTY COURT HOUSE (1767)
East King Street at Court Street
Edenton, North Carolina

Gilbert Leigh, architect

A small but skillfully proportioned two-story courthouse, perhaps the finest Georgian court-house in the South. Its discreetly projecting and pedimented central bay, the relation of this three-windowed bay to the one-windowed (per floor) sides, the cornice and pediment with prominent modillions, and a competent cupola atop the hip roof make a nicely taut building. In front, a bowered village green slopes down to Edenton Bay and the Albemarle Sound. The courtroom on the ground floor was in use until 1979—in addition to court work, it accom-modated a variety of public meetings. Note the apsidal bay at the rear on which stands the por-tentous judge's chair. The second floor contains an unusually tall (13 feet/4 meters) and siz-able (30 x 45 feet/9.1 x 14 meters) white-pine-paneled assembly room, reputedly the largest in the colonies at that time. This served for town festivities, banquets, and similar gatherings. Its paneling rises to the ceiling to meet its cornice.

In constant use for over two hundred years, the courthouse is in excellent condition. The brick stringcourse across the front was formerly painted white, as were the lintels over the win-dows. Authorities attribute the design of the building to one Gilbert Leigh, a local man who originally came from Williamsburg. The influence of the Virginia Capitol is evident. Outstand-ing—and a National Historic Landmark.

The exterior was restored in 1991. Restoration of the interior, begun in 1994, is still in progress; it will return the building to its c. 1850 condition, with the exception of the east wing, which will hold modern facilities. The courthouse will continue to be used for various public events.

The interior is currently closed to the general public. The interior and exterior are included on a five-building tour given by the Historic Edenton Visitors Center. April 1–October 31, tours given Monday–Saturday at 9:30 A.M., 11:00 A.M., 1:00 P.M., and 2:30 P.M., Sunday at 1:30 P.M. and 2:30 P.M. November 1–March 31, tours given Monday–Saturday at 10:30 A.M., 12:30 P.M., and 2:00 P.M., Sunday at 1:30 P.M. The cost is $5 for adults, $2.50 for children grades K–12. For more information call the Historic Edenton Visitors Center at (919) 482–2637.

TRYON PALACE (1767–70/1952–59)
610 Pollock Street at George Street
New Bern, North Carolina

John Hawks, architect
Perry, Shaw, Hepburn & Dean, architects of restoration

New Bern—named by Swiss settlers in 1710—possesses in Tryon Palace the most significant Colonial restoration in the United States after Williamsburg. The ambitious restoration of Governor William Tryon's palace is due to the energy and resources of Maude Moore (Mrs. James Edwin) Latham, who was born in New Bern and who from early childhood had wanted to rebuild the state's first "permanent" capitol. The superb result involved the complete rebuilding and furnishing of the palace and its flanking buildings. (A 1798 fire destroyed the main building, and though the east dependency survived the fire, it at some unrecorded time "disappeared"; the stable adjunct to the west remained structurally sound.) In addition to the rebuilding of the house, the extensive gardens—today one of the delights of the place—had to be carefully replanted. The problem was further complicated by the fact that fifty-four houses, which for 150 years had naturally encroached on the old domain, had to be removed by the state, which by then had title to the area.

The restoration, like that at Williamsburg, was not conjectural. It was built on the excavated foundations of the eighteenth-century buildings, with the aid, unbelievably, of the architect's original drawings, which were found in New York and London. The whole project has been sumptuously carried out, from house to furnishings to gardens. The refurnishing of the palace was enormously simplified by a precise inventory—discovered in England in 1953—made for Governor Tryon in 1771 when he was appointed Royal Governor of New York and left New Bern. (The furnishings of the governors of the colonies were their personal properties and went with them when they were transferred.)

Tryon Palace derives, as would be expected, from Andrea Palladio, interpreted by John Hawks via James Gibbs's *A Book of Architecture* (1728). Plate 63 of his book shows a similar dwelling with raised two-story centrally pedimented block attached by quadrants to flanking two-story dependencies. The use of quadrants—the most graceful of hyphens—was puzzlingly rare in the American colonies (Mount Airy near Richmond and Mount Vernon [see page 94] are the only two surviving prominent examples). Hawks was brought from England by Governor Tryon to design and supervise the building of his "palace." The site's guidebook claims that Hawks was "the first professional architect to remain in America," but little is known of his subsequent activities except for two houses in New Bern, of which the John Wright Stanly House (1780) is open to the public. (Peter Harrison, 1716–75, Yorkshire-born, is generally considered the States' first "professional" architect.) In any case Hawks, with the usual books, turned out a more than distinguished building.

As one approaches the palace, one notes the 1741 English wrought-iron gates. A second gate (of little interest) and a wrought-iron fence enclose the semi-ovoid compound of the palace, the main building flanked by a stable dependency at the right (west), with kitchen and office at the left. The royal coat of arms of George III stands colorfully forth in the pediment. The roof parapet on either side of the pediment was rare for its time. Most of the lower floor of the palace is given over to "official" rooms, climaxed by the council room in the southeast (far left) corner. This room, which also doubled as a ballroom, is filled with distinguished furniture and chandeliers. Several kings and a queen supervise affairs of state from their canvases. The state dining room, adjacent to the council room, is equally rich. It should be noted that all of the mantels and much of the molding (chair railing, etc.) came from a series of eighteenth-century English mansions either directly or via antique dealers. Even the brass locks were found abroad. In spite of the resulting lack of consistency, all of the interior was restored to its period of greatness. The upper floor formed the governor's residence and, like the lower, has been meticulously restored and beautifully furnished. Note, on going upstairs, the skylight that Hawks used to illuminate the interior.

In addition to seeing the house—informed hostesses escort one through and guidebooks are available—the visitor should explore the elaborate series of gardens that occupy much of the grounds. These range from intricate geometrical compositions, to kitchen gardens, to "wildernesses" found on each side of the smooth and ample south lawn, which once rolled down to the Trent River. The outbuildings, too, should not be missed, for they have been just as carefully restored as the mansion. Note the several "blind" windows in these dependencies. Perry, Shaw, Hepburn & Dean of Boston, who restored Williamsburg, were the restoration architects for Tryon Palace. It might indeed be "The Most Beautiful Building in the Colonial Americas" as the brochure proclaims: Hugh Morrison adds—from studying the drawings before the rebuilding—"Beyond question the finest house in North Carolina, and perhaps in any of the Colonies" (*Early American Architecture*, Oxford University Press, 1952).

Located 1 block south of US 17 (Broad Street). Open Monday–Saturday 9:00 A.M.–4:00 P.M., Sunday 1:00–4:00 P.M. Closed New Year's Day, Thanksgiving, and 24–26 December. Admission prices vary. Free tour with admission; tours given every 30 minutes. For more information, call (800) 767–1560.

SAN JOSÉ MISSION (1768–82)
Mission Road
San Antonio, Texas

The Mission of San José y San Miguel de Agüayo—the last name belonging to the then-governor of Texas and the patron of the church—was the most important, as well as the best fortified, in New Spain. It has been referred to as the "Queen of Missions." Earlier and sometimes more elaborate than the California missions, and more sophisticated than the primitive adobe churches of New Mexico, the five Spanish- and Mexican-influenced stone missions in and south of San Antonio form a vital chapter in Spanish architecture in the United States. Of these San José is by far the most impressive. The mission (which had been founded in 1720 but moved twice) forms a large compound, approximately 500 x 550 feet/152 x 168 meters. Its eighty-four apartments for Christianized Native Americans (Payayas) line three walls of the enclosure, a granary stands in the northwest corner, a prefecture and quarters for the few soldiers make the fourth wall, and the present church is inset at the northeast. The buildings along the walls, which were, of course, windowless on the exterior, are of relatively little architectural interest except for the vaulted and buttressed granary.

But the church, at least its facade, is one of the glories of the Spanish contribution to building in this country. The main entrance sparkles with its Spanish Baroque or Churrigueresque richness of ornament played off against the simple stuccoed walls of its semi-Moorish facade. The church's external elaboration did not, however, stop at the superbly rich entry and portal window, for most of the building was—originally—covered with stucco decorated with painted geometric patterns. A small sample of this can still be seen near the lower right-hand corner of the tower. This strong use of color, like that which once brightened Athens's Parthenon, is now nothing but a monochromatic reflection of former glories. The highly accomplished carvings of the so-called "rose window" on the south wall are traditionally held to be the work of Pedro Huizar, a Mexican born in Aguascalientes in 1740, according to most sources. Hugh Morrison writes that this is "the finest Spanish colonial facade in the United States" (*Early American Architecture*, Oxford University Press, 1952), though others might opt for San Xavier del Bac (Arizona, see page 117). The church now standing—an earlier one was torn down to make way for this—was not started, according to most authorities, until 1768 and not finished until 1782. Built of thick walls of local tufa and roofed with four groin vaults and one dome (over what would be the transept), the church forms a simple and today unprepossessing rectangular interior, but one unquestionably covered with frescoes when built. A three-bay baptistry lies along one side, while behind the sanctuary stretch the intriguing ruins of the monk's vaulted cells and the cloister.

All, however, did not go well with San José—or with its sister missions. Upon complete secularization in 1824 by the now-independent Mexicans, all uncultivated mission lands were subdivided and sold. The San José Mission church dome collapsed sometime between 1868 and 1870. Meanwhile the magnificent portal sculpture was used for target practice and, more recently, chopped at by souvenir hunters. The original cedar front door was stolen but later reconstructed from old photographs. Then in the 1930s sentiment for the mission's reconstruction became effective and through the combined efforts of the San Antonio Conservation Society, the Archdiocese of San Antonio, the State of Texas, and the Works Progress Administration—in conjunction with architect Harvey P. Smith—the complete compound was rebuilt and the church restored (except for the decorated stucco on the exterior and the frescoes within). In 1941 it was made a National Historic Site, full restoration was completed

in 1949, and in 1978 it became part of the San Antonio Missions National Historic Park. This is one of the outstanding examples of Spanish architecture in the United States.

Located 5 miles/8 kilometers south of city off US 281 (Roosevelt Avenue). Open 9:00 A.M.–6:00 P.M. in summer, 9:00 A.M.–5:00 P.M. in winter. Closed Christmas and New Year's Day. Admission is free. Tours available in summer at 11:00 A.M., 12:00 noon, 3:00 P.M., and 4:00 P.M., and in winter at 10:00 A.M., 11:00 A.M., 2:00 P.M., and 3:00 P.M. For more information call (210) 229-5701.

POHICK CHURCH (1769–74)
9301 Richmond Highway
Lorton, Virginia

The Pohick Church forms a compact hip-roofed rectangle, unlike many towered and gabled churches of the New World Georgian era that favored a Greek cross or transept plan. And although it is almost domestic in outward appearance, it possesses probably the most sophisticated interior of its time in the colonies. The quietly stated outer walls, laid in the usual Flemish bond are relieved by prominent white stone quoins, well-pedimented doors (the main one in the long wall, two others at the west end), fifteen roundheaded windows, and a firmly denticulated cornice. The round-topped, keystone-less windows deliver a syncopation to the facades. The sandstone enframements of the doors are capable interpretations from standard English architectural books. Upon entering one encounters an elegant single chamber, totally comprehensible, whose only break is a gallery (restored) at the western end. Directly facing the main entrance from the opposite wall rises the pulpit, with a wineglass base and a cantilevered canopy sounding board above. A broken pedimented plaque at the chancel end, with a small altar below, contains the usual scriptural references, while a grid of waist-high box pews with two long aisles fills most of the rest of the church. All elements have been fused by the clarity of the space and by being painted the same putty color. The results are admirable.

George Washington, who was a member of the vestry at Pohick, had a strong hand in its design; in 1859 Benson J. Lossing published a plan and elevations that he claimed were drawn by Washington. William Buckland, who designed most of Gunston Hall in Mason Neck, Virginia (see page 92) for George Mason (who, in his turn, was also on the vestry at Pohick), was responsible for the completion of the church, according to parish records. He was probably involved in the interior carving, and possibly its completion, while James Wren, some believe, was the architect and builder who worked with Washington. The church was damaged in the Civil War and much of the interior gutted—hence most of what we see today dates from the restorations of 1874 and 1906, the latter putting the church as near its original condition as possible for the state's tricentennial in 1907.

Located immediately east of US 1, and west of Fort Belvoir. Open Monday–Friday 9:00 A.M.–4:30 P.M., Saturday 10:00 A.M.–5:00 P.M. Sunday services held at 8:00, 9:15, and 11:15 A.M. Tours can be arranged by calling (703) 550–9449.

MONTICELLO (1769–1809)
Charlottesville, Virginia

Thomas Jefferson, architect

Thomas Jefferson was the nation's most talented self-trained architect, almost a professional. He had spent five years in France (1784–89) as United States foreign minister, and during that time he studied as many buildings as his duties would allow. This exposure to architectural sophistication and French visionary design and philosophy gilded his book learning, and its influence can be clearly seen in Monticello. Moreover he went out of his way to meet the most distinguished avant-garde architects of his day, Etienne-Louis Boullée and Claude-Nicolas Ledoux among them. Though smitten by the Classicists, Andrea Palladio, and the new French approach to domestic life (the Hôtel de Salm, 1782–89, in Paris was particularly pertinent), Jefferson was no copyist (except, in part, with the Virginia State Capitol, see page 120). As with his glorious University of Virginia (see page 163), he was inspired but not fettered either by what he had seen and sketched or by the books in his extensive architectural library. Although Jefferson's architectural direction was strictly Classical, his taste in gardens ran to informal English landscaping, a fashion then also popular in France.

Upon his return to the States (1789), although his beloved wife and four of his six children had died (Mrs. Jefferson plus three of the children died before he went to France), he began a considerable expansion of his early house and garden, a process that was only partially interrupted when he was president from 1801–09.

At Monticello he was perceptive in his recognition of the microclimate, for his "little mountain" provides a site 567 feet/173 meters above the Rivanna River and hence boasts cool, clean air as well as fine views. He was also sharply analytic in his deployment of serving versus served areas (compare the theories of Louis I. Kahn), and was finally a capable tinkerer in building mechanics.

For the basic plan of the "new" Monticello he used the flanking dependencies typical of Palladian architecture, but instead of flaunting these wings on the approach side of his hilltop house, he moved the dwelling near the east edge of the judiciously leveled site, on which work had begun in 1768. There he projected his dependencies to make an angled U-shaped plan with the house in the center but with the two long, parallel utility wings half-tucked into either side of the grade drop-off. Thus service buildings are virtually invisible from the mansion except for their roofs, which form low terrace decks—one on the north, its twin on the south, the two connected by passages underground, extended from the basement of the house proper. By this means views from the house open in all directions. Not only is the servicing of the house (servants, kitchen, dairy, smokehouse, stables, etc.) accommodated on its own totally separated level, but also the terraces extend the space of the dwelling outward to smooth the transition of house to gardens (which Jefferson also originally designed and which were properly restored in 1939–40). The terraces, framed by "Chinese" railings, terminate in pavilions. The ingenious embrace of the west lawn by the house and its two arms provides one of the meaningful contributions of the overall plan.

In the design of the dwelling itself some ambivalence appears, perhaps inevitably. For this house, this "laboratory" house, was put together, taken apart, and gradually fashioned over a period of forty years. Its site utilization and its incredibly original design are masterful; its scale at times disturbing. On the east (approach) side, two floors masquerade as one (the second-floor window frames touching those below), while on the garden side there is some lack of clarity as to what goes on inside. The porticoed parlor flanked by the dining room and Jefferson's bedroom/study—the three forming the first (that is, original) section of the

house—are of two stories. The six "compressed" rooms of the second floor are largely invisible from the west and the three bedrooms of the top floor are windowless but skylit, with the prominent dome containing two half-round and six round windows. The problem was to coordinate all of these elements into a coherent whole. The purist might have reservations concerning the sometimes awkward result; the rest of us will rejoice in its freshness, even if it is aesthetically vulnerable. Note that Monticello is a building whose design urges one to perambulate about its circumference (a factor stemming largely from its lopped corners, perhaps an influence from the Hammond-Harwood House in Annapolis, see page 116); it is not fully grasped from a single point.

The interiors, particularly the parade of Roman-inspired details, are for many the most intriguing parts of the house. Almost every room disports an entablature or frieze from an ancient temple, as published in one of the late-eighteenth-century French or English books on the antique. (An excellent account of the house and its evolution is contained in *Monticello* by Frederick D. Nichols and James A. Bear, Jr., published by the Thomas Jefferson Memorial Foundation, 1967, and available at the gift shop at entry.) As Jefferson wrote, "The Hall is in the Ionic, the Dining Room is in the Doric, the Parlor is in the Corinthian, and the Dome in the Attic. In the other rooms are introduced several different forms of those orders, all in the truest proportions according to Palladio." An education in architecture of the period.

Jefferson died in 1826 in near poverty, partly because public duty had kept him from properly managing his estate, but also because, against his better judgment, he had signed a note for a cousin in 1820 who then went bankrupt, taking Jefferson with him. The house was sold five years later, the furniture even earlier. It was not until 1923 that the house and grounds, which had been reasonably maintained (except for the period during and after the Civil War), were acquired by the Thomas Jefferson Memorial Foundation. The often frustrating efforts to raise funds for the purchase of the property were spearheaded by the Moscow-born Theodore Fred Kuper. In 1954 structural restoration was undertaken, much furniture was retrieved from descendants, and Monticello's pleasures opened to a grateful public.

Located southeast of town via VA 53, 5 miles/8 kilometers from downtown. November–February open daily 9:00 A.M.–4:30 P.M. March–October open daily 8:00 A.M.–5:00 P.M. Closed Christmas. Admission is $8 for adults, $7 for senior citizens, $4 for children ages 6–11, free for children under 6. Thirty-minute guided tours are given every 5 minutes. For more information call (804) 984–9822.

FIRST CHURCH OF CHRIST, CONGREGATIONAL (1771–72)
75 Main Street (CT 10) at Church Street
Farmington, Connecticut

Captain Judah Woodruff, designer/builder

In contrast to the nave-dominant, altar-accented houses of worship of the Virginia Colony (usually of brick)—virtually all of which belonged to the Church of England—the great majority of the late-seventeenth- and eighteenth-century meeting houses of the Northeast were simple, gabled boxes with, at times, a stair hall attached to the end but often without towers and steeples. In plan they formed a compact rectangle with three doors; the main entry was on the longer side facing the pulpit. This arrangement delivered maximum contact between parson and congregation (as the New Liturgy seeks today). The prominent pulpit was elevated to reflect the centrality of the Bible, and so that the divine could oversee the gallery, which wrapped around three sides. Most of the early New England colonists were anti-Church of England, and their architecture logically and functionally reflected this. Whereas house building—in all the colonies—closely followed designs and trends of the areas of England from which the early settlers came, the meeting house, which combined both religious and secular functions (in some cases as late as the early nineteenth century), with almost no prototypes, evolved its own form independent of Europe. Some consider it to be the only American contribution to architecture until the balloon frame for house building of the mid-nineteenth century or the skyscraper of the latter part of that century.

One of the finest meeting houses—the third for its members—is this at the southwest edge of Farmington. The relation of the First Church of Christ to its green-carpeted site, the tower's relation to the church, and the joyfulness of light within mark this as an outstanding eighteenth-century ecclesiastical building. The rectangular body of the church resembles others of a similar size (it measures 74 x 50 feet/23 x 15 meters), but the belfry and spire atop its tower (150 feet/46 meters high) are superior; the open octagon of the belfry is duplicated in the base of the spire and then fairs with a curve into the graceful spire (which was built on the ground and somehow hoisted into place). Towers were rare in the early part of the eighteenth century, but later they began to sprout in many New England towns, as this example proclaims (many, indeed, were added to existing churches). However, when tower and steeple abut the end of a meeting house—as here—a visual dichotomy is set up because the tower outpulls the main door: where does one enter? It might be said that the Farmington shrine epitomizes and terminates an architectural era, doing so with uncommon style. The American Revolution began shortly after it was completed and there then followed a period when virtually no building was undertaken. When matters perked up, financially and otherwise, in the last decade of the eighteenth century, the new plans—under a variety of influences—became distinctly longitudinal with tower unambiguously over and proudly marking the entry, with the result, as has often been said, that the Puritan meeting house "became a church."

The First Church of Christ interior is as rewarding as the outside. Suffused with light, it has been accurately restored. Until 1952 the 1901 organ dominated and almost threatened the pulpit; it has now been put in its correct place, and the whole east wall attended to. Other earlier changes had been made—the Greek Revival portico dates from 1834—but today all is in proper order.

Sunday services held at 10:00 A.M. Open by appointment only. Tours can be scheduled by calling (203) 677–2601.

CORBIT-SHARP HOUSE (1772–74)
Main Street at 2nd Street
Odessa, Delaware

Robert May, architect

A sophisticated city house—directly inspired by the original owner's stay in Philadelphia. If it seems urbane in its country-town setting it is nonetheless extremely handsome outside and in, and is one of the finest colonial houses open to the public in Delaware. The house remained in the family of William Corbit, for whom it was built, until 1938, when it was purchased by H. Rodney Sharp, who meticulously restored and refurnished it with Delaware Valley antiques. In 1958 Sharp gave it to the Winterthur Museum, which now administers this and the adjacent David Wilson Mansion. The Corbit-Sharp House presents a refreshingly lively facade, and much of this vitality stems from its details. Note, for instance, the paneled blinds: the lower four windows that bracket the front door have solid shutters painted white, while the upper five have louvered shutters—which permit ventilation with privacy in the upstairs rooms—and are dark green, a solution as logical as it is handsome (and one seen often in the state). The bold slash of the granite belt course, which is echoed by the keystoned lintels and the prominent mutule blocks of the cornice, adds a strong accent to the facade. The end of the house nearest the road is windowless. Four dormers, the two in front differing slightly from the two at left, transfer the eye to the delicate Chippendale balustrade of the roof deck. The two-story kitchen wing at left was added in 1790 (the first kitchen was in the basement). Robert May, a master carpenter, is credited with the overall design, aided without question by Abraham Swan's *Collection of Designs in Architecture* (1757) and *The British Architect* (1745).

The interior lives up to the front of the house. It is well proportioned and discriminately detailed. The upstairs "long room" with its pediments, pilasters, and paneling is the most elegant single chamber. The other rooms, while simpler, make their own contributions. An inventory of the original furnishings enabled Sharp to approximate the ambiance of the interior as it was over two hundred years ago. And in recent years descendants of William Corbit have donated many pieces of the original furniture to the house. A garden, designed in 1938 in the Colonial style, extends from the kitchen wing. It, too, is well worth seeing.

Located east off US 13 at Main Street. Open March–December Tuesday–Saturday 10:00 A.M.–4:00 P.M., Sunday 1:00–4:00 P.M. Closed Easter, Independence Day, Thanksgiving, 24–25 December. Admission is $4 for adults, $3 for senior citizens, students, and children ages 5–11, free for children under 5. Two-hour tours given every half hour. Combination admission tickets for the Corbit-Sharp House as well as two other historic Odessa houses are available at reduced rates. For more information call (302) 378-4069.

FIRST BAPTIST CHURCH (1774–75)
75 North Main Street at Waterman
Providence, Rhode Island

Joseph Brown, builder/architect

Roger Williams, that admirable gladia-
tor for religious freedom ("soul liberty")
of the early colonies, founded not only
this "the First Baptist Church in
America," and served as its short-term
pastor, but also the city in which it
stands (1636). The latter was named by
him for his deliverance, after banish-
ment from Massachusetts. Williams
died in 1683, and in a way this splendid
church, though completed almost a century after his death, can be considered
his metaphoric memorial. Joseph
Brown, of the still-famous Rhode Island
family, remains the acknowledged designer—he was a merchant by profession—but James Gibbs, late of London,
was vicariously by his side via his 1728
Book of Architecture. The elegant steeple
of the church was indeed basically
copied from Gibbs's book. Incidentally,
the spire's 185-foot/56-meter height was
raised into position from within the
church by means of telescoping sections, with one James Sumner in
charge. An excellent Tuscan portico

adds the other distinguished note to the facade. The body of the First Baptist is in the New
England wooden tradition with sand-colored clapboarding, quoins in imitation of stone, and a
double row of unshuttered roundheaded windows. The interior, which measures approximately 80 feet/24 meters square, suggests a compromise between the short-axis meeting
house and the long-aisle Church of England. In any case it lives up to the excellence of the exterior, its restrained exuberance revealing its late Colonial date. An elaborate Waterford chandelier (1792—its Irish provenance is not authenticated) hangs from the center of the vaulted
nave; its richness is enhanced by the well-detailed sanctuary wall. The church, which seats
eight hundred on the main floor and six hundred in the balconies that encircle three sides, was
made larger than necessary for its congregation so that commencements for nearby Brown
University (until 1804 Rhode Island College) could also be accommodated. The building, from
foundation to spire, was beautifully restored with funds provided by John D. Rockefeller, Jr.,
who taught Sunday school in the church when he was a student at Brown.

Open Monday–Friday 10:00 A.M.–3:00 P.M. Closed for holidays. Sunday services held September–June at 11:00 A.M., July–
August at 9:30 A.M. Tours given Sunday after services. Tours can also be arranged by calling (401) 751–2266. Tours are free,
although a donation is requested.

HAMMOND-HARWOOD HOUSE (1774–80)
19 Maryland Avenue at King George Street
Annapolis, Maryland

William Buckland, architect

Considered "without doubt one of the finest medium-sized houses of the world," Hammond-Harwood represents the ultimate contribution of William Buckland, who planned and supervised it. It also represents his best in its breadth of concept and fastidiousness of detail. It is unlikely, however, that any of its wondrous woodwork was carved by him. (Unfortunately Buckland died in 1774, when only forty years old, and before the Hammond-Harwood House was finished.) The dwelling has a fine sense of scale, proportion, and even detail, while the almost pulsating profile of its three sections, connected by hyphens, carries great sophistication. The dependencies on either side—note the semioctagonal front ends—were designed for a law office (left) and kitchen (right). The nearly square central block is quietly understated except for its impeccable front door, the framing of the window above it, and the bulls-eye window in the pediment (the latter inspired by a plate in James Gibbs's *A Book of Architecture*, 1728). The entry ranks as one of the finest in U.S. Georgian architecture. Note that it garners extra attention because the windows alongside are modest (with the upper central exception) and shutterless. On entering one finds a front hall lit only by a fanlight. However, a few steps farther on, beyond the smallish front rooms and the separate stair passage at right, one enters—or encounters—the superb dining room, Buckland's masterpiece. The wood carving here reached an apogee, from the framing of the doors, windows, and interior shutters up to the intricate cornice encircling the ceiling. Note that one of the windows also doubles as a door to the garden; its lower section is hinged to form a jib door. The ballroom on the second floor is almost as fine as the dining room, as, indeed, are the airy bedrooms. There is an Adamesque influence in the plasterwork, but historians disagree as to whether this was Buckland's design or an addition made after his abrupt death. Although the monumentally pilastered garden facade of the Hammond-Harwood House cannot equal the elegance of the front, mostly because of its heavy pediment, altogether it lays claim to being one of the most beautiful town houses in America. Fortunately it has been superbly restored.

Although Matthias Hammond commissioned the house, he never actually lived in it. It was owned by Judge Jeremiah Townley Chase, and his granddaughter inherited the house after she married into the Harwood family—descendants of architect William Buckland—and occupied the house for most of the nineteenth century. St. John's College purchased it and used it as a Colonial museum beginning in 1926. The Hammond-Harwood House Association, organized in 1938, purchased the property from St. John's and has cared for the mansion ever since.

Open Monday–Saturday 10:00 A.M.–4:00 P.M., Sunday 12:00 noon– 4:00 P.M. Closed Thanksgiving Day, Christmas Day, and New Year's Day. Admission is $4 for adults, $3 for children ages 6–18, and free for children under 6. Forty-five minute tours are given on the hour. Group tours should be scheduled in advance by calling (410) 269-1714. While in the neighborhood, be sure to visit the Chase-Lloyd House (1769–74), another fine Georgian home designed by William Buckland and located directly across the street from Hammond-Harwood.

SAN XAVIER DEL BAC (1776–97)
1950 West San Xavier
Tucson, Arizona

Spain took the Baroque movement in architecture—which began in Rome in the mid-seventeenth century—and molded it to fantastic and at times overreaching heights. This Iberian melding of Gothic, Renaissance, and Baroque influences—spiced by a bit of Islamic influence as well—eventually reached these shores. When the Spanish, accompanied by their extraordinarily dedicated priests, explored and conquered Mexico (1519–1821) and what is now the southwest United States, they dotted these lonely regions with a series of missions and churches that enrich this country's cultural heritage enormously. Their architectural expression varied both chronologically and geographically, particularly in those outposts farthest from Mexico, such as northern New Mexico, where limited materials (mostly adobe) and unskilled Native American labor produced more primitive—but also more indigenous—results. In almost all of the Spanish churches outside of Mexico, sharp contrasts are apt to appear, with plain walls erupting into great facade accents of exuberant carving, with dazzling light-colored exteriors against dark, mysterious naves, with simplicity versus elaborateness, with piety next to semi-idolatry.

Epitomizing these tendencies, and resting like some strange ship tethered to a desert mooring, San Xavier del Bac rises as the pinnacle of Spanish religious architecture in this country. It was founded in 1692 by the incredible explorer and Jesuit, the Tyrolean Eusebio Francisco Kino (or Chini). But the chapel for which Father Kino laid foundations in 1700 (eleven years before his death) was never built, and the church we see today was constructed much later. In 1776 under the direction of the Franciscans, who in 1768 replaced the "troublesome" Jesuits (whose order was "suppressed" by monarchs in Iberia and France in the mid-eighteenth century), the startlingly ambitious mission we now see was begun under Father Velderrain and finished by Father Llorenz. Recent evidence seems to show that the architect, or "master mason," was Ignacio Gaona.

The church with its adjoining mortuary chapel is constructed of an inner and an outer wall of burnt brick, with local volcanic stone filling the space between. The foundations are also of

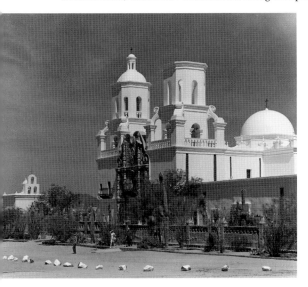

local volcanic stone. Its facade derives from Mexican prototypes (compare the Cathedral of Chihuahua and SS Prisca y Sebastián in Taxco, among others). It is divided into almost equal thirds, with two plain, blindingly white square towers, topped by belfries, rising as guardians beside the intricately carved, soft red brick central portal. This ornately scrolled, boisterous (at times primitive) centerpiece leaps from its quiet white frame to provide a startling introduction to the church. Note that the vertical scrolls that contain the portal's two sides (and that are echoed at the top where the portal projects as a false front) are repeated as a horizontal stringcourse with their ends curling

upward on themselves to tie the whole front together. Note, too, the strange "scroll" buttresses at each corner of the towers, where they lend support to the octagonal belfries (one is incomplete). The portal announces the reredos within, or, as William H. Pierson, Jr., succinctly put it in volume 1 of *American Buildings and Their Architects* (Doubleday, 1970), "One of the most Baroque aspects of the San Xavier portal is the direct relationship it bears with the reredos behind the altar... the two are similar in design, both in [their] general shapes and divisions of space."

The dark and cool, vaulted and domed interior (compare the flat-roofed Spanish churches in New Mexico) is dominated by an incredible carved brick and polychrome stucco *retablo mayor*, or reredos, flanked by richly treated transepts. This cavalcade of carving and decoration includes a cloth-draped statue of San Xavier in the center, with the Virgin above, saints flanking the two, angels and putti hovering about, all within firm architectural organization. There is no church interior north of Meso-America that can touch this sensational mixture of architecture and sculpture. It derives, via saltwater transmutation, straight from the Spanish work of José de Churriguera, his architect father, four architect brothers, three architect children—and pupils. (The family, not surprisingly, added the word "Churrigueresque" to our panoply of architectural terms. The movement reached its climax in Salamanca, then traveled to Mexico, to Arizona and, more modestly, to other Spanish possessions in the Southwest.) The "European" plan of San Xavier is roofed by four low ovoid domes (one over each transept) and one high circular one over the crossing. There are four windows in the high dome and in the nave walls, but none in the transepts. The nave itself suffers from a ponderous "cornice" that runs along the spring line of the vaults, but this heaviness evaporates before the power of the *retablo*.

The church bid farewell to its Spanish missionaries in 1828 when the Franciscans were expelled following Mexico's independence. Its history throughout the rest of the nineteenth century was one of intermittent use, minor repairs, and considerable neglect, conditions complicated by the fact that no one was in full charge. Though earthquakes and lightning created minor damage, and weather took its toll, it was not until cracks in the dome appeared that the Catholic bishop of Arizona authorized (1906) overall repairs and a sprucing up and expansion of the ancillary buildings. In 1949 a restoration under the aegis of a professional architect, E. D. Herreras, was undertaken, including retouching of some of the paintings by Henry Milan. A more comprehensive interior restoration by an international team of conservators began in 1992 and is scheduled to be completed in 1997. The only intact survivor of the seven missions founded in Arizona, San Xavier is soon to be visible in all its original glory. Spain's architectural efforts in Mexico may reveal more expertise and finesse, but this, by far, is their greatest effort in the United States.

Located 1.3 miles/2 kilometers west of I-19 at the San Xavier exit, 9.5 miles/15 kilometers south of Tuscon. February–October open daily 8:00 A.M.–6:00 P.M. November–January open daily 8:00 A.M.–5:00 P.M. Closed for major holidays. Sunday services are held at 8:00 A.M., 9:30 A.M., 11:00 A.M., and 12:30 P.M. A recorded self-guided tour is available at no charge.

ROCKY HILL MEETING HOUSE (1785)
4 Portsmouth Road
Amesbury, Massachusetts

The Rocky Hill Meeting House is not only a prime example of its type, it is also fairly accessible, open to the public by appointment—unlike most of its cloistered sisters. Thus the Spartan interior of one of the finest and most characteristic New England places of worship can be fully savored. Worship, however, was only one function of these bare-boned, heatless boxes: they also served secular purposes. Rocky Hill was first used to inaugurate a town meeting; its last years of public activity were also for this purpose. The interior, which measures 61 x 49 feet/19 x 15 meters, follows the usual pattern, with balcony on three sides, and organ and choir in the center of the gallery facing the magisterial pulpit. The design of this properly elevated rostrum, topped by a well-turned sounding board, with table and deacon's seat in front, ranks high among its peers. The marbleizing of the pulpit's pilasters and of the columns upholding the balcony should be noted, as should the warm color of the unpainted pine pews. The church, with its spireless, simply gabled, almost clinical exterior resembles the slightly earlier (1773), smaller meeting house at Sandown, New Hampshire, as do the interior handling and details. Some authorities believe that one Timothy Palmer, a master carpenter, was responsible for both. Though the last services were held over one hundred years ago (in the 1870s) and town meetings ceased in 1886, Rocky Hill miraculously managed to survive as built, unmolested by later stylistic foibles or recent vandalism. In 1942 it was given to the Society for the Preservation of New England Antiquities, which now carefully guards it.

Located southeast on Elm Street to Portsmouth Road, about 1.4 miles/2.3 kilometers from town (or about .5 mile/.8 kilometer north of I-95 Amesbury exit) Open by appointment only; call the Society for the Preservation of New England Antiquities at (508) 462–2634 or (617) 227–3956. Admission is $2 per person.

VIRGINIA STATE CAPITOL (1785–92)
Capitol Square, between 9th and Governor streets
Richmond, Virginia

Thomas Jefferson, architect

Thomas Jefferson's Virginia State Capitol introduced Classical architecture to the budding nation. The country never recovered. This extraordinary statesman/architect, who honed his architectural wits while in Europe as the United States Minister to France (1784–89), despised the Georgian—its British derivation obviously influenced his post-Revolution taste—and considered the Christopher Wren-designed building at William and Mary an uncouth "brick kiln" and the facades of Independence Hall "puny." He turned more and more to the Roman Classical and its Palladian interpretations for his inspiration. Though Jefferson never visited Rome or Greece, one wonders what would have happened to the architecture of this country if he had studied great Classical buildings at first hand, instead of via books. The Maison Carrée in Nîmes in the south of France was the only major Roman temple he ever saw, though he traveled as far as Genoa to study rice cultivation.

In any event, Jefferson was the first architect anywhere to fit a major workaday building into a Classically derived temple form—though not without difficulties. It was also the first building to include both houses of the legislature in a single structure. In this he was influenced by Charles-Louis Clérisseau, the architect who, interestingly enough, also influenced Scotland's famous Adam brothers, Robert and James.

The temple at Nîmes might have been the inspiration for the Richmond capitol, but it was not altogether the model, for the latter was far larger, with Ionic capitals instead of more elaborate Corinthian, and unfluted columns instead of fluted. Neither does the Capitol have pseudo-peripteral, attached columns like those that embrace the side of Nîmes, nor (originally) steps up the front like its Roman model. To quote the Virginia Historic Landmarks Commission, "It might also be noted that Jefferson *intended* that the building have front steps, they are shown in his drawing and model. Jefferson did not supervise the construction, and apparently the contractor took the liberty of leaving off the steps because the portico door led directly into the Supreme Court chamber. Only when that space was partitioned off to make a central corridor were the front steps finally erected."

The capitol was, however, an extremely important and influential building, a pioneer in the evolution of architecture in this country, even if aesthetically not comparable to Jefferson's brilliant University of Virginia (see page 163) or his piquant Monticello (see page 110). It should also be borne in mind that only the central part of the building we see today belongs to Jefferson, for the two wings housing the Senate (west) and the House of Delegates (east) were added at the early part of this century (1904–06), and the south portico transformed to the main entrance, its steps installed and the intrusive pediment windows removed (see the plaster model of the original). Minor remodeling occurred in 1962–63. The interiors, because of the changes, are handsome but not completely harmonious. Note Jean-Antoine Houdon's famous statue of George Washington in the domed entry hall. The stately siting of the capitol, its landscaping, and even its fence (1819) are all excellent.

April–December open daily 9:00 A.M.–5:00 P.M. December–March open Monday–Saturday 9:00 A.M.–5:00 P.M., Sunday 1:00–5:00 P.M. Closed Thanksgiving, Christmas, and New Year's Day. Admission is free. Half-hour free tours given. Tours can be scheduled in advance by calling (804) 786–4344.

BOLDUC HOUSE (c. 1787)
125 South Main Street
between South Gabouri and Market
St. Genevieve, Missouri

The French, working first as explorers, then as fur traders, moved from what is now Canada and Wisconsin down the Mississippi in the late seventeenth century, claiming the land for France (Sieur de LaSalle in 1682). By 1749 they had established their first permanent base at St. Genevieve in what later became Missouri, and then settled in St. Louis in 1764. The Spanish acquired all of what was then called "Louisiana" by 1763 but secretly retroceded it to France in 1800. In 1803 through Thomas Jefferson's far-sightedness, the great Louisiana Purchase was put through and the entire area (roughly to the Rocky Mountains) came to the United States, more than doubling the size of the country. French influence, however, continued in Missouri for years—as it did in New Orleans—where we still find souvenirs of French culture.

The small town of St. Genevieve, 61 miles/98 kilometers down river from St. Louis, is one of the most rewarding centers of French influence, and the Bolduc House one of the finest Creole buildings. The dwelling was constructed around 1787, using wood (possibly only large beams) harvested as early as 1746. Behind the mandatory palisade, which not only kept out Native Americans and stray cattle, but also stray eyes, the typical angled-hip-roofed (originally probably of thatch), wide-galleried house was built of massive oak logs placed vertically on a stone foundation, a system called *poteaux sur sole*. Straw mixed with clay and animal hair (*bousillage*) filled the interstices between the uprights. A heavy oak-trussed roof, reflecting Norman regionalism, covers the 48 x 82-foot/15 x 25-meter house. A simply supported veranda—probably enlarged around 1846—encircles it on three sides to provide protected open-air work and rest areas, and to preserve the whitewashed walls. The house was acquired by the National Society of the Colonial Dames of America in the State of Missouri (1949), and carefully restored (1956–57) outside and in, along with outbuildings and garden, by Dr. Ernest Allen Connally. It is now a national historic landmark. An outstanding building of its type.

Open 1 April–1 November Monday–Saturday 10:00 A.M.–4:00 P.M., Sunday 11:00 A.M.–5:00 P.M. Closed Easter. Admission is $2 for adults, $1 for students 17 and under. All visits are guided; half-hour tours given throughout the day. For more information call (314) 883–3105.

The Amoureux House (c. 1792), located south on St. Mary's Road (US 61), is similar to the Bolduc and will interest the specialist. Built by Jean Baptiste St. Gemme Beauvais, the house was purchased by Benjamin Amoureux in 1852 and was owned by successive generations of his family. It uses the *poteaux-en-terre* method of construction, in which cedar logs are set upright directly in the earth to form the walls. The floor is supported on a series of stone piers. The steeply-pitched roof is in a French Canadian style. In 1995 the house was donated to the State of Missouri and is presently part of the Felix Valley House State Historic Site.

Plans are currently underway to open this building to the public. For more information, contact the Felix Valley House State Historic Site at (314) 883–7102.

ROCKINGHAM MEETING HOUSE (1787–1800)
Meeting House Road
Rockingham, Vermont

As an isolated structure the Rockingham Meeting House stands as a well-proportioned, white clapboard box with auxiliary entries and stairs at each end. Measuring 56 x 44 feet/17 x 13 meters, it carries the proper number of windows on its four sides and a good main door. However, when studied in relation to its hilltop site and adjacent cemetery (1782) and even its frail picket fence, the whole, to paraphrase Paul Valéry, almost bursts into song. (It is a rare building that can be properly assayed out of its context.) This chaste house of worship is lifted above routine interest in its proportions, its sweeping command of the countryside, and its very vibration with nearby tombs. As regards its location, "In voting to place the Meeting House on a hill, the town carried out the usual custom of early days of locating such buildings on some eminence, where they could be seen for miles around, and where, in addition, they would be strategically located for defense from hostile Indians" (Lyman S. Hayes, *The Old Rockingham Meeting House*, 1915). The meeting house, the oldest in the state and the second for its congregation, reflects the straightforward characteristics of contemporary buildings in remote areas, following cautiously architectural developments along the seaboard. During its early years, in the usual tradition, it was used for both religious and secular offices. In 1839 the building ceased to be used as a church, and in 1869 was abandoned as a town meeting hall. In 1906 it was fully restored, after interior vandalization, and rededicated the following year. The interior is scarcely more elaborate than the Spartan white pine exterior. Highlights are the box pews of natural wood with delicately spindled tops (restored); those around the periphery are slightly higher than those toward the center. The usual balcony surrounds the three sides above.

Located on hill above village, off VT 103 (1.4 miles/2.3 kilometers northwest of exit 6 of I-91). During the summer, open daily 10:00 A.M.–4:00 P.M. Closed in winter. Admission is 50¢ per person.

GREENERY AND WATER (1791–)
Washington, D.C.

Major Pierre Charles L'Enfant, basic plan

The Mall provides its informal formalization, Potomac Park spreads its greenery artfully between waters, while Rock Creek Park, with its miraculously untouched river, meanders until it blossoms northward. Close at hand dozens of ellipses, squares, triangles, and circles add geometric testament. When these are combined with the prodigality of trees—infinite trees— and the grasses and unspoiled waters, Washington (in its public areas) becomes the country's loveliest city. And the bowered residential streets of the ancient (1751) port of Georgetown, the numerous lessons of mid-city openness, grass, flora, and shining waters should remind every visitor that cities are not brutal when people work with nature downtown, mid-town, and uptown.

Williamsburg in 1699 and Washington not quite a hundred years later (1791) are perhaps the only, and certainly the earliest, urban plans that identified their capital status on a major scale, with monumental avenues, cross-axes, terminal vistas, and specific locations for impor-

tant buildings. Major Pierre Charles L'Enfant's greatest contribution in planning the Federal City was that he sought to create an interrelation between town and nature (including the Potomac River). Indeed, he thought first not of broad avenues but of parks, "two coordinate axes of parks," one stretching from the Capitol to the Potomac to form the Mall, and the other from the White House to the river, with the Washington Monument at their axial intersection. By this strategy, the park imprimatur—the glory of the city—was set. He then laid out the diagonal Baroque geometry of the rest of the city, influenced by Christopher Wren's bold but never constructed plan for London (1666) and by the work of André Le Nôtre in France, particularly at Versailles (L'Enfant had spent much of his youth at Versailles where his father was a royal artist). Additionally, the cross-axial plan of Williamsburg could have influenced the layout for Washington: Capitol for Capitol, Duke of Gloucester Street for the Mall, William and Mary College for the Lincoln Memorial (here obviously a questionable hypothesis, as the swamp area had not yet been filled in), and, on the cross-axis, the Governor's Palace and Green for the White House and its green. L'Enfant's inability to work with others, however, soon caused the word terrible to be coupled with his name and he was fired (January 1792); only the name of Andrew Ellicott, his successor, appeared on their famous plan later that year.

Although Ellicott, an engineer and highly regarded surveyor, remained faithful to the Frenchman's plan (until he, too, was replaced, by J. R. Dermott in 1797), Washington itself, as it burgeoned through the years, did not, since there was, seemingly, no real authority in charge. President Andrew Jackson placed the new Treasury Building (1836) so that any expansion of the building would block the view of the United States Capitol from the White House, while the Smithsonian was allowed to poach on the Mall, and much of the rest of the city simply accreted. In the middle of the nineteenth century, President Millard Fillmore laid the cornerstone for the lateral extensions of the Capitol (1851) (see page 128) and, at about the same time, retained Andrew Jackson Downing, then the country's premier landscape architect, to pull together the Mall in front of the Capitol and the grounds around it. Downing's "natural style of Landscape Gardening" was small scaled, romantically oriented, and was therefore in conflict with L'Enfant's broadly classical urban layout. Thus it is fortunate that upon Downing's death in 1852 relatively little of his plan had been put into effect. The Civil War then curtailed all activity.

In 1871 Alexander R. Shepherd (a builder and a part-owner of the *Washington Star*), abetted by C. S. Noyes (another owner of the paper), was made head of the newly appointed Board of Public Works and began a furiously active campaign to spruce up the city with new roads, sidewalks, sewers, water supply, "scores" of new parks, and thousands of trees. Visual holes are apparent in Shepherd's plan and its scale at times got out of hand, but Washington was enormously improved by his efforts until they were halted by the depression of 1873. The Senate Park Commission later took over and its report of 1902 reestablished L'Enfant's plan and the development of the Mall area—"then no better than a common pasture"—and planned the nearly 1,800 acres/728 hectares of Rock Creek Parkway, whose valley had been purchased in 1890, and extended Potomac Park. Planning for the revitalization of Pennsylvania Avenue between the Capitol and the White House began under the Kennedy Administration. That rebuilding is almost complete; it includes new open spaces, new buildings, the Pennsylvania Quarter mixed-use community, and the recycling of landmark buildings. The National Capitol Planning Commission prepared a new plan for an expanded Monumental Core, published in 1995. But forget the names, the dates, and the incidences, and lose yourself in those lovely sections of Washington that balance nature and man in determining our cities and suburbs. In what other city—here or abroad—can one encounter canoeing, jousting on horseback, field hockey, and polo, to say nothing of minor diversions, on a half-mile walk along the river of a Sunday afternoon?

OLD CONNECTICUT STATE HOUSE (1792–96)
800 Main Street at State Street
Hartford, Connecticut

Charles Bulfinch, architect

The Old State House will, of course, recall Charles Bulfinch's Massachusetts State House in Boston (see page 133), designed in 1787 but not built until 1795–97, roughly the time when this much smaller sister in Hartford was constructed. Many of the same basic architectural elements are common to each (but at different scales): brick loggia on the lower floor of a projected center bay or pavilion, Classical portico above, and golden dome atop. In Hartford the dome is vestigial on a small cupola and was added in 1827—possibly not by Bulfinch. And, as in Boston, English influence—here Federalized—is apparent. (Harold Kirker's encyclopedic *The Architecture of Charles Bulfinch*, Harvard University Press, 1969, illustrates this graphically.) Whatever the inspiration the result is skillful. The State House became the City Hall (1879) following the building of the new capitol, then underwent a period of decline when municipal functions moved out in 1915. A partial restoration—which stabilized the building—was undertaken in 1921. Much of the original interior had been so drastically altered that the restorers had to go to the Boston prototype for details. Then in 1978–79 a complete renovation, including both structural and mechanical updating, took place, spurred and largely financed by the non-profit Old State House Association. (Roger Clark was the architect.) Another full-scale renovation was begun in 1992, to be completed in spring 1996: the senate chamber is now restored to Bulfinch's design, including ceiling rosette, paneled shutters, and color scheme, the council chamber is restored to the 1879–1915 period, and the exterior has returned to its original cream color. The building now shines brightly, serving as a Visitors Center and for exhibitions, concerts, and other cultural activities. Designated a historic landmark in 1961, it is one of the nation's oldest state houses.

Open Monday–Friday 10:00 A.M.–6:00 P.M., Saturday 10:00 A.M.–5:00 P.M. Admission is free. Self-guided tour available.

SAN CARLOS BORROMEO (1793–97)
3080 Rio Road
Carmel, California

The church we see today so verdantly set in a gardened court was, one hundred years ago, a lonely wreck, its roof fallen in, its mission buildings destroyed. The second of the series of twenty-one missions founded by Father Junípero Serra—who lies buried near its altar—the church itself was stoutly constructed of stone, with an unusual vaulted roof whose three ribs of stone, properly buttressed on the outside, support a half-barrel ceiling of lateral wood planks laid atop the arches. An inverted boat shape results, climaxed by a recent (1957) reredos. The exterior, with two unequally sized towers (the larger of Ibero-Moorish inspiration), a fine Baroque star-shaped window over the prominent door, plus the asymmetrical approach and its garden setting, create a comely ambiance. Secularized in 1834, the church nearly collapsed shortly thereafter: the roof did fall in 1851 and was incorrectly replaced in 1884. Finally in the 1930s it was given a complete restoration.

In summer, open Monday–Saturday 9:30 A.M.–7:00 P.M., Sunday 10:30 A.M.–7:00 P.M. In winter, open Monday–Saturday 9:30 A.M.–4:30 P.M.; Sunday 10:30 A.M.–4:30 P.M. Admission is free but a $2 donation for adults ($1 for children) is suggested.

UNITED STATES CAPITOL
(1793–1863)
Capitol Hill
Washington, D.C.

William Thornton,
Benjamin Henry Latrobe,
Charles Bulfinch,
Robert Mills,
Thomas Ustick Walter,
architects

The United States Capitol—"the spirit of America in stone"—achieves greatness in spite of its oft-troubled and interrupted history (which includes burning). Its Classical influence and its spirit of boldness—even its use of cut stone instead of brick as a facing material—were of enormous importance in the development of the young country, and the lengthy evolution of its construction is itself fascinating. As Glenn Brown put it in his monumental two-volume *History of the United States Capitol*, "The Capitol is not a creation, but a growth, and its highest value lies in the fact that it never was, and it never will be, finished" (Government Printing Office, 1900). Moreover as the father-image of most United States state capitols, it was, of course, of seminal importance.

The construction of the building covered four major and several minor stages. The first occurred in 1792 when Thomas Jefferson, with President George Washington's approval, proposed a competition for a capitol. The winning design was that submitted (late) by William Thornton, a West Indies-born, Edinburgh-educated, non-practicing doctor with an impressive range of interests, including a surprising (for a self-taught amateur) grasp of architecture. Jefferson said of the winning project, "It is simple, noble, beautiful, excellently arranged" and "had captivated the eyes and the judgment of all" (quoted in I. T. Frary, *They Built the Capitol*, Garrett and Massie, 1940).

The principal element of Thornton's sophisticated design was a prominent porch with eight Corinthian columns, simple pediment above, and low dome on stepped drum—highly similar to the Roman Pantheon (A.D. 124). But as Thornton was not a professional architect, troubles arose to plague the building's erection, many continuing to the present day. Stephen (Etienne Sulpice) Hallet, a capable French-born architect, who had won second prize, was appointed superintendent of construction and he immediately attacked the technical inadequacies in his rival's plans. He was discharged in November 1794 for taking "excessive liberties" with Thornton's design. George Hadfield, a promising English architect, succeeded Hallet but he lasted only until May 1798. Work, however, continued and Congress occupied one wing (the north) in 1800. The building's construction was managed by three commissioners—of which Thornton was one—until 1802.

Stage two commenced in 1803 when Benjamin Henry Latrobe, a highly trained English architect and engineer, was made surveyor of public buildings with the chief responsibility of completing the Capitol. Latrobe completed the House wing and repaired the Senate wing, which at the time were connected by a covered walkway with no central portion built. He also introduced his imaginative "corncob capitals." Then in 1814 (during the War of 1812) the British burned the building, and the next year Latrobe was charged with repairing what he termed "a most magnificent ruin." As Talbot Hamlin remarked, "The burning of the Capitol . . . was architecturally far from an unmixed catastrophe. It gave Latrobe a free hand in rebuilding much of the interior, while preserving Thornton's exquisite walls" (*Greek Revival Architecture*, Oxford University Press, 1944). Latrobe redesigned the hall of representatives (now statuary hall), completed the two wings, as mentioned, and made drawings for the central domed mass and added cupolas—really low domes—over each wing. However, he, too, encountered disagreements and resigned in November 1817. He died three years later of yellow fever while supervising engineering work in New Orleans.

Stage three began in 1817 when President James Monroe, on seeing Charles Bulfinch's famous Massachusetts State House in Boston (see page 133), persuaded Bulfinch to come to Washington as architect of the Capitol. Bulfinch first finished some repairs needed on the Senate and House (Congress moved back into them in 1819), and in 1818 began construction of the central portion, thus joining the hitherto lonely wings to make one substantial building; the rotunda link was finished in 1826. Most of the work that Bulfinch designed followed Latrobe's earlier sketches, but when it came to the dome that Thornton had originally drawn up, Bulfinch was pressured by the president and cabinet to make it higher. This was done with results that suggest an unhappy compromise between the dome of the Roman Pantheon and that of Bulfinch's own Massachusetts State House. Bulfinch also designed the west front, on the Mall side, that also recalls his state house, and landscaped the grounds. The Capitol then entered a tranquil phase from 1829 until the mid-1850s. Robert Mills, who had won the competition (1833) for the Washington Monument (see page 216), became architect and engineer for the government in 1836; his occasional concerns with the Capitol were heating, ventilating, lighting, and acoustics.

By 1850 the rapidly growing country needed more space for its governmental offices, and Congress approved a competition for the Capitol's extension. Though five prizes were awarded for this, the results were inconclusive, and President Millard Fillmore appointed Thomas Ustick Walter on 11 June 1851. Walter designed the two large additions for the House (occupied in 1857) and the Senate (occupied 1859), placing—with great skill—their axes at right angles to the main axis of the building and connecting them with proper hyphens. Equally important, he replaced the copper-sheathed masonry and wood dome, which Bulfinch had designed, with one far higher and bolder, made of cast iron (1855–65). Walter realized that his broad extensions, which almost doubled the building's length—to 725.8 feet/221 meters—and nearly tripled its size, demanded a higher dome to maintain proper proportions. For maximum buildup, he placed the dome on a two-story pilastered drum encircled by a one-story peristyle. Walter, with Montgomery Meigs the supervising engineer and August Schoenborn his assistant, wanted to build the dome's structure of iron for fire protection. However, as Carl Condit points out, "The only example of an iron-framed dome in existence at the time was that of the Cathedral of St. Isaac in St. Petersburg, Russia" (*American Building Art*, Oxford University Press, 1960). Walter, Meigs, and Schoenborn therefore carefully studied the documentation on the Russian structure and came up with their daring result. They were also highly influenced by St. Isaac (1817–57)—with its multitude of freestanding columns—in the design of their drum. The Washington dome, beautifully engineered, consists of two cast-iron shells, a high one for exterior silhouette nesting over a low one for interior scale (originally a concept of the Italian Renaissance). The Capitol dome, while a structural triumph, is for some finicky on the interior, especially in its coffering. It lacks the boldness of concept behind its hidden structure.

Except for a few details the Capitol was finished in 1863 and Walter—during another power struggle—resigned two years later. The building remained basically untouched until 1959–62, when the east front was extended 32.5 feet/9.9 meters. The length of time taken to complete the Capitol is underscored by the fact that three of the cornerstones were laid by presidents in three different centuries: Washington, 1793; Fillmore, lateral extensions, 1851; and Eisenhower, east front extension, 1959.

Frederick Law Olmsted was in charge of landscaping the Capitol grounds from 1874 to 1892, including the addition of the terraces. Thomas Wisedell, an architect, worked with Olmsted on the design of the west stairways and terraces.

Chief among the artists who decorated the interior of the building was Constantino Brumidi (1805–80), an Italian who spent twenty-five years working on the Capitol, most conspicuously in the rotunda. His fresco, *The Apotheosis of George Washington*, which fills the concave canopy of the dome, was very enthusiastically received upon its completion in 1866.

Brumidi also began the great 8-foot-/2.4-meter-high frieze around the base of the Rotunda dome. This depicts highlights in the history of the nation from its "discovery" by Christopher Columbus to William Penn's treaty with the Native Americans, begun by Brumidi and continued after his death by Filippo Costaggini. Allyn Cox completed the frieze in 1953 with a representation of the Wright brothers at Kitty Hawk. Some of the corridor decorations in the first-floor Senate wing tend to flamboyance and—for some—questionable taste. And if, as Talbot Hamlin wrote, the statuary hall is marred "by some of the world's least appealing sculpture," it ranks as a detail. Architecturally there are many moments of grandeur in the Capitol of the United States.

Open daily 9:00 A.M.–4:30 P.M. Admission is free. Free tours given daily 9:00 A.M.–3:45 P.M.; tours begin in the rotunda every 15 minutes. Gallery passes to the Senate and House sessions available when Congress is in session. For more information call (202) 225–6827.

SHAKER VILLAGE (1794–1847)
Sabbathday Lake
Poland Spring, Maine

Austerity has always marked Shaker activities, to the point of celibacy in their personal lives. (The growth of the movement, which reached a peak of more than six thousand members in the middle of the nineteenth century, was a result of conversion and adoption.) Shaker architecture and furniture naturally reflect this purity and pared-down directness. It is unfortunate that of the nineteen settlements that descended from Mother Ann Lee and her Band of Eight, who landed in New York in 1774, this is the only active Shaker group that still exists. It is worth mentioning that the United Society of Believers in Christ's Second Appearing celebrated their bicentennial two years before that of the United States. Several notable Shaker communal villages, which are discussed in this book, can be seen, but these have by now passed into other hands. The unadorned meeting house (1794) at Sabbathday Lake—perhaps the only building of the group of sixteen that can claim architectural merit—constitutes a basic response to isolated, even primitive, building conditions shaped by liturgical demands. Moses Johnson of New Hampshire reputedly built it and ten other meeting houses—each with gambrel roof, two separate but equal doors (for brethren and sisters) and upper-floor apartments—in New England between 1785 and 1794. Though these buildings are not of "stylistic" significance in architectural terms, they give good insight into the "purity and plainness" of Shaker design. Note, too, the sinewy furniture.

Some of the most successful commercial products of Sabbathday Lake—as in other Shaker communities—were its extensive herbs; here the herb industry was housed in a separate clapboarded Herb House (1824). Though trade is of course not as active as it was one hundred years ago, it is still carried on with a resident herbalist in charge.

Located 3 miles/5 kilometers south of Poland Springs—take exit 11 east off the Maine Turnpike, then north on ME 26 at Gray. Memorial Day–Columbus Day open Monday–Saturday 10:00 A.M.–4:30 P.M. Admission is free. A one-hour tour is available at a cost of $4 for adults and $2 for children ages 6–12. A two-hour tour is available at a cost of $5.50 for adults and $2.75 for children ages 6–12. For more information call (207) 926-4597.

FIRST HARRISON GRAY OTIS HOUSE (1795–96)
141 Cambridge Street at Lynde Street
Boston, Massachusetts

Charles Bulfinch, architect

The restrained, almost severe facade of the Otis House—the first of three in Boston for the growing wealth of the same appreciative client—proclaims with dignity the emerging Federal Style of planar red brick front, white marble stringcourses, and discriminating touches of Classical detail. Both the entry and the Palladian window above partially withdraw into the wall, while the other openings are almost flush with its outer surface. The cornice that traces the top is a model of discretion. Even the shutters are inside, not out: the integrity of the wall is paramount. It is the representative of an architecture of sophisticated proportions that reaches a climax in Samuel McIntire's Gardner-Pingree House in Salem (see page 143), a dwelling inspired by the Otis House (which in turn was inspired by work in Philadelphia and London). The Society for the Preservation of New England Antiquities purchased the house in 1916—it had fallen on evil days, having been used as a tenement—and began restoration. There are a few details on the exterior, such as the second-floor windows, that do not match Bulfinch's elevational drawing, but it is generally agreed that economy dictated double-hung windows instead of the "French style" he favored. The restoration of the museum rooms of the Otis House interior is now substantially complete: one should notice in particular the delicate mantels of the dining room, the delightful 1826 painting in the hall, and the withdrawing room on the second floor. The SPNEA, which has done so much to preserve the area's enormous heritage, uses the Otis House as its headquarters.

Open Tuesday–Friday 12:00 noon–5:00 P.M., Saturday 10:00 A.M.–5:00 P.M. Admission is $4 for adults, $3.50 for senior citizens, $2 for children ages 6–12. 45-minute tours given on the hour; the last tour is at 4:00 P.M. For more information, call (617) 227–3956.

MASSACHUSETTS STATE HOUSE (1795–98/1895/1917)
Beacon Street at Park
Boston, Massachusetts

Charles Bulfinch, architect

The famous State House was designed by America's first native-born professional (really semiprofessional) architect, Charles Bullfinch, who was born in Boston (1763) and educated at Harvard. (Peter Harrison, 1716–75, is generally considered our first architect, but he was born in Yorkshire, coming to this country in 1740. Charleston's Robert Mills was born in 1781.) The State House was for many years the most important public building in the United States, and was directly responsible for Bulfinch's appointment as architect of the Capitol in Washington, D.C., (see page 128) in 1817. British design via Andrea Palladio obviously inspired the design of the State House, as Bullfinch himself was the first to admit. We find here a bold structure crowning the hill and proclaiming, via its dazzling gilded dome, that democracy dwells within. (The dome was original-

ly shingled, then copper-clad by Paul Revere in 1802, and finally gold-leafed in 1874.) The horizontal main block of the building might well have been architecturally more correct without the addition of its pedimented element and towering golden dome; although it would be a less busy building, it would also be a less dashing capitol. The pediment of the upper portion, with its frustrated verticality, is at odds with the horizontality of the columned porch directly beneath it, while the dome seems ready to take off and ascend heavenward. But though the separate elements may play too much their separate games, a stately quality still remains. The central block is flanked by two Federal wings and topped by a continuous balustraded cornice (which was neither continuous nor fully balustraded in the first design). Note that the seven arches of the loggia are more widely spaced at the two ends than in the center; this subtle feature is coordinated above by coupling the wooden Corinthian columns for the end bays of the open porch. On either side of the porch recessed, roundheaded windows, the central ones Palladian, marry the arches below, unifying the 172-foot-/52-meter-wide facade.

As soon as one enters the building and crosses the Doric Hall one encounters the frippery of the 1889–95 addition to the State House. However, hasten up the steps to the domed Senate Chamber (until 1895 the House of Representatives) and the barrel-vaulted Senate Reception Room (the former Senate Chamber): both are basically untouched since Bulfinch's day (a few fireplaces and back windows filled), and both are superior public rooms. The 55-foot-/17-meter-square Senate Chamber was, as Professor Buford Pickens has pointed out, greatly influenced by James Wyatt's London Pantheon of 1772. An enormous extension to the rear of the building was completed in 1895, and the white wings on either side were added in 1917 (Chapman, Sturgis & Andrews, architects).

Open Monday–Friday 9:00 A.M.–5:00 P.M. Closed for holidays. Free 45-minute tours given Monday–Friday 10:00 A.M.–4:00 P.M.; tours should be scheduled in advance by calling (617) 727–3676.

HOUSES OF CHARLESTON (late 18th/early 19th century)
South of Broad Street between Ashley and Cooper rivers
Charleston, South Carolina

On Charleston's triangle of land, formed by the meeting of the Ashley and Cooper rivers, stretches an unparalleled regional response to urban living. Meandering down Church, Tradd, or Meeting streets— to name only a few—the visitor will encounter urban felicity of the highest order. This patrician region has not been spoiled by commercial development or exploitation. Then too, the Civil War left most of the once comfortably off citizens financially depleted, so that they could not afford late-nineteenth-century architectural extravagances.

Since 1931 this twenty-block, 144-acre/58-hectare delight has been protected by a city ordinance. By 1966 the boundaries incorporated 412 acres/166 hectares and the site was declared a National Register Historic District; in 1975 this was increased by 377 acres/152 hectares. While preservation zoning is practiced today by over one hundred cities, the 1931 Charleston action was the first of its kind. (The first legal historic zoning was that of the Vieux Carré in New Orleans.) It should be added that in the area south of Broad Street relatively little restoration has been necessary: most of the houses are basically as they stood 150–200 years ago; they were not rehabilitated as was much of Savannah nor rebuilt as, for instance, was most of Williamsburg.

The houses in Charleston provide a unique solution to sun, rain, dampness, and heat—and occasional floods, hurricanes, and earthquakes. Though surprisingly packed together, each manages to include a private garden, generally in the back. This clustering may stem from similar town-house groupings frequently found in the Caribbean, especially Barbados, with which early Charlestonians were very familiar. Before the Revolution many English settlers came to the Carolinas from this semitropical part of the world, and after it a number of Royalists went back. The West Indies' domestic influence was logically echoed in Charleston, where ground, insect, and flood conditions are largely similar, which led to the use of masonry for the lower floor even when the upper two are of wood. This base was generally stuccoed for greater protection against ground moisture. Another factor leading to urban density was that the city used walled fortifications until the early 1700s. Also, in the East Bay commercial sections, many people lived over stores until around 1800. The most intriguing—and the most functional—of the Charleston houses is the so-called "single house," which includes a single room made wide for greater ventilation. The rooms extend onto double-deck porches measuring about 10 feet/3 meters wide, forming piazzas for open-air living. In general the porches grace the south or westerly sides of the houses, and were often added to older dwellings.

Almost all of the lots in this peninsula area of the city are fenced, many handsomely (note the ironwork on their gates). Most houses have their narrow end to the street, and the typical front door, often of distinguished design, somewhat startlingly opens onto the piazza and not the front hall. In back of the houses are (or were) the outbuildings containing kitchens, in many cases, plus stables and servants' quarters. Gardens for both flowers and vegetables fill much of the remaining open space—the city is famous for them. *Quaint Old Charleston* (Legerton, 1965) mentions that "Two of our best known flowers are named after Charleston people. The gardenia was named by Linnaeus after Dr. Alex Garden, and the poinsettia was named after Dr. Joel Poinsett, who introduced the flower from Mexico."

It is gratifying to note that an enlightened group of citizens and politicians is determined that historic Charleston will not be allowed to become commercialized. The Preservation Society of Charleston, the "Charleston Ordinance" of 1931, the Historic Charleston Foundation that buys up old houses, renovates them, and resells them with controls—all of these are inspiring, and inevitably are involved in dedicated work. Only recently the above groups blocked an interstate highway that engineers wanted to run through a key historic area.

On the peninsula area lies the Ansonborough neighborhood (Hasell, Meeting, George, Laurens, and East Bay streets), whose restoration was sponsored by the Historic Charleston Foundation. This was one of the first neighborhood preservation/restoration projects in the country. Since 1958 hundreds of houses, mostly from the mid-nineteenth century, have been or are being rehabilitated. Because of the success of Ansonborough, a number of other neighborhoods have been revitalized in more recent years, among them Canonborough, Wraggborough, Radcliffeborough, and Harleston Village. The City of Charleston, Historic Charleston Foundation, and Charleston Affordable Housing are currently working on restoring the area of Elliotborough, which contains several hundred pre-Civil War single houses built during the cotton boom.

Most of the homes in the historic peninsula of Charleston are closed to the public except during spring and fall tours. They can, however, be seen from the street. For tours in March and April contact Historic Charleston Foundation, 11 Fulton Street, telephone (803) 723–1623; for tours in September and October contact the Preservation Society of Charleston, 147 King Street, telephone (803) 722–4630.

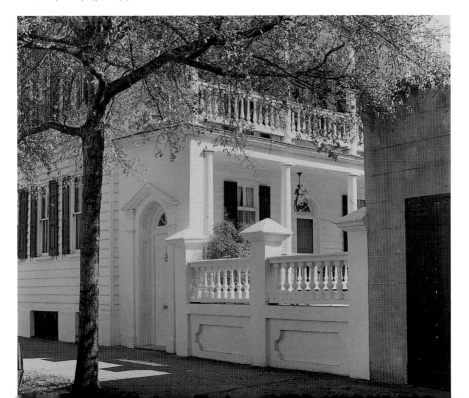

FARMERS' MUSEUM AND VILLAGE CROSSROADS
(1796–1840)
Lake Road
Cooperstown, New York

Frank Whiting and others,
architects

Brilliantly focused on the re-creation of early nineteenth-century village life, of farmers working in a demanding climate with an obdurate soil, the Farmers' Museum and Village Crossroads poignantly reveal a segment of United States history that is too comfortably forgotten today. Concerned with the agrarian needs of upstate New York, the museum and crossroads rise to expository heights in giving a socioeconomic depiction and understanding of a vanished era. The museum, established in a capacious stone dairy barn (1918, Frank Whiting, architect), provides an enlightening, even exciting, introduction to the village with its craft presentations (such as broom-making and weaving), its chronological depiction of New York agriculture, and its evolution of tool design. One then strolls onto the green and the crossroads of this microcosmic village. Its "highway" is an engaging path lined with thirteen buildings, all of which are original, all from the upstate area, and mostly pre-1840. These are not dead relics, but buildings actively staffed with knowledgeable attendants. The major units are the prominent Bump Tavern (built in 1796, but with Greek Revival porch from 1840); the sprawling Lippitt Farmstead of 1797, which has been miraculously preserved, meticulously restored, and enlivened with appropriate animals; and the church (finished in 1821, remodeled in 1861). The latter forms the strategic terminus, architecturally and otherwise, of the village. A country store, well stocked with the miscellany of its time (1850), a one-room school (1810), and a blacksmith shop (1827—in use until 1934) are among the other units. Note that an unusual number of the buildings are of stone, rather than the more typical wood, reflecting the nearness of local quarries.

Located on NY 80 at the north edge of Cooperstown. Closed January–March. April open Tuesday–Sunday 10:00 A.M.–4:00 P.M. May open daily 10:00 A.M.–4:00 P.M. June–Labor Day open daily 9:00 A.M.–5:00 P.M. Labor Day–October open daily 10:00 A.M.–4:00 P.M. November open Tuesday–Sunday 10:00 A.M.–4:00 P.M. (closed Thanksgiving weekend). December open Friday–Sunday 10:00 A.M.–4:00 P.M. (closed Christmas). Admission is $9 for adults, $4 for children ages 7–12. For more information call (607) 547-1400.

Diagonally across Route 80 from the museum stands Fenimore House Museum (1932—Harry St. Clair Zogbaum, architect), the headquarters of the New York State Historical Association. Its superb exhibits of folk art complement the museum and crossroads, and should by all means be visited. This Neo-Georgian structure was expanded in 1995 with a new Native American wing, designed by architect Hugh Hardy. Designed to house a collection of Native American art, the addition is comprised of two large main galleries as well as an education room and auditorium.

READ HOUSE (1797–1801)
42 The Strand
New Castle, Delaware

George Read, Jr., architect

The Read House is one of the most handsome early Federal-style dwellings in Delaware. Mr. Read designed the house himself and supervised its construction. It is set off by its garden on one side and the Delaware River in the front. One striking feature of the well-detailed exterior is the compact richness of the woodwork in the entry and the window above. The flair of the angled lintels above the windows gives an upward lift to the facade, while two slender dormers and the captain's walk on the roof (note the urns) are tautly contained by the broad doubled chimneys at each end. There is a slight heaviness of detail in the Palladian window above the entry, which is in part due to the fact that the molding that defines the half-round of the upper section is approximately the same width as the molding around the much wider doorway directly below. On the interior an elegant arched double doorway divides the front and back parlors. The detailing of its framework and fanlight (by Peter Crouding) is superior. The plaster work should also be noted. The garden, occupying the site of a house that had earlier burned, was laid out in 1847. Its original design, attributed to Robert Buist of Philadelphia, includes three divisions with a vegetable garden at the rear. The property was acquired in 1975 by the Historical Society of Delaware and opened to the public the same year. (The shutters shown in this photo were removed in 1978.) Both the interior and the exterior were completely restored in 1985.

Open Tuesday–Saturday 10:00 A.M.–4:00 P.M., Sunday 12:00 noon–4:00 P.M. January and February open weekdays by appointment only. Closed for holidays. Admission is $4 for adults, $3.50 for senior citizens and students ages 13–21, $2 for children ages 6–12. All visits are guided; tours are given every half hour. For more information call (302) 322–8411.

OCTAGON (1799–1801)
18th Street NW at New York Avenue
Washington, D.C.

William Thornton, architect

The American Institute of Architects regards this chaste early Federal style building as its hall-mark. One of the first substantial houses in the new city, it was planned for Colonel John Tayloe III by Dr. William Thornton, who had won the competition for the design of the Capitol six years earlier. During the War of 1812 when the White House was burned, the Tayloe mansion served briefly as the home of President James Madison. (Incidentally, the city was not incorporated as "Washington" until 1802.) The brilliance of Thornton's work can be immediately grasped when one sees how the building dovetails onto its difficult, seventy-degree angled plot. Although the site was open country when the dwelling was put up, the street pattern had already been laid out by Charles Pierre L'Enfant. The angled sides of the house parallel the two streets, while the wider front bay breaks out with a near semicircular entry. (The plan is, of course, not a pure octagon as one face is arced.) The commanding result is unorthodox but masterful. The partially raised porch (eleven steps) leads to a circular vestibule—note the fanlight—with dining room at left, stair hall on axis, and drawing room at right. These front rooms are virtually identical in size (they differ by a few inches), measuring 20 x 28 feet/6.1 x 8.5 meters. Each has an inset fireplace at the far end so that the windowless rear walls could be flush on the outside. The ground-floor room disposition is repeated on each of the two upper levels. Servant area and wine cellar occupy the basement.

After the death of Mrs. Tayloe in 1855 and the departure of the family, the house was used as a school and as offices, and eventually deteriorated into a tenement. In 1897 the American Institute of Architects, then located in New York City, rented the building—in the process removing ten indigent families—and therewith transferred its headquarters to Washington. After thorough cleanup and repair, the AIA moved in (1899) and found the accommodations so suitable that it purchased the entire property and outbuildings three years later from the Tayloe family. With the growth of the AIA from roughly 3,000 members in 1940 to 8,374 in 1949, long-standing plans were implemented, all staff offices were removed from the Octagon (1949) to a nearby office building, and the first major renovations of the house were undertaken. With the explosive increase of members in the 1960s (there are approximately 56,000 today) larger headquarters became essential. (The sophisticated new building—designed by The Architects Collaborative in 1971–73—stands on the same property as the Octagon, which, for administrative reasons, was acquired by the American Architectural Foundation in 1968.) The house itself was then restored (1968–70) by the firm of J. Everette Fauber, Jr. of Lynchburg, Virginia, and reopened to the public in 1970 as a museum. Between 1990 and 1995 the firm of Mesick Cohen Waite gave the building a more comprehensive restoration—when fresh documentation became available—intended to reflect the changes and furnishings made during the 1801–28 Tayloe family occupancy. The Octagon represents the early Federal style at its best, with a simplicity of wall statement, a delicacy of detail, and a quiet elegance that evolved as a reaction to the increasingly rich late Georgian style—and its English connotations.

Open Tuesday–Sunday 10:00 A.M.–4:00 P.M. Closed for holidays. Admission is $3 for adults, $1.50 for children, students, and senior citizens. One-hour tours are available. For more information call (202) 638–3221.

WOODLAWN PLANTATION (1800–05)
9000 Richmond Highway
Mount Vernon, Virginia

William Thornton, architect

Located a few miles from Mount Vernon, Woodlawn asserts a style of architectural cohesion and elegance lacking in its earlier neighbor. Dr. William Thornton was the architect. (In 1793 he had won the competition for the United States Capitol and had also designed the Octagon, 1799–1801 [see page 138] in Washington.) Thornton incorporated a key feature of the James River plantations in his new work but gave it an unusual direction for that time. Instead of a house block with flanking but unattached dependencies on either side, he connected the central block with hyphens to the kitchen dependency at right and the plantation office at left, with both units presenting a gabled end to the approach. He then extended this frontage by partially attaching the dairy beyond the kitchen and the smokehouse (left of the office) with a high wall, thus creating an imposingly long facade. It should be added that the hyphens and wings were enlarged early in the twentieth century, with dormers added to the hyphens to accommodate bathrooms, making these once inconspicuous elements compete with the main facade.

The interiors of Woodlawn are excellent. The central hall—used for the living area in hot weather, as was often the practice—is not distinguished, but the music room, the parlor, and the downstairs bedroom are well turned out and decorated and furnished with many original pieces. Since 1951 the house and the nearby Pope-Leighey House by Frank Lloyd Wright (1940–41, see page 393) have been administered by the National Trust.

Located northwest off US 1 at VA 235, 14 miles/23 kilometers south of Washington, D.C. Open daily 9:30 A.M.–4:30 P.M. (January and February closed Monday–Friday). Closed New Year's Day, Thanksgiving, and Christmas. Admission is $6 for adults, $4 for children ages 5 and up, students, and senior citizens. A combination ticket for admission to Woodlawn Plantation and the Pope-Leighey House is $8 for adults, $5 for children and senior citizens. All visits are guided; tours given every half hour. For more information call (703) 780-4000.

FIRST RELIGIOUS SOCIETY MEETING HOUSE (1801)
26 Pleasant Street
Newburyport, Massachusetts

The meeting house of the First Religious Society of Newburyport gives satisfaction outside and in. Though difficult to grasp fully because of its crowded urban site (try viewing it from the public parking area directly behind), the exterior shows careful detailing, from its fanlight door to its finely chiseled cornice and elaborate spire. The famous church architect Ralph Adams Cram (1863–1942) described the four-stage steeple as "the most beautiful wooden spire in New England." The long-aisled interior with extended balcony on two sides and with its prominent and very accomplished Palladian-inspired pulpit on axis is typical of the early-nineteenth-century Federalist period. The nave, with low box pews, is full of graceful light and space. Tradition holds that ships' carpenters were active both in the construction and in the delicate carving. Timothy Palmer oversaw the construction and is thought by some to have designed the church. However, Samuel McIntire had a hand in it, as church records show that he was paid for the carving of the ornamentation on the pulpit and balcony. (There is also a similarity with McIntire's now destroyed South Church in Salem.) In any case the result is very, very fine.

Open by appointment only. Sunday services held at 10:30 A.M. (no services in July or August). Visits can be scheduled by calling the church office at (508) 465–0602; the office is open Monday–Friday 9:00 A.M.–2:00 P.M.

NEW YORK CITY HALL (1803–12)
City Hall Park between Broadway and Park Row
New York, New York

Joseph François Mangin and John McComb, Jr., architects

New York's City Hall is marked by both an outer and inner delicacy. One of its architects—
Joseph François Mangin—was of French descent and probably received French training.
Hints of Ange-Jacques Gabriel's Petit Trianon (1762–68) appear on the exterior, and the
splendid stair within owes a small debt to Gabriel's École Militaire (1751–82) and to James
Paine's Wardour Castle in Wiltshire of 1770–76 (as Clay Lancaster brings out in a perceptive
article in the *Journal of the Society of Architectural Historians*, March 1970). But whatever the
background, the results at the Federal style City Hall are distinguished or, as Henry James put
it, in "perfect taste and finish." The commission for the building's design was won by competition, but the award-winning project—berated by Benjamin Henry Latrobe (who had obviously lost)—was scaled down because of costs, and Mangin took no further part; it was completed by the New York-born John McComb, Jr.

 The entrance hall startles with its geometric counterpoints: the circular sweep of the twin
stairs, and the contrast of horizontals (floors) versus verticals (the Corinthian columns semi-
silhouetted on the second floor), with a dome climaxing these elements. The governor's room
on the second floor, with five rhythmic roundheaded windows (marked on the exterior above
the Ionic entry porch), provides a sunny portrait museum, with many distinguished paintings
(including one of McComb himself). The delicate interior of this room was completely
restored by Grosvenor Atterbury (1912), and stops short of being finicky. On the outside, the
Justice-topped cupola encounters difficulties in adjusting to its rectangular base, but overall
this is one of the city's prizes. A complete restoration, including replacement of all exterior
walls (which were disintegrating), was carried out in 1954–56 by Shreve, Lamb & Harmon; in
1983 the governor's room was restored to the period of Atterbury's work.

Open Monday–Friday 10:00 A.M.–4:00 P.M. Closed for holidays. Free 45-minute tours can be arranged Monday–Friday for
groups of 10–30 people; smaller groups can join an already scheduled tour. For tour information call (212) 788–6865.

GARDNER-PINGREE HOUSE (1804–05)
128 Essex Street
Salem, Massachusetts

Samuel McIntire, architect

Samuel McIntire at his peak—as he is here in the brick Gardner-Pingree House—attained an architectural sophistication that few practitioners, before or after, ever reached in domestic design. The exquisitely tensioned elements of this facade represent nothing less than perfection. The understated semicircular portico quietly pulls one to the dwelling, and its cornice is picked up to embrace the house in the lower stringcourse. A second stringcourse above completes the division of the front into three horizontal elements, each a bit narrower than the one below. Into these bands are set three rows of windows, the bottom two of identical size, the top smaller. Their proportions, their white keystoned lintels, and their dark shutters make them coordinated accents in this pinkish brick front; a white wood balustrade across the top ties it all together. Some of this design is influenced by Charles Bulfinch's First Harrison Gray Otis House of 1796 in Boston (see page 132), but the orchestration here is on a far purer plane. The almost severe elegance of the exterior relaxes within, and opulence, still in check, can be seen throughout. The most memorable feature is the wood carving, for which McIntire was justly famous. The carved framing of the sliding doors between the two parlors should be noted, but the finest work is in the mantels, where the rhythm of elements is often overlooked in favor of their technical virtuosity. One of the superior houses in the United States, it was given to the Essex Institute by the Pingree heirs in 1933.

The Gardner-Pingree House is part of the Peabody Essex Museum, open Monday–Saturday 10:00 A.M.–5:00 P.M. (Thursday until 8:00 P.M.), Sunday 12:00 noon–5:00 P.M. November–Memorial Day closed on Mondays. Closed Thanksgiving and Christmas. Admission is $7 for adults, $6 for students and senior citizens, $4 for children ages 6–16, $18 per family. All visits to the Gardner-Pingree House are guided; tours are included with museum admission. Call (508) 745-1876 for more information.

SHAKERTOWN AT PLEASANT HILL (1805–59)
3500 Lexington Road
Harrodsburg, Kentucky

Micajah Burnett, planner and architect

This extensive and informative restoration of a village of thirty-three buildings is the western-most outpost of the United Society of Believers in Christ's Second Appearing, otherwise known as the Shakers. The community numbered as many as five hundred in the early nine-teenth century, and these worshipful, industrious, and celibate Kentuckians—converted by Shaker missionaries from New York and New England—constituted a phalanx in developing scientific agriculture (especially seeds), handicrafts, and cattle breeding. All property was communal, and growth of the sect was maintained, for a while, by the conversion of adults and the adoption of orphans. The group disbanded in 1910 but many buildings remained in use, though most slipped into quiet neglect. To stop this erosion and save the buildings, a public-spirited non-profit group was incorporated in 1961, the entire settlement purchased, and restoration begun in 1963.

All of the buildings have now been restored for a variety of adaptive uses, and their collective impression, strung along a cobbled lane, is one of harmony and brotherhood. Local wood, stone, and brick were used for construction, and the proverbial Shaker simplicity and thoroughness are manifest throughout. The Meeting House (1820), a building used only for the four services formerly held each Sunday, is perhaps the most intriguing: its entire second floor is suspended from roof trusses so that the meeting room below, which measures a surprisingly large 44 x 60 feet/13.4 x 18.3 meters, constitutes one open space for the believers' famous dancing. This was an architectural/engineering achievement of a high order. The twin circular stairs in the Trustees' Office (by Micajah Burnett, 1839—Burnett was also responsible for the layout of the village and the design of most of its buildings) rank with the finest in the country. The largest structure (and the one shown in the photograph) is the three-story, T-shaped Center Family House (1824–34), whose front section measures 55 x 60 feet/16.7 x 18.3 meters, with kitchen/dining wing extending 85 feet/26 meters behind.

The competition of mass-produced factory items after the Civil War, the drastic decline of Southern markets, and the lure of the city initiated Pleasant Hill's decline. Hastened, too, by celibacy and dissension, it finally closed down, as mentioned, at the beginning of this century. (The last Sister died in 1923).

Other Shaker settlements of architectural interest and open to the public are the Hancock Shaker Village in Pittsfield, Massachusetts (see page 171) and the Shaker Village near Canterbury, New Hampshire. Both, because of a more demanding climate, are even more Spartan than Shakertown, with its basic but appealing buildings and furnishings. All combine simplicity of conception and refinement of detail with probity of construction. A unique attraction of Pleasant Hill is that lodging for the public (in sixty-three air-conditioned rooms) is available in twelve of its restored buildings, while excellent meals from Shaker recipes can be had in the Trustees' Office. It is, thus, very much alive, and worth a visit. The restorations, which opened in 1968, were under the direction of James Lowry Cogar, with Washington Reed, Jr., chief architect.

Located on US 68 at KY 33 (22 miles/35 kilometers southwest of Lexington, 7 miles/11 kilometers northeast of Harrodsburg). April–October open daily 8:00 A.M.–6:00 P.M., November–March open daily 8:00 A.M.–5:00 P.M. Closed Christmas Day. Summer admission is $8.50 for adults, $4 for children ages 12–17, $2 for children ages 6–11. Winter admission is $6 for adults, $3 for children ages 12–17, $2 for children ages 6–11. Tours can be arranged by calling (606) 734-5411.

GORE PLACE (1805)
52 Gore Street
Waltham, Massachusetts

New England society, with wealth based primarily on shipping, manufacturing, and finance, was largely urban-oriented, unlike the plantation-based (that is, agricultural) South. One thus finds relatively few rural or semirural mansions, at least until the nineteenth century. Outstanding among them, and one of the finest Federal houses in the country, is the elongated (204 feet/62 meters) Gore Place. The Gores, who lived in England for eight years while Christopher Gore was commissioner under Jay's Treaty, had been impressed by the south facade of Heaton Park, a house reconstructed by James Wyatt in 1772. However, as Charles Hammond, the former curator of Gore Place, wrote, "The house was designed by the Gores in collaboration with Jacques-Guillaume Legrand (1743–1807) as Gore's letters dated 1801 from Paris indicate."

The central block of the mansion bows out gracefully to mark the one-and-one-half-story oval reception room with the family parlor above. Hyphens—one for the billiard room, the other for the servants' hall—extend from either side of the main structure to be terminated by right-angled pavilions housing the library at one end and the kitchen at the other. Note in these wings the fine geometry of the lower windows and their shutters with the half-round windows above, both tightly contained in shallow arched recesses. The overall result is elegant, though there is confusion at the entry with one door leading to the front hall and its twin to the butler's pantry. Used (and somewhat abused) as a country club in the 1920s, the mansion was purchased by the Gore Place Society in 1935 and thoroughly restored and furnished. The once extensive grounds are down to 45 acres/18 hectares from an original 400 acres/162 hectares, but the spaces are wide and invitingly open—with an obvious influence from the work of Humphry Repton (1752–1818), the famous English landscape architect.

Located south off Main Street (MA 20). 15 April–15 November open Tuesday–Saturday 10:00 A.M.–5:00 P.M., Sunday 2:00–5:00 P.M. Admission is $4 for adults, $3 for students and senior citizens, and $2 for children ages 5–12. A one-hour tour is available. For more information call (617) 894-2798.

ADENA—THOMAS WORTHINGTON HOUSE (1806–07)
848 Adena Road
Chillicothe, Ohio

Benjamin Henry Latrobe, architect

Dominating a plateau northwest of the town, and itself almost dominated by oaks and mag-
nolias, the Worthington House and Garden make a handsome team. Considering building
conditions at the beginning of the nineteenth century in Ohio—it was called Northwest
Territory until 1803 when Ohio became a state (with Chillicothe its first capital)—the mansion
represents an impressive achievement. Benjamin Henry Latrobe, who was at one time architect of the Capitol in Washington, designed the house, having met Colonel Worthington when
the latter was serving as Ohio's senator. As Talbot Hamlin points out in his biography of
Latrobe (Oxford University Press, 1955), the plan of the house with its projected wings resembles that of "Old West" at Dickinson College in Pennsylvania, which Latrobe designed in 1803.
The results here, built with local sandstone and walnut, are commendable, though they proclaim a certain rusticity. The house—the gift of the daughter of the late owners—became a
state memorial in 1946 and has been restored to its early-nineteenth-century condition, as
have the numerous outbuildings and the gardens.

Located off Pleasant Valley Road, off OH 104. Memorial Day–Labor Day open Wednesday–Saturday 9:30 A.M.–5:30 P.M.,
Sunday 12:00 noon.–5:00 P.M. Labor Day–end of October open Saturday 9:30 A.M.–5:00 P.M., Sunday 12:00 noon–5:00 P.M.
Memorial Day, July 4, and Labor Day open 12:00 noon–5:00 P.M. Admission is $4 for adults, $1 for children ages 6–12, $3.20
for senior citizens and AAA members. For more information, call (614) 772–1500.

CONGREGATIONAL CHURCH (1806–09)
Main Street and Route 7
Middlebury, Vermont

Lavius Fillmore, architect

Lavius Fillmore's masterpiece, the Congregational Church, was carefully located to face the town green and to be seen obliquely from two of its main streets. For many observers the finest church in the state, it epitomizes, outside and in, a New England urban house of worship of the early nineteenth century. The projected, column-less entry and pediment are almost identical to the Old Bennington Church, which Fillmore had just finished. However, the tower, belfry, and spire at Middlebury are more accomplished and better tied to the mass of the building; only the setting is less prepossessing. The steeple is composed of square on square, octagon on octagon, with a short spire on top. The interior, too, resembles the Bennington church but is larger. Like its predecessor, it is light, airy, and dignified. An unusual feature of both churches can be seen in the four semifreestanding Ionic columns that support the edge of the balcony and rise uninterruptedly to fair into the ceiling vaults. Note in the Middlebury example the painted ceiling with its symbolism of the cross surrounding the orb of the world. Altogether a gracious setting for worship.

Open Sundays 9:30–11:30 A.M. for church services. Tours can be scheduled during the week by calling (802) 388–7634.

BASILICA OF THE NATIONAL SHRINE OF THE ASSUMPTION
OF THE BLESSED VIRGIN MARY (1806–21/1863)
(Baltimore Cathedral)
Cathedral and Mulberry streets
Baltimore, Maryland

Benjamin Henry Latrobe, architect

This, the first Roman Catholic cathedral in the United States, calls on ancient Rome (mostly) for its architectural inspiration with imposing results. It is this church that broke the English-inspired Colonial pattern of church design that had dominated most religious architecture—other than meeting houses—in the northeast part of the country in the seventeenth and eighteenth centuries. Its importance is thus seminal, and the great Nikolaus Pevsner calls it "North America's most beautiful church" in *An Outline of European Architecture* (Penguin Books, 1943). The Baltimore Co-Cathedral, its second name, was designed by the British-born (1764), English- and German-educated architect and engineer Benjamin Henry Latrobe, who came to the United States in 1796, becoming one of its most distinguished early architects; Talbot Hamlin called him "the father of the American architectural profession" (*Benjamin Henry Latrobe*, Oxford University Press, 1955).

For the Baltimore Cathedral, Latrobe submitted—gratis—two designs, one of Gothic derivation, the other Roman. A cross section of the chosen design reveals a strong parallel with his earlier (1798) Bank of Pennsylvania in Philadelphia: Classical portico, low entry, high-domed central chamber. The cathedral is, of course, much larger and more imposing than the bank, but the basic arrangement of parts is the same. (The church's portico was added in 1863 by Eban Faxon.) The awkwardness in this church layout is that, whereas it generates a potent development of spaces on the interior, primary focus belongs to those worshipers seated under the brilliantly engineered dome. The buildup of spaces is good as long as one is walking down the center aisle, but when seated in the nave (as opposed to the circular crossing) the lateral spaces seem dissipated and semi-isolated. Moreover, in 1890 the chancel was extended to the rear, almost doubling the size Latrobe had designed, and providing open side aisles instead of the original closed niches, which further vitiates spaces that should be the climax of the church. (The onion-shaped domes atop the towers—not those of Latrobe's proposal—were added in 1862–63.) But don't let these criticisms restrain you: visit the cathedral and enjoy what Professor William H. Pierson, Jr., calls "one of the most extraordinary moments in American architecture" (*American Buildings and Their Architects*, Doubleday, 1970).

Open Monday–Friday 7:00 A.M.–5:00 P.M., Saturday–Sunday 7:00 A.M.–6:30 P.M. Guided tours given Sunday at noon. For more information call (410) 727-3564.

NATHANIEL RUSSELL HOUSE (1808–09)
51 Meeting Street
Charleston, South Carolina

High on the list of elegant town houses in the United States stands the Nathaniel Russell House in Charleston. Outside and, particularly, within, the house exults in style. Set in a tree-girted lot with a garden about it, the building enjoys more space than most of its peers along the historic streets of this area. Its narrow end faces the road, and this facade is marked by an energetic play of verticals and horizontals. The three very tall windows of the second (main) floor are set in recessed red-brick arches with white keystones; the thinness of these windows, their tightly recessed framing, and their keystones all emphasize verticality. Prominent white lintels atop the windows and a narrow white stringcourse (aided by a subtle double-brick stringcourse above) set up a horizontal motion. Finally, the three top floor windows push upward only to be countered by the horizontality of the parapet across the top. A light wrought-iron balcony, which breaks out in a semicircle before each of the second-story windows, pirouettes across the front (note Nathaniel Russell's initials in the center one). At left is an angled, four-sided bay, also with balcony. The plan reflects the Charleston "single house" (that is, one room deep).

On entering one is swept, almost before realizing it, to the floor above by a flying stair of mahogany that coils upward to the third floor without touching a wall. The rooms on the second floor—where the main living areas were placed to catch more breeze and light, and to avoid the damp and mosquitoes—are radiant with a flood of daylight from windows that virtually touch the floor; the half-circle balconies outside enable them to be opened safely. Many elements reflect the new England (Rhode Island) background of Russell. The atmosphere of space and light can be seen especially in the ovoid drawing room, or music room, opposite the ovoid stairway. The use of ovals for room shapes is Adamesque, while the decoration epitomizes the Adam-inspired Federal style then coming into fashion. From fireplaces to doors to cornices, both design and workmanship are exemplary. Used as a boarding school, then as a convent school at the end of the last century, and again as a home for many years, the house was purchased in 1955 by the Historic Charleston Foundation, aided by many friends, as its headquarters. Upon being sumptuously restored, it was opened to the public the following year. Although the architect is not known, the house numbers among the very great.

Open Monday–Saturday 10:00 A.M.–5:00 P.M., Sunday 2:00–5:00 P.M. Admission is $6, free for children under 6. All visits are guided; 30-minute tours given throughout the day. For more information call (803) 724–8481. AF 12/61

FAIRMOUNT PARK WATER WORKS (1812–15)
Philadelphia, Pennsylvania

Philadelphians claim that Fairmount Park (William Penn's "Faire Mount") is the largest city park in the United States (presently 4,319 acres/1,748 hectares). Starting at John F. Kennedy Plaza near the middle of the city, it heads for the Schuylkill River, which it warmly embraces on both banks, and then meanders northward up Wissahickon Creek for a total distance of some 10 miles/16 kilometers. Size, however, pays homage to quality, for this is one of the loveliest spreads of urban greenery to be seen, accented by the placid river that flows between its largely unspoiled banks. Even from the windows of a speeding train this carefully tended series of hills, plains, treed areas, and playgrounds (and, unhappily, the Schuylkill Expressway, I-676) is refreshing. The riverside Water Works—suggestive of temples in a landscape by Nicolas Poussin—form a more than engaging group of Greek revival buildings. Built between 1812 and 1815 they were designed by engineer Fredrick C. Graff—probably with help from Benjamin Henry Latrobe or Robert Mills. (Latrobe and Graff in 1799–1801 designed the city's first waterworks system; their neat, domed pumping house was torn down in 1827.) The Water Works are currently undergoing an extensive restoration scheduled to take more than a decade. The enormous art museum on the hill behind was designed by Zantzinger, Borie & Medary together with Horace Trumbauer (1916–28).

Park open daily 24 hours. Water Works open by appointment only; call (215) 592–4908. AR 7/27

NEW HAVEN TOWN GREEN AND ITS CHURCHES (1813–15)
Temple Street between Elm and Chapel
New Haven, Connecticut

The three churches lined up like so many saints on New Haven's green underscore the stylistic dichotomy of nineteenth-century (and, indeed, twentieth-century) Protestant approaches to the house of God, while delighting us with their serenity amid the moil of a city center. This New England common stands in sharp contrast to today's downtown chaos. The space and visual peace of the green are even more valuable now than when laid out—with strict biblical planning precepts and a single church—as the center of nine squares in 1638. It is still the

essence of New Haven. (The eight surrounding squares, measuring 825 feet/251 meters— roughly 500 Old Testament royal cubits—on a side, were then further subdivided by other roads. Strangely, both harbor and river were almost ignored in the planning of the green.)

The dichotomy mentioned stems from the fact that Trinity Episcopal at the southwest end of the Green is Neo-Gothic—and one of the country's earliest essays into this style—while the other two, with their more independent (that is, Congregational) background, are basically Georgian. All were finished within a year or so of each other, Trinity and Center Church by the same architect/builder, Ithiel Town. (As an index of versatility—aided by his library, which reputedly had over eight thousand books—Town became famous with his subsequent partner, Alexander Jackson Davis, for their Greek Revival work.)

The first of the trilogy, Trinity, has been so drastically changed both outside and in since it was finished in 1814 that it is scarcely recognizable as the church seen in early watercolors and engravings. Part of the exterior (including the upper tower) was initially of wood, later replaced in stone. However, further liberties, simplifications, and expansions continued through the years. When built Trinity was, as mentioned, one of the first examples of the Gothic Revival in the United States, and one of Ithiel Town's most precocious designs.

Ithiel Town's role in the erection of the second, the First Church of Christ in New Haven (generally called Center Church, at left in photo) remains somewhat unclear, but most authorities believe that Town himself designed the building with assistance to the plan from Asher Benjamin of Boston, to whom Town had been early apprenticed. All agree that Town was in charge of construction. The National Register of Historic Places stated in 1976 that its design "was initiated by Asher Benjamin and completed by Ithiel Town." (Isaac Damon, who had probably worked in Town & Davis's New York office, actually received the church commission.) In any case the results are splendid; it is by far the handsomest church of the lot. It was called a meeting house for its first few years until the separation between church and state in Connecticut became law in 1818. Its rich portico and pediment, confident well-engineered steeple (with a bit of James Gibbs here), and urn-topped parapet make this one of Connecticut's finest buildings. The interior—used until 1895 for Yale's commencement exercises— does not live up to the exuberance of the facade. In addition, it underwent changes and counterchanges with the years (the 1894 Davenport window in the pulpit wall is simply anachronistic). The crypt (currently undergoing restoration) with its 135 ancient tombs is, however, intriguing. It exists because the present church (the fourth on this same site) not only covers more ground than its predecessor, but part of its cemetery as well.

The third of the group, the United Church or Old North (at right in photo), was built under the supervision of David Hoadley, who designed a number of competent churches throughout the state. However, the architect of this meeting house remains somewhat a mystery: it is generally supposed that Ebenezer Johnson, Jr., produced the final plan, very likely aided by preliminary work by John McComb in New York and Asher Benjamin in Boston (especially on the interior). Of the same red brick and Federal style as Center Church, the United Church suffers from propinquity with the richness of the latter. The audience room (nave), its pulpit wall originally flat, underwent a series of changes through the years.

But see them all. The churches and their green are an incalculable visual and spiritual asset to the city.

Trinity Church open Monday 9:00 A.M.–12:00 noon, Tuesday 9:00 A.M.–5:00 P.M., Wednesday 9:00 A.M.–3:00 P.M., Thursday 9:00 A.M.–5:00 P.M., Saturday 8:00 A.M.–2:00 P.M., Sunday 7:00 A.M.–1:00 P.M. Sunday services held at 8:00, 9:00, and 11:00 A.M. Tours can be scheduled by calling (203) 624–3101. Center Church open Tuesday–Saturday 10:30 A.M.–2:30 P.M. Closed for holidays. Sunday services held at 10:00 A.M. Tours given Sunday at 11:00 A.M. Tours can also be scheduled by calling (203) 787–0121. United Church open by appointment; tours can be scheduled by calling (203) 787–4195. Sunday services held at 10:30 A.M. (10:00 in summer).

LA PURÍSIMA MISSION (1813–18/1934–39)
2295 Purísima Road
Lompoc, California

Secularization (in 1834), earthquakes, and vandalism have largely destroyed the original mission; almost all of the buildings seen here today stem from the rebuilding of 1934–49. Yet the overall impression is of well-researched authenticity. Moreover at La Purísima, as opposed to some of the more pretentious California missions, the visitor can clearly grasp from the unusual in-line (as opposed to quadrangular) architectural layout the full cycle of mission life. This involved houses and schools for Native Americans; shops and living quarters; facilities for accommodating travelers; and, of course, the church. Occupying an unspoiled little valley, La Purísima was first established (1787–88) some 4 miles/6.4 kilometers southwest of its present location but was destroyed by an earthquake in 1812. In 1813 it was moved to the present site on the famous El Camino Real. It became the eleventh of twenty-one Franciscan missions stretching 650 miles/1,046 kilometers from San Diego to Sonoma—each a day's good march from another—which the energetic Father Junípero Serra (1713–84) planned for Alta California. (He lived to see nine established.) Mexico's freedom from Spain (1821) sparked the mission's Chumash tribes to revolt (1824), and from then on the establishment went downhill, particularly after secularization. What was left was sold by Mexican Governor Pio Pico in 1845.

Used as a sheep ranch and sharecrop farm in the last century, and sadly weakened by weather, the ruins and 507 acres/205 hectares were acquired by the state in 1935, and, under experts and the Civilian Conservation Corps, work was commenced on its reconstruction. (The

Union Oil Company donated part of the land, including that on which the buildings stand.) The foundations and crumbled walls of the old mission enabled all buildings to be precisely located, while early sketches were useful in restoring their appearance. All materials used in the rebuilding, from 250,000 adobe bricks to hand-adzed beams, were authentically produced. Though not as architecturally sophisticated as several of the other missions, La Purísima gives a fuller understanding of mission life. It is, incidentally, one of the most ambitious reconstructions in the West.

Located off CA 1 and 246, 3 miles/4.8 kilometers northeast of Lompoc. Open daily 9:00 A.M.–5:00 P.M. Closed Thanksgiving, Christmas, and New Year's Day. Admission is $5 per vehicle. Group tours can be arranged by calling (805) 733-1303. For more information call (805) 733-3713.

OLD ALBANY ACADEMY (1815–17)
Academy Park
Albany, New York

Philip Hooker, architect

The Old Albany Academy, also known as the Joseph Henry Memorial for the great scientist who was educated and taught there, is one of a handful of buildings of architectural character in the city of Albany. Its reserved lines, two-story pilasters, red sandstone ashlar walls, and copper-topped cupola give quiet, Federal style distinction to the exterior. Built as a boys' school (which moved to larger quarters in 1931), it has been owned since 1930 by the Albany City Board of Education. In 1935 it was thoroughly restored and remodeled by Marcus T. Reynolds. Though the rooms on the main floor are of little interest and are crowded with offices, the former chapel on the second floor—with its two-story height, cove ceiling, and Corinthian pilasters—is very dignified. Strangely, one Thomas C. Taylor—of whom little is known—was, according to some official records, the architect of the academy, while Seth Geer (also spelled Gier) is quoted by another state source. However, the dedication stone is inscribed "Ph. Hooker, architect," and there are receipts for payments to him for his services. Geer, it seems, was the master builder while Taylor submitted an earlier design that Hooker— it is thought—substantially changed and improved upon. As Edward W. Root tantalizingly put it in his book *Philip Hooker* (Charles Scribner's, 1929), "Whichever way it was we have no means of telling."

Located off Eagle Street, adjacent to New York State Capitol. Open Monday–Friday 8:30 A.M.–4:30 P.M. Closed for holidays and school recess periods. Visits can be arranged in advance by calling the assistant superintendent at (518) 462–7302.

Directly behind the academy on Washington Avenue stands the State Education Building (1908–12), designed by Henry Hornbostel. It flourishes a parade of thirty-six enormous hollow Corinthian columns with a terra-cotta entablature that represents the apotheosis of cooked earth in the Americas. Lobby open during business hours

Just across Washington Avenue from both education building and academy rises the cheerless bulk of the New York State Capitol, begun in 1867, partially occupied by 1879, but not completed until 1899. Augustus Laver and Thomas W. Fuller—both English-born—won the competition for its design but this was subsequently changed (above its lower floors) by Leopold Eidlitz and H. H. Richardson, and finished by Isaac G. Perry. Though the exterior is bedeviled, parts of the interior are very rewarding, the most notable being Richardson's smashing senate chamber (1881–82) designed with the assistance of the young Stanford White. This colorful, baronial, near-square room was brilliantly restored in 1978–79 by architects Mendel-Mesick-Cohen and now shines as a city highlight.

Free tours are given on the hour Monday–Friday 9:00 A.M.–4:00 P.M. and Saturday–Sunday 10:00 A.M.–4:00 P.M. Located diagonally across the park on Eagle Street stands Richardson's City Hall (1881–82), competent but not sparkling. Open during business hours.

MAISON OLIVIER (1815)
(Acadian House)
Longfellow Evangeline State Commemorative Area
St. Martinville, Louisiana

Cypresses, pines, and a monumental live oak, all heavy with Spanish moss, make a marvelously regional setting for this Creole raised cottage. Though of small stylistic significance, the house, its outbuilding, and its grounds provide an informative and romantic vignette. The Acadian area of Louisiana was named for its French-Canadian settlers—locally the "Cajuns"— who were forced from Acadia, Nova Scotia, in the mid-eighteenth century when they would not swear allegiance to the British who had captured the area. They are still a group apart, speaking today a French patois. (Louisiana at the time of the Acadian migration was French, and its churches were administered until 1763 by the diocese of Quebec, which is why this far-off land was chosen for resettlement. During the French Revolution, the early Acadians were joined by many titled French families.) This house in the Longfellow Evangeline Commemorative Area has the usual masonry lower story, with upper floor and a half framed in cypress with bousillage and moss walls clapboarded, and put together with pegs in place of nails. (It is, thus, a Creole-type dwelling, not Nova Scotia Acadian.) In plan it is a room and a half deep with a gallery across the front and, until the 1850s when it was enclosed for added rooms, one also across the rear. The state purchased the dwelling in 1931 and restored it, opening it to the public as a museum in 1933.

Be sure to see the Acadian Craft House, also in the area. Note the chimney construction (notched wood and mud) and the steep stair to the boys' room in the attic. The little house is a reproduction of the one-front-room version of the Creole-Caribbean cottage that was adopted in Louisiana by the Acadians. The house type is now known as "the Cajun cabin."

Located off LA 31, just north of St. Martinville. Open daily 9:00 A.M.–5:00 P.M. Closed Christmas and New Year's Day. Admission is $2 for adults; free for children under 12 and senior citizens. Free tours given daily. For more information call (318) 394-3754.

DAVENPORT HOUSE (1815–20)
324 East State Street
Savannah, Georgia

Isaiah Davenport, master builder

The Davenport House stands as a monument to historic preservation and what such preservation can do for a house, a square, a section of town—indeed, a city. The building was saved from imminent destruction—to become the inevitable parking lot—then purged from being a tenement (eight families were occupying it before its purchase in 1955 by the Historic

Savannah Foundation). Sensitively rehabilitated on the exterior, and completely restored and refurnished within, it was the first—and key—purchase and restoration in the rescue operation to save Savannah's great but dwindling architectural heritage. Restoration, while extensive, was completely authentic.

The dwelling, measuring 46.1 x 37 feet/14 x 11.3 meters, occupies a corner site facing Columbia Square, which had been laid out in 1799 and which recalls the domestic squares of London and New England. Isaiah Davenport himself was born in Rhode Island and trained in Massachusetts; he favored exposed red brick and suppressed but elegant detail. Note the delicacy of the wrought-iron railing of the double stair that curves and rises to the equally fine front door. (Most Savannah houses rest on raised basements against dampness and street dirt.) The windows, with brownstone lintels, have exterior shutters, creating alternate bands of wood and glass across the facade. The interior, though maltreated through the years, is largely intact, even including the plaster cornices. Davenport used an unusual proliferation of low arches, starting with the front door and continuing with the entrance hall, where freestanding Ionic columns uphold a richly detailed arch that sets off the three-story elliptical stair hall at rear. Arches continue boldly in the drawing room, where each end is framed by an ellipse. The light color of the walls and the quality of the furniture make the interior uncommonly attractive. Very fine Federal style architecture.

Open daily 10:00 A.M.–4:00 P.M. Closed for major holidays. Admission is $4 for adults, $3 for children ages 6–18, free for children under 6. All visits are guided; tours given every half hour. For more information call (912) 236–8097.

The success of the Historic Savannah Foundation with the Davenport House sparked a movement that no other city in the country can match. Charleston is beautifully preserving its patrician enclave and is beginning to broaden its activities elsewhere; New Orleans is conspicuously consuming its once unique inheritance; San Francisco fluctuates; but Savannah is reaching out to purchase, reconstruct, and resell (with controls) its hundreds of worthy, if badly undernourished and often vacant, buildings. Almost all of these would have disappeared otherwise. The foundation has done a fantastic job, which was, until federal help in the 1970s, accomplished with private funds operating on a non-profit basis. Over eight hundred houses (plus a wedge of commercial structures) of historic merit have been directly or indirectly resuscitated by the foundation's efforts, largely with non-profit revolving funds. Thus, a house, having been bought by the foundation, is sold under strict conditions of rehabilitation. The citizens of Savannah are turning back to the city instead of turning their backs on it. Along with most of the rest of the population the tax collector is beaming. Seven women—led by Anna Hunter—saw the Davenport House in its slum condition, grabbed it before it was too late, then supervised its reconstruction; they went on to establish the Historic Savannah Foundation, Inc. in 1955. In addition, Leopold Adler II, the foundation's onetime president, was a driving force. It is no overstatement to declare that they have transformed the city's present and future by its past.

FIRST CHURCH OF CHRIST (1816–17/1881)
Village Green on Main Street
Lancaster, Massachusetts

Charles Bulfinch, architect

One of the great Federal style churches in the country, this masterpiece by Charles Bulfinch—rather, Bulfinch and his job captain Thomas Hearsey—should be seen by all interested in the architectural developments of the early nineteenth century. It established a new creativity in church building, reflecting both the architect's increased sophistication and the design changes effected by Hearsey, who came from Boston to supervise the job. (Bulfinch himself supposedly never visited the church—see Harold Kirker's encyclopedic *The Architecture of Charles Bulfinch*, Harvard University Press, 1969.) Hearsey's most prominent changes involved making the three arches of the portico of equal height, adding the volutes on the tower base, and reducing the size of the cupola—all design changes for the better, particularly the equalization of the portico arches. (Bulfinch had proposed one large arch flanked by two smaller.)

The church stands parallel to the street, facing a well-kept green, which it shares with several spatially disjoined municipal buildings. The proportions of the well-projected portico (which boasts an arch on each side to match the three in front), the exquisite thinness of its brick piers, and the refinement of its white-painted pilasters and entablature are masterful. The knife-like flatness of the arches and their interaction with the shadowed spaces behind and with the black-faced clock above (only a touch smaller in diameter than the arches) create a rhythm unmatched by any other church entry. A vestibule, not quite as wide as the nave proper, stands directly behind the portico, with a modest, almost cubic, brick tower surmounting it, with identical clocks adorning its three other sides. White wooden volutes marry the tower's narrow width to the block on which it rests. A temple-like cylindrical wooden cupola capped by a small dome weighs (heavily?) on the tower base. Altogether this is a facade liberated from prototypes, one bringing fresh design ideas into the young country. The interior follows the usual squarish meeting house plan and does not share the exterior's architectural venturesomeness. The balconies, for instance, push themselves into the space of the worship room instead of being as one with it, and while the north wall boasts an elaborate, almost magisterial, high pulpit, the elements of the sanctuary end do not work harmoniously together. Some of this is due to the fact that this end of the church was altered when the chapel was added in 1881, necessitating the closure of its chancel windows; plaster decorations also date from this period (and probably the prominent stovepipes). Strangely enough there was no artificial lighting until indirect broad-beam lamps were installed in the balconies (c. 1970).

Sunday services held at 8:30 A.M. and 10:30 P.M. Also open by appointment at other times; call (508) 365–2427. Tours can be scheduled in advance by calling the above number.

OWENS-THOMAS HOUSE (1816–19)
124 Abercorn Street, Oglethorpe Square
Savannah, Georgia

William Jay, architect

William Jay, a bright English architect, arrived in Savannah in 1817 at the age of twenty-four to supervise the final design and the construction of this spirited Regency house for Richard Richardson. (The house is now known by the names of its last two owners.) He is said to have received the commission because Richardson's brother-in-law married Jay's sister. Jay went on to design several distinguished—but not fully regional—buildings both in Savannah and Charleston before returning in 1824 to his native England (and eventually to Mauritius, where he died).

The exterior of the Owens-Thomas House reflects some of the flair of Jay's native Bath, where John Wood the Younger's Circus and Royal Crescent (1764 and 1769) would have given any architecturally inclined young man memorable ideas. John Nash's work in London, where Jay studied, also stirred his ambitions. The distinguished features of the facade are twofold. First is the graceful one-story portico that bows subtly out in plan, with an entablature that wraps around the house as an outsize belt course. Second, the front entry is set in an arched niche reached by twin curving stairs: good early Regency design. Note that the approach is within a low-walled garden, unusual for Savannah. The busy sides are less well articulated, but examine the cast-iron balcony (possibly made in England) on the south facade.

One enters a ceremonial front hall with two gold-capped Corinthian columns visually slowing the progression up the stairs. These stairs split at the landing, double back on either side, and are bridged at top. The drawing room, decorated with elaborate, liberated-Greek plasterwork that fans out like palmettos onto the ceiling from the corners, is the most unusual room. The mantel, too, should be noted. Furnishings throughout the house are superior. The basement walls of the Owens-Thomas House are made of tabby (burnt oyster shells for lime, crushed seashells for aggregate, water, and sand), further waterproofed by natural cement, finished with stucco, and given a light ocher wash.

It might be said that in spots the interior shows more imagination than mastery of detail, but William Jay in his seven years in Georgia and South Carolina left a definite imprint on United States architecture. Would that he had stayed. Many consider this to be the finest Regency house in the country. The house was willed to the Telfair Museum of Art in 1951 and opened to the public three years later. The garden, designed in 1954 by landscape architect Cleremont Lee, is also well worth inspection. In 1995 a Visitors Center was opened in the carriage house, once used as slave quarters and stable.

Open Tuesday–Saturday 10:00 A.M–5:00 P.M., Sunday 2:00–5:00 P.M. Closed for holidays. Admission is $5 for adults, $3 for students, $2 for children ages 6–12. All visits are guided; half-hour tours given daily. For more information call (912) 233-9743.

FIRST UNITARIAN CHURCH (1817–18/1893)
Charles and Franklin streets
Baltimore, Maryland

Maximilian Godefroy, architect

The French-born Godefroy (c. 1765–1845) is little known in the United States, but his impact as an architect and an architectural professor (among the earliest) was strong in Baltimore, to which city he fled (1805) after Napoleon proclaimed himself emperor. Chief among his few surviving works is this church, which confidently occupies its corner site. The three arches of the pedimented entry bay on Franklin Street are echoed by the arched windows on Charles. The unusual and effective burnt-clay *Angel of Truth* in the pediment was sculpted by Antonio Capellano (and upon its deterioration was renovated in 1954 by Henry Berge). Note the bold geometric simplicity of the attic above the cornice line. The exterior remains essentially as originally built. The nave, 53.5 feet/16.3 meters square, is no longer as Godefroy designed it, with Pantheon-inspired dome producing unfortunate acoustics, despite several corrective attempts made through alterations of the chancel. Thus in 1893 a false barrel-vaulted ceiling was installed by J. E. Sperry, a prominent Baltimore architect of the time, and the church rededicated. A Tiffany mosaic is located in the chancel, and the six side windows contain Tiffany stained glass, all installed between 1895 and 1904.

Sunday services held at 11:00 A.M. Group tours given every third Sunday at 12:30 P.M. The rest of the week, open by appointment only; tours can be arranged by calling (410) 685–2330.

ACADEMICAL VILLAGE (1817–26)
University of Virginia
Charlottesville, Virginia

Thomas Jefferson, architect

For a nation that has few successfully composed urban spaces, the Lawn and Rotunda of Thomas Jefferson's "academical village" offer lessons just as valid today as they were when laid out. For here is one of the world's great architectural conceptions, probably the finest since Giovanni Lorenzo Bernini's embracing forecourt to St. Peter's (1656–67). Those wanting to savor masterfully handled space, as well as every architect and planner, should make their hegira here. The greatest rewards are not from the Neo-Classical mold of the architecture, for this, fine though it be, belongs to another era, but from what this architecture does in creating and delimiting three dimensions.

Jefferson was interested in education as an essential element of democracy—his tombstone inscription ends with "the Father of the University of Virginia"—and when he retired from the presidency in 1809, much of his energy was directed toward creating the nation's first non-religious university. He sought to mold an educational system in a "village" with faculty and student body united in closely related buildings. "Corporate humanism," Kenneth Clark called it, cast architecturally in a Classical, not Georgian, frame.

The plan of the university takes one up a short flight of compacted stairs to an inner refuge containing the Lawn and Rotunda, unfolding in a revelation of ordered greenery and buildings. The rows of trees are doubled so that the central open space is bordered with tall trees to create an appropriate horizontal scale, while a smaller row behind eases the scale to the buildings. The colonnades along each side allow one to participate in enclosure or move out to observe it; one can walk enframed by building, by building and trees, or by trees alone. Each option has its rewards. From the south end, the broad terraces as they step up toward the Rotunda create a descant in the rhythm of the whole (reflecting the inclined profile of the site), giving an upbeat to the colonnades and pavilions on each side and emphasizing the crowning of the Rotunda.

Ten two-story "pavilions," five to a side, housed classrooms on the lower floors and unmarried professors' quarters above; dormitories for students are spaced in between. The red brick pavilions are all different—they are a museum of Classical architecture based on Roman temples as well as Palladian interpretations. Their spacing, moreover, is not static but a brilliant progression of four, six, seven, and eight living units between the five pavilions, those more closely grouped standing nearest the Rotunda. Behind these two rows that frame the "grounds" (not "campus"), and separated from them by gardens with Jefferson's famous serpentine walls, stand two more rows of students' quarters interlarded with dining quarters, called "hotels." Jefferson had the foresight here to enlist professional architectural advice from both Dr. William Thornton and Benjamin Henry Latrobe. Both contributed to the design of the arcade and pavilion facades. In addition, Latrobe realized that a dominant element was needed to pull the rows of buildings into a unified composition, and therefore suggested that a substantial domed structure would add enormously to the grouping. This idea appealed to Jefferson, who placed the Rotunda, containing the library and six oval meeting rooms, across the north end of the Lawn, thereby bringing the rows into superb unity. Based on the Roman Pantheon—a cylindrical, domed mass with a pedimented porch in front, but here at half scale—the Rotunda, Jefferson's "capstone of the University," superintends the great space in front, sending out low lateral terraces across its end to connect the center with the two nearest rows of housing.

The Rotunda was heavily damaged by fire in 1895 but was rebuilt with alterations by Stanford White, who took out the second floor to make one larger inner space and replaced Robert Mill's bulky 1850–51 Annex, which had been attached to the north, with a portico to match that facing the Lawn. (White—with McKim, Mead & White—also was responsible for the 1896–98 building, which unfortunately closed the once open end of the Lawn, thus blocking the vista of the distant mountains.) With the late Professor Frederick D. Nichols, the Jeffersonian scholar and architect, working with the firm of Ballou & Justice, the Rotunda was restored to Jefferson's interior design for the 1976 Bicentennial. Although the pavilions and quarters also underwent some changes through the years, a comprehensive thirty-year restoration of the Academical Village begun in the early 1980s is moving ahead. One of the nation's greatest architectural experiences.

Open daily 9:00 A.M.–4:45 P.M. Closed Thanksgiving weekend and for winter recess (mid-December–mid-January). Guided tours given daily at 10:00 A.M., 11:00 A.M., 2:00 P.M., 3:00 P.M., and 4:00 P.M. Special tours can also be scheduled by calling (804) 924-1019 or (804) 924-7969.

HYDE HALL (1817–35)
Glimmerglass State Park, Mill Road
Cooperstown, New York

Philip Hooker, architect

It comes as a distinct surprise to find an early-nineteenth-century mansion as sophisticated as this in an area that was then barely settled. But then George Hyde Clarke, its owner—and probable co-designer with Philip Hooker—was no ordinary squire. The first part of the building, the so-called Stone House, was begun in 1817 then extended to the north in 1819, along what is now the rear. The office, kitchen, and service wing date from 1819–23. The foundations for the main dwelling—the distinguished structure that now dominates the site—were put in during 1819, but it was not until eight years later that Hyde Clarke began above-ground construction and not until 1835 that it was completed. There is an intriguing scale in its Federal-influenced facade, primarily from the four square windows across the front. This unusual fenestration quietly states that a square commands. Discreet inset panels both above and below the windows extend their influence, with a stringcourse binding all together. At center four unfluted Doric columns project to mark the entry, with a small, temple-fronted second floor above in plane with the facade. Inside, the drawing room (left) and dining room(right) are impressively proportioned, particularly their lofty coved ceilings. Both rooms are currently under restoration. Hyde Hall had been lived in continuously by Clarke heirs until shortly after World War II. The state purchased the house in 1963. Rot and mildew had taken their toll and a long-term program of restoration began in 1971, the roof rightly receiving top priority. Rehabilitation depends on the Friends of Hyde Hall, an organization that in 1988 acquired a thirty-year lease of the site and is responsible for restoration and management. Hyde Hall is a National Historic Landmark. Glimmerglass State Park—of which Hyde Hall is a part—offers rewards itself. Designed by the Central New York State Parks Commission and opened in 1966 (bathhouses, 1968), the park provides spacious facilities for picnicking, boating, and swimming on grounds that once belonged to the mansion.

Located 10 miles/16 kilometers north of Cooperstown on Country Road 31 (4.4 miles/7 kilometers south of NY 80 at East Springfield, also on 31). Tours of Hyde Hall are given from June to September Saturday–Sunday at 1:00, 2:00, 3:00, and 4:00 P.M.; during the week by appointment. Admission is $5 for adults, $4 for senior citizens. For more information call (607) 547–5098.

SECOND BANK OF THE UNITED STATES (1819–24)
420 Chestnut Street between 4th and 5th streets
Philadelphia, Pennsylvania

William Strickland, architect

The Second Bank is one of the key buildings in the development of the Greek Revival—a revival that had a marked influence on the design of public buildings in the United States in the first half of the nineteenth century. William Strickland won the commission for the bank in a competition (1818), and though some feel that Benjamin Henry Latrobe's entry, which placed second, was subsequently used to modify Strickland's design (Strickland had earlier worked with Latrobe), most authorities attribute the building completely to young Strickland and to the English books on ancient Greece that he possessed. The bank's gabled ends were directly inspired by the Parthenon without the sculpture—as Strickland himself proclaimed—but its sides, because of interior space demands, lack the fifteen lateral Doric columns that embrace the home of the virgin Athena. Actually the competition itself called for "a chaste imi-

tation of Grecian architecture," and the result is the earliest "pure" example of this style in the United States. The main banking room, which occupies the entire center of the building extending from side to side, is a well-proportioned chamber with freestanding Ionic columns upholding a vaulted ceiling. Note on the exterior the arched windows on the sides.

In 1836 the federal charter for the Second Bank expired and its renewal was vetoed by President Andrew Jackson. A state charter was granted for a private bank to operate in the building, but in 1841 the bank failed, and from 1844 to 1932 the building was used by the federal government as a customhouse. For the bicentennial it was transformed into a portrait gallery of the nation's leaders from the 1775–1825 period. The bank forms a major asset to the Independence National Historical Park.

Open daily 9:00 A.M.–5:00 P.M. (July–August until 6:00 P.M.). Admission is free. Guided tours are available. For more information call (215) 597–8974.

BETHESDA PRESBYTERIAN CHURCH (1820–22)
502 De Kalb Street (US 1)
Camden, South Carolina

Robert Mills, architect

The Bethesda Presbyterian Church, sitting back on its green lawn from the main street in Camden, is one of the most comely Greek Revival churches in the country. It is doubtful that one will encounter a finer religious building on US 1 from Madawaska, Maine to Key West, Florida. The church, one of the earliest examples of the Greek Revival in the state, is curiously double-ended, with an excellent four-column Tuscan portico facing the avenue, and a three-column portico at rear, now the main entry. (Mills himself made no mention of a rear portico, and its design makes it unlikely that he had anything to do with it.) The avenue facade is distinguished by a large, arched, framed panel, stuccoed and painted white, with two roundheaded, shuttered doors (rarely used) on either side. Originally this recess was of plain brick with a white arch over its top and over the two doors. A small rectangular plaque, also white (again, originally of plain brick), is placed above each door and is repeated atop the five windows along the sides. The entrance end is unusually complicated by twin flights of external stairs, which meet and then double back as they rise to the gallery above, with the two main doors placed under their landings. Six doors in one small church seem redundant, but the two at front were probably primarily for ventilation. The church is topped off by what Mills termed a "neat" spire.

The interior, which was restored in 1937, is white, chaste, and a little dry, and, as Mills wrote, "is so arranged that the floor and pews rise as they recede from the pulpit, giving every advantage to the audience in seeing and hearing." Mills also added, "it is far easier to harm than to benefit church architecture in the making over" (quoted in H. M. Pierce Gallagher, *Robert Mills*, Columbia University Press, 1935). The chancel wall is marked by repetition of the framed recess seen on the facade and by the recesses of the two flanking doors. The central, raised pulpit is reached by twin flights of curved stairs. The five windows on either side carry out the round-head motif seen in front.

Note, also, the *Monument to De Kalb* (1825), which Mills also designed, on the avenue front of the church. (General Johann De Kalb, a German-born hero of the American Revolution, was killed [1780] in the Battle of Camden.)

Open Monday–Friday 8:00 A.M.–5:00 P.M. Sunday services held at 9:00 and 11:15 A.M. Guided tours are available through HisToury, (803) 432–1723.

FIREPROOF BUILDING (1822–26)
100 Meeting Street
Charleston, South Carolina

Robert Mills, architect

The advantage of having so much timber proved to be an architectural liability to the American colonies at times, certainly in crowded cities, where the threat of fire was high. Most large communities, even as early as the late seventeenth century, outlawed any but stone or brick construction in town, at least for the outside walls. However, the country's first structure for the fireproof storage of records was Charleston's County Record Building. Though it has been nicknamed the "Fireproof Building" since the time of its construction, Robert Mills himself always referred to it as the "Fireproof Office." Mills also convinced the city to surround the building with a small park to act as a firebreak as well as to add more light and air.

As the structure had to accommodate a number of state agencies, easy inner circulation was necessary. The nearly square plan was therefore divided into three banks of barrel- and groin-vaulted, squarish rooms separated by two barrel-vaulted longitudinal corridors. A skylit stair hall illuminated the middle and stimulated a flow of air. Only two of the three floors are fireproof because the top floor was initially rented out for private offices; it was later used for personnel but not for the storage of important official records. The upper walls are of masonry but roofed with a wood truss. Actually only four of the rooms, those on the ends of the center bank of the lower floors, are *totally* fireproof (and without fireplaces). The others, however, lag not far behind in incendiary security; even the original casement windows and shutters were made of iron.

The Fireproof Building is the most noted existing structure that Mills designed for his native town. Mills, who was born in Charleston (1781) and initially educated there, was one of the country's first native-born, adequately trained architects (James Hoban, Thomas Jefferson, and Benjamin Henry Latrobe all helped his education). He was also an accomplished engineer, climaxing his career with the Washington Monument in the nation's capitol (see page 216). What we now see at the Fireproof Building was watered down from his original design which had clean-cut pediments over its two Doric porticos (one at each end) instead of the awkward parapet that now tops the building; fluted columns instead of dull stuccoed ones; and graceful curved twin stairs instead of the right-angled ones (the stairs were replaced after the famous 1886 earthquake, when part of the pediment also fell off; these apparently were the only damages the building suffered). Some of these design changes might well have been carried out by John George Spidle, a local Charleston architect who was hired to supervise construction when Mills was away. Though good, the building is not an esthetic triumph—due to its straying from Mills's drawings—but it is very definitely a technical triumph. It now houses the South Carolina Historical Society.

Only the Historical Society's research library is open to the public: open Tuesday–Friday 9:00 A.M.–4:00 P.M., Saturday 9:00 A.M.–2:00 P.M. Closed for holidays and the Saturdays before holidays. Admission is $5 per person. Group tours can be scheduled by calling (803) 723-3225.

Though closed to the public, take a look at the gate and exterior of Hibernian Hall (1839–40) across Meeting Street (105), designed by Thomas Ustick Walter. It is a fine example of the Ionic Greek Revival.

ROBERT MILLS HISTORIC HOUSE AND PARK (1823–25)
1616 Blanding Street between Pickens, Henderson, and Taylor streets
Columbia, South Carolina

Robert Mills, architect

Robert Mills (1781–1855) was South Carolina's most noted architect. He was also one of the nation's most distinguished designers, in addition to being a highly talented engineer. His most renowned work is the Washington Monument (see page 216), but, in Pennsylvania, he designed what was at the time the longest single-span bridge in the world. (See H. M. Pierce Gallagher, *Robert Mills*, Columbia University Press, 1935.) Mills's domestic output was limited, so this Federal Style/Greek Revival mansion he designed for Ainsley Hall is particularly valuable. That it exists at all is due to the efforts of historic preservationists, who later founded the Historic Columbia Foundation and who, at the last moment, saved the property (1960) from becoming one vast parking lot. Upon reconditioning and refurnishing, the Ainsley Hall House was opened to the public (1967) as the Robert Mills Historic House and Park.

The mansion, which is of brick, rests on a white-painted raised "basement" with a squarish two-story dependency (reconstructed) on either side. The dwelling's two facades differ markedly: that on the north—the main entrance—carries the usual pedimented two-story portico, here with four slender Ionic columns; that to the south or garden side has a distinctly original, seven-arch, projected colonnade across the entire front, with smaller brick arches, flush with the edge, at the lower level. The south front is further distinguished by an intriguing arched niche, almost a small exedra, which accommodates the twin doors from the twin drawing rooms on this side.

The building, incidentally, was never used as a residence by Ainsley Hall or anyone else. Shortly after completion it was sold (1829) to the Columbia Theological Seminary, which occupied it for almost one hundred years. Thus, although only repair work was necessary on the structurally intact interior, the furnishings have had to be collected from various sources in recent years. The restoration of the house and the reconstruction of the two dependencies (on their old foundations) was carried out by Simons, Lapham, Mitchell & Small of Charleston and Reid Hearn Associates of Columbia. Directly across the street at 1615 Blanding stands the Hampton-Preston Mansion, built in 1818. It will interest the specialist both outside and in.

Both houses open Tuesday–Saturday 10:00 A.M.–4:00 P.M., Sunday 1:00– 5:00 P.M. Closed for holidays. Admission is $3 for adults and $1.50 for students. For more information call the Historic Columbia Foundation at (803) 252–1770.

ROUND BARN (1826/1864)
Hancock Shaker Village
US 20 at MA 41
Pittsfield, Massachusetts

Shaker building, as can be seen in Maine, New Hampshire, and Kentucky, has always been characterized by an appealing directness and simplicity. It has, on the other hand, only occasionally risen to the architectural distinction that Shaker furniture attained in its design field. However, the Round Barn (1826, roof and interior rebuilt in 1864 after fire) is one of the great functional examples of early American agricultural building, a timeless and eloquent structure. A three-level cylinder of local gray limestone 95 feet/29 meters in diameter forms this vernacular bastion, and is topped by a twelve-sided, white-painted wooden clerestory and lantern, the latter replacing the pre-fire conical roof. (A red brick abutting wing, tacked on in the late 1860s, is a sore intrusion.) The simple mathematics of stone cylinder and dodecagonal clerestory erupt inside with a startling geometric fanning of chestnut rafters, beams, and posts. The barn's round shape was chosen so that hay wagons could enter, deliver their load from the ramped top level to a central hay deposit, then exit at the same door. Fifty-two cows occupied the wedge-shaped stalls on the floor below, and a circumferential manure pit took up the lowest level. This tri-level functional design created a farming sensation, and creaking copies (in wood) can be seen to this day in the Plains States. In 1932 Massachusetts law ruled that the cows must go as the barn did not have a concrete floor (which could be properly cleaned). When the warmth that the cows had brought to the interior vanished, freezing winter weather attacked and seriously cracked the walls (a process already inaugurated by inadequate footings).

The rest of the twenty buildings of the community, which was the third Shaker settlement in the United States, merit a look, even if the exteriors are not inspiring. (The last Shakers left in 1960 and the village was officially closed, to be reestablished as Shaker Community Inc.) Forget, for instance, the outside of the five-story Brick Dwelling (1830) but do sample its authentically furnished period rooms. The 1793 Meeting House, moved here from the Shirley Plantation (see page 67), should also be seen—as should the extensive gardens. When leaving look back at the Round Barn: it is one of the country's greatest autochthonous buildings. It owes its existence today to the generosity of Mr. and Mrs. Frederick W. Beinecke, who donated a substantial sum to save it from collapse, and to restore it (1968) to its condition of over one hundred years ago. Terry F. Hallock was architect of the restoration.

Located just west of MA 41, 5 miles/8 kilometers west of Pittsfield. April–November open 9:30 a.m.–5:00 p.m. Admission is $10 for adults, $5 for children ages 6–17, free for children under 6, $25 for families. Tours are given from 1 April to Memorial Day and from late October to 30 November. To arrange a visit during the winter months, call (413) 443-0188.

ARCADE (1827–29)
130 Westminster Street and 65 Weybosset Street
Providence, Rhode Island

J. C. Bucklin and Russell Warren, architects

The multistory arcade as an urban link and architectural adjunct was not widely employed in the early nineteenth century in the United States, in spite of the successful examples of the Royal Opera (1790) and Burlington (1819) arcades in London. Structural demands and the necessity for substantial panes of glass inhibited widespread use here until a bit later. Among the earliest examples in this country is this arcade in Providence, 216 feet/66 meters in over-all length. Introduced at each end by a stalwart line of granite Ionic columns—for years the largest monoliths (22 feet/6.7 meters high and weighing 13 tons/13.2 metric tons each) in the United States—this Greek revival arcade provides to this day a pleasant milieu for shopping. Note that the Westminster Street end has a pediment while the other does not. Some feel that arcade shops anticipated the department store and that this Rhode Island example was one of the first enclosed shopping centers in America. Its lateral tightness and modest dimensions deny it the grandeur of the much later Arcade in Cleveland (1890—see page 286), but it is a pleasure to find a weather-protected "street" (recently reconditioned) where one can stroll and shop at leisure in the fast-moving turmoil of downtown Providence. It is also rewarding to see that contemporary architects and planners, impressed by such elderly prototypes, are recognizing the delights of top-lighted covered spaces—as many of today's covered mall shopping centers attest.

Open during business hours. For more information call (401) 272–2340.

OLD CUSTOM HOUSE (c. 1827–46)
115 Alvarado Street
Monterey, California

The king of Spain made Monterey the capital of California in 1775, but no structures of that era remain (other than the Royal Presidio Chapel, site of the area's first mission). The newly created Republic of Mexico acquired this part of California in 1822, and the first stage of the Old Custom House (the north end) was built soon after (1827–28)—it is now California's oldest secular building. Americans captured much of the state in 1846 (raising the flag on this building), but it was not until four years later that California actually became part of the Union as its thirty-first state. The Old Custom House, expanded from 1841–46, continued to serve its original functions until abandoned by the United States government in 1867. Subsequent commercial uses did not help the building's condition, but beginning in the late 1890s some restoration was made of its adobe and stone walls, and finally, in 1938, it came under the state's purview and was fully restored. Though more of historic than architectural importance, the building is a good index of its time and place. It is listed in the National Register of Historic Places.

Located on plaza at Fisherman's Wharf. Open daily 10:00 A.M.—5:00 P.M. in summer and 10:00 A.M.—4:00 P.M. in winter. Admission is free. Park guides available to answer questions. Group tours can be arranged by calling (408) 649-7118.

FIRST CONGREGATIONAL CHURCH (1828–29)
21 Torrington Road
Litchfield, Connecticut

Litchfield, its hilltop location (1,100 feet/335 meters) sparing it the blessings of a main-line railroad and nineteenth-century industrial development, merits its reputation as one of New England's few unspoiled towns, as this common and church attest. The town was founded in 1719 and platted the same year. North and south streets were offset, rather than continuous, to define thus a small green central square. Each of these two streets merits a stroll, for both have buildings (private) of merit. (It must be added that the green fades away into commercialism at the west end.)

First Congregational Church was carefully placed to command the uphill approach to the village while its facade proudly holds down the green outstretched in front. The church's exterior is distinguished by its massing and its sharp detail, with harmony rising from portico to tower to octagonal belfry to conical steeple (restored). It is the three-dimensional merit of these parts that lends the exterior distinction both when approaching from the hillside or from the green. The outside of the Litchfield church has relatives around the state, the closest being those in Milford and Cheshire, designed by David Hoadley. A church booklet suggests that Levi Newell and Selah Lewis may have had a hand in its design, but nothing definite is known about the architect. The interior is flooded with light from windows on both sides of its longitudinal plan. Yet it falters at the sanctuary, where centrifugal forces pull the eye from the spidery mahogany pulpit to the rear corners where side galleries merge into doors. The church was moved from its original site to one several hundred feet up Torrington Road (where it once operated as a movie house), and a new Victorian edition was erected (1873) in its place. When truth dawned this upstart was demolished (1929), and the old meeting house put back where it first sat and restored (1930) to pristine condition by Richard H. Dana, Jr.

Church open weekdays 9:00 A.M.–1:00 P.M. Admission is free, although a donation is suggested. Tours can be scheduled by calling (203) 567–8705.

SOMERSET PLACE (c. 1830)
2572 Lakeshore Road
Creswell, North Carolina

The house at Somerset plantation falls more into the category of upper-bracket, low-country tradition than that of a mansion of architectural distinction. However, the dwelling and the numerous outbuildings (some still in the process of restoration) give an excellent idea of the size and complexity of large-scale farming operations in this region early in the last century. The plantation began in the 1780s as a 100,000-acre/40,469-hectare cooperative for raising rice. Much of the land was swamp and had, with great difficulty, to be drained. The grandson of the principal founder was willed the plantation and around 1830 began constructing (or reconditioning) the house we see today, adding many more outbuildings and new canals, and shifting from rice to corn as a cash crop.

The house—which grew through the years—was used primarily as a winter home, as the heat and mosquitoes dictated summers in the North. Note the proliferation of double-decked porches (added after 1830)—typical of the Carolina coast—to shade the dwelling by day and afford refreshing sitting places in the breezes at dusk. (Moreover, the second level was more apt to be free of plant- and ground-loving mosquitoes.) T-shaped in plan, the house has fourteen rooms, enough to accommodate numerous guests, many of whom stayed for a month. Sliding doors allowed the two parlors to be thrown together, but there is no major salon.

After the Civil War the family was forced to sell the plantation and the house was eventually vandalized. Acquired by the federal government in the 1930s, it was transferred to the state as Pettigrew State Park, and a careful restoration of the house was undertaken. In 1969 the renewed plantation was opened to the public. Although few of the furnishings are original, all are of the 1850 period. Somerset Place is administered by the Division of Archives and History of the Department of Cultural Resources.

Located 7 miles/11.3 kilometers south of US 64 at Creswell. April–October open Monday–Saturday 9:00 A.M.–5:00 P.M., Sunday 1:00–5:00 P.M. November–March open Tuesday–Saturday 10:00 A.M.–4:00 P.M., Sunday 1:00–4:00 P.M. Closed for major holidays. Admission is free. One-hour guided tours are available. Groups should schedule tours in advance by calling (919) 797–4560.

CHAPEL, UNIVERSITY OF GEORGIA (1831–32)
off Broad Street, central campus
Athens, Georgia

Athens's Classical inheritance can be traced back to this Greek "temple," which served as chapel and, for almost one hundred years, as assembly hall for the university. The picturesque exterior (of stuccoed brick) presents six sharply cut, unsubtle (no entasis, primitive capital) Doric columns upholding a simplified entablature. The interior is dominated by an enormous painting (23.5 feet/7.2 meters wide) of the interior of St. Peter's in Rome, the work of George Cook (1783–1857).

Open Monday–Friday 8:00 A.M.–5:00 P.M. Visits should be arranged in advance by calling the Office of the Vice President for Academic Affairs at (706) 542-5721.

OAKLEIGH (1831–32)
350 Oakleigh Place at Savannah Street
Mobile, Alabama

James W. Roper, architect

Oakleigh's masonry ground floor and its wood-porticoed main floor above identify it as a clear member of the French-influenced antebellum houses that stretch along the Gulf of Mexico. Some historians believe that this "raised cottage type"—often with Greek Revival details—originated with the French in Alabama, then gravitated to Louisiana, where it achieved its greatest popularity. Though planned without benefit of a trained architect—its original owner, James W. Roper from South Carolina, designed it—the house has a highly functional *T*-shaped plan that permits cross ventilation (generally from three exposures) in the major rooms. It is elevated above ground because of dampness and insects, and is reached by an unusual curved

outside stair set within the portico. The kitchen was placed in the rear, as was the custom. Its setting, a 33-acre/13-hectare portion of an original Spanish land grant of some 400 acres/162 hectares, is surrounded by fine old live oaks (hence its name), azaleas (which were introduced by the French), and camellias (which are generally at peak blossom from mid-February through March). A number of changes were made in the house by its various occupants—it once even served as a youth center. Oakleigh was acquired by the city in 1955 and, after full restoration and furnishing in the pre-1850 fashion, was made into a museum-house.

Located south off Government Street, 4 blocks on George or 3 on Roper. Open Monday–Saturday 10:00 A.M.–4:00 P.M., Sunday 2:00 –4:00 P.M. Closed holidays and the week of Christmas. Admission is $5 for adults, $4.50 for senior citizens, $2 for children ages 6–11. All visits are guided; one-hour tours given daily. Tours can also be scheduled by calling (334) 432–1281.

OLD CATHEDRAL—BASILICA OF ST. LOUIS (1831–34)
209 Walnut Street at 2nd Street
St. Louis, Missouri

Joseph C. Laveille and George Morton, architects

Near the south leg of the Gateway Arch (see page 486)—in an area once crowded with aged buildings—stands the Basilica of St. Louis, King of France, the fourth church on this site, and the first major example of the Greek Revival in Missouri. (The style was more seriously explored five years later in the nearby Old Court House.) Most of the church's Classical "Revivalism" resides in the tawny, chaste, Doric portico at the entry. Several details in the cornice are elementary, as are the sides of the church, but note the 135-foot-/41-meter-high, well-proportioned steeple. The interior was brightly renovated (1958–64) by Murphy & Mackey, who removed a great number of accumulated statues and a weighty altar and reredos. His Holiness, the late Pope John XXIII, elevated the church to a basilica in 1961.

Open daily 6:30 A.M.–6:00 P.M. Sunday services held at 7:30, 9:00, and 10:30 A.M., 12:00 noon, and 5:00 P.M. The Old Church Museum is open Sunday–Friday 9:30 A.M.–4:00 P.M., Saturday 9:30 A.M.–6:45 P.M. Closed Christmas. Admission is 25¢. Tours available Monday–Friday 9:00– 11:00 A.M. and 1:00–3:00 P.M. For more information call (314) 231–3250.

SHADOWS-ON-THE-TECHE (1831–34)
317 East Main Street (LA 182) at Weeks Street
New Iberia, Louisiana

One of the major Louisiana antebellum houses open to the public, Shadows-on-the-Teche is the slightly eclectic, up-country mansion of a wealthy Delta planter. The building is oriented to the town, and so its street facade, rather than the one facing the bayou, provides the main entrance. The house is divided vertically into seven well-proportioned bays by eight stuccoed brick Tuscan columns (with high bases and thin capitals), and emphasized horizontally by its second-floor veranda or gallery, and, above, by an unusually triglyphed cornice (which encircles the house): a most satisfying interplay is set up. Three dormers and two inset chimneys add their own touch. The two end bays are screened from top to bottom by green-painted wood blinds and lattices to conceal the outside stair behind the west bay (there is no stair at the other). This architectural sleight-of-hand, which also knits the entire front more compactly together, is thought by some—probably apocryphally—to stem from a Spanish edict taxing inside stairways. The Bayou Teche facade of the Shadows is less enticing than the front, having a simple loggia inset at the upper floor over a three-arched service area. The former steamboat landing lies only a few hundred yards beyond the landscaped informal grounds.

The interior is highly compartmentalized, and there is no inside hall—a reflection of the no-hall, raised-cottage plan previously popular in Louisiana. Thus the dining room that occupies the center of the lower floor is reached only via the front porch or the back loggia. The upper floor, which contains the parlor, sitting room, and bedrooms, also lacks an interior hall; the veranda provides access.

The house was commissioned by David Weeks, who unfortunately died before moving in. James and Jotham Bedell were the master builders who put it together. The house remained in the Weeks family, undergoing a few ups and many downs, until William Weeks Hall, the great-grandson of the builder, began restoration of both house and grounds in 1922. Before his death in 1958, Hall generously gave the mansion, including all the furniture and appointments plus an endowment, to the National Trust for Historic Preservation. Aided by the Weeks Family Papers, a collection of approximately 17,000 letters and invoices, the National Trust restored the house to the antebellum era and opened the museum to the public in 1961.

Open daily 9:00 A.M.–4:30 P.M.; closed Thanksgiving, Christmas, and New Year's Day. Admission is $6 for adults, $3 for children ages 6–11, free for children under 6. Group rates are available. Free one-hour tours are given daily. Tours for large groups can be scheduled by calling (318) 369–6446.

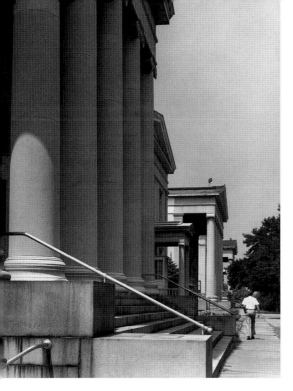

SNUG HARBOR CULTURAL CENTER
(formerly Sailors' Snug Harbor)
(1831–81/1976)
1000 Richmond Terrace at
Snug Harbor Road
New York (Staten Island), New York

Minard Lafever, principal architect

Financed by the will of Captain Robert R. Randall, a boldly successful privateer in the Revolutionary War, Snug Harbor was built to house over 1100 "aged, decrepit and worn-out sailors." Most of Randall's fortune was wisely invested in his Manhattan farm and real estate, and the land rental of some 130 acres/53 hectares of what is now the Washington Square section of New York built and supported Snug Harbor. The alignment of five interlocking Greek Revival buildings at Snug Harbor produces the most extraordinary parade of temples in the United States. The domed administration building at center (1831–33) opposite the Richmond Terrace Gatehouse, sports eight two-story-high, unfluted Ionic columns of marble. This is accompanied on either side by two narrower units (1839–44) each with a simple Classic portico, and these, in turn, are protected by end "temples" (1880–81) with six columns but otherwise similar to the central mass. (The two end wings were added to house additional sailors.) All five are laterally connected by low hyphens. Dormitories occupied the four "side" buildings with chapel and services in separate structures behind. The resulting impression is on the chilly side architecturally—a fact emphasized by the buildings facing north—but nonetheless here stands probably the most ambitious moment of the Classic Revival in the United States (one curiously slighted by the late Talbot Hamlin in his *Greek Revival Architecture in America*).

In 1976, with only 120 "decrepit sailors" in residence, the harbor moved to new and smaller quarters in Sea Level, North Carolina. The city then purchased the buildings and grounds and established the Snug Harbor Cultural Center in the structures, keeping the exteriors intact. The facilities include a children's museum, botanical garden, art lab, and theater and conference facilities, with an institute of arts and sciences planned for the future. An 1892 theater building is currently being restored and will be reopened as a music hall in 1997. In addition to the Greek Revival major buildings, there are also fine examples of the Italianate, Victorian, and French Second Empire. Earlier attributed to Martin E. Thompson, the Main Hall (which was partially renovated in 1994 and now houses the Newhouse Center for Contemporary Art) is certainly the work of Minard Lafever according to an erudite article by Barnett Shepherd of the Staten Island Institute of Arts and Sciences (*Journal of the Society of Architectural Historians*, May 1976). A prodigious statement of the Greek Revival, much of Snug Harbor can be seen from the road itself, with Manhattan's downtown in the distance—along with Bayonne's refineries across the Kill van Kull.

The grounds are open daily from dawn to dusk. Newhouse Center open Wednesday–Sunday 12:00 noon–5:00 P.M. Admission to the grounds is free; a $2 donation is suggested for admission to the exhibitions. On Saturday and Sunday free tours are given. Tours can also be scheduled in advance; the cost is $5 per person. For more information call (718) 448-2500.

JEFFERSON PLACE (1833)
(formerly Sweetsprings Resort)
VWA 3 at VA 311
Sweetsprings, West Virginia

Jefferson Place began as the the Sweetsprings Resort "watering place" in 1792. Its main building (the second on the site) was obviously influenced by the work of Thomas Jefferson. (Some claim, without documentation, that it was based on a design by Jefferson.) Situated in an angle of the state abutting the road between Roanoke and White Sulphur Springs, the impressively long facade consists of a white arcaded base on which rest the two upper floors of red brick. Three double-height Doric porticos grace this considerable expanse, adding a welcome relief to the brick walls behind. Half-round windows in their three pediments pick up the geometry of the arcade, tying the facade together. Used for many years as a spa, then closed in 1930 for a long time, it recently served as an old people's home; currently the building is empty. The interiors today are not of interest. It is listed in the National Register of Historic Places.

The interior is closed to the public.

MOBILE COUNTY DEPARTMENT OF HUMAN RESOURCES
(1833–36) (formerly Old City Hospital)
850 St. Anthony Street at Broad Street
Mobile, Alabama

William George, architect

Comprised of two stories on a raised basement, this rangy example of the Greek Revival is one of the most original in the country— "naive but impressive," wrote Talbot F. Hamlin (*Greek Revival Architecture in America*, Oxford University Press, 1944). The naivety lies in some of the proportions, particularly the low pediment with unusual Federal window, the too-narrow entablature, and the stretched Tuscan columns. The east and west wings, incidentally, were added in 1907–08. Designed, among other things, to keep off the heat of the Southern sun—which it does well—the building served as a hospital until 1968, when a new medical center was opened. Following the termination of its medical function, then desultory municipal use, the future of the building—an important example of its kind in the South—was long in doubt. Then in 1972 a civic-minded business executive, Joseph Linyer Bedsole, thoughtfully established a half-million-dollar trust for the building's restoration in memory of his sister, the late Lorraine Bedsole Tunstall, the first director of the Alabama Child Welfare Department. The building has been totally rehabilitated with matching city and county funds, and it is now used as offices for the Mobile County Department of Human Resources. Grider & Laraway were architects for the reconstruction, with George M. Leake consultant. This superb adaptive use gives Mobile not only a fine building but one of the most stalwart lineups of Tuscan columns—fourteen in all—in the United States.

Open Monday–Friday 7:30 A.M.–4:30 P.M. Closed for holidays.

OLD ARKANSAS STATE HOUSE (1833–42/1867/1885)
300 West Markham Street at South Center
Little Rock, Arkansas

Gideon Shryock, architect

Rightfully the pride of Arkansas, this ranks among the freshest Greek Revival examples in the country. Firm in profile, inventive in detail (note the unusual paneling in architrave and frieze), the building has great personality. It was erected to serve as the territorial capitol, replacing the tavern that served in that capacity. The Old State House was designed by Gideon Shryock, who had completed the state capitol of his native Kentucky at Frankfort just a few years earlier. It should be added that Shryock never personally visited Arkansas, and his clerk of the works, George Weigart, took charge locally, reducing the size of the building (with the aid of the governor) to meet the budget, keeping however the fine basic proportions. Although occupied in 1836, it was not fully completed until 1842. The brick stuccoed central block was originally connected to its two wings by "wooden houses" (probably porches), but these were replaced in 1867 (west) and in 1885 (east) by office structures to provide more clerical space. The cast iron seen today dates from these additions. At the same time the rear of the central building was extended toward the river. When the increasing population of the state outgrew these facilities, the legis-

lature commissioned the scandal-heavy capitol (1900–17) located nearby. (George R. Mann was the original architect, Cass Gilbert his successor.)

The Old State House was threatened with destruction until given a temporary reprieve for use as a medical school. Then in 1947—its quality finally recognized—complete restoration to its original nineteenth century state was begun under the architectural direction of H. Ray Burks and Bruce R. Anderson; since 1951 it has served as an Arkansas history museum. The triple-tiered cast-iron fountain in front came (in part) from the Philadelphia Centennial Exposition: the first tier is original, the top two are replacements (1947).

Open Monday–Saturday 9:00 A.M.–5:00 P.M., Sunday 1:00–5:00 P.M. Admission is $2 for adults, $1 for senior citizens, 25¢ for children grades K–12. Tours can be scheduled by calling (501) 324-9685.

NORTH CAROLINA STATE CAPITOL (1833–40)
Union Square at Edenton, Salisbury, Morgan, and Wilmington streets
Raleigh, North Carolina

William Nichols, Jr., Town & Davis, and David Paton, architects

Wayne Andrews, in his handsomely illustrated *Architecture in America* (Atheneum, 1960), calls this "the most distinguished of all our state capitols." Situated at the center of important crossroads in the approved fashion of the day, and occupying only the small center section of its square, the North Carolina State Capitol is not only commanding urbanistically, but is also of great interest architecturally. The history of the building is curious. The initial structure was a two-story state house constructed on this site between 1792 and 1796. Architect/builder William Nichols, the state architect, vastly expanded this core in 1820–24, adding two wings to make a cross plan, a third floor, and a central domed rotunda to contain a treasured statue of Washington (in Roman armor) sculpted in 1820 by the famous Antonio Canova. In June 1831 Nichols's building burned to the ground (Washington's statue was also destroyed—a duplicate was installed in the rotunda in 1970), and William Nichols, Jr., as agent for his father (who then worked in Alabama and Mississippi), was retained to devise plans for a replacement, keeping the cross plan but making it larger. Young Nichols completed the initial plans before he was succeeded in August 1833 by the more experienced Ithiel Town of New York's Town & Davis, who significantly refined the Nichols proposal. (Ithiel Town, incidentally, was probably the best engineer in the country at that time, inventing and patenting the much-used Town lattice truss for wooden bridges in 1820. The royalties from this sustained him when architecture was depressed.) In 1834 Town & Davis, having completed design work, hired David Paton, a young Scot who had worked for Sir John Soane in London, to supervise construction for the state. Paton not only supervised, he also made numerous changes on the interior (the outside walls of gneiss had been largely completed), with, it is pertinent to note, some design consultation (1836–37) with William Strickland. From this mixture of talents evolved the building we see today.

North Carolina's Capitol adds a solid note to the Greek revival with its sturdy, cruciform dimensions of 160 x 140 feet/49 x 43 meters. Its well-detailed porches on east and west fronts, with Doric columns above a sharp-edged rusticated "basement," rest beneath the low copper dome floating above the central rotunda. A restraint bordering on dryness characterizes the interior of the central rotunda, but the second-floor gallery is boldly cantilevered over the lower hall. The Senate chamber is not well knit, but the semicircular House of Representatives hall with two-story Corinthian-derived columns comes out handsomely. The columns and details on both Senate and House were copied from specific Greek temples, though some liberties were obviously taken. In a more up-to-date fashion the Supreme Court chamber (gallery added c. 1858) and the state library were designed in the Gothic style.

The grounds encircling the capitol are particularly herbaceous, bursting with over two score varieties of trees, almost all native to the state, and all carefully identified. In front an unusually composed, realistic statue by

Charles Keck (dedicated in 1948) presents the three Presidents North Carolina has given the nation: James K. Polk, Andrew Jackson, and Andrew Johnson. While the building's functions have been taken over by the new State Legislative Building one block north (see page 469), the capitol continues to house the offices of the governor and secretary of state. The legislative chambers, formerly the Supreme Court chamber (restored to the 1850s, when it functioned as the state geologist's office), and state library are intact and open to the public. The entire building is currently being restored and refurnished.

Open Monday–Friday 8:00 A.M.–5:00 P.M., Saturday 9:00 A.M.–5:00 P.M., Sunday 1:00–5:00 P.M. Closed Thanksgiving, Christmas, and New Year's Day. Admission is free. Tours by appointment only; call the Capital Area Visitors Center at (919) 733-3456.

VERMONT STATE HOUSE
(1833–38/1857–59)
115 State Street (US 2)
Montpelier, Vermont

Ammi B. Young, architect

An appealing, competent state house for the nation's smallest capital. The original building, designed by Ammi B. Young in 1833, burned in January 1857, but it was soon rebuilt largely on the same lines, though with a bay added at each end and at the rear, plus a higher dome. (Young went on to become the first supervising architect of the U.S. Treasury Department following the famous Robert Mills, who had been federal architect.) Thomas W. Silloway was the architect of the reconstruction for a year, followed by Joseph R. Richards. The scale of the projected Doric portico—which survived the fire and which is more or less straight from Athens's Theseion of 465 B.C.—tends to overwhelm even the extended side wings and dome. However, the spacious maple-shaded lawn in front, the spritely, gold-leafed dome topped by the 14-foot/4.3-meter statue of Agriculture, and the backdrop of trees on the hill behind make one soon overlook any discrepancy of parts. Close at hand the excellent detailing takes over. The capitol's granite construction, its careful upkeep, and what must be its pollution-free environment make it appear newly minted in spite of nearly a century and a half of use. On the interior the *D*-shaped House of Representatives with 150 seats is a bit crowded, but the Senate (at east end), with Corinthian columns and ovoid domed ceiling, carries atmosphere. Most of the interiors have been carefully restored to their nineteenth-century appearance.

Open Monday–Friday 8:00 A.M.–4:30 P.M. July to mid-October tours available 10:00 A.M.–3:30 P.M.; also open Saturday 11:00 A.M.–4:00 P.M. Closed for holidays. For more information or to schedule tours call (802) 828–2228.

FOUNDER'S HALL (1833–47)
Girard College
Girard and Corinthian avenues
Philadelphia, Pennsylvania

Thomas Ustick Walter, architect

Founder's Hall was designed by the Philadelphia-born Thomas Ustick Walter when he was twenty-nine, with precise instructions from Stephen Girard's will, which stipulated length "at least one hundred and ten feet [33 meters] east and west, and one hundred and sixty feet [49 meters] north and south. It shall be three stories in height, each story at least fifteen feet [4.6 meters] high in the clear from the floor to the cornice. It shall be fire proof inside and outside." And so the will goes, down to details such as wall thicknesses and stair details. There were probably suggestions also from the Hellenophile Nicholas Biddle, whose Greek Revival Andalusia Walter was designing at roughly the same time. Moreover Pierre Vignon's Church of the Madeleine (begun in 1806 in Paris), a temple form with eight Corinthian columns across the front, must have been of influence. In any event Founder's Hall is one of the monuments of the Greek Revival in this country, a substantial step beyond William Strickland's Second Bank of the United States (see page 166).

With its four flanking buildings, two per side, the hall initially constituted the complete "college" for "poor male white orphans ... born in the City of Philadelphia ... in any other part of Pennsylvania ... the City of New York ... [or] the City of New Orleans." (Girard, 1750–1831, first landed from his native France in New York, while New Orleans was the first port at which he traded as "first officer, and subsequently as master and part owner of a vessel." He was subsequently enormously successful as a merchant and banker.) However, the "simple, chaste and pure architecture of the ancients" that Walter used encountered difficulties in housing a school for young boys, and problems of heating, humidification, and acoustics arose at every turn; these recurred during the following sixty-six years until other buildings more appropriate for school purposes were erected. As Robert Dale Owen, chairman of the Building Committee for the Smithsonian Institution, put it, "So serious are the obstacles presented by the rigid and uncomplying forms of the classical school, that internal convenience is often sacrificed upon the altar of antique taste" (*Hints on Public*, 1849, De Capo reprint, 1978). The second and third floors were—and still are—divided into four rooms (formerly for classes). A low, precisely calculated vault covers each, and the top four were skylit (though now closed off). Since the early part of this century the main building has been used as a memorial to its founder, with a museum and recreational and social facilities occupying the remaining space. With its authoritative massing at the head of the street, abetted by the bold scale of the columns of Founder's Hall (54.5 feet/16.6 meters high), this group of five buildings—"the most sumptuous example of the Greek Revival in the country" (Agnes A. Gilchrist)—exerted a powerful architectural influence on the nation.

Though originally limited by Girard's will to white orphan lads, "whiteness" was ruled unconstitutional in 1968 and "functional male orphans" (not receiving adequate care from one or both of their natural parents) were admitted in 1977. Today almost four hundred students, male and female, receive free boarding and tuition. Some enter in the first grade and can stay through high school—or, indeed, remain for 365 days a year if there is family need. Extraordinary.

Open to the public Wednesday–Thursday 10:00 A.M.–2:00 P.M. Closed for holidays. Tours can be scheduled by calling (215) 787–2602; the fee is $3 per person.

LARKIN HOUSE (1834–35)
Calle Principal at Jefferson Street
Monterey, California

This simple, hip-roofed adobe house with its three-sided, two-story veranda—one of the first in the state—is generally regarded as an unusual example of the merging of American and Mexican building techniques. Built as a combined store and home, it later became the United States Consulate when its owner, T. O. Larkin, served here as consul to Mexico from 1844 to 1848. Its walls are of thick adobe in the Mexican-Spanish fashion long familiar throughout the Southwest. Note that the Larkin House, because of its second-floor wood balcony (included primarily for access to the bedrooms) and its balustrade, gives a light, even delicate impression, very different from one-story, solid masonry structures. Harold Kirker writes in his thoroughly researched *California's Architectural Frontier* (Peregrine Smith, 1973) that even "San Francisco was without a frame structure until 1836." As Kirker also mentions, Larkin, though he hailed from Massachusetts, spent ten years in North Carolina before he journeyed west. Thus it seems almost inevitable that the traditional tidewater dwellings of the Carolinas (Edenton, Beaufort, and Wilmington, let alone Charleston) with their "routine" double verandas influenced Larkin more than his native New England. (Interestingly, many believe that the Carolina double porches themselves evolved from Caribbean prototypes.) In any case the combination of sturdy and well-insulated Mexican adobe with the tensile airiness of wood make the Larkin house unique for its time. The house was given to the state of California in 1957 by Larkin's granddaughter, Alice Larkin Toulmin.

June–August open Wednesday–Monday 2:00–5:00 P.M., September–May open Wednesday–Monday 1:00–4:00 P.M. Closed Thanksgiving, Christmas, and New Year's Day. Admission is $2 for adults, $1.50 for children ages 12–18, $1 for children ages 6–12. All visits are guided; 45-minute tours are given every hour on the hour. For more information call (408) 649-7118.

FEDERAL HALL NATIONAL MEMORIAL (1834–42)
(formerly Custom House)
26 Wall Street at Nassau Street
New York, New York

Town & Davis and John Frazee, architects

There are many individual Greek Revival "temples" in the United States—where, actually, the style attained its most widespread popularity—but few are as pure or as dramatically sited as this. (Note also the siting of nearby Trinity Church, see page 202, just at the end of Wall Street.) A few yards from the New York Stock Exchange, topping the end of Broad Street, ringed with buildings many times its own height, the building maintains its own identity with aplomb. And when shafts of sun bore in like searchlights to inch over its Parthenon-like facade, splashing light and shadow up and down its steps, and wreathing a nimbus on George Washington's statue, 26 Wall Street, is animated by chiaroscuro. Though designed by masters of the Greek Revival—Ithiel Town and Alexander Jackson Davis, who won its

commission by competition—John Frazee (1790–1852), an early American architect, sculptor, and mason, came on the scene and over a period of almost seven years redesigned the building inside and out. As Talbot Hamlin explains, "The Commissioners in charge of the work were perhaps rightly frightened at the lightness of the construction indicated on the Town & Davis plan" (*Greek Revival Architecture*, Oxford University Press, 1944).

The facade rests on a high plinth because of the drop in grade from back to front, necessitating a steep flight of entry steps. Note that this is softened by the statue of Washington (by J. Q. A. Ward, 1883), rising directly from a sidewalk podium. (Washington took his oath as president of the new country at this spot in 1789.) As mentioned, the front of the building is directly modeled on the Parthenon, omitting only the sculpture in the tympanum and metopes. As the *New York Commercial Advertiser* put it, "Its general dimensions, compared with those of that ancient temple, are as eleven to twelve" (13 July 1842). The sturdy development of the Nassau Street side (178 feet/54 meters long) should also be noted. The interior, with its strikingly domed rotunda, comes as a surprise because of its richness and because of the incongruity of a shallow Roman dome within a Greek temple. (The arch and dome were, strangely, almost never used by the Greeks. Town & Davis's original design had a dome bursting through the roof.) The entire building is fireproof, with brick vaulting in both basement, which should be seen, and in dome. Beginning in the 1950s the structure was fully reconditioned and given its new name.

Open daily 9:00 A.M.–5:00 P.M. Closed Thanksgiving, Christmas, and New Year's Day. Free tours can be arranged by calling (212) 825–6888.

FIRST ALABAMA BANK (1835)
216 West Side Square at Fountain Row
Huntsville, Alabama

George W. Steele, architect

Clearly designed by a Greek Revival cognoscente, (with reputedly an outstanding architectural library), this expertly pedimented bank is one of the finer—and one of the lesser known—buildings of its period. Its six two-story Ionic columns were shipped to Huntsville by river barge from Baltimore; the limestone slabs comprising the front are thought to be local. All stonework is finished so smoothly that no mortar was used at the joints. The entire building was, indeed, so meticulously polished that the town's early settlers dubbed it the "Marble Palace." Originally built as the Huntsville Branch of the State Bank of Alabama, it has been continuously used for banking purposes ever since (the present name dates from 1971). Since the 1950s the interior has been carefully adapted to modern conditions by a bank that obviously cares about its building.

Open Monday–Friday 9:00 A.M.–2:00 P.M. Closed for holidays. Half-hour tours can be scheduled by calling (205) 535–0103.

ACTORS THEATRE (1835–37/1972/1994)
(formerly Old Bank of Louisville)
316 West Main Street
Louisville, Kentucky

James H. Dakin, architect

Though a mere 38 feet/11.6 meters wide (and the same dimension to the cornice), James Dakin's Greek Revival bank is surprisingly monumental. At one time used by the Louisville Credit Men's Association, it has been the Actors Theatre of Louisville since October 1972 . The august quality of its facade is achieved by two towering Ionic columns *in antis* (columns set within enclosing side walls), by the "unequal" space divisions in the porch, and by the strategic inward angling of the outer edges of the "pylon" of the facade. These measures give the illusion of greater height and scale. The composition is topped by an acroterion (of cast iron), an opulent note that is repeated at a smaller scale on the front door (no longer used as an entrance).

Until recently it was thought that Gideon Shryock was the designer of the bank, but with the discovery of some 180 original drawings by James Dakin, it is clear that the latter was the architect, with Shryock supervising. (See Arthur Scully, Jr., *James Dakin, Architect*, Louisiana University Press, 1973.) In any case we have not only a jewel of the Greek Revival (with a tinge of the Egyptian) but the viable adaptive reuse of a great building.

The interior, carefully restored by Harry Weese & Associates, is bathed with daylight from an oval oculus above the old banking floor, and forms a cheerful lobby to the theater. The original offices behind the banking room (of no architectural interest) were removed and the 637-seat Pamela Brown Auditorium theater, almost a semicircle in plan, was put in by expanding into the nineteenth-century warehouse adjacent; the Victor Jory Theatre soon followed. In 1994 the 332-seat Bingham Theatre, also designed by Weese, opened, completing this extraordinary facility.

Open for evening performances September–May. Tours can be arranged by calling (502) 584–1265.

ST. PHILIP'S CHURCH (1835–38/1848–50/1921)
146 Church Street between Queen and Cumberland
Charleston, South Carolina

Joseph Hyde and Edward B. White, architects

On the exterior St. Philip's bears more than a casual relationship to St. Michael's, also in Charleston (see page 89). Both have roughly similar spires (St. Philip's is 201 feet/61 meters high), and each has a prominent portico. Their resemblance is no coincidence, inasmuch as both were strongly influenced by eighteenth-century London buildings, primarily the works of Christopher Wren and James Gibbs. At St. Philip's the base of the tower is embraced by three identical pedimented Tuscan porches, while at St. Michael's the tower partly disappears into the body of the building.

However, on the interior the two churches are startlingly dissimilar: St. Philip's is more architecturally coordinated and more airy, with a parade of opulently topped two-story Corinthian columns (very Gibbsian) supporting arches that uphold the roof and plaster-vaulted nave (the lateral ceilings are flat). The interior is thus woven into a unity of verticals and horizontals, arches and vaults. This is emphasized by the horizontal galleries tying into the two-story columns at their midpoints. St. Michael's, on the other hand, tends to produce a layered or stratified space, its almost flat ceiling (supported by unseen trusses) hovering over the entire nave width, while its *U*-shaped balcony establishes a strong horizontal as it rests on its one-story columns.

The first St. Philip's—the first Anglican church in the Carolinas—was built of wood in 1681 (ironically on the site now occupied by St. Michael's), but by the early eighteenth century it proved inadequate and was replaced (1710–23, final touches 1733). This building burned in 1835 but was almost immediately rebuilt, largely to the design of its predecessor but with some changes, including the chancel, made by its architect, Joseph Hyde. The steeple—much improved over the original—was added in 1848–50 by Edward B. White. The chancel was expanded in 1921 after another fire.

It is provocative to note that the 1723 building, according to Dr. Frederic Dalcho's *History of the Church in South Carolina* (quoted in the folder entitled *History of St. Philip's Church*), had "three porticos before the west, south, and north doors." This, of course, is some thirty years before the building of St. Michael's, which, it has been long claimed, had one of the first monumental porticos in the colonies. An ancient print of the 1723 St. Philip's shows the three porticos almost precisely as they are today, with the exception that the earlier ones do not project as far, and are topped by an ungainly tower. Moreover Edward McCrady's *A Sketch of St. Philip's Church* (1901) states, concerning the 1838 building, that "in regard to its external sittings, the *new* differs not greatly from the *old* building. The three characteristic porches, north, south, and west, were repeated, each with four columns supporting entablature and pediment" (his italics). It would thus seem that not one but three monumental porticos appeared in Charleston in 1723 on the second St. Philip's Church.

A major restoration has recently been completed, following damage brought about by 1989's Hurricane Hugo.

Open Monday–Friday 10:00 A.M.–12:00 noon. Services held Wednesday at 5:30 P.M. and on Sunday morning for three services (times vary). For more information call (803) 722–7734.

MINT MUSEUM OF ART (1835–40/1846/1983–85)
2730 Randolph Road
Charlotte, North Carolina

William Strickland, architect

In the earlier part of the nineteenth century the Charlotte area was the largest producer of gold in America. The descriptive folder of the Mint Museum of Art states, "There were, at one time, between 75 and 100 mines within a 20 mile [32 kilometer] radius of Charlotte. One . . . had a main shaft 350 feet [107 meters] deep, and 3,500 feet [1,070 meters] of levels." So that the ore could be minted near the source, the U.S. Congress in 1835 commissioned William Strickland to design a U.S. Branch Mint. Strickland was the country's leading exponent of the Greek Revival, as evident in his Second Bank of the United States in Philadelphia (see page 166) and his Tennessee State Capitol in Nashville (see page 210). Here, however, he edged toward the Federal style in this nearly flat, centrally pedimented facade. The building was partially destroyed by fire in 1844, but was rebuilt two years later as Strickland had designed it, it is thought (except perhaps for piazzas in the rear). Minting was stopped in 1861, and the building was employed as a hospital during the Civil War, then as a federal assay office from 1867 to 1913. Old Mint was then utilized for various civic functions until threatened (1933) by the expansion of the downtown post office. Concerned citizens banded together and had it moved to its present site—which was donated—in the southern section of the city. Since 1936 it has served as a museum of the arts, the interior remodeled for this purpose. The relaxed, almost domestic scale of the exterior is highlighted by the 14-foot/4.3-meter eagle, with its wings spread, in the pediment. In 1983–85 the museum was expanded to three times its original size, and a new front entrance was created. Strickland's original facade has been kept intact at what is now the rear of the building.

Take I-77 to I-277, exit on Third Street, then follow signs. Open Tuesday 10:00 A.M.–10:00 P.M., Wednesday–Saturday 10:00 A.M.–5:00 P.M., Sunday 12:00 noon.–5:00 P.M. Closed Thanksgiving, Christmas Eve, Christmas, and New Year's Day. Admission is $4 for adults, $3 for senior citizens, $2 for students, free for children 12 and under. Free admission Tuesday 5:00–10:00 P.M. and the second Sunday of each month. Free one-hour tours given daily at 2:00 P.M. For more information call (704) 377–2000.

JEFFERSON COUNTY COURT HOUSE

(1835–60)
527 West Jefferson Street
between 5th and 6th
Louisville, Kentucky

Gideon Shryock, original architect

Gideon Shryock's Jefferson County Court House stands strong in its three-dimensional statement, albeit weak in some details. (Shryock was not responsible for many of these. Recent research reveals that his attribution is limited to the 1835–42 period. He resigned from the project, or was forced out, in 1842.) Note, for instance, the ramrod Doric columns (no entasis or subtle curvature of profile) and their understated capitals. Moreover the cornice was drastically simplified in 1932 because of crumbling stone. It is the building's blunt positiveness of form and its setback from the sidewalks that lends force to the street and to the city.

Construction took an abnormally long time because of difficulties with funding. Engineer/architect Albert Fink (1821–97) is credited with altering, expanding, and completing the building (1858–60)—and with adding the tetrastyle porticos, constructing the unusually handsome rotunda and dome, and finishing the upper floor. He also changed the planned hexastyle front portico to tetrastyle and omitted completely (possibly wisely) the towering cupola that Shryock had designed. Following a fire in 1905, Brinton B. Davis redid (1912) much of Fink's interior except the rotunda gallery, and most of the detailing is ascribable to him. A complete interior renovation to its 1906 appearance, as well as some mechanical updating, was undertaken in the early 1980s.

From its earliest days, the building has not been without criticism. The *Daily Courier* (1 September 1858) termed it an "elephantine monstrosity of architecture" and less than a year later the *Daily Louisville Democrat* said, "It stood like a gigantic stone scare-crow on the most beautiful square in the city" (1 July 1859). The *Herald-Post* predicted (31 January 1926) "that antiquated pile on Jefferson Street, known as the courthouse . . . is going to be razed. That is the pile's destiny as surely as the sun shines on a cloudless day." In addition to verbal abuse, the building, like many of its peers across the country, was threatened with physical demolition as facilities became inadequate and/or civic aspirations demanded the latest in architectural fashions. Fortunately pragmatic rehabilitation won the day and Louisville thus is a more abundant city.

Lobby open daily 24 hours. Free tours can be scheduled Monday–Friday 8:00 A.M.–5:00 P.M. by calling (502) 574–5761.

Facing the court house across 6th Street stands the City Hall (1870–73), designed by John Andrewartha. Because only the east wing was built, it appears an uncommonly mixed-up structure. Note the sculpted locomotive yclept *Progress* in its tympanum.

GOVERNMENT STREET PRESBYTERIAN CHURCH (1836–37)
300 Government Street at Jackson
Mobile, Alabama

Gallier, Dakin & Dakin, architects

Classical Revival devotees will want to include in their itinerary this sturdy church in down-town Mobile. The exterior falls into one of the standard patterns of its time with inset (*in antis*) porch, a form used here simply but boldly. The interior shows greater freedom with its diago-nally coffered ceiling and confidently elaborate chancel wall with rich retable. Its tapered sides hint of the Hellenistic and even the Egyptian. The entire church was handsomely restored in 1975–76 for the Bicentennial. (Its original steeple—hit by lightning in 1852—was not replaced.) There has been dispute concerning the architects of the church, with some histori-ans crediting the design to Thomas F. James of Mobile, who did a number of Greek Revival buildings in the city. However, James Gallier, Sr.'s diary claims that he and the Dakin broth-ers were the architects of both church and nearby Barton Academy. Arthur Scully, Jr., in his *James Dakin, Architect* (Louisiana State University Press, 1973) dismisses James as "merely one of the contractors." Professor Scully also suggests that the chaste exterior of the church prob-ably reflects the hand of Gallier, while the sumptuously detailed interior is more likely the work of the Dakin brothers. It is pertinent to note that the Irish-born Gallier and the New York State-born James and Charles Dakin had all worked together in Town & Davis's office in New York before moving south, where each remained (Charles unfortunately died there at the age of twenty-eight). Mobile, and the South, are richer for their efforts.

Open Monday–Friday 8:30 A.M.–4:30 P.M., Sunday 8:00 A.M.–1:00 P.M. Sunday services held at 11:00 A.M. (June, July, and August at 10:00 A.M.) Tours can be arranged by calling (334) 432–1749.

D'EVEREUX (1836–40)
160 D'Evereux Drive (US 61/84)
Natchez, Mississippi

James Hardie, architect

D'Evereux, the most pristine, most elegantly gracious Greek Revival house in the state, is also one of the most satisfactory anywhere. Of compact design, it has a temple-like quality, with pedimented front and six carefully fluted Doric columns. (Note, too, the small, feathery, wrought-iron balcony.) A like number of columns, but unfluted and supporting a full-width upper veranda, line the back or garden side; facing south, the veranda was—and is—a much-used open-air room. The building's sides are relieved by simple pilasters, with a quiet entablature encircling all. An observation cupola, surrounded by a wooden balustrade, tops the hip roof. The four downstairs rooms (the only ones open to the public because the house is a private residence) have been superbly restored, and are marked by great refinement. Note, especially, the crystal chandeliers. Supposedly all dimensions in the house are divisible by three, from the number of columns to their height (24 feet/7.3 meters) to the dimensions of all rooms—an early precursor of Le Corbusier's "modulor."

The house, like so many throughout the South, fell on difficult days after the Civil War until purchased in 1923, when partial restoration was undertaken. In 1962 it was acquired by T. B. Buckles and returned to its magnificent early condition. James Hardie (also spelled Hardy) is generally credited as being the architect.

Located 1 mile/1.6 kilometers northeast of Natchez. Open April–Labor Day daily 3:00–6:00 P.M. Admission is $5 per person. All visits are guided; tours given generally every half-hour. For more information call (601) 446–8169. Also open in the fall and spring for "pilgrimage" tours; call Natchez Pilgrimage Tours at (601) 446–6631 for more information.

KAWAIAHAO CHURCH (1836–42)
957 Punchbowl Street
Honolulu, Oahu, Hawaii

Reverend Hiram Bingham, designer

Kawaiahao Church is a surprisingly competent house of worship, considering that its design-er was a Vermont-born missionary and ad hoc architect. The church is the fifth on its site; its smaller predecessors were made of thatch. The trim facade combines a white-painted, Classical, attached "portico" with tanned and weathered Gothicizing coral tower and walls; the ambiance excuses all architectural naiveté. (Note the entry piers and gates.) The simple interi-or is more accomplished, even though its galleries and small windows reflect New England, not the semitropics. The walls are made up of some 14,000 blocks of coral, or "reef rocks" as they are locally known, cut from the reef that stretches from Waikiki to Pearl Harbor. A Congregational service is held at 10:30 A.M. every Sunday, in which both the English and Hawaiian languages are used. The building is a National Historic Landmark.

The Reverend Doctor Abraham K. Akaka, pastor emeritus of the church, thoughtfully sent me the following excerpts from the diary of Dr. Gerritt P. Judd, written in 1840–42:
8 July 8, 1840, "Having received the promise of a mano or two [a mano is 4000] of mamaki kapa and 200 cattle from the king [to be exchanged for shingles for the church], I started for Waialua to hire 100,000 shingles made."
27 April 1841, "Punihaole [a deacon] went to Ewa to measure timber."
12 June 1841, "Timber for meeting house being brought."
27 August 1841, "Wrote contract for roof of church . . . Commenced in good earnest. Sawing going on."
11 November 1841, "Raised last rafters."
10 January 1842, "Roof of Hale Pule finished. Paid off the carpenters."

Open Monday–Saturday 9:00 A.M.–3:00 P.M.; Sunday 8:00 A.M.–4:00 P.M. Half-hour guided tours can be arranged on week-days by calling (808) 522–1333.

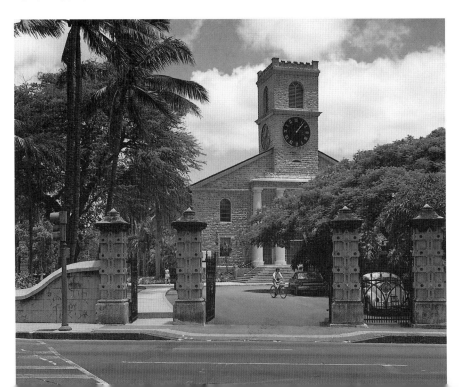

OAK ALLEY PLANTATION (1837–39)
3645 Highway 18
Vacherie, Louisiana

Gilbert Joseph Pilié, architect

Much of the Classic Revival—that pristine but sometimes desiccated style that hypnotized American architects for roughly the first half of the nineteenth century—would not be entered in a functionalist's notebook. Its visual rewards were often great, it certainly stood for law and order, but too many buildings, especially in the North, were straitjacketed into temple formations. Oak Alley, however—like many of its type throughout the South—is a superbly logical, semi-Greek Revival answer to the imperatives of its environment. An enormous (70 feet/21 meters square) parasol of a hip roof, supported by twenty-eight two-story Tuscan columns, protects the house from merciless sun and lashing rains. Its double galleries are so wide that windows can be kept open almost all the time, while in fair weather each veranda forms an open-air living room. In front, spaced a precise 80 feet/24 meters apart as they advance to the Mississippi, stretch the unbelievable oak trees (twenty-eight in number, like the columns), which understandably changed the name of the house from Bon Sejour—and which antedate the mansion by at least a century. George Swainey was the builder of the house, not the architect as sometimes claimed.

The thick brick stuccoed walls of Oak Alley are painted pink, as are the brick columns— proper mates to the fern-covered trees (*Polypodium incanum*). The dwelling, like most great houses in the South, fell on more than hard times following the Civil War, and early in this century it was deserted and in danger of falling apart when Mr. and Mrs. Andrew Stewart purchased it (1925) and began a restoration (really a renovation) under the direction of the late Richard Koch, FAIA, who did much work in rehabilitating Louisiana's magnificent architectural inheritance. Though the interior furnishings do not match the quality of the outside and its setting—what could?—this remains one of the United States' greatest estates. As Clarence J. Laughlin wrote concerning southern Louisiana plantations, "There is in many of them an architectural feeling as close to being truly indigenous as anything that can be found in the United States—not omitting New England" (*Architectural Review*, June 1947).

Located 2.5 miles/4 kilometers west of Vacherie. March–October open daily 9:00 A.M.–5:30 P.M.; November–February open daily 9:00 A.M.–5:00 P.M. Closed Thanksgiving, Christmas, and New Year's Day. Admission is $7 for adults, $6 for military personnel, $4 for children ages 12–18, $2 for children ages 6–11. All visits to the house are guided; tours given every half hour. Visitors are free to walk around the grounds. For more information call (504) 265–2151.

LYNDHURST (1838/1864–65)
635 South Broadway
Tarrytown, New York

Alexander Jackson Davis, architect

Lyndhurst was one of the first and is probably the most picturesque of Neo-Gothic mansions in the United States. Set on undulating acres that drop down to the Hudson River, unrolling the proper mixtures of vistas, lawns, and trees, the original house was begun in 1838 but was substantially expanded between 1864–65 by the new owner, who fortunately used the same architect, the talented Alexander Jackson Davis. It is typical of their times that Davis and his illustrious partner, Ithiel Town, were active in both the Neo-Classical and Neo-Gothic movements in this country. The interior of the house, after the somewhat strained exterior, bursts with intensity accented by the "vaulting" of most ceilings. The rooms, with the exception of the second-floor gallery (once the library), seem surprisingly small, an effect intensified because they are intricately decorated and are full of furniture and pictures that have come down from each of the three families that lived in the house (the last until 1961), thus displaying a cross section of the tastes of the occupants. The dining room, especially, should be noted; Davis himself designed much of the furniture for it. Also on the grounds was an enormous (380 feet/116 meters long) and once stunning greenhouse, which is currently undergoing restoration. The house was left to the National Trust in 1964, was fully restored where necessary, and is immaculately maintained.

Located off US 9 just south of Tappan Zee Bridge. May–October open Tuesday–Sunday 10:00 A.M.–5:00 P.M., November– April open Saturday–Sunday 10:00 A.M.–5:00 P.M. Closed Christmas and New Year's Day. Admission is $7 for adults, $6 for seniors, $4 for children ages 6–16. Admission to the grounds only is $3 per person. One-hour guided tours are given daily 10:30 A.M.–3:30 P.M. Group tours can be scheduled by calling (914) 631–4481.

AMOSKEAG MANUFACTURING COMPLEX (1838–1915)
East bank of Merrimack River
Manchester, New Hampshire

To the student of American socioindustrial economy the Amoskeag millyard makes possibly the most extraordinary architectural statement on nineteenth-century manufacturing in this country. Stretching in tiers for almost a mile along the Merrimack River and tapping its Amoskeag Falls—named by the Native Americans, "a place of much fish"—an integrated and continuously abutted series of factories proliferated for some seventy-five years. (The first building on the east side of the river dates from 1838, the last from 1915.) From its beginning the complex embraced decent workers' housing, here placed at right angles across from the upper canal. (Compare the lack of these amenities in most European and American industrial slums in the nineteenth century.) Growth of the Amoskeag plant and subplants had been planned as a full community by Ezekial Straw as engineer, with Samuel Shepherd and John D. Kimball generally cited as the first architects. Water supply and transportation ingeniously determined the basic layout, with two lines of canals and two of railroad sidings dividing the ranks of buildings paralleling the curves of the river. The resulting industrial, even urban, unity is unique. In effect an instant city with all amenities for ten thousand people sprang up. Although products included such hardware as fire engines and locomotives, the Amoskeag enterprise was known primarily as being the largest manufacturer of cotton textiles in the world, turning out 50 miles/80 kilometers of cloth an *hour* at peak production. The company collapsed during the Depression. The multiple lines of red brick factories, simple in form and highlighted occasionally by a Victorian tower, angle and curve along the river, and still create a powerful scene, although many units are not in top condition.

Beginning in 1969, a federal urban renewal program took steps to remove many of the older buildings in the millyard (unfortunately including some of the finest) and fill the canals to create roadways. Many of the remaining millyard buildings are vacant, as the city lacks a coherent plan to develop this area and encourage new uses for these spaces. The debate on whether to raze these buildings for parking lots continues today. Amoskeag was the grandfather of the enterprises that developed the industrial might of New England; a substantial portion should be maintained for posterity. Or is it even now too late?

Contact the Manchester Historic Association at (603) 622–7531 regarding tours of the millyard. The cost is $5 per person.

OHIO STATE CAPITOL
(1839–61/1901)
High, Broad, State, and 3rd streets
Columbus, Ohio

Henry Walter, Alexander Jackson
Davis, W. R. West, Nathan B. Kelly,
Isaiah Rogers, Thomas Ustick Walter,
and Richard Upjohn, architects

Although it required seven architects (four designing, three consulting), twelve governors, and twenty-two years to design and complete this state house, the effort was not in vain. Low-haunched, compact, and powerfully molded, with conviction showing on all sides and the top, the Ohio State Capitol is a virile member of the Greek Revival elite. In spite of its modest two-story height, its length of 304 feet/93 meters and breadth of 184 feet/56 meters fill its city block with an authority marred only by the 1901 annex at the back. The limestone building is crowned—refreshingly—by a substantial cylinder instead of a dome. (A drum, incidentally—and fortunately—was demanded by the legislators because of disagreement about and the expense of the once-intended dome.) Because the porches on each of its four sides are recessed, the entablature wraps around the building in an unbroken line, binding and compacting the mass into a sturdy block. This solid rectangularity then plays against the cylindrical drum above, while the low triangular pediment above the main entry adds a geometric touch.

The design of the capitol was begun with an 1838 competition won by Henry Walter of Cincinnati. The officials, however, were not wholly satisfied and got Alexander Jackson Davis, the apostle of Greek Revival, to consult with Walter, whom they kept as resident architect. The cornerstone of the Walter-Davis plan was laid in 1839. But all was not settled: W. R. West replaced Walter, who retired, in 1848, while Nathan B. Kelly took over in 1854, to be replaced by Isaiah Rogers in 1858 (apparently Kelly's interiors were too romantic). Rogers, a well-known architect of the period, was aided by consultations with two of the country's great designers, Thomas Ustick Walter and Richard Upjohn, whose advice, obviously useful, primarily concerned the size and nature of the drum. The exterior of the building, in spite of the tribulations of its construction, came off with aplomb. The interior, because of them, and because of the multiplicity of the hands that touched it, is less satisfactory. But all in all the building is one of the United States' great capitols, and one of the few with a distinctive personality.

A major restoration (over $100 million) under the direction of Schooley Caldwell Associates is currently underway, to be completed by July 1996: the Senate building and atrium have been completed, walls added to the statehouse at a later date have been removed, skylights have been reopened, and the interior has been painted with the original colors. A new enclosed atrium links the original structure with the 1901 annex.

Open Monday–Friday 9:00 A.M.–5:00 P.M. Closed for holidays. Free one-hour tours can be arranged by calling (614) 752–6350. For general information call (614) 752–9777.

ORTON PLANTATION (c.1840/1910)
9149 Orton Road SE
Winnabow, North Carolina

Orton Plantation is a nostalgic witness of an era long past. In the spring it is one of the most glorious spots in the United States. The only survivor of several score of plantations that once lined the Cape Fear River, the plantation and its house evolved over many years. The first building was a small (60 x 75 feet/18 x 23 meters), one-and-one-half-story house dating from around 1725. Timber and its by-products, such as turpentine, formed the basis of the economy of the surrounding area. Following independence, with the need to supply the British navy no longer pressing, rice was introduced, and the nineteenth-century fields of Orton eventually stretched for some 6 miles/9.6 kilometers along the river's tidal waters, which were so vital to its cultivation. The quality of the cereal grass grown along this river—the northern limit of the rice belt—attained such renown that it was used as seed rice throughout the South. In 1840, with growing affluence and the peak of the Greek Revival period of architecture, the old house was expanded to two stories and a properly gabled, sharply detailed portico with tall Doric columns (of cement on brick) was added to the river (east) side. During the Civil War the house was used as a hospital by Northern troops, fortunately for its preservation. With the abolition of slavery and the ensuing lack of capital, rice could be grown only with difficulty, and Orton languished.

Later in the nineteenth century the house was restored, and in the early part of this century it was purchased by the James Laurence Sprunt family, who still own it and who added the two side wings (1910—designed by Kenneth M. Murchison) and the chapel (1915—a memorial to Luola Sprunt), and extended the gardens. A further expansion of the gardens was undertaken in the early 1930s, largely under the direction of R. S. Sturtevant, the landscape architect. Sturtevant, and the late Churchill Bragaw who succeeded him, related house to garden to river masterfully, establishing a series of paths to strengthen the mutual interrelationship. As one approaches, the house reveals itself on one side while the broad view of the marsh—previously the rice fields and now a wildfowl sanctuary—opens to the right, climaxing with the distant river. Close at hand paths meander through live oaks with Spanish moss, pause by the brown but clear waters of a cypress swamp-lake, and cross a lagoon, which once led to the river that provided the main access to the house until the 1920s. The parterred Scroll Garden, visible from a small bridge, injects a formal note to counterpoint hedonistic nature. In between

are vistas and, in season, millions of azaleas and camellias alternating with a variety of other plants (note the Chinese wisteria) and flowers: 12,000 acres/4,856 hectares of another world. Go in spring if possible, but go.

Travel west across river on US 17, 74, or 76, then south on NC 133 18 miles/29 kilometers (near Wilmington). March–August, grounds open daily 8:00 A.M.–6:00 P.M. September–November, grounds open daily 10:00 A.M.–5:00 P.M. Admission prices vary; call (910) 371–6851 for details. The house is not open to the public.

TRINITY CHURCH (1841–46)
74 Trinity Place at Broadway and Wall Street
New York, New York

Richard Upjohn, architect

Of all the Gothic Revival churches in this country, none can match either the dramatic location—terminating Wall Street (which once marked the site of the Dutch wall around the town)—or the grounds of this intriguing, self-confident house of worship. By virtue of the hoary, beautifully planted cemetery on either side (note the extraordinary variety of trees and shrubs), the church even today has sufficient breathing space to successfully withstand the competition of the towering buildings that encircle it. (The cemetery, incidentally, was a burial ground before Trinity was founded; its oldest stone carries the date of 1681—for a lad of five.) Ironically, Trinity was for forty-two years the tallest structure in New York at 280.5 feet/85 meters, until St. Patrick's Cathedral was built—see page 223. The first Trinity, built in 1698, burned at the time of the Revolution, while the second (1788–92)—with a few spiky Gothic details—was torn down (1839) because of structural weakness. (It is worth noting that domestic Gothic Revival suggestions were evident as early as 1799 in Benjamin Henry Latrobe's Sedgeley Mansion, near Philadelphia, long destroyed.)

The present Trinity was designed by the British-born Richard Upjohn (who became the principal founder [1857] and first president of the American Institute of Architects). Upjohn developed his reputation with St. John's Church in Bangor, Maine, which was finished in 1839, and almost immediately he was called to New York to design Trinity. (Upjohn's Gothic "conversion" was largely due to the work and writings in England of A. W. N. Pugin and the proselytizing of the Cambridge Camden Society.) When Trinity was completed in 1846, it received immense acclaim, inspiring a host of imitations. In effect, it launched the Gothic Revival in the United States (aided by the same architect's contemporaneous but more remote New St. Mary's Church in Burlington, New Jersey, see page 211). It also launched Upjohn. The exterior was once marvelously blackened by soot, its dark walls a proper foil to the snows of winter and the bright greens of summer, with the weathered white tombstones engaged in their own pirouette around the brownstone hulk. (In 1992 the exterior received a complete cleaning.) The interior does not live up to the fascination of the outside. It is, of course, highly competent, but almost coldly so, an effect that the chancel window seeks vainly to ameliorate. (The stained-glass windows were among the first in the country and were designed by the architect.) Though Horatio Greenough (1805–52) termed it "the puny cathedral of Broadway," Wayne Andrews considers this "one of the greatest, if not the greatest, church erected in America" (*Architecture, Ambition and Americans*, Harper, 1955). The reredos was designed by Frederick C. Withers in 1877. While Upjohn's design was accepted by the church in 1839, the cornerstone was not laid until 1841, and some feel that changes, mostly influenced by Pugin, occurred in the final design. All Saints' Chapel, Thomas L. Nash, architect, was added in 1913; the Manning wing with sacristy and museum added in 1966.

Open Monday–Friday 7:00 A.M.–6:00 P.M., Saturday 8:00 A.M.–4:00 P.M., Sunday 7:00 A.M.–4:00 P.M., holidays 8:00 A.M.–4:00 P.M. Services held Monday–Friday at 8:00 A.M. and 12:05 P.M., Saturday at 9:00 A.M., Sunday at 9:00 and 11:15 A.M. Free tours given daily at 2:00 P.M. Tours can also be scheduled by calling (212) 602–0872.

WAIOLI MISSION HOUSE (1841)
off HI 56
Hanalei, Kauai, Hawaii

Surrounded by lanais, this picturesque former church now serves
the ex-port of Hanalei as a community center. Because its design so
capably solved the problems of a
sometimes wet and windy climate by
means of wide skirting and sturdy
plastered walls, the whole topped by
a well-pitched roof, this evolutionary
building epitomizes the Hawaiian
vernacular. The rainiest spot on earth at 40.5 feet/12.3 meters per annum lies only 12 miles/19
kilometers inland, while the occasional high winds were strong enough to have blown down
the original thatched church. The interior is now of little architectural consequence. The building was restored in 1921 and again in 1994 following Hurricane Iniki.

Interior visible by appointment; call (808) 826–6253.

ASHLAND-BELLE HÉLÈNE (1841)
Ashland Road
Geismar, Louisiana

James Gallier, Sr., architect

A plantation near the edge of the
Mississippi, Ashland-Belle Hélène
forms a peculiarly nostalgic, proud
remembrance of a vanished era.
Entirely surrounded by a peristyle of
twenty-eight square Doric columns
or piers, eight to a side—and square
in plan itself—the house states its case with conviction. Much of this positiveness stems from
its heavy entablature and its "invisible" roof, which seem to propel the hard-edged colonnade
toward the observer. It is illuminating in this regard to compare Ashland with the more delicate Oak Alley in Vacherie (see page 197), also square in plan and surrounded by twenty-eight
round columns (not piers) and with high hip roof and dormers. The rotundity of Oak Alley's
columns creates less of a barrier than do piers, while the receding geometry of its prominent
roof pulls one on. Ashland has great strength; Oak Alley great grace. The house with its 20-
foot-/6.1-meter-wide galleries and 30-foot-/9.1-meter-high piers, is a stalwart building, having
barely survived a period of almost total neglect. In 1992 it was purchased by Shell Chemical
Company; they have stabilized the house to prevent further deterioration, but unfortunately
there are no current plans for restoration.

Located off LA 30: 2.5 miles/4 kilometers southeast of Geismar via LA 73 from US 61; 6 miles/9.7 kilometers northwest of
Darrow via LA 22 from US 61. The interior is closed to the public.

GAINESWOOD (1842–60)
805 South Cedar Street (US 43)
Demopolis, Alabama

Nathan B. Whitfield, architect

Though Gaineswood is disjointed and of a scale that makes the house appear larger in photographs than in reality, it carries itself with grace. This unusual Greek Revival mansion was designed by its owner, General Nathan B. Whitfield, an amateur architect and engineer who took a minute interest in every facet of the building, to the point of personally constructing some of the shop machinery for the production of parts. The plan of the house, which is of two stories with only secondary bedrooms above, is unusual. The entry is not through the prominent portico across the front, but by the porte cochère at right. The balustraded parterre and the portico (with round Doric columns of wood and inset square ones of masonry) are matched by a low portico at rear, also with balustraded parterre. In plan these are axially offset. A drawing room occupies the front of the house with master bedroom beyond and the "family" bedroom with half-round bay is appended to this. On the back side of the hall are the parlor and dining room, each dominated by a large and elaborately decorated domed ceiling of Italianate detail, with oculus for daylight in the center (the parlor is almost windowless).

The design of each room is sumptuous; the drawing room in particular contains some of the richest detailing to be seen in the waning days of the Greek Revival. Influenced, obviously, by various handbooks on the subject, the columns, capitals, cornices, and ceilings are wondrously intricate, pushed to the limit. The decoration of the domed ceiling in dining room and parlor are also of this type.

Though heavily damaged by vandals, the house fortunately survived and is one of the most remarkable examples of its style in the country—and unquestionably the finest house open to the public in Alabama. The dwelling was purchased by the state in 1971 and completely restored by the Alabama Historical Commission in 1975. Descendants of the builder have furnished the mansion with original family pieces.

Open Monday–Saturday 9:00 A.M.–5:00 P.M, Sunday 1:00–5:00 P.M. Admission is $3 for adults, $2 for students, 50¢ for children. Informal tours available. For more information call (334) 289–4846.

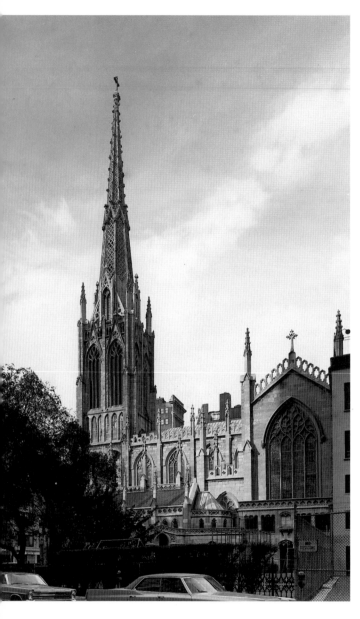

GRACE CHURCH
(1843–46)
802 Broadway
at East 10th Street
New York, New York

James Renwick, Jr., architect

James Renwick, Jr., won the competition for Grace Church when he was only twenty-three. Though he went on to design the more oracular St. Patrick's Cathedral (see page 223) and the Smithsonian Institution Building in Washington, D.C. (see page 214), the Municipal Art Society places the white marble Grace Church on its list of eight New York City landmarks "which are of National Importance" (St. Patrick's is in category 2). Renwick at Grace Church achieved greater "authenticity," plus more correlation of interior to exterior, than Richard Upjohn did with Trinity Church, which was finished the same year. As Phoebe B. Stanton wrote in her book, *The Gothic Revival and American Church Architecture* (Johns Hopkins, 1968), "Grace Church is more tightly knit, less rigorous, and less dry than Trinity." Though the site is slender (compared to that of Trinity), the steeple, its original wood replaced by marble, was placed so as to be visible up and down Broadway, which angles at East 10th Street. Whether the Gothic is appropriate for Protestant houses of worship—the style was developed in the Middle Ages for Roman liturgy—injects another question, but for an influential, indeed romantic, example of its revival visit Grace Church: Renwick himself worshipped there most of his adult life. Note the sense of lateral openness connecting nave and transepts.

Open Monday–Friday 10:00 A.M.–5:00 P.M., Saturday 12:00 noon–4:00 P.M. Sunday services held at 9:00 A.M., 11:00 A.M., and 6:00 P.M. Tours given after Sunday 11:00 A.M. services. Tours can also be arranged by calling (212) 254–2000.

TAYLOR-GRADY HOUSE (c. 1844/c. 1900)
634 Prince Avenue
Athens, Georgia

Although the interior of this outstanding Greek Revival house is not open to the public every day, a look at the exterior can be had at any time and at any time is worth it. The well-scaled porch wraps around the front and sides, upheld by thirteen Roman Doric columns, leading to the supposition that they represent the original states of which Georgia was the last proclaimed (1732)—and the largest. (The east side porch has four columns, that on the west five: note the variation in intercolumniation across the front. The columns wrapped both front and sides of the original house; the rear section was added c. 1900.) Whatever the symbolism, the architectural effect is regal.

The house was purchased by the city in 1966, then leased to the Athens Junior Assembly, which restored and furnished it throughout with period pieces. Note the anthemion motif on the pilasters flanking the entry and the four curved "corners" within. The original smokehouse and kitchen are on the grounds. A boxwood garden lies to the east.

As Talbot Hamlin wrote, "nowhere did the Greek Revival produce a more perfect blending of the dignified and the gracious, the impressive and the domestic, than in the lovely houses of the thirties and forties in upstate Georgia and Alabama" (*Greek Revival Architecture in America*, Oxford University Press, 1944).

Open Tuesday–Friday 10:00 A.M.–3:30 P.M. Closed for holidays. Admission is $2.50 per person (free for children under 6). Half-hour tours available. For more information call (706) 549–8688.

EGYPTIAN BUILDING (1845)
1223 Marshall Street at College Street
Richmond, Virginia

Thomas S. Stewart, architect

From its battered walls to its cavetto cornice, and from its scarabaeus to its lotus-capped columns, the Egyptian Building rates as one of the great examples of the Egyptian Revival in the United States. (Another is William Strickland's Downtown Presbyterian Church in Nashville, Tennessee—see page 220.)

Built originally as the first unit of the Medical College of Virginia (now the Medical College of Virginia Campus of Virginia Commonwealth University), it has been in continuous use since it opened. In 1939 the building was completely restored, outside and in, through the generosity of Bernard Baruch, whose father had been an alumnus. In the early 1980s the upper three floors were renovated, and research laboratories were converted into classrooms and offices. On the ground floor, a colorful lobby leads to an auditorium (of little interest). Note the details of the cast-iron fencing: the posts are in the form of mummies.

Lobby and grounds open Monday–Friday 8:00 A.M.–5:00 P.M. Closed for holidays.

GROVE STREET CEMETERY GATES (1845–48)
227 Grove Street at Prospect Street
New Haven, Connecticut

Henry Austin, architect

This diverting foray into ancient Egypt is a nostalgic example of a little-seen style. Henry Austin (1804–91), who got his start working for Town & Davis, evolved into a facile designer on his own, establishing, in the process, a long and successful practice. He first favored the Greek Revival when it was popular (up to the 1840s), then espoused the newly imported Tuscan Villa or Italianate Style, ending with Ruskinian Neo-Gothic and the Neo-French Imperial. These gates represent probably his only excursion into the land of the pharaohs. Richard G. Cartott's book *The Egyptian Revival* (University of California Press, 1978) offers an excellent survey of the style. Measuring approximately 48 feet/14 meters wide by 25 feet/7.6 meters high and constructed of red sandstone, the gates provide a Nilotic entry to the cemetery. They exhibit two pylons rightly battered and two columns with reasonable lotus-bud capitals, the whole topped by solar disc and protective vultures. The burial ground itself was opened in 1797, and is locally held to be the earliest in the country to be laid out in family lots.

TENNESSEE STATE CAPITOL (1845–59)
Charlotte Avenue between 6th and 7th avenues
Nashville, Tennessee

William Strickland, architect

Dominating a piece of elevated land (the highest in the city), and boldly conceived to be observed from all four sides, the Tennessee Capitol ranks with the most original in the nation. The perceptive Paul F. Norton, on the other hand, considers it "Strickland's worst monument" and "ludicrous" (*The Arts in America: The 19th Century*, Scribner's, 1969). Porticos with eight Ionic columns and blank pediments—atop a rusticated Doric basement—fill the two gable ends. Flat porticos of six similar columns project from the long expanse of the two sides. The influence of Athens's Erectheion is strong. Loftily (perhaps too loftily) perched atop the roof and serving in lieu of the traditional dome sits a rusticated square tower base surmounted by a circular lantern (total height 170 feet/52 meters). Its design was inspired by the often-mimicked Choragic Monument of Lysicrates in Athens (335 B.C.) (but with eight columns instead of six, as Agnes Gilchrist points out in her estimable book *William Strickland, Architect and Engineer*, Da Capo Press, 1969). The House of Representatives with its two lateral galleries (and offices under the galleries) stretches across the south end of the building, while the Senate shares the north end with the state library. A substantial lobby fills the middle. The building measures 238 x 109 feet/72 x 33 meters.

The talented Strickland died in 1854, when the Capitol had already received its first legislative session, but before the completion of many details, including the tower (1855) and the terraces (four years later). Appropriately he was buried in the north wall of the building that climaxed his distinguished career. Strickland's son, Francis, supervised the work from 1854–59. In 1958 and again in 1984–87 major restorations were made of the entire area.

Open Monday–Friday 8:00 A.M.–4:00 P.M. Closed Easter, Thanksgiving, Christmas, and New Year's Day. Admission is free. Free half-hour tours given at 9:00, 10:00, and 11:00 A.M. and 1:00, 2:00, and 3:00 P.M. Tours can also be arranged by calling (615) 741–2692.

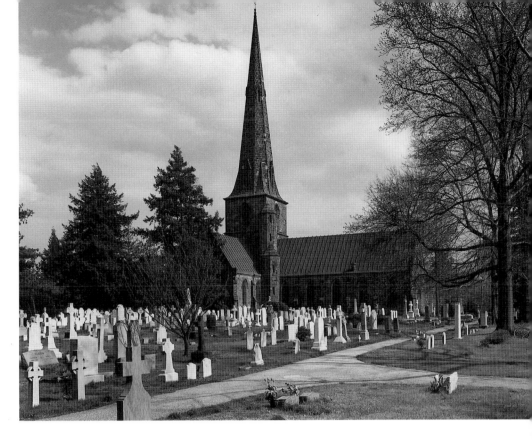

NEW ST. MARY'S CHURCH (1846–54)
145 West Broad Street between Wood and Talbot streets
Burlington, New Jersey

Richard Upjohn, architect

Having outgrown its original church, built in 1703 and still standing adjacent to New St. Mary's, the congregation asked Richard Upjohn—the apostle of religious Gothic Revival—to design a larger house of worship in 1846. Upjohn responded, producing a handsome example of the mid-nineteenth-century fashion very much in the English tradition. (Upjohn himself was born in England in 1802, and came to the States in 1829. He was, incidentally, a founder and the first president of the American Institute of Architects.) Surrounded by an ancient churchyard, the church rises gracefully from it, using its ashlar sandstone not only for the walls and square tower base but for the steeple (144 feet/44 meters high) as well, creating thus an unusual exterior harmony. (Note the fairing and broaching of the spire, which changes from a square to an octagon.) The most impressive features of the interior are the four powerful stone piers that support the tower and steeple. Marking—even jostling—the four corners of the crossing of nave and transept, these give tremendous structural and visual strength to the church.

The church was severely damaged by fire in 1976, and most of the interior woodwork was destroyed. Basic reconstruction, under the direction of architect Richard Murphy, was completed in 1979. The stained glass has also been completely restored.

Open daily 9:00 A.M.–5:00 P.M. Sunday services held at 7:30 and 9:00 A.M. Free tours can be scheduled by calling (609) 386–0902.

OLD LOUISIANA STATE CAPITOL (1847–49/1880–82)
North Boulevard at St. Philip Street
Baton Rouge, Louisiana

James H. Dakin, architect

There are few entrance halls of any architectural period that can match the sheer inebriety of this one in the Old State Capitol. An umbrella of multicolored panes, spewing glass fireworks from the top of the central column, provides a domed ceiling, while the exposed structure (cast iron) and decoration (intricately colored and fabricated glass) are fused with it. Gothic Revival arches and arcades mark each level of the hall, from which the major rooms open.

James H. Dakin won a competition with his design for the Old Capitol. Dakin had for several years been a member of the New York firm of Town & Davis, famous for their Greek Revival structures. Here, however, he opted boldly for the "newer," more up-to-date, Gothic Revival style because the former "appeared in every city and town of our country." He practiced the rest of his life in Louisiana except for brief excursions to Mobile, Alabama.

The building was gutted by fire during the Civil War (1862), but was restored twenty years later under the direction of William A. Freret, who included a new dome and lantern (the original design possibly had a dome) and added the fourth floor and spiral stair. The Old State Capitol served in its original capacity until 1932, when the new Capitol was built. After a recent large-scale restoration, the building reopened in 1994 as the Center for Political and Governmental History.

The exterior of the Old Capitol is tame, formed by a stiffly symmetrical block with two towers standing beside both river and land entrances. The water approach, with a long straight stairway leading to the arched door hemmed by octagonal turrets, is perhaps the better from an architectural point of view. The street turrets are square (and vaguely Assyrian). A machicolated "cornice" runs around all. Though the outside is thus reasonably quiet, the exuberant central hall is the finest civic Gothic Revival interior in the United States.

Open Monday–Saturday 10:00 A.M.–4:00 P.M., Sunday 12:00 noon.–4:00 P.M.; October–March closed Monday. Closed for major holidays. Admission is $4 for adults, $2 for students, and $3 for senior citizens and veterans. Children under 6 admitted free. Guided 90-minute tours can be scheduled by calling (504) 342–0500.

OLD COURT HOUSE (1847–50)
7 North Main Street
Dayton, Ohio

Howard Daniels, architect

Ralph Adams Cram called this august Greek Revival courthouse "the finest thing of its kind in America" (*Dayton Evening News*, 6 September 1923). It is lifted above the ordinary by its set-back corner location, tawny limestone walls, unfluted Ionic columns, and by its unique "scallops" bitten off the two rear corners (these indentations functionally reflect the shape of the great oval courtroom that fills the rear third of the structure).

Its style supposedly derives from a copy of James Stuart and Nicholas Revett's famous book *The Antiquities of Athens* (1762), which a local dignitary possessed. A copy of the plate showing the Theseion was sent to the architects invited to compete for the Court House commission. Howard Daniels, the winner, used only the temple front (and changed the Doric columns to Ionic), with pilastered instead of columned sides (to admit proper light and air), and, as mentioned, took logical bites out of the rear corners. He also put a coffered Roman dome over the two-story courtroom. The building itself is of solid masonry (even the original roof was of stone until it leaked too much); only the window sashes and inner doors are made of wood (the outer doors are metal). The vaulting of the basement is of interest, as is the spiral stair to the visitors' gallery of the courtroom. Very impressive of its kind.

Its civic functions long ago (1884) superseded by a larger building, the Old Court House was in danger of destruction, but preservationists and the energetic Montgomery County Historical Society saved it. Beginning in 1973, the building was then transformed into a living museum of the area and its history. The previously hemmed-in building was "liberated" on one long side and back by a richly patterned Plaza in 1974 by architects Lorenz Williams Lively Likens & Partners, making the Old Court House a more contributory member of Dayton's resurgent downtown.

Located at the northwest corner of Third Street and Main Street. Open Monday–Friday 10:00 A.M.–4:30 P.M., Saturday 12:00 noon–4:00 P.M. (Labor Day–Memorial Day closed Mondays). Free tours can be scheduled in advance by calling (513) 228–6271.

SMITHSONIAN INSTITUTION BUILDING (1847–55)
The Mall, 1000 Jefferson Drive
between 9th and 12th streets SW
Washington, D.C.

James Renwick, Jr., architect

James Renwick, Jr., was catapulted into national prominence when at the age of twenty-three he won the competition for the design of Grace Church (see page 206)—a church considered by many to be the finest example of Gothic Revival in the country—in his native New York. In 1846, a year after its completion, he was commissioned as architect—over a sizable number of firms consulted—for the Smithsonian Institution Building. James Smithson, an Englishman who died in 1829, left the United States a munificent bequest of more than half a million dollars for "the increase and diffusion of knowledge among men." After years of inexcusable delay the government accepted, but it was not until 1846 that Congress finally chartered the Smithsonian Institution. (Smithson's only trip to America was in his coffin to be buried in the museum he had made possible.) The institution's many functions are now housed in a potpourri of scattered buildings, but this whimsical pile, a "red stone castle," strung along (and intruding into) the Mall, remains its administrative and sentimental heart. The building has been described as twelfth-century Italian Lombard Romanesque style— reputedly the first such in the country—but with hints of the Gothic that Renwick used at Grace Church. But the rich, red sandstone, "medieval confusion" (Horatio Greenough) of the Smithsonian is the free interpretation of an architectural style that has only recently escaped from ridicule. (Nathan Reingold characterized the Smithsonian as "early Robin Hood.") This was an era when Victorian taste preferred the complicated to the simple, the picturesque or "artful" to regularity, the variegated to the plain—in other words, it was a total rejection of the formal Greek Revival period it superseded. The plan, it is surprising to note, is almost completely symmetrical; it stretches 447 feet/136 meters.

A fire destroyed part of the building only ten years after its completion (1865), and what we see today was partly rebuilt by Adolph Cluss, who finished the job in 1867. Numerous changes were made through the years, the most recent alteration dating from 1967–70 when the entire building was mechanically updated and restored (Chatelain, Samperton & Nolan, architects). The Smithsonian is architecturally one of the delights of its improbable period.

Open daily 9:00 A.M.–5:00 P.M. Closed Christmas. Admission is free. Much of the building is currently closed to the public. Tours can be arranged by calling (202) 357–2987.

Be certain to visit the adjacent polychrome brick, "modernized Romanesque" Arts and Industries Building (1879–81—Adolph Cluss and Paul Schulze, architects; General Montgomery C. Meigs, consulting engineer). The finely engineered dome over its four 56-foot-/17-meter-high "naves" and the colorful confusion of the interior spaces hold great excitement. It came into being largely to house the exhibits from the Philadelphia Centennial Exhibition of 1876, for which it had no existing space available. The rotunda and four naves were sparklingly restored (1974–76) for the nation's bicentennial by the Smithsonian's Office of Facilities, Planning, and Engineering Services with Hugh Newell Jacobsen, architect.

Open daily 9:00 A.M.–5:00 P.M. Closed Christmas. Admission is free.

LOG CABIN VILLAGE (1848–70)
2100 Log Cabin Village Lane
Fort Worth, Texas

A small, documentary group of frontier cabins with the architectural directness that characterizes the primitive building of the region. Brought together by the Texas Pioneer Heritage Committee and the Tarrant County Historical Society, these seven original cabins have been meticulously restored. The Isaac Parker Cabin (1848) is so authentically furnished inside and out that it suggests its inhabitants have momentarily dropped everything and gone to repel an

attack by Native Americans—as they probably often had in the past. Note its dog run or possum trot for channeling the breeze and for providing a covered open-air work space. The cabins date from 1848 (the Parker Cabin) to 1870 (the tiny Isaac Seela Cabin). Although their corner mortising would not pass the critical eye of a sixteenth-century Swede—there is a whole science to this joinery—the logs are smartly trimmed and straight.

Located 1/2 block south of the intersection of University Drive and Colonial Parkway. Open Tuesday–Friday 9:00 A.M.–5:00 P.M., Saturday 10:00 A.M.–5:00 P.M., Sunday 1:00–5:00 P.M. Closed for holidays in winter. Admission is $1.50 for adults, $1.25 for senior citizens and children ages 4–17. For more information call (817) 926–5881.

WASHINGTON MONUMENT (1848–84)
The Mall off Constitution Avenue or 15th Street
Washington, D.C.

Robert Mills, architect

Senmut, Queen Hatshepsut's architect, erected more obelisks than anyone before or since. However, he probably never dreamed that this polished marble symbol would, some 3,400 years later, stand 555 feet/169 meters high on a green-swathed hill. But what more noble monument to the father of our country? The Washington Monument as erected is superb in its simplicity. It is the least-quarreled-with memorial to be found in America. However, the purity one sees today was not of the original design. Robert Mills, who won the competition—organized by private citizens—for its design (1833), planned to build an obelisk 600 feet/183 meters high atop a 100-foot-/30-meter-high circular Greco-Roman temple 250 feet/76 meters in diameter! (Mills, incidentally, had won an earlier competition for a monument to Washington in Baltimore, one in the form of a modified Tuscan column atop a large base that was also vastly simplified between original design in 1815 and completion in 1824.) The monument in Washington got off to a slow start, as, initially all money for the project was privately donated, although the land was given by Congress. The cornerstone was not laid until 1848 and its height had only reached 152 feet/46 meters when lack of funds and subsequently the Civil War postponed construction. However, its location at the intersection of axes south from the White House and west from the Capitol (which Pierre Charles L'Enfant had suggested) had to be moved 371 feet/113 meters east of the north-south axis and 123 feet/37 meters south of the Capitol axis because of unsatisfactory soil conditions (the Potomac River was then much closer). The west-east axis was reshifted by the McMillan Report of 1902 so that Capitol, Monument, and site would align for a proposed major memorial. One hundred years after the Declaration of Independence work on Washington's needle was again commenced, this time under the direction of Lieutenant Colonel Thomas L. Casey of the Army Corps of Engineers, who found the obelisk out of plumb, necessitating further delays to shore it up and install a 13-foot-/3.9-meter-thick pad of concrete underneath. Also at this time, due to the research of G. P. Marsh, then U.S. Minister to Italy, the height was fixed at 555 feet 5.125 inches/169.3 meters to match the usual ancient Egyptian proportions of ten modules of height to one of base, the base line being 55 feet 1.5 inches/16.8 meters. And through Marsh's enlightenment, Mills's nearly flat capping was changed to a proper pyramidion, and the "temple" desecration at its base omitted—causing one critic of the day to term the result a "stalk of asparagus ... the refuge of incompetence in architecture." Mark Twain wrote that "It has the aspect of a factory chimney with the top broken off."

The resulting slender, hollow shaft has walls that taper in thickness from 15 feet/4.6 meters at base to 18 inches/.46 meter at top. Marble facing with rubble masonry fill was used for the first portion (completed prior to the Civil War), and marble with granite backing above except for the last 103 feet/31 meters, which is all marble. The exterior is sheathed entirely with Maryland marble, from two different stratums of the same quarry, hence the mismatched "band" around the middle at the 152-foot/46-meter level. There are 897 steps inside plus elevator and entry ramp for the handicapped. It is the highest all masonry (no steel) structure in the world, and certainly the States' finest legacy from Egypt. More sensitive landscaping is needed, but the Washington Monument itself might well be the world's finest memorial in the pure, albeit impersonal, sense. One of the best times to ascend it is at dusk.

September–March open daily 9:00 A.M.–4:45 P.M. April–August open daily 8:00 A.M.–11:45 P.M. Closed Christmas. Admission is free. Free tours given every 5 minutes. Tours can also be scheduled by calling (202) 426–6841.

BEAUVOIR (1848–51)
2244 Beach Boulevard
Biloxi, Mississippi

Beauvoir is a relaxed example of the function-bred raised cottage found along the Gulf Coast and the lower Mississippi, where the problems of flooding, dampness, and insects are always a threat. Following the usual response, the elevated basement is of masonry, with the cypress-built house above, surrounded by porch or gallery on three sides. In addition to shielding the dwelling from the hot sun, the piazza provides the most popular living "room" in the house in the cool of the evening. Shaded by live oaks and a scattering of cypress and cedar, Beauvoir directly faces the Gulf of Mexico—and was among the very first southern waterfront buildings to do so.

Within, the basically square front section can be opened to catch even the suspicion of a zephyr, while the 15-foot-/4.6-meter-high reception hall that runs down the middle acts as a breezeway. This area often doubled as a banquet hall, extending, as it does, from the front entry to the rear service porch. Connecting onto the central hallway are the front and rear parlors to the left of the entrance and two bedrooms to the right; their frescoes have recently been restored. Two additional bedrooms occupy the left (northwest) corner at the rear and are matched by a wing on the opposite side containing dining room and pantry. Connecting doorways and triple-hung windows almost anticipate the "open plan" so favored today. The dwelling is flanked by twin cottages, the east one of which was used as an office and also a study/schoolroom (now the Library Cottage), while the western dependency (enlarged) was used for guests.

Occupied by Jefferson Davis after the former president of the Confederacy retired (1877), the house remained in the family until 1903 when Mrs. Davis sold the estate to the Mississippi Division, Sons of Confederate Veterans (who still own and operate the site). It was operated

by the state as the Beauvoir Jefferson Davis Soldiers Home 1903–56. In 1940, in accordance with Mrs. Davis's earlier-expressed wishes, it was turned into the Jefferson Davis Shrine and opened to the public as such the following year, having been properly restored, and with many of the original furnishings recovered. A Davis museum occupies the basement. House and cottages were reputedly designed by James Brown, the original owner.

Open daily 9:00 A.M.–5:00 P.M. Closed Thanksgiving and Christmas. Admission is $5 for adults, $4.50 for senior citizens and military personnel, $2.50 for children ages 6–15. Guided tours can be arranged by calling (601) 388–1313.

SAM HOUSTON PARK HERITAGE BUILDINGS
(mid–late nineteenth century)
1100 Bagby Street at Lamar
Houston, Texas

The Harris County Heritage Society has given downtown Houston a series of buildings that together re-create an architectural perspective of the early days of this city. The group and its greenery provide a welcome respite to the concretion of skyscrapers so near by. Anchored by the Kellum-Noble House—the only unit that stands on its original site—five other houses, a church, a fine plantation cabin with cedar frame (1824), and a reconstructed row of shops have been brought together (with slightly unfocused disposition) and rehabilitated. All of the buildings came from Harris County, and though several were in parlous shape, and the shops—Houston's earliest—totally rebuilt from early documents, all are now in mint condition. No original furniture was left in the dwellings, but appropriate period pieces have been used.

Note the functional porch of the Kellum-Noble House, undoubtedly influenced by adjacent Louisiana, which shields all four sides and both floors from the sun and weather. Built in 1847, it is thought to be the oldest brick dwelling in the city. At one time it served as a private school, and it was restored in 1954 as the first unit in the park. The Nichols-Rice-Cherry House (c. 1850) possesses an elaborate entrance, while an unexpected richness of wood detail within belies the chaste Greek Revival exterior. It shows some influence from upstate New York, since its builder, Ebenezer B. Nichols, was a native of Cooperstown. St. John's Church was built by German Lutheran farmers in 1891; it is simple on the outside, but the interior is spacious and pleasant. Altogether a fine lot to which, it is hoped, subsequent additions will be made.

Open Monday–Saturday 10:00 A.M.–4:00 P.M., Sunday 1:00–4:00 P.M. Closed for major holidays. Admission is $6 for adults, $4 for senior citizens and for children ages 13–17, $2 for children ages 6–12, and free for children under 6. One-hour tours are given on the hour. For more information, call (713) 655–1912.

DOWNTOWN PRESBYTERIAN CHURCH (1849–51/1881–82)
154 5th Avenue North
Nashville, Tennessee

William Strickland, architect

Nashville's Downtown Presbyterian Church unveils the most engaging extant Egyptian Revival interior to be seen in this country. Although perhaps more suited to *Aïda* or even corporate worship than infant baptism, it is a design of such power as to place it high among the various revivals that characterized American architecture of the nineteenth century and almost half of this. (It might also be kept in mind that Egypt is mentioned in the Old Testament more than any country except the Holy Land, hence this Christian adaptation of Egyptian architecture is not too farfetched.) William Strickland had timidly used the Egyptian revival in his Mikveh-Israel Synagogue (1822–25) in Philadelphia, a building long demolished, but this Nashville example uses the style with great conviction.

The hypostyle "halls" of massive Egyptian columns and lotus-bud capitals *à la* the Temple of Karnak—both in relief and in painted perspective—that frame the chancel are daringly conceived and boldly painted. The windows along the two sides each carry the proper cavetto cornice, while overhead painted clouds once wafted by. Measuring 80 x 136 feet/24 x 41 meters, the nave and balcony accommodate 1,300.

However, it must be brought out that the two end "walls" seen today framing the sanctuary were not designed by—or at least not put in by—Strickland, but are additions dating from 1881–82. At that time "the church underwent a major redecoration to bring a richer Egyptian flavor to the interior. The Egyptianesque colors, patterns, scenes and symbols were added to the auditorium" (James A. Hoobler, *Tennessee Historical Quarterly*, Fall 1976). Because the church records for those years have been lost, it is not known who was responsible for the design, but Strickland's influence was certainly strong. Renovations undertaken from 1955 to 1957 have changed some of the original design of the sanctuary. The church was called First Presbyterian until 1955, by which time most of the congregation had moved to the suburbs.

Open Monday–Friday 10:00 A.M.–3:30 P.M. Sunday services held at 11:00 A.M. Closed for holidays. During April–November, free 20–minute tours can be scheduled by calling (615) 254–7584.

ST. JOHN CHRYSOSTOM CHURCH (1851–53)
Church Street
Delafield, Wisconsin

Richard Upjohn, architect

Nineteenth-century "Village Gothick" in wood is still found in numerous states. Among the better examples is this Episcopal church—named for the famous fourth-century Antiochean—some 25 miles/40 kilometers west of Milwaukee. Painted a reddish color, the church is set in an old cemetery and punctuated by a detached wood belfry that owes a debt to Swedish bell towers. The nave—note the trusswork built by English shipwrights—is on the dark side, but, fortunately, neither the interior nor the exterior has been seriously altered through the years. (The elaborately carved barge boards are well worth noticing.) A complete restoration inside and out took place from 1973–76.

Recent research almost definitely confirms that Richard Upjohn was the architect, even though this is not mentioned in *Richard Upjohn, Architect and Churchman* by Everard M. Upjohn (Da Capo Press, 1968). *Upjohn's Rural Architecture*—which helped so many small communities build their Gothic revival churches and other rural structures—was published in 1852, a year after St. John Chrysostom was commenced, and the church bears a very strong resemblance to examples in this volume. It might well be that this Wisconsin chapel was thus Upjohn "designed" —that is, its drawings sent by him to the parish. Whatever the attribution, let us be grateful for the result.

Located west off Genesee (just north of I-94 and adjacent to St. John's Military Academy). Open for services Wednesday at 9:00 A.M., Sunday at 8:00 and 10:00 A.M. Tours can be scheduled by calling (414) 646–2727.

MALLORY-NEELY HOUSE (c. 1852/1883)
652 Adams Avenue
Memphis, Tennessee

The Victorian Village Historic District of Memphis comprises one of the nation's finest collections of mid- and late-nineteenth-century dwellings. Though most of these period houses are private, those that are open to the public merit exploration. The Mallory House, built circa 1852 for a banker named Isaac Kirtland, underwent substantial changes after 1883 when James Columbus Neely purchased it and added a third floor, along with his name. He also changed the facade to incorporate the then-fashionable Tuscan central tower; note its carefully dissimilar, strangely gabled flanks. A pale salmon stucco covers its brick walls. The interior, almost untouched for one hundred years, is one of the Victorian prides of America.

The parlor in particular is sumptuous almost beyond belief, while the library and dining room are not far behind. The colored glass windows in the front door are possibly unsurpassed, while the French window on the stair-landing facing it is almost as fine (all were

purchased at the 1893 Chicago World's Fair). Moreover the house was continuously lived in from 1852 to 1969. The furnishings are all of the Victorian period, and belonged to the Neely and Mallory families.

The dwelling and carriage house behind were given in 1972 by the children of the late Mrs. Barton Lee Mallory (née Neely) to the local chapters of the Daughters, Sons, and Children of the American Revolution. It is currently owned by the city of Memphis, which is overseeing its restoration. A new slate roof has been installed to protect the fabric of the house, the porches have been rebuilt, and the carriage house has been renovated. On the interior, the dining room has been completed, and work continues as funds materialize. One of the finest of its period to be seen.

Open Tuesday–Saturday 10:00 A.M.–4:00 P.M., Sunday 1:00–4:00 P.M. Closed Thanksgiving, Christmas Eve, Christmas, and in January and February. Admission is $4 for adults, $3 for senior citizens and children ages 5–college age. Guided tours given every half hour. For more information call (901) 523–1484.

ST. PATRICK'S CATHEDRAL
(1853–88/1901–08/1941–42)
5th Avenue at East 50th Street
New York, New York

James Renwick, Jr., architect

James Renwick, Jr.'s earlier Grace Church (see page 206) is finer, and more "organic," in its architecture, but St. Patrick's Cathedral unquestionably establishes a more commanding urban presence. When the church's location was originally settled upon, it was criticized as being "too far out of town," but never was urban prescience—plus urban lottery—more gratifyingly justified. Thanks primarily to the building of Rockefeller Center in the 1930s, the church now forms part of the core of New York City: for its parishioners, especially the Irish, it is the core. Renwick, having designed Grace Church, pulled out all the stops at St. Patrick's. He, questionably, took

as his prototype Cologne Cathedral, which the famous Banister Fletcher termed "a conspicuous instance of the adoption of the details of a style, without having assimilated the spirit that created it" (*A History of Architecture*, Charles Scribner's, 1896 *et seq.*). There is, thus, a certain dryness in St. Patrick's, particularly in its exterior fabric (as opposed to its podium setting); it is too "petrified" for the vital Gothic of the Middle Ages. (Incidentally, the "Gothic" got its name from the Italians, who considered it so uncouth that they named it for a tribe of barbarians.)

St. Patrick's interior reveals its most successful architectural aspect, a potent, if for some an overdramatic, stage for worship, a proscenium activated by a constant ebb and flow of people. Much of this puissance stems from a remodeling in the early 1900s, when Charles T. Mathews pushed out Renwick's originally flat east nave termination, fashioning it into a polygonal lady chapel and adjacent chapels (1901–08). Then in 1941–42 a new high altar and 57-foot-/17-meter-high, bronze baldacchino by Charles D. Maginnis were added, climaxed by theatrical down-lighting, to create a numinous setting. The buttresses receive no load from the roof, and the marble within turns to plaster higher up, but what a stage set—and, at 330 feet/101 meters, what spires. The church's conversation with one avenue and two streets is brilliant. (William H. Pierson, Jr., devotes a long and fascinating chapter to the development of St. Patrick's in his volume *American Buildings and Their Architects, The Corporate and Early Gothic Styles*, Doubleday, 1978.)

Open daily 6:30 A.M.–8:45 P.M. Free group tours can be scheduled by calling (212) 753–2261.

GOVERNOR'S MANSION (1853–56), 1010 Colorado Street
NEILL-COCHRAN HOUSE (1855), 2310 San Gabriel Street
Austin, Texas

Abner Cook, architect

These two Greek Revival houses were designed by the same master builder/architect and constructed within a few years of each other. Most dwellings of this style are characterized by
white columns and white walls (whether of masonry or wood), but the Neill-Cochran House
is refreshingly "local" in that behind its stately row of six two-story Doric columns stands a wall
of 18-inch-/46-centimeter-thick buff-colored limestone. Opening onto the porch, which
extends across the entire front, are four floor-to-ceiling windows that give both scale and ventilation. Since 1958 the house has belonged to the National Society of the Colonial Dames of
America in the State of Texas, which has carefully restored both house and garden to their century-old appearance (the building at one time having served as a hospital, then as an institute
for the blind, and still later as a home first for the Neills and then the Cochrans). The entrance
hall with its circular stair is perhaps the most competent single room, but the level of design
is high throughout.

The Governor's Mansion (shown in the photograph) follows the basic disposition of the
Neill-Cochran House, but with Ionic columns, a full-width, second-story porch, and a bit more
finesse in detail. It is a stalwart example of the Greek Revival and, having been maintained in
prime condition throughout its life, the mansion, as well as its lovingly tended gardens, is well
worth a visit.

The Neill-Cochran House is open Wednesday–Sunday 2:00–5:00 P.M. Closed for holidays. Admission is $2. Guided tours are
given. For more information call (512) 478–2335. The Governor's Mansion is open Monday–Friday 10:00–11:40 A.M. All visits
are guided: free tours given every 20 minutes. For more information call (512) 463–5518.

CAST-IRON ARCHITECTURE (mid to late nineteenth century)
SoHo district: south of Houston Street, north of Canal,
between Crosby and West Broadway
New York, New York

Daniel D. Badger, James Bogardus, and others, architects/builders

Cast-iron architecture in the United States developed well over one hundred years ago as a technique that presaged not only today's curtain-wall construction, but also much of the theory of skyscraper design—to say nothing of prefabricated, standardized, demountable, and transportable building. Admitting far more daylight than masonry construction, cast-iron fronts revolutionized commercial architecture in much of the United States, becoming so popular that shipments of demountable buildings, or at least their facades, were regularly made to the West Coast (traveling around South America) following the Gold Rush.

Iron casting was, of course, an early historic development: the Book of Genesis, 4:22, says that Tubal-cain "was the forger of all instruments of bronze and iron"; L. Sprague de Camp in his book *The Ancient Engineers* (Doubleday, 1963) ascribes the invention of cast iron to the Chinese in the fourth century B.C. But until controlled smelting was mastered during the Industrial Revolution, cast iron was largely employed only for firebacks, grave slabs, balusters, and decorative features because of its friability. Robert and James Adam used it often. Norman Davey in *A History of Building Materials* (Phoenix House, 1961) writes, "The first structural cast-iron beams by Charles Bage (1774–1822) were used in a five-story flax mill built at Shrewsbury in 1796 and 1797." William Fairbairn's Iron Flour Mill of 1839–41 was probably the world's first completely iron building (although it may have had wood floors). Of three stories and measuring 27 x 50 feet/ 8 x 15 meters, it was erected and dismantled in London and then shipped to Istanbul. In the early nineteenth century rapid technological developments took place in Europe, and cast iron was used frequently as a structural component, particularly in hollow columns, often even for trusses. Joseph Paxton's Crystal Palace in London (1851), of course, stunned the world with its cast (and wrought) iron. It remained for America, however, to go into large-scale production of whole building fronts of this material, the iron modules of the facade replacing the masonry that once upheld the floors, hinting at later skyscraper construction with its completely independent columnar grid frame. (Most, if not all, early cast-iron buildings had only iron fronts: sides and backs and often partitions were of masonry. Such was the case with John B. Corlies and James Bogardus's famous—but now destroyed—Harper & Brothers Building of 1854 in New York.) Daniel D. Badger and Bogardus were leading advocates in developing cast iron structures in this country. Badger was head of the Architectural Iron Works and turned out in his plant an almost endless variety of cast iron; Bogardus, more an architect, was "inventor and patentee," who designed buildings but had others build them. His most stupendous work was a warehouse he sent to Cuba measuring 400 x 600 feet/122 x 183 meters!

It is not within the scope of this book to explore further the background of this exotic phase in American architecture. However, two more general remarks concerning the "style" might be in order. Cast iron, successful because of the repetitive copies it could turn out in a fire resistant form, possessed as a consequence a ready adaptability to ornament. Thus most of its examples—for better if one is a romantic, for worse if a misanthrope—are at times lively with fantastically intricate capitals and decoration. It finally developed such popularity that stone construction began to imitate iron. (The energetic Friends of Cast-Iron Architecture gives small magnets to all new members so that they can themselves determine what lurks behind the paint.) Secondly, the nature of cast-iron framing logically developed a sharply defined metronomic beat, at times of great vitality, thus anticipating the modular construction of today. Cast iron began to meet serious challenges when Andrew Carnegie introduced inexpensive rolled steel members. Steel has far greater tensile strength, hence greater reliability in long spans, and could be employed for beams as well as columns. Thus a total structural skeleton of one material, wrapped in fireproofing, was made feasible. (Exposed steel is more vulnerable to fire than cast iron, but it can be more easily fireproofed. Tile fireproofing for metal construction basically dates from the early 1870s.) However, a few examples of cast iron date from the early 1900s.

The greatest remaining single monument to cast iron—and now a National Registered Landmark—is New York's former E. V. Haughwout Store (see photograph below) at 488 Broadway, northeast corner of Broome Street, by J. P. Gaynor and Badger's Architectural Iron Works (1856–57). As Paul Goldberger wrote in his extremely useful book *New York, The City Observed* (Vintage Books, 1979), "It is one of those rare pieces of architecture in which everything fits together perfectly and yet with room for passion." The Haughwout Store combines the modular and the rich decoration mentioned above in its two extraordinarily handsome facades, which are largely copies of Jacopo Sansovino's library in Venice of 1536. The building is further notable in that Elisha Otis here installed the country's first "safety elevator," with this invention making the skyscraper possible. Beyond Haughwout, so to speak, lies a vast sea of cast iron in a thriving area transformed by the artists' community. This once-forgotten midriff section of the island was formerly rarely experienced by the routine New Yorker, sandwiched as it is between the financial district and Greenwich Village. Sir Nikolaus Pevsner calls this

SoHo (south of Houston) area "a veritable museum of cast iron, a greater concentration than anywhere else in the world." In 1973 it was designated a historic district by the Landmarks Preservation Commission. Here whole streets of smartly profiled cast-iron buildings, many with enormous panes of glass, frame city blocks, their later-added fire escapes (dating from the 1870s following the Chicago fire) only partially blurring their hundred-year-old precision. Greene Street has several gutsy columned facades. Broadway (427 to 691), Broome, and Mercer streets have fine examples. Farther uptown on 23rd Street (32 to 46), a bit west of 5th Avenue, an imposing white-painted former department store lines the south side of the street. There are also three iron fronts in the Ladies Shopping Mile Historic District on Sixth Avenue: the Ehrich Brothers Building at 24th Street, the O'Neill Building at 22nd Street, and the B. Altman Building at 19th Street.

An excellent recycling of an old cast-iron building can be seen at Broadway and 11th Street (see photograph above). Designed with Venetian overtones in 1868 by John Kellum, it once housed the McCreery Department Store (among other uses—including a shoe factory). In 1973 the structure was imaginatively remodeled by architect Stephen B. Jacobs to produce 144 luxury apartments. As the side facade is 221 feet/67 meters long, its white-painted four floors of cast iron (a fifth, set back on the top, is new) are a sparkling asset to the street. The building's salvation and transformation was initiated by the community, the Landmarks Preservation Commission, and the Friends of Cast Iron Architecture, and, through their petitioning, code variances were granted by the Board of Standards and Appeals. Everybody—including the owners—benefited.

For more information on this extraordinary richness, see *Cast-Iron Architecture in New York* by Margot Gayle and Edmund Gillon, Jr. (Dover, 1974), or contact the Friends of Cast Iron Architecture, 235 East 87th Street, New York, New York, 10128. They are doing a wonderful job in documenting and propagandizing this too little-known lode.

JOHNSTON-FELTON-HAY HOUSE (1855–60)
934 Georgia Avenue at Spring Street
Macon, Georgia

Thomas Thomas and Son, architects

This opulent, cubic, Italianate palazzo adds a startling note to the architecture of the region. The mansion was originally built for W. B. Johnston, a hugely successful merchant and investor, who took his bride to Italy for their honeymoon, where the two probably decided on the "style" of their new home. Its red brick walls glow against the green of the grounds and the white stone steps that splay from the front facade. The main floor is sheltered behind a porch that extends across the facade, breaking into a semicircle at the entry. The windows of the second floor bear heavy pediments (note the central one especially), while those on the third-floor "attic" frieze are round, somewhat like those in Andrea Palladio's Basilica (Palazzo della Ragione) in Vicenza. Statuesque chimneys, two per side, add a note to the roof, which is climaxed by an outsize, octagonal cupola, banded by scrolled buttresses.

The interior, which is even more lavish than the outside, boasts two dozen rooms, most of them with Carrara marble mantels. Walnut, oak, and rosewood graining, trompe l'oeil marbleizing, painted ceilings, sparkling chandeliers, and opulent furnishings complete the scene. It is said that the architect brought over Italian workmen to construct this extraordinary house. It is doubtful whether local talent could match their craftsmanship. In 1977 the dwelling and its contents were acquired by the Georgia Trust for Historic Preservation and are now managed by them. The interior is currently under renovation.

Open Monday–Saturday 10:00 A.M.–5:00 P.M., Sunday 1:00–5:00 P.M. Closed for major holidays. Admission is $6 for adults, $5 for senior citizens, $2 for students over 12, $1 for children ages 6–11, free for children under 6. Tours are given every half-hour; the last tour is at 4:30 P.M. Note: the Greater Macon Chamber of Commerce, 640 1st Street, offers a free self-guiding map of the historic spots of the city. Though most are private they merit a look either from car or on foot.

VICTORIA MANSION
(1858–60)
109 Danforth Street
at Park Street
Portland, Maine

Henry Austin, architect

"The finest and least altered example of a brown stone Italian villa town house in the United States" (as the plaque proclaims) was acquired in 1939 by the Victoria Society of Maine Women, and is now operated as a historic museum by the Victoria Society of Maine. Long in need of repair, the roof and the once scaly exterior were restored (1974–79) with matching funds from the Department of the Interior, the National Park Service, and the Maine Historic Preservation Commission. Designed as a summer home by Henry Austin of Yale Library (1842) fame, this is one of the most opulent of Victorian mansions; it must be seen to be believed. A variety of ideas and motifs—with a deep bow to the bracketed Italianate—have been hurled at this two-story brownstone, but hurled

with accuracy. In spite of the prominence of individual parts, it achieves a marvelous unity. (The reddish stone, incidentally, was shipped from Connecticut.) The interior offers an astounding parade of mid-nineteenth-century opulence, all in a variety of styles, with many walls and ceilings painted by Giuseppe Guidicini and eleven assistants. The lofty entrance hall provides an unexpected spatial welcome—and a prominent, freestanding, hand-carved mahogany stair. But the real delights are found in the rooms, particularly the reception room to the right, where every square inch, including the ceilings, has been attended to. The interior of the square tower, which rises imposingly above the well-modeled, well-articulated facade, was furnished in Turkish style. Also known as the Morse-Libby House, the building was designated a National Historic Landmark in 1972.

Memorial Day–Labor Day open Tuesday–Saturday 10:00 A.M.–4:00 P.M., Sunday 1:00–5:00 P.M. Labor Day–late October open Friday–Sunday 1:00–5:00 P.M. Admission is $4 for adults, $3.50 for senior citizens, $1.50 for children ages 6–17. 45-minute tour included with admission. For more information call (207) 772–4841.

UNITED STATES COURT HOUSE AND FEDERAL BUILDING (1858–61)
(formerly Customs House)
20th Street at Avenue E
Galveston, Texas

Ammi B. Young, C. B. Cluskey, and Edwin Moore, architects

This former Customs House established a surprisingly elegant Greek Revival beachhead in Galveston, one undiminished by well over one hundred years of hurricanes and man-made batterings. The north and south facades are distinguished by inset porches on both floors, the whole suggestive of Inigo Jones's Queen's House (1616–35) near London; the two-story portico on the west, on the other hand, projects prominently. Almost all of the exterior details are of cast iron (reputedly from New York), including the window frames and the columns (Ionic on the ground floor, Corinthian above). Cast iron was also used for the interior stairs. Willard B. Robinson in his excellent book *Texas Public Buildings of the Nineteenth Century*, with photographs by Todd Webb (University of Texas Press, 1974), points out that although the redoubtable Ammi B. Young, then supervising architect of the Treasury Department, initially designed what was for his output a dull, three-story structure, work stopped in 1859 because of the Civil War. The Customs House was then reduced by one story and finished by C. B. Cluskey and Edwin Moore with, it should be added, more finesse than Young's earlier design. (The National Register of Historic Places [1976] cites Ammi Young as the architect.) During the Battle of Galveston (1863) it was used as Confederate headquarters. Handsomely restored in 1967, it is one of the highlights of the Gulf Coast. Inside, the ground floor has been divided into offices and is of little interest, but the second floor beautifully houses the old courtroom and ancillary chambers.

The interior is not open to the public.

RENWICK GALLERY
(1859–60/1972)
(formerly Corcoran Gallery)
Pennsylvania Avenue
at 17th Street NW
Washington, D.C.

James Renwick, Jr., architect

The facade of the Renwick Gallery is of the exuberant Second Empire period—and its first example of consequence in the United States. It is also probably the first building in the States to be designed as a museum. The skill evident in this rich and assured structure can be seen on the exterior by the powerful buildup of forms. This is apparent in the prominent curved mansard roof of the central pavilion versus the small straight-sided flanking mansards, and in the emphasis of the pedimented entry bay where paired, free-standing "Corinthian" columns (with corn motif capitals) are used instead of the flat corner pilasters on the second floor. (A facade influence of the Paris Louvre has been noticed by most historians.) On entering one pushes open the etched glass front doors (added when the building became a part of the Smithsonian Institution) and marches straight up red-carpeted stairs to the Grand Salon. This sedate chamber, top-lit to show its pictures best, offers an imposing background for the art on its mulberry walls.

Originally built to house the collection of William W. Corcoran, the gallery was used as a warehouse during and after the Civil War (1861–69), and it was not fully restored and formally opened to the public until 1874. In 1897, Corcoran's collection having outgrown its premises (he built the "new" Corcoran down the street), the building was sold to the federal government. The U.S. Court of Claims occupied it from 1899 until 1964, inflicting some damage in partitioning the major spaces. In 1965 it was added to the Smithsonian Institution's "family of national museums" for the purpose of displaying crafts and decorative arts, and full restoration was undertaken in 1972 as a public institution. (The windowed entry level, originally the sculpture hall, is for temporary exhibitions; the second floor holds the permanent collection.) John Carl Warnecke & Associates, with the assistance of Universal Restoration, was charged with repairing the fabric of the building, including replacing most of the time-eroded exterior ornament. Hugh Newell Jacobsen & Associates restored the interior in the spirit of its day. They did an admirable job, the American Institute of Architects' Honor Award proclaiming it "a masterpiece of creative restoration." And how appropriate to have the building renamed in honor of its architect.

Open daily 10:00 A.M.–5:30 P.M. Closed Christmas. Admission is free. Tours can be arranged by calling (202) 357-2531.

CENTRAL PARK (1859–76)
between 5th Avenue and Central Park West (8th Avenue)
between 59th and 110th streets
New York, New York

Frederick Law Olmsted and Calvert Vaux, designers

It is important to realize when strolling, sitting, boating, biking, playing, or seeing plays that Central Park's cornucopia of delights, while seemingly almost spontaneous, owes its creation to the same functional analysis that goes into the design of a major building complex. Soil conditions, drainage and irrigation, water supply, sewage disposal, classification of circulation (pedestrian, horse, bicycle, vehicular, urban cross-town), provisions for the young, provisions for the old—let alone tree, shrub, and plant characteristics—are merely obvious program elements that helped fashion the extraordinary heart and lungs of Manhattan Island. As Frederick Law Olmsted wrote, "Every foot of the park's surface, every tree and bush, as well as every arch, roadway and walk has been fixed where it is with a *purpose*" (from Henry Hope Reed and Sophia Duckworth's highly recommended *Central Park, A History and a Guide*, Clarkson N. Potter, 1972). With the help of Ignaz Anton Pilat, an Austrian-born botanist,

Olmsted and Vaux supervised the installation of several million trees, bushes, and plants (Reed mentions "four or five million" by 1873) representing hundreds of species.

Central Park was not just a piece of fortuitously available open land in mid-nineteenth-century New York that the city simply "fenced off," as Reed, its former curator, so succinctly put it. It represents landscape architecture at its technical and esthetic peak, the work of true professionals designing the first significant park in this country. Its 843 acres/341 hectares were acquired by the city in spite of political shenanigans, the infighting of vested interests, and even the objections of many bankers and real-estate men. But dedicated civic—and a few political—leaders, William Cullen Bryant leading the clan, backed it as an essential component for the rapidly expanding city. The concept was officially approved in 1856, with Frederick Law Olmsted hired to supervise the clearing of the rough, hovel- and hog-infested land, and to drain its swamps. (The site at this time already included the old, rectangular Croton Reservoir, built in 1842, with 106 acres/43 hectares of land for a new reservoir—the present—acquired in 1852. The Arsenal, by Martin E. Thompson, had been completed in 1851.) A competition was then announced (1858) for the design of the new park, but Olmsted, because of his in-house position, did not consider entering it until urged to collaborate by and with his friend Calvert Vaux, an English-born architect. (Olmsted also got permission to compete from his boss.) That theirs was the finest of thirty-three entries was due to Olmsted's passionate, if self-taught, background in landscaping, plus his immense grass-roots knowledge, buttressed, of course, by Vaux's professional know-how and sense of spatial modeling. (Vaux had come to the United States in 1850 to work with Andrew Jackson Downing, the famous horticulturist, who died in a tragic accident in 1852. Olmsted himself had studied at first hand Downing's "picturesque" or romantic school of design and expanded his horizons by also examining the English school of landscaping from the work of Capability Brown to Humphrey Repton to Joseph Paxton.) Moreover the two had tramped over every millimeter of the acreage.

In effect there are two Central Parks, the reservoir (roughly between 86th and 96th streets) nearly cutting it in two, with the northern section rougher than the southern, and with its topography left more natural. The southern part also has about fifty percent more land area and far more amenities. The main entrance is at 59th–60th streets and 5th Avenue where it could serve as the gateway for the greatest number of people, for when the park was laid out there were few buildings in its area. This entry also leads to the Mall, double-lined with elms—and one of the few formal elements of the entire design. This promenade, which is almost .25 mile/.4 kilometer long, contrasts usefully with the picturesque naturalness around it. The Mall is punctuated by the Naumburg Bandshell and climaxed by the Terrace and Bethesda Fountain, which overlook the rowing pond with the Ramble on the far side. So as not to interfere with cross-town traffic—and vice versa—there are four transverse roads (65th–66th, 79th, 85th, and 97th streets) that were mandated by the competition and that Olmsted and Vaux depressed across much of the width of the park. There are, of course, surface carriage and automobile roads that can also be used. (Roads, underpasses, and bridges—the cast-iron ones especially—all merit attention.)

One might say that the only problem with Central Park is its overwhelming success, for although most physical encroachments have been kept in check, the place is so wonderful it is being almost trampled to death. (Crime and drugs continue to be problems.) It is almost impossible to imagine New York City without the park: indeed America's concept of urban living was never the same after it was opened; cities across the country emulated the example. Olmsted took his humanism and technology, his "social democracy" it has been called, as far as California, becoming one of the first advocates of Yosemite Valley and its preservation (1864), a forerunner of the National Park concept that was initiated at Yellowstone in 1872. (He also came back to California to be the landscape architect of Berkeley in 1866, with Vaux, and of Stanford University in 1888, with his son.) Olmsted's concern for man in the wilds or in the city was matched only by his ability to implement this concern: no one has physically enriched the nation more.

Open daily 6:00–1:00 A.M. Central Park tours given by the park rangers; for more information call (800) 201–PARK. For specialty tours or additional information on Central Park call (212) 360–3444.

Prospect Park (1866–74) in Brooklyn is New York's other great monument to Olmsted and Vaux's skills. Though only 526 acres/213 hectares versus 843/341 for Central Park, it is more felicitously landscaped. McKim, Mead & White's formalistic Brooklyn Museum (1895–1914) is set adjacent to the park off Eastern Parkway at Washington Avenue. In January 1980 a thorough rehabilitation of the park began: most of the park structures have already been repaired, the entrance at Grand Army Plaza (also by McKim, Mead & White) has been restored, and the ravine area is soon to be rehabilitated as part of the ongoing upkeep of the landscape.

Take the IRT No. 2 or 3 to the Grand Army Plaza stop. Open daily dawn to dusk. For information on Prospect Park events call (718) 965–8951. The Brooklyn Center for the Urban Environment offers tours of Prospect Park at a cost of $8 for adults and $4 for senior citizens and children under 16; for more information call (718) 788–8549.

LONGWOOD (1860–61)
140 Lower Woodville Road
Natchez, Mississippi

Samuel Sloan, architect

The never-finished Longwood—construction stopped when its Philadelphia workmen has-tened home at the start of the Civil War—is the most impressive (and the largest) of the few remaining houses that were inspired by the architectural philosophy of Orson Squires Fowler. Fowler was a successful phrenologist who preached that the "spherical" or the octagonal was the most logical plan for a house, and in 1848 wrote an influential book on the subject—*A Home for All*—which went through many printings. Though his geometry never approached Etienne-Louis Boullée's (1728–99) fantastic proposal for a 500-foot-/152-meter-high spherical tomb for Isaac Newton, Fowler's persuasive arguments found some echo, almost one hundred years later, in Buckminster Fuller's hexagonal Dymaxion House of 1927, and, of course, in Fuller's geodesic domes, which reached a climax in the 250-foot-/76-meter-diameter sphere at the Montreal Expo '67. Maybe historians have underrated Orson Squires Fowler. (Octagonal plans were, of course, well known in the history of architecture; San Vitale in Ravenna—526–47—is one of the first great examples.)

In 1860 Dr. Haller Nutt commissioned Samuel Sloan—"one of the most distinguished of early American architects" (Henry F. Withey, *Biographical Dictionary of American Architects [Deceased]*, Hennessey & Ingalls, 1970)—to design Longwood: would that it had been finished. To compound the tragedy, Nutt died in 1864. Although only the basement level had been fully enclosed, it and the two main floors are still in excellent condition. If the six-story dwelling (basement, three main floors, solarium, and observatory—all crowned by an onion dome or an East Indian *amalaka*) had been completed as designed, the towering central hall, which runs through the house, would have been staggering, for Sloan had planned an elaborate system of translucent panels to allow sunlight to reach the basement level. He also had planned to ven-tilate the house in summer by drawing cool air in from the lower level and exhausting it at the top. All thirty-two major rooms have two exits plus cross ventilation.

John Nash's famous Royal Pavilion at Brighton (1815–22) might have influenced Nutt and Sloan to produce what could be termed a "Moorish-Tuscan" mansion; in any case Longwood is one of the most fascinating houses in the country. Fortunately it was pur-chased (1968) by the Kelly E. McAdams fam-ily. The McAdams Foundation generously gave it and 5 acres/2 hectares in 1970 to the Pilgrimage Garden Club, which is repairing and preserving it, having acquired 82 acres/33 hectares of additional land as pro-tection. Unique—and since 1970 a National Historic Landmark.

Located south of J. R. Junkin Drive (US 65 by-pass). Open 9:00 A.M.–5:00 P.M. During March and October pilgrimages hours vary; call (601) 442–5193 for more information. Admission is $5 for adults, $2.50 for students ages 7–17, free for children under 7. Forty-minute tours are given daily.

SALT LAKE TABERNACLE (1863–70)
Temple Square
Salt Lake City, Utah

Concept by Brigham Young
William H. Folsom and Truman O. Angell, architects

A 10-acre/4-hectare walled compound in the heart of Salt Lake City—whose street numbering pattern originates here—Temple Square is unquestionably the most remarkable religious enclave in the United States. The buildings of architectural interest are the Temple (which is open only to Mormons), the famous Tabernacle, and the Neo-Gothic Assembly Hall (the latter two are open to visitors).

The Tabernacle, with straight sides and semicircular ends, has been dear to radio audiences since 1929 for its superb 375-member volunteer choir and its organ recitals. (Recitals are given Monday–Saturday at noon, Sunday at 4:00 P.M., throughout the year; from mid-June to mid-September also nightly at 7:30 except Sunday. Choir rehearsal Thursday 7:30 P.M., public welcome.) The Tabernacle's turtle-back form—subject of much folklore—was erected, like the nearby Temple, under the most primitive conditions (that is, by oxcart). The result is somewhat scaleless, both on the exterior, with its uninterrupted aluminum roof (originally of wood shingles), and on the inside, with its smooth inverted bowl ceiling. However, the auditorium's inner space is stunning. (The form must have been stupendous during construction, when its arches and bracing were fully revealed.) Overall, the building measures 250 feet/76 meters long and 150 feet/46 meters wide, with a periphery of forty-four masonry piers (ashlar sandstone) upholding its daring carapace. Note the Classical capitals on the piers. According to Paul L. Anderson, the manager of the Historic Buildings and Sites Section of the Church, "The roof structure is made up of elliptically arched lattice trusses that act as rigid curved beams. There is no lateral thrust, so no tie rods are needed." The nine trusses are spaced 12 feet/3.6 meters apart and span a 132-foot/40-meter clear inner width. Trusses in half-arch form rise from the semicircular ends, their "fanned" juncture with the straight arches ingeniously butted (to judge from the drawings). A plaster ceiling shell hangs from the trusses. The 10-foot-/3-meter-deep, bridge-like arches—Henry Grow, the building's engineer, had designed lattice-truss bridges in Pennsylvania, New Jersey, and elsewhere in Utah before tackling the Tabernacle's roof—are fastened together with wooden dowels and reinforced with rawhide in case the wood split. Little metal was employed until some handmade bolts were added later. (Iron was scarce in Utah before the coming of the railroad.) The wide *U*-shaped balcony, put in by Truman O. Angell in 1869–70, not only increased the seating capacity to approximately 8,000, it made the acoustics—for choirs—superb. (Some authorities believe that the horsehair in the plaster helps control echoes.) The slight blandness of the plastered interior is offset by an ebullient organ of 10,814 pipes (twice rebuilt and enlarged, most recently in 1948–49). Architecturally impressive, the Tabernacle from the constructional point of view ranks among the wood engineering masterpieces of the past century. William H. Folsom, the father of one of Brigham Young's wives, drew the original floor plan of the Tabernacle, but the arched roof was Young's idea, engineered by Grow. Angell was responsible for the exterior cornice and the interior woodwork, in addition to the gallery.

The Temple, standing in adjacent splendor, was begun in 1853 but not finished for forty years. Its basic design, like that of the Tabernacle, is largely attributable to Brigham Young—a carpenter and cabinetmaker by trade—with the help of Angell as architect. Joseph Don Carlos Young, Brigham's son, took over in 1887 upon Angell's death. The Temple measures 186.5 x 118.5 feet/ 56.8 x 36 meters, with a 210-foot/64-meter east center tower. Many believe that the Temple is the most impressive religious edifice in the West.

It might be useful to digress here for a moment on Mormon temples and their religious and architectural derivation, for although they are not open to the public (after their dedication), they form an impressive element on the Utah landscape and their exteriors and grounds can be seen by all. Beginning in 1820 Joseph Smith, then a lad of fourteen in western New York State, had, the faith holds, a series of visions. Six years later he was led by an angel's instructions to a hill in Palmyra, New York, and there he found a neatly packed series of thin gold plates incised with inscriptions. Their characters resembled, it is said, those used by the ancient Egyptians. Joseph Smith miraculously translated these plates—which the angel retrieved in 1829—calling them the Book of Mormon, and thenceforth establishing The Church of Jesus Christ of Latter-day Saints. This Egyptian-Hebrew background, evident in the language of the Book of Mormon (which supplements the Old and New Testaments), is slightly suggested in the architecture of Mormon temples. It would seem—at least to some observers—that an influence from the Near East was sought when the Salt Lake Temple was designed. Its towered ends and crenellations, for instance, recall, if vaguely, the Palace of Sargon at Khorsabad (722–705 B.C.). In addition there are certainly Gothic Revival influences in the buttresses, and, according to some, Masonic touches. Note, incidentally, the profusion of symbolic representations of the earth, sun, moon, and stars on the temple's exterior walls.

The separate Assembly Hall, 1877–80, is an example of Victorian Neo-Gothic with seemingly dozens of spires piercing the heavens. Obed Taylor was the architect. It is employed for public worship and as a conference center, and is also used by the community. Altogether, Temple Square is one of the world's most unusual architectural complexes, a compact, fascinating religious compound.

Temple Square (which includes the Tabernacle and the Assembly Hall) is open daily 9:00 A.M.–8:30 P.M. Admission is free. Free tours are given every 5–10 minutes. Tours can also be scheduled by calling (810) 240–4872.

PLUM STREET TEMPLE (1865–66)
8329 Ridge Road
Cincinnati, Ohio

James K. Wilson, architect

Relatively restrained and Saracenic on the exterior but filled with a glorious outburst of Middle Eastern and Gothic architectural motifs and influences within, the Isaac M. Wise Temple (to use its other name) is one of the few of its "style" remaining in the United States. Beautifully maintained—the roof was replaced and the decorative plaster work restenciled as part of a $2 million restoration in 1994–95—it is an outstanding monument; would, only, that it were open more frequently. There is little "formal" architectural tradition for the design of a synagogue, and, as with churches, early temples in the United States followed the various architectural fashions (Georgian in Providence, Greek Revival in Charleston, etc.). However, in the mid-nineteenth century, a mantle of details of vaguely Moorish origin cloaked most temples. At Plum Street they abound, and even include minarets—but all within a homogeneous context. The famous Rabbi Isaac Mayer Wise (1819–1900), who founded Reform Judaism in this country—and had a hand in the temple's design—claimed the Alhambra as its inspiration. It is one of the States' great religious buildings, both outside and in, and is, of course, listed in the National Register of Historic Places.

Open for services. Tours are given on Mondays and Thursdays. Call (513) 793–2556 for hours of services or to arrange a visit.

TEXTILE MILLS (1865–80)
I-195
Fall River, Massachusetts

The granite textile mills of Fall River comprise a sterling chapter in the history of American industrial building, the post-Civil War era sparking its most prolific development. The uniqueness of their appearance stems from the fact that the city rests on an extensive granite ledge. The cheapness and availability of this stone has bequeathed us a series of enormous mills of this handsome material instead of the often-depressing brick found almost everywhere else at this time. Though only the specialist will be concerned with a detailed inspection of the individual buildings—most of which have now lost their textile manufacturing—even the hurried motorist will be impressed while driving along the interstate highway that cruelly bisects the city. The interstate, it should be added, was formerly the Quequechan (that is, "falling water") River from which the mills once drew their power, as it stepped down to Mount Hope Bay. Rarely will one encounter such non-industrial-appearing industrial buildings: with their gray granite walls, white-trimmed windows, and dark roofs, many resemble gigantic barns. Technically they are put together with precisely cut blocks to build up their 3-foot-/1-meter-thick lower walls and the vibration-damping bases required for heavy machinery. The large looms usually occupied the first two floors, with carding, spinning, and dressing above. Dozens of the mill buildings have been reopened as retail stores and/or multiuse buildings, and thus the interiors have been fairly extensively renovated. With such expert workmanship, general feeling for proportion, tower accents, 400 feet/122 meters or more of length, plus often good spatial interaction, they also constitute fine architecture.

Turn off interstate on Pleasant Street or Plymouth Avenue and Rodman Street. Open Monday–Saturday 9:00 A.M.–6:00 P.M., Sunday 12:00 noon–5:00 P.M. Closed Easter, Thanksgiving, and Christmas.

TERRACE HILL (1867–69)
2300 Grand Avenue
Des Moines, Iowa

William W. Boyington, architect

Terrace Hill epitomizes its period—surprisingly so because Des Moines's population was only some 12,000 when this house was built. It bears rewarding comparison with any Victorian mansion in the country. Commissioned by Benjamin Franklin Allen, the state's first million-aire (largely from life insurance), the house and extensive grounds (once 30 acres/12 hectares) are monuments of and to their period. The building's superb present state of preservation is due to the fact that it was occupied until 1956 (except for a period when Allen went bankrupt), generally by presidents of the Equitable of Iowa Insurance Company. Internal changes were made toward the end of the nineteenth century when the kitchen was moved, steam heat installed, stained glass added, and a rock-crystal chandelier of suitable presumption hung in the drawing room, all carried out in the ornate spirit of the time. Upon the death of the last owner—who left a trust fund for its maintenance—most of the contents of the house were given to various descendants and the building closed, none of the heirs electing to live there. But interest in the mansion was so substantial that by 1960 a process of refurnishing got under way. Today its interior is again sumptuous, with some pieces original to the house and all others of the period. In 1971 it was given to the state of Iowa. In 1984 the carriage house was restored; it is currently used for offices and a visitors center. The landscape and formal gardens have also been restored to their Victorian splendor. The architect of this "country residence in modern French design with Mansard roof" was William W. Boyington, probably Chicago's most famous practitioner around the time of that city's great fire (1871), and chiefly remembered today for his Gothic water tower (see facing page) in that city. His Terrace Hill is equally memorable, one of the few remaining masterpieces of its giddy era.

March–December open Tuesday–Saturday 10:00 A.M.–1:30 P.M. Closed for holidays. Admission is $3 for adults, $1 for children ages 6–12, free for children under 6. Guided tours given on the hour and half hour. For more information call (515) 281–3604.

OLD WATER TOWER (1867–69)
806 North Michigan Avenue at East Chicago Avenue
Chicago, Illinois

William W. Boyington, architect

This castellated nugget arose through no Arthurian whimsicality, or because its designer simply liked towers; it was built to contain a standpipe 138 feet/42 meters high and 3 feet/.9 meter in diameter. This cylinder took up the pulsations and pressure variations in the old Corliss engines that once powered the pumps that are still housed across the street. Water to supply Chicago's pumping stations, of which there are twelve, comes from the lake via "cribs" placed several miles offshore, then piped underground. Though this tower is no longer needed (electric pumps have long ago replaced George Corliss's invention), its Gothic Revival fancifulness is still very much needed as an architectural celebration.

It is one of the few structures (the only public "building") that withstood the 1871 fire; it also survived the street-widening of 1918. The limestone tower and the pump house were both restored in 1913–16. As Carl Condit observed in his book *The Chicago School of Architecture* (University of Chicago Press, 1964), it is "as sacred as a religious symbol." The Water Tower was renovated (1978) into a Visitors Information Center; then from 1985 to 1992 it was used as administrative offices for the Chicago Office of Tourism. In 1994 it was renovated once again and reopened as Chicago's Historic Water Tower Visitor Welcome Center.

Open Monday–Friday 9:30 A.M.–6:00 P.M., Saturday 10:00 A.M.–6:00 P.M., Sunday 1:00–5:00 P.M. (June–August open Monday–Saturday until 7:00 P.M., Sunday until 6:00 P.M.) Closed for holidays. For more information call (312) 744-2400. The building is included on the Chicago Architecture Foundation's Michigan Avenue tour; the cost is $5. The building is also included on the CAF's bus tour; the cost is $25. For more information on CAF tours call (312) 922-3432.

EADS BRIDGE (1867–74)
Washington Avenue, St. Louis, Missouri to
East River Front, East Saint Louis, Illinois

James B. Eads, engineer

The Eads Bridge—the Great Illinois and St. Louis Bridge—represents one of the supreme developments of America's early technical know-how. On 4 July 1874, it opened a new phase in spanning spaces (center arch 520 feet/158 meters, the two adjacent arches 502 feet/153 meters each). By so doing it accelerated the push of the railroads towards the Pacific, and thus the opening of the West. The struggles that James Buchanan Eads (1820–87) went through— he had never built a bridge before, let alone an "impossible" one of this scope—make fascinating reading. Eads immediately recognized that the bridge's foundations would have to be on bedrock (in places 103 feet/31 meters deep), and placing these footings in a powerful, swift (up to 12 mph/19 kph), arbitrarily shifting river proved no simple matter. Legend has it that Eads at the age of twenty-two had invented a diving bell (to recover—highly successfully— cargo from sunken river steamers); although this has never been proved, he certainly had underwater expertise that served him well when he had to devise the large caissons necessary to protect workmen building the bridge's foundations. (Eads pioneered caisson use in the United States on this job.) Moreover he had *walked* over much of the bottom of the Mississippi with his diving apparatus, and knew its forces and treacheries at first hand. He also knew iron, steel, its producers, and metal-skilled labor from building a series of remarkably successful iron-clad gunboats for Union use in the Civil War; his first was launched a year before the Monitor slid down the ways.

However, Eads was only a self-trained engineer, and for him to attempt to design and construct the then-longest bridge in the world was a staggering undertaking. (The three combined arches of his bridge made it the longest: Thomas Telford's Menai Suspension Bridge of 1819–26 in Wales spanned 579 feet/176 meters, while Charles Ellet's suspension bridge at Wheeling, West Virginia covered 1,010 feet/308 meters in 1849.) Although the bridge was constructed largely of wrought iron, Eads also used chrome alloy steel, a material whose economical production was untried as a major structural element. This was, indeed, the first structural use of alloy steel for bridges in the country—"one of the great calculated risks of engineering history," as Joseph Gies put it in his *Bridges and Men* (Doubleday, 1963). (Cast iron and wrought iron, including wrought-iron wire cables, had, of course, been employed earlier.) For his bridge Eads used steel tubing, 18 inches/46 centimeters in diameter and 2.5 inches/64 millimeters thick for the enormous supporting arches. By erecting scaffolding atop his previously constructed masonry piers, he was able to cantilever his tubed trusses foot by foot from each side of the piers until they met heroically in the center of their spans. (The mean high water clearance was 55 feet/17 meters.) The two decks of the bridge (the top for vehicles and pedestrians, the lower for railroads) are supported on double-tube arches by multiplane, Warren truss triangulations, which anticipated the space frame so popular today. The Eads Bridge is one of the signal monuments of the evolving technical ability—"the innocent daring" (Gies)—of the United States. Its esthetics are also potent. The spidery, lattice lightness of the supporting members against the Roman aqueduct grandeur of the granite-faced limestone piers, plus the fact that the center arch is slightly wider than the other two (to give more visual life), combine to make this the outstanding non-suspension bridge in the country. It is appropriate that one of the significant contributions of nineteenth-century engineering lies only a few hundred feet away from one of the most poetic of the twentieth—the Gateway Arch (see page 486), also of steel. Colonel Henry Flad was Eads's constant assistant; Charles Pfeifer and Professor William Chauvenet of Washington University were structural consultants. The bridge was declared a National Historic Monument in 1965.

In 1974 train traffic stopped using the bridge until the early 1980s, when it was restored for rail use; Metrolink began using it for light rail use in 1993. The vehicular deck was closed to automobile traffic in the late 1980s due to structural conditions. It is currently under reconstruction and is scheduled to be open for passenger traffic in 1997. A sidewalk for pedestrians and bicycles should also be in use by that date.

FORT CONCHO (1868–81)
213 East Avenue D
San Angelo, Texas

The fort buff will want to see these sixteen original buildings, five reconstructed buildings, and one stabilized ruin. Most are made of local limestone, with beams of pecan—the state tree—and wood shingles. The fort was an important base during the Indian Wars and at times housed several distinguished black cavalry regiments, nicknamed the "buffalo soldiers." Fort Concho was founded by the Fourth Cavalry in 1867. Abandoned in 1889, the fort experienced ups and downs in private hands until the Headquarters Building became a museum in 1930 and a restoration campaign was begun. It currently features exhibits and restored interiors focusing on the Indian Wars period. Fort Concho is a registered National Historic Landmark.

Open Tuesday–Saturday 10:00 A.M.–5:00 P.M., Sunday 1:00–5:00 P.M. Closed Thanksgiving, Christmas, and New Year's Day. Admission is $2 for adults, $1.50 for senior citizens, $1.25 for students ages 6–18. Walking tours available. For more information call (915) 657-4444.

LADD & BUSH BANK (1869/1967)
302 State Street at Commercial Street
Salem, Oregon

John Nestor, architect
Skidmore, Owings, and Merrill, architects of renovation

A marvellous building which possesses facades with some of the most superb cast-iron work in the country. The bank was established as an independent downstate bank with architectural influence from the Ladd & Tilton Bank (1868) in Portland—probably through commonality of partial ownership by William S. Ladd. The Salem design was based directly on the Portland prototype; the Willamette Iron Foundry produced the original molds and shipped them to Salem, where they were probably cast by the Drake Iron Works. In 1954 the Portland building was replaced by a new and larger structure, but its cast-iron front was carefully preserved. When the Salem bank needed to be expanded in 1967, having been acquired by the United States National Bank, the cast-iron sections of the Portland building were purchased, moved some 40 miles/64 kilometers south, and added to the Salem core; almost nothing of the old was altered except its length, depth, and cornice. (The facades now measure 102 x 165 feet/31 x 50 meters. Note that the bay width of the addition is a tiny bit narrower.) During the renovation and expansion the structural frame was changed from brick to reinforced concrete, over which the cast iron was meticulously relaced. Skidmore, Owings & Merrill were the architects for the expanded building. The garlanded, emblazoned, and "rusticated" main pilasters, the rich keystones and flanking voussoirs, and the solid balustrade on top—all wrapped in recollections of Venetian glory and painted to resemble stone—are superb testaments to the skill and development of cast-iron workmanship in the United States, even under "frontier" conditions. The interior has of necessity been altered, but the beautifully designed and maintained exterior (diminished by the sign over the front door) ranks among the masterpieces of its kind.

Open Monday–Thursday 10:00 A.M.–5:00 P.M., Friday 10:00 A.M.–6:00 P.M. Closed for holidays. Free tours can be arranged by calling (503) 399-4035.

PIONEER POST OFFICE (1869–75)
520 Southwest Morrison Street between 5th and 6th streets
Portland, Oregon

Alfred B. Mullett, architect

Century-old government buildings are a vanishing species in the United States, and this—the oldest standing federal structure in the Northwest—is of value partly because it still exists, but more so because of its capable architecture. Designed in Washington, D.C., it was begun only ten years after Oregon attained statehood. Alfred B. Mullett was later (1888) responsible for that gutsy exaltation in Washington known as the Executive Office Building (see page 251), but here in Portland he worked more timorously with a subdued Classically girdled rectangle topped by a slightly discordant cupola. The post office's two upper stories, neatly divided by Tuscan pilasters, rest on a slightly rusticated ground floor; its projected pediments on the long sides and chaste detailing all combine to produce a patrician structure. Note the diminution of the windows with the rising floors. The building is also used for the Federal Court House, but the Custom House moved to its own quarters in 1901. A wing was added to the west side (1903–05) to create greater square footage, primarily for the post office. Once threatened as "surplus" because of the completion of new facilities, the Pioneer Post Office was carefully remodeled in 1973 for judicial use by Allen, McMath & Hawkins. The large, very dignified courtroom on the second floor for the United States Court of Appeals is the finest single room.

Open Monday–Friday 8:00 A.M.–4:00 P.M. Closed for holidays. Free tours can be arranged by calling (503) 326–2107.

BROOKLYN BRIDGE (1869–83)
City Hall Park, Manhattan; Cadman Plaza, Brooklyn
New York, New York

John Augustus Roebling, Washington Roebling, and Emily Roebling, engineers

The Crystal Palace in London (1851), the Brooklyn Bridge in New York (1869–83), and the Eiffel Tower in Paris (1889) constitute the greatest spatial conquests of the nineteenth century, as Sigfried Giedion (*Space, Time and Architecture*, Harvard University Press, 1941 *et seq.*) and James Marston Fitch (*American Architecture: The Historical Forces*, Houghton Mifflin, 1966), among others, have so excitingly shown us. The exhibition hall covered vast spaces with an all-glass prefabricated system (the building was later dismantled and moved to another site; sadly, it burned in 1941); the bridge spanned a staggering horizontal space (1,595 feet/486 meters); while the tower's height of 984 feet/300 meters was unmatched for years—until New York's own Empire State Building (see page 368) was finished in 1931 at 1,250 feet/381 meters (without TV mast). Architecture and architectural engineering would never be the same: the development of the Modern Movement was inevitable. The study of history is the study of the shape of the tool, and these heroic structures employed "tools" never previously deemed possible.

The Brooklyn Bridge established a scale so gigantic that one gasped—and one still does. A walk along its centrally placed, elevated pedestrian way ranks among the great urban experiences, with the warp and woof of the cables weaving the sky together to envelop the astounding backdrop of Manhattan or Brooklyn. (The impression by car is disappointing because of the boxed-in structure of the vehicular level.)

John Augustus Roebling (1806–69), who came to this country in 1831 from his native Germany, arrived here with a splendid education and a burning faith in steel suspension bridges. The Chinese had used iron chain spans before the seventh century (Carl Condit mentions A.D. 580), and it is certain that a chain bridge of wrought iron, the 70-foot/21-meter Wynch Bridge, was erected in England by 1741. Wrought iron reached its peak with Thomas Telford's startling Menai Straits Bridge (1819–26)—"the grandfather of all modern suspension bridges" (David B. Steinman)—which spans 579 feet/176 meters. James Finley and Charles Ellet in the United States had also done pioneering work, and Marc Séguin in France in 1824 had erected near Tournon the world's first "wire rope" bridge, a foot span still in use. Roebling was, of course, familiar with all of these and the others they inspired, but he had greater and more improbable notions in mind. His first American effort (1845) was in Pittsburgh, and, as he progressed, he developed the concept of spinning and tightly binding with a jacket the multitude of cables that stretched their catenaries over vast rivers. (Previously the cables had been only partially clamped and rarely covered.)

The Brooklyn Bridge's center span of 1,595 feet/486 meters was more than fifty percent longer than the previous record, which was that of the Wheeling Bridge in West Virginia. Its

double-arched, 276.5-foot-/84-meter-high, Gothic towers may seem quaint today (actually their shapes approximate the forces acting on them), while Montgomery Schuyler felt (1883) that the "disappearance" of the cables into the tower head was an act of "architectural barbarism." The employment of both vertical and inclined cables as floor stays (to uphold the deck) represented unnecessary complexity—widely "fanned hangers" are today obsolete—but their spreading angles do reach out to clutch, like some giant web, both decking and pedestrians. The bridge, almost needless to add, conquered the world.

Tragically, John Augustus Roebling's foot was crushed soon after the bridge was begun, and he died from gangrene. His talented son, Washington, supervised the construction, only himself to suffer from caisson disease (although he did not die until 1926), leaving his wife Emily to mediate on-site. Roebling, his son, and his daughter-in-law revealed new concepts of space; their Brooklyn Bridge was not substantially exceeded until the George Washington Bridge of 1931.

Open twenty-four hours to both vehicular and pedestrian traffic. PA 10/58

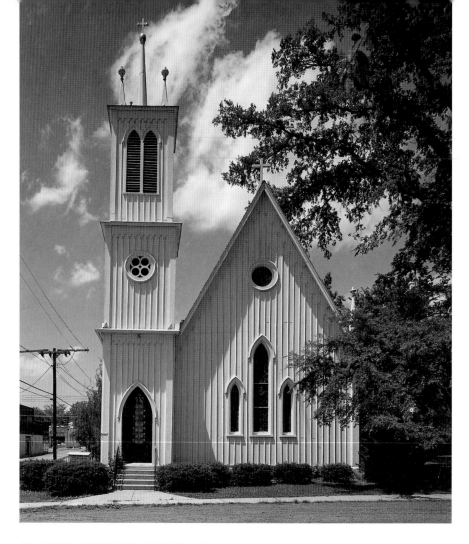

ST. PAUL'S EPISCOPAL CHURCH (1870–71)
East Reynolds Street at Knob
Ironton, Missouri

Epitomizing the small-town, all-wood, Victorian Gothic Episcopal church of one hundred and more years ago, St. Paul's remains refreshingly untouched in the twentieth century. Its steeply pitched roof—unexpectedly decorated with a large chevron pattern—its white, vertical batten sides, and its unspoiled interior with hand-carved pews combine to make the church an architectural autograph of another era. A locally prominent judge donated the land and, apparently, the design, though it is doubtful that he drew it up himself. There were, of course, the usual English and American architectural handbooks and magazines that all builders could—and did—turn to and copy from. Wooden village Gothic was popular for churches from New England (there is a fine one in Ipswich, Massachusetts) to the South (Talbotton, Georgia), thence irregularly across the country. But this beautifully preserved exemplar in a Missouri town ranks with the best. It was listed in the National Register of Historic Places in 1969.

Open Monday–Saturday 9:00 A.M.–4:30 P.M. Sunday service held at 11:00 A.M. Half-hour tours can be arranged by calling (314) 546–2397.

OLANA (1870–74/1888–90)
Route 9G
Hudson, New York

Frederic Edwin Church, architect
Calvert Vaux, consulting architect

Olana's opulent architecture matches its spectacular site some 500 feet/152 meters above the Hudson River. This thirty-seven-room mansion is one of the key houses of the freewheeling "Oriental" school of the latter part of the nineteenth century. In an era when anything went, everything happened at Olana, at least everything that a lover of the Near East could contrive, collect, and attach to vertical walls. Kublai Khan himself could hardly have outdone Frederic Edwin Church, professionally aided by Calvert Vaux. (Church added the studio wing and gallery himself in 1888–90.) Fortunately the heirs of this century-old house lived in it until recently so that its emblazoned interior has been well maintained. All the furnishings are original; there are even ancient photographs to show the furniture arrangements. Fortunately, also, the state of New York, together with concerned private individuals, purchased the house, its contents, and the inspiring hilltop site of 250 acres/101 hectares on which the mansion rests. (Also included were a substantial number of Church's unbelievably popular paintings of the geographic majesty of many sections of the world.) In 1967 it was opened to the public.

Located .8 mile/1.3 kilometers south of Rip Van Winkle Bridge (NY 23). April 15–Labor Day open Wednesday–Saturday 10:00 A.M.–4:00 P.M., Sunday 12:00 noon–4:00 P.M. Labor Day–October 31 open Wednesday–Sunday 12:00 noon–4:00 P.M. Admission is $3 for adults, $1.50 for children ages 5–11. All visits are guided; 50-minute tours given regularly. Grounds are open daily 8:30 A.M.–sundown; admission is free. For more information call (518) 828–0135.

GRAND OPERA HOUSE
(1871/1976)
(formerly Masonic Hall)
818 North Market Street
between 8th and 9th streets
Wilmington, Delaware

Thomas Dixon and Charles L. Carson, architects

Wilmington's old Masonic Hall has been totally restored outside and in as the Grand Opera House, creating a focus for the city's pedestrian mall (1974, David Crane & Partners, landscape architects). The building is a notable addition to the city, its late nineteenth-century Parisian-inspired facade projecting a rich and well-composed example of cast-iron work. Built by the Masons as a performance hall (their offices and recreational facilities still occupy the top floor), there are Masonic details throughout: note, for instance, the eye in the pediment of the central bay. The ground-floor shops, all brightly refurbished, were part of the original design, as was the prominent filigree of cast iron capping the slate of the mansard roof. The 1,100-seat horseshoe-shaped auditorium is now used by the Delaware Symphony, the Wilmington Opera Society, and a number of both nonprofit and corporate groups. Whereas the exterior needed only a moderate amount of cleaning and restoration, including the recasting of some pieces of cast iron, the interior, which had been cannibalized, required a complete technical updating, fire protection, and the provision of general amenities. These improvements—including the replacement of the frescoed ceiling—were completed with the aid of the original drawings. Grieves-Armstrong-Childs were the architects of the restoration; Steven T. Baird, consulting architect for cast iron; Roger R. Morgan, theater consultant; and Klepper, Marshall, King, acoustic consultants. A fine facility of which city, citizens, and the professionals concerned can be proud. It is listed on the National Register of Historic Places and is a charter member of the newly formed League of Historic American Theatres.

Open for performances. Tours can be arranged by calling (302) 658-7897.

EXECUTIVE OFFICE BUILDING (1871–88)
Pennsylvania Avenue at 17th Street NW
Washington, D.C.

Alfred B. Mullett, architect

The former State, War and Navy Building is unfortunately only open to the public for limited Saturday tours. However, as its prime architectural attraction lies in the almost palpitating outside walls that encompass this vast pile, much of the building can be appreciated by strolling by. Symmetrically and compositionally holding down a whole block with a vigor that would do credit to European grandezza, the English-born Alfred B. Mullett's handling of scale, modulation, and site rank this building high among Second Empire buildings in this country. There are, reputedly, nine hundred Tuscan columns on the outside and 2 miles/3.2 kilometers of corridors within. Moreover, it is claimed that this was the largest office building in the world when built. (Mullett, who was supervising architect of the Treasury Department, 1865–74, also designed the somewhat similar Old Post Office in St. Louis [see page 254] and the San Francisco Mint. In ill health toward the end of his life, he committed suicide in 1890.)

Open Saturday 8:30 A.M.–12:00 noon. Closed the Saturdays of Thanksgiving weekend, Christmas weekend, and New Year's weekend. All visits are guided. Free 90-minute tours given each Saturday on the half hour; advance reservation is required. To reserve a tour call (202) 395–5895.

PENNSYLVANIA ACADEMY OF THE FINE ARTS (1872–76)
118 North Broad Street at Cherry Street
Philadelphia, Pennsylvania

Frank Furness and George W. Hewitt, architects

Frank Furness (1839–1912)—"fearless Frank" he has with reason been called—was probably the gutsiest architect who ever walked the North American continent. His extraordinary buildings, of which, sadly, many have been demolished, apotheosize boldness, exude power even when small in size, and clearly anticipate what is now called the New Brutalism—they are preposterously wonderful. The buildings are, indeed, like the man himself, who won the Congressional Medal during the Civil War as Captain Frank Furness of the 6th Pennsylvania Cavalry, for carrying a heavy box of live ammunition to a beleaguered outpost, an action that necessitated directly exposing himself to enemy fire; he is probably the only architect in the United States to win the nation's highest military honor. Furness, who was born in Philadelphia, worked for the famous Richard Morris Hunt in New York before returning home, thus acquiring a practical, French-influenced background. (Interestingly the young Louis Sullivan worked briefly for Furness until the depression of 1873—the two reputedly became great friends. Sullivan, it should be added, was also undoubtedly influenced in Philadelphia by William J. Johnston's eight-story-plus cupola Jayne Building of 1849–51, then probably the tallest structure in the world. It had a materials hoist but no passenger elevator. The building was destroyed in 1958.) Furness's architecture in his heyday was an amalgam of late Victorian Gothic plus the Queen Anne style, with a bit of H. H. Richardson, his contemporary, in the background. The writings of John Ruskin (*The Stones of Venice*, 1851–53) and of Eugène-Emanuel Viollet-le-Duc were also influential. However, Furness manipulated and sublimated these fashionable facets with the force of a pile driver, achieving an intensity and compaction rarely seen.

His greatest surviving building is that for the Pennsylvania Academy of the Fine Arts, the oldest institution of its kind in the country (founded in 1805), combining a distinguished art school (on the lower floor) with a first-rate museum. Its commission was won by Furness and George W. Hewitt through an invited competition. Though Hewitt left Furness a year after the academy was finished (to set up an office with his brother William D.), his contribution to its design perhaps has been underplayed. For Hewitt's work—including some fifty churches—reveled in the polychromatic Neo-Gothic style so apparent in the Academy, particularly in the stunning stair hall. Observe on the building's facade—probably largely by Furness—that although each element is prodigiously detailed, the whole has been orchestrated with tremendous authority. (Robert Venturi in his provocative book *Complexity and Contradiction in Architecture* [Museum of Modern Art, 1966] wrote of an equally "violent" but now destroyed Furness building that "it is an almost insane short story of a castle on a city street." For a thorough and up-to-date review of Furness's work, see George E. Thomas, Jeffrey A Cohen, and Michael J. Lewis, *Frank Furness: The Complete Works* (Princeton Architectural Press, 1991). The building was formally opened to the public during the nation's Centennial Exposition in Philadelphia; let us hope that it graces its three hundredth birthday.

Hyman Myers, an architect and Furness scholar working with the firm of Day & Zimmermann, was responsible for the restoration of the building; it was sumptuously carried out in 1974–76. The interior is almost phosphorescent with its newly renovated richness.

Open Monday–Saturday 10:00 A.M.–5:00 P.M., Sunday 11:00 A.M.–5:00 P.M. Closed Thanksgiving, Christmas, and New Year's Day. Admission is $5.95 for adults, $4.95 for students and senior citizens, $3.95 for children ages 5–12, free for children under 5. Tours are given Saturday–Sunday at 12:30 and 2:00 P.M. Self-guided audio tours also available. For more information call (215) 972–7600.

OLD POST OFFICE (1872–84/1984)
801 Olive Street between 8th and 9th streets
St. Louis, Missouri

Alfred B. Mullett, architect

Designed by the doughty architect of the old State, War and Navy Building in Washington (now the Executive Office Building, see page 251), with "War and Navy" and the then-recent Civil War possibly influencing its stronghold aspect, this robust number has only recently been reprieved from a fate worse than a parking lot. Though it might faintly suggest a forti-fied building, the 30-foot-/9.1-meter-deep areaway surrounding it is *not* a moat but a light well; and the inside iron shutters were for fire protection, *not* against mob violence, their circular holes for pressure release (in case of fire), *not* gun ports. Moreover there is no truth to the rumor that there was a well in the basement to slake defenders in case of attack. (However, it was expected that gold bullion would be stored there.) Actually little short of an eight-point Richter scale earthquake could harm its granite walls, so substantially was it built. Erected par-tially on quicksand, some 4,400 Missouri pine pilings 34 feet/10.4 meters long, topped with 4 feet/1.2 meters of concrete, were needed for its foundations. But this solidity, which fills an entire downtown block, was realized with eminent architectural skill in scale buildup and an almost Sansovinian play of light and shade (plus a share of local scandal). Built as a combined Custom House and Post Office, its design reflects Second Empire France—appropriate in a city dedicated to that country's Louis IX, or St. Louis (1214–70). Note on the 8th Street pedi-ment the copies of the statues of *Peace* and *Vigilance* by Daniel Chester French (the originals are now located inside the building).

The federal courts having moved out in 1935 (the Post Office in 1913), the building was declared surplus and its future began to be in doubt, particu-larly as local real-estate interests eyed the site. But concerned citizens, led by Austin P. Leland and buttressed by the indomitable George McCue of the *St. Louis Post-Dispatch*, and backed by the National Trust, the American Institute of Archi-tects, and the Society of Architectural Historians, effected its saving. The General Services Admini-stration, which owns the building, has been most solicitous regarding its future, and conducted a limited competition for its adaptive use. This was won by Patty, Berkebile, Nelson Associates of Kansas City in a joint venture with Harry Weese & Associates of Chicago. It was finished in 1984, the hundredth anniversary of its opening. The Old Post Office now houses both federal offices and com-mercial tenants. It is, without question, one of the finest of its period in the country and high among the fifty or so structures designed by Alfred Butt Mullett when Supervising Architect to the Treasury Department (1866–74).

Open Monday–Friday 8:00 A.M.–5:00 P.M. Closed for holidays.

PHILADELPHIA CITY HALL (1872–1901)
Market Street at Broad Street
Philadelphia, Pennsylvania

John McArthur, Jr., architect

Pride of city fathers has never been more exuberantly expressed than in this glorious mastodon that dominates downtown Philadelphia. (One might add that questionable city and county finances and patronage have rarely been more conspicuously monumentalized.) Ossa on Pelion pales beside it, and the United States Capitol in Washington reputedly could fit inside with ease. Ambition has been matched by performance. The central bays are splendiferous, the corners magnificent—all in a late Second Empire "Louvre" Style—and the tower outrageous, so outrageous in fact that the building took thirty years to complete. The 511-foot/156-meter tower (without statue) claims to be the tallest all-masonry construction (that is, with no steel) achieved; its tremendous weight demanded walls 22 feet/6.7 meters thick at the bottom. (It is, in fact, 45 feet/14 meters lower than the Washington Monument, which, however, was not finished until 1885. Moreover, Philadelphia City Hall's tower is of brick and masonry up to the level below the clock, and its upper stages were of cast iron painted to match the gray granite. In the course of a recent restoration, the cast iron was covered with approximately two thousand pieces of steel.)

William Penn, all 37 feet/11 meters and 53,348 pounds/24,200 kilograms of him, surveys from his vantage point atop the tower the legacy of his enlightened leadership that did so much to plant the city's seed of growth in "the virgin settlement of this province." The building stands on the precise spot selected for it by Penn in 1683. Binoculars are recommended to study Penn and the smaller sculptures that leap from every cranny of the outside. All continents, all races, and practically all animals can be seen, carved by Alexander Milne Calder, who, like John McArthur, Jr., the building's architect, was a Scot immigrant. (Calder's grandson and namesake, of course, ranked with the most noted sculptors of the twentieth century.) The evidence also seems conclusive that Thomas Ustick Walter had a hand in the design of the tower and inner decoration, for in 1865, upon resigning as architect of the Capitol, he returned to Philadelphia and joined forces with McArthur.

In plan City Hall describes a hollow square with all rooms facing either outward or onto the inner courtyard. The interior attains perhaps its greatest architectural impact in the six-story-high open stairwells located at the four corners. The council chamber, the caucus room, the mayor's reception room, and the conversation hall, in all their glory, should also be seen. There will never be another city hall like this one. Fortunately a 1957 committee of the American Institute of Architects, in strongly recommending renovation over destruction and "modern" replacement, said "City Hall is perhaps the greatest single effort of late-nineteenth-century American architecture" (quoted by John Maass in an excellent article in the *AIA Journal*, February 1965). A major renovation is currently under way, to be completed in 2001.

The tour information center and the observation deck are open Monday–Friday 9:30 A.M.–4:30 P.M. Closed for holidays. Admission is free. Free tours are given Monday–Friday at 12:30 p.m. For more information call (215) 686–2840. JAIA 2/65

IOWA STATE CAPITOL (1873–86)
East Locust at East 9th Street
Des Moines, Iowa

Cochrane & Piquenard, architects

The architects of state capitols—obviously with the enthusiastic support of their clients—were seemingly as much concerned with the dome as with office square footage. Thomas Ustick Walter's 258-foot-/79-meter-high bubble in Washington, D.C. (see page 128) had established an almost irresistible precedent. So it is in Des Moines, where a 23-karat gold-leafed dome, 275 feet/84 meters high, shines throughout the day, a lighthouse of politics, so to speak, warning and/or reassuring as the case may be. This, the state's fifth capitol, succeeds doubly, or rather quintuply, for its one great dome has a scale-intensifying backup dome at each corner. On the inside a vast rotunda, decked with appropriate murals and flags and twenty-nine different marbles, introduces one to the glories of the state. The commission for the Capitol was awarded by a competition, with the New Hampshire-born John C. Cochrane teaming with the French-born Alfred H. Piquenard to capture first place. There is an obvious similarity between the Des Moines Capitol and that which Cochrane designed for Springfield, Illinois.

Open Monday–Friday 8:00 A.M.–4:30 P.M., Saturday–Sunday and holidays 8:00 A.M.–4:00 P.M. Admission is free. Free tours of the building (40 minutes) and the dome (10 minutes) are given daily; call (515) 281-5591 for times.

MARK TWAIN HOUSE (1874/1881)
351 Farmington Avenue
Hartford, Connecticut

Edward T. Potter, architect

The Mark Twain House embodies a period of architecture that is only now being properly appreciated. Its fanciful Stick Style contains hints of the Bernese Oberland in Switzerland, of a hill station in Simla, India, and of the work of H. H. Richardson and his compatriots in the United States. For roughly two decades (the 1870s and '80s) the style gloried in the expression of wood, particularly with structural outrigging, and in a prominent covering of shingles. When structure became more contained and shingles more prominent the style was then termed the "Shingle Style." Though Edward Potter specialized in churches, primarily in a Romanesque vein, here he persuaded Mark Twain to let him design "a poet's house." After Louis Comfort Tiffany and Associated Artists added their embellishments to the interior (1881), the result became one of the most important dwellings of its period; a form of Stick Style fireworks. A servants' wing was also added in 1881 under the direction of Alfred H. Thorp, Potter's assistant. Reputedly all of the Clemens family dearly loved this house, and the care, affection, and money that they lavished on it can be seen today. Note, incidentally, the picture window through the dining room fireplace. Because of heavy personal debts (in the basement is the typesetting machine on which Mr. Clemens lost a fortune), the house was sold in 1903 (Mark Twain died in 1910), and subsequently was used as a private school, warehouse, apartments, and a branch public library. Threatened with destruction in 1929, it was purchased by friends, but it was not until 1955 that sufficient funds were raised to undertake the complete restoration necessary, including the restenciling of the Tiffany decorations.

Open Monday and Wednesday–Saturday 9:30 A.M.–5:00 P.M., Sunday 12:00 noon–5:00 P.M. From Memorial Day to Columbus Day and in December, also open Tuesday 9:30 A.M.–5:00 P.M. Closed Easter, Thanksgiving, Christmas Eve, Christmas, and New Year's Day. Admission is $6.50 for adults, $6 for senior citizens, $2.75 for children ages 6–16. Guided tours are available; the last tour leaves at 4:00 P.M. For more information call (203) 493–6411.

TRINITY CHURCH (1874–77/1897)
Copley Square
Boston, Massachusetts

Henry Hobson Richardson, architect

The stalwart ruggedness, even majesty, of Trinity rightly places it among the country's signal churches. Although its commission was won in an invited competition in 1872, many changes—fortunately—were made before the church was completed. Its front porch (not by Richardson but based on his design) was not finished until eleven years after the architect's untimely death (at forty-eight) in 1886. Trinity's exterior massing reaches an almost thundering climax in a series of scale buildups culminating in the enormous turreted tower at the crossing. Richardson wanted a strong central tower—"the main feature," as he put it—to hold down the visual approaches to the church from any angle. His studies, drawn after winning the competition, continually enlarged the tower's bulk, in the process changing it from an octagon to a more compelling square form. In the meantime engineers determined that the landfill on which the church stood could not support the reputed 18 million pounds/8.2 million kilograms to be placed upon it in spite of 4,500 piles already (1873) driven into the ground. Though some weight was pared from the tower, most reduction was achieved by lowering the walls, a move that caused Richardson proper anguish. Not until 1875, after the adjacent parish house had been completed, did the tower reach its final form, and above-ground construction on the church itself commence.

In the design of Trinity references to medieval France are obvious: its Louisiana-born, Beaux-Arts-trained architect, who spent five years in Paris, wrote that "the style of the Church may be characterized as a free rendering of the French Romanesque, inclining particularly to the school that flourished in the eleventh century in Central France" (*Trinity Church in the City of Boston, 1733–1933*, Boston, 1933). However, Ann Jensen Adams writes in *The Art Bulletin* (September 1980) that HHR was also impressed by G. E. Street's description and illustration of the Old Cathedral of Salamanca in his book *Gothic Architecture in Spain* (London, 1865), a copy of which Richardson possessed. But these influences constituted no mere copying. In an age of architectural eclecticism the introduction of "new" architectural forms, here freely adapted from eleventh- and twelfth-century Europe, occasioned an esthetic revolution in the United States, one that gave buildings a vivid—if at times overworked—imprimatur known as the Richardsonian Romanesque. This was, it should be added, a uniquely American development, refreshingly untouched by contemporary influences from Europe. As Wayne Andrews wisely put it, "Richardson... brought order out of chaos" (*Architecture, Ambition and Americans*, Harper, 1955).

The interior of Trinity, in plan a compact Greek cross plus apse, proclaims a unity—once one adjusts to its dim level of natural light (compared to the

radiance of early meeting houses)—that surprises by its oneness and by its sweep upward. This stems from the prominence of the inner void of the square tower, which gathers the spaces together from nave and transepts, pauses before the chancel (refurbished by Charles D. Maginnis in 1938), then shoots heavenward 103 feet/31 meters. This three-dimensional journey is enlivened by polychromy (of complex iconography) by John La Farge, and magnetized by the stronger light from the tower windows. The resulting "color church" forms one of the most successful collaborations between architect and artist in this country. (It should be added that the famous Phillips Brooks, the rector, also made many suggestions.) It is important to note that the interior is transformed when the artificial lights are turned on: without them the church approaches the gloomy; with them it almost bursts into song. The boldness of the inside (restored in 1956–57) thus matches that of the exterior—and Richardson was always bold. Hugh Shepley, of Shepley, Rutan and Coolidge, completed the west towers and the porch in 1897.

Open daily 8:00 A.M.–6:00 P.M. Closed Thanksgiving, Christmas, and New Year's Day. Sunday services held at 8:00, 9:00, and 11:00 A.M. and 6:00 P.M. Free tours given after Sunday 11:00 A.M. services.

RAEDER PLACE (1874/1978)
(formerly Christian Peper Tobacco Company Building)
727 North First Street
St. Louis, Missouri

Frederick W. Raeder, architect

Sigfried Giedion, the Swiss architectural historian whose book *Space, Time and Architecture* (Harvard University Press, 1941) opened the eyes of the contemporary world to the meaning and contribution of the buildings of the past, described the St. Louis waterfront area and its cast-iron architecture as "a witness to one of the most exciting periods in the development of America. Some of its commercial buildings—fur and china warehouses, Pony Express offices, ordinary business blocks—exhibited an architecture far in advance of the ordinary standards at the time of their erection." Hundreds and hundreds of cast-iron-fronted and supported buildings were put up following the great fire of 1849 (which started in Laclede's Landing Area), as the city sought to recover quickly to maintain its position as the gateway to the West. (The California Gold Rush also took place in 1849.) The speedily erected, more or less fireproof, cast-iron facades and framing were ideal for the job. Alas, today only a pitiful few remain, the great majority having been destroyed, ironically, for the Jefferson National Expansion Memorial and its arch. Among the best is the six-story Raeder Place. Possessed of good scale and resolute detail, it is a century-old structure of great value in the history of the city. Note the round-headed windows of its well-lit east facade. Laclede's Landing Area underwent a startling "rediscovery" in the late 1970s, and many of its sturdy but shabby structures have been brightly rehabilitated into a variety of tempting shops, offices, and restaurants. Raeder Place was renovated in 1978 into restaurants on the ground floor with office space above by architects Kimble A. Cohn & Associates.

Lobby open to the public daily 8:00 a.m.–11:00 p.m. Restaurants also open to the public.

JEFFERSON MARKET BRANCH LIBRARY (1875–77/1967)
425 Avenue of the Americas at West 10th Street
New York, New York

Frederick C. Withers and Calvert Vaux, architects
Giorgio Cavaglieri, architect of rehabilitation

Refulgent on the exterior with almost all the architectural trappings that the High Victorian possessed, and highlighted within by parades of original stained-glass windows and doughtily carved black walnut doorways, the Jefferson Market Branch Library offers a nostalgic rallying point for Greenwich Village. (Some of this Ruskin-influenced design can be traced to the fact that both architects were British born.) The building was not always an amiable forum, for a courthouse (with a few overnight cells) occupied its premises until 1932, while the notorious Women's House of Detention remained next door until 1973 (its cleared site is now a cheerful community garden). Threatened with destruction when it became redundant (1958), the courthouse's venerable charms were saved by dedicated friends (including then-Mayor Robert Wagner) to become a local library. Its legal chambers were transformed to bright, lofty reading rooms by the skill and imagination of architect Giorgio Cavaglieri. He preserved where possible, put in a catwalk to conform to the building code, accented the dark woodwork with light walls, and installed new light fixtures. He also sandblasted the brick vaulting in the basement to turn this once lugubrious spot into a fine reference room (note the light fixtures). The multicolored exterior was thoroughly cleaned, reinforced where necessary, but left basically as it was to let us savor, one hundred years later, one of the wildest periods of architectural hedonism. The tower, typical—indeed almost mandatory—of its era (note the gargoyles), was not mere whimsy; its 98-foot-/30-meter-high deck served as a fire lookout for the neighborhood. One of the delights of a vanishing species.

Open Monday 10:00 A.M.–6:00 P.M., Tuesday 12:00 noon–6:00 P.M., Wednesday 12:00 noon–8:00 P.M., Thursday–Friday 12:00 noon–6:00 P.M., Saturday 10:00 A.M.–5:00 P.M. Closed Sundays and holidays. For more information call (212) 243-4334.

MITCHELL BUILDING (1876–78), 207 East Michigan Street
MACKIE BUILDING (1879–80), 225 East Michigan Street
Milwaukee, Wisconsin

Edward Townsend Mix, architect

Two of the most ebullient office buildings of the 1870s—designed by the same architect and built within a few years of each other—stand adjacent and lightly connected in downtown Milwaukee. Their architectural hedonism, the frenetic modulation of their facades, and their presumptuous ambitions bring cheer to the central business district—they are a veritable Damon and Pythias of office buildings. The window treatment alone furnishes a handbook for the stop-at-nothing school, achieved nonetheless with knowing talent. Note in each that the fenestration in each progresses from one large pane of glass at street (elevated basement) level, to coupled windows on the main floors, two separate windows above, and finally three at the top, all crowned with both broken segmental and triangular pediments. The entrances, too, are glories of their kind. That on the Mackie (also known as the Chamber of Commerce Building—at left in photograph) suggests the influence of Frank Furness. The more restrained, semi-Baroque front door of the Mitchell Building (at right in photograph) is flanked by griffins at the ready. Well preserved inside and out (except for two inexcusable signs), they are examplars of their improbable era. W. A. Holbrook was associated with Mix in the design of both.

The lobby and grain exchange are the only areas open to the public. Open Monday–Friday 8:30 A.M.–5:00 P.M.; also occasionally open on Saturday. Admission is free.

AMES MEMORIAL LIBRARY (1877–79)
53 Main Street
North Easton, Massachusetts

Henry Hobson Richardson, architect

H. H. Richardson combined three elements at North Easton: one, his subsequently famous, almost Dantesque arched opening (here used by him for the first time); two, an offset tower that serves as a vertical agglutinator; and three, an extended horizontal wing with a row of clustered windows. Generated by requirements of the plan, these elements have been put together to form a simple but skillful hillside composition. Even more important, the building works well inside. Note in approaching that the only breaks in the solidity of the granite base beneath the stringcourse (on which the windows "rest") are the deep-set entry and two slit windows flanking it: a powerful introduction that monumentalizes penetration. The profuse sandstone-framed windows that light the stacks at left combine with those in the entry projection to roll across the facade. The openings in the tower join in by repeating at a smaller scale their round-headed (that is, Romanesque) framing.

The interior's finest feature is the room of stacks, with a barrel-vaulted butternut ceiling with applewood strapping designed by Stanford White, who started his architectural career with Richardson and worked with him for six years (1872–78). White also helped with the design of the library fireplace and much of the exterior carving. The Ames Library, with its clarity and monumentality, combined with directness of function, numbers among the key small buildings of the 1870s and '80s. Frederick Law Olmsted was the landscape architect.

Open Monday 10:00 A.M.–8:00 P.M., Tuesday–Wednesday 1:00–8:00 P.M., Thursday–Friday 10:00 A.M.–5:00 P.M., Saturday 10:00 A.M.–4:00 P.M. July–August closed Saturday. Closed holidays. Admission is free. Tours can be arranged by calling (508) 238–2000.

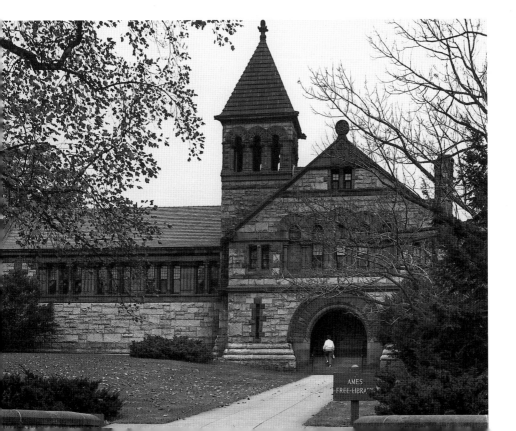

MANTI TEMPLE (1877–88)
us 89 at the north edge of town
Manti, Utah

William H. Folsom, architect

Surveying the Sanpete Valley, Manti Temple's exterior—like the Temple, Tabernacle, and Assembly Hall in Salt Lake City, Utah (see page 236)—combines a variety of architectural influences with hints of the Gothic Revival, topped by a mixture of mid-nineteenth-century motifs in the Second Empire manner. When the Mormons first moved into this section of central Utah in 1849, they entered a land that had been a backwater of Mexico. Even though the Mexican War had ended a year earlier—with the Southwest and California ceded to the United States—the area long remained undeveloped. Thus the building of the Manti Temple represents an especially difficult achievement. The oolitic limestone of which the temple is built was quarried from the hill on which its stands. The exterior (95 x 171 feet/29 x 52 meters), with its elevated position (properly east-facing) and beautifully kept grounds, is the most impressive of the temples of the Church of Jesus Christ of Latter-day Saints. In 1985 a complete restoration was undertaken.

As with other temples (but not tabernacles) of the faith, non-Mormons cannot enter the Manti Temple, but they are welcome to its grounds. (As was explained to the author, a Mormon temple is not strictly a "house of worship." Temples are used for the performance of certain ordinances in favor of both the living and the dead. Congregations do not meet for worship purposes in the usual sense of the word.)

Interior closed to the public.

VILLAGE BANDSTAND (1879)
Public Square off Main Street
Bellville, Ohio

Abraham Lash, architect

Though not the most momentous shelter in Ohio, this village bandstand nostalgically recalls a time when entertainment came from the community, not to the community via airwaves and cable. The pavilion's exuberant Victorian and Eastlake detailing conjures the innocence of a long-vanished era of architecture. As the *Richland Star* wrote of its dedication, "The benediction was

offered and a volume of music broke upon the air, which continued loud and long. We are pleased to note the excellent manner in which Mr. Bell performed this part in calling the people to order and introducing the speakers and also the tasty and orderly method in which the ceremonies were performed" (18 September 1879). Measuring 20 feet/6.1 meters in both diameter and height, it may well be the best bandstand in the country. Pure delight. Both Bandstand and Town Hall (1876) are registered National Historic Sites.

'IOLANI PALACE (1879–82)
King and Richards streets
Honolulu, Oahu, Hawaii

T. J. Baker, C. J. Wall, Isaac Moore, architects

Suggesting the Renaissance gone tropic, with hints of Second Empire France, the 'Iolani Palace, though modest in size (100 x 140 feet/30 x 43 meters), is architecturally fascinating. It is, moreover, the country's only state residence for royalty. Only two monarchs occupied the building: King Kalākaua, who lived there with Queen Kapi'olani from 1882 until his death in 1891 (having survived a revolution in 1887), and his sister Queen Lili'uokalani who ruled only two years, and did not survive the 1893 revolution that ended the monarchy. (Hawaii was annexed as a territory by the United States on 12 August 1898, and the palace was used as the capitol until the new one—see page 510—was built.) It is an essential document of Hawaii, especially its throne room. Designed by T. J. Baker, and modified by C. J. Wall and Isaac Moore "after a serious flaw was discovered in the original plans," the palace, which replaced an earlier one, is constructed of stuccoed brick and numerous well-made cast-iron columns. Two-story lanais embellish each side. The 'Iolani, which means "Bird of Heaven," has recently been beautifully restored as a museum. Many of the artifacts were acquired by King Kalākaua on a trip around the world, the first such tour, it is said, made by a king. (The chandeliers are American.) Stroll, also, through the well-kept grounds with a giant banyan tree (*Ficus bengalensis*) in one corner and an octagonal bandstand, built (1883) as the king's Coronation Pavilion in the other (and rebuilt, largely of termite-proof concrete, in 1920).

Open for guided tours only. Open Wednesday–Saturday 9:00 A.M.–3:00 P.M. Closed for holidays and during the beginning of September. Admission is $6 for adults, $1 for children ages 5–12. All visits are guided; 45-minute tours are given every 15 minutes until 2:15 P.M. For reservations or more information call (808) 522–0832.

PEOPLE'S NATIONAL BANK (1881)
Washington Street
McLeansboro, Illinois

Reid & Reid, architects

Half the architectural motifs in the latter part of the nineteenth century (plus the striped awnings of the twentieth) were gathered together for this marvelous bank. Among the more prominent elements of its design cornucopia are "blocked" or banded columns, a segmental central pediment, roundheaded windows, red brick and white stone facade and sides, a richly decorated frieze, several cornices, outward-splaying chimneys, and a Mansard roof enthusiastically punctured by dormers, all topped by a clocked, squared dome surmounted by filigreed ironwork. There is a compactness of elements here that even hints of the work of Frank Furness. As one of the most ebullient statements of late-nineteenth-century "cultural aspirations" in the United States, its photograph rightfully graces the cover of *Illinois Architecture* by Frederick Koeper (University of Chicago Press, 1968).

Located opposite courthouse. Open Monday–Friday 8:30 A.M.–4:00 P.M., Saturday 8:30 A.M.–12:00 noon. Closed for holidays. Tours can be arranged by calling (618) 643–4303.

AMES MONUMENT (1881–82)
I-80 at Veedauwoo exit
Laramie, Wyoming

Henry Hobson Richardson, architect

This lonely pyramid on a desolate summit (8,640 feet/2,633 meters high) surveys the land that Oakes and Oliver Ames opened to settlement when they pushed through the nearby Union Pacific Railroad (1865–69)—the first to span the continent. It is H. H. Richardson's only work west of the Mississippi, the commission stemming from his library for the Ames family in North Easton, Massachusetts (see page 263). Its angled mass of random ashlar, 60 feet/18 meters high, and 60 feet/18 meters square at the base, suggests the influence of the Bent Pyramid at Dahshur of Egypt's IV Dynasty (2680–2565 B.C.), while in its powerful silhouette—visible from the railroad (which is now relocated)—it vividly recalls the great mountains around it. Near its top, on opposite sides, are plaques to the Ames brothers designed by Augustus Saint-Gaudens. Henry-Russell Hitchcock, in a phrase of early enthusiasm, wrote that "this is perhaps the finest memorial in America" (*The Architecture of H. H. Richardson and His Times*, Museum of Modern Art, 1936; MIT Press, 1966).

Located 18 miles/29 kilometers southeast of Laramie and 31 miles/50 kilometers west of Cheyenne.

TIPPECANOE COURT HOUSE (1881–84)
Main, 3rd, 4th, and Columbia streets
Lafayette, Indiana

Elias Max, architect

The battle between General William Henry Harrison's troops and Chief Tecumseh's Shawnees (7 November 1811) made Tippecanoe famous, but this courthouse gives its county distinction. It possesses a lateral ferment—recessions, progressions, angles, returns, porches, and pilasters—that makes this one of the most three-dimensional building blocks in the country. And like Andrea Palladio's famous Villa Rotunda, all four facades are basically alike. This is no sleek envelope for the *citoyens de Lafayette* (the town was named for the general), but a gutsy limestone monument to their taste and their pocketbooks. The interior was restored in 1992. Although Elias Max is credited with the design (as per cornerstone), local opinion holds that his superintendent, James F. Alexander, was responsible.

Open Monday–Friday 8:00 A.M.–4:30 P.M. Closed for holidays. One-hour tours can be scheduled by calling the Greater Lafayette Visitors Bureau at (800) 872–6648; there may be a fee.

NATIONAL BUILDING MUSEUM (1882–87)
(formerly Pension Building)
401 F Street NW between 4th and 5th streets
Washington, D.C.

General Montgomery C. Meigs, architect

Sangallo's and Michelangelo's Palazzo Farnese in Rome (1517–89) obviously inspired the facades of this aged delight. However, Montgomery C. Meigs replaced stucco and travertine with 15,500,000 red bricks, and belted the building's enormous girth with probably the longest (1,200 feet/366 meters)—and certainly the most tedious—sculptured frieze known to mankind. Its terra-cotta panels by Caspar Buberl depict Civil War military units (note even the covered wagons). But whereas the exterior is semiarcheological, the titanic inner court (159 feet/48 meters to ridgepole) is a space all its own. Thirteen United States presidents have held inaugural balls here. Eight freestanding Corinthian columns 75 feet/23 meters high—each, supposedly, of 70,000 bricks—uphold the central portion of the roof, their stucco-covered massiveness playing against the delicacy of the wrought-iron rod trusses (which should also be noted). Four floors of museum gallery space and offices surround this core. An arcaded clerestory crowns the top of the court and floods the interior with light. Note that the arch motif carries through the interior. From any level the effect is mighty.

Open Monday–Saturday 10:00 A.M.–4:00 P.M., Sunday 12:00 noon–4:00 P.M. Closed Thanksgiving, Christmas, and New Year's Day. Admission is free. Free one-hour tours are given Monday–Friday at 12:30 P.M., Saturday–Sunday at 12:30 and 1:30 P.M. For more information, call (202) 272–2448.

BILLINGS STUDENT CENTER (1883–85)
University of Vermont, Main Campus
University Place via Colchester Avenue
Burlington, Vermont

Henry Hobson Richardson, architect

The Richardson buff will want to see the Billings Student Center (ex-library) on the ridge over-looking the main campus mall. One of five libraries HHR designed, it combines almost all his trademarks: pivotal tower jostling vertical with horizontal, large arched entrance almost demanding that one enter (compare Frank Lloyd Wright's often hidden entries), strip and gathered windows, and polygonal (here octagonal) end bay, the whole pulled together into its rosy sandstone mass. The interior has been restored to its original condition and, with the library stacks removed, the full glory of Richardson's interior design is revealed. As part of the restoration, furniture designed by Richardson specifically for this building has been repaired and refinished or, in some instances, replaced with custom-made duplicates. The building now serves as a student center, and the ground-floor rooms serve as lecture and concert halls and for small student, faculty, and public gatherings. The tower room, open from floor to roof beams, is occasionally used for student theater productions.

During the academic year, open daily 8:00 A.M.–midnight. During the summer, open Monday–Friday 8:00 A.M.–4:30 P.M. Tours can be arranged by calling (802) 656-2060.

CARSON MANSION (1884–86)
143 M Street at 2nd Street
Eureka, California

Samuel and Joseph C. Newsom, architects

The eighteen-room Carson Mansion is owned by the private Ingomar Club—and not open to the public—but the exterior alone is such a spectacular example of gung-ho Queen Anne and nineteenth century eclecticism in general that it more than merits a drive by. It is, indeed, probably the finest late Victorian exterior in the country, a culmination of profligate fancies haughtily—but gloriously—dispensed. Mary Mix Foley describes it as "a valedictory to every style which had gone before and a harbinger of others to come" (*The American Home*, Harper & Row, 1979). A complete restoration is currently under way.

The interior is not open to the public.

ALLEGHENY COUNTY JAIL
AND COURT HOUSE
(1884–88)
436 Grant Street between 5th
and Forbes avenues
Pittsburgh, Pennsylvania

Henry Hobson Richardson,
architect

Brawn in American architecture reached its apogee in these Allegheny County buildings, which are H. H. Richardson's (and the era's) masterpieces. We find here a climax of stone construction combining guts with sophistication: the lessons of the cut-stone masonry in the jail are imperishable. It recalls, appropriately, Giovanni Battista Piranesi's *Carceri* as it rises as an unfractured bastion to fill its block. Its wall, broken only by a grilled entrance and a few windows in front, and a service gate on the side, wraps masterfully around the almost triangular block as it envelops the three-armed jail and its yard. No base, no cornice jars this wall's authority. The junctures of the wall, as it rises flush to fair into the ends of the jail wings and as it meets the towers, provide one of architecture's greatest statements in undressed ashlar granite. Here, indeed, is the primeval strength of the inner earth.

The more formal court house (finished a year later) is handsome, but more routine. Attached to the jail by its Bridge of Sighs (on Ross Street), it shelters an elaborate group of functions. Though somewhat fractured on the exterior, except for a superior tower, it achieves strength within, especially in the two entrance halls, where parades of arches uphold the floors above. Note, too, in the entry the vitality of the main stairs and the variety of capitals atop the columns. The design of the court house—which was won by competition—was planned so that its high, wide courtrooms alternate with narrow "double-decked" judges' rooms, most of which are marked on the exterior by half-round turrets. Thus the problem of public versus private scale has been imaginatively handled. With a continuous corridor on each of its five floors encircling the open courtyard of the center, a highly functional building results. Incidentally, step into this courtyard to see the rhythm of the window and wall arches there. The yard itself was refurbished in 1977 with new brick paving, a fountain, a number of planting boxes with trees, and sixteen teak benches. The great tower that rises above yard and building was designed for storage of legal documents and—an advancement for the time as well as a reflection of the city's atmosphere—as fresh-air intake for the whole building. Richardson, the building's genius, saw only the jail section of his masterpiece completed: he died in April 1886 at the age of forty-eight just two years before the court house was opened. The supervisory work was completed by Shepley, Rutan and Coolidge. A new, larger jail has recently been built in the area, and thus Richardson's jail will be closed to the public while its future is determined; at least one section will eventually house additional courtrooms. One of the greatest buildings of the nineteenth century.

Open Monday–Friday 8:30 A.M.–4:30 P.M. Closed for holidays.

QUEEN ANNE COTTAGE (1885)
(E. J. Baldwin Guest House)
Arboretum of Los Angeles County
301 North Baldwin Avenue
Arcadia, California

A. A. Bennett, architect

Among the non-bosky benefits of the Arboretum of Los Angeles County are several buildings
that illustrate the early architecture of this region—all that remains of a 13,000-acre/5,260-
hectare ranch. The oldest—though reconstructed—is the house originally built in 1840 by
Hugo Reid. Immediately adjacent stands a Gabrielino wickiup. Across the small lake and built
almost as a *folie* is the Queen Anne Cottage, a guest house for the most famous owner of the
property, E. J. "Lucky" Baldwin. Its Victorian stick-work, including its original colors, has been
carefully renovated. Baldwin's matching coach barn (1879) stands nearby. A good group, fortunately acquired by the arboretum in 1947.

The grounds are open daily 9:00 A.M.–4:30 P.M. Closed Christmas. Admission is $5 for adults, $3 for students and senior citizens. The cottage is open once a year, a different day each year; call (818) 821-3222 for more information.

MIAMI COUNTY COURT HOUSE (1885–88)
201 West Main Street at South Plum Street
Troy, Ohio

Joseph Warren Yost, architect

Troy's court house proffers bifurcated whimsy of astounding ingenuity. The three-story building, whose four facades are similar in size and treatment, resembles in color and texture—and
perchance even in architecture—a gigantic cube of gingerbread. Atop this cavorts a cornucopia
of white temples and domes of Classical and would-be-Classical inspiration, the whole surmounted by a raised drum and central dome topped by the statue of Justice. Nestled between
four corner, domed "attics" peak four richly pedimented (and half-hidden) temples, their triangulations adorned with greenish copper figures, that on Main Street holding up five books
of law.

Although government offices still occupy the court house, the offices of the county elected
officials, as well as the sheriff's department and jail, are now housed in a consciously quiet
three-story Safety Building adjacent. It was designed in 1972 by Hart-Ruetschle-Hart, with
John F. Ruetschle partner-in-charge.

Open Monday–Friday 8:00 A.M.–4:00 P.M. Group tours can be arranged by calling (513) 332–7000.

HAAS-LILIENTHAL HOUSE (1886)
2007 Franklin Street
San Francisco, California

Peter R. Schmidt, architect

An outstanding example of the Queen Anne style, this house escaped the 1906 earthquake
and fire virtually intact. Perhaps even more remarkable, its all-redwood construction has withstood man-created depredations for the ninety years since nature revolted. Its wondrously
gabled, turreted, and bracketed exterior sports mandatory stylistic asymmetry and projected
window bays, that on the corner topped by a round shingled tower with conical roof. The interior, its ground-floor rooms sensibly connected by sliding doors in the fashion of the day, was
modified at the turn of the century; though more subdued than the outside it still merits a
look. The house was generously donated by the Haas-Lilienthal heirs to the Foundation for
San Francisco's Architectural Heritage; it may well be the finest example of its style open to
the public in the United States.

Open Wednesday 12:00 noon–3:15 P.M., Sunday 11:00 A.M.–4:15 P.M. Admission is $5 for adults, $3 for senior citizens. All visits are guided; tours last one hour. Tours can also be arranged at other times by calling (415) 441–3004.

GLESSNER HOUSE (1886–87)
1800 South Prairie Avenue at 18th Street
Chicago, Illinois

Henry Hobson Richardson, architect

Although he was born in Louisiana, Henry Hobson Richardson's contribution to American architecture toward the end of the past century—either directly or by influence—can be seen over much of the northern half of the country. Seeking a virile robustness, unlike the effete pseudo-Classicism that was soon to mold Chicago's World's Columbian Exposition of 1893, Richardson injected a forcefulness into domestic architecture, as into all his buildings, that is still revered today. The Glessner House, on the once finest residential street in Chicago (now in the Prairie Avenue Historic District), demonstrates this well. It exhibits more than the normal Richardsonian strength, appearing almost as a granite arsenal (note the stonework). Richardson skillfully turned the house inside out by putting the small-windowed halls and service quarters on the 18th Street side and opening the principal rooms onto a private garden court away from the north wind, noise, and dirt—one of the earliest examples of truly functional planning. Most of the house itself has been (and is being) restored and refurnished with original pieces. The court has already been renovated.

   Saved from impending destruction by the heroic efforts of the Chicago School of Architecture Foundation (now the Chicago Architecture Foundation), the dwelling—occupied by the family until John J. Glessner's death in 1936—is today operated as a museum by Prairie Avenue House Museums (an offshoot of CAF). Richardson himself unfortunately died a month before the ground breaking of his greatest house. His Chicago work left a lasting impression on John Root and Louis Sullivan (and Frank Lloyd Wright) of the famous "Chicago School," which did so much to launch what we call Modern, as opposed to eclectic or back-to-the-past, architecture.

Open Wednesday–Sunday 1:00–4:00 P.M. All visits are guided; one-hour tours are given at 1:00, 2:00, and 3:00 P.M. The cost is $5 per person. For more information call the Prairie Avenue House Museums at (312) 326–1480.

FLAGLER COLLEGE (1886–88)
(formerly Hotel Ponce de León)
King Street at Cordova
St. Augustine, Florida

Carrère & Hastings, architects

The east coast of Florida was developed as a winter refuge for ice-bound Northerners by the perceptive Henry Morrison Flagler. As a background on his profitable acumen, Flagler, while clerking in Ohio, joined forces with a fellow upstate New Yorker named John D. Rockefeller,

and the two became the prime founders of the Standard Oil Company (1870). Later, to seek further fields and especially to demonstrate that a tropical sandbar could be transformed into a tropical Eden, Flagler established a hotel beachhead in the quaint village of St. Augustine. This salient—one incomprehensively removed from any beach, water, or view (except from upper floors)—was the Hotel Ponce de León, named for the explorer who reputedly spent five days in the area in 1513. Realizing that a first-class railroad would be necessary to fetch his guests, the astute Flagler built the Florida East Coast Railroad (starting at Jacksonville), which he pushed down the peninsula as far as Palm Beach by 1894, Miami two years later, and finally Key West. For architects of his mid-city snuggery (his first of eleven in Florida), Flagler selected the untried but promising firm of John M. Carrère and Thomas Hastings, two young

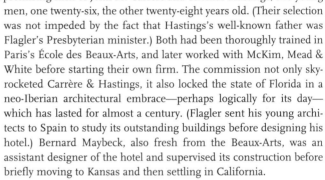

men, one twenty-six, the other twenty-eight years old. (Their selection was not impeded by the fact that Hastings's well-known father was Flagler's Presbyterian minister.) Both had been thoroughly trained in Paris's École des Beaux-Arts, and later worked with McKim, Mead & White before starting their own firm. The commission not only sky-rocketed Carrère & Hastings, it also locked the state of Florida in a neo-Iberian architectural embrace—perhaps logically for its day—which has lasted for almost a century. (Flagler sent his young architects to Spain to study its outstanding buildings before designing his hotel.) Bernard Maybeck, also fresh from the Beaux-Arts, was an assistant designer of the hotel and supervised its construction before briefly moving to Kansas and then settling in California.

The result, though not without pastiche, is a functionally planned hotel constructed of solid reinforced concrete (six parts coquina to one of cement)—one of the first concrete buildings in the country—and trimmed with brick and terra-cotta. Moreover, the hotel, again ahead of the trade, generated its own electricity and boasted electric lights and steam heat, while its towers contained water tanks holding 8,000 gallons/36,370 liters for fire protection. The Ponce de León documents with éclat the eclecticism that characterized most American architecture for the last hundred and more years. Note, on entering, the dazzling 80-foot-/24-meter-high rotunda and its murals (those in the dining room by George W. Maynard), and the many chandeliers by Louis Comfort Tiffany.

In 1968 the hotel's sturdy bulk was transformed into Flagler College, a 1,350-student, accredited liberal arts institution, its hotel rooms now serving as dormitories.

The campus and rotunda are open to the public Monday–Friday 10:00 A.M.–4:00 P.M. May–August free tours are given daily 10:00 A.M.–4:00 P.M. on the hour. The rest of the year, tours can be arranged by calling (904) 829-6481.

Directly facing the college is the former three-hundred-room Alcazar Hotel (1887–89) also designed by Carrère & Hastings but in a simpler yet equally solid manner. The hotel closed in 1930, and now serves partly as the Lightner Museum (open daily 9:00 A.M.–5:00 P.M., closed Christmas; admission is $4 for adults, $1 for children ages 12–18) with an exposition of toys and dolls, while the remainder of the building houses the St. Augustine City Hall.

LAST CHANCE GULCH (1886–89)
Helena, Montana

Toward the end of the nineteenth century, before American architecture became timid, there existed a handful of gutsy practitioners, the most accomplished of whom was Frank Furness of Philadelphia. These men, some influenced by H. H. Richardson, produced many of the most powerful—if at times outlandish—buildings that this country has spawned. Among a few lonely nuggets in the Northwest are the burly examples found along Last Chance Gulch, this capital city's main street—so named because weary prospectors took one last poke (1864) into a stream here and came up (eventually) with some $20 million worth of gold. Sudden wealth erupted, as did sudden death, and in 1888 it is said that Helena was the richest city per capita in the United States. In its early days the city sought to attract a variety of businesses and settlers from the East to lessen its mining dependency. It concentrated on substantial, in some cases exotic, commercial buildings to act as bait and also to fill local needs. Despite fires and a major earthquake (1935), a scattering of the hoary delights remains. An urban renewal program during the 1970s did target certain buildings for rehabilitation, yet allowed hundreds of historic structures in the heart of the city to be demolished.

Ingloriously, the most fascinating structure in the city, the Novelty Building (1888), John Paulsen, architect, is no more. Heavy rains in 1975 undermined the rear, which collapsed. Then in an act of official vandalism the still-standing facade—almost a history of architecture by itself—was torn down. Admittedly the building was in parlous condition, but with foresight instead of neglect it could have been saved. Among the principal buildings of interest (remaining), listed by street number, are:

Atlas Block (1888), 7–9. Shaffer & Stranahan, architects. Although one of the tamer buildings, its ground floor boasts a stout arch—reminiscent of a Richardsonian library—while on a platform that rises above the eaves a determined metal salamander does battle with unlikely reptiles. The building was built for an insurance company, hence its name—with a small statue of Atlas at midpoint. The fire-resisting myth of the salamander is expanded by the stylized flames of the cornice. Although it once faced the street (as seen in the photograph at left), today it looks onto a pedestrian mall.

Power Block (1889), 58, 60, 62. Willetts and Ashley, architects. Architecturally the Power Block, a six-story pile of rusticated granite that holds down its corner site with authority, is the most accomplished building along the Gulch. Its design stems largely from the upper half of Richardson's Marshall Field Wholesale Store (1885–87—now destroyed). Its march of windows is set in roundheaded reveals, topped by a stringcourse, and finished with an "attic" band of small windows, also roundheaded (the corresponding ones at Marshall Field were squared). The expression of the large-windowed shops of the ground floor versus those of the office above recalls Louis Sullivan. The interior framing is of heavy timber construction. Once marred by signs (as seen in the photograph above), but restored in recent years, 58 Last Chance Gulch is a worthy mountain cousin of the Chicago School. Fortunately it is in good structural condition.

A smaller example of the same Richardsonian ilk that will interest the specialist will be found in the Securities Building (1886) at 101 North Main Street at Grand, Hodgson, Wallingford & Stem, architects. Though now bereft of its tower, it possesses some good detailing, along with free-wheeling fenestration.

Building interiors open during business hours. A free booklet on the history of Helena, which includes a self-guided walking tour, is available from the City of Helena Planning Department at (406) 447-8490.

ROOKERY BUILDING
(1886–88/1905/1930s/1992)
209 South LaSalle Street
at Adams
Chicago, Illinois

Burnham & Root, architects
Frank Lloyd Wright, architect
of lobby

The exterior of this squarish, doughty, eleven-story building (179 x 167 feet/55 x 51 meters) is knobbly and dark, but its capaciously domed, skylit lobby is full of light. Measuring 71 x 62 feet/22 x 19 meters, the first renovation of this "graceful, semiprivate square" (to quote the Chicago Landmarks Commission) was done by Frank Lloyd Wright in 1905, at which time were added the touches of marble and gold leaf that make the place refulgent under his geometric lamps. (Wright's ornamentation for the lobby was actually based on John Wellborn Root's original designs.) The elaborate structure of the perforated *I*-beam trussing, indeed the whole lacy atmosphere, should not be missed. In *The Meanings of Architecture, Buildings and Writings by John Wellborn Root*, collected by Donald Hoffman (Horizon Press, 1967), the central court is termed "an example of interior spatial organization without parallel in the architecture of the Chicago School." The building's foundations, incidentally, represent one of the first uses of crossed railroad rails embedded in concrete to form a steel grillage.

In the early 1930s a remodeling of the ground floor interior was carried out under the direction of William Drummond; he destroyed the original two-story entrance lobbies, added a semicircular stair in the light court, changed the mosaic floor to marble, and created the bronze entrances and the elevator lobby. In 1992 an extensive restoration of the exterior and the public spaces along with a rehabilitation of the office spaces was completed by the McClier Corporation, architects, for the current owner, Baldwin Development Company. Except for the elevator lobby and the bronze entrances, all of Drummond's changes were removed and the building returned to its Root/ Wright appearance. The two-story lobby spaces and the mosaic floor were reconstructed, and the light court was restored to Wright's design and covered by a new skylight at the top of the building in order to protect the terra cotta and the historic space below.

Open Monday–Friday 8:00 A.M.–6:00 P.M., Saturday 8:00 A.M.–2:00 P.M. Closed for holidays. The Chicago Architecture Foundation gives a one-hour tour of the building; the cost is $3. The building is also included on the CAF's walking tour of early Chicago skyscrapers; the cost is $10. For more information on CAF tours call (312) 922–3432.

HOTEL DEL CORONADO (1887–88)
1500 Orange Avenue
Coronado, California

Reid & Reid, architects

This *grande dame* of resort hotels, one of the few remaining of its genus, still holds sway with almost regal assertiveness. Turrets and balconies, along with a reputed two million shingles (nailed down by hundreds of Chinese carpenters) embellish this behemoth of wood, while its interiors, especially the monumental 1,000-seat dining room and the bars, are of a quality that any seaside resort today could envy. The hotel was planned, largely by James W. Reid, about a large court (150 x 250 feet/46 x 76 meters) filled with a garden of tropical trees, shrubs, and flowers, with its public rooms overlooking the ocean and bay. Its 399 guest rooms each had a fireplace originally, plus a wall safe (steam heat was installed in 1897). Moreover they were—as was the rest of the hotel—illuminated by both electricity (the largest hotel in the West so supplied) and gas, this latter never needed. Although several of the public rooms have been changed through the years (notably—rather not notably—the grand ballroom), the oak-lined lobby with its wonderful elevator, the sugar pine dining room, and the bars remain substantially as built, and all beautifully maintained. Some 30,000 sprinkler heads were put in in 1916. The hotel's centennial was celebrated in 1988; may it hold sway over the Pacific well into its second century. Coronado (near San Diego) needs a structure of quality such as this, as a look up and down the strand at present-day buildings will confirm. Shingle-Queen Anne-Eastlake: architectural divertissement of a high order.

Open daily 24 hours. Tours available Thursday–Saturday at 10:00 and 11:00 A.M.; the cost is $10 per person. Self-guided audio tours available daily during daylight hours; the cost is $5 per person. For more information call (619) 435-6611.

AUDITORIUM BUILDING (1887–89/1967)
430 South Michigan Avenue at Congress Parkway
Chicago, Illinois

Adler & Sullivan, architects

Behind this unlikely facade hides one of the finest auditoriums in the United States; Frank Lloyd Wright termed it the finest "in the world—bar none." Yet the exterior of the building is a model of homeliness and confusing scale. One expects more from Louis Sullivan, even if his client's program did call for a building to house office space, a hotel, and a theater, the first two intended to pay for most of the overhead. The load-bearing exterior, as is obvious, denies the building's largest space (the commercial rooms wrap around the auditorium), which is unfortunate but perhaps inevitable. Moreover, the top six floors reference H. H. Richardson's Marshall Field Wholesale Store, built in 1885–87 and demolished in 1930, heavily. (This, seemingly without question, can be ascribed to the Auditorium directors' admiration of the Richardson building.)

However, inside lies one of the country's most dazzling interiors. There is a golden glow to this auditorium that visually captures festivity; aurally it rewards with acoustics that are nothing short of sensational. As Sigfried Giedion wrote, it is "the finest assembly hall of its period." The design of the room, which seats as many as 4,237, was almost all Sullivan's; the ingenious engineering, flexibility (rear sections can be closed off), and acoustics were by Dankmar Adler—whose reputation for acoustics got the firm the job. The detail flanking the proscenium employs arches set in panels (foreshadowing Sullivan's Transportation Building of 1893) to fill the spaces between the ends of the projecting boxes and the stage. This is distracting, and it can be argued that the precise rectangle of the proscenium itself stands uncomfortably under the soft arch that embraces it, but these obliquities vanish in the overall triumph. Young Frank Lloyd Wright reputedly detailed the ornament sketched by Sullivan.

Harry Weese and his associates restored the building in 1967 with keen sensitivity, down to matching its carbon-filament bulbs. Crombie Taylor and George Izenour were key consultants. The heavy money needed for the restoration was raised by the energetic Auditorium Theater Council; Harry Weese graciously contributed his services. The lobby was restored in 1992. Since 1946 the offices and hotel have been occupied by Roosevelt University.

Open during performances. Tours can be scheduled by calling (312) 922–2110; the cost is $4 for adults, $3 for students and senior citizens. The Chicago Architecture Foundation offers a two-hour tour of the building; the cost is $8. The building is also included on the CAF's walking tour of early Chicago skyscrapers; the cost is $10. For more information on CAF tours call (312) 922–3432.

OLD RICHMOND CITY HALL (1887–94)
1001 East Broad Street at 10th Street
Richmond, Virginia

Elijah E. Myers, architect

The exterior of Old City Hall—the commission for which was won by competition—stands hard and chiseled in the late Victorian Gothic manner. Having been cleaned, its immutability stands boldly forth. Of itself, the exterior is not unusual. The four-story interior stair hall and "court," however, provide us with tiers of Neo-Gothic levels, some gilded, some crocketed, all potent. Although the new City Hall is now completed, this older bastion has not been destroyed—as was the previous City Hall by Robert Mills (destroyed in 1874)—but has instead been converted into office space. The building is listed in the National Register of Historic Places.

Lobby open Monday–Friday 9:00 A.M.–4:00 P.M. For more information call (804) 782–1019.

ARCADE (1888–90)
401 Euclid Avenue
Cleveland, Ohio

John M. Eisenmann and George H. Smith, architects

The Cleveland Arcade forms a mid-block urban nexus between two major avenues; its design is unparalleled in the United States. (See also the Arcade of 1827–28 in Providence, Rhode Island, page 173.) Not only does it provide a protected pedestrian link between two downtown thoroughfares, it mediates—keenly—the change in level between them. In early-nineteenth-century Europe, skylit arcades (as opposed to covered sidewalks) began to grace Paris, London, Milan, and Naples as smart meeting and shopping locales—so successfully, it might be added, that all are still going strong. Cleveland was influenced by them and also by an example in Toronto. With this distinguished lineage, it furnishes us with a perpetual urban amenity, one particularly suitable in a lakefront city buffeted by wintry gales. The constituent fact of the arcade's excellence lies in its breadth of conception—at 290 feet/88 meters long, 60 feet/18 meters wide, and 104 feet/32 meters high, only the Galleria Vittorio Emanuele II in Milan (1867) is longer (but not quite as wide or high)—and in the excellence of its design.

Lightness and air fill the interior, while a subtle scale buildup lends it character. Note that as the arcade rises it steps backward on successive floors, thus admitting the maximum of sunshine. Because of the 12-foot/3.7-meter change in level between the two outside avenues, there are two main "streets" or shopping levels in the arcade (providing for scores of shops); the stepped-back third level forms a secondary street. The two upper floors are primarily for professional and office use. With the setbacks of the floors establishing a horizontal emphasis and the skylight-capped roof attracting the eye upward, an energetic horizontal/vertical activity results. Note, too, that none of the floors is treated precisely like the one below.

One of the chief structural achievements trussing the glazed roof so that the usual tie rods—which would have detracted from the inner lightness—could be dispensed with. John M. Eisenmann, who had been trained as an engineer and had studied in Germany, developed a trussed arch, supported on knee braces, which transmits the roof load to the outer masonry walls, a solution so daring that only a bridge-building firm—the Detroit Bridge Company—would undertake it. The span of the three-hinged arches is 49.9 feet/15.1 meters with a 23 foot/7 meter rise. The supporting columns and beams are of cast iron, the intricately detailed railings of wrought iron. (Note the beam-end beasties; they once held incandescent bulbs in their mouths.)

The five-story arcade connects two nine-story office buildings, bringing light and revenue-producing shops into their midst; the arcade itself is almost swallowed up when seen from either street. All of this intensifies the contrast when one steps within (preferably from the angled Euclid entry—modernized in 1939) and encounters its inspired light and lightness. A success from its opening day, the Cleveland Arcade is still one of the country's greatest urban achievements. In 1979 the skylight was reglazed and the arcade thoroughly renovated and updated mechanically.

Alternate entrance at Superior Avenue. Open Monday–Saturday 7:00 A.M.–8:00 P.M. Closed Sunday. Shop hours vary. For more information call (216) 621–8500. PA 9/40

OLD VANDERBURGH COUNTY COURT HOUSE (1888–91)
201 Northwest Fourth Street
Evansville, Indiana

Henry Wolters, architect

In most of the larger (and many minor) cities of Indiana, the courthouses were conceived with Medici-like grandeur, and the Vanderburgh County building is no exception. Its limestone pile set stiff competition for its neighbors, in trade and prestige. (The smaller towns splurged on their courthouses, hoping to be named the county seat.) The building was designed by a German-born architect educated at the École des Beaux-Arts in Paris. The profligacy of architectural motifs at Evansville testifies to civic pride and a willingness to part with public money. The 216-foot-/66-meter-high cupola and central bay alone must be seen to be believed. When to these are added the domed, half-round bays, their circular windows at top suitably wreathed, the building overflows with varietal fashions. Its exuberant sculpture by Franz Englesmann is worthy of binocular scrutiny.

Though the interior is cut up in places, Wedgewood Hall (formerly the law library) is not only good, but is also available for public and private functions. When the courthouse became inefficient for municipal usage, its future remained unclear until the nonprofit Conrad Baker Foundation (now known as the Old Courthouse Preservation Society) acquired the building in 1969 on a ninety-nine-year lease. It is now using the restored structure for an office building housing a variety of tenants, two theaters, a few shops, and other *pro bono publico* functions. One wishes the society and the citizens of Evansville the greatest of success; this is one of the most distinguished buildings in the state.

Open Monday–Friday 7:00 A.M.–6:00 P.M. Closed for holidays. Tours can be arranged by calling (812) 423-3361; the cost is $1 for adults and 50¢ for children.

MARBLE HOUSE (1888–92)
Bellevue Avenue and Cliff Walk
Newport, Rhode Island

Richard Morris Hunt, architect

The Colonial inheritance of Newport, samples of which we have already seen, was overshadowed by villas of proper Veblenian presumption in the late nineteenth and early twentieth centuries. Quaintly called "cottages," Newport's summer houses find no equal in the Western world: their interiors, indeed, must be seen to be believed. Fortunately the most pretentious are open to the public during much of the year. Richard Morris Hunt's Marble House for William K. Vanderbilt—its name reflecting the unrelenting use of its material—recalls with its Corinthian columned and balustraded shape the garden facade of the Petit Trianon (1662–68) at Versailles, except that Hunt's projected portico and roundheaded windows lack the compact authority of Ange-Jacques Gabriel's earlier building. But Hunt, who studied for nine years at the École des Beaux-Arts in Paris—the first American to do so—and who afterward worked at the Tuileries in Paris, put together a highly skillful small palace. Chastely white on the exterior, the house erupts with unrestrained hedonism

within. The Neronian richness of the dining room is established by roast beef-colored marble walls, while the ballroom—the gold room—projects its aureate charms from panels gilded in red, green, and yellow gold and set off by wondrous chandeliers and by a gold-leaf and bronze mantel. And so it progresses, from entry gates (which should be noted) to the black walnut and silk details upstairs—where almost all major bedrooms unaccountably face the land. The architect himself is remembered by the grateful owner with a bas-relief on the stairs—he should be.

In addition to designing several of the most sumptuous houses in the United States, plus the facade of the Metropolitan Museum of Art and one of the first skyscrapers with elevators (the 230-foot-/70-meter-high, wall-bearing Tribune Building, 1875, in New York), Richard Morris Hunt—by helping also to establish the American Institute of Architects—fathered professional architecture in this country.

April–October open daily 10:00 A.M.–5:00 P.M. November–March open Saturday–Sunday and holidays 10:00 A.M.–4:00 P.M. Closed Christmas Eve and Christmas Day. Admission is $6.50 for adults, $3 for children ages 6–11. 45-minute tours available. For more information call (401) 847–1000.

BOSTON PUBLIC LIBRARY (1888–95)
Copley Square
Boston, Massachusetts

McKim, Mead & White, architects

The late Talbot Hamlin, a noted architectural historian, said of this library, "its perfect harmony makes it one of the best loved of all modern American architectural masterpieces" (*The Enjoyment of Architecture*, Duffield, 1916). Charles Follen McKim of McKim, Mead & White was partner-in-charge of the building. And as it sits facing H. H. Richardson's Trinity Church (see page 258), completed just eleven years before, it asserts more than "perfect harmony": it heralds the beginning of a new era in American architecture. The Boston Library was the first expert public building in this country to espouse the Neo-Italian Renaissance: Richardson's gutsy Neo-Romanesque was doomed by the strictly ordered new style. (McKim's Paris-trained, Neo-Classical style reached its apogee five years after the library was started at the Chicago World's Columbian Exposition of 1892–93, in which he played a leading role. Drolly enough, he also worked with Richardson on the design of Trinity.) It might be pointed out that in addition to the challenge of the new Renaissance-inspired style made popular by the library, Richardson's magnificent labors in stone were also "threatened" by constructional steel, then becoming an economical material.

Under the library's quiet green tile roof a caravan of thirteen arched windows marches across the facade—and picks up the arch motif of Trinity—expressing well that one great room, the reading room, lies behind. As has been pointed out, the facade of the library was based on the Italian Renaissance, as well as on Pierre-François-Henri Labrouste's Bibliothèque Sainte-Geneviève (1839–50) in Paris—on which Richardson himself worked—though McKim's library has more panache (on the exterior). However, William H. Jordy points out the

great influence of the side wall of San Francesco in Rimini, which Leon Battista Alberti transformed c. 1450 (*American Buildings and Their Architects, Progressive and Academic Ideals,* Doubleday, 1972). At each of the two stringcourses the building steps back a few inches to lessen visually the overall mass. The chief points of interest within are the sumptuous stairway and quiet Roman courtyard at entry level, the great (218 feet/66 meters long) reading room inspired by a Roman bath, the Puvis de Chavannes gallery and the Edwin Austin Abbey room on the second floor, and the muraled John Singer Sargent hall on the third. After this elegant effort Boston puzzlingly dozed and did not produce another building of distinction for almost eighty years, until its new City Hall of 1969 (see page 494) (if one excepts Welles Bosworth's classical MIT complex in Cambridge of 1912–15).

In 1969–72 the adjacent Public Library Addition, Boylston Street at Exeter, was built to the design of Philip Johnson and John Burgee. It is a smoothly working circulating library addition (holding 750,000 volumes) to McKim's 1895 palazzo, the earlier now used primarily for research. (A large-scale renovation of the main building is currently under way, to be completed in the year 2000.) The new building of nine structural bays, nearly square in plan, does not eschew monumentality outside or in, the exterior favoring a muscular scale while the center of the structure, the granite-revetted great hall, rises through seven floors to a skylight at top. (The new does pick up the cornice and stringcourse line of the old.) The entry level, mezzanine, and second story are devoted to open stacks, with staff occupying the third and book stacks the fourth to seventh floors. The third through sixth floors are hung from 16-foot-/4.9-meter-deep trusses to eliminate all interior columns. The lower-level concourse houses the higher education and audio-visual departments, a lecture hall, and public lavatories. The Architects Design Group were associates, William LeMessurier the structural engineer.

Open Monday–Thursday 9:00 A.M.–9:00 P.M., Friday–Saturday 9:00 A.M.–5:00 P.M.; also open on Sunday 1:00–5:00 P.M. from October to May. Free tours are available Monday at 2:30 P.M., Tuesday and Wednesday at 6:30 P.M., Thursday and Saturday at 11:00 A.M., and Sunday at 2:00 P.M.

MABEL TAINTER MEMORIAL BUILDING
(1889–90)
205 Main Street
Menomonie, Wisconsin

Harvey Ellis, architect

Henry Hobson Richardson was the godfather of this accomplished structure. Its great carved sandstone arched narthex—which opens onto an Italian marble and mahogany lobby—would not be to his discredit. Nor, indeed, would the massing of the turreted facade. The building, much of which is occupied by a library/reading room, was built as a community center by a local timber baron and his wife in memory of their daughter, who died at the age of nineteen. A fully restored, compact theater forms an integral part of the building and should also be seen. It is still in active use. This assertive example of rural Romanesque Revival is on the list of the National Register of Historic Places.

Open Monday–Friday 8:30 A.M.–5:00 P.M., Saturday 12:00 noon–5:00 P.M., Sunday 1:00–5:00 P.M. Closed for holidays. Admission is free. One-hour tours are given at 1:00, 2:00, 3:00, and 4:00 P.M.; the cost is $3 for adults, $2 for children ages 6–12, free for children under 6. For more information call (715) 235-9726.

MONADNOCK BUILDING

(1889–91/1893)
53 West Jackson Boulevard at Dearborn Street Chicago, Illinois

Burnham & Root, architects of north half Holabird & Roche, architects of south half

The Monadnock is a dinosaur among skyscrapers. It is the last of a species in that its floors are upheld not purely by iron or steel—as were its cohorts then rising in Chicago, including others by Burnham & Root—but also by wall-bearing masonry. (The walls on the perimeter are load bearing, while certain of the columns in the center and the beams in the floors are steel.) Its client, apparently, distrusted the potential longevity of steel columns, though this is what the architects originally proposed throughout. Thus the Monadnock's sixteen-story-high outer walls are enormously thick at street level (6.3 feet/1.9 meters) to support a load that could easily have been carried on fireproofed metal columns of considerably smaller size. Burnham & Root lightened this bulk visually by creating a lively oscillation of windows and bays, and by employing a pared-down simplicity (also the client's wish); in this they succeeded with aplomb. It is one of the first major buildings in this country to eschew all ornamentation; its smooth flanks are totally free of embellishment. The elegance and finesse of its brickwork—many special molds were employed—and its flared base find imitators even today. Note the chamfered corners and details of the projecting bay windows. When completed it was the largest office block in the world. The south half of the building was added (using steel) in 1893 by Holabird & Roche. Its interior was remodeled in 1938 by Skidmore, Owings & Merrill. Much of the building was restored in the 1980s.

BROWN PALACE HOTEL (1889–92/1959)
321 17th Street between Tremont Place and Broadway
Denver, Colorado

Frank E. Edbrooke, architect

Few voids have ever been as positive as this nine-story, top-lit, 56-foot-/17-meter-wide, squarish column of properly conditioned air, which is the essence and genius of the Brown Palace Hotel. Here, indeed, nothing is everything. For this delightful space—whose most prominent grandchildren are the Guggenheim Museum in New York (see page 431) and the Hyatt Regency Atlanta Hotel (see page 518)—demonstrates what cagily handled, sparklingly illuminated, and people-animated space three dimensions can produce. Tracing its origins to the atrium house of Pompeii, the *cortile* of Italian Renaissance palaces, and more recently the old Palace Hotel in San Francisco, 1873–75 (destroyed by the earthquake and fire of 1906, and though rebuilt, not as was), Denver's masterpiece ranks with them all in spatial élan. The exterior of the hotel was influenced, like so many buildings, by H. H. Richardson's now demolished Marshall Field Warehouse of 1885–87. However, as some historians rightly point out, the Brown Palace design also shows a suasion from Adler & Sullivan's Auditorium Building in Chicago (see page 284), begun in 1886. Incidentally, the Brown Palace's architect was from Chicago, but stayed to design many of Denver's important works. Though the exterior is of moderate architectural interest, a step into the lobby is *épatant*. Internal changes and modernization (with varying degrees of success) have kept the public rooms, bedrooms, and services up-to-date, but the great lobby has remained largely untouched. Note, too, the onyx-lined lower floors, the enormous stained-glass skylight, and the bronze balcony panels, all of which are scrupulously maintained. This "ancient" hostel—which was commenced in the heyday of Colorado's mining boom—has been so successful that a twenty-two-story addition was made in 1959 (William B. Tabler Associates, architects), more than doubling the number of rooms.

Lobby open daily 24 hours. Free tours are given Wednesday and Saturday at 2:00 P.M. For more information call (303) 297-3111 or (800) 321-2599.

WAINWRIGHT BUILDING (1890–91)
111 North Seventh Street at Chestnut Street
St. Louis, Missouri

Adler & Sullivan, architects

The problem of the tall building—that uniquely developed American building type—had been solved in technical terms a few years before the Wainwright Building. However, the first metal-framed "skyscrapers" (roughly twelve stories or more), involving as they did drastically new design problems, were almost an embarrassment to their early architects, who proceeded to drape them with confused historic trappings of timidly neutral disposition. William LeBaron Jenney is generally credited with the first high-rise use of skeletal metal construction in his famous but now destroyed Home Insurance Company (1884–85) in Chicago, an eleven-story pioneer of cast and wrought iron and steel, but no gem to gaze upon. Holabird & Roche's far more advanced Tacoma Building (1886–89), also in Chicago and also destroyed, had thirteen floors, all marked by a daring use of glass, but it was a lumpish, layer-cake building.

Louis Sullivan, however, the designer of the Wainwright, asked, "what is the chief characteristic of the tall office building? And at once we answer, it is lofty. This loftiness is to the artist-nature its thrilling aspect. . . . It must be in turn the dominant chord in his expression of it, the true excitant of his imagination. It must be every inch a proud and soaring thing, rising in sheer exultation that from bottom to top it is a unit" ("The Tall Office Building Artistically Considered," reprinted in his *Kindergarten Chats*, Wittenborn, 1947). And so it is. Just as Sullivan himself has been rightly called "the father of modern architecture," so the Wainwright, in its expression of verticality and unity, is the progenitor of the skyscraper as it was subsequently to develop—the first "to pay attention to the voice of steel" (Nikolaus Pevsner, *Pioneers of Modern Design*, Museum of Modern Art, 1949). Or as Fiske Kimball put it, in the Wainwright the "wall surface was abandoned for a system of pier and spandrel" (*Architectural Record*, April 1925).

For more than a generation this cohesive, nine-story-plus-"attic," U-shaped structure influenced the tall buildings of the world. (In plan it measures 127 x 114 feet/39 x 35 meters.) Sullivan wanted to express on the exterior precisely what went on inside (though he fudged in making his non-structural piers as heavy as the structural). Thus the two lower floors state their commercial character: the ground level is largely plate glass for the shops that occupy it, and the second is masonry for walk-up offices and stores. Above the first and second floors, which are sheathed in reddish brown sandstone, a pronounced string course emphasizes the separation of the commercial from the seven floors of professional offices, the whole boldly capped by a tenth-floor utility level with small circular windows peeking from its fantastic cornice. (The building's many copiers transmuted these logically expressed elements into a "Classic" column of base, shaft, and capital.) The Wainwright's verticality is expressed by the corner columns (of exaggerated size), and by the seven-story-high, red brick piers between the ranks of windows. Prominence is given to these piers by their smoothness (in contrast to the intricately ornamental spandrel panels between them), by their rounded "rope" edges, and by the fact that the spandrels are set back from the pier face so that, from an oblique view especially, verticality is the dominant expression. (From acute angles the piers actually recall a parade of Classically derived pilasters, possibly referencing Sullivan's experience in the École des Beaux-Arts.) The red terra-cotta spandrels were not culled from historical antecedents, which most subsequent skyscraper architects espoused, but grew from Sullivan's incredibly facile pencil and Celtic imagination. Note that the panel design differs on each floor. The Wainwright, even at ten stories, dominated downtown St. Louis for years, and its basic design was shortly afterward (1894–95) used by Sullivan for the Prudential (Guaranty) Building in Buffalo, New York (see page 308). The latter shows more finesse than the Wainwright; its entrances are better integrated, and it attains finer overall proportions because of the increased number of office floors (ten versus seven) between the two-story base and elaborately corniced roof. It does, however, have decorated piers, which, for many, does not represent an improvement. But the simpler, sturdy Wainwright ranks among the country's greatest buildings of the nineteenth century. As Hugh Morrison wrote, "In the Wainwright Building, Sullivan gave esthetic form—for the first time in America—to the comparatively new problem of the tall office building" (*Architectural Record*, June 1956).

In 1974 the building was purchased by the State of Missouri, which also sponsored a national competition for the rehabilitation of the entire block for a state office complex. The competition was won by Mitchell/Giurgola of Philadelphia, with Hastings & Chivetta of St. Louis as associates. Renovations have now been completed, and a three-story annex was added in 1979–80.

Open Monday–Friday 8:00 A.M.–5:00 P.M. Closed for holidays.

RELIANCE BUILDING (1890–91/1894–95)
32 North State Street at Washington
Chicago, Illinois

Burnham & Root and D. H. Burnham & Company, architects

The cluster of new skyscrapers on nearby Dearborn Street, several of which can be seen behind the Reliance Building, are lineal descendants of this fourteen-story, nineteenth-century masterpiece. The Reliance, many believe, is the most advanced skyscraper of the Chicago School. In it we find skeletal steel construction with internal wind bracing, prodigious panes of glass, curtain walling (here a narrow band of glazed terra-cotta, reputedly its first high-rise use)—all prototypes of the new technology. The Reliance epitomizes steel skeleton and glass skin more than any of its contemporaries. Glass here forms a wall, not a hole in a wall, and as a consequence it rises with a refined lightness that its masonry-freighted friends could not match. As Sigfried Giedion points out in *Space, Time and Architecture* (Harvard University Press, 1967), the Reliance Building was a direct precursor of Mies van der Rohe's 1920–21 project for an all-glass-sheathed, thirty-story skyscraper. In addition, it refined the bay window treatment of earlier high rises, all seeking light on narrow streets. The Reliance's white terra-cotta is perhaps fussily detailed, but this one-hundred-year-old veteran is still one of the United States' very greatest pioneers.

The building had a curious construction history, which is told by Donald Hoffman in his informative book *The Architecture of John Wellborn Root* (Johns Hopkins University Press, 1973). The site of the Reliance Building (including a previous structure) had been purchased in 1882 by a developer who wished to put up a high-rise (fifteen to sixteen stories) office block, but the lease of the ground floor and basement did not run out until May 1890, while that of the upper three (originally four) continued until 1894. Burnham & Root waited until 1890 and then cranked up the top three floors, laid a new spread foundation, constructed upon it a glass-lined shop—taken by Carson, Pirie, Scott & Company—and established a full-service basement. In January 1891 young John Root died—he was forty-one. Moreover his design for the remainder of the building has never been discovered. The distressed Daniel H. Burnham, after consulting friends, took on the Massachusetts-born, Harvard-educated Charles B. Atwood. (Atwood made substantial contributions to the 1893 World's Columbian Exposition of which Burnham was Director of Works. This brilliant, too-little-known architect also died young—at forty-seven.) Early in 1894 Atwood—soon to become the design partner of the firm—produced the drawings for the thirteen floors to go atop the new base, and when the lease of the old floors was up that May they were removed and the tower we now see was erected. The steel was topped out, in record time, on 1 August 1894, at exactly 200 feet/61 meters.

The structural plan of the Reliance is unusual in that its supporting column grid is not uniformly aligned to form square bays, and though columns frame each of the three projecting or oriel bays per floor (that in front slightly wider than the two on the side), this is not indicated on the exterior. On the interior, the corridors on the upper seven floors are almost completely intact; notable are the cast-iron stairs, the Carrara marble wainscoting, the mahogany trim, the Florentine glass, and the terrazzo floors. There have been changes to the building over the years: the lower floor has been remodeled several times, the mezzanine was added in 1927, and in the late 1940s the cornice was removed, probably for safety reasons. A 1995 restoration was carried out by the McClier Corporation, architects and engineers.

The interior is presently closed to the public. The building is included on the Chicago Architecture Foundation's State Street tour. For more information on CAF tours call (312) 922–3432. PA 8/93

CITY AND COUNTY BUILDING (1891–94)
451 South Street
Salt Lake City, Utah

Proudfoot, Bird & Monheim, architects

A Neo-Romanesque bulwark of officialdom that presides over a flowered and treed setting with determined, almost fortified solidity (which withstood a 1934 earthquake). Its sandstone bulk is energized by a dramatic change of scale at the entry, progressing from tripartite arches (note the polished granite columns)—in the H. H. Richardson manner—to a four-part tall and airy loggia. Three squared towers soar above, and conically capped half-turrets anchor either side. Behind, and turreted itself, rises the five-story central tower, which pulls all forces together and also provides a strong silhouette for the city. The building originally served as territorial capitol (1894–96), then as the first capitol of the state from 1896 to 1916, while the present capitol was completed. (Utah finally attained statehood in 1896, in part due to the Mormons' renunciation of polygamy six years earlier.) The north half of the building now serves as City Hall, the south as County Courthouse. The interiors were restored between 1987 and 1989, and they now feature the marble fireplaces, hand-tiled floors, and red and green color scheme that were originally present. Considering the eclecticism of its era, the City and County Building is by far the best of the end-of-the-century buildings in the state and one of the finest in the West.

Located on the block of 4th South, State, 5th South, and 2nd East streets. Open Monday–Friday 9:00 A.M.–5:00 P.M. Free tours are given from March through November by the Utah Heritage Foundation on Tuesday at 12:00 noon and 1:00 P.M. and on Saturday at 10:00 and 11:00 A.M.; group tours can be arranged by calling the UHF at (801) 533–0858.

BILTMORE (1891–95)
One North Park Square
Asheville, North Carolina

Richard Morris Hunt, architect
Frederick Law Olmsted, landscape architect

There is not another house in the United States that unfurls wealth in a more princely fashion than George Washington Vanderbilt's Biltmore, all 250 rooms and 780 feet/238 meters of
it. There is no other that approaches it in size. Even Hunt's other "vacation houses" for the
Vanderbilts at Newport, Rhode Island—Marble House (1888–92, see page 289) and Breakers
(1895)—seem almost modest beside it, while the Loire chateaux on which Biltmore is based
are amiable transatlantic peers. Richard Morris Hunt did not spend nine years studying, working, and traveling in France in vain. It should be added that Vanderbilt himself had more than
a cursory interest in architecture, in addition to a smart array of languages.

For some observers there is a lack of coordination in the main facade as it peers across its
smooth green parterre, double-lined with trees. This is largely because the central entry with
its pronounced projection and richness dominates the adjacent elements instead of coordinating with them. Most prominent is the stair attached to the left of the front door, basically a
copy, here glazed and reversed, of the famous Francis I double-spiral, towered stair at Blois
(c. 1525).

However, it is on the interior that Biltmore staggers, particularly the incredible six-story-
high (70 feet/21 meters) banquet hall with barrel-vaulted ceiling hovering over all. Beautifully
proportioned and acoustically excellent, this baronial refectory is embellished with thrones,
tapestries, halberds, rugs, *ad infinitum*, with a triple fireplace emblazoning the end. The smaller but even more lavish library—which holds some twenty thousand volumes, mostly rare,
seemingly often read—is also not to be missed. But visit all the rooms open to the public, each
as originally furnished. There will never be another house like it.

The landscaping was laid out by Frederick Law Olmsted, who designed among other great
works New York's Central Park (see page 232). Chauncey Delos Beadle took over the grounds
after Olmsted's death in 1903, having begun with him in 1890. He stayed on at Biltmore for
sixty years. The approach road that Olmsted and Beadle plotted from gate to house is serpentine and highly effective, taking one through the closeness of a forest, then bursting onto an

esplanade. A series of garden terraces escort one from the formality of the mansion to the freedom of nature with a progression that merits study. In addition to the Italian garden next to the house, there is a 4-acre/1.6-hectare walled garden in the English style, plus rose garden and azalea gardens beyond.

Although only 8,000 of the 125,000 acres (3,239 of 50,586 hectares) of the original estate remain—much of it having been deeded to the government as part of Pisgah National Forest and some of it sold—the house itself stands as built and furnished. It was opened to the public (by Vanderbilt heirs) in 1930. The music room, strangely never finished with the rest of the house, was completed in 1976 under the skillful guidance of Alan Burnham, FAIA, a longtime student of Hunt's work.

Located west off US 25, 2 miles/3.2 kilometers south of Asheville. Open daily 9:00 A.M.–5:00 P.M. Closed Thanksgiving, Christmas, and New Years Day. Admission is $24.95 for adults, $18.75 for children ages 10–15, free for children under 10. Guided tours and self-guided audio tours available for an additional fee. Tours can also be arranged by calling (800) 543–2961.

CORN PALACE (1892/1965)
604 North Main Street
Mitchell, South Dakota

This paean to corn affirms that agriculture is South Dakota's leading industry. (Some ninety-two percent of the state's land is occupied by farms.) Originally built in 1892, the Corn Palace was rebuilt on this site in 1921, was completely remodeled in 1965, and now serves primarily as a civic auditorium. The facade of the "palace" is redecorated each fall by a South Dakotan artist. Only natural-colored corn, wheat, and Sudan grass are used—some 350–400 bushels/12,300–14,100 liters of corn and 2 tons/1.8 metric tons of grains and grasses. It is probably the world's largest "living" mural.

Memorial Day–Labor Day open daily 8:00 A.M.–10:00 P.M.; May and September open daily 8:00 A.M.–5:00 P.M., October–April open Monday–Friday 8:00 A.M.–5:00 P.M., except holidays. Closed Thanksgiving, Christmas, and New Year's Day. Admission is free. Memorial Day–Labor Day, free 20-minute tours available twice an hour. For more information call (605) 996–7311.

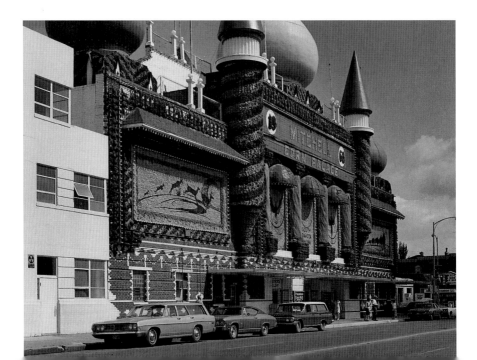

WAINWRIGHT TOMB (1892)
4947 West Florissant Avenue
St. Louis, Missouri

Louis H. Sullivan, architect

Ellis Wainwright, whose famous office building (see page 294) was also designed by Louis H. Sullivan, lost his lovely wife at a tender age (he outlived her thirty-three years). Deep in sorrow, he asked Sullivan to design her (and eventually his) tomb. Sullivan complied with one of the country's most sensitive mausoleums, one forming almost a cube in shape, topped by a dome stepped back at its springing. In front, to soften the transition of its almost Claude-Nicolas Ledoux-like geometry to the landscape, he extended a "porch" with seats at each end and four low steps in front. A rinceau of exquisite plant forms traces across the front, outlining the form of the limestone mass while emphasizing the door. There is quiet, even peaceful eternity here. Its entombment of death has few equals.

Located at the southeast corner of Bellefontaine Cemetery. The cemetery is open daily 8:00 A.M.–5:00 P.M.

UNION STATION (1892–94)
1820 Market Street
between 18th and 20th
St. Louis, Missouri

Theodore C. Link, chief architect

A picturesque pile, whose design was won by invited competition, this terminal reigned for a short time as the largest railroad station in the world. On the exterior, influence of H. H. Richardson's Romanesque Revival, plus other French touches, are evident in a facade that stretches over 600 feet/183 meters, its turrets bristling bravely upward with what the late Carroll L. V. Meeks aptly termed "romantic scenery" (*The Railroad Station: An Architectural History*, Yale University Press, 1956). E. A. Cameron may have had an early hand in the design but he resigned before construction began. There is some thought that the elusive Harvey Ellis also made contributions. The barrel-vaulted grand hall on the second floor today serves as a waiting room and as the Hyatt Regency Hotel lobby. In 1985 the station interior was renovated and redeveloped as a mixed-use building.

A seemingly endless train shed, designed by engineer George H. Pegram, stretched behind. The original thirty-one rows of tracks, plus ten more added in 1929–30, once efficiently handled up to 260 mostly long-distance trains a day. Pegram's shed uses a low-profile, five-arch roof to span its width, hence the space lacks that overwhelming impact delivered by several of the dramatically vaulted stations in London and on the Continent. But the St. Louis shed at 606 feet/185 meters wide by 700 feet/213 meters long still achieves an awesome expanse of roof.

Open Monday–Thursday 10:00 A.M.–9:00 P.M., Friday–Saturday 10:00 A.M.–10:00 P.M., Sunday 11:00 A.M.–7:00 P.M. Tours can be arranged by calling (314) 421-6655.

Carl Milles (1875–1955) was the master of the play of urban waters and a pioneer in injecting spray, in addition to "solid" jets, into fountains. Here in the Aloe Plaza Fountain (1941), representing the allegorical marriage of the Mississippi and the Missouri—whose union some 15 miles/24 kilometers to the north sired St. Louis—we have a civic celebration. (The village was founded in 1764 below the river junction because of higher ground.) This meeting of the waters could also be described as the marriage of bronze and water, so intimately conceived are the statues and their spray. When the water is off, the group stands disjointed and kithless. The angles of the jets and their grouping are complemented by the figures, ranging from the fish-sized fish to the more than life-sized couple. The seriousness of the demure bride (the Missouri) and the eagerness of the groom (the Mississippi) are offset by several outlandishly gleeful sea scoundrels, a total cast of fourteen. One of the few great urban fountains.

UNITED STATES POST OFFICE (1892–94)
621 Kansas Avenue at 7th Street
Atchison, Kansas

Treasury Department, Office of the Supervising Architect, architects

In the 1890s, as increasingly today, the federal government sought high-caliber architectural advice for its buildings. This post office obviously stems directly from the work of H. H. Richardson, and, equally obviously, has been "handled in an unusual and creative manner," as the National Register puts it. Note, for instance, that the left-hand tower is taller, the better to "pivot" the corner. The building's soft, light-colored limestone walls—carved on the site—are showing signs of weathering, and the once lofty interior had its ceiling dropped in the mid-1950s, concealing the inner balcony, but structurally it is as sturdy as when built. The carved oak detailing in the lobby is of particular interest. A thorough restoration was completed in 1993. The nearby Court House (1896–97), Parallel Street at 5th, is in the same Neo-Romanesque mold.

Lobby open daily 5:30 A.M.–8:00 P.M. Window hours are Monday–Friday 8:00 A.M.–5:00 P.M., Saturday 9:00–11:00 A.M.; closed for holidays. Tours can be scheduled by calling (913) 367–6303.

BRADBURY BUILDING (1893)
304 South Broadway
Los Angeles, California

George H. Wyman, architect

Spritely in spite of its years, and surviving the inconveniences of fire, earthquake, and semi-neglect in a once deteriorating section of downtown, this five-story building is one of the few commercial treasures of any period. Its top-lit central court, though somewhat cramped on the entry floor, radiates light and space above, while its lavish use of wrought iron (some think made in France) is wonderfully inventive, especially on the "open" elevator cages. Once one of an endangered species of central-court, sky-lit "skyscrapers" (compare the Brown Palace Hotel in Denver, Colorado, page 293), the Bradbury through a variety of happy circumstances has come down to us basically intact. In 1991 the building was handsomely restored and brought up to current fire and earthquake codes under the direction of architect Brenda Levin. All has been returned to pristine glory, including the 50 x 120-foot/15 x 36-meter skylight. A storage area was converted into a rear entrance, and sprinklers and lighting sconces added, but otherwise the interior now looks as it did one hundred years ago. The exterior, of brick and sandstone (also restored), will not stop traffic, but step inside to see what a young draftsman—bolstered reputedly by a Ouija board—did with space, light, and loving attention to detail. It is listed in the National Register of Historic Places.

Ground floor open to the public Monday–Saturday 9:00 A.M.–5:00 P.M. The building is included on a walking tour given on Saturday mornings by the L.A. Conservancy; for more information call (213) 623–2489.

ST. NICHOLAS ORTHODOX CHURCH (1893–94)
326 5th Street
Juneau, Alaska

This minute and architecturally modest church is of Russian parentage but includes some Victorian details. The octagonal body, with gabled entry on one side (note belfry), is topped by a bold octagonal roof with an onion-domed (or flame-shaped) cupola atop and a cross above. The tiny interior, almost half sanctuary, is of interest chiefly for its collection of iconic paintings. The church was built primarily by Native Americans who converted to the Russian Orthodox religion. St. Nicholas, the oldest parish church building in southeast Alaska, is listed in the National Register of Historic Places.

Open mid-May to mid-September daily 9:00 A.M.–6:00 P.M. The rest of the year, open for services Saturday 5:00–7:00 P.M. and Sunday 9:00–11:30 A.M. A $1 donation per person is requested. In summer, tours can be arranged by calling (907) 586–1023.

JEFFERSON HOTEL (1893–95/1907)
Franklin and Adams streets
Richmond, Virginia

Carrère & Hastings, architects
J. Kevan Peebles, architect of remodeling

The sumptuous Jefferson Hotel, a prime example of the French Beaux-Arts style, first opened to the public in 1895. In 1901 a fire destroyed a large portion of the building, and the subsequent remodeling by J. Kevan Peebles altered much of the original interior. The hotel reopened in 1902 and accommodated guests until 1980, when it was closed until 1986 for an extensive restoration to bring much of it back to its Beaux-Arts appearance. Its cream-colored brick exterior is graced by a campanile ornamented with decorative terra-cotta detailing. The palm court, used as the main lobby, is surrounded by a Pompeian-style colonnade and capped by a faux stained-glass skylight. Closed to the public between 1949 and 1980, this room has largely been restored to its original 1895 appearance. The lower lobby, also known as the rotunda, speaks with nothing less than Neronian splendor: massive columns of marbleized masonry topped by capitals rich with gilt and flowered swags, mezzanine walls refulgent with red and gold. If the fates are ever so unkind as to phase out this 274-room Betthaus, let us hope that the rotunda will always be kept; no hotel could have a finer introduction. Behind this sturdy Classicism are grouped unobtrusive but efficient hotel facilities.

Lobbies open to the public daily 24 hours. Group tours can be arranged by calling (804) 788–8000.

MUSEUM OF SCIENCE AND INDUSTRY (1893/1933–40)
(formerly Palace of Fine Arts)
57th Street and South Lake Shore Drive
Chicago, Illinois

D. H. Burnham & Company, architects

Chicago's famous World's Columbian Exposition of 1892–93 was the most momentous fair ever held in the Americas. Not only was the gleaming White City of overwhelming beauty to most of its viewers (but not all of its critics) by day, it was magically illuminated at night—the first time buildings of such scale had been floodlit. Moreover the fair's mostly "Roman" stage-set gave an imprimatur to Neo-Classical architecture, which thereafter was a decisive factor in shaping a large share of the "official" buildings (and banks) throughout the United States. Classical influence continued for more than the fifty years that Louis Sullivan mournfully predicted. Though the fair's other building and most of its lagoon (by Frederick Law Olmsted) are gone, the Palace of Fine Arts, designed by Charles B. Atwood in Burnham's firm, is still with us. It is important, and surprising, to note that the building "was not constructed as a temporary structure; the main walls are of solid brick and perfectly sound, and the foundations of brick and concrete and the entire structural features are [today] in good condition" (*Architectural Forum*, July 1921).

Chicago's former Palace was initially used after the fair as a natural history museum with much of its collection coming from the fair itself. It was first known as the Field Columbian Museum, then the Field Museum of Natural History. However when the present Field Museum in Grant Park was completed in 1920, Graham, Anderson, Probst & White, archi-

tects, the old Palace was deserted. In 1921 Julius Rosenwald, who had been deeply impressed by Munich's Deutsches Museum—the greatest technical museum in the world—offered to contribute $1 million if the city would establish a similar institution. Though Rosenwald's offer was not acted upon at this time, it planted a seed, for on 9 June 1922, the American Institute of Architects staged a banquet in the great 1893 Rotunda to focus public attention on saving the building. In 1925 a substantial bond issue was passed to rehabilitate (with a museum in mind) the only relic of its famous fair, and the next year the ever-generous Rosenwald offered $3 million if the city would make it a museum of science and industry. (He later doubled his gift.)

This largesse was, of course, welcomed, and the long-term process of reconditioning and planning begun, the museum opening in the spring of 1933 for Chicago's Century of Progress Exposition. It was not until 1940, however, that all of the interior and its installations were completed. The architects rehabilitating the exterior of this Athenian-inspired, Classical Revival example were Graham, Anderson, Probst & White, with Shaw, Naess & Murphy responsible for the interior. Whether (as claimed of the original) the building constituted "a result unequaled since the days of Pericles" is a moot question, but at least we have one of America's most fascinating museums and a souvenir of the country's most famous fair.

Memorial Day–Labor Day and during the holiday season open daily 9:30 A.M.–5:30 P.M.; the rest of the year open Monday–Friday 9:30 A.M.–4:00 P.M., Saturday–Sunday and holidays 9:30 A.M.–5:30 P.M. Closed on Christmas. Admission is $6 for adults, $5 for senior citizens, $2.50 for children ages 5–12. Free admission on Thursdays. For more information call (312) 684-1414. The building is included on the Chicago Architecture Foundation's bus tour; the cost is $25. For more information on CAF tours call (312) 922-3432.

ELLIS COUNTY COURT HOUSE (1894–97)
Main Street (US 287)
Waxahachie, Texas

J. Riely Gordon, architect

Towered and turreted, this is "one of the most interesting and literate of all the Richardsonian court houses" (*Court House*, Richard Pare, ed., Horizon, 1978). We find here a bastion of granite (gray for base, pink above), sandstone, and terra-cotta that will interest the specialist. The interiors are unprepossessing. J. Riely Gordon (1863–1937), incidentally, supposedly designed sixty-nine courthouses in his long career, and was even commissioned to do the Texas Pavilion at the New York World's Fair of 1939–40.

Open Monday–Friday 8:00 A.M.–5:00 P.M. Free 30-minute tours can be arranged by calling (214) 923-5000.

GUARANTY BUILDING (1895–96)
(also known as the Prudential Building)
34 Church Street at Pearl Street
Buffalo, New York

Dankmar Adler and Louis H. Sullivan, architects

There are many Guaranty buildings across the United States but none commands the serenity of this 1896 masterpiece by Louis H. Sullivan. (Sullivan parted with Dankmar Adler in 1895
and finished the Guaranty Building alone.) He was the country's first "modern" architect
("form ever follows function"), designer of several of the United States' greatest early skyscrapers, and Frank Lloyd Wright's *lieber Meister*. As Henry-Russell Hitchcock wrote, "Almost
miraculously one genius, Louis Sullivan, was able to cope with the skyscraper, in the fullest
architectural sense, functionally, technically, and aesthetically" (*Architectural Review*, July
1937). Yet he was also a man who died in 1924 spurned and neglected—an American Mozart.
Although planned as the H. L. Taylor Building, Taylor died before construction began, and the
thirteen-story building was named for its subsequent owner, Guaranty Construction Company
of Chicago. However, it was known as the Prudential—its next financial backer—from 1898
until it was rededicated in 1982.

The structure possesses a unity, a wholeness, that few of today's even modest skyscrapers
carry. (The facade does not, however, reveal which piers are structural.) Note, first, the doubling of the bay on the two lower floors. On the street level the structural columns are explicitly revealed behind huge sheets of plate glass: the second floor, devoted to walk-up retailing
and not offices, carries its own statement. Above this two-story base rises a ten-story cage of

divisible offices. At top the
combined office and utility
floor, illuminated by startling
round windows (oval on
Pearl Street), terminates all
with its glorious cornice.
Sullivan colored the terra-
cotta skin needed for fire
protection in earth tones
when most architects were
opting for white.

Sullivan's famous orna-
ment, or rather Sullivan's and
George Elmslie's ornament
(Elmslie worked for Sullivan
for twenty years), was used
with elaborate skill on the
Guaranty Building; terra-cotta
and steel never have been so
artfully wedded. (As regards
terra-cotta, Karl Friedrich
Schinkel, 1781–1841, is generally credited with its first
"contemporary" use in his
Berlin Academy of 1835; the

material's origins go back at least to Assyrian times.) As the famous Montgomery Schuyler (1843–1914) wrote, "I know of no steel-framed building in which the metallic construction is more palpably felt through the envelope of baked clay" (*Architectural Record*, February 1896). However, it should be noted that Sullivan used decoration on the *piers* of the Prudential, whereas on the earlier Wainwright in St. Louis (1891—see page 294) he wisely left these vertical structural elements in pure brick with slight edge molding. Postmodern architects—for whom ornament is fashionable—find Sullivan's ornament an unparalleled achievement.

In 1975 the Guaranty was made a National Historic Landmark. In 1974, a fire damaged the top floors, and although it caused little exterior damage, it helped push the building into receivership. After a five-year preservation campaign it was saved and fully restored inside and out by Cannon Design, architects, in 1982–83. The exterior was cleaned, and windows and broken terra-cotta repaired or replaced. The interiors of the first two floors have been returned to their original appearance, including restoring or recreating light fixtures, mosaics, stained glass, and cast-iron work. The upper floors were remodeled into modern offices, which unfortunately included filling in the central light well to create additional floor space.

Lobby open to the public Monday–Saturday 9:00 A.M.–5:00 P.M.

MINNESOTA STATE CAPITOL (1896–1905)
75 Constitution Avenue
St. Paul, Minnesota

Cass Gilbert, architect

Other states have their dome-bedecked capitols, and some boast interiors of no small grandeur, but it is doubtful if any can equal the Roman-bath splendor of the upper halls and grand stairways of this one in Minnesota. It was designed by an Ohio-born, Minnesota-educated (with one year at MIT) architect, Cass Gilbert. Gilbert went on to greater fame with his "Gothic" Woolworth Building (1911–13) in New York (see page 336), then regressed, some feel, with his Supreme Court Building (1935) in Washington, D.C.; but overall the Minnesota State Capitol ranks high among structures surfeited with political megalomania. The dome itself, a scaled-down copy of Michelangelo's atop St. Peter's—the last epistle of the Romans to St. Paul—dominates the countryside as domes are wont to do. (Note the quadriga at its base.) The building's length is 434 feet/132 meters. Inside, the executive offices fill, with only moderate inefficiency, the first floor, while Supreme Court, House, and Senate occupy the second. Unfortunately Interstate 94 cuts a swath (at least sunken) across the front edge of the capitol complex, thereby isolating government from downtown. Obvious to all except the Bureau of Public Roads, it would have been far better located north of the capitol.

Open Monday–Friday 9:00 A.M.–5:00 P.M., Saturday 10:00 A.M.–4:00 P.M., Sunday 1:00–4:00 P.M. Free tours are given every hour on the hour. Group tours can be scheduled by calling (612) 296–2881.

BLAIR HALL (1897)
Princeton University
Princeton, New Jersey

Cope & Stewardson, architects

The use of pure Gothic for universities, from paradigms in Oxford and Cambridge, began in this country in the late 1880s, not, it should be pointed out, as a continuation of the much earlier Gothic Revival, an altogether different aspect of Victorian eclecticism. The so-called "Collegiate Gothic" was the outcome of a movement that sought to return to the traditions of medieval humanism and learning, where the scholars could enjoy close relations with their masters in a setting conducive to contemplation and freedom from architectural rigidity. Walter Cope and John Stewardson were among the pioneers of this style, and their work for Bryn Mawr (c. 1886) is probably its first significant essay. (The slightly earlier designs by William Burges for Trinity College in Hartford and by Henry Ives Cobb for Rockefeller University in Chicago were similarly directed but less pure and only partly finished.)

Princeton's Blair Hall (pictured below), however, established the Collegiate Gothic movement for decades to come, a movement that reached a "spiritual" climax in Ralph Adams Cram's memorable Graduate School for Princeton (1913) (pictured on the following page)—and perhaps chilled with his University Chapel (1928). (Cram, not unexpectedly, was architect of the university from 1904–27.) James Gamble Rogers's notable Harkness Quadrangle for Yale (1921)—plus others to follow— and Horace Trumbauer's Duke University Campus (1923–32) were of the same ingratiating— and, in their day, even functional—persuasion.

But back to Blair Hall and the quadrangle it faces. Far more permanent than the building's initial impact—and with a force that will outlive any cycle of architectural fashions—is the molding of its architectural spaces. There are vertical spaces created by changes in level that are experienced via the almost theatrical steps at the arch and in the landscaping, and horizontal

spaces in the pulsations of Blair and the buildings extending from it. The Blair Hall family of structures narrows closely at the south end (faltering a bit at the southeast corner), then the spatial continuum broadens into the elongated, eminently relaxed quadrangle framed by a series of dormitories (all from the early 1920s). This three-dimensional excursion is climaxed by the sensitive Dodge Memorial Gateway (1933—Day & Klauder). Through the years these buildings were interwoven to produce a masterful three-dimensional experience, one with unforgettable spatial, textural, and landscaping lessons: even the geometry of the paths is important. Altogether an exhilarating experience

Alexander Hall stands diagonally to the northeast from Blair Arch. W. A. Potter used Richardsonian detailing in what became this movement's swan song, for the hall was dedicated in 1894, just three years before the new Collegiate Gothic rose to reduce the Neo-Romanesque's once prominent role to stylistic limbo.

Blair Hall and Alexander Hall are closed to the public. The exteriors of Blair Hall and Alexander Hall are part of a free campus tour given by the Orange Key Guide Service. Tours given Monday–Saturday at 10:00 A.M., 11:00 A.M., 1:30 P.M., and 3:30 P.M., Sunday at 1:30 and 3:30 P.M. No tours given on major holidays or during winter or spring recesses. For more information call (609) 258–3603. AF 12/25

BROADWAY AND ITS BUILDINGS (1897–99)
Skagway, Alaska

Skagway—the Home of the North Wind—was the once-thriving entry port for the Yukon Gold Rush, that stampede of perhaps 30,000 or more determined men and women struggling into Canada's Klondike in 1897–98. At its zenith the town reputedly reached a population (mostly transient) of some 8,000–10,000, the largest in the territory. However, it declined rather quickly to less than 1,000, primarily because more and more accessible gold was discovered (1899) across Alaska at Nome on the Bering Sea. Skagway almost collapsed (the population was reportedly 492 in 1930, while the adjacent village of Dyea did disappear), but it fortunately revived somewhat during World War II as a supply base for constructing the Alaska Highway. (The Japanese had captured Attu and Kiska islands in the Aleutians in 1942–43, and the highway, more than half of which traverses Canada, was a vital U.S. supply line.) Then in the mid-1960s mineral wealth in the Yukon began to be shipped out in huge quantities and Skagway became a prominent shipping point for ore concentrate, its White Pass and Yukon Railroad (daringly built during the Gold Rush) finally coming into its own. (The railroad shut down when the mine closed in 1982; reopened in 1988, it has been running during the summer months—May to September—as a spectacular tourist excursion.) Throughout these ups and downs the buildings of the late 1890s survived, many thanks to the work of the National Park Service (which owns and has restored a number of these structures), and this legacy, though modest, is important in any review of the architecture of the state. There is no significant individual structure, but Broadway as a street will reward the dedicated, as well as followers of Jack London and Robert W. Service. Note that Broadway had long been a gravel street—it was paved in 1984—and the sidewalks are still of wood. The most frenetic structure is the Arctic Brotherhood Building (built 1899—currently the Visitors Center, it is open daily 8:00 A.M.–5:00 P.M. in summer) near the harbor end of the street, with a facade totally decorated with sticks of driftwood, looking like some giant match king's last fling. A half block up the street stands the Golden North Hotel (1898, open year-round); its "dome" was removed to add a third story and then replaced when the hotel was moved down the street in 1908. Within is displayed a hair-raising collection of photographs of endless lines of miners attacking the murderous snows of White Pass and Chilkoot trails, which lead over the Canadian border and then to the gold fields of the Yukon, still some 500 miles/800 kilometers away. A number of rooms of the Golden North have been comfortably restored as originally furnished (but with modern plumbing). There are other interesting buildings of the era along Broadway, but more important is the general, relatively unspoiled, total character of the street. The Trail of '98 Museum (open May–September, daily 9:00 A.M.–5:00 P.M.; winter months by request), just off Broadway, is on the second floor of the McCabe College building (1899); the ground floor houses the City Hall. Though no architectural sensation, it was the first stone structure in the state, and the museum has a kaleidoscope of memorabilia of the Gold Rush period. Fortunately the Skagway Historic District has been entered in the National Register of Historic Places so that this unique town will be preserved.

Visitors may want to stop by the National Park Service Visitors Center; it is located at Broadway and 2nd Avenue and is open late May and September daily 8:00 A.M.–6:00 P.M., June–August daily 8:00 A.M.–8:00 P.M., with free 45-minute walking tours from mid-May to September at 9:30 A.M., 11:00 A.M., 2:00 P.M., and 4:00 P.M. For more information call the Visitors Center at (907) 983–2921.

CARSON, PIRIE, SCOTT STORE (1899/1903–04/1906/1961)
(formerly Schlesinger and Mayer Department Store)
1 South State Street at Madison
Chicago, Illinois

Louis H. Sullivan, architect

In addition to the balloon frame, the skyscraper, and Frank Lloyd Wright's open-plan "prairie houses," Chicago gave the world "the Chicago window." This consists of an enormous fixed glass pane flanked by smaller, double-hung sash windows for ventilation on one or both sides. No enterprise could employ these windows to greater advantage at the time of their development than a department store, and the great Sullivan here used glass to maximum advantage. Today's fluorescent lighting and year-round air conditioning have transformed mercantile emporia into windowless boxes, except for the ground-floor showcases, but at the end of the nineteenth century the Carson, Pirie, Scott Store achieved a fenestrated grandeur (while directly reflecting its structural frame) that has never been equaled.

To give relief to the building's basic plainness, and to entice customers into the main entrance (on the corner), Louis H. Sullivan traced out, and George G. Elmslie detailed, a filigree of incredible cast-iron ornament—"coiling thickets of iron ribbons" (Vincent Scully)—that traces along the lower two floors and blossoms at the entry. Take a long look at this entrance ornament: the world is not apt to see such inventiveness and such craftsmanship again.

The building began in 1899 under Sullivan as the three-bay, nine-story unit to the east (nearest the lake) on Madison Street; then in 1903–04 Sullivan designed a twelve-story addition, attaching three more bays along Madison, the rounded corner, and seven bays on State

Street; D. H. Burnham & Company added a matching extension on State in 1906, as did Holabird and Root in 1961. There were later additions and alterations, but the great contribution lies in the Sullivan facade and the entry at northwest corner.

In 1979 the city completed the State Street Mall in front of Carson's and other important stores. Traffic on this nine-block landscaped "great street" is currently limited to buses and emergency vehicles. The street is scheduled for redevelopment beginning in 1996; the plan, designed by Skidmore, Owings & Merrill, will include sidewalk repaving, increased landscaping, lighting on building facades, and the reintroduction of 1920s-era streetlights. One hopes the result will be sympathetic to the historic architecture it faces.

Open Monday–Friday 9:45 A.M.–7:00 P.M., Saturday 10:00 A.M.–6:00 P.M., Sunday 12:00 noon–5:00 P.M. Closed Thanksgiving and Christmas. For more information call (312) 641–7000. The Chicago Architecture Foundation offers a two-hour tour of the building; the cost is $5. For more information on CAF tours call (312) 922–3432.

THE ELMS (1899–1901)
Bellevue Avenue between Bellevue Court and Dixon Street
Newport, Rhode Island

Horace Trumbauer, architect

Though removed from the sea (and questionably close to the avenue) The Elms establishes intimate contact with nature on its garden side through André Le Nôtre-inspired landscaping by C. H. Miller and E. W. Bowditch, working in close cooperation with the architect. The gardens are probably the finest to be seen in Newport. The house itself wears the mantle of a stylistically "correct" eighteenth-century French chateau, though the result might be said to be on the dry side. The little-known Chateau d'Asnieres (1751, on the southwest edge of Paris), built for the Marquis de Voyer d'Argenson, is mentioned as inspiration—as indeed it is—but Horace Trumbauer, who at that time had never even been to France, cut The Elms' wings to four bays and added a pediment. The interior of the house, beginning with its foyer and entry hall, rises with relaxed opulence and even excitement, with elaborate furnishings carried out by two French decorating firms. The resulting impression, however, tends to be of a series of highly furnished, almost competitive rooms. One of the most sophisticated houses of the early twentieth century, it had been scheduled for demolition and its furnishings had been sold when the Preservation Society of Newport County raised enough money to purchase it (1962) and to collect and borrow sufficient furnishings to refit it in proper style. A major restoration of the grounds is currently in progress.

May–October open daily 10:00 A.M.–5:00 P.M. November–April open Saturday–Sunday 10:00 A.M.–4:00 P.M. Closed Christmas Eve and Christmas Day. Admission is $7.50 for adults, $3 for children ages 6–11. 45-minute tours available. For more information call (401) 847–1000.

ROSECLIFF (1899–1902)
Bellevue Avenue at Marine Avenue
Newport, Rhode Island

McKim, Mead & White, architects

Restrained grace, as opposed to inescapable opulence, characterizes Rosecliff. This "decorative confection," as it has been called, is also, more than any other "cottage" in Newport, highly livable. Almost all major rooms are in visual contact with the sea and with light and air coursing through the ballroom, which forms the "bar" (appropriately) of its *H*-shaped plan. This sunny chamber ranks with Newport's finest. In designing the mansion, Stanford White—the partner-in-charge—freely recalled J. H. Mansart's Grand Trianon at Versailles (1688), but added a second floor and extended the end wings.

April–October open daily 10:00 A.M.–5:00 P.M. Admission is $6.50 for adults, $3 for children ages 6–11. 45-minute tours available. For more information call (401) 847-1000.

FLATIRON BUILDING (1901–03)
(Fuller Building)
175 5th Avenue and 949 Broadway at 23rd Street
New York, New York

Daniel H. Burnham, architect

Daniel H. Burnham's practice had been overwhelmingly successful—he had for one thing been chief planner and coordinator for the 1893 Chicago World's Columbian Exposition—when he came to New York to design its then tallest building. With the exemplary Reliance Building in Chicago (see page 296) behind him and the Classical shades of the exposition affecting his taste buds, he put together one of the city's first all-steel frame skyscrapers. He draped its twenty floors with a profligate amount of decoration, all arranged in the Classical pattern of attic, shaft, and basement. From the top down we find in layers a balustrade, a bold cornice, a band of maidens peeping out of blocks between windows, two-story roundheaded window framing, and finally a clutch of lions' heads—all in the four floors of the attic. Then come a row of one-story roundheaded windows (all others have flat lintels) and twelve floors of shaft broken on each side by three eight-story vertical bands of slightly projecting windows or oriels. One contemporary article claims "that the eight-story hanging oriels which diversify his [Burnham's] front are so spaced as on the one hand not visibly to destroy their own purpose of gaining sidelong views out of certain favored offices, and, on the other, as agreeably to diversify the monotony of the wall without impairing the effect of the repetition of its equable fenestration" (*Architectural Record*, October 1902). The relatively mild four floors of the "basement" begin with an energetic band of decoration and meet the ground with a sharply incised entry level with proper front door(s). Rustication characterizes most of the stonework (and terra-cotta). It is small wonder that the Flatiron (technically the Fuller) Building was "the most notorious thing in New York, and attracts more attention than all the other buildings now going up put together" (*ibid.*). Lavish decoration aside, the Flatiron was a local structural pioneer. Its triangular plan, mandated by the meeting of 5th Avenue and Broadway, is such "that, during a storm, people are sometimes whirled off the sidewalk and plate-glass shop-windows shivered" (Karl Baedeker, *United States*, 1909).

Lobby open to the public Monday–Friday 8:00 A.M.–6:00 P.M. Closed for holidays. AR 10/02, AR 7/15

NEW YORK PUBLIC LIBRARY, CENTER FOR THE HUMANITIES (1902–11)
5th Avenue between 40th and 42nd streets
New York, New York

Carrère & Hastings, architects

The facade of the New York Public Library represents the Beaux-Arts School of architecture at its best, but it is the building's extraordinarily sympathetic relation to the street that is beyond compare—and beyond the veils of any style. Set back 75 feet/23 meters from 5th Avenue (Thomas Hastings fought for more), every foot has been carefully developed: note that the planting begins at the sidewalk itself on either side of the gentle steps (and seating alcoves), with E. C. Potter's famous lions standing guard. (The planting is, of course, much finer today than when the library was finished.) We are then introduced to a relaxed parterre that stretches the full length of the 390-foot-/119-meter-long building to terminate in well-landscaped retreats at each end. Planting—here backed by good-sized trees—is picked up again to frame the terrace on its inner edge and soften the flanks of the building. On either side and slightly in front of the triple-arched entry stands a monumental urn. A fountain adorned by statues of Truth and Beauty by Frederick MacMonnies (1920) is set in each angle of the projected portico. The coupled Corinthian columns obviously establish a commanding entrance, but do not intimidate or become too serious, primarily because of the treatment of the terrace and the invitation extended from the street itself.

On entering the lobby we are confronted with what many would hold to be the architects' only serious error: to get to the books on the third floor "it was expected that the public would be required to use the stairs"—all seventy-three of them—or wonder and wander down the corridor to find two half-hidden elevators, then walk back to midpoint on the top floor. The

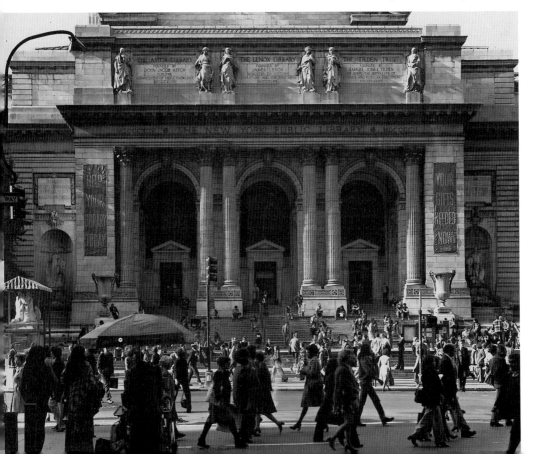

great reading room itself is one of the finest spaces in the city; its lofty proportions and the beautifully tempered quality of its bilateral lighting make it virtually a perfect reading and research spot. Moreover it is not disturbed by masses of books; it has only a modest band of reference volumes around three sides. A service spine divides the room into halves, but the spine's height was kept low so as to allow spatial unity—and a full view of a ceiling of prodigious richness. This central service facility is placed directly over the stacks on the lower floors so that efficiency of book retrieval is excellent.

The library, which is privately and municipally supported, represents the 1895 consolidation of the Astor and Lenox libraries and the Tilden Trust. Occupying the site of the old Croton Reservoir, the building's design was reached by a 1897 competition won by two architects who had formerly worked for McKim, Mead & White (who had also entered the competition and, one gathers, did not relish third place). John Merven Carrère (1858–1911) was unfortunately killed in an automobile accident just a few months before the library was dedicated, but it was sufficiently finished for him to appreciate its sterling qualities. G. H. Edgell in his book *The American Architecture of Today* (Scribner's, 1928) contends that Hastings was not satisfied with the central pavilion, and made a proposal for doubling the single end columns and statues, and elaborating its corners—which Edgell fully illustrates—and "made a provision in his will for the means to carry out the change." This, as can be seen, was never done.

Open Monday, Thursday, Friday, and Saturday 10:00 A.M.–6:00 P.M.; Tuesday and Wednesday 11:00 A.M.–6:00 P.M. Closed for holidays. Free one-hour tours are given Monday–Saturday at 11:00 A.M. and 2:00 P.M. Tours can also be scheduled by calling (212) 930–0911. For general information call (212) 340–0849; for library hours call (212) 661–7220; for exhibition information call (212) 869–8089.

Directly behind the library, on the site occupied by New York's Crystal Palace from 1853 until it burned five years later, lies Bryant Park (1884–1995). Covering two-thirds of a block (9.6 acres/3.9 hectares) it was named for William Cullen Bryant. Its scope is of unexpected interest in that it technically wraps around the library and extends to 5th Avenue itself to include the entrance terrace to the library. Thus Thomas Hastings, one of the architects of the library, was also responsible for the park's basic architectural design, notably the raised terrace adjacent to the library at the rear and the two stone kiosks (originally comfort stations) at the west end. The park was neglected beginning in the 1920s, until in 1933 during the Depression, the Architects' Emergency Committee held a competition—limited to unemployed architects and draftsmen—for its rejuvenation. This was won by Lusby Simpson, and the landscaping and planting was carried out in 1934 by the Parks Department under its new commissioner Robert Moses, with Aymar Embury, Jr., architect to the department. This small bit of urban delight was designated a Scenic Landmark by the Landmarks Preservation Committee in 1974. In 1992 Bryant Park was reopened after its landscaping was completely refurbished by Hanna/Olin, Hardy Holzman Pfeiffer, and Kupiec & Koutsomitis, with recommendations from urbanist William H. Whyte and funding from the Bryant Park Restoration Corporation. It presently consists of a large central lawn bordered by two 300-foot/91-meter gardens and rows of trees to the north and south. The Lowell Memorial Fountain (by Charles A. Platt, 1912) stands on a rebuilt plaza to the west; on the terrace directly behind the library is a statue of William Cullen Bryant (by Herbert Adams, 1911) along with a restaurant and café overlooking a transverse promenade. The modest changes in levels, the definition of circulation, the degrees of separation from active to passive, and the quality of planting make this a distinguished small mid-city park.

September–May open daily 8:00 A.M.–6:00 P.M., June–July open daily 7:00 A.M.–9:00 P.M., August open daily 7:00 A.M.–8:00 P.M. AR 9/10, LA 12/92

OLD FAITHFUL INN (1903–04/1913/1928)
opposite Old Faithful Geyser on Yellowstone Loop
Yellowstone National Park, Wyoming

J. C. Reamer, architect

The Swedes introduced the log cabin into the American colonies in 1638, but it is doubtful if any of them could have envisioned a log (and frame) structure as mammoth as Old Faithful Inn. With 325 bedrooms, 248 baths, and public areas pyramiding to an eight-story overall height in the center, it would be imposing of almost any material. There is an authentic rustic quality to the inn's log, boulder, and lava block construction, which typifies a high-mountain, Western, resort hotel at the turn of the century. It has, indeed, potent architectural validity today. (If only we could find workmen as dedicated as those who erected this in extremes of cold and snow, handling difficult material logistics.) The interiors of the public rooms form an almost unique period piece: to quote a 1908 guidebook, "Windows of diamond-shaped panes and dainty French curtains are exquisitely beautiful against the setting of rough logs. Elbows of natural branches from the neighboring forests form braces for the numerous gables and frame the many balconies and stairways surrounding the office while timbers braced this way and that support the high roof" (reprinted in *Wyoming History News*, May 1975). J. C. Reamer, a Seattle architect, added the east wing in 1913 and the west wing in 1928. Listed in the National Register of Historic Places, the inn forms an environmentally sympathetic introduction to the nation's first (1872) national park.

Open May–September daily 24 hours. Tours given daily. For more information call (307) 344–7311. W 10/04

UNION STATION (1903–08/1976/1985–88)
40 Massachusetts Avenue NE at Louisiana and Delaware avenues
Washington, D.C.

Daniel H. Burnham, architect

Daniel H. Burnham was one of the founding architects of, and chief of construction for, Chicago's World's Columbian Exhibition of 1893—an exhibition both famous and infamous for its influence. (Louis Sullivan said of its Neo-Classic architecture, "The damage wrought by the World's Fair will last for half a century"—quoted in Hugh Morrison, *Louis Sullivan*, Norton, 1935 & 1962.) Burnham's Union Station was obviously influenced by the Roman Classicism of the fair that he had had so much to do with, but Burnham also carefully studied important depots in Europe and saw to it first that his design for Washington was a splendidly working railroad station. It would be Classical obviously, but not a building plucked from the pages of architectural history with function compromised accordingly.

The setting was also designed by Burnham, who with Charles F. McKim, Frederick Law Olmsted, and Augustus Saint-Gaudens comprised the laudable McMillan Commission (Senate Park Commission), whose report of 1902 did so much to shake up laissez-faire

Washington. The report forcefully pointed out that a full return to Pierre Charles L'Enfant's original plan should be made, and, despite considerable opposition, this was largely effected. The new station and its plaza relate completely to the L'Enfant concept, providing a stimulating and immediate view of official Washington from the main entrance. Moreover, the reverse is also true: the building holds down its position with dignity as one approaches it. (The previous station, 1873, penetrated the Mall itself with its tracks—at 6th Street—almost at the foot of the Capitol.)

The monumental Burnham facade is dominated by three almost triumphal arches, with statues by Louis Saint-Gaudens on top of its Ionic columns, and with long, lower arcaded wings on either side. Union Station, particularly its main terminal level, where canopied platforms along its tracks once led to a 760-foot-/232-meter-long concourse with an airily vaulted roof, functioned extremely well. Its circulation pattern was spontaneously clear to any traveler. The great, deeply coffered, barrel-vaulted waiting room—reminiscent of, but not a slave to, the tepidarium of a Roman bath—provided one of the country's few monumental interior spaces.

With the decline of rail travel the station lost much of its traffic and was remodeled at vast expense (1976) as a controversial National Visitors Center. However, in 1978 the Visitors Center was closed, and in 1981 Congress requested that a plan be drawn up for the structure's future. Thus the Union Station Redevelopment Corporation was created as a partnership between the government and three private firms: LaSalle Partners (corporate real-estate developers), Williams Jackson Ewing (retail developers), and Benjamin Thompson & Associates (restoration architects). The restoration and revitalization project (1985–88) returned rail service to the building, while also creating retail space in a style sympathetic to the existing architecture, to make the station financially self-sufficient. This change sagely reflects the burgeoning interest in high-speed rail traffic in the BoWash corridor—and appreciation of Dan Burnham's claim that "this station [is] superior to any structure ever erected for railway purpose" (*ibid.*).

Open daily 24 hours. Group tours can be scheduled by calling (202) 371–9441; the cost is $2 per person. AR 7/15, AR 6/77, ARev 7/77, PA 11/77, JAIA mid-5/78, PA 5/78, A 1/80, PA 2/88, PA 8/93

GRAND CENTRAL TERMINAL (1903–13)
89–105 East 42nd Street at Park Avenue
New York, New York

Warren & Wetmore, Reed & Stem, architects

Grand Central Terminal—an amusingly egregious title—is far more than a building; it is the most important nodal point and transportation interchange in New York City and a fulcrum for the entire East Side. Moreover, as the multitude of tracks that feed the terminal demand considerable lateral and linear space, its urban impact has been immense. The first Grand Central (1869–71), with a 200-foot-/61-meter-wide arched train shed, was vastly expanded in 1899–1901; both stations were served by surface steam trains that chugged in and out by the hundreds to make a grimy slash of what was then a very depressing 4th Avenue. In 1902 a smoke-generated accident prompted the state to require electric locomotives for passenger service into the city after 1910. Spurred by the 1901 decision of the rival Pennsylvania Railroad to tunnel under two rivers into Manhattan (it had previously terminated its southern line in Jersey City and its eastern branch in Queens), the directors of the New York Central/New Haven railroads decided on an ambitious new terminal. The result was so momentous that Carl W. Condit wrote, "The New York terminals of the Pennsylvania and the New York Central railroads are not only the greatest works of construction ever undertaken anywhere for the purpose of handling rail traffic, they are also the most extensive and most impressive civic projects in the United States built by private capital" (*American Building Art, The Twentieth Century*, Oxford University Press, 1961). This referred, of course, to the time before Rockefeller Center.

The boldness of the new Grand Central Terminal transformed an eyesore—the noisome, open trench of trains on 4th Avenue—into the city's finest residential street—Park Avenue, with its two lanes of traffic divided by a central landscaped mall. (Interestingly, the street was christened Park Avenue in 1888, well before Grand Central was built, in anticipation of future changes.) This avenue, in turn, later housed the most prestigious office building lineup in New York, with much of the property, incidentally, owned by the railroads via air rights. Beneath this comely boulevard are nearly fourteen full blocks of tracks—from near Lexington Avenue almost to Madison and from 42nd Street to 50th, where they squeeze together—a process that involved a fantastic amount of clearing, excavating, and eventually tunneling. Colonel William John Wilgus (1865–1949), the brilliant engineer who was responsible for almost all of the rail layout, looped some of the tracks around the terminal itself so that trains could exit without reversing, and double-decked many of the rest, with express trains utilizing the upper level and suburban commuter trains the lower. Freight and mail—a major post

office is adjacent—have their own spurs. In all there are over one hundred platforms, and in the 1940s as many as 600 trains a day used the station; even today they number over 400 with some 500,000 people reputedly passing through the terminal.

On top of this maze of underground rails sits the notable Grand Central Station, the design competition for which was won in 1903 by Reed & Stem of St. Paul, Minnesota, architects who had specialized in railroad stations. (Also atop this rail net rises a clutch of office buildings and hotels supported by a veritable forest of enormous steel piers—as Colonel Wilgus envisioned.) According to Carl Condit, William K. Vanderbilt more or less forced his cousin, Whitney Warren, along with Warren's partner Charles D. Wetmore, onto the Reed & Stem design team, and when Reed died in 1911, Warren & Wetmore took over and considerably altered the original plans, moreover taking credit "as sole architects of the terminal." (Stem, adds Condit, sued for damages and collected $400,000. Wilgus, incidentally, had left the project in 1907, owing to a disagreement.) Whoever was chiefly responsible for the final design, it seems likely that the École des Beaux-Arts-educated Warren and the Harvard-educated Wetmore were the prime architects of the main concourse, inside and out. The plaque outside Grand Central reads, "Completed in 1913 from plans of Warren & Wetmore and Reed & Stem." In any case a more than distinguished building resulted, even though it has to contend with an elevated roadway across its front and around its sides. This raised road was designed contemporaneously with the station but not finished until 1920. The former New York Central Building, since 1978 the Helmsley Building, straddles Park Avenue at the 46th Street ends of the two ramps and skillfully accommodates them in its facade. Designed by Warren & Wetmore, it was finished in 1929. The building has been thoroughly renovated and regilded in the proper places. Note, *en passant*, the pyramidal roof complete with cupola.

But whereas the exterior, highlighted by a bravely wing-borne statuary group and clock by Jules-Félix Coutan, is merely quietly authoritative in a Classical vein, the main concourse is one of the greatest spaces—anywhere—of the twentieth century. Measuring 120 x 375 x 125 feet high/37 x 114 x 38 meters high, it elevates rail travel, both on arriving and departing, into an almost noble ceremony. Overhead on the barrel-vaulted ceiling—suspended from the trusswork—floats Paul Helleu's painting of the heavens. Note the elegantly embellished lunettes at the window reveals. Not only is the concourse a glorious space, all about it works superbly, which, one might add, the previous New York City station picturesquely stuffed into a Roman bath did not. Grand Central's clarity and ease of circulation, no matter where one enters, is extraordinary for a structure of such complexity: much of this is probably due to Reed & Stem. In addition it is conveniently connected underground with three subways plus numerous office buildings and hotels. The Biltmore (1913—demolished 1981) and Commodore (1916—remodeled in 1980 as the Grand Hyatt) were also designed by Warren & Wetmore. According to Harmon H. Goldstone and Martha Dalrymple, this maze of weather-protected corridors "was the inspiration for the concourse system built later under Rockefeller Center" (see their fascinating *History Preserved*, Schocken, 1976).

Threatened for years to be either demolished or surmounted by a fifty-nine-story skyscraper, Grand Central won a historic reprieve in June 1978, when the U.S. Supreme Court ruled that its landmark status must not be infringed upon. In 1990 the firm of Beyer Blinder Belle drew up a master plan for the revitalization and restoration of the entire building. Some parts of the project have already been completed, with much of the plan currently under way or scheduled for the near future.

Open daily 5:30 A.M.–1:30 P.M. The Municipal Arts Society offers free tours of the interior; tours meet Wednesdays at 12:30 P.M. in front of the bank on the main level. For more information call (212) 986–9217. Grand Central Partnership offers free walking tours of the area; tours meet Fridays at 12:30 P.M. in front of the Philip Morris Building at 42nd Street and Park Avenue. For more information call (212) 818–1777. JAIA 10/82, A 11/88

UNITY TEMPLE (1906–08)
875 Lake Street at Kenilworth Avenue
Oak Park, Illinois

Frank Lloyd Wright, architect

Throughout the nineteenth century in both the United States and Europe, Christian religious architecture in the main was strangely content to dust off past historical styles (as, of course, were most building types). The greatest periods of church building—Early Christian, Byzantine, Romanesque, Gothic, Renaissance, and United States Colonial, to name only the most obvious—had always looked forward. The Gothic age especially exhibited a fierce ambition to build higher and more boldly with each new cathedral. (It was, of course, named for wild men, the Goths.) Against the eclectic stagnation of the nineteenth and early twentieth centuries a shock arose when Frank Lloyd Wright designed this Unitarian-Universalist Church with almost no historical reference—and very little money ($45,000). The walls of solid concrete—"the first concrete monolith in the world" (FLW)—and the high, smallish windows materialized from Wright's desire to screen out disturbances from the church's busy corner. The economy of concrete—until then almost never so frankly used in a "dignified" building—was also a factor.

The church is divided into two conjoined units, the 64-foot-/20-meter-square worship room (most prominent from Lake Street), and a rectangular parish house; both are entered via a low nexus off Kenilworth Avenue. As one approaches the entry the spatial involvement generally found in penetrating Wright's buildings develops, here with both ambiguities (as to which section is which) and excitement (at the multilevel interaction). Once hesitancy has been resolved and one turns left to the church proper, another manipulation of spaces begins, for one enters behind the chancel at a half-level below the nave floor via a "cloister," or ambulatory, which allows glimpses of the auditorium while permitting latecomers to enter without disturbing others. The church room itself, though intimate in feeling (it seats four hundred), attains, however, a strangely monumental quality. Pews in the central, squared floor area are framed on three sides by two levels of alcoves. This produces both liturgical closeness and a stage-like emphasis on the sanctuary, a theatrical effect intensified by the fact that most of the daylight floods down from amber-colored roof skylights (with artificial lights placed behind them). The resulting room is probably the first in centuries to establish a totally fresh church interior. Whether it conjures a religious ambiance depends upon what one brings to it, remembering that the church is a Unitarian house of worship. Architecturally the auditorium

reveals, and revels in, a sequential family of squares—from its overall plan, down to its lighting fixtures, and to its surprisingly Mondrianesque treatment of the glass in the roof monitors. Some find too much visual restlessness in this treatment and the restored (1961) colors too strong; others might object to the fact that a large proportion of the congregation is relegated to balcony seats. Still Unity Temple represents a decisive step in architecture in the United States and in religious architecture of the twentieth century. Money, however, is sorely needed for its upkeep, indeed its preservation.

Take I-290 West, exit on Austin Avenue North, left on Lake Street. Open daily 1:00–4:00 P.M. Closed Thanksgiving, Christmas, and New Year's Day. Sunday services held at 12:30 P.M. A 20-minute taped tour is available Monday–Friday 1:00–4:00 P.M.; the cost is $3 for adults, $2 for senior citizens and children ages 18 and under. Guided tours are given Saturday–Sunday at 1:00, 2:00, and 3:00 p.m.; the cost is $5 for adults and $3 for senior citizens and children ages 18 and under. For more information call (708) 383–8873. The building is included on the Chicago Architecture Foundation's "Frank Lloyd Wright in Oak Park" tour; the cost is $9. For more information on CAF tours call (312) 922–3432. AR 3/08, AF 35/38, AR 10/60, AF 6/69, PA 11/87, A 3/88, AR 1/91

Note: The Frank Lloyd Wright Home and Studio is not far distant.

NORWEST BANK OWATONNA (1907–08)
(Formerly National Farmers' Bank)
101 North Cedar Street at Broadway
Owatonna, Minnesota

Louis H. Sullivan, architect

Few buildings—of any period of architecture—measuring a mere 67 feet/20 meters on a side hold down a corner site with more authority than this masterpiece. It was the first—and remains the finest—of a small but glorious series designed by Louis H. Sullivan after he unfortunately left Dankmar Adler (1895) with whom he had enjoyed fifteen wonderfully productive years.

In Owatonna, Sullivan's well-known arch-set-in-a-rectangle motif is employed on each of the two street facades, which are virtually identical except for the main entrance on the west. (Sullivan used a more elaborate form of an arch in a rectangle in his famous Transportation Building at Chicago's World's Columbian Exposition of 1893.) However, Hugh Morrison writes that "the idea of the single great arches of the facade" was George G. Elmslie's (*Louis Sullivan*, Norton, 1935). Elmslie himself claimed not only "every last detail of decoration, inside and out, but the main motif as well" (*ibid.*).

The 36-foot/11-meter half-circles of the arches (and the square windows below them) are sharply incised in the two flat planes of brick (not set back in radiating bands as in the Transportation Building). The faces of the bank, abutting each other decisively, rest on a firm sandstone base (at the spring-line of the arches) and are crowned on top by a boldly corbeled cornice. A running polychrome terra-cotta mosaic decorative band frames each "panel" of the facades, with two monumental cartouches per side giving a pharaonic imprimatur to the upper corners. The windows that fill each arch are of opalescent leaded glass. These facades are unmatched. Fortunately they are still exactly as Sullivan (and Elmslie) created them.

The lofty, square, and colorful interior is highlighted by decorated arches (structural mirrors of the exterior), which support the well-tended ceiling. Four cast-iron chandeliers of intriguing complexity, painted to match the green decor, hang in the skylight. The bank's interior, which had been ill-used for years, was remodeled with great sensitivity (and some simplification) in 1956–58 by Harwell H. Harris, thanks to the enlightened attitude of the president, Clifford C. Sommer. He showed the same foresight that a previous president, Carl K. Bennett, exhibited when he bravely commissioned Sullivan to design the bank in 1907. One of the delights of its era, it constitutes a milestone in the development of a banking architecture that had hitherto sought refuge in monumental imitations of ancient Rome.

Open Monday–Friday 9:00 A.M.–3:30 P.M. Tours can be scheduled by calling the Owatonna Visitors Bureau at (800) 423–6466. AR 10/08, AF 7/58

DAVID B. GAMBLE HOUSE (1907–08)
4 Westmoreland Place
Pasadena, California

Greene & Greene, architects

Charles Sumner Greene (1868–1957) and Henry Mather Greene (1870–1954)—both trained at MIT—designed for David and Mary Gamble one of the provocative houses of the early twentieth century. Charles had a deep interest in Far Eastern art and Buddhist philosophy, and both Greenes had been impressed by the "medieval" Japanese Pavilion at the World's Columbian Exposition of 1893, along with the aborning Shingle Style. At a time when wealthy clients unhesitatingly regarded dusted-off "styles" of European vintage or United States Neo-Colonial as absolutes in house design, the brothers Greene erected a shingle house—"neo-Stick," writes Vincent Scully—let it grow from the ground, projected outriggings of porches to catch the view and enjoy the breeze, and topped all by climactic sun-shielding roofs. The subtle progression from restrained to exuberant, particularly at the east end, is stunning: the lucid expression of structure, from rafter resting on beam down to minute junctures, is meticulous. The architects not only solved the problems of site, sight, and room layout, they did so with style, homogeneity, and integrity, while never forgetting function. Equally outstanding is the building's craftsmanship. Each joint, each beam end, and every detail, including furniture and kitchen cabinets (at that time disdained by architects), are unsurpassed for workmanship. Note, particularly, the metal straps and wedges for binding beams together. An infatuation with intricacy of detail may at times take over, but take over with consummate elegance and regard for material. Incidentally, the green color of the shingles is not original, resulting from paint applied in the 1930s.

The house, although of two full stories, popularized the California bungalow style—though here both large and expensive—bearing as it does resemblance to the wide-roofed, veranda-wrapped Bengali *bangla* of India (from which, of course, the name "bungalow" comes). The Greene brothers themselves designed over 150 bungalows in their long and busy practice. Fortunately in 1966 the Gamble House—one of their finest—was given by the heirs of Cecil and Louise Gamble to the city of Pasadena in joint agreement with the University of Southern California, a gift for which all can be thankful. In addition to being open to the public, the house is used for seminars and special events related to historic preservation and architecture. It was designated a National Historic Landmark in 1978.

Located off North Orange Grove Boulevard, a half block north of Walnut Street. Open Thursday–Sunday 12:00 noon–3:00 P.M. All visits are guided; tours are given every 20 minutes. The cost is $4 for adults, $3 for senior citizens, and $2 for students. AR 5/48, AF 10/48, PA 11/72

CARL SCHURZ HIGH SCHOOL (1907–10)
3601 North Milwaukee Avenue at West Addison Street
Chicago, Illinois

Dwight H. Perkins, architect

Assured and dignified and with a fine assortment of angles and planes, the Carl Schurz High School possesses a character that time has not eroded. A slight influence from Hendrik Petrus Berlage and the Dutch brick tradition (and even from Sir Edwin Lutyens) can be felt. The Tennessee-born, MIT-educated Dwight H. Perkins stated his solution of massing and of imaginative detail with confidence and skill. Most of the architect's professional life was concerned with school design with a strong input of the philosophy of John Dewey and "education as a tool." Although formalism can be seen here, particularly in plan, those interested in early-twentieth-century architectural developments will certainly want to see this school. Originally designed as a technical high school, the building underwent several changes and additions through the years.

Open Monday–Friday 7:30 A.M.–3:00 P.M. Closed for holidays. Visitors must obtain a pass from the main office. AR 6/10

BOLEY BUILDING (1908–09)
1124–1130 Walnut Street at 12th Street
Kansas City, Missouri

Louis S. Curtiss, architect

Though not sensational considering today's architectural developments, this six-story building is nonetheless an extraordinary, but too-little-known pioneer. Its walls (except at the corners) are enclosed by continuous bands of glass, accented slightly by glazed French doors, above painted steel spandrel strips. This is probably the world's first expression of steel-mullioned strip-windows and uninterrupted metal spandrels forming a facade. (Walter Gropius and Adolf Meyer's Fagus Factory dates from 1911–13; Willis Polk's glass-sheathed Hallidie Building in San Francisco—see page 344—from 1917–18.) The continuous glass was made possible by a 5-foot/1.5-meter cantilever beyond the structural columns. Although the lower floor has been savagely handled, the building remains a landmark in architectural development. The original research on the work of Louis S. Curtiss was undertaken by Fred T. Comee, of U.S. Steel Corporation. The Boley Building is listed in the National Register of Historic Places.

Lobby open to the public Monday–Friday 8:00 A.M.–5:00 P.M. PA 8/63

FREDERICK C. ROBIE HOUSE (1908–10)
University of Chicago
5757 South Woodlawn Avenue at 58th Street
Chicago, Illinois

Frank Lloyd Wright, architect

In the history of twentieth-century domestic architecture there are two houses that are of transcending importance: the Robie House in Chicago and the Villa Savoye (1927–31), some 17 miles/27 kilometers west of Paris, by Le Corbusier, the Swiss-French architect. Both pioneered directions in domestic shelter that subsequently changed the shape of many of the world's dwellings. The Robie House's immortality—a word not casually used—lies in the fact that it, and other houses by Frank Lloyd Wright that led up to it, transformed the typical house plan comprising a cluster of boxlike rooms into a free-flowing series of interrelated spaces. Each of the major rooms has its own identity, but it is a shared identity that extends a hand to the next room: space is a continuum, not a closet. This "liberation" of the plan, this demolition of the

box cincture, the "cellular sequestration" as Wright called it, is today a constituent concept in the planning of even our tract houses, but in the early part of this century, house planning was an uptight affair, and it was every room for itself.

Wright also used in the exterior of the Robie House a concept that he had been nurturing for years, but had hitherto been unable to express so fully; he tied the house to the land so that it rises as an extension of the plain, a house in league with its setting. (His first client house, the Winslow of 1893, hints of this.) This partnership of man and land was always part of Wright's concerns: its most spectacular manifestation leapt a waterfall—see Fallingwater, Mill Run, Pennsylvania, page 382. The "binding to the soil" process of the Robie House was accomplished by boldly cantilevered roof lines of sharp eaves (whose steel-braced extensions were calculated to admit low winter sun, but not the high and hot sun of summer), and by unbroken low walls of brick alternating with continuous strips of windows. (The "window wall" across the front of the living room and dining room is 56 feet/17 meters long.) Note the finesse with which these broadly etched bands and walls of brick "slow down" and develop their ends with a series of stabilizing shapes—reminding one of the diminishing velocity of the figures of the Parthenon frieze as they approach the corners. The low outer wall marking, indeed nudging, the property line and the shadow-casting balcony over the billiard room and children's playroom on the lower level accent this horizontality. The stretched hipped roof planes cap all, and establish subtle tensions with their cross-axis.

The entrance to the house, like so many of Wright's entrances, is convoluted: on entering for the first time one does not know whether one will end up above or below. Once inside, however, the sequence of spaces commences. They are liberated outward via the window wall (whose sash head is near ceiling height), and they jog upward in the angled ceiling planes. The focus of the living room—a half-flight above ground (compare the Villa Savoye)—is the large fireplace that acts as a divider between it and the dining room, making the seating arena around the fire partially a circulation area—hence somewhat restless—but creating a masterful flow laterally. (Note that one can "see through" the top of the fireplace into the dining room.) The bedrooms on the upper floor are routine, but there is nothing routine on the two lower floors.

Wright stunned the world with the Robie House: domestic architecture was never again the same. *Chicago's Famous Buildings*, edited by Arthur Siegel (University of Chicago Press, 1969), calls it "one of the most brilliant designs in the history of architecture." The house was saved from immediate destruction in 1956 by a flood of telegrams from concerned architects.

One-hour tours are given daily at 12:00 noon. The cost is $3 for adults, $1 for students and senior citizens, free for children under 5. Closed for holidays. Group tours can be scheduled by calling the University of Chicago Office of Special Events at (312) 702–8374. The building is included on the Chicago Architecture Foundation's Hyde Park tour; the cost is $6. The building is also included on the Chicago Architecture Foundation's bus tour; the cost is $25. For more information on Chicago Architecture Foundation tours call (312) 922–3432. AF 6/28, AF 10/58, Int 5/69, AF 6/69

FIRST CHURCH OF CHRIST, SCIENTIST (1910–12)
2619 Dwight Way at Bowditch Street
Berkeley, California

Bernard R. Maybeck, architect

On first entering this church one must pause and move slowly, for its subtle ambiance unfolds with measured grace. The wide, horizontally couched auditorium (the Christian Science term for the nave), built in an era of vertical pseudo-Gothicism, envelops one in an atmosphere of inner architectural harmony. Yet this joyous, peaceful quality—one elusive in any period of religious building—cannot be pinpointed, nor does it lie in a study of details. The building's excellence lies in the triumphant mantle of the interior and in the transcendence of its unity, not in the assemblage of its parts. Bernard R. Maybeck completely synthesized the "oneness" mandate that the church's building committee had given him. The auditorium is so artfully woven together, one forgets that whispers of the Byzantine, the Gothic, Art Nouveau, and the Japanese—to name the most prominent—are all apparent. More importantly, they are all working together to produce an intricate whole, not a potpourri of styles. Moreover, Maybeck called for utilitarian concrete, asbestos cement board, and factory sash in the construction; he was one of the first to use such industrial materials for a prominent building. (Compare Frank Lloyd Wright's Unity Temple of 1908 near Chicago, page 326.) The huge, unplaned timber, double trusses rest on freestanding concrete columns, their diagonal lines throwing a focus on the chancel and its centrally placed podium. Their angled lower chords and the modest touches of color in their gold-painted plaster inserts keep these massive roof supports from seeming oppressive. Other touches of color, plus accents of richly modeled concrete capitals atop the concrete piers, and the indirect bowl lights of hammered steel fuse happily together. There is a slight glare problem from the two side windows—the auditorium is finer with the lights

on—but there is no problem with religiosity or architectural glory. The exterior builds up intriguingly at the entrance though the sides tend to an amalgam of influences that at times becomes disjointed and even labored (such as the extravagant pergolas atop the columns). But this is carping; the church is one of the greats—a seminal building in the development of California's architecture. The Sunday school wing was added in 1929 by Henry Gutterson.

Open for services Wednesday at 8:00 P.M. and Sunday at 11:00 A.M. Also open to the public at 12:15 P.M. on the first Sunday of every month; a one-hour tour is given at this time. Group tours can be arranged by writing to the church office at 2619 Dwight Way, Berkeley, CA 94704. AR 1/48, AR 1/49, AR 12/56, AF 7/61, SAHJ 3/84

MERCHANTS NATIONAL BANK (1911–12)
102 East 3rd Street at Lafayette Street
Winona, Minnesota

Purcell, Feick & Elmslie, architects

Though William G. Purcell and George G. Elmslie worked with Louis Sullivan, they were always in his—and sometimes Frank Lloyd Wright's—shadow, even after they had left to set up shop for themselves (1909). Elmslie, as has been mentioned (see Norwest Bank Owatonna, page 328), was at one time Sullivan's right hand and often personally drafted the master's intricate ornament. The two architects were of the same mind, favoring broad, plain wall surfaces highlighted by decorative accents of power and color, emphasizing the static and the dynamic. It is thus with this bank—Purcell, Feick & Elmslie's finest non-domestic work. Note above the enormous windows of the two facades the boldly expressed lintel, with each broad brick fascia or panel resting on two brick piers that are carefully separated by a panel of glass from the adjacent wall spurs. In the center, between sharply cut lower windows, stands the entry surmounted by an exquisitely designed, arched motif—"the play work in the architect's day, his hour of refreshment" wrote Elmslie. Square in plan, the bank's interior is as elegantly simple as the outside. Sympathetically expanded (1969–70) by Dykins & Handford, this beautifully preserved building was thoroughly restored in 1972. One of Minnesota's notable pieces of architecture.

Lobby open to the public Monday–Thursday 9:00 A.M.–4:00 P.M., Friday 9:00 A.M.–5:00 P.M. Closed for holidays. Free tours can be arranged by calling (507) 457-1100. A+A 2/67, NWA 1–2/74.

WOOLWORTH BUILDING (1911–13)
233 Broadway at Park Place
New York, New York

Cass Gilbert, architect

The Houses of Parliament are the godfathers of this famous "Cathedral of Commerce" (as an amused member of the cloth termed it), because Frank Woolworth, on his many trips to London, admired them extravagantly. When he commissioned this monument to enterprise, he asked Cass Gilbert to design his office building "in Gothic style." The results startled the world—because of its fifty-eight-story height and structural bravura, not monastic cloaking. Whereas we may now smile at its flying buttresses, gargoyles, and other medieval trappings, the structure represents a conquest of sizable technological problems, for never before had a skyscraper soared to such a wind-exposed height (792 feet/241 meters) on non-bedrock foundations. (The previous tallest building was New York's Metropolitan Life Insurance Building, 1907–09, by Napoleon Le Brun and Sons. This reached 700 feet/213 meters but the wind factor on it was less and the subsoil conditions better.) Gilbert and his engineers, the Gunvald Aus Company, came up with a brilliantly successful result: innovative struts and knee bracing for the wind, 110-foot-/34-meter-deep caissons filled with concrete for the foundations. It was the tallest building in the world from 1913 to 1930, when the Chrysler Building took title for a few months until the Empire State Building was topped off. Esthetically there is a conviction in the boldness of the tower that transcends its details. Be certain to see the lobby: it is dazzling. A complete overhaul, including replacement of the 4,400 old windows with new aluminum sash (operable), was completed in 1980.

Lobby open daily 7:00 A.M.–6:00 P.M. AR 2/13

LA JOLLA WOMAN'S CLUB (1913–14)
715 Silverado Street at Draper Avenue
San Diego (La Jolla), California

Irving J. Gill, architect

The far too little-known Irving J. Gill (1870–1936) was one of the brilliant early advocates of the Modern Movement in the United States. His work reflected the "morality" and "down with the past" thinking of Louis Sullivan, for whom he worked (1890–93); his affection for Southern California and the arcaded geometry of its Spanish missions, though then in partial ruins; plus an anti-ornament perspective that he shared with his exact contemporary, the Austrian Adolf Loos (1870–1933). The two conceivably exerted a cross-fertilizing influence on each other, but their mutual admiration for Sullivan's writings more likely accounts for some similarities in their work. Gill's work thus possesses a potent simplicity and in many cases, such as here in La Jolla, a rhythmic movement of multiple arches. His architecture might be described as shaved Spanish, flat-roofed and without moldings, but shaved at a time when most Iberian-inspired buildings were on the shaggy side. As Esther McCoy points out in her valuable *Five California Architects* (Praeger, 1975), Gill's professional popularity suffered markedly after the heavily decorated Churrigueresque style became fashionable following the 1915 Panama-Pacific Exposition in San Francisco and the 1915–16 Panama-California International Exposition in San Diego. (McCoy also illustrates the very advanced tilt-slab concrete construction of the Woman's Club.) Gill's greatest building, the Walter L. Dodge House (1914–16) in Los Angeles, was wantonly destroyed in 1970, but this clubhouse in downtown La Jolla shows how advanced he was for his day. One can get a good grasp of his buildings' simple elegance at any time from the sidewalk; the interiors are of less interest. The building is listed in the National Register of Historic Places.

Open daily 9:00 A.M.–1:00 P.M. and 2:00–4:00 P.M. Closed Thanksgiving weekend, the last two weeks in December, and New Year's Day. Admission is free. Tours can be scheduled by calling (619) 573-1516. AR 12/13

PALACE OF FINE ARTS (1913–15/rebuilt 1965–67)
3301–3601 Lyon Street at Bay
San Francisco, California

Bernard R. Maybeck, architect

Bernard R. Maybeck (1862–1957) was at heart a romantic eclectic, and though his Beaux-Arts training in Paris had given him a Classical foundation, he generally essayed a more organic idiom, as in his houses and his First Church of Christ, Scientist at Berkeley (see page 334). For the Roman pomp of the Panama-Pacific International Exposition of 1915, however, nothing would do but back to the forum—with Giovanni Battista Piranesi standing in the wings. For this he created an intoxicatingly rich octagonal temple and colonnade with an arc-shaped gallery—for the art of the nations of the world—directly behind. The sketch for this thrilled the fair's commissioners, as did the building.

The Palace of Fine Arts indeed became so popular that when the fair was over (December 1915) and the buildings ready to be demolished, some 33,000 visitors begged for its preservation. The trouble was that the "temple" was made for short-term use, having a wood frame encased with plaster of paris and hemp fiber in a mixture called "staff." The gallery and rotunda, however, were spared, and as they gradually crumbled—as Maybeck once wished—the place became increasingly dear to San Franciscans. Bond issues to save it were put up but initially defeated when, in 1959, Walter S. Johnson, a generous local executive and philanthropist, offered $2 million toward its reconstruction in permanent materials. (Johnson eventually gave close to $4 million for the project. The bond measure did eventually pass and was also a valuable source of funds, as were the many public donations.) This munificence sparked both city and state. Under the direction of William G. Merchant, and, after his death, of Hans U. Gerson—both former Maybeck partners—aided by Welton Becket & Associates, architectural work was begun to rebuild it from the ground up for the ages.

The Palace of Fine Arts, in particular the rotunda and colonnade, can be said to epitomize and terminate Roman opulence in architecture in the United States, a style that had been launched so successfully (but, as some say, with disastrous results) at an earlier fair, Chicago's World's Columbian Exposition of 1892–93. Behind the rotunda—screened by the spatial intermedium of the colonnade—stands the quarter-circle gallery building, which once housed the exhibits of the nations. This large building is today filled with provocative exhibits of the Exploratorium plus the 1,000-seat Palace of Fine Arts Theater. The 5-acre/2-hectare gallery was divided for the fair into 120 separate exhibition rooms. Having a sturdy steel frame it survived the years (once serving for indoor tennis courts), and its structure was used in the remodeling.

Grounds open daily 24 hours. The Exploratorium is open Memorial Day–Labor Day daily 10:00 A.M.–6:00 P.M. (Wednesday until 9:30 P.M.); Labor Day–Memorial Day open Tuesday–Sunday 10:00 A.M.–5:00 P.M. (Wednesday until 9:30 P.M.). Closed Thanksgiving and Christmas. Admission is $8.50 for adults, $6.50 for college students and senior citizens, $4.50 for children ages 6–17, $2 for children ages 3–5. Free architectural tours can be scheduled by calling (415) 561–0360. The Palace of Fine Arts Theater is open for performances. For more information call the box office at (415) 567–6642. AR 11/15

LINCOLN MEMORIAL (1915–22)
23rd Street NW and Constitution Avenue on the Mall
Washington, D.C.

Henry Bacon, architect

The Lincoln Memorial so epitomizes the interrelation between architecture, landscape architecture, and sculpture that it must not be considered an isolated building, but one that synthesizes a meridian of media working in respectful harmony. And just as the setting of axis, reflecting pool, and built-up acropolis of green ennoble the building, so the interior bows discreetly to the majesty of Daniel Chester French's statue. It should be pointed out that this is not a Greco-Roman temple, as often termed, but a rectangular marble box peripherally framed by thirty-six Doric columns. It presents its broad side as its entry and does not have the mandatory gable roof, while the cella, or enclosing, walls rise in a straight projection "through" the embrace of its columns and entablature. The columns do not support the roof in a Classical statement of structure, nor does the entablature frame its eaves. Thus Henry Bacon inventively—many think brilliantly—modified a Greek prototype.

The reflecting pool—recalling those at Versailles and the Taj Mahal—projects the image, if not the substance, of the memorial into the Mall, further binding building to nature. Finished in 1923, the pool measures 2,027 feet/618 meters long, 160 feet/49 meters wide, and 3 feet/.9 meter deep. The memorial stands at a spot that was once a swamp, but that, at the urging of the McMillan Report of 1902, had been filled in from 17th Street to beyond 25th to form West Potomac Park. The Lincoln Memorial Commission pinpointed the building's precise spot in 1913 over other proposals for a location near the U.S. Capitol or Union Station.

Initially, in a signed drawing dated 29 September 1911, Bacon proposed to place the building on a rectangular stepped "pyramid" of thirteen steps, named for the original states. The proportions were so awkward, however, that he used instead the traditional stylobate of three giant steps of 7.8 feet/2.4 meters total height, with eighteen normal risers at entry. The memorial thus rests on a terrace with retaining wall 15 feet/4.6 meters high, 256.9 feet/78 meters long, and 187 feet/57 meters wide made of North Carolina granite.

The thirty-six white Colorado-Yule marble columns, which give the building's periphery such chiaroscuro and spatial interaction, are 44 feet/13 meters high, and though rumor has it that they represent the number of states at the time of Lincoln's death, the fact is that this happened to be the number that Bacon rightfully thought architecturally desirable—twelve on the long sides, eight on the short. The "attic" on top carries plaques for the forty-eight states, listed in order of joining the Union, existing when the memorial was completed. (A proposal to add Alaska and Hawaii—additions requiring more than casual changes—was dropped, fortunately, due to the dedicated work of Leslie N. Boney, Jr., FAIA.)

It is pertinent to note that the fluted columns of nine drums each do not stand precisely perpendicular, but tilt in slightly toward the wall, those on the corners tilting 3.5 inches/89 millimeters, the second ones 2 inches/50 millimeters. The outer wall, too, has a slight inward tilt. Moreover, the end columns are closer together than the others to compensate optically for the bright light usually showing between them—while the two marking the center entry are farther apart (optical refinements reminiscent of the Parthenon). The naos, or "shrine" proper, measures 60 feet/18 meters wide and high, and 74 feet/23 meters deep, and is finished with Indiana limestone.

French's majestic statue, resting in that monumental chair, faces the rising sun, supplemented by a built-in "sun" that artfully spotlights Lincoln throughout the day and much of the night. (The ceiling is of thin slabs of Alabama limestone made translucent with beeswax.

Above it are skylights and a battery of artificial lights.) Though constructed of twenty-eight blocks of white Georgia marble, the chair and figure seem almost monolithic. The statue, incidentally, was originally proposed to be only 10 feet/3 meters high but was later—and wisely—enlarged to 19 feet/5.8 meters. It was carved over a four-year period by the Piccirilli Studio in New York's Bronx, utilizing a 5-foot/1.5-meter clay model from French and assistance by him. Its 175 tons/159 metric tons were sent in eleven freight cars to Washington in 1922. On either side of this main room are less satisfactory chambers—that at left of entry with a plaque with the Gettysburg Address, that at right with Lincoln's Second Inaugural Address (each difficult to read). Their allegorical murals on canvas, measuring 60 feet/18 meters long, were painted by Jules Guerin.

There are, of course, those unmoved by both building—"this white dream of a forgotten Acropolis"—and its setting. Some hold the landscaping to be old-fashioned, the architecture a refuge of Classic design, and the statue unimaginatively realistic. Robert Lowell writes of "the too white marmoreal Lincoln Memorial." Moreover, what is a man of Lincoln's reputed warmth and concern for humanity doing wrapped up in these cold white walls—or do they represent what he was up against? Even Lewis Mumford queried, "Who lives in that shrine— Lincoln, or the men who conceived it?" (*Sticks and Stones*, Dover, 1955). However, such stray thoughts tend to vanish for most when wrapped in the magic of Bacon's creativity. It is unquestionable that this building has added appreciably to Lincoln's position in United States history. With gracious thoughtfulness, President Harding, on the steps of the memorial, presented Henry Bacon with the Gold Medal of the American Institute of Architects upon the dedication of his masterpiece (30 May 1922). Bacon died less than two years later, deeply grateful for the building's reception and justly proud of the building in which he had put so much care and ten years of his time—contributions far beyond normal professional duties.

Open daily 24 hours. Rangers are available to answer questions daily 8:00 A.M.–midnight. AR 6/23

INDIANAPOLIS-MARION COUNTY
PUBLIC LIBRARY (1916–17/1975)
40 East St. Clair Street
Indianapolis, Indiana

Paul Philippe Cret, architect
Kennedy, Brown and Associates, architects of addition

A limestone Doric library that is generally considered the French-born Paul Philippe Cret's finest work. Bound strictly to Hellenism, here with freshness, it stands high in the period of the eclectic development of architecture in the United States. It has, indeed, been called "the best classic building in America." The main reading room approaches the grandiose. Zantzinger, Bone & Medary were associate architects. The main, east, and west reading rooms underwent a complete restoration in 1985.

In 1975 a five-story addition designed by Kennedy, Brown and Associates was opened to the public. A black glass wall marks the transition between the patterned limestone facade of the new edifice and Cret's structure.

Open Monday–Friday 9:00 A.M.–9:00 P.M., Saturday 9:00 A.M.–5:00 P.M., Sunday 1:00–5:00 P.M. Closed for holidays. Free tours can be arranged by calling (317) 269–1729. AF 9/18

WOODBURY COUNTY COURT HOUSE (1916–18)
620 Douglas Street at 7th Street
Sioux City, Iowa

William L. Steele and Purcell & Elmslie, architects

William L. Steele, George Grant Elmslie, and William G. Purcell had worked together in Louis Sullivan's office in Chicago. (Steele acquired the court house commission—and remained the executive head of the project—but he at once got Elmslie to collaborate with him and to take charge of overall design.) This background in Sullivan's office, with perhaps a touch of influence of the Dutch early modernist Hendrik Petrus Berlage (1856–1934), and a hint of Frank Lloyd Wright, are fused in this courthouse on the western edge of Iowa. Whatever the influences and inspirations, the result produced one of the United States' freshest public buildings of the early twentieth century.

The exterior presents a two-story, square block of subdued form, with a six-story tower rising from the center. The detail of the Roman brick piers that envelop the exterior are accented at the entry by a sculptured group by Alfonso Iannelli. However, it is the interior, illuminated by a glass "dome" and alive with terra-cotta decoration, that provides the real glory. The rotunda (square) is, indeed, a triumph of terra-cotta; used with unity and appositeness, it produces a symphony, not a cacophony. Even the genre painted wall panels (by John W. Norton) contribute their period bit. The building is currently undergoing a $2 million restoration. One of the finest examples of its architecturally groping time, and, indeed, the present.

The first and second floors are open to the public Monday–Friday 9:00 A.M.–4:30 P.M. Closed on holidays. Free tours can be arranged by calling (712) 279–6539. PP 9/41

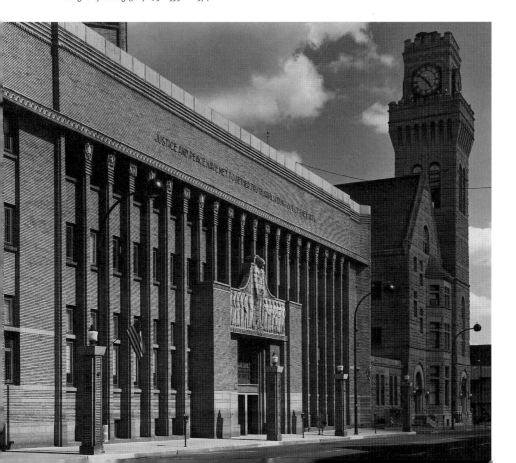

HALLIDIE BUILDING (1917–18)
130 Sutter Street
San Francisco, California

Willis Polk, architect

One of the most remarkably advanced buildings of its time, the seven-story Hallidie Building still stands as a monument to the use of boldly scaled glass. Its facade is all glass with the exception of four fanciful bands of superimposed cast-iron decoration and fire escapes. The structure of the building—the concrete columns and girders across the front—is set back 3.3 feet/100 centimeters from the glass wall. Triangular brackets support the thin floor slab next to the glass, the slab increasing in thickness behind the midpoint of the columns. Onto the outer edge of these floor slabs (at every third horizontal mullion) is affixed a mullion that carries the glass. The "curtain wall" was widely heralded in the 1950s as a new method of construction, the skin being conveniently independent of the bones. However, Willis Polk, almost forty years before, had pioneered the all-glass facade in this country with results that still command the utmost admiration. (There are other curtain-wall antecedents, of course, from Joseph Paxton's Crystal Palace of 1851 to

Walter Gropius and Adolf Meyer's Fagus Factory of 1911.) Wisely the Hallidie Building was declared an Official Landmark by San Francisco's Board of Supervisors in 1971, against the will of the owners at the time. It was the first so designated because of its architectural, as opposed to its historic, significance. The building was sold in 1975 and very carefully restored to its original condition the following year by Kaplan/McLaughlin/Diaz, so that we can once again enjoy this blistering wall of glass, side to side and top to bottom, its admirable speculum set off by festooned nostalgia.

The interior is closed to the public. AR 10/18, SAHJ 12/71, AR 3/76, PA 11/81

PEOPLES FEDERAL SAVINGS & LOAN ASSOCIATION (1917–18)
101 East Court Street at Ohio Street
Sidney, Ohio

Louis H. Sullivan, architect

A jewel of a bank, and one of Louis H. Sullivan's last works. His familiar arch—which he first used to acclaim in the Transportation Building at the Chicago World's Columbian Exposition of 1893—here graces the north-facing narrow end of the bank, with sculptured ornament of great intricacy greeting the customers. (Sullivan almost undoubtedly picked up this arch motif from Moroccan gates he saw in publications while a student at the Paris École des Beaux-Arts—compare the Bab el-Khemis at Meknes.) The strong cornice belting, polychromed arch, griffins, wiry lettering, and the low belt course that ties all together produce an overall richness. The long side of the building—possibly Sullivan's finest wall and the bank's most coordinated feature—parades a line of opal-glass windows, elevated to throw natural light deep onto the banking floor. The details of the terra-cotta sculpture echo the other delights of the facade.

The interior is austere, indeed a bit flat, compared to Sullivan's Norwest Bank at Owatonna, Minnesota (1908—see page 328), and the Merchant's National Bank at Grinnell, Iowa. However, he makes a compelling feature of the vault door (probably the first time this was done), setting its intriguing mechanism behind a glass wall. (Compare Skidmore, Owings & Merrill's Chemical Bank in New York of 1953, page 414.) Sullivan also used indirect lighting (in the vases) and an early form of air conditioning. Both interior and exterior of the Sidney bank have been beautifully maintained. Sullivan himself considered it one of his finest buildings. This rebuffed idealist, the "father of modern architecture," died tragically a few years after the bank's completion (1924), without work, and largely without friends.

Open Monday–Wednesday 9:00 A.M.–4:00 P.M., Thursday 9:00 A.M.–12:00 noon, Friday 9:00 A.M.–6:00 P.M., Saturday 9:00 A.M.–12:00 noon. Free tours can be arranged by calling (513) 492–6129. AR 4/25

HOLLYHOCK HOUSE (1919–21)
Barnsdall Art Park
4800 Hollywood Boulevard
Los Angeles (Hollywood), California

Frank Lloyd Wright, architect

Wright's famous Hollyhock (Barnsdall) House is the first of ten residences he designed in the Los Angeles area. It clearly shows his early interest in Mesoamerican architecture with its plain canted walls (here of wood plastered with stucco and trimmed with cast stone) set off by a band of rich decoration. Hollyhock House (note the flower in the frieze) dominates a hill—which forms Barnsdall Art Park—on the eastern edge of Hollywood. Its cross-axial plan is of almost Roman monumentality, but its appearance, especially around its garden court and circular pool, is domestic in scale. (The court was later used for outdoor theatrical performances.) With its projecting wings semi-enclosing space, the plan recalls that of the Imperial Hotel in Tokyo, on which Wright was working at the same time. On the interior note the dropped living room, the cathedral ceiling, and the indirect lighting. Observe, too, the channel of water from an upper outdoor pool to a lower one with its detour around the fireplace. It is an interior more of units rather than of the spatial flow seen in Wright's Frederick C. Robie House in Chicago (see page 332)—but what units!

Barnsdall Art Park occupies a site that Aline Barnsdall once planned for a center for the performing arts, but this never materialized, and in 1927 she gave house, guest residence, and grounds of the former estate to the city "for recreation and cultural purposes." For some years (1927 to the early 1940s) the California Art Club was headquartered at the house, but as the plaque in front states, "In 1947 this building was reconstructed, furnished and equipped . . . by the Olive Hill Foundation, which was founded and endowed by Dorothy Clune Murray, in memory of her son." In 1971–75 further restoration was undertaken—termites having done great damage—and the house is now open for escorted tours. One of the greats.

The entry building at the Barnsdall Arts Center (1920–21) was designed by Rudolph M. Schindler (while in Wright's employ), who also supervised the construction of the main house (Wright himself being mostly in Japan at the time). The center was originally a guest residence, one of a group that Barnsdall proposed.

Located just west of Vermont Avenue. One-hour tours of the Hollyhock House given Tuesday–Sunday at 12:00 noon, and 1:00, 2:00, and 3:00 P.M. The cost is $2 for adults, $1 for senior citizens, free for children ages 12 and under. Closed Thanksgiving, Christmas Eve, Christmas, and New Year's Day. For more information call (213) 662-7272. SAHJ 3/79, PA 11/79, PA 11/85

HEARST CASTLE—SAN SIMEON (1919–47)
750 Hearst Castle Road (CA 1)
San Simeon, California

Julia Morgan, architect

San Simeon was named for Saint Simon by the San Miguel Mission, which once owned these lands. William Randolph Hearst himself called his beloved retreat *La Cuesta Encantada*, the Enchanted Hill. San Simeon is not so much a unitary house as an incredible collection of elements, most of them of startling quality. This glorious *palacio*—here its parts almost greater than the whole—stands as the crowning refuge of perhaps the last of the prodigal spenders. Besides building his castle, Hearst spent considerable sums on embellishing it with works of art. Designed—perhaps fitted together would be more accurate—by the noted Julia Morgan (the first woman to enter Paris's École des Beaux-Arts and among the first registered female architects in California) in collaboration with Hearst himself, Hearst Castle merits more than a casual look, for one must savor, not skim, its unbelievable richness. (There are several separate tours; all are recommended.)

Hearst Castle grew organically, like a well-loved garden, around Hearst's staggering rooms, many by Miss Morgan. The three guest houses (containing an average of fifteen rooms each) were the first constructed, with work on the main house commencing in 1922 and basically finished in 1947; Hearst died in 1951. The main building, framed in reinforced concrete, carefully incorporates 115 rooms (38 bedrooms), almost all with priceless art and furnishings. San Simeon forms a veritable museum of architecture, furnishings, art, and books; it must be experienced to be believed. Almost equally impressive—and a true index of Morgan's skill—

are the terraced grounds and gardens, climaxed by the Neptune Pool with its sweeping stairs and Hellenistic temple assembled from genuine Roman elements. As the *Saturday Evening Post* wrote in 1968, "all the pleasures of infinity are to be found here and now." San Simeon was given to the State of California by the Hearst corporation. In 1957 it was officially designated a state monument, and in 1976 it was declared a National Historic Landmark.

Located midway between Los Angeles and San Francisco. Open daily 8:20 A.M.–5:00 P.M. in winter; hours vary in summer. Closed Thanksgiving, Christmas, and New Year's Day. All visits are guided. Four different two-hour day tours are available year-round; the cost is $14 for adults, $8 for children ages 6–12, free for children under 6. Evening tours are available in spring and fall on Friday and Saturday; admission is $25 for adults, $13 for children ages 6–12, free for children under 6. Tour times vary. For reservations or for more information call (800) 444–4445. JAIA 6/76

GENERAL MOTORS BUILDING (1920–22)
3044 West Grand Boulevard between 2nd Avenue and Cass Street
Detroit, Michigan

Albert Kahn, architect

Albert Kahn (1869–1942) arrived in the United States as an eleven-year-old in an impoverished family. Though never undergoing further schooling in his adopted land he eventually made an enormous impact on it. For he developed in his Detroit office innovative factory concepts and startling planning efficiencies that helped make this city—and this country—the motor capital of the world. Some believe, indeed, that Detroit might well have not become the Motor City if it had not been for those two contemporary geniuses: Albert Kahn and Henry Ford. Kahn's greatest work was in industrial building, and in this field—which had been spurned by other architects and left completely to engineers until World War II—he was the first to demonstrate to tough industrial executives that the space-organizing ability of a perceptive architect brings an essential talent to major plant planning. He was so successful that he not only won over Detroit and much of the nation, he built several billion dollars' worth of factories—reportedly some five hundred—in the USSR in the late 1920s and early 1930s. Kahn's 1905 plant for the Packard Motor Company—in which he was helped by his engineer brother—was the first of concrete in the field; his Pierce-Arrow factory in Buffalo (1906) introduced the novel one-story concept for a giant-scale production facility whose plan in effect diagrammed an assembly line, the whole properly daylit by skylights; his famous Rouge Plant (1917–22) for Henry Ford was probably the single most impressive industrial installation in the country; and in 1937 he built an airplane assembly building for Glenn L. Martin with clear floor area of 300 x 450 feet/91 xi 37 meters.

Almost all of Kahn's great industrial buildings have been so altered since erected—or are not open to the public—that little of his personal contribution can now be seen. However, this General Motors Building—the largest corporate office block built at its time—is unchanged on the exterior after more than a half century of use. Its restrained Classical touches were modest in an era when most city buildings were encrusted with every imaginable frosting of architectural sleight of hand. (It must be added that Albert Kahn's architectural predilections for domestic work were strictly historicist.) The General Motors Building is one of the important skyscrapers of its time. Always well kept up, in 1970 it underwent extensive renovation to maintain it in top condition.

The General Motors Building lobby is open to the public daily 24 hours. Showroom open Monday–Friday 8:00 A.M.–4:00 P.M. Free tours can be scheduled by calling (313) 556–1676. AF 8/38

In 1978 General Motors Corporation began a joint private and public revitalization of the neighborhood—now an eighteen-block area known as New Center Commons—that adjoins its world headquarters. The master plan is by Johnson, Johnson & Roy. Almost nine hundred housing units, both houses and apartment buildings, have been built or restored, new streets and parks have been created, and stores and restaurants line the streets of this previously crime-ridden and neglected area.

SIMON RODIA TOWERS—WATTS TOWERS (1921–54)
1765 East 107th Street
Los Angeles, California

Simon Rodia, architect/builder

Vladimir Tatlin (1885–1953), the Russian painter/sculptor, is generally credited with the birth of Constructivism. His work in making "void" as much an element as "solid" was carried to impressive heights in his 1920 project for a monument in Moscow, a design in which the spatial interpenetrations of the Eiffel Tower might well have been influential (he had visited Paris in 1913). Whereas Simon Rodia—who was born in an Italian village in 1879 and came to the United States some twelve years later—had undoubtedly heard of the Eiffel Tower, it is more than doubtful that he knew of Tatlin's work. Yet Rodia, untutored and long unrecognized (he was indeed early mocked), was creating his own constructivism at almost the same time as Tatlin but along the railroad tracks of south Los Angeles. Rodia, a tile-setter by trade, sought to give something to his adopted country in kindly recognition of what it had given to him—a sentiment invigorated no doubt by a not unworthy desire to be remembered.

Working always alone, with incredible dedication, Rodia erected with castoff steel reinforcing rods, wire mesh, and concrete—and without drawings or scaffolding—two major towers (104 and 100 feet/32 and 30 meters high) and several lesser ones. Rodia gave thirty-three years of his spare time to the towers. When he finished them in 1954, he left Watts, never to return. All were encrusted with what the art world would now call "found objects": bottle bottoms and pieces of glass from junkyards, shells (some seventy thousand) from nearby beaches, colored tile fragments from construction sites, barrel hoops, broken plates—the ingredients are almost endless. However, this is no rubbish collection, no casual assemblage, but a carefully conceived esthetic achievement of fantastic imagination, fashioned lovingly through the years. If it seems more folk art than museum work, as of course it is, who cares? This is a museum in itself. But do not remain content with viewing the Rodia Towers from the sidewalk. Experience their spatial dynamism—this "participation in infinity" (Reyner Banham)—by walking in and about and through this dazzling web of three-dimensional virtuosity. Ingenious from the tensile engineering standpoint, the towers are also absorbing as sculpture. Rodia made much from little, and the country is far richer for his labors. Whether we term it architecture or sculpture is secondary. The end product is molded space for the delectation of humanity. Here the trivial has lost its triviality. Simon Rodia has given us the finest example of large-scale folk art in the Americas: an "extreme conception of an architecture without skin" (Ulrich Conrads and Hans G. Sperlich, *The Architecture of Fantasy*, Praeger, 1962).

Neglected and partly vandalized after Rodia's departure, the towers were purchased by two concerned admirers, William Cartwright and Nicholas King. They then organized the Committee for Simon Rodia's Towers in Watts, a volunteer effort to save them when the City Building Department condemned the towers (1959) as unsafe and "not conforming to building regulations." The outcry of architects, engineers, art lovers, and museum directors stayed their execution until tests by experts were made. When all the county's horses couldn't budge the towers—one shell fell off—reprieve was granted. The committee was in charge of the towers until 1975, when they were given to the city of Los Angeles. In 1978 title was transferred to the state of California, but administered by the city's Cultural Affairs Department.

East off Harbor Freeway (CA 11) on Century Boulevard, south on Central Avenue, east on 108th Street, follow signs. Largely visible from the street. Interior open Saturday 10:00 A.M.–4:00 P.M., Sunday 12:00 noon–4:00 p.m. Closed for holidays. Admission is $1 for adults, free for children under 16. For more information call (213) 485–1795. ARev 3/52, AF 1–2/69, PA 7/85, A 8/85

NEBRASKA STATE CAPITOL (1922–32)
Centennial Mall at 1445 K Street
Lincoln, Nebraska

Bertram Grosvenor Goodhue, architect

Bertram Grosvenor Goodhue (1869–1924) was one of the last of the great romantic and eclectic architects, and this capitol is his greatest building. Goodhue began his architectural life at fifteen, worked for James Renwick for six years in New York (he never went to college), then moved to Boston where he worked with Ralph Adams Cram. The pair eventually teamed up to "revolutionize ecclesiastical architecture." In 1914 he withdrew from Cram, Goodhue & Ferguson, and for a while from the Gothic, to set up shop on his own in New York. Having received a firm schooling in the Gothic under Renwick, and in the Byzantine and even Spanish with Cram and Ferguson, it is extraordinary that Goodhue could come up with such a total break in his competition entry for this state capitol. (There are suggestions of Eliel Saarinen's Helsinki Railroad Station, 1906–14, in the design.) For Nebraska, Goodhue wisely wanted a lofty building, "a Tower on the plains," that would soar above the flat landscape. The notion of another of the domes from Rome that dot most states was anathema. (His first sketches were far more Classical than his competition winner. The competition was held to select an architect, not a final design, from the ten competitors.) The result is a beacon—literally and figuratively—of a building, 400 feet/122 meters high, surmounted by Lee Lawrie's 19-foot/5.8-meter bronze figure of a sower.

The significance of the capitol lies not only in its advanced architectural quality, but in the fact that it constituted a magnificent, pioneering break with a long-outworn tradition. Moreover it integrated architecture and sculpture, particularly in its buttressed piers, to a degree rarely seen since the Gothic. In overall concept, Goodhue's design created a low mass, 437 feet/133 meters on a side, its tower rising in the center. The periphery is efficiently double lined with offices, pierced at midpoints by four entrances. These entries connect to form a Greek cross within the square framed by offices, with open courtyards filling the four corners. The majestic (95 feet/29 meters high) main entrance hall (north side) occupies one arm of the cross, the legislative chambers the east and west, while the Supreme Court chamber and law library fill the south. The tower itself rises skyward on piers that mark the central crossing. Goodhue had originally planned to utilize much of the tower for the library stacks, but working offices, not books, were substituted after his death (Goodhue died in 1924 and the capitol was completed by his associates). There is a slight dryness in the exterior, but considering that the competition for its design was won in 1920, the Nebraska Capitol is one of the key forward-looking buildings in America. There is, one hastens to add, no dryness in the interior: it boasts symbolic mosaics on the floors and ceilings by Hildreth Meiere, as well as murals, paintings, multicolored tiles, and hanging lamps, all coordinated with magniloquent scale. The building is extraordinary both in its daring and in its intimate coordination between architect and artist.

Open Monday–Friday 8:00 A.M.–5:00 P.M., Saturday and holidays 10:00 A.M.–5:00 P.M., Sunday 1:00–5:00 P.M. Closed Thanksgiving and the following Friday, Christmas, and New Year's Day. Admission is free. Free half-hour tours given on the hour (no tours at 12:00 noon). For more information call (402) 471-0448. JAIA 10/76

TRIBUNE TOWER (1923–25)
435 North Michigan Avenue
Chicago, Illinois

John Mead Howells and Raymond M. Hood, architects

For "the most beautiful office building in the world," the Chicago Tribune staged the most famous international architectural competition (1922) ever held in the United States at that time. Not only were there 285 entries from 23 countries, but in many respects it marked a turning point in America's architectural outlook. As the *Tribune* itself proclaimed in assessing the entries, the designs submitted "may be considered an encyclopedia of the architecture of the skyscraper."

John Mead Howells and Raymond Hood's prize-winning eclecticism occasioned doubts when contrasted with many of the more advanced entries from Europe, especially the design of Eliel Saarinen from Finland, which won second prize. There were many who thought that his project should have placed first, and Saarinen's "non-historic" design versus the "Gothic-inspired" winner had a strong influence on many younger architects, including, it might be fairly hypothesized, Hood, the co-winner. Louis Sullivan, with his well-known foresight, wrote in reviewing the competition winners, "The Finnish master-edifice is not a lonely cry in the wilderness, it is a voice, resonant and rich, ringing amidst the wealth and joy of life. In utterance sublime and melodious, it prophesies a time to come, and not so far away, when the wretched and the yearning, the sordid and the fierce, shall escape the bondage and mania of fixed ideas" (*Architectural Record*, February 1923). Perhaps equally important for the development of architecture in this country, the competition brought Eliel Saarinen (1873–1950) and his son Eero (1911–61) to the United States, where the latter's short-lived genius bequeathed many of the United States' most stimulating structures.

None of the above background seeks to deny virtue in the Howells-Hood design, for it is a clever building even if the rationale of using a steel frame in a medieval stonemason's garb seems oblique. Its strength lies not in its Tour de Beurre (A.D. 1485) remembrances of profile nor in its "Gothic" drapery (compare the Woolworth Building, page 336) of top and base. Much of its neglected contribution can be seen in the wrap-around "oneness" of its main shaft (not the adjuncts), a three-dimensional design concern that is finding imitators today. Important, too, are the rhythmic pier-and-mullion variations (which most contemporary skyscraper fenestration simply does not possess) that lend a briskness to its limestone and glass exterior. It is not irrelevant to note that Raymond Hood was subsequently one of the chief designers of the RCA Building in New York's Rockefeller Center (see page 374), whose fenestration and pier pattern were possibly foreshadowed here.

Lobby open to the public Monday–Friday 8:00 A.M.–6:00 P.M. Closed Christmas. The building is included on the Chicago Architecture Foundation's Michigan Avenue tour; the cost is $5. The building is also included on the Chicago Architecture Foundation's river cruise tour; the cost is $15 on weekdays, $17 on weekends. For more information on Chicago Architecture Foundation tours call (312) 922–3432. AF 2/35, PA 7/74

LIBERTY MEMORIAL (1924–26)
100 West 26th Street
Kansas City, Missouri

H. Van Buren Magonigle, architect

One of the most imaginative memorials to the American dead of World War I is located atop the hill overlooking Kansas City's Crown Center. On the downtown side, the Liberty Memorial—a national competition winner—presents an enormous inscribed flat wall (488 feet/149 meters long by 48 feet/15 meters high) to the city side (north). On the hill behind and above this rises its towering shaft. It makes a particularly impressive sight from the doughty Union Station almost at its feet. (The near vestigial station, 510 feet/155 meters long, was built in 1910–14 with Jarvis Hunt as architect.) On the main, upper, park approach side of the memorial a landscaped allée, 600 feet/183 meters long, provides a proper introduction, leading to a low podium guarded by two sphinxes, their eyes covered against the shame of warfare. The semirounded shaft of the memorial rises 217.5 feet/66 meters above, with flat facets alternating with curved ones that climax in four slightly abstracted figures at top. (There is an elevator to the observation platform.) An "eternal flame" of steam and colored lights—"the Flame of Liberty"—burns above. The side buildings, their "shaved Classic" architecture far ahead of their time, contain a museum at left and memory hall to right. The museum contains memorabilia of World War I, while the memory hall is noted for a series of gigantic murals—the south and west walls were painted by Daniel MacMorris; the north wall, 69 feet/21 meters long, was restored by MacMorris in 1958–59 but was originally painted during the war by French artists. The *In Memoriam* on the east wall was done by Jules Guerin, the French artist whose murals can also be seen in Washington's Lincoln Memorial (see page 340).

Park always open. Museum closed for restoration until late 1996. It will be open Wednesday–Sunday 9:30 A.M.–4:30 P.M. Admission will be $2 per person. For more information, call (816) 221-1918. PA 11/33, PA 11/34

LOS ANGELES PUBLIC LIBRARY, CENTRAL LIBRARY (1925–26/1993)
630 West 5th Street between Flower and Grand
Los Angeles, California

Bertram Grosvenor Goodhue, architect
Hardy Holzman Pfeiffer, architects of renovation and expansion

One of Goodhue's last works (he died in 1924), Central Library not only represents a bold step forward but hints strongly of Proto-Modern architecture. The smooth stucco walls are almost totally bereft of the historical motifs that typified the eclecticism of its day, while the window sash is the type used in industrial buildings. Goodhue, with associate architects Carleton Monroe Winslow, has put the elements together with great skill, topping all with a colorful mosaic pyramid on the central tower. Lee Lawrie created the sculptured figures. Though the interiors—even the rotunda and reading rooms on the second floor—exhibit only modest spatial grandeur, their walls are richly covered with murals. Those in the rotunda were painted on canvas (1927–32) by Dean Cornwell, and represent scenes from the "four great eras" (*Discovery, Mission Building, Americanization,* and *Founding of Los Angeles*) in the history of Los Angeles. In the dome are geometric decorations by Julian E. Garnsey. The Children's Literature Department has a fine series of pictorial canvases by Albert Herter (1871–1950), while the other reading rooms have elaborately painted ceilings.

An over $200 million restoration and expansion project—initiated by a need for more space and accelerated by a devastating fire in 1986—was completed in 1993 by Hardy Holzman Pfeiffer. The new Thomas Bradley Wing—named for a former mayor and advocate for the library—has been sensitively attached to the old building, half of its eight floors placed underground so as not to challenge Goodhue's landmark pyramidal top. A light-filled, eight-story atrium forms the core of the new. The new auditorium can be entered from outside or in. Norman Pfeiffer was architect in charge; Lawrence Halprin beautifully restored the landscaping. Altogether Los Angeles's pride and mid-city delight.

Note: the advent of electronic cataloging made obsolete some 7,000,000 old library cards: thousands of these mementos are imaginatively used behind glass to educate the elevators.

Open Sunday 1:00–5:00 P.M., Monday 10:00 A.M.–5:30 P.M., Tuesday–Wednesday 12:00 noon–8:00 P.M., Thursday–Saturday 10:00 A.M.–5:30 P.M. Closed for holidays. Free tours given Monday–Friday at 12:30 P.M., Saturday at 11:00 A.M. and 2:00 P.M., Sunday at 1:30 and 3:30 P.M. Free specialized or group tours can be arranged by calling (213) 228–7168. For general information call (213) 228–7000. AF 5/31, A 11/93, A 4/94, PA 9/94, A 5/95

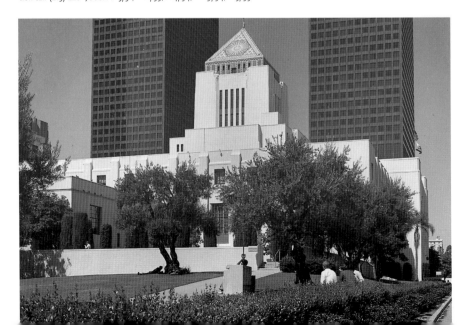

CRANBROOK EDUCATIONAL COMMUNITY (1925–42)
1221 North Woodward Avenue
Bloomfield Hills, Michigan

Eliel Saarinen, architect

Architecture, waterscaping, sculpture—a triumphant triumvirate. The main mall at the Cranbrook Educational Community is not only an example of superior campus planning, it is one of the highlights of American architecture in the early 1940s. It was also one of the first educational institutions in this country to eschew the threadbare Neo-Colonial and the Collegiate Gothic. Eliel Saarinen (1873–1950), who designed the Cranbrook buildings for the farsighted George G. Booth, came to this country from his native Finland in 1923 upon winning second prize in the famous Chicago Tribune Competition (which many thought his design should have won, see page 354). His impact on United States architecture and architectural education was significant, while the achievements of his son, Eero (1910–61), are legendary. At Cranbrook Eliel was helped by the Swedish-born Carl Milles (1875–1955), who collaborated with the elder Saarinen in the water design of the mall, and who made all the sculpture there. Milles stayed for twenty years as the academy's resident sculptor.

The buildings at Cranbrook, with a sensitive spatial relationship between units, a quietly civilized brick simplicity, and a splendid emphasis on craftsmanship, recall the best of Scandinavia and Finland of that period. Whereas formalism (especially that of the museum and library at the head of the mall) is present, the community grounds and its museum are well worth a visit. The Cranbrook Academy of Art (1925–42), the Cranbrook Campus (1927), the Kingswood Campus (1931), the Institute of Science (1938), and the Saarinen House (1928–30) also show Saarinen's Northern Country tradition of feeling for and respect for massing and site, one highlighted close up by many inventive, even playful, details. As Ian McCallam thoughtfully put it in his book *Architecture USA* (Architectural Press, London, 1959) Cranbrook is "one of the first important inroads made by a European architect on the American scene since Colonial times."

Located 7 miles/10.8 kilometers north of I-696. Cranbrook's Art Museum is open Wednesday, Friday, and Saturday 10:00 A.M.–5:00 P.M., Thursday 10:00 A.M.–9:00 P.M., Sunday 12:00 noon–5:00 P.M.; admission is $4 for adults, $2 for students. Saarinen House and Gardens open May–October for tours at various times, admission is $6 for adults, $4 for students and seniors. Cranbrook's Institute of Science open Monday–Thursday 10:00 A.M.–5:00 P.M., Friday and Saturday 10:00 A.M.–10:00 P.M., and Sunday, 1:00 P.M.–5:00 P.M.; admission is $5 for adults and $4 for children. For more information call (810) 645-3000. AF 12/38, PP 12/43, PA 7/74, AF 1/83, AP 8/83, AR 6/84

YWCA LANIAKEA CENTER (1926–27)
1040 Richards Street
Honolulu, Oahu, Hawaii

Julia Morgan, architect

The considerable talents of Julia Morgan (1872–1957) fortunately now are being recognized. Her work for William Randolph Hearst's San Simeon (see page 347) was outstanding, but in some respects it represented a highly skilled organization of existing parts. This YWCA building reflects her design ability and is, many think, her finest achievement. It directly faces the 'Iolani Palace (see page 265) while on the other side its gardens, designed by Catherine Thompson, once extended to the street behind. Morgan was the first woman accepted by the Paris École des Beaux-Arts, and the Y's facade and details thus reflect a restrained semi-Classical derivation, but one put together with freedom. Its surprise, and delight, is the unanticipated courtyard in the center of the building, with a sizable open-air swimming pool on one side of the two-story central arcade, and a garden patio, alive with umbrellas, on the other. This latter adjoins a small restaurant open for breakfast and lunch. In addition to clarity of organization, note the details and the handsome wrought-iron work. The building serves as executive headquarters of the YWCA, and in addition provides meeting rooms, a gymnasium and recreational facilities, and educational functions (arts, crafts, cooking). Residential accommodations are provided in another building.

Located opposite the 'Iolani Palace. Open Monday–Thursday 6:30 A.M.–9:00 P.M., Friday 6:30 A.M.–10:00 P.M., Saturday–Sunday 8:30 A.M.–4:30 P.M. Admission is free. Free 20-minute tours can be arranged by calling (808) 538–7061. JAIA 6/76

HONOLULU ACADEMY OF ARTS (1926–27)
900 South Beretania Street
Honolulu, Oahu, Hawaii

Bertram Grosvenor Goodhue, architect

A domestically scaled, quiet building that tactfully encourages exploration of its extensive galleries, its five open-air courtyards, and its sculpture garden. Together they present an outstanding collection of the arts of China, Japan, Korea, and India (the galleries to left on entering), plus a representative input from America and Europe (galleries to right). In addition to the collections, there are classes in art practice and history, lectures, concerts, films, and a well-stocked library. Note the gentle upturned eaves of the prominent roof and its soft gray tiles; the arc of the individual tiles is echoed in the wall vents at the end. The scale throughout is excellent. The granite paving stones of the Oriental court reputedly came from China as ballast; sandalwood for incense was shipped back. The academy was one of Bertram Grosvenor Goodhue's last designs (he died in 1924), and was also one where the client and generous donor, Mrs. Charles Montague Cooke, had a contributory hand. The building was finished by Hardie Phillips after Goodhue's death. Albert Ely Ives added the Robert Allerton Library wing in 1956 and an educational wing in 1960. The Clare Boothe Luce Wing, designed by John Hara, was opened in 1977 in celebration of the museum's fiftieth anniversary. This serves largely for the contemporary collection and also includes a 290-seat theater plus administrative offices.

Open Monday–Saturday 10:00 A.M.–4:30 P.M., Sunday 1:00–5:00 P.M. Closed for holidays. Admission is $5 for adults, $3 for students, senior citizens, and military, free for children under 12. Guided tours available Tuesday–Saturday at 11:00 A.M. The garden cafe (behind the central court) is open during museum hours. For more information call (808) 532–8700. JAIA 3/82

BOSTON AVENUE UNITED METHODIST CHURCH (1927–29)
1301 South Boston Avenue at 13th Street
Tulsa, Oklahoma

Rush, Endacott & Rush, architects

One of the country's most daring churches when it was opened over sixty-five years ago, the Boston Avenue United Methodist Church continues to command respect. With a faint architectural reference to Gothic aspirations and a touch of Art Deco, there is sturdy architectural forcefulness in proclaiming faith, while its 255-foot/78-meter tower, topped with copper and glass, creates a dramatic urban focus. The three large figures over the north entrance represent John Wesley (1703–91), who in 1784 founded the Methodist Church, his brother Charles, and their mother Susanna, who had a strong influence on the brothers' lives. Above the south entrance is carved a circuit-riders' group. A series of abstracted praying hands crown the tower, main building, and educational wing as they "point to the receptivity of divine grace." Robert Garrison was the sculptor.

The plan of the building consists of a semicircular auditorium symmetrically attached to a rectangular four-story educational/social/office block. The worship room, which seats 889 on the main floor and 461 in the balcony, carries out the motifs of the exterior with commendable consistency. Its semicircular raking pews focus on the pulpit "which signifies the centrality of the preaching of the Word," with a vaguely Gothicized but effective rood screen and a symbolic mosaic behind. The educational wing with nursery and preschool facilities was added in 1965. It was designed by M. Murray McCune of McCune McCune & Associates.

The design of the church has been credited in many publications solely to Bruce Goff, then a twenty-two-year-old member of the firm of Rush, Endacott & Rush. However, a personal letter from the church (September 1979), in referring to early documents, states "that Miss Adah Robinson, artist and art teacher, was asked by the Building Committee to present designs for a Church which would express definitive modern Christianity in mid-America . . . [and] that

Rush, Endacott & Rush was contracted on Miss Robinson's recommendation because Bruce Goff, a former student, worked as draftsman for the firm. She thought he could best translate her drawings into architectural terms." Robinson is mentioned in the architectural contract of June 1926, as being responsible for "all artistic features, interior finish, exterior design." A landmark of its kind, the Boston Avenue Church was listed in the National Register of Historic Places in 1978.

Open Monday–Friday and Sunday 9:00 A.M.–5:00 P.M. Occasionally open Saturday. Closed for holidays. Sunday services held at 8:30 and 11:00 A.M. Free tours given Sunday at 12:00 noon. Free tours can be arranged during the week by calling (918) 583-5181. AR 12/29, AD 5/57

FOSHAY TOWER (1927–29)
821 Marquette Avenue
Minneapolis, Minnesota

Magney & Tusler, architects

The notion of a habitable obelisk—even a nine-to-five one—is, of course, *divertènte*: Senmut, the ancient Egyptian obelisk maestro, would undoubtedly applaud. And though Wilbur B. Foshay wanted his office tower to "be accepted as the west's memorial to George Washington," he saw to it that his own name in letters 10 feet/3 meters high appeared on the four sides of the top. This extraordinary excursion in high-rise design was—until the completion of the nearby IDS Center (see page 556)—the tallest structure (at 447 feet/136 meters) for hundreds of miles. But height is secondary to its unforgettable profile. The building itself, though a beacon to the idiosyncratic, was solidly built. In addition to offices, the building furnished Foshay's office and apartment, including three bedrooms and three baths with marble tubs and gold-plated fixtures, on the twenty-seventh and twenty-eighth floors. Alas, the former art student turned utilities magnate was star-crossed. Before he could move into his personal pylon, the Depression struck and by December 1929 the tower was in receivership. Shortly thereafter Foshay and his chief aide were in Leavenworth Prison for fraudulent financial practices. The Foshay Tower is attached to Minneapolis's famous Skyway System, which links buildings of the fifteen-block heart of the city, thus creating desirable office space. In 1977–78 it was completely updated and refurbished, including sandblasting the exterior, and an extensive renovation of the lobbies, elevators, and common spaces was completed in 1991.

Lobby open during business hours. Foshay Museum and observation deck open April–October Monday–Friday 12:00 noon–4:00 P.M. and Saturday 11:00 A.M.–3:00 P.M., weather permitting. There is a minimal admission fee. Tours available; call (612) 341–2522 for more information. AD 5/48

NEW YORK SUSPENSION BRIDGES (1927–64)
New York, New York

Othmar H. Ammann, chief engineer

The great suspension bridges of New York City (with the exception of the Brooklyn Bridge—see page 246), along with those of San Francisco, account for five of the seven mightiest spans in the United States. Moreover, all five show some imprint of Othmar H. Ammann, who was born in Schaffhausen, Switzerland in 1879 and came to the United States—like John Augustus Roebling before him—because of its almost unlimited opportunities compared to his native Europe. Not long after he began work with the Port Authority of New York and New Jersey in 1925, his lyrical monuments could be seen lacing the city together. The Outerbridge Crossing Bridge (1928), Goethals (1928) (both cantilevers), Bayonne (1931, still the largest arch bridge in the world), the George Washington (1927–31), Bronx-Whitestone (1937–39), Throgs Neck (1961), and Verrazano-Narrows (1964) (four suspension bridges) all show his hand, often as chief designer. (The bridges in San Francisco, where he served as adviser, are the Golden Gate (1937—see page 380) and the double-span San Francisco-Oakland Bay Bridge [1936]).

The George Washington Bridge (shown in photograph) first captured public and professional admiration when the length of its main span (3,500 feet/1,067 meters) almost doubled that of any other in existence. Comprising over 25,000 individual, parallel wires made up into 61 strands, with it 3-foot/.9-meter diameter cables (still to be surpassed), this bridge stunned the world by its technology. Its towers were to have been revetted with stone but fortunately were spared this fate. Cass Gilbert was the consulting architect.

The Bronx-Whitestone, whose span (2,300 feet/701 meters) is much less than that of the George Washington, has captured the eye of the purist by virtue of the elegance of its towers. The sparse mathematics of these pylons are incomparable. Sad to relate, however, the boldly honed original deck has been compromised by the introduction of trusses along its upper edge to prevent wind oscillation. This wind factor has also put a load on other recent bridges.

The Verrazano-Narrows Bridge is, as is well known, the longest in the world (4,260 feet/1,298 meters—just 60 feet/18 meters more than Golden Gate), and while superb to experience—like any great span—it does not carry the magic of Golden Gate, due in large part to the setting of the latter. Structurally it does not represent any noticeable advance in bridge design over the California example of over a quarter century earlier, and there is a heaviness at the top of the towers of the Verrazano Bridge, whose arched portals seem excessive at 87 feet/26 meters deep at center by 28 feet/8.5 meters wide, especially when compared to the Bronx-Whitestone. As a detail, the Verrazano lamp standards are of insensitive design.

But try all of New York's bridges; each has its rewards, and each represents a staggering achievement. Moreover the firm of Ammann & Whitney was associated as structural engineers with architects on a number of the most important buildings in this book. Rest in peace, Dr. Ammann (1879–1965): you have vastly enriched the world by your gossamer imagination in steel.

AF 9/39

SWAN HOUSE (1928)
3099 Andrews Drive Northwest
Atlanta, Georgia

Philip T. Shutze, architect

The decade of the 1920s was perhaps the most indecisive in the development of American architecture. Freewheeling eclecticism had long been the only "acceptable" approach to building in this country, and it was epitomized by the work following World War I. (This took place when much of Europe was eagerly exploring the future in an architectural development we now call the International Style. The phrase, incidentally, infuriates Europeans: their pioneering was not a style, it was a religion.)

For wealthy Americans, with no design restraints and considerable fortunes (and little income tax), the sky was the architectural limit. Among the outstanding mansions of this period is the Swan House. Designed by local architect and Prix de Rome winner Philip T. Shutze, it was built for Mr. and Mrs. Edward Hamilton Inman. The quiet exterior gives little hint of the richness that awaits within. There is, to be sure, a Doric porte-cochere on the entry side and an elaborate door on the garden (approach) facade, but basically the exterior forms a simple, well-ordered mass. The interiors, however, are sumptuous and among the most beautifully detailed that one will see. Virtually all the rooms merit thorough study. The house is currently part of the Atlanta History Center.

Open Monday–Saturday 10:00 A.M.–5:30 P.M., Sunday and holidays 12:00 noon–5:30 P.M. Closed Thanksgiving, Christmas Eve, Christmas Day, and New Year's Day. Admission to the History Center is $7 for adults, $5 for senior citizens and students 18 and over, $4 for children ages 6–17, free for children under 6. Tours of the Swan House are an additional $1 per person; tours are given every half hour Monday–Friday 10:30 A.M.–4:30 P.M., Sunday and holidays 12:30–4:30 P.M. For more information call (404) 814–4000. PA 12/82

450 SUTTER BUILDING (1928–29)
San Francisco, California

Timothy L. Pflueger, architect

The Four Fifty Sutter Building is probably the most sophisticated skyscraper of the Art Deco period, a twenty-six-floor building full of elegance and subtleties. The exterior (above the seventh floor) emphasizes via its chamfered corners that the building is not solely a facade on Sutter Street but one that wraps around three sides. Note, too, the slight suggestion of the San Francisco bay window in the fenestration. The gilded entry with its incised tile extends a lively if compacted welcome. The lobby more than lives up to the promise of the exterior with a corbeled ceiling, elevator doors highlighted with touches of gold and silver, and rich Mesoamerican motifs. Dark marble walls furnish the background. The building, moreover, was one of the very first with an in-house garage, here holding 450 cars. A complete modernization and upgrading was carried out in 1978–79. From its beginning the building has been directed to the medical and dental professions.

Lobby open during business hours. A+A 3/26

CHRYSLER BUILDING (1928–30)
405 Lexington Avenue between 42nd and 43rd streets
New York, New York

William Van Alen, architect

In the century of development of high-rise design probably no skyscraper has so unabashedly explored (and exploited) a current fashion—here the Art Deco—with such success. (Art Deco is a useful vulgarization of the Exposition Internationale des Arts Decoratifs et Industriels Modernes of 1925 in Paris.) That the fashion in the United States was ephemeral may, indeed, be due to the fact that the seventy-seven-story Chrysler Building said it all; with it the style peaked (as did the Depression). A lance-like finial (185 feet/56 meters high) jabs the clouds above the multiple arcs of the dome that flash in the sun; gargoyles of wondrous spread poke from the high corners. Not only did a new material—stainless steel—cap a building, a new esthetic was stamped on New York's skyline. Moreover the Chrysler Building briefly set a new structural height (1,046 feet/319 meters). (Reputedly a miniature of the building's top also crowned Walter Percy Chrysler's automobile hood.) Glazed enamel white brick (more than 3,500,000) faces the building; note its patterns, its automotive abstractions, and the black striping near top. For at least one generation it was thought only proper to smile wryly at such stylistic exercises, but with the years we have become more tolerant and now regard what was once considered an aberration with avuncular affection. Whether we like it or not—most do— the city's architectural bouillabaisse is far richer for Chrysler's monument. (Across the top grille of a few of the building's elevator cabs are—it is not too much to suggest—the abstracted initials of Walter Percy Chrysler.) The lobby ceiling is covered with a mural by Edward Trumbull; appropriately, it concerns energy.

The building encountered financial difficulties in 1975 and was taken over by the insurance company that held its mortgage. However, in March 1978 a complete overhaul of the entire structure and its mechanical equipment was begun, including a thorough renovation of its handsome lobby and murals. As Paul Goldberger, the distinguished critic of the *New York Times*, put it, "There, in one building, is all of New York's height and fantasy in a single gesture" (18 August 1980).

Lobby open Monday–Friday 8:00 A.M.–6:00 P.M. Grand Central Partnership gives free walking tours of the area; tours meet Fridays at 12:30 P.M. in front of the Philip Morris Building at 42nd Street and Park Avenue. For more information call (212) 986–9217. AF 10/30, AP 5–6/74, PA 11/78

RADBURN (1928–31)
Plaza Road North, Radburn Road,
Howard Avenue
Fair Lawn, New Jersey

Henry Wright, Sr., and Clarence S.
Stein, architects and planners

The planning/architecture team of Henry Wright, Sr., and Clarence S. Stein did much to influence the development of urbanism in this country. Their example would have been of greater impact if the Depression had not occurred shortly after the birth of Radburn, their foremost work. Influenced by Ebenezer Howard (1850–1928), Raymond Unwin (1863–1940), Patrick Geddes (1854–1932), and the Garden City movement, which commenced in England at the turn of this century, Wright and Stein fought valiantly—generally against municipal and corporate indifference—to make large-scale professional planning an essential ingredient of urban expansion. The most famous of their efforts is, as mentioned, the modest-sized community of Radburn—approximately 670 families/3,000 population with 430 single-family houses, 92 apartment units, 60 town houses, 30 row houses, and 54 duplexes—"the town for the motor age," located 12 miles/19 kilometers northwest of the George Washington Bridge.

The layout—which was initially intended to be much larger—has a number of elements: the superblock; a community center (including library, gymnasium, senior citizens room, and youth provisions) with shopping facilities adjacent; residential cul-de-sacs with clusters of houses placed away from the noise and danger of automobiles; separation of the vehicular and the pedestrian; the park rather than the street as the core of the neighborhood; and houses turned "outside-in" to face the park, not the access road. The houses are reached by car from the rear or garage-kitchen side via a short cul-de-sac, the street servicing two rows of houses. (A single built-in, narrow garage and no curb parking create problems with today's two-car families.) Circulation on foot occurs on the other side where the houses open onto gardens, with a walkway in the center leading both to a private park and to (Ebenezer) Howard or (Robert) Owen avenues. An underpass between the superblocks allows children to walk to school or their numerous playgrounds or sports facilities without crossing a street. Radburn today is a well-treed community, comfortably lived in. Twenty-three of its 149 acres (9 to 60 hectares) form interior parks, all well maintained by a house assessment. Its lots are small, hence the houses (of non-scintillating architecture) close together. However, this cluster "compaction" makes the surrounding parks economically feasible. For the seeker of a basic pattern for a superior environment for family life, for the historian of the suburb, and for planning enlightenment, Radburn stands as one of the United States' precious few planning contributions of the early twentieth century.

Frederick L. Ackerman worked closely with Wright and Stein in developing the basic idea of Radburn. Clarence Stein, though he died in 1975 (Henry Wright in 1936), will also live on via his book *Toward New Towns for America*, while Henry Wright's literary contribution can be seen in his *Rehousing America* (Columbia University Press, 1935).

Free tours can be arranged by calling (201) 796–1300. AF 4/36, AF 7–8/71

NEWS BUILDING (1929–30)
(formerly Daily News Building)
220 East 42nd Street
New York, New York

Raymond M. Hood with John Mead Howells, architects

Raymond M. Hood and John Mead Howells won—with a Gothic-draped proposal—the 1921 competition for the design of the Chicago Tribune Tower (see page 354), one of the pivotal international architectural competitions of this century. The American architectural profession was much impressed by Eliel Saarinen's second-place entry, plus the squared-off design by Max Taut, and it seems without question that these two had a particularly strong impact on the pragmatic Raymond Hood. Thus, in 1928, when the *New York Daily News* commission came to Hood and Howells—the *News* being owned by the cousin of the proprietor of the *Chicago Tribune*—the Gothic was forgotten and a boldly cut thirty-seven-story skyscraper resulted, with Hood in charge of design.

The setbacks mandated by zoning laws played their part in the building's design, but the basic statement of the News Building is all Hood and all very fresh. The numerous setbacks—seen later in Rockefeller Center, on which Hood also worked—develop a convincing, well-scaled mass, one that takes off directly from the sidewalk and ends with a squared-off top to conceal elevator housing and water tanks (among the first to do so). The white brick verticality with terra-cotta and black-colored brick spandrels—backed by red venetian blinds—almost electrified 42nd Street. Rumor holds that its "vertical ribbons" of white suggest rolls of newsprint. (Walter H. Kilham, Jr.'s, *Raymond Hood, Architect*, Architectural Book Publishing Company, 1973, gives a fine account of this and Hood's overall contribution.) It should be

pointed out that while only every other pier is structural, the others are filled with utilities. In any event the News Building ushered in a new phase of high-rise rationality, one liberated from historic cliché and one rightly confident in its geometric statement. As Henry-Russell Hitchcock wrote for the Modern Architecture International Style exhibition at the Museum of Modern Art in 1932, it "remains the most effective skyscraper in New York." Take a look, too, at the relief at the entry and the towering lobby with its dramatically lit, revolving globe. A substantial annex was added in 1958 on the east side (Harrison & Abramovitz, architects).

Lobby open Monday–Friday 8:00 A.M.–6:00 P.M. Closed for holidays. AF 2/35, AP 10/73

The following year and down the same street (330 West 42nd) Hood pioneered another direction when he emphasized the horizontal instead of the vertical, and took the use of color to a new high in the old McGraw-Hill Building (1930–31). A partial industrial building in that its lower floors incorporated printing presses (until 1933), the thirty-four-story skyscraper, though economical—and in some respects profiled by the building code (except the Art Deco top)—achieves high marks, especially its blue-green terra-cotta facing and its lobby.

Incidentally, Raymond Hood's first essay in color was the American Radiator Building (1923–24), 40 West 40th Street, where black brick for the walls was touched at the top with gilt paint. (The budget would not permit gold leaf.) From the design point of view this use of black was to neutralize the "holes" of the windows "so they wouldn't show" and make the twenty-story, slightly Gothic structure appear more massive.

EMPIRE STATE BUILDING (1929–31)
350 5th Avenue between 33rd and 34th streets
New York, New York

Shreve, Lamb & Harmon, architects

The pharos of Manhattan has maintained its civic dignity and fulfilled its urban function (as radio and TV beamer) for over three score years. It stands as a determined sentinel in a lonely niche of the island, and its nearly foursquare, stepped-back design (tower seven by nine bays) rises to meet almost any challenge. (In 1945 a B-25 bomber unfortunately hit the 79th floor while traveling at an estimated 200 mph/322 kph. It inflicted no structural damage to the building.) The Empire State Building is, in short, a mnemonic addition to New York's profile, an almost timeless milestone of distinguished architecture in the United States. (It was George Washington who in 1784 reputedly termed the state of New York the "seat of empire.") That it was also our tallest structure from 1931 to 1971 (when the World Trade Center, see page 522, surpassed it) gave it the useful cachet as "New York's most distinguished address" (as, of course, was planned). The building contains eighty-five floors of offices—with primary setbacks at the 6th and 72nd levels—topped by observation platforms at the 86th and 102nd floors, with a pylon above intended as a dirigible mooring mast, but used only twice as such. The mast on top was extended in 1951–52—without touching the structural frame below the 102nd floor—to serve as the consolidated television antenna for all of New York's stations. Total height is 1,250 feet/381 meters, with television tower 1,445 feet/440 meters. H. G. Balcom was the too-little-recognized structural engineer.

Lobby open daily 8:00 A.M.–midnight. Observation decks open daily 9:30 A.M.–midnight; admission is $4 for adults, $2 for children ages 5–12, senior citizens, and military personnel. For more information call (212) 736-3100, ext. 314. AF 1/31, AF 4/31

PSFS (PHILADELPHIA SAVING FUND SOCIETY) BUILDING (1929–32)
1212 Market Street at South 12th
Philadelphia, Pennsylvania

Howe & Lescaze, architects

The superb thirty-six-story PSFS Building was one of the germinal office towers in the country. Considered by many as the most important tall structure from the 1890s to the 1930s, it was the United States' first truly "modern skyscraper" (*Architectural Review*, May 1957) and one that influenced subsequent buildings for years. The evolution of its design is elusive but there is more than a hint of the European International Style in it. (Architect William Lescaze was himself born in Switzerland.) Richard J. Neutra's office building of c. 1925 for Rush City Reformed had similar cantilevered horizontal bands of fenestration in front and vertically expressed structure on the side. However, PSFS stands as an advanced design to the bank. Note, in this regard, the low (and expressed) twenty-first floor, which houses air-conditioning equipment. Air conditioning— here only the second installation in a high rise in the United States—made the building far more attractive to potential tenants. The narrow band of fenestration of the mechanical floor, moreover, gives subtle scale to the facade. The rounded corner base might be considered mannered today, and there is some fussiness at the top, but PSFS will always remain prominent in the hierarchy of office buildings and in the development of Modern American architecture. (William H. Jordy in the fourth volume of *American Buildings and Their Architects*, Doubleday, 1972, has an excellent chapter on PSFS and its architects.) Not only is the exterior of great merit, the interiors—down to the design of the clocks and the colors used—are admirable. In 1992 the bank failed and the building was seized by the government; it is currently being renovated and will reopen as a Hyatt Hotel.

Lobby open to the public during business hours. ARev 5/57, SAHJ 5/62, AF 5/64, SAHJ 12/68, A 3/96

MUSEUM CENTER AT UNION TERMINAL (1929–33)
1301 Western Avenue
Cincinnati, Ohio

Fellheimer & Wagner, architects

Railroad passenger stations in the United States trace over a century-and-a-half career, reflecting through the decades a valuable mirror of architectural and spatial development. As the railroads themselves prospered many outdid themselves to take care of and impress their passengers. The Cincinnati Union Terminal—built during the Depression—was one of the last moments of glory in this cavalcade. Little of substance in the field was built after it. (The sizable Los Angeles Union Station, finished in 1939, was the last of the great depots.)

The building itself climaxes an elevated plaza and drive with a monumental semicircular facade. Measuring 200 feet/61 meters in diameter, it is "the unchallenged giant of station portals" as the late Carroll L. V. Meeks put it in his authoritative book *The Railroad Station* (Yale University Press, 1956). Its apsidal entry, keyed by a band of murals by Winold Reiss wrapping the semicircle of the room, forms one of the highlights of the Art Deco movement. Numerous decorative touches, including even the terrazzo paving, brighten the rest. The enormous entrance exedra leads, with unexpected diminution—almost a spatial siphon—onto a lengthy, slightly arched concourse that spans and that once gave access to the tracks below.

That the Cincinnati station is even standing today, passenger operations having ceased in 1972, is a tribute to stout-hearted preservationists, local and nationwide. There were early attempts at turning the station into a shopping mall, but they succumbed to the recession of the early 1980s. Then in 1986 the Hamilton County voters approved a bond issue to restore the terminal as a museum. With state, city, corporate, and private funds it reopened in 1990 as the Museum Center at Union Terminal under the joint auspices of the Cincinnati Museum of Natural History and the Cincinnati Historical Society. With primary emphasis on the natural history of the Ohio Valley, and with its displays taking advantage of the latest exhibition techniques, the museum has proved to be a dramatic success. As a fine by-product the railroad section is now open to Amtrak service.

Open Monday–Saturday 9:00 A.M.–5:00 P.M., Sunday 11:00 A.M.–6:00 P.M. Closed Thanksgiving and Christmas. Admission is $4.95 for adults, $2.95 for children ages 3–12. Free one-hour tours are given Saturday–Sunday 11:00 A.M.–4:00 P.M. on the hour. For more information call (513) 287-7000. The Cincinnati Historical Society Museum also offers tours; for more information call (513) 287-7095. AF 6/33

PARAMOUNT THEATRE (1931)
2025 Broadway
Oakland, California

Miller & Pflueger, architects

The Oakland Paramount Theatre is a delirious example of Art Deco. Its exterior with its 110-foot-/34-meter-high tile mosaic of enormous figures bifurcated by the projecting Paramount sign—which can be seen up and down the street—gives a hint of the prodigious, but it is the interior that rises to unequaled heights. A 58-foot-/18-meter-high lobby—with side walls made of alternating vertical bands of warm artificial light panels and muted red piers, and with both ends and ceiling decorated with an almost luminescent grillwork—forms a regal introduction. The grille, 12 inches/30 centimeters in depth, is made of carefully composed metal leaves, behind which indirect light shines with a greenish cast. As one moves about the lobby the depth of the patterning evokes the play of sunlight through a canopy of dense foliage. But whereas the foyer relies on stately luxuriance, the auditorium is unmatched for its refulgent splendor. Its gilded galaxies of whorls, patterns, and stylized figures are unbelievable. Furthermore this largesse extends over the stepped ceiling, while a solid-color curtain with silver and green appliquéd design calls attention to the stage. Outside and in, the Paramount radiates the dream-world escapism with which the movies sought to beguile their customers. There will never be another like it. Timothy Pflueger was chief of design.

After years of desultory life the theater was thoroughly reconditioned and restored in 1973 to serve as the home of the Oakland Symphony and Oakland Ballet, as well as for other cultural events. New seats were installed (reduced from 3,434 to 2,998 more comfortable ones), new rugs woven, and the whole brightly refurbished. Skidmore, Owings & Merrill were consultants for the restoration, with Milton Pflueger & Associates assisting. Michael Goodman was the interior designer. The building is now in the National Register of Historic Places.

Open for performances. Two-hour tours are given at 10:00 A.M. on the 1st and 3rd Saturdays of the month; the cost is $1 per person. Private tours can be arranged by calling (510) 893–2300. AP 3–4/74, PA 7/74

HOOVER DAM (1931–36)
US 93, on Nevada-Arizona border
near Boulder City, Nevada

U.S. Bureau of Reclamation, engineers

Hoover Dam rises in a wild, intractable landscape, spun overhead with a gossamer net of high-tension wires. It comprises one of the country's boldest achievements of man harnessing nature to the advantage of each. Floods that once ravaged California's Imperial Valley and regional farmlands have been contained and water shortages largely eliminated by the controlled release from the dam's reservoir, the 110-mile-/177-kilometer-long artificial Lake Mead. The lake also serves as a key recreation facility for the region. In addition to the stabilized irrigation that the dam and lake make possible, a process augmented by the Parker and Imperial dams downstream, some 1 billion gallons/3.8 billion liters of water a day are supplied for domestic and industrial uses to Southern California (via a 242-mile/389-kilometer aqueduct and five pumping stations to lift it over the mountains) and to central Arizona (via a 335-mile/536-kilometer aqueduct and fourteen pumping plants). Moreover, its hydroelectric production, created from the non-polluting force of gravity, was for ten years (1939–49) the greatest in the world. At 2,080,000 kilowatts generating capacity it is still one of the largest.

Hoover Dam itself measures 726.4 feet/221 meters in total height above stream bed, with a crest length of 1,244 feet/379 meters and a bottom thickness of 660 feet/201 meters of solid concrete. Throughout the great mass 1-inch/25-millimeter pipes with a total loop of 582 miles/937 kilometers were embedded to cool the concrete so that in pouring—which began in June 1933—it would cure properly and speedily. There are also five inspection galleries laced through it to monitor the dam's behavior, a feature subsequently adopted for most large-scale dam construction. Clamped on the rocky vise of restless hills, its smooth mathematics relay stunning splendor to the beholder. Moreover the architectural and engineering aspects of powerhouse and substations (with the exception of some details) are good. Altogether, dam and setting are enormously impressive. John Lucian Savage was the brilliant chief engineer, as he was for the Bureau of Reclamation up to World War II.

In 1995 a Visitors Center was opened, vastly expanding an understanding of the role of hydro-electricity in today's world. Its two high-speed elevators descend 53 stories to the generators below. At top a theater shows films of the dam's construction.

Located 7 miles/11 kilometers east of Boulder City, Nevada. Open daily 8:30 A.M.–6:30 P.M. Closed Christmas and Thanksgiving. Admission is $5 for adults, $2.50 for senior citizens and children 10–16, free for children under 10. Forty-minute tours given throughout the day. Call (702) 293–8421 for more information, (702) 293–8367 for tour information. A 1/96

ROCKEFELLER CENTER (1931–40)
5th–6th avenues, 47th–51st streets
New York, New York

Reinhard & Hofmeister, Corbett, Harrison & Macmurray,
Hood & Fouilhoux, principal architects

The essential lesson of Rockefeller Center is its careful grouping of harmonious buildings about a scintillating central focus. This has been so obvious for so long that it is more than puzzling that subsequent multi-skyscraper developments have ignored this, including, it should be added, Rockefeller Center's own expansion westward (post-1940) across 6th Avenue (the design of which is not relevant here). The thirteen original buildings are, more than sixty years after birth, a bit dated with their limestone facing and cast aluminum spandrels, but they are so mutually respectful, their buildup of scale from six stories to seventy so adroitly handled, and the "waste space" of the lower plaza and its promenade so fascinating, that this has become the spontaneous core of New York City, just as the agora was in ancient Greece, and the piazza is in today's Italy. The seasonally planted *passeggiata* from 5th Avenue down the promenade to the plaza, where the umbrellas of summer alternate with the ice skaters of winter, where the flags of the United Nations emblazon the sky (and welcome foreign visitors), together produce a free, non-stop, open-air theater. And however we may regard Paul Manship's *Prometheus* in the light of today's sculptural excursions, it furnishes an extremely important visual termination of the mall axis. With its forward location, this gold-leafed figure sparkles in the sun long after the facades of the skyscrapers behind it have been left in darkness.

As a group of buildings Rockefeller Center heralded a whole new concept of coordinated city development: each building working with the others and with the street. The seventy-story GE (ex-RCA) Building is the pivot, while the thirty-three-story One Rockefeller Plaza building was oriented north-south to cast minimum shadow on the plaza. Note that part of the buildings' subtlety comes from the varying widths of the vertical bands of limestone, reflecting (generally) the column spacing behind. (The uniform solid-glass-solid striping of the new units is lifeless in comparison.) An underground pedestrian concourse—which boasts a grand selection of shops and restaurants—ties the entire complex together. (This was completely refurbished in 1979 by the Walker Group.) More greenery in the center would have been in order, but in its tiny mall and its lively plaza—and in the celebration of space between them— we find a few strategic square feet becoming the core for acres of building. People come alive here, participants, even if vicariously, as they observe, are observed, and absorb. This imperishable lesson was well ahead of its time.

It is useful to recall that Rockefeller Center was initially planned as a complex based on a new Metropolitan Opera House, the opera having outgrown its quarters on 39th Street. Benjamin W. Morris III and Harvey Wiley Corbett—both architects familiar with large-scale enterprises—made grandiose schemes. The Depression, among other factors, killed this; to salvage the investment in the already assembled land, John D. Rockefeller developed the beginnings of the Rockefeller Center we see today. L. Andrew Reinhard and Henry Hofmeister are generally credited with its basic scheme, with Raymond Hood contributing significantly to the design of the main buildings.

No discussion of the complex would be complete without mention of its inside Mecca, Radio City Music Hall, a theater that half the nation—and much of the world—either has seen or would like to see. Entering under a low but roomy ticket sale area, one is thrown into a breathtaking lobby 60 feet/18 meters tall and 150 feet/46 meters long, chandeliers dangling,

mirrors sparkling, and broad stair tempting at the end. With the entry thus set, one proceeds into the great auditorium to encounter an aurora of semicircular bands of light spreading outward and upward with geometric rapture. There is no theater interior that can match it. The hall was designed in part by the then twenty-nine-year-old Edward Durell Stone, bolstered, one understands, by the hall's impresario, Samuel "Roxy" Rothafel. Donald Deskey was responsible for the interior decoration.

In the 1970s the music hall's 6,200 seats were rarely filled and the theater lost vast sums annually. In April 1979 a master plan for a completely new entertainment approach was announced—one stressing live productions—relieving fears that the Hall would be closed and the site used for an office block. As a *New York Times* editorial (10 January 1978) had put it, "If Radio City Music Hall really closes . . . it will be a little like closing New York." A thorough internal restoration of the Art Deco magnificence of the former movie palace (the largest in the world) was also announced, and in June of that year the completely renovated theater reopened to tumultuous acclaim.

Lobbies of buildings open during business hours. Self-guided walking tour available in seven languages from the information desk. Monday–Friday 9:00 A.M.–5:00 P.M. AF 4/31, AF 10/31, AF 1/32, AF 7/32, AF 2/33, AF 6/65, AF 1–2/66, AR 3/74, PA 7/74, JAIA 2/78, JAIA 9/78

FOREST PRODUCTS LABORATORY, USDA FOREST SERVICE (1932)
1 Gifford Pinchot Drive
Madison, Wisconsin

Holabird & Root, architects

As an example of early Depression Moderne and Art Deco, this laboratory is one of the country's adventurous pioneers. Its symmetrical composition atop a hill and its corner windows countering the verticality of its profusion of fins are all dated now. But this was one of the first large "contemporary" structures in the country when it was built, an exciting statement of its time. The original setting has been marred by unsympathetic additions, the exterior color scheme has been changed, and a nearby expressway does not help matters, but the laboratory still maintains much of its original vanguard conviction.

Lobby open to the public Monday–Friday 8:00 A.M.–4:00 P.M. Closed for holidays. AF 8/33

CHATHAM VILLAGE (1932/1936/1956)
Bigham Street, Virginia Avenue, and
Olympia, Sulgrave, and Pennridge roads
Pittsburgh, Pennsylvania

Clarence S. Stein & Henry Wright, Sr., planners

The Buhl Foundation built the 45-acre/18-hectare Chatham Village as a rental housing development at the depth of the Depression; it is still a model full of lessons for the developer and architect. Its site planning directly responds to the steep topography, and every change of level has been used functionally and for visual variety. Services are confined to the periphery while groups of attached houses form a ring around beautifully landscaped and scaled central greens. Unobtrusive yet convenient garage compounds accommodate many cars, while other parking is incorporated under some of the houses when grade permits. The first section of 129 simple, red-brick, modified Georgian, two-story houses was completed in 1932 (R. E. Griswold, landscape architect), and the second phase of 68 more in 1936 (T. M. Kohankie, landscape architect). A former mansion (1844) used as a clubhouse and a small group of commercial buildings occupy the northeast corner. In 1956 the Buhl Foundation added a nineteen-unit apartment building (Frederick Bigger, planner; Ingham, Boyd, and Pratt, architects). Recreation facilities abound; a public park lies adjacent. Chatham Village is admirable—and a highly successful private undertaking. It was purchased by its devoted tenants as a cooperative in 1960.

Located in the Mount Washington area of Pittsburgh. Tours can be scheduled by calling the management office at (412) 431–4300. The Pittsburgh History and Landmarks Foundation also offers tours of Chatham Village for a fee; call (412) 471–5808 for more information. AF 4/33, AF 4/35, AF 5/60

NORTH DAKOTA STATE CAPITOL (1933–34)
1200 East Divide Street
Bismarck, North Dakota

Joseph Bell De Remer and W. F. Kurke, architects
Holabird & Root, associates

The North Dakota State Capitol ranks among the more daring and more successful buildings of its time in the United States. It is the outstanding governmental structure of the 1930s. As the official leaflet states, "The average visitor to North Dakota's state capitol is not immediately impressed with the exterior, for it is different. It is not what he expected, after viewing other state capitols. The building has a style of architecture entirely its own. No other capitol building in all the world approaches it in such considerations as simplicity, practicability, and usability." The folder adds that the building cost $2 million at 46 cents per cubic foot, an extraordinarily low figure.

The early 1930s were a difficult time for architecture both philosophically and financially. The beginnings of "contemporary" architecture were being seen in the United States, generally expressed by what we now call the "Moderne" or even "Modernistic," the latter with its jazzed game of angles. It was a searching-out process with little background material to bolster the exploration. And the Depression of course ended almost all major construction. Thus when the architects evolved the design for the Bismarck capitol, replacing one destroyed by fire in 1930, it was probable that a businesslike efficiency rather than glamour would result. The capitol measures 389 x 173 feet/119 x 53 meters and is accented by a nineteen-story office tower. The profile is perhaps influenced by Bertram Grosvenor Goodhue's famous Nebraska State Capitol (see page 352), but the influence—except in bravery for both—is slight. The low section at left contains legislative chambers, the Senate with 52 seats and the House with 116. These rooms are restrained but elegant, and are particularly noted for their fine wood paneling. A memorial hall 150 feet/46 meters long by 40 feet/12 meters high stretches across the entry. Steel-frame construction is used throughout with limestone facing. Strangely, there is no art in the building—no murals, mosaics, or sculpture. Although Joseph Bell De Remer from Grand Forks and W. F. Kurke from Fargo are listed as the principal architects, it is likely that Holabird & Root had more than an "associates'" role.

In 1980–81 a Judicial Wing and State Office Building were added to the capitol. Ritterbush Associates and Foss Engelstad Foss were associated architects and engineers.

Open daily 8:00 A.M.–5:00 P.M. Free 45-minute tours given Monday–Friday 8:00–11:00 A.M. and 1:00–4:00 P.M. on the hour; Memorial Day–Labor Day tours also given on Saturday 9:00 A.M.–4:00 P.M. and Sunday 1:00–4:00 P.M. Tours can also be scheduled by calling (701) 328-2480. AR 4/32, AF 2/35

NORRIS DAM (1933–36)
Highway 441
Norris, Tennessee

BULL RUN STEAM PLANT (1962–66)
Edgemore Road (Highway 92)
Clinton, Tennessee

Tennessee Valley Authority, architects and engineers

The Tennessee Valley Authority (TVA)—centered in Knoxville, Tennessee—has changed the face of much of the southeast, overwhelmingly for the better. Its success has spawned similar developments not only in this country but in many of the developing nations of the world. It is rightly upheld as an example of what can be done to salvage a region. This once-depressed, erosion-ravaged section of Appalachia was not even "developing" fifty to sixty years ago. It was moribund, with a per capita income, unbelievable as it now seems, of around $168 per annum in 1933 and with only 3.5 percent of its farms having electricity. (Tennessee's per capita income in 1993 was over $17,600.) It can be said, indeed proclaimed, that TVA was largely instrumental in saving the South, for its plants provided inexpensive power that attracted industry and raised employment, its twenty-nine dams helped control flooding, and its stabilized rivers aided transportation. And however history will judge the atomic bomb and atomic energy, they were created in Oak Ridge, Tennessee because of the power capacity of TVA. Though electric power, flood control, and year-round navigation are TVA's chief concerns, "community development" and recreational use of its waters are of increasing importance. In brief it can be said that TVA is "the world's boldest venture in regional reconstruction" (*Architectural Review*, London, June 1943).

Norris Dam was the first to be constructed (1933–36), and it was here that a momentous breakthrough in architectural philosophy occurred. The earliest design proposals for the powerhouse and non-dam facilities were in a so-called "Colonial style" when David Lilienthal, TVA's first director, asked Roland Wank (1898–1970), who had been retained as town planner for the expansion of Norris, "to take a look." Wank took a look for two weeks, came back to Lilienthal, and said, "This is the way I think it should be," and then outlined the sparse, powerful, unencumbered, dateless lines that have made TVA design the great exemplar in architectural-engineering terms. Wank, fortunately, got the job as chief of design (1933–44), producing a superlative series of structures from power plants to gantry cranes. Norris Dam itself was a good beginning but the work of the next eleven years was finer. The chief engineer during the early developing period was Arthur E. Morgan.

Located on the Clinch River about 21 miles/34 kilometers north-northwest of Knoxville. Take I-75 to Highway 61 to 441. Closed until summer 1996; it will be open Monday–Friday 8:00 A.M.–3:30 P.M.

The earliest sources of TVA energy were river based, but when the full water-power potential of its seven-state region had been harnessed, the Authority—to keep up with the growing demand for electricity—augmented this source with steam, as here at Bull Run (shown in photograph) and at Paradise, Kentucky (see page 459). By 1978 TVA had increased its generating capacity 100 per cent over its pre-1968 level, primarily with nuclear plants, of which Browns Ferry in Alabama is the first of seven anticipated. No more sizable dams are planned. The Bull Run Steam Plant (1962–66), like most of its confreres, rises above routine industrial force with coordinated strength and stark simplicity of line. It is dominated by an 800-foot-/244-meter-high chimney (equal to a seventy-story building), anchored by its powerhouse (950,000-kilowatt capacity), and tethered to the land by its giant covered conveyors. These feed it coal at over 5 tons/4.5 metric tons per minute from a 123-foot-/37-meter-high silo. Though the complex is not as overwhelming as the coal-fired plant at Paradise, with its hyperbolic cooling towers, it is still very powerful. The lake formed by the Melton Hill Dam supplies the 400,000 gallons/1,818,435 liters of water a minute needed for cooling. On design terms, Bull Run reestablished TVA's reputation for excellence, a reputation that had slipped a bit following Wank's departure. As with most of its undertakings, Bull Run was designed and constructed by the Authority's forces.

Located northwest of Knoxville. Take Alcoa Highway to 275 north to Clinton Highway exit, after 7 miles/11.2 kilometers turn left onto Edgemore Road, plant is 2 miles/3.2 kilometers on left. Open Monday–Friday 7:00 A.M.–3:30 P.M.

Tours of both sites available on an informal basis. Group tours can be scheduled by calling (615) 632–1825. AF 9/35, AF 8/39, PP 11/39, AF 9/41, PP 1/45

GOLDEN GATE BRIDGE (1933–37)
US 101 above the Golden Gate
San Francisco and San Rafael, California

Joseph B. Strauss, chief engineer
Othmar H. Ammann, Leon S. Moisseiff,
Charles Derleth, Jr., and Irving F. Morrow, consultants

The spatial experience of traversing the Golden Gate Bridge—especially in a car with the top down (if such can be found)—ranks supreme among bridge crossings, or any other form of highway exhilaration. Much of this is due to its incomparable setting: the unsullied nature of the winding southbound approach, the intervening hills that permit only snatches of the top-rigging, the capricious veilings by wisps of fog, then the personal confrontation with those

mammoth red pylons and their skein of yard-thick cables, the whole transformed from a study in statics into sculpture at car speed. The George Washington Bridge (1927–31), the Bronx-Whitestone (1937–39), and the Verrazano-Narrows (completed 1964), all in New York (see page 362)—for all three of which the Swiss-born Othmar Ammann was designer or consultant—are inspired spans, but none carries the sheer intoxication of the Golden Gate and its approaches. Its 4,200-foot/1,280-meter suspension length when completed in 1937 was the longest in the world until 1964 when the Verrazano surpassed it by 60 feet/18 meters. Its two steel-plate tower legs, 33 x 54 feet/10 x 16 meters and slightly stepped back in stages as they rise, are braced horizontally at four spots above the decking, topping off at 746 feet/227 meters above the bay. One of the chief problems in the bridge's erection was the building of the south (San Francisco side) pier in swirling water 85 feet/26 meters deep and over 1,100 feet/335 meters from land. Moreover the bridge, both in construction and after completion, was and is exposed to full blasts of wind from the Pacific, and is often fog-shrouded, while the earthquake belt that has notably tossed the city is only a half-dozen miles (10 kilometers) away. Fortunately the bridge has serenely weathered everything that nature and sometimes man (via ships) has been able to throw against it. It can be crossed on foot or bicycle as well as automobile. One of the greatest sights.

Bridge open daily 24 hours to automobile traffic. Pedestrian sidewalk open daily 5:00 A.M.–9:00 P.M. Vista and informational displays located on southeast side of bridge. A 3/85

MUNICIPAL AUDITORIUM (1934–36)
301 West 13th Street
between Central and Broadway
Kansas City, Missouri

Alonzo H. Gentry Voskamp & Neville
Hoit, Price & Barnes, architects

This large-scale, limestone-sheathed, Moderne auditorium is a classic example of its period. Note the excellent Art Deco detailing. The carving on the friezes depicts the intellectual and social purposes for which the building is used. Combining music hall, arena, little theater, and exhibition hall, the Municipal Auditorium is a synopsis of an era and its architecture. There is an underground connection with the Bartle Exhibition Hall.

Lobby open to the public during business hours. Also open for events. Tours can be scheduled by calling (816) 871-3700. AF 3/37

Frank Lloyd Wright, architect

Nature and architecture, embraced and embracing, are here, and unless people work intimately with and respect the environment—as Frank Lloyd Wright did—the one will wither as the other immolates itself. Pyrrhus is the name. This is no perfect house. Perfection in terms of domestic choice and complexity does not exist. But Fallingwater stands on a pinnacle in its interlock—indeed in its clannish conspiracy—with its setting. Providentially, this house and the Robie House in Chicago (see page 332)—two of Wright's greatest works—survive and are open to the public even if some formalities are necessary to enter each.

Fallingwater, or Bear Run as the family called it, is approached via a winding path that reveals mere snatches of the house through the trees. It is only upon crossing a modest bridge that the whole building is seen and the waters that tumble and swirl at its feet are perceived. The dominant elements that one first grasps are the pale ocher concrete cantilevered terraces, resembling enormous shallow trays, the upper set at right angles to the lower and jutting with magnificent authority over the falling waters. The house itself, its local sandstone walls, its glass, and the slender cantilever of its roof—all of its elements agitating and complementing each other—then materialize, and the space games begin. The waters gurgle and splash—"the noise of which is presumably welcomed by the occupants," an irate critic (Royal Cortissoz) once remarked—while above this the tensions of the terraces, intensified by the vibrancy of their right-angle placement, take over and contrast first with nature and then as counterpoint with the other components, fieldstone and glass. Space is embraced, and stone, concrete, and glass dance.

Within, the music continues with Wright's famous "free plan," wherein, as the Italian critic Bruno Zevi perceptively remarked, "the same tendency is apparent: to amalgamate the rooms, to animate the building as if it were a continuous spatial discourse rather than a series of separate words." The boundaries between people and nature are architecturally slender here—and purposefully so; rooms flow outward onto terraces and almost evaporate in the mists of the waterfall, while the boundaries between one room and the next are almost nonexistent. No room in this smallish house is a foursquare box, the major ones do not even have a single-plane ceiling. A certain fracturing of space can be said to result, and in the living room a lack of focus is apparent even with the potent accent of the great fireplace and the living rock that rises through the floor and nestles against the chimney breast. But no more quibbling: see this stone and concrete poem—and see, too, the Guest House (1939) on the small ridge behind the main dwelling. As the Museum of Modern Art's 1965 exhibition and catalog entitled *Modern Architecture U.S.A.* said, "in no other building, even by Wright, do poetry and technique fuse in a vision so hypnotic." As to its background, FLW himself wrote, "The Gale

House built in wood and plaster in 1909 was the progenitor, as to general type, of Fallingwater, 1936" (*A Testament*, Horizon Press, 1957).

Built for the late Edgar J. Kaufmann as a weekend retreat from Pittsburgh, some 60 miles/97 kilometers to the northwest, Kaufmann's son, Edgar Kaufmann, Jr., gave the house and its extensive grounds (1,543 acres/624 hectares) to the public (1963) with an endowment to keep it up. It is now open to the public under the Western Pennsylvania Conservancy. The conservancy has since added considerable more ground to safeguard the watershed, and in 1976 completed a major restoration of the dwelling.

A Visitors Center was built in 1978 to accommodate the numerous tourists to the house. Designed as a series of pods projecting from a central open but covered information core, it provides a display pod illustrating the background of Fallingwater, its geology, flora, and fauna. There is also a toilet pod, a children's pod (those under twelve cannot visit the house), and a service pod. Well separated from the house, the center has been carried through with "invisibility" in mind plus sharp attention to detail. Paul Mayen was the designer, with Curry, Martin & Highberger the architects.

Located 3.5 miles/5.6 kilometers north of Ohiopyle. April 1–November 15 open Tuesday–Sunday 10:00 A.M.–4:00 P.M. November 16–March 31 open Saturday–Sunday 10:00 A.M.–4:00 P.M. Admission is $12 per person on weekends and $8 during the week. All visits are guided; the tour lasts 45 minutes. For more information call (412) 329–8501. AF 1/38, JAIA 8/81, A 11/89

S. C. JOHNSON OFFICES (1936–39)
S. C. JOHNSON LABORATORY (1947–50)
1525 Howe Street off 14th
Racine, Wisconsin

Frank Lloyd Wright, architect

Pietro Belluschi wrote of the Johnson complex, "These buildings shine in uncompromising purity and deliver all that the spirit may wish" (*Architectural Record*, July 1956). Of all its influential parts, it is the interior of the main administrative unit that gleams the most. This magnificently fashioned room was modern architecture's first substantial administrative beach-

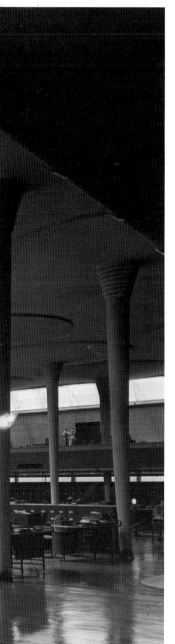

head on the then-reactionary shores of United States corporate wisdom (Frank Lloyd Wright's demolished Larkin Building excepted). It was, and is fifty-six years after its completion, one of the great spaces—and there are precious few.

The fifty-eight (thirty-two freestanding) dendriform columns (the tallest are almost 31 feet/9.5 meters high) uphold the 128 x 228 foot/39 x 69 meter ceiling—structurally they hold up mostly themselves. In shape they vaguely recall those that supported King Minos's Palace in Crete of about 2000 B.C., and they were so beyond the building code concept of base size to load that they were immediately challenged by the state. Thereon, Wright—who studied engineering before beginning architecture—had a prototype column constructed and piled with sandbags until it exceeded by twelve times the load it was calculated to carry. The city engineer was among the first in hailing FLW's triumph. (The columns are hollow and were poured integrally with steel mesh.) Though this forest of columns with conical necks and lily-pad tops (18 feet/5.5 meters in diameter) do not support as much as they appear to, the fact remains that their exquisitely tapered shapes with their glass tube interstices provide a noble, suffusedly illuminated hall. It is also one intended to create a "family" ambiance for work in a non-stimulating industrial environment.

One of the essential features of the spatial quality of the two-story-with-balcony room can be seen in the juncture of three of its sides with the ceiling plane. This is effected by a continuous glass tube clerestory that lends spatial freedom to the enclosed volume while delivering a glowing emanation outside at night. (The extensive exterior use of 2-inch/50-millimeter Pyrex glass tubing, in 5- and 10-foot/1.5- and 3-meter lengths, occasioned initial leakage problems, but these have been solved by a silicone rubber sealant.) The cabinets of the typing and accounting activities at the column bases—all designed by the architect—are finished in a cheerful Cherokee red. Note that, as has been already mentioned in connection with many of Wright's buildings, the entrance rarely announces itself; here at Racine it is mischievously tantalizing. There is no ambiguity about the great forested work space, however: it is masterful. As Samuel C. Johnson, chairman and chief executive officer of the company, adds, "We became a different company the day the building opened. We achieved international attention because that building represented and symbolized the quality of everything we did in terms of products, people, the working environment within the building, the community relations, and—most important—our ability to recruit creative people" (*AIA Journal*, January 1979).

Behind the administrative building rises the fourteen-story Research Tower (currently closed), best known for its unique "tap root" structure. Swathed in slightly streamlined bands of glass tubing and red brick, its vertical accent is welcome amid the low units about it.

Building open Monday–Friday during business hours. March–November tours given Tuesday–Friday at 10:00 A.M., 11:15 A.M., 1:00 P.M., and 2:15 P.M. December–February tours given Tuesday–Friday at 11:15 A.M. and 1:00 P.M. Memorial Day–Labor Day tours given Saturday–Sunday at 1:00 and 2:15 P.M. Tours are free and last 30 minutes; reservations are required. Call (414) 631–2154 for tour information. AR 1/38, AR 1/48, AF 1/51, AR 7/56, AR 10/60, JAIA 5/74, JAIA 1/79, JAIA 7/80

WINGSPREAD CONFERENCE CENTER (1937)
4 Mile Road
Racine, Wisconsin

Frank Lloyd Wright, architect

Wingspread, the former Herbert F. Johnson residence and "the last of the Prairie Houses," was named by Frank Lloyd Wright himself for its four wings, which spring toward the cardinal points from an octagonal core. One wing was for the master bedrooms, children occupied the second, guest rooms and carport filled the third, while kitchen and services took up the fourth. (Compare the windmill plan of Wright's Isabel Roberts House of 1907 and Mies van der Rohe's 1923 plan for "a brick country house.") It provides a fascinating spatial experience. One enters via a somewhat cautious front door into a purposefully low entry hall, then steps into the towering, climactic great hall, literally crowned with rings of light at the top, while garden vistas lure one at eye level. Banked around the periphery of an immense chimney-bulwark are living, reading, dining, and music areas set off by changes in levels and by low screens or built-in furniture. A flood of light, slanting in through a triple clerestory, gives dramatic emphasis to the visual role of the fireplace so that whatever the hour the sun is out it puts a spotlight on this great brick core, "a massive kernel," as Sigfried Giedion summed up Wright's centricity. Repose from this exciting and inevitably somewhat restless communal space can be sought in the quiet study rooms in the wings.

Fortunately, the house and sensitively landscaped grounds were given to the Johnson Foundation as a high-level international conference center. With the exception of a few minor changes to adapt it to group sessions, the dwelling and grounds are as Wright designed them.

Located east off wis 32 (Main Street), on the northeast edge of Racine. Open Monday–Friday 9:00 A.M.–2:00 P.M. unless a conference is taking place. Call (414) 639-3211 to schedule a visit or for more information. AR 1/38, JAIA 1/79

MUSEUM OF MODERN ART (1938–39/1964/1979–84)
ABBY ALDRICH ROCKEFELLER SCULPTURE GARDEN (1953/1964)
11 West 53rd Street
New York, New York

Philip L. Goodwin & Edward Durell Stone, architects of original museum
Philip Johnson, architect of addition and garden
Cesar Pelli, architect of renovation and expansion

When Philip L. Goodwin and Edward Durell Stone designed the Museum of Modern Art they revolutionized the self-important, Classical-inspired, warehouse concept of displaying art. The museum was designed to show to best advantage its pictures—not itself. Goodwin and Stone entice visitors in with, instead of the usual awesome flight of steps followed by a puzzling series of closets for pictures, a glimpse of a garden behind an all-glass wall, and then surround them with art before they know it. Moreover, this pioneering building—fortified by a series of electrifying exhibitions—was to make "Modern" architecture (and art, design, and photography) acceptable, even fashionable. It played thus an incalculable role in the development of the whole spectrum of contemporary culture in this country. Philip Johnson added the western annex to the Goodwin-Stone core in 1950 (now demolished) and the exquisitely detailed east wing in 1964.

The museum trustees realized from the beginning that the natural light of an outdoor garden would be the most expositive for the display of sculpture. Thus when additional space became available just before the museum opened (May 1939)—less than two weeks remained—a quickly designed garden was run up by John McAndrew, the curator of architecture, with suggestions from Alfred Barr, the museum's polymathic first director. Goodwin redesigned this in 1942 when he also installed a small garden pavilion-restaurant.

In 1953 the entire garden was replanned by Philip Johnson, with a hand from the director Rene d'Harnoncourt, as the Abby Aldrich Rockefeller Sculpture Garden in memory of Mrs. John D. Rockefeller, Jr., one of the museum's three founders. An L-shaped 2-foot/.6-meter drop-off creates an entrance "surveying" terrace from the main museum floor. (Compare the contemplation veranda of the fifteenth-century Ryoan-ji at Kyoto, Japan.) Ground cover of ivy eases and accents the grade transition. A 14-foot-/4.3-meter-high gray brick wall establishes

enclosure along the long north side; note the two grilled openings—one a gate—that give visual relief to the expanse of wall. Two "canals" laterally bisect most of the main sculpture garden level and are offset so as not to become dominant. Four differently scaled contiguous spaces result in this "roofless room" (see also Johnson's Roofless Church in New Harmony, Indiana, page 451). A careful lack of rigidity is evident throughout the garden except for the rectangles of the two pools, one of which carries Aristide Maillol's *The River*; note that even the planting areas are irregularly delimited by the Vermont marble paving modules. The predominant tree is the weeping beech.

The result is that sculptured metal, sculptured stone, and sculptured greenery are interwoven to mold sculptured spaces, making this not just a garden for art but a most perceptively calculated series of outdoor haunts, lairs, and delights. Sculpture, placid waters that sometimes erupt into fountains, quiet nooks, busy bridges, seats in the sun, and seats in the shade—intertwined with mobile humans—are among the elements that garrison this greenery of trees, bushes, and ivy. Each activity, or lack of activity, is carefully plotted, with a modest level change underscoring their division. In spite of limited size there are spatial surprises around every clump of trees as one turns and confronts some of the world's greatest contemporary sculpture. In winter, though the spaces are diminished as the greenery is lost, the sculpture gains new aspects when topped with snow. As Philip Johnson describes his work here, "What I did was to make a processional, using canals to block circulation and preserve vision, greenery to block circulation and block vision too, and bridges to establish the route. Always the sense of turning to see something. The Garden became a place to wander, but not on a rigidly defined path" (quoted by Elizabeth Kassler, *The Sculpture Garden*, MoMA brochure, 1975).

In 1979–84 Cesar Pelli enlarged the museum, almost doubling its exhibition space. The largest new portion is the six-floor west wing, with a forty-four-story privately developed residential tower above it. The existing north wing was completely renovated, and a garden wing replaced a terrace built in 1964. Escalators just beyond the museum entrance overlook the garden and carry visitors from one floor to the next.

Open Saturday–Tuesday 11:00 A.M.–6:00 P.M., Thursday–Friday 12:00 noon–8:30 P.M. Closed Wednesday. Closed Thanksgiving and Christmas. Admission is $8 for adults, $5 for students and senior citizens, free for children under 16. Thursday and Friday 5:30–8:30 P.M., pay what you wish. Various tours available. For more information call (212) 708–9480. A 10/34, AF 8/37, AF 8/39, ARev 9/39, AR 3/81, A 10/84, AR 10/84

FLORIDA SOUTHERN COLLEGE (1938–58)
Johnson Avenue and McDonald Street
Lakeland, Florida

Frank Lloyd Wright, architect

Time has not always dealt gently with the FLW buildings on the 1,800-student campus of Florida Southern College, the first plans for which were drawn as early as 1938, while the last building dates from 1958 (the year before Wright's death). It is difficult to be enraptured by them. First, their broken, angled planes and surfaces do not take kindly to the insidiousness of their hot and humid climate that periodically drowns them with rain, occasionally lashes them with hurricanes, and in between bakes them with sun. Second, the first structures (all but two of the original eight) were built largely by student labor with on-site production of concrete blocks, so that the buildings' native naivety to environment has been compromised by material frailty. (The college was built on a minimum budget.)

From the design standpoint there are questions too. The Ann Pfeiffer Chapel (1941, pictured here) beckons from its prominent location, with its dramatic play of roof angles, but its chancel is amorphous. The adjoining Danforth Chapel (1955) is scarcely better, having an uneasily compacted shape, while behind the altar strips of red and yellow glass alternate with clear panels to provide a view of the parking lot. (It is reported that Wright himself was unhappy with this glass.) The Lucius Pond Ordway Building (1952) on McDonald Street and the Polk County Science Building (1958) are more satisfactory. The covered walkways are highly useful in tying the buildings together and in providing weather protection.

However, in spite of this criticism, and with the cheerful note that the buildings were renovated in 1980, take a look, for they form the most extensive grouping—anywhere—of the maestro's work. And beyond the above negative remarks, the buildings do constitute a closely knit and harmonious grouping. Unfortunately, Wright's complete plan, with outdoor theater and contact with Lake Hollingsworth, all set in orange groves, did not materialize.

Via South Florida Avenue, east on McDonald Street to Johnson Avenue. Some buildings are closed on weekends and when school is not in session. Self-guided walking tour available at the Visitor Centers. Guided group tours can be scheduled by calling (813) 680–4118; the cost is $5 per person. AF 1/48, AF 1/51, AF 9/52, F 5/53, AF 4/55, F 5/73

TALIESIN WEST (1938–59)
12621 North Frank Lloyd Wright Boulevard
Scottsdale, Arizona

Frank Lloyd Wright, architect

Frank Lloyd Wright always was concerned with what he called the "kinship" of architecture with its setting, admonishing students, for instance, not to build on top of a hill in dominance, but beside it in partnership. Taliesin West—named for a Welsh bard who lived around the sixth century A.D. (FLW was of Welsh descent)—is the Arizona setting for Wright's winter-spring headquarters. To carry out this project he purchased from the government 800 acres/324 hectares of land upon which he promptly set to work. Of the land he wrote, it "is a grand garden the like of which in sheer beauty of space and pattern does not exist, I think, in the world" (quoted in *On Architecture*, Frederick Gutheim, ed., Duell, Sloan & Pearce, 1941).

For the harsh, "savage," yet strangely haunting light and geography of this choice bit of Arizona, Wright designed a series of interacting, in-love-with-the-desert buildings that rank among his exalted works. (Reyner Banham, the perceptive but oft acerbic English architectural critic, called it "a tribal encampment.") The Taliesin nucleus, prominent in its geometry of both plan and space, comprises the famous drafting room, with the private quarters linearly attached behind, and a theater to the left. Though the complex was begun in 1938 it was added to and refined for over twenty years, becoming in the process more permanent, more lived-in, more subtle. Originally used for only a few months in winter, occupancy gradually has increased. Since 1959 (the year of Wright's death) it has served, for extended periods, Taliesin Architects, the maestro's very busy successors, plus the Frank Lloyd Wright School of Architecture.

The most striking units of Taliesin West are fortunately those nearest the entry: the drafting room mentioned above—note its assured roof angle—and the theater detached at left. The latter burned in 1964 but has been completely restored. When most of the structures were first built they were roofed with canvas, which transmitted a soft enveloping luminosity. However, as substantial upkeep was required in an often harsh climate, cloth has been replaced by translucent plastic panels, with steel-reinforced rafters supporting them. Note the base of native boulders and mortar, in fine contrast to the lightness overhead. These slightly inclined, horizontally striated walls—reminiscent of the Mayan stonework that FLW admired so much—constitute the most sumptuous masonry of the twentieth century. Partake, also, of the artful changes in levels, the programmed angles of circulation, and the quality of space in and between buildings—and, of course, the silence and beauty of the desert mesa. One of the country's greatest complexes. As the distinguished architect Pietro Belluschi put it, "The years have not diminished the elemental quality of Taliesin West. More than other works by the master, it shows how to grasp the mood of the land and transform it into a place of harmony and beauty" (*AIA Journal*, May 1973).

North on Scottsdale Road, east on Shea Boulevard 4.8 miles/7.7 kilometers to gate. All visits are guided: one-hour tours given on the hour. October–May tours given daily 9:00 A.M.–4:00 P.M.; the cost is $10 for adults, $8 for students and senior citizens, $3 for children ages 4–12. June–September tours given daily 8:00–11:00 A.M.; the cost is $8 for adults, $6 for students and senior citizens, $3 for children ages 4–12. Other tours also available. Closed Easter, Thanksgiving, Christmas, and New Year's Day. For more information call (602) 860–8810. AF 1/38, AF 1/48, AF 6/59, JAIA 5/73, AF 7/73, A 3/84, A 12/87

CROW ISLAND SCHOOL (1939–40/1954)
1112 Willow Road at Glendale Avenue
Winnetka, Illinois

Saarinen & Saarinen, architects
Perkins, Wheeler & Will, architects of addition

The Crow Island School, which helped revolutionize the architecture of elementary education, is still in fine shape, fifty-five years after its completion. Its evolution, which started with the design of an ideal classroom—as opposed to the monumental self-important building then popular—still has lessons to teach. Note its children's scale, its L-shaped rooms with ample window seats, and its close association with nature. (Much of this innovative designing was inspired by the school's superintendent, Carleton Washburne.) Pedagogical shelter has changed abruptly in the past few decades—the classroom unit itself has largely given way to an undefined flexible teaching space—but Crow Island lies behind much of the evolution. One of the far-reaching pioneers. It was added to in 1954 by Perkins, Wheeler & Will.

Located 2 miles/3.2 kilometers east of I-94. Open during school hours. Free one-hour tours must be arranged in advance by calling (708) 446–0353. AF 8/41, AF 10/55, AR 9/56

POPE-LEIGHEY HOUSE (1940–41)
Woodlawn Plantation
9000 Richmond Highway
Mount Vernon, Virginia

Frank Lloyd Wright, architect

Frank Lloyd Wright began the Usonian houses—small houses for people with limited incomes—in 1937. These began with the Herbert Jacobs House in Wisconsin, then expanded into a whole series in the 1940s to form a key part in the development of domestic architecture in the United States. It should be remembered that FLW was one of the few architects in this country to concern himself with developing a house for moderate-income clients. When pneumatic "Colonial" and other so-called "styles" were peppering every suburb at that time, these modestly priced dwellings introduced the carport, low or flat roof, natural wood finish, and basement-free living, while the interiors of most of them were characterized by Wright's famous flow of internal spaces plus his well-known furniture. The Pope-Leighey House, saved from destruction by being moved to this site in 1965, is not the most successful of these, primarily because the brick utility core housing the kitchen and heater is, from the outside, not well integrated with the rest of the house. It is, however, a revealing, inexpensive house, and in it one can glimpse some of the master's delight with three dimensions.

When the Pope-Leighey House was hastily moved from its original site in 1965, its foundation was placed on soft clay, which has caused the base to warp and crack over the years. Therefore it is currently being moved to a site 30 feet/9.15 meters away from its present location. After the move is complete, much of the interior will be restored to the 1940–45 period, when Loren Pope occupied the house; one room will become a gallery space. The "hemicycle" (the landscaping surrounding the house) will be returned to Wright's design.

Located northwest off US 1 at VA 235, 14 miles/ 23 kilometers south of Washington, D.C. The house is scheduled to reopen to the public in the spring of 1996. Open daily 9:30 A.M.–4:30 P.M. (January and February closed Monday–Friday). Closed New Year's Day, Thanksgiving, and Christmas. Admission is $5 for adults, $3.50 for children ages 5 and up, students, and senior citizens. A combination ticket for admission to the Pope-Leighey House and the nearby Woodlawn Plantation is $8 for adults, $5 for children and senior citizens. All visits are guided; tours given every half hour. For more information call (703) 780–4000.

VILLAGE GREEN (1940–41)
(formerly Baldwin Hills Village)
5300 Rodeo Road
Los Angeles, California

Reginald D. Johnson and
Wilson, Merrill & Alexander,
architects
Clarence S. Stein, consultant
and site planner

Village Green is an outstanding example of urban land usage for domestic building—like the other communities with which Clarence Stein was associated. Fifty-five years ago it triumphantly proclaimed lessons that we incredibly ignore today—and will tomorrow. Built with Federal Housing Association financing, it shows what an enlightened developer with top-bracket designers can do with 64 acres/26 hectares of open farmland. Its principles are so simple that one marvels that it has not spawned reasonable facsimiles across the nation, especially when those principles have been so financially rewarding that there has scarce been a day when one of its 629 apartments has been empty.

The success of the development, like that of the earlier and influential Radburn in Fair Lawn, New Jersey (see page 366), stems mainly from the fact that people and automobiles should each have their separate place, and that the former and their children and pets should not be menaced by the latter. Thus the overall plan was laid out as a superblock with seventeen garage courts (generally at right angles to the street) projecting inward about the periphery, and with low-density row housing zigzagging around these service areas. The main rooms of the houses—and their front doors—face onto the open parks that meander through the length of the development. Greenery and flowers are everywhere. The "town houses" comprise both duplexes and one-story-over-ones—plus some one-story bungalows—which are entered from opposite sides. There are 275 one-bedroom units, 312 two-bedroom, and 42 three-bedroom houses, all of which have a private patio. (Brick serpentine-walled patios were added to those units without patios after World War II.) Though not architecturally inspired, they are competent and direct, their several muted colors giving quiet accents. A bit formalistic in overall plan and now lacking sufficient community facilities and shopping—many of the original shops were converted to living units—Village Green has yet many lessons for us today. In 1972 the project received the 25-Year Award for Excellence from the American Institute of Architects. Fred Barlow and Fred Edmonson were the landscape architects.

Since its conversion to condominium status in 1978, its popularity has continued. However—and perhaps ironically—its initial family orientation has vanished. Village Green is now an all-adult community with no children and no pets.

Located between Sycamore Avenue and Hauser Boulevard (south off I-10 on La Brea Avenue). The property is not formally open to the public. PA 9/44, PP 10/44, A+A 8/64, JAIA 7/72, A 7/85

RED ROCKS AMPHITHEATER (1941)
COL 93
Morrison, Colorado

Burnham Hoyt, architect

In a setting of palpable grandeur in the red sandstone outcroppings west of Denver, Burnham Hoyt tidied up the hillside with sixty-nine quietly regimented curved ranks of seats, installed a stage and related services, and produced the most spectacular outdoor amphitheater in the United States. Downtown Denver vibrates on the distant plain. Cradled between Creation Rock and Ship Rock, with Stage Rock as backdrop—their partial enclosure producing excellent acoustics—some eight thousand seats have been eased into the wild beauty of this natural bowl, every millimeter of which was preserved where possible. Retaining walls are of local stone, the seats of natural wood, and the stepped ranks of concrete. (The rows of seats range in length from 135 feet/41 meters to 230 feet/70 meters.) The stage, altered from its original design and now a bit intrusive, is double-decked, with services hidden on the lower floor. Parking is totally out of view.

In 1990 the city of Denver began to draw up a master plan for the repair of Red Rocks Park and Amphitheater. Although the project is not yet under construction, plans include a complete renovation of existing seating, walkways, and under-stage service areas, restoration of the old lighting fixtures and addition of new lights, restructuring of the existing stage cover to improve stage lights and rain protection, and construction of an improved loading area. Projected new structures include a first-aid and security building and a two-story hospitality center with restrooms and concessions at the top of the amphitheater. Sink Combs Dethlefs were the architecture consultants; Wenk Associates were landscape consultants.

Located about 16 miles/26 kilometers west-southwest of Denver via 6th Avenue, then west on I-70, south on COL 93. Park open daily 24 hours. Admission is free. Performances held on summer evenings as scheduled; there is an admission fee for performances. AF 5/45

BAKER HOUSE (1947–48)
Massachusetts Institute of Technology
362 Memorial Drive
Cambridge, Massachusetts

Alvar Aalto, architect

Alvar Aalto's preoccupation with the curve—always functionally generated—began with the ceiling of his library in Viipuri, Russia (1935). The lyric undulations, which were used for acoustic betterment, were continued in the memorable Finnish Pavilion at the 1939 New York World's Fair, and reached a climax—at least in scale—in MIT's Baker House for over 300 undergraduates. Wishing to give each student a view up or down the Charles River flowing in front of the building, yet circumscribed by a plot of limited length, Aalto curved his building onto the site by using a double bend. This graceful curved facade contrasts with the refreshingly angular entry side, where an extraordinary V of projected stairs steps down to the front door with unabashed utilitarianism. Down with the uniform, tidy box. In front (on the Memorial Drive side) rises a two-story dining hall, squarish in plan. Perry, Shaw & Hepburn were associate architects.

Open Monday–Friday 8:00 A.M.–4:00 P.M. Closed for holidays. Free tours can be scheduled by calling the Baker Dormitory manager at (617) 253-3675. AF 8/49, AP 7/73

COMMONWEALTH BUILDING (1947–48)
(formerly Equitable Building)
421 Southwest 6th Avenue between Stark and Washington streets
Portland, Oregon

Pietro Belluschi, architect

The innovations of the Equitable Building influenced subsequent skyscraper design throughout the country, yet many of its contributions have not been sufficiently appreciated. Four years before Lever House in New York City (see page 408), it used, probably for the first time, a flush curtain-wall skin whereby the structural frame, spandrels, and glass are virtually on the same plane (maximum difference .875 inch/22 millimeters). Moreover, the doubling of the plate glass and its sealing in a fixed frame were both innovative measures. (The bay proportions of two large panes and three spandrel divisions are superb.) In addition, the subdued but effective use of color revived a skyscraper note that had been largely dormant since Raymond Hood's ex-McGraw Hill Building (1931) on New York's 42nd Street. In Portland, aluminum-covered concrete—another first—was used with light-brown cast aluminum spandrels and combined with blue-green glass to produce a quiet, sophisticated, twelve-story building. (A thirteenth story was subsequently added.) The building was sold and renamed, but the basic suavity is still there. As an innovative skyscraper the Equitable/Commonwealth ranks very, very high.

In the early 1970s the lobby was completely remodeled in a style unsympathetic to the original building, and in 1987 Soderstrom Architects, with the help of Belluschi himself, were hired to renovate it. Although the current lobby (completed in 1990) is not a true restoration, it attempts to incorporate as much of the original design as possible, and strives to recreate the feel of the original. A 27-foot/8-meter mural, which was originally designed by Belluschi in 1948 for the lobby but was not actually painted, has been added.

Lobby open Monday–Friday 7:00 A.M.–6:00 P.M., Saturday 8:00 A.M.–4:00 P.M. Closed for holidays. Free guided tours can be scheduled by calling (503) 228–0812.

The Roman Revival building at right in the photograph above is the U.S. National Bank, designed by A. E. Doyle (1917). Its four-story-high Corinthian columns and pilasters are topped by an unusually rich entablature and balustrade (and bear a more than casual resemblance to McKim, Mead & White's slightly smaller Knickerbocker Trust Building of 1902–04 in New York City—now demolished). Note the bronze front door. The main banking room is one of the city's finest of its period. Belluschi worked with Doyle's firm from 1927–43.

Lobby open Monday–Thursday 9:30 a.m.–5:00 p.m, Friday 9:30 a.m.–5:30 p.m. Closed for holidays. AF 9/45, AF 4/47, AF 9/48, ARev 12/48, AF 6/68, JAIA 7/82, PA 4/89

UNITED NATIONS SECRETARIAT BUILDING (1947–50)
1st Avenue between 42nd and 48th streets
New York, New York

Wallace K. Harrison, director of planning
Max Abramovitz, deputy director
Le Corbusier, Sven Markelius, Oscar Niemeyer,
N. D. Bassov, members of advisory committee

This assured building changed the pattern of skyscraper design in more ways than have been generally recognized. Firstly, the architects—partly under Le Corbusier's influence—made the building a pure, unflinching slab in form, with no breaks or setbacks, with its broad sides of glass and its narrow (72 feet/22 meters) ends solidly sheathed in marble. Secondly, they were the first to recognize that the mechanics of air conditioning in a tall structure needed more accommodation than a basement or rooftop could provide. Its designers thus—startlingly for the time—boldly introduced four service floors between roof and ground (sixth, sixteenth, twenty-eighth, and thirty-ninth floors), and expressed them as esthetic and scalar assets instead of camouflaged mechanics. Thirdly, for better or worse, they gave an imprimatur to the curtain wall, a prefabricated skin enclosure totally independent of structure. (Compare the Hallidie Building of 1918 in San Francisco, page 344.) At the UN this curtain wrapping used greenish tinted glass (to screen the sun's heat) and greenish glass spandrels, the two together reflecting the changing skies and the dapplings of sun on adjacent buildings, an effect then unheard of. The features mentioned above are now, more than two generations later, routine, but they were largely pioneered on the banks of the East River by the staff mentioned above buttressed by over a dozen other international consultants.

It should be added that Le Corbusier (1887–1965), the Swiss-born French representative on the design team—and probably the greatest architect since Michelangelo—was by temperament not team-oriented, and his sessions with his United Nations confreres were rarely harmonious, in spite of the dedicated efforts of Wallace K. Harrison. For instance, Corbu championed vigorously for *brise-soleils*, or louvers, to protect the broad west side from the hot afternoon sun. These work admirably in semitropical Rio de Janeiro's Ministry of Education (1942)—fine echoes of which can be seen here—for which Corbusier was consultant and Oscar Niemeyer architect, and in Le Corbusier's first proposal of *brise-soleils* (1933) for a project in Algiers. However, movable exterior blinds would not be practical in New York's snow and ice, while the sun's heat load could be solved by beefing up the air conditioning on the west side and by the use of tinted glass, as has become standard practice.

The final Secretariat Building, the thirty-nine-story nerve center (tombstone?) for the hopes of the world, nonetheless possesses a poetry that even the flaccidity of the Assembly scarce diminishes. Details of the curtain wall and grilles of service floors are fussy by today's tastes— "a Christmas package wrapped in cellophane" wrote Lewis Mumford (*New Yorker*, 15 September 1951)—and some of the interior decisions regarding office space were questionable. Lamentably, Sven Markelius's proposals for an approach mall westward to connect the UN Building with Lexington Avenue never materialized. But from the river (one of the finest boat trips available), from the FDR Drive (preferably northbound), or even from the street, there is greatness here.

Secretariat Building not open to the public. The UN complex is open to the public daily 9:00 A.M.–5:00 P.M. Closed Thanksgiving and Christmas. In January and February, closed on weekends and holidays. Tours of the UN complex given every half-hour; the cost is $6.50 for adults, $4.50 for senior citizens, $3.50 for children grades 1–8. Group tours can be scheduled by calling (212) 963-4440. For general information call (212) 963-7713. AF 6/49, AF 5/50, AF 11/50, AF 4/52, AR 7/52, AF 10/52

CIRCLE GALLERY (1948–49/1983)
(formerly V. C. Morris Shop)
140 Maiden Lane
San Francisco, California

Frank Lloyd Wright, architect

Frank Lloyd Wright's use of the helix started with his love for the chambered nautilus. Its architectural manifestation began with his never-built planetarium for Sugar Loaf Mountain (1925) near Frederick, Maryland, sprang from the desert in his Arizona house (1952) for his son David, took off with this work, and reached a climax in his Guggenheim Museum in New York (see page 431)—for which this shop/gallery was a miniature prototype. The stimulus of its spaces as one winds up and down its spiral ramp makes the second floor both an attractive prospect and a rewarding reality. The circle framed by the ramp—which almost fills the width of the building—is echoed by a two-thirds circle offset at left rear. The ceiling is composed of a galaxy of plastic circles and half domes—a "female ceiling," writes Vincent Scully, surveying its mastoidal forms—from which pours a flood of both natural and artificial light. (The skylight is the only source of daylight, other than the glass door.) The interior was renovated and restored in 1983 under the direction of architect Michel Marx.

The solid wall of the facade is of meticulously laid Roman brick. Most merchants would, of course, have insisted on plate glass. Its radiating arch recalls Louis Sullivan's well-known Transportation Building of the Chicago Fair of 1893, and its entry is taken almost straight from H. H. Richardson's Glessner House of 1887 (see page 277). We are enticed into this enigma and giddily treated for our excursion.

Open Monday–Saturday 10:00 A.M.–6:00 P.M., Sunday 12:00 noon–5:00 P.M. Closed on New Year's Day, Easter, Thanksgiving, and Christmas. For more information call (415) 989–2100. AF 2/50, A 11/86

860–880 LAKE SHORE DRIVE APARTMENTS (1948–51)
Chicago, Illinois

Mies van der Rohe, architect

Two of the first buildings by Mies van der Rohe to excite the American scene—which had been alerted by the S. R. Crown Hall of the IIT campus (1955–56, see page 422) and the concrete Promontory Apartments (1946–49)—are these twenty-six-story apartment buildings overlooking Lake Michigan. Identical in form (though the south building contains only six-room apartment buildings and the north three-and-one-half-) these two three-by-five-bay apartments stand at right angles to each other, carefully offset by one bay, with a flat, column-free canopy connecting them. In plan they measure 64.9 x 106.9 feet/19.7 x 32.5 meters. The frame is steel, with poured concrete floors and concrete used for fireproofing the skeleton, while steel cover plates encase the concrete and were used as part of its formwork. Steel "wallframes" of combined mullions and spandrels were prefabricated and lowered into place, while the light-colored aluminum window frames were installed from within.

The buildings have been criticized because the vertical steel mullions that divide the windows

also appear on the columns, where, of course, they are not structural. Mies explained these "rhetorical I-beams" (Robert Venturi) as necessary to maintain "the rhythm which the mullions set up," and also to stiffen the steel plates covering the other face of concrete fireproofing. Rationalized or not, the result is stunning. (Note that in order to maintain the constant 5.25 feet/1.6 meters on center of mullion spacing, the two end windows of each bay are slightly narrower than the two center ones.)

The twin blocks' exterior airiness comes from their elevation above largely open ground floors through which the sun streams and confinement evaporates. Their dark, impeccably understated elegance—monastic severity—carries on above. (The penthouse treatment for the water tanks is, however, not satisfactory.)

From within, the lobbies are classic entries, while the apartments themselves, with windows from ceiling to within a few inches of the floor, provide heady accommodations. The exterior curtains are all the same gray color to maintain harmony from without, but the tenants, who own their apartments, can hang inner curtains if desired. Air conditioning should have been installed initially—the recent individual units are not coordinated—and there might have been another elevator per building. But the apartments have become so popular that anyone fortunate enough to have had one when the buildings were first opened could now sell it at considerable profit. PACE Associates and Holsman, Klekamp & Taylor were associate architects of the project.

It is illuminating to compare 860–880 Lake Shore Drive with the adjacent Mies structure at 900–910 Lake Shore Drive completed five years later (1956). The newer buildings are even more refined in detail (note window treatment), have central air conditioning and more facilities, but the use of dark plate glass (for sun control) and the dark window framing tend to sap the vitality of their facades.

Located on Lake Shore Drive between Chestnut Street and Delaware Place. The interior of 860–880 Lake Shore Drive is visible by appointment only; call (312) 943–0432. The interior of 900–910 Lake Shore Drive is closed to the public. The buildings are included on the Chicago Architecture Foundation's bus tour; the cost is $25. For more information on Chicago Architecture Foundation tours call (312) 922–3432. AF 1/50, AF 10/52, A+BN 4/54, AF 11/55

HARVARD UNIVERSITY GRADUATE CENTER (1949–50)
Everett Street at Oxford Street, just off Massachusetts Avenue
Cambridge, Massachusetts

The Architects Collaborative, architects

The buildings belong to an earlier—and pioneering—generation of the Modern Movement, but the spaces between them speak to no single generation. This seminal effort by TAC, with Walter Gropius as "job captain," advanced educational architecture in the United States immeasurably by demonstrating that its oldest university could call on one of its most advanced architectural firms. The center is composed of seven dormitories housing approximately six hundred students; its Harkness Commons is able to feed over one thousand at a sitting. Note that although the space is limited, no dormitory faces its neighbor. A milestone in the development of the Modern Movement in this country.

Interiors generally closed to the public. Harkness Commons open Monday–Friday 7:00 A.M.–7:00 P.M. when school is in session. The grounds are also open to the public. AF 12/50, AF 9/60, AF 12/69, JAIA 1/79

CHRIST CHURCH LUTHERAN (1949–50)
3244 34th Avenue South at East 33rd Street
Minneapolis, Minnesota

Eliel Saarinen, architect
Eero Saarinen, associate

This ingratiating church, one of the finest contemporary examples in the country, was among the earliest to break with historic traditions. The last work of Eliel Saarinen (1873–1950), it bears some resemblance to his North Christian Church, finished in 1942, in Columbus, Indiana (see page 488), but it has more warmth and cohesion. The nave, which seats six hundred, provides a high central volume with low expansion areas on either side. Thus with less than a full congregation the church will not seem sparsely occupied. A thirty-six-seat chapel at the rear, behind the

open narthex and placed at right angles to the nave, provides for overflow services and accommodates its own conjunctive functions. The choir and organ are placed in a balcony directly over the narthex, while the baptistry is at the forward end of the nave at left. A low curved wood screen at right ties the nave to the sacristy, enabling direct passage to the chancel for the pastor and also forming a backdrop for the pulpit. Note the slightly angled panels of open brickwork high along the right-hand side, where they play both an acoustic and a visual role. The ceiling is angled for similar considerations. Daylight pours in from tall narrow windows lining the low side aisles, their glazing set on the outer face of the brick piers whose depth minimizes glare. The sanctuary receives a dramatic shaft of midmorning sun from a floor-to-ceiling chancel window concealed behind a projecting louvered wood grille. The chancel wall is angled and curved at the right side to reflect this light and is given emphasis by having its brick painted white and then sanded. Artificial illumination is provided by spoon-shaped indirect fixtures and ceiling downlights.

A courtyard separates the church from an education and fellowship building with administrative offices designed by Eero Saarinen and erected in 1962. An arcade connects the two and provides weather protection. The exterior of Christ Church Lutheran lacks total coordination but its nave is one of the finest. Hills, Gilbertson & Hayes were associate architects.

Open Monday–Thursday 9:00 A.M.–3:00 P.M., Friday 9:00 A.M.–12:00 noon. Tours can be arranged by calling (612) 721–6611.
AF 7/50, JAIA 5/77

WAYFARERS' CHAPEL (1949–51)
5755 Palos Verdes Drive South
Palos Verdes, California

Lloyd Wright, architect

The architectural expression of the relationship among God, man, and nature has been eloquently achieved in this small, one-hundred-seat chapel on picturesque hills that tumble down to the Pacific. Designed by the famous (and eldest: 1890–1978) son of an even more famous father, the structure was kept to a discreet minimum. The congregation is scarce aware that it is enveloped on the sides and most of the roof by panes of clear glass set in a simple, triangulated, redwood frame resting on a base of local stone. The chapel's laminated wood arches, four per side, open to a Y shape at spring point to make a roof of triangular (that is, Trinity) planes. This religious greenhouse is in turn wrapped and shielded by a wide variety of trees and plants, samples of which—plus a tiny waterfall—are also found within. Inasmuch as the chapel is basically transparent, with solid roof panels kept to a minimum, there is no problem with glare (though solar heat gain was troublesome in the early years before the anticipated planting had matured). The 60-foot-/18-meter-high campanile dates from 1954, and the cloister and library from 1957, their interconnection based on thirty-degree triangles. The chapel belongs to the Church of the New Jerusalem, a sect based on the tenets of Emanuel Swedenborg (born Svedberg, 1688–1772), a remarkably learned Swedish scientist and theologian, who was much impressed by the Book of Revelation. He believed that there is a spiritual basis in all nature—a philosophy that Lloyd Wright beautifully interpreted. (Wright was trained as a landscape architect by Frederick Law Olmsted.) One of the few genuinely sensitive houses of worship.

Located 1 mile/1.6 kilometers east of Marineland. Open daily 9:00 A.M.–5:00 P.M. Closed Christmas. Self-guided tours available. For more information call (310) 377–1650. AF 8/51

FIRST UNITARIAN MEETING HOUSE (1949–51)
900 University Bay Drive
Madison, Wisconsin

Frank Lloyd Wright, architect

This famous Unitarian church settles on its low ridge, quietly *simpatico* with nature, like all of
Frank Lloyd Wright's buildings. Symbolically its green copper prow-roof suggests—as Wright
was wont to point out with his elegant fingers—hands folded in prayer; indeed "the whole edifice is in the attitude of prayer" (FLW). However suggestive the exterior might be, the interior
is, in some respects, disappointing—at least to this observer. This is because of the source and
treatment of natural light. Wright wanted to express Unitarian "open-endedness" and "to
make the outdoors a part of the room," but as the large windows behind the pulpit supply
almost the sole source of daylight some glare results. (Because of the church's triangular
"prow" there is no chancel in the regular sense of the term, only a pulpit.) It should be immediately added that, according to the minister, this is not the general point of view. The triangular plan of the interior develops a brilliant intimacy between minister and congregation and
among the congregation itself. The very flexible auditorium, which seats 250, can be turned
into a parish hall, with its seats reversed, when it then faces the hearth room that opens off the
rear. An educational wing, a large assembly room, and offices complete the church.

Located one block north of University Avenue at western edge of University of Wisconsin campus. Open mid-May–
September Monday–Friday 10:00 A.M.–4:00 P.M. Tours given daily. Visits can be arranged year-round by calling (608)
233–9774. Admission and tours are free but a $3 donation is suggested. AF 1/48, AF 12/52

FIRST PRESBYTERIAN CHURCH (1950–51)
216 South 3rd Street at Adams Street
Cottage Grove, Oregon

Pietro Belluschi, architect

The relaxed neighborhood atmosphere of the First Presbyterian (also known as United Presbyterian) Church commences at the sidewalk, where a simple wood fence and gate establish domain. The great locusts and oaks in front draw one to this gate, whose open vertical slats merely suggest enclosure, letting the eye into the temenos where it is greeted—both from sidewalk and within—by a magnificent boulder directly on axis. This huge mossy stone carries an inscription from Psalm 122: "I was glad when they said to me, 'Let us go into the house of the Lord.'" One makes a short left-hand turn, then a right—both under a covered walk—past the rock and a small but careful planting area. A wood bell standard, simply carved at top (by the former pastor), holds down the far end of this forecourt. The manipulation of progression, the trees outside and in the enclosure, the stone and planting, the band of gravel and small rocks along the nave, the understated bell mount—all against the background of the natural fir boards and battens of the church itself—make a rewarding introduction to the church. It is a prelude that provides both an esthetic experience and a religious transition when approaching or leaving the church.

The nave is entered directly from the narthex, and faces due north as it overlooks the garden. A high, large louvered window (with the famous Pietro Belluschi scale handling in the grille design) gives an accent of slightly tinted light to the chancel and receives further emphasis from the graceful swoop of the spruce ceiling. The natural-finish wood on the ceiling and on rear and garden walls contrasts with the white plaster on walls at front and left. Note the pattern of downlights in the ceiling. The chancel is slightly marred by the half-height projection of the vestry wall at left with vertical louvers for the pipe organ behind (not apparent on exterior), but this is only a detail of an otherwise worshipful and in-touch-with-nature nave. And, it is important to realize, religious ambiance was attained without traditional religious trappings: the cross alone may be said to be the only element from the past. Emphasizing this freshness, the choir is placed on one side of the congregation to underscore the Presbyterian non-structured "family" approach. A parish hall, juniors' room, Sunday school, small chapel, and minister's office (separately enterable from Adams Street) wrap around the nave on three sides. The church is listed in the National Register.

Belluschi designed several other distinguished churches contemporary with this one in Cottage Grove (notably Zion Lutheran [1952], 1015 Southwest 18th Avenue, and Central Lutheran [1951], 2104 Northeast Hancock Street, both in Portland), but this local-wood Presbyterian example—with its inspired, stepped-up profile rising toward the chancel, its simple, dedicated nave, and its incomparable parvis—lift it very high among the early modern churches of the United States. Belluschi's use of wood, whether as here in a simple barn tradition, or with sophisticated laminated wood arches (which he greatly helped to popularize) as in the two Portland examples mentioned, was very influential in church design throughout the entire country.

Open Tuesday–Friday 9:00 A.M.–12:00 noon. Sunday services held at 10:00 A.M. Tours can be arranged by calling (503) 942-4479. PA 3/52

LEVER HOUSE (1950–52)
390 Park Avenue between 53rd and 54th streets
New York, New York

Skidmore, Owings & Merrill, architects

Lever House, diagonally opposite the Seagram Building (see page 420), was a pivotal sky-scraper when built, and though its visual strength has been vitiated by a neighbor's unflatter-ing imitation, Lever's contribution was great. Its chief legacy to the city—and to architecture—lies in its seemingly profligate use of its site. As a one-company headquarters (there is no rental space), a certain freedom was built in: SOM seized the opportunity to make this the first

"prestige" office block, and to free most of the ground level of enclosure so that the pedestrian could stroll through and under; an open-to-sky garden court fills the center. A one-story computer and stenographic floor stretches across the Park Avenue frontage, airily perched on pilotis. Then soaring above all, a slen-der slab, visually de-tached from the horizon-tality below, rises eigh-teen floors in a precisely rectangular, blue-green glass package that just skirts the flashy. The contrast of the vertical with the horizontal is great, while the "libera-tion" of the site is superb. Gordon Bunshaft was chief of design; Raymond Loewy Associates, interi-ors; Weiskopf & Pick-worth, structural engin-eers. One of the gener-ative pioneers.

Lobby open to the public Mon-day–Friday 10:00 A.M.–5:00 P.M., Sundays and holidays 1:00–5:00 P.M. Closed July 4, Labor Day, Thanksgiving, Christmas, and New Year's Day. AF 6/50, AF 6/52, AR 6/52, JAIA 3/80

MOUNT ZION TEMPLE (1950–54)
1300 Summit Avenue at South Hamline
St. Paul, Minnesota

Erich Mendelsohn, architect

Erich Mendelsohn (1887–1953) led a peripatetic and at times frustrating architectural life. He first startled the world with a series of superlative sketches, which he began in the trenches of World War I. Though tiny affairs they have a power and expressionism that still grip. (Some of these sketches, it is proper to add in discussing Minnesota, were of grain elevators.) His boundless imagination took concrete shape in 1920 with the expressionistic Potsdam Observatory, which still stands southwest of Berlin, a building that skyrocketed him to prominence, and enabled him to enjoy a very active practice in his native Germany until the Nazis entered the scene. Mendelsohn traveled to England (1933–36 and 1937–39), and back and forth to Palestine (1934–38), and in 1941 to the United States, where he finally was able to get considerable work, primarily designing synagogues. Yet none, good though they be, live up to his work abroad. Mount Zion Temple is, many feel, the finest in this country, being particularly notable on the exterior for the relation, indeed the spatial tension, set up between the large sanctuary and the smaller chapel placed separately at a right angle to it. These copper-clad, almost windowless boxes enjoy a keen relation to each other as they project boldly above the brick walls that form a pinkish base, tying the center together. (Mendelsohn's first sketches were for two accordion-pleated forms; the simple rectangular ones finally used are much more potent.)

The interiors of both main sanctuary and chapel lean to the Spartan, even claustrophobic, due to the tight enclosure and to the fact that the only windows are behind and above the congregation, but as a group in space they set up vibrations. Beside the two worship halls there is a large community room (with small stage and kitchen), which can double as an extension of the main chapel on high holy days. There are also administrative offices and, at a slight angle, a classroom wing. After Mendelsohn's death, the temple was completed by his associates, Bergstedt & Hirsch.

Open Monday–Friday 9:00 A.M.–5:00 P.M. Closed for holidays (including Jewish holidays). Tours can be arranged by calling (612) 698–3881. AF 2/55

YALE UNIVERSITY ART GALLERY (1951–53)
1111 Chapel Street at York Street
New Haven, Connecticut

Louis I. Kahn, architect

The architectural revolution that shook the Gothic and Colonial mantles off Yale University's conservatism came largely during the presidency (1950–63) of the late A. Whitney Griswold, who died in office at the age of fifty-six. The vitality he encouraged brought many of the finest architectural talents in the country to the campus. The resulting buildings (some two dozen) make Yale a Mecca for architects from all over the world. A limited cross section of their work is included here—the process of excellence continues.

The structure that inaugurated Yale's new approach is this four-story art gallery—really an addition to Egerton Swartwout's 1928 building—by Louis I. Kahn (1901–74). Appropriately, his posthumously finished Yale Center for British Art (1972–77, see page 588) stands directly across the street. The Chapel Street facade and entry to the gallery are quietly stated—the late Philip L. Goodwin's pioneering project for the museum in the 1940s (halted by the war) was more inviting—but once inside the excitement of Kahn's building begins. The chief impacts come from the flow of space and the intriguing tetrahedral ceiling. This ceiling, 2.2 feet/.67 meter deep (and possibly inspired by Buckminster Fuller's geometric excursions), delivers a textured, triangulated canopy that hovers over exhibition and work floors. Its alternately open, alternately closed tetrahedrons enable all spot- and down-lights to be recessed yet installed and projected at will, and also allow the air-conditioning ducts to be laced through with appropriate acoustic insulation above. Equally important, almost complete flexibility in installing partitions is assured. There is, however, one problem in the gallery: the busy diagrammatic ceiling can distract from the works of art. On the main floor this impingement rarely occurs—depending somewhat on the type of exhibition beneath—because the ceiling height is sufficiently high. Here it works wonders. But in the upper galleries, where the ceiling is lower, the geometric "pressure" tends to compete with the art below. But linger on the main floor, stroll into the small garden behind: rewards are there. Douglas Orr was the associate architect; Henry A. Pfisterer was the structural engineer.

An addition containing 2,000 square feet/186 square meters of exhibition space and a lecture hall was added in 1976 (Herbert S. Newman Associates, architects). In 1979 the Gallery was the recipient of the prestigious "25-Year Award" of the American Institute of Architects.

Open Tuesday–Saturday 10:00 A.M.–4:45 P.M., Sunday 2:00–4:45 P.M. Closed in August. Admission is free. Free one-hour tour of the building and art collection given Wednesday and Saturday at 1:30 P.M. For more information call (203) 432–0600. PA 5/54, JAIA 5/79

GENERAL MOTORS TECHNICAL CENTER (1951–56)
Mound Road, just north of Twelve Mile Road
Warren, Michigan

Eero Saarinen & Associates, architects

An interrelation between architecture, landscaping, and waters—both still and active—forms the dominant impression of this magnificent layout (compare Cranbrook Educational Community in nearby Bloomfield Hills, page 357). There is a partnership here between forty-one buildings and nature (some of which is man-fashioned nature) that has earned the center the sobriquet of an industrial Versailles. The second impression recognizes the businesslike efficiency, colorful positiveness, and flexibility of its individual buildings. There are six major groups on this campus: Design Center (with dome), Engineering Center, Manufacturing Center, Research and Development, North American Operations Headquarters, and Technical Center Service Section, all with several subunits. The central restaurant building, one of the best from the design point of view, stands between Engineering and Manufacturing. The low structures (three floors maximum) are deployed about a rectangular 22-acre/8.9-hectare lake, approximately 1,800 feet/549 meters long by 550 feet/168 meters wide, embellished by four islets containing weeping willows. The lake acts as a spine for the layout and, in addition to giving orientation and visual pleasure, serves as a thermal pond for the center's air-conditioning system. The feeling of orientation is highlighted and the basic horizontality of the complex energized by the elegant, three-legged, stainless-steel-clad water tower that rises from the waters. Its upward thrust is repeated by the fountains, particularly when their computerized ballet—designed and programmed by the sculptor Alexander Calder—erupts. Landscaping and trees (some 13,000 altogether) have been imaginatively used to shield cars from view and sun from cars.

The technically advanced buildings are almost all of curtain-wall construction (porcelain panels over a fireproof core), with a basic 5-foot/1.5-meter module throughout. The pungent end walls, however, are of brightly colored glazed brick, a Saarinen innovation inspired by ancient Assyrian tiles. The Technical Center was begun under Eliel Saarinen, but the present version was developed by Eero Saarinen after his father's retirement, then death in 1950. An influence from Mies van der Rohe is apparent. Smith, Hinchman & Grylls were associate architects-engineers; Thomas D. Church was the landscape architect.

Buildings and grounds closed to the public. AF 11/51, AF 11/54, PA 2/55, AF 5/56, AR 5/56, AF 6/71, A 4/85

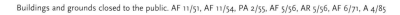

J. S. DORTON ARENA (1952–53)
1025 Blue Ridge Road
Raleigh, North Carolina

Matthew Nowicki and William Deitrick, architects
Fred N. Severud, engineer

The architects took two enormous and opposing concrete arches, raised the arc of each at a twenty-two-degree angle to the ground, abutted their open ends, and elevated their juncture on two low triangular supports. (This deceptively extended their thrust lines—compare Mies van der Rohe's Barcelona chair.) They then stretched cables between the arches to create support for the roof and for lateral stability and thus designed the first stressed-skin roof system in the United States. It is a brilliant concept. Moreover Matthew Nowicki—who died in a plane crash before construction began—and William Deitrick plotted the seating arrangement to create the greatest number of places toward the center, and reflected this undulation of seats both inside and out. The resulting elliptical, column-free "great room" measures 221 feet/67 meters long by 126 feet/38 meters wide and contains 5,500 permanent seats and 4,400 portable ones. Agricultural, industrial, and commercial clientele are its chief users. In 1979 a thorough renovation and updating was carried out by engineers Buffaloe, Morgan & Associates. The arena is listed in the National Register of Historic Places.

Located west of city on State Fair Grounds. Open for performances. Tours can be arranged by calling (919) 733–2626. AF 4/54, AR 11/56, JAIA 9/80

CHURCH AT EDMOND (1953)
(formerly Hopewell Baptist Church)
5801 NW 178th Street
Edmond, Oklahoma

Bruce Goff, architect

The admirers of Bruce Goff have rightly lamented that his architecture is so extremely personal that his commissions were mainly limited to private houses of sympathetic friends. This small church (three hundred seats) is one of only several nonresidential buildings available to the public. (See also the Boston Avenue United Methodist Church in Tulsa, Oklahoma, page 360.) The Church at Edmond seeks an architectural symbolism to tie the religious activities of its parishioners to their working life—one largely connected with oil wells—a successful enosis, but one no easier in architecture than in daily living. In addition there was probably in the back of the architect's mind the indigenous tepee form that once dominated this landscape.

Bruce Goff was adept at utilizing inexpensive—often surplus—material, and here he employed reconditioned 2.5- and 4-inch/6.4- and 10-centimeter pipes used in the oil industry for the supporting trusses of his twelve-sided church (note their refinement), with simple corrugated aluminum for the sides. The pastor then corralled the pipe fitters and riggers from his flock and put the whole piece together for an unbelievable twenty thousand dollars. Windowless against the road noises outside, the interior basks in light from a clerestory at its peak. (This interior is currently out of view to the public. In the early 1970s it was sprayed with asbestos for insulation. As a result the building has been closed and is slowly falling into disrepair while its fate is decided.) In addition to the intimate nave, there are an assembly room plus meeting rooms in the half-basement. Some fussiness can be seen around the sanctuary, and a few awkward junctures occur on the exterior (and more upkeep is needed), but this is a *multum in parvo* achievement by a too-little-understood architect.

Located 8 miles/13 kilometers west of US 77 (Broadway Expressway) via 3rd Street West in Edmond, which is a northern suburb of Oklahoma City. The interior is closed to the public. AF 12/54

CHEMICAL BANK (1953–54)
(formerly Manufacturers Trust Company)
510 5th Avenue at 43rd Street
New York, New York

Skidmore, Owings & Merrill, architects

Skidmore, Owings & Merrill's reputation for innovative architecture—for years no firm could touch them in this regard—gained much of its initial credibility with Lever House (see page 408) and this five-story branch bank. For the architects not only shattered the then-lingering myth that banks must hide behind Roman columns, they even took the sacred vault out of the basement and put it almost on the sidewalk (a sheet of .5-inch/13-millimeter plate glass is the only protection provided). Needless to say, this iconoclasm revolutionized the art of bank design—and also elevated vaults, here the work of Henry Dreyfuss, into mid-twentieth-century sculpture. In addition, since the working floors are wrapped solely in glass—at the time the largest ever installed at 22 feet/6.7 meters high by 9.8 feet/2.9 meters wide—the interior, aglow with an unbroken luminous ceiling (of sufficient lumen output to minimize external reflections), extends an invitation for all to enter. The bank's entrance has been criticized as being "incidental," and "not on 5th Avenue," but this is carping: the main item on 5th Avenue is the view of the stainless-steel and bronze vault door. On the inside, the first floor, which once served for speedy banking services, is soon to be remodeled and rented as retail space, while the loftier second floor, reached by escalator, was used for more lengthy bank transactions and is now a Chemical Bank branch. This floor is actually a mezzanine, inset on the two street sides so that spatially the two public floors are in visual league, and share, actually, the same two-story-tall curtains. This mezzanine is highlighted by a 70-foot-/21-meter-long golden sheet-metal screen by Harry Bertoia, an elegant piece of sculpture that establishes a magnificent partnership with the architecture. The upper floors are leased to outside tenants. Charles E. Hughes III won an SOM office "competition" for the initial design; Gordon Bunshaft, as chief of design, carried it through; Eleanor Le Maire was interior design consultant; Weiskopf & Pickworth, the structural engineers.

Lobby open to the public during business hours. Chemical Bank open Monday–Friday 8:30 A.M.–3:30 P.M. The vault is visible from the street. AR 11/54, AF 12/54, AR 4/57, PA 6/73

CHAPEL (1953–55)
Massachusetts Institute of Technology
Cambridge, Massachusetts

Eero Saarinen & Associates, architects

The problems that Eero Saarinen (1910–61) had to face in designing this small (130-seat) chapel—a building that ranks high in his memorable output and from which he himself was buried—involved creating a "religious atmosphere" to accommodate a variety of faiths or no faith at all. Instead of an interior that homogenizes active and passive religion into a bland, multifaith, convertible box, we find a spiritual retreat, a retreat directed mostly to a place where one can contemplate things larger than oneself, yet one with no references to organized religion. (A cross or other symbol can be used or not, as desired.) Saarinen walled off the busy, traffic-heavy world outside with a windowless cylinder of deep red brick that rests on light arches in an encircling moat. The inner wall, also of brick, instead of assuming the pure circle of the exterior, undulates rhythmically against the outer so as to lessen any psychological feeling of geometric compaction or acoustic feedback. Both outer and inner walls rest on the

same low arches, and they extend sufficiently beyond the circumferential bench-high base of the chapel to allow the insertion of a narrow glazing strip between inner wainscot and the encircling walls. Through this reverse clerestory (which might have been wider) reflections bounce from the sun shining on the pool, thus delivering an evanescent light. The main illumination (daylight and artificial), however, pours down from a shielded roof oculus and onto a masterful reredos whose short, flat, multiangled gold facets play with and reflect the light. This grille by Harry Bertoia represents a consummate example of the rewards of architect and sculptor working together. A simple cube of marble standing on a low circular dais in front of the screen serves as altar. A forceful aluminum spire by Theodore Roszak tops the chapel; Anderson, Beckwith & Haible were associate architects. Landscaping beside it is good, the combination superb.

Located off Massachusetts Avenue and Amherst Street. Open daily 7:00 A.M.–11:00 P.M. Visitors are not allowed to tour the chapel during services. For more information call (617) 253–3913. AF 1/53, AF 1/56, AR 1/56, PA 1/56, AF 3/56

H. C. PRICE TOWER (1954–55)
501 South Dewey Avenue at East 6th Street
Bartlesville, Oklahoma

Frank Lloyd Wright, architect

Frank Lloyd Wright's dream of a mile-high skyscraper for Chicago never, alas, got further than his inimitable drawings; nor did his 1929 plan for the twenty-story St. Mark's Tower (a prototype for the H. C. Price Tower), which he proposed for New York. However, in 1955 he finished his first and, unfortunately, his last skyscraper, a nineteen-story combined office and apartment block that invigorates the undulating prairies of northeast Oklahoma in no small fashion. It is an enigmatic work by a genius, a building not easily understood or readily forgotten. Among other attributes, it stands as a manifesto against the smooth-skinned, curtain-clad high rise—a not unpopular trend today. And in spite of the Price's complicated appearance, its plan basically forms a square broken on each side by angled projections.

The structure of the building, which can be partially grasped on the ground floor, consists of a spine, a "tap-root" foundation, of four vertical concrete fins set in a squared windmill formation but not touching at the center, thus leaving core spaces for the lobbies. These 18-foot-/5.5-meter-long arms, each with one elevator, are rotated at sixty degrees to the outer skin of the building and are contained within this skin. From each pair of their right-angled intersections the floors are boldly cantilevered, eliminating completely the need for exterior columns. The facade treatment was therefore liberated from the typical grid of steel or concrete imposed on almost all tall buildings. Wright made the most of this. The rotating of an X-shaped structural core within a square exterior, then the cantilevering of hollow floor slabs from the arms, is technologically ingenious (and expensive). (Rotated-plan buildings are today favorably regarded by several prominent architects.)

The Price Tower provides space for three offices and one duplex apartment per floor (though a number of the eight original apartments have been changed to offices). The apartments (which originally all had fireplaces) are immediately identifiable by their double-height vertical louvers, which provide sun protection in the afternoon. Though the arms of the structural core do not project beyond the building's face, the cantilevered floor slabs do; that of the living rooms in the southwest corner of the tower forms the largest of the angled protrusions from the building's square shape. The projection of the apartments' kitchens abuts that of the living quadrant, with fire stair on the windmill diagonal on the opposite side of the building. The two other projections are minor and contain, on either side, lavatories for the offices, which are marked by copper louvers placed horizontally against sun and sky glare.

The glass is gold tinted (among the first so treated) and the masonry tan, so there are, along with the 20-inch-/51-centimeter-wide copper tinning and sculpted spandrels, chromatic touches. The overall exterior nourishes a whirlwind of activity considering that it spans only some 45 feet/14 meters per side. The top, which sports roof terraces, is characterized by hyperactivity (and some indelicacy of detail). Some find this architectural nervousness fascinating, by day as well as night; others consider it excessive. Many, however, regard the Price Tower as both a structural and an esthetic celebration. In any case it is the only skyscraper—non-skeletal at that—by the greatest native-born architect in the United States. The more one analyzes its rationale, the more one understands Wright's "romantic" rejection of what he termed the "fascist derived" typical skyscraper.

Lobby open during business hours. Tours given Thursday at 1:15, 1:45, and 2:15 P.M.; a donation is requested. Tours can be scheduled by calling (918) 661–7471. AF 5/53, AF 2/56, AR 2/56, JAIA 7/82

CIGNA CORPORATION BUILDINGS
(formerly Connecticut General Life Insurance Buildings)
Wilde Building (1954–57/1971); North Building (1962–63)
900–950 Cottage Grove Road
Bloomfield, Connecticut

Skidmore, Owings & Merrill, architects

The Wilde Building (formerly known as the South Building), was pivotal in establishing large-scale corporate headquarters in the suburbs (here 5 miles/8 kilometers northwest of Hartford). (In 1982, Connecticut General merged with INA Corporation to form CIGNA, and in 1984 the South Building was renamed in honor of Frazar Wilde, Connecticut General's president from 1936–61.) This complex and the Reynolds Metals Corporate Headquarters in Richmond, Virginia (see page 425)—each designed by Gordon Bunshaft of SOM within a year of each other—changed both city and country. (Central business districts have now "regrouped" and are fighting back, in many cases successfully.) While the CIGNA Corporation Buildings are important from a socioeconomic standpoint, their architecture is equally cogent. The three-story design (with separate but attached five-story executive block) represents the early "classic" development of SOM and is carried out with their usual thoroughness, from curtain wall to detailing. Its flexible interiors open outward to the countryside and inward to six garden courts designed by Isamu Noguchi. The Wilde Building was expanded by approximately fifty percent in 1971 and a low but three-level garage was built as a berm unobtrusively across the street. It remains one of the key buildings of its period, while its 280-acre/113-hectare, beautifully landscaped site with red granite sculptured group by Noguchi looks better every year.

The North Building, originally designed for Emhart Manufacturing Company five years after the Wilde Building (and acquired by Connecticut General in 1977), lies directly across Cottage Grove Road and shows graphically the progression of Skidmore, Owings & Merrill toward more structural expression (especially in concrete). A serene detachment characterizes the North Building. Poised on stilts along the brow of a hill amid a well-tended, 100-acre/40-hectare lawn, the drive toward it curves so that the 378-foot-/115-meter-long building only gradually reveals itself. This introduction is intensified close up by the spatial magnet of the atrium, or entrance court, framed on three sides by an elevated wing of executive offices and on the fourth by the mass of the main building. As all but the central block is poised on stilts, the lawn seemingly flows through, integrating the building with nature. The elevation of the office floor above grade also permits parking for employees under the building, thus removing an unsightly array of cars, minimizing walking, and providing weatherproof access. The towering concrete "umbrellas" on which the office part is supported form floor sections 42 feet/13 meters square. Windows are set back 3 feet/.9 meter from their edge for sun protection—and, of course, for design richness. One of the country's most impressive headquarters buildings. Gordon Bunshaft was design partner in charge.

GRAIN ELEVATORS (mid-twentieth century)
West Gordon Street on the north bank of Kansas River
Topeka, Kansas

It is perhaps no accident that Kansas's most impressive monuments to its wealth should be found in housing the source of its income rather than in sheltering the recipients thereof. (Kansas is the largest producer of wheat in the United States.) The smaller grain elevators that pepper the state's countryside—as, of course, they do all the Plains States and farming belts— shine encouragingly in the sun as they bulk-handle their grain vertically, while the staggeringly large complexes like those around northern Topeka cannot fail to excite with their interplay of geometric forms. (Reputedly the longest grain elevator in the world—.5 mile/.8 kilometer in length—can be seen at Hutchinson in mid-Kansas.) Here is unadorned functionalism—both material and economic—that yet becomes sculpture at a giant's scale. Would that the buildings by the people and for the people even approached this fundamental excellence. Or, as Le Corbusier put it in an article in *L'Esprit Nouveau* of October 1920, "Thus we have the American grain elevators and factories, the magnificent first-fruits of the new age. The American engineers overwhelm with their calculations our expiring architecture" (reprinted in *Towards a New Architecture*, Frederick Etchells, trans., John Rodker, London, 1931; originally *Vers une architecture*, Cres, Paris, 1923).

SEAGRAM BUILDING (1954–58)
375 Park Avenue between 52nd and 53rd streets
New York, New York

Mies van der Rohe and Philip Johnson, architects

The Parthenon (454–438 B.C.) evolved from a series of prototypes that can be traced back to wood; its first primitive "mock-up" in stone was manifested with the Heraion at Olympia (700 B.C.) and continued at Paestum and Sicily in the 6th–5th centuries B.C. The same refining process might be said of that Parthenon of skyscrapers, the Seagram Building, for Mies van der Rohe's background in steel—he rarely designed in any other material—seemingly was but preliminary homework for this triumph on Park Avenue. (Mies's twin apartments at 860–880 Lake Shore Drive in Chicago, 1951—see page 401—are similar in approach to the Seagram.)

Much of the authority of the thirty-eight-floor Seagram Building—Mies's first major office building—derives from its 100-foot/30-meter setback from Park Avenue and from its side streets, lending it imperial detachment together with elegant monumentality. (The building occupies only fifty-two percent of its site.) Then the openness of its precisely double-height ground floor adds airiness to the entry, which if solid would be dead. (It is fair to say that Mies's work must always be raised or partially raised aboveground, as here, to develop lightness, otherwise it will stifle. His famous one-story S. R. Crown Hall in Chicago, see page 422, and the Farnsworth House achieve this by being transparent.) The low granite-paved podium on which the Seagram Building rests—and which adjusts to Park Avenue's slight change in grade—creates dominion, while fountains and a pool on either side keep matters from becoming too serious; a touch of greenery also helps.

Behind rises the pure and incredibly dignified building. (At least it is pure on the front and two sides; on the back the geometry of the massing becomes complicated and is far less satisfactory.) The Seagram also proclaims more eloquently than any other skyscraper before or since the ultimate expression of the divisible cube—that is, total flexibility in office partitioning behind a cage facade. Far more than a proclamation, however, it is a poem. An office floor provides an open work space that may or may not demand subdivision, and the Seagram exterior says just this. Other tall buildings may stress the vertical or the horizontal; the Seagram states neutrality, but neutrality with éclat—and, of course, within the verticality of 525 feet/160 meters height.

The architects of the Seagram Building pioneered several features that have now become part of the skyscraper vernacular: the "prestige" concept of a plaza with building rising behind, the plaza here actually flowing into the lobby, thus allowing the shaft of the tower to rise without setbacks (compare the Lever House diagonally opposite, page 408, and its different use of site); brown tinted glass (its first use) to reduce sun load within and lend a solemn majesty without; bronze mullions and bronze-colored Muntz metal spandrels (a rash of dark skyscrapers has arisen in imitation); and floor-to-ceiling windows made feasible by utilizing a new low-profile (11 inches/28 centimeters high) air-conditioning unit. However, the five-by-three structural bays of the tower (which are not expressed) meet some difficulties in accommodating the utility core on each floor. As regards the bronze exterior, building codes demanded

fireproof construction (which unprotected metal cannot meet); therefore the structural frame of the Seagram is steel encased in concrete—as is routine—the whole wrapped in a skin of metal and glass of meticulous detail (note corners especially). "God is in the details," wrote Mies. He is obviously no stranger to 375 Park. The Four Seasons Restaurant and bar, located inside the Seagram Building and designed by Philip Johnson, take interior elegance to a new high. Kahn & Jacobs were associate architects; Severud-Elstad-Krueger, structural engineers.

Note that the building sets up an entertaining colloquium with McKim, Mead & White's Racquet & Tennis Club (1916–19) directly opposite (not open to public); the latter expresses the formalism of the Italian Renaissance.

Lobby open to the public during business hours. Tours given Tuesday at 3:00 P.M. (speak to the guard). An art gallery on the 4th floor is also open to the public. AR 7/58, AF 7/58, ARev 12/58, JAIA 1/59, PA 6/59, Int 12/59, PA 12/59

S. R. CROWN HALL (1955–56)
Illinois Institute of Technology
3360 South State Street
Chicago, Illinois

Mies van der Rohe, architect

Crown Hall represents an ultimate in steel construction, the most keenly honed ferric exercise that will be seen today, or even tomorrow. It is, thus, a procreant building in the development of contemporary architecture, a building with an exhilaration of its large-scale inner space that is matched by the small-scale meticulousness of its detailing. When Mies van der Rohe said that "God is in the details," and "simplicity is not simple," he must have had Crown Hall foremost in mind. The building, the design of which began in 1950, comprises only one vast, transparent, upper enclosure resting 6 feet/1.8 meters above grade on a semi-raised basement containing classrooms, workshops, and services. The major room is completely wrapped in glass, clear in the top part, translucent below. Note that the framed height of the translucent section when added to that of the lower window (in basement) exactly equals the dimension of the clear glass above. The steel-framed concrete roof of this great rectangular structure, which measures 120 x 220 feet/37 x 67 meters, is hung externally from four mammoth plate-girder trusses 120 feet/37 meters long, 6.3 feet/1.9 meters deep, and 60 feet/18 meters on center, with a 20-foot/6.1-meter cantilever at each end. This system completely eliminates the need for interior columns—and thus achieves Mies's total universal space. Peripheral *I*-beam mullions and the supports for the trusses occur every 10 feet/3 meters. It is a totally explicit assertion of structure. As the building has only one main floor above ground, there was no need to fireproof the steel (as at 860–880 Lake Shore Drive, page 401); it is thus the material's ultimate expression.

The interior, liberated of supports (there are two utility ducts), is unobtrusively subdivided into exhibition space (at main entrance), drafting rooms (on either side), and administration (behind central area), with 8-foot-/2.4-meter-high movable oak partitions creating an undulation of space beneath the 18-foot-/5.5-meter-high ceiling. This space mates with the lateral limitlessness of the glass exterior walls. The sweep that results is visually potent—and pedagogically stimulates interchange between the older and younger architectural students. Noise transmission can be a nuisance at times, and the acoustic ceiling, venting, and lighting are not distinguished (largely because of economics). But walk up those twelve tensioned travertine steps (whose tread separations lend weightlessness to the whole), pause to take in the detail of steel on steel (note ventilators) and steel meeting glass, then step into this chamber of transparency and you will have encountered one of the United States' great buildings. PACE Associates were associate architects.

In 1939, two years after his first arrival in the States, Mies was also asked to plan the entire IIT Campus (31st–35th streets, along State Street). Ludwig Hilberseimer, a Bauhaus associate of Mies, helped with this. The overall campus that resulted is for many observers static, with too much of a oneness (a 24-foot/7.3-meter module runs throughout). As for Crown Hall itself, "Not since the Gothic has there been such clarity of expression"—Philip Johnson (*Architectural Record*, July 1956).

Open Monday–Friday 9:00 A.M.–5:00 P.M. Tours can be arranged during the school year by calling (312) 567-3104. The building is included on the Chicago Architecture Foundation's 3.5 hour bus tour; the cost is $25. For more information on Chicago Architecture Foundation tours call (312) 922-3432. AF 11/43, AR 1/55, AR 8/56

HILLSDALE HIGH SCHOOL (1955–56)
3115 Del Monte Street between 31st Avenue and Hillsdale Boulevard
San Mateo, California

John Lyon Reid & Partners, architects

Hillsdale was a bold and unorthodox—but prophetic—school when it opened. Now, over a generation later, it is still impressive. Taking advantage of the gently sloping site, the architects placed the large block of general classrooms at the upper end and developed a sizable court in the center. A three-hundred-seat theater (near entry) and cafeteria close one side of this open space, with workshops on the other, while two top-lit gymnasia and an auditorium seating one thousand are aligned across the bottom. Covered galleries provide weatherproof open-air circulation and also help knit the complex together. Though all units are of one story, the gym-auditorium end is, of course, higher, helping—with the change in grade—to develop a well-scaled rhythm along the 720-foot/219-meter total length.

The most unusual aspect of the school, and one that has been influential in subsequent educational plants throughout the country, is the classroom concept. Here a "loft plan" embraces all general instructional rooms under two almost square, mammoth roofs separated by an atrium circulation area. Though all but peripheral classrooms are windowless, they are each illuminated by four 6-foot-/1.8-meter-square, prefabricated skylights that are finned

to admit only north and low south light. The resulting industrial-like space, 12 feet/ 3.6 meters high with a structural module of 28 feet/8.5 meters square, can be readily changed by relocating its movable partitions. Questions will of course arise as to the advantages of having a series of classrooms where students cannot see out, but such rooms have wall surface flexibility in themselves and establish a variety of spatial experiences among themselves. Touches of color and, outside, good planting accent the complex. Burton Rockwell was partner in charge; Alexander G. Tarics the structural engineer—note the earthquake bracing strongly expressed on the gym end.

Open September–June Monday–Friday 7:30 A.M.–3:30 P.M. Closed for winter and spring recess. Visits can be arranged by calling (415) 574-7230. AF 1/56, AF 8/56

REYNOLDS METALS CORPORATE HEADQUARTERS BUILDING (1955–58/1968)
6601 West Broad Street (US 250) at Dickens Road
Richmond, Virginia

Skidmore, Owings & Merrill, architects

Skidmore, Owings & Merrill's elegant Reynolds Building and Wilde Building (Bloomfield, Connecticut, 1954–57—see page 418) gave an impetus to establishing corporate headquarters in the suburbs, which has had a profound effect on American business and its architecture. Other headquarters have been built since—some of the best by SOM—but Reynolds and Connecticut General were significant innovators. Reynolds's site is a rolling tree-rich countryside with ample room for expansion and parking yet only a short ride from downtown. The three-story building, square in plan around a hollow court, rests on a low podium. A 250-foot-/76-meter-long reflecting pool stretches in front; willow oak allées on either side. Two sides of the entry level are partly open and two

closed by the L-shaped wing for reception and executive offices. A freestanding auditorium for 140 stands at the left of the entry. The two upper floors of offices describe a full square, while a basement accommodates services and a cafeteria, which, because of the slope in grade, enjoys a sunny terrace to the south.

On approaching the inner, open courtyard, one is pulled to the entry and tempted beyond to the fountain court itself. The courtyard is divided into sections of brick, grass, and water by narrow bands of white concrete that mark the column spacings, producing thus a well-scaled mosaic. A tall magnolia and a five-jet fountain lend their accents, while the east side is left open as a loggia and spatial keyhole to provide views of distant Richmond. The reception lobby is a glazed extension of this court, even to the red Virginia brick flooring. The two office floors, which are columnless, are protected on east and west from the low sun by 880 vertical aluminum louvers, anodized gray on their south faces and painted blue on their north. The louvers (14 feet/4.3 meters high and 1.9 feet/.56 meter wide) are automatically operated and programmed by a master clock and photocells. Set out from the face of the building, they offer not only sun protection—with a consequent economy in air conditioning—but also provide platforms for window washing. The south front is shielded from the high sun by the horizontal projection of these platforms. Details throughout the building received meticulous attention, down to the hardware, the fabrics, and the numerous works of art of museum caliber. Aluminum was, of course, used whenever feasible.

The original headquarters was joined in 1968 by a six-story annex, which one sees to the right on approaching, and which is connected by underground tunnel to the main building. Designed by the same architects, it forms a trim building. Gordon Bunshaft was partner in charge of design; Marcellus Wright and Baskervill & Son, associates; Ebasco Services were consultants.

Located 5 miles/8 kilometers northwest of downtown. Interior closed to the public. AF 9/58, JAIA 12/58

CONCORDIA THEOLOGICAL SEMINARY (1955–58)
6660 North Clinton Street
Fort Wayne, Indiana

Eero Saarinen & Associates, architects

North European vernacular, particularly Scandinavian, influenced this unexpectedly romantic academic village from the Eero Saarinen office. The seminary is grouped about an artificial 9-acre/3.6-hectare lake and develops a homogeneity of small, simple units dominated by its chapel. Approximately 250 students attend the seminary, almost all of whom will enter the Lutheran ministry (Missouri Synod). Its 198-acre/80-hectare site, northeast of Fort Wayne, was formerly farmland.

The 575-seat Kramer Chapel, triangular in section, rests on a terraced podium at the head of the lake, where its geometry and location make it the visual dominant at the circulation crossroads of the campus. The chapel interior is effectively illuminated by a skylight that runs the length of the ridge, plus a panel of glass from ridge to floor on the right side of the chancel, with peripheral indirect bands of light (in the Saarinen fashion) along the base of each side. As a result, light flows in, enlivening the somewhat austere architectural treatment of the interior. The church's sharp roof angle measures 23.5° from the vertical, those of the secular buildings 23.5° from the horizontal. All thus are geometrically locked together, and all are covered with dark gray tiles The slender, triangular bell tower, 103.5 feet/31.5 meters high, adds the proper vertical accent. A variety of art (mosaics, wall carvings, bronzes, terra-cottas, and wood carvings) is found throughout.

Located 1.6 miles/2.5 kilometers north of US 30. Open Monday–Friday 8:00 A.M.–4:30 P.M. 90-minute campus tours can be arranged by calling (219) 481–2100. AR 12/54, PA 12/58

ST. LOUIS AIRPORT TERMINAL BUILDING (1956/1968)
I-70 (Mark Twain Expressway)
St. Louis, Missouri

Hellmuth, Yamasaki & Leinweber, architects

The day it opened the airy, spacious concourse of the St. Louis Terminal won deserving acclaim. Its three groin vaults, each 110 feet/33 meters on a side, form one of the country's first thin-shell dome constructions. (A fourth was added in 1968 as part of an expansion plan.) Their interplay creates an airy, sprightly interior. Moreover the vistas out are excellent as they partake of the field and its activities. The lower level is less appealing and walking is a chore, while, to the specialist, the exterior supports for the vaults are curiously concealed. Minoru Yamasaki was original partner in charge of this pioneering design. Hellmuth, Obata & Kassabaum were the architects of expansion and for recent improvements.

Located northwest from downtown. Building open daily 24 hours. One-hour tours available Monday–Friday 10:00 A.M.–4:00 P.M.; tours should be scheduled in advance by calling (314) 426–8162. AR 4/56, AF 5/56

CHAPEL OF THE HOLY CROSS (1956)
780 Chapel Road
Sedona, Arizona

Anshen & Allen, architects

In the Chapel of the Holy Cross, the architects have carefully introduced an evocative memorial chapel in a setting suggestive of the not-distant Grand Canyon, and with a background of towering, vigorously sculptured red sandstone cliffs. From the approach the building almost appears to be extruded from its dramatic site, forming a pinnacle instead of being a mere adjunct of the cliff behind. The prominent (90-foot-/27-meter-high) cross, which fits into and slightly projects beyond the end walls, commandingly rises from the ground between two outcroppings on which the chapel's sides rest. A partially elevated road leads up the cliffside to the parking area just below the chapel, unfolding a succession of panoramas as it goes. One then takes a footpath that snakes around the bluff, permitting glimpses of the chapel. The path and, at top, the carefully convoluted balustrades that double as outdoor benches establish a contrast against the sharp geometry of the chapel.

The cross, which projects one third of its depth into the nave itself, is sufficient to act as a sunshield for the dark glass that fills the chancel end; the cross thus is also dominant inside the church. A 13-foot/4-meter steel crucifix, gaunt but impressive, by Keith Monroe is attached to its inner face, while the altar is cantilevered directly from its lower part. The church's side walls are parallel in plan but angle upward in profile toward the sanctuary while inclining slightly inward toward the roof. The 12-inch-/30-centimeter-thick reinforced concrete walls were poured in place in 8-foot/2.4-meter sections. The nave measures 62 feet/19 meters long by 26 feet/8 meters wide. Both ends are of glass. The nave accommodates approximately fifty souls in permanent pews that line the two sides and part of the rear, with chairs available for the open center section if needed. Sacristy, office, and services fill the basement.

The chapel was a gift of Marguerite Brunswig Staude to the Roman Catholic Church in memory of her parents. It forms a dramatic memorial, one that grows with majesty from its cliffside setting. The profusion of sculptural forms in the natural red rock site and the towering cliffs embracing the building defied human competition; the dynamic simplicity of the chapel provides a counterpoint to them.

Located off AZ 179, 3.8 miles/6.2 kilometers south of intersection with US Alt 89. Open daily 9:00 A.M.–5:00 P.M. Closed Easter, Thanksgiving, and Christmas. No regular services held. For more information call (602) 282-7545. AR 10/56, AF 12/56

FIRST PRESBYTERIAN CHURCH (1956–58)
1101 Bedford Street off Hoyt Street
Stamford, Connecticut

Wallace K. Harrison, architect

The exterior of First Presbyterian Church is of boldly angled planes that envelop its parishioners and visitors in a glorious colored glass mantle that produces a unique experience. Almost the entire body of the church—from the floor to the very ridge itself—is enclosed by walls and roof made of multicolored pieces of glass set in 152 precast concrete panels (which also form the supporting structure). The effect of the sun shining through these 22,000 chunks of 1-inch-/25-millimeter-thick *betonglass* is stunning. As the glass is faceted (on its inner face), the moving sun darts jeweled rays into the building, bringing some elements to intense life while fading others only to shine again later; when one walks down the nave the colors pulsate with every step. Gabriel Loire of France, working in close cooperation with the architect and his overall design, produced the glass with eighty-seven colors, and although there is abstruse symbolism in each of its sections (for example, the crucifixion on right and the resurrection at left when entering), one's enjoyment of this multicolored canopy is not impaired by not knowing about it. (A folder giving an explanation of the symbolism is available at the church.) A few details are questionable, and the plan might be too attenuated for liturgical intimacy, but the nave of the First Presbyterian, which seats 670 below and 50 in the balcony, is highly moving. Sherwood, Mills & Smith were associate architects, with Willis N. Mills partner in charge of both church and the adjacent educational complex. Felix J. Sammuely was consulting engineer; Bolt, Beranek & Newman, acoustic consultants.

Open Monday–Friday 9:00 A.M.–5:00 P.M. (July and August open 9:00 A.M.–3:00 P.M.) Closed for holidays. Sunday services held at 10:00 A.M. Tours can be scheduled by calling (203) 324–9522; a donation is requested. AF 4/58, PA 4/58, PA 5/59, JAIA 6/59

D. S. INGALLS HOCKEY RINK (1956–58)
Yale University
73 Sachem Street at Prospect
New Haven, Connecticut

Eero Saarinen & Associates, architects

Take one gigantic arched spine of reinforced concrete with a 228-foot/69-meter clear span, abut a horizontal concrete arch on either side just above the ground, stabilize them with three guy cables per side, lace the three frames together with catenaries of steel cables 6 feet/1.8 meters on center, and on this lay a wood roof deck. The result is a brilliant tensile structure with a plan of optimum shape for 2,900 spectators. Moreover the building's graceful profile makes it acceptable in its near-campus location, where the typical barrel-vaulted rink would not be relished. With chairs in (and ice out) the Ingalls Rink can seat up to 5,000 for commencements and even dances and concerts (acoustics are excellent).

The esthetics of the entry are worth noting, as one moves through low front doors sheltered under the sweep of the projected roof, advances under the still low lobby, and then confronts the dramatic plenum of the interior. The rink is set 10 feet/3 meters below the entry level, while the arched spine rises to 75 feet/23 meters above the ice. Precast concrete bleachers envelop the 200 x 85-foot/61 x 26-meter rink with maximum number of seats near center line (and with dressing rooms beneath). The underside of the cable-supported, neoprene-covered roof was left as natural wood "boat construction" but with a plaster soffit immediately over the peripheral spectator area for fire protection. Fred N. Severud of Severud-Elstad-Krueger Associates worked closely with the architect in developing the tensile structure. Douglas W. Orr was associate architect. Oliver Andrews designed the lighting fixture projected over entry.

Upper sections open to the public daily 9:00 A.M.–4:30 P.M. (June–August closed Saturday and Sunday). Closed for holidays. Lower sections can be seen on a free tour, which can be scheduled by calling (203) 432–0877. AR 8/57, AR 10/58, AF 12/58

SOLOMON R. GUGGENHEIM MUSEUM (1956–59/1992)
1071 5th Avenue between 88th and 89th streets
New York, New York

Frank Lloyd Wright, architect
Gwathmey Siegel & Associates, architects of addition

Frank Lloyd Wright was early interested in organic forms, especially those with a pronounced geometric basis—a heritage, Wright students believe, from his childhood Froebel teaching. (FLW was also a great admirer of Buckminster Fuller's geometrically generated work.) Triangles and hexagons can be seen in many of his projects and some buildings, and from these he explored what he called "the ultimate in flexibility—the circle." Wright's earliest essay with the spiral and "a continuous flow of movement" was probably that for the never-built Sugar Loaf Mountain Planetarium of 1925—a circular ziggurat (compare the minaret at Samarra). Wright continued in this vein with his startling proposal for Huntington Hartford's mountain-top country club (1947); while one of his last radius-generated projects was the never-built cultural complex for Baghdad (1957). Wright's Annunciation Greek Orthodox Church in Milwaukee (1959–61, see page 452), however, is one of the important demonstrations of the built circle, while the small ex-V. C. Morris shop in San Francisco (1948–49, see page 400) whirls its own circular ramp. Though the Morris shop was finished ten years before the Guggenheim

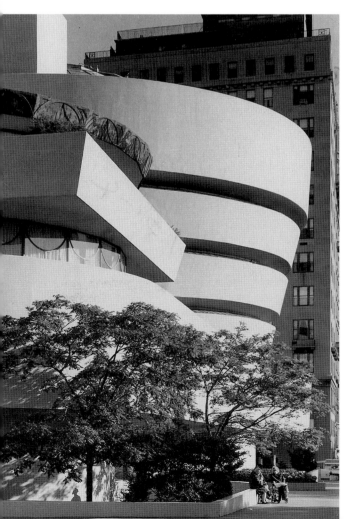

Museum, the latter's design was first presented and published in 1944. (Construction of the museum was delayed by World War II and Solomon R. Guggenheim's death in 1949.) And the circle with ramp, via *Nautilus pompilius*, is, of course, the rationale of the Guggenheim; the scheme was perhaps assisted by Baroness Hilla Rebay, the museum's first director, and Rudolf Bauer, Guggenheim's early artist-protégé. In the museum Wright sought by means of a fantastic expanding helix to create a "reposeful place in which paintings could be seen to better advantage than they have ever been seen" (to quote Wright in the museum booklet issued by the Solomon R. Guggenheim Foundation, 1975).

There are those who believe that Wright cared little for art, other than a few Japanese prints and pieces, and that this museum reveals his prejudices. Moreover, some hold that he considered the building far more important than the art. Granted the Guggenheim's walls—and the original lighting—are not always cooperative, the museum itself is so exciting as a sculptured space that people come to experience the building and find themselves captured by the art—art that in many cases the museum has indeed glorified. The progressive impact on the visitor is breathtaking as one advances under a purposefully low, even insignificant entrance (a great many of Wright's entries are conspiratorially subordinated) to a centrifugal explosion of inner space. Here one is wrapped, almost like Laocoon, in a coil of serpentine spirals that finally leap through the glazed roof—no small museum introduction. Peter Blake, the distinguished architect, editor, and educator, calls this "one of the most beautiful spaces created in this century" (*Architectural Forum*, December 1959). It is also one of the few monumental rooms of our time; somehow architects have almost lost this art. (The open four-story core of Wright's 1904 Larkin Building—destroyed in 1950—foreshadowed the Guggenheim's heady inner space.)

The gallery-goer has the option of strolling up the ramp or taking the elevator (inadequate) to the top and gliding—on a slice of infinity—to the bottom, a process of gravitational advantage but, like walking up, only via a controlled circulation—a very un-Wrightian path—not to everyone's liking. Lewis Mumford called it "Procrustean." (One can exit, however, at several levels by means of stairs or elevator.) In the process of unwinding, as it were, the silhouettes of the visitors opposite add animation to the interior, while the observer has the pleasure of seeing most pictures both at a distance and close up. The width of the picture-hanging bays, predicated by the building's structural frame, is relatively inflexible for some gallery installation, especially for large canvases. The "fins" defining the bays occur at each 30 degrees, thus there are twelve in plan, and they widen as they rise to give lateral structural stability. But on the other hand, art and building become almost one, the building's bays serving as extended frames for the pictures, often only one per section, and thus lending preciosity to them. The hanging spaces, in a revolt against the flat-walled mentality, are angled behind the pictures so that the canvases stand free; they float, hence developing a liaison or immediacy with the spectator that other museums with pictures possessed by the walls do not engender.

The original lighting was unusual—and ineffective. Wright wanted the major source to be natural (but glaring) illumination emanating from the glazed band that rings his continuous spiral, its light bathing the pictures angled against the wall. Upon James Johnson Sweeney's accession as director in 1959 this was supplemented by an angled band of fluorescent lights that wraps around the entire periphery—note the notches of the backs of the fins to permit continuity—and by direct incandescent trough fixtures. The domed sky-light, it should be noted, bears strong organizational similarity to a Tiffany glass dome designed in 1908 by George B. Post and Sons for the Cleveland Trust Company.

One of the spatial by-products of the Guggenheim's one-room design lies in the fact that one always knows where one is and which is the way out, comfortable knowledge not found in labyrinthine complexes that encase much art. And when one looks across the museum, especially from an upper (deeper) bay, the hypnotic continuity of the sweep of the ramp is punctuated by the tangible compartmentation, while the near-horizontal coil of the spiral is visually crosshatched by these short vertical divisions. The interaction of these two geometric determinants creates quiet dynamism in the interior. In addition it is visually refreshing—if hair-raising for some—to look over the parapet (which leans slightly outward) to see the fountain and sculpture on the main floor.

A circular, 299-seat auditorium occupies much of the basement. The Justin K. Thannhauser Collection of seventy-five works was installed in 1965 as a permanent loan in a separate second-floor wing; it greatly expands the scope and depth of the original Guggenheim collection.

The exterior of the Guggenheim has its awkward moments, and a few junctures are not only difficult, they are nearly impossible. But as Wright, with his characteristic wit, exclaimed, "When the first atomic bomb lands on New York [the museum] will not be destroyed. It may be blown a few miles up into the air, *but when it comes down it will bounce!*" (*Architectural Forum*, January 1964). Though faults appear, the Guggenheim is loaded with rewards. George N. Cohen was the brave builder who constructed this difficult masterpiece.

In 1992, after years of discussion, an addition by Gwathmey Siegel & Associates was made, a nine-story, largely blank-walled oblong whose shape is very similar to the windowed proposal Wright himself had suggested forty years earlier. Substantial changes and improvements were also carried out inside. Criticism has been made of the new work—as, indeed, was Wright's original plan—but the addition is probably as sympathetic as exigencies demand. The museum is still a glorious adventure.

Open Sunday–Wednesday 10:00 A.M.–6:00 P.M., Friday–Saturday 10:00 A.M.–8:00 P.M. Closed Thursday. Closed Christmas. Admission is $7 for adults, $4 for students and senior citizens, free for children under 12. (Admission is free on Friday 6:00–8:00 P.M.) A recorded audio tour is available. Guided tours can be arranged by calling (212) 423–3555. For general information call (212) 423–3500. AF 1/46, AF 4/52, AR 5/58, AF 6/59, AF 12/59, Int 12/59, AR 3/86, PA 4/89, A 8/92, AR 8/92, AR 10/92

ST. JOHN'S UNIVERSITY CHURCH (1956–61)
St. John's University
Collegeville, Minnesota

Marcel Breuer, architect

Exuding strength, St. John's University Church is one of the most intriguing religious buildings in the United States. Its orientation is north, hence the main facade is sunless for most
of the year. This posed problems of visual vitality, which the architects imaginatively solved by
a stupendous—there is no other word—freestanding "bell banner" 117 feet/36 meters high by
99 feet/30 meters wide. The structure rests on four sculpted supports that straddle the entry
to the church. By piercing this trapezoidal banner with a horizontal rectangle for bells and a
vertical opening for a cross, the southern sun picks up facets of bells and cross, and with its
reflections—abetted by the positive-negative of solids and openings and the parabolic curves

of the supports—creates a masterful introduction to the shadowed entry. Moreover the honey-combed concrete and stained-glass facade of the church reflects the sun bouncing from the south side of the bell banner. Thus the banner brings added life to the front much of the day and also helps light the church interior through the latter's windows. (Incidentally, the final design of the banner—which suggests the church plan in its shape—represents careful evolution over Breuer's initial sketches. The rectangular opening with bells was inspired, we are told, by Greek village churches.) Hamilton P. Smith was associate architect, Pier Luigi Nervi, structural consultant.

The shrine is entered via a top-lit baptistry, also trapezoidal in plan, attached to the front of the building with sunken font symbolically in center. Directly on stepping into the fabric of the church proper, one finds oneself under the freestanding balcony; on moving forward into the nave one encounters the staggering force of the full interior. Its roof is constructed of enormous folded concrete plates that span the room laterally; their weight and thrust are carried down to an edge beam on either side by triangular pleated side walls. (The influence of the

Conference Building in the UNESCO Headquarters in Paris, designed by Pier Luigi Nervi, Marcel Breuer, and Bernard Zehrfuss—and very similar in size and shape—can be seen at St. John's.) An airily suspended baldacchino gives focus to the altar and helps define the spaces for clergy and congregation (1,700 seats).

This enormously powerful room, a spiritual redoubt, does have a few minor shortcomings. Chief among these is the handling of natural light, for below the great concrete cap are bands of almost unshielded windows along either side, producing a glare that tugs at the eye. Moreover, the sanctuary and the brothers' and priests' choirs, whose three hundred seats describe an extended semicircle about the altar, seem unanchored because of the passages and spaces behind the chancel. But these are details: the experience of this great church should not be missed. It is perhaps most impressive at dusk.

St. John's University is located north off US 52/I-94, 12 miles/19 kilometers west of St. Cloud. Open daily 6:00 A.M.–midnight. Sunday services held at 10:30 A.M. 90–minute tours can be scheduled by calling (612) 363–2573. AF 7/54, AR 11/61, AF 5/68, JAIA 5/68, F 5/68

Directly facing stands the Alcuin College Library (1967), by the same architects, which should also be seen. The interior brandishes two eight-armed "trees" of concrete that uphold—with an intriguing degree of structural arm flexing—the roof, which measures 200 x 120 feet/61 x 36 meters. These trees make a dynamic room as well as free the floor space for maximum flexibility.

When school is in session, open Monday–Friday 8:00 A.M.–midnight, Saturday–Sunday 10:00 A.M.–midnight. When school is not in session, open Monday–Friday 8:00 A.M.–4:30 P.M.

AIR FORCE ACADEMY (1956–63)
Academy Drive
Colorado Springs, Colorado

Skidmore, Owings & Merrill, architects

The Air Force Academy presides over one of the most dramatic sites of any building group in the country. The academy itself is sharply etched on a podium atop hills that fade into the plains to the east; the Rampart Range of the Rocky Mountains juts immediately as a backdrop. On a partially natural, but mostly man-chiseled, acropolis, a knife-edge collection of buildings—by the Chicago office of SOM—stands at military attention in this setting of grandeur. Harmon Hall, the three-story administration building, defines the upper (mountainside) limit of the academy, and is raised on pilotis so that space snakes through its largely open ground floor to bind site and architecture together. From the terrace in front of Harmon—the Court of Honor—the public can survey the entire layout. Arnold Hall, a large social center used for festivities, stands immediately at the left of Harmon. It contains a theater, exhibition space, and recreational facilities. Vandenberg Hall, six stories high and a quarter mile (1,337 feet/407 meters) in length (at left in photograph), provides quarters for over 2,000 cadets. Forming a hollow rectangle about two major central courts with cadet rooms lining both sides of its corridors, this building, too, is on pilotis, thus lessening its vast extent as fingers of space penetrate both at ground level and at the "empty" floor between the two top decks and the two lower ones. The field house, with its own road, stands separate northeast of Vandenberg Hall. Across the far (east) side of the campus, parallel to the Court of Honor and at right angles to Vandenberg, stretches (985.8 feet/300 meters) the Library and Academic Complex, the two in line but not directly joined above ground. The ramp down to the parade ground is adjacent. Mitchell Hall, the dining hall—which can seat approximately 4,400 cadets at one time—rises at the southwest corner of the class bank, partially framing the "air garden" in front. It boasts an enormous, column-free interior, 252 feet/77 meters square, with a ceiling height of 24 feet/7.3 meters. Only four columns per side support this great Warren-truss umbrella, whose overall dimensions, with a 22-foot/6.7-meter cantilever on all four sides, measure 308 x 308 feet/94 x 94 meters.

The Cadet Chapel is the only structure regularly open to the public. In addition to filling spiritual needs, it provides the architectural marrow of the campus, its heaven-thrusting spires—like the folded plane wings on the flight deck of an aircraft carrier—dramatically relieving the horizontality of its neighbors. Without its serrated verticality mobilizing the group to unity, unity would be diminished. The chapel was the last major building finished at the academy, and though it is not a church that everyone will like (a football coach has been quoted as saying, "we don't know whether to pray in it, for it, or at it"), many will find it fascinating. The structure, composed of contiguous units of triangulated tetrahedrons, two facing out, one in, is ingenious technically. These forms, with steel tube structure and aluminum facing, complement each other so that when the two outer ones come to a point, the inner face reaches maximum width, and vice versa. Narrow (1-foot/.3-meter) bands of stained glass mark their junctures. These intriguingly angled forms, seventeen to a side, spring from freestanding, concrete buttresses, leaving a covered passage along both sides and the front of the chapel. The Protestant chapel occupies the entire upper "platform" and provides pews for 1,200, with a 100-seat choir loft over the entry. The Roman Catholic worship space (500 seats) and the Jewish (100) are placed beneath and half below the grade of the surrounding terrace. There is also a tiny, non-denominational meeting room on the lower level.

Regarding the architecture of the Air Force Academy as a whole, we find an enormous undertaking, authoritatively sited to counterpoint the mountains, not blend with them, asserting people's place in nature. Its buildings are obviously—and intentionally—on the mechanistic side, as are the instruments its cadets will eventually fly. Some critics have suggested that the buildings belong more in a metropolitan setting than in wild nature, but this no-nonsense academy is one of the potent complexes of the century, the epitome of its period. *Sic itur ad astra.*

The 19,100 acres/7,733 hectares of grounds (but not the buildings) are in large measure open to the driving public, but the central architectural emphasis is found, of course, in the Academy buildings mentioned above. Walter A. Netsch, Jr., was in overall charge of design, with Kenneth Naslund structural engineer. Dan Kiley was landscape architect.

Located at exit 156B off I-25, about 8 miles/13 kilometers north of Colorado Springs. Grounds open daily 6:00 A.M.–10:00 P.M. Visitors Center open daily 9:00 A.M.–5:00 P.M. Self-guided tours available at the Visitors Center. June–Labor Day, guided tours are given every half-hour from 9:15 A.M.–3:45 P.M. at the Visitor Center. For more information call the Visitors Center at (719) 472–2025. The Cadet Chapel is open Monday–Saturday 9:00 A.M.–5:00 P.M., Sunday 1:00–5:00 P.M. Sunday services are held in the Catholic and Protestant chapels at 9:00 and 11:00 A.M.; Friday services are held in the Jewish worship space at 8:00 P.M. For more information call the chapel at (719) 472–4515. AF 6/55, AF 9/57, AF 6/59, AR 6/59, AF 12/62, AR 12/62

ALFRED NEWTON RICHARDS MEDICAL RESEARCH BUILDING (1957–61)
GODDARD BIOLOGY LABORATORY (1962–64)
University of Pennsylvania
3700 Hamilton Walk, next to Medical School
Philadelphia, Pennsylvania

Louis I. Kahn, architect

The Richards Research Building and the slightly later conjoined Goddard Biology Lab number among the influential buildings in the development of mid-twentieth-century architecture. Wilder Green of the Museum of Modern Art in a special brochure termed Richards "probably the single most consequential building constructed in the United States since the war" (1961). The reasons for this accolade lie in the conceptual, humanistic, and technical achievements of its architect, Louis I. Kahn. First of all he sought the "humanity" of clusters of smallish labs instead of an impersonal attenuated corridor plan. He then stated—some believe overstated—the division of what he called the "served" spaces from the "servant" to emphasize their differing functions. (Frank Lloyd Wright had closely studied and expressed "servicing requirements" in his Larkin Building of 1904.) The scientists and professors who work in Richards use a number of noisome gases and fumes, but instead of treating the necessary air-change and air-dissipation problem as an embarrassing nuisance to be swept under the architectural rug, Kahn seized upon it as the rationale of the whole building. To this end he designed four separate but coupled eight-story blocks comprising three served laboratory towers grouped around and plugged into a windowless concrete servant unit that houses animals used in research plus mechanical services. On the south side of the servant unit are attached four dramatic brick air-intake stacks whose sheer walls rise two stories above the roof. Pure air is taken in near the bottom of these stacks, then conditioned and ducted to the distribution shaft on every floor and piped into the laboratories. Fumes and exhausted air from each lab are voided high above the roof by ventilation ducts rising in brick towers attached to the laboratories. On the opposite side of each laboratory block a similar brick tower containing emergency stairs is affixed. The 45-foot-/14-meter-square laboratories, with their air-exhaust stack and fire stairs on the outside, are thus completely free of vertical obstruction, hence can be subdivided as needed. Altogether there are eleven ten-story stacks—four intake, four exhaust, and three emergency stairs—clutching the eight-story servant and three served towers and creating the most romantic group of towers big and small since San Gimignano. (Kahn had spent 1950–51 at the American Academy in Rome.) The structure of the laboratory towers—which was closely worked out with Dr. August E. Komendant and the Keast & Hood Company as consultants—consists of a framework of both prestressed and post-tensioned concrete beams, designed, fabricated, and put together with imagination and precision, as can be seen at the entry. The open webbing of these 3-foot-/.9-meter-deep floor trusses enables the extensive pipe runs to be woven through as needed. Note also the drop-off in the size of members as the spandrel beams cantilever to the corners.

The Goddard Biology Laboratory, respectfully tied to Richards, was constructed later and shows more finesse, especially in window detailing, and also more economy. Lacking the soaring grandeur of Richards, it is nonetheless impressive. One of its most sensitive features is the fact that one wing of its ground floor is raised on pilotis, which not only lets the southern sun stream through to give life to the northern (and entrance) facade, but also provides visual contact with the garden beyond.

Richards has not been without critics. Some of the professors like it very much, others not. The perceptive Reyner Banham termed it "picturesquely heroic" (*Architectural Review*, March 1962). Many of the complaints stem from changes made after original construction cost bids came in substantially over the budget and the building was completed economically without reducing its size. Some of the building's users believe that there is too much visual intimacy

between labs in one tower and the one adjacent, and too much aural intimacy within one's own tower (over the partitions and through the trusses) and not enough flexibility to accommodate change. Moreover there have been problems with sun control—which have been largely corrected in the biology lab. But with any complex undertaking, there are bound to be problems; when the effort is a pioneering one, such likelihood increases. Richards' contribution, however, shines and here is where we all benefit; it is a brilliant demonstration of turning the utilitarian, the architectural nuisances, into logical and vital elements of design.

The interior is not regularly open to the public. Tours can be arranged by calling (215) 898–2876. AF 7/60, AR 8/60, ARev 2/61, A+A 7/61, PA 9/64

CHASE MANHATTAN BANK (1957–61)
1 Chase Manhattan Plaza: Nassau Street between Pine, Liberty, and William streets

MARINE MIDLAND BUILDING (1967–68)
140 Broadway between Cedar and Liberty streets

ONE LIBERTY PLAZA (1970–72)
165 Broadway at Liberty Street

New York, New York

Skidmore, Owings & Merrill, architects

Downtown Manhattan boasts three skyscrapers by SOM, all more or less aligned, and all making contributions to the evolution of postwar high-rise design. Two of the three are enriched by outstanding pieces of sculpture, the third by a small park.

The Chase Manhattan Bank (see photo below) virtually "saved" the financial district by building its headquarters downtown (a decision urged by David Rockefeller in 1955), thus reestablishing the area's pre-World War II importance. The building also injected a hard-edged profile into the melange of turrets, domes, crockets, and finials that bedeck most of its older eclectic neighbors. Chase was the first of downtown's "slab" skyscrapers, and its boldness stands out. Its two-block site was assembled by a trade-off with the city, whereby the city permitted the bank to close (and build over and under) one block of Cedar Street and the bank gave the city sidewalk perimeters on much of four sides so that street widening could be carried out. The architects then took this challenging site and established a podium over all but one corner (occupied by Chase's former headquarters). On this sweeping terrace, which equalized the drop-off in grade down to William Street, they erected the 280-foot-/85-meter-long skyscraper, running it up without breaks for sixty floors. The result is not only extraordinarily powerful visually—the building's "arcaded" meeting with the horizontal is masterful—it was far more economical to construct than a building with a series of setbacks. Note that the structural frame is expressed on the exterior; its great piers give both scale and vitality to the long facades and effect an uninterrupted wall within for flexibility in partitioning.

To give identity to customer banking operations, which occupy the lower level off William Street, the terrace has a large circular opening that enables all using the building to gaze into the banking floor and to look down onto a landscaped pool by Isamu Noguchi. The opening also permits views into this pool area for those on the banking floor. The crowning touch of the plaza is the 42-foot-/13-meter-high walk-through *Group of Four Trees* by Jean Dubuffet, installed in 1972. A work of both strength and delicacy, the sculpture is constructed of epoxy-coated fiberglass and aluminum over a steel frame. This closes the space of the podium when approaching from Nassau Street (it had previously leaked out), acts as an intriguing magnet from Pine and William streets, and establishes the territory of the terrace with élan. The interior works of art are equally distinguished. Gordon Bunshaft was partner in charge of design; Weiskopf & Pickworth, structural engineers.

Lobby open Monday–Friday 9:00 A.M.–5:00 P.M. Closed for holidays. AF 7/51, AF 4/57, AF 7/61, AR 7/61, AF 4/68, F 11/72

In the Marine Midland Building SOM sought to create a building that would not impinge on or be in conflict with Chase Manhattan across the street. They therefore evolved a dark, smooth-skinned (black anodized aluminum and bronze glass) skyscraper rising straight from the ground. To give its fifty-two-story height breathing space (and to enable it to rise without setbacks) more than half of the site was treated as a plaza and paved with travertine. This terrace is made eloquent on the Broadway side by Noguchi's brilliant orange-red cube (28 feet/8.5 meters on a side)—which, like Chase's Dubuffet, is one of the United States' finest pieces of urban sculpture—and given accents by circular seaters/planters on Cedar Street. Briefly challenged by a slightly irregular trapezoidal street pattern, the architects came up with a symmetrical trapezoidal shape for their building, avoiding awkward street relationships and maximizing allowable office space. The main banking floor is on the second level (compare Philadelphia's pioneering PSFS of 1932, page 370), and its extra tallness (18 feet/5.5 meters) tends to push the lower entry floor into the ground; here the building suffers in comparison with Chase Manhattan. The treatment of the top of the building, by contrast, with an inset marking the utility level, is unsurpassed. For an economical commercial office block Marine Midland is hard to equal. Gordon Bunshaft was chief of design.

Lobby open 24 hours. F 4/68, AR 7/73

The startling quality of the fifty-four-story One Liberty Plaza (see photo on following page) lies in its daringly exposed steel framework. Its great spandrel girders exhibit a brooding yet confident virility that no other high rise has approached. (The girders are approximately 52 feet/16 meters long on the three-bay ends and 47 feet/14 meters on the five-bay sides, all measuring 70 inches/1.8 meters deep.) Its structural development was arrived at after almost a year of collaborative exploration between U.S. Steel, the architects, and the engineers. U.S. Steel's Applied Research Laboratory felt that there were new structural possibilities in skyscraper design, particularly the ability to express steel more vividly, and the result—after a minute examination of the pros and cons of nine potential means (such as weight of steel versus cost of enclosing it and free bay size versus weight of steel) was the solution seen here.

The most extraordinary aspect of the exterior, both technically and aesthetically, can be seen in the exposed spandrels mentioned, for steel, of course, buckles when subjected to intense heat unless it is properly fireproofed—as the building code requires. Yet there is visible metal here. The architects and their consultants developed a flame shield for the built-up girders, wrapping their flanges first with insulation then with 14-gauge steel but leaving the deep web almost totally exposed on its exterior face. Moreover, the shield's width was extended some 8 inches/20 centimeters beyond the spandrel girder's flange to deflect outward any fire that might occur—and also to give greater sun protection (2.3 feet/.7 meter overhang) to the vertically pivoted windows. (The client-requested operable sash is a U.S. Steel design to facilitate window washing.) The proposal for flame shielding the exposed steel structure required considerable testing with a full-size mock-up before it was accepted by the New York City Board of Standards and Appeals. Another unusual facet of the building's design can be seen in the fact that the solid and void are almost precisely equal, making the exterior half steel (all exposed) and half glass.

Unfortunately, because of the pronounced grade falloff the setback entrance is lower than the street, while the entry floor is far shorter than the second (banking) floor, so that the structure seems to be subsiding into the ground, an effect intensified by its somber color and dark gray glass. (The west side terraces down to Church Street.) It is reported that the architects initially wanted to leave the entire ground level unenclosed except for the elevator lobby, but this notion gave way to rental consid-

erations. In plan the building is framed directly from outer periphery to inner circulation and service core, producing a column-free interior. The landscaped park opposite the Liberty Street side, known as Trinity Park, was acquired so that the building could rise without setbacks. Ernest Flagg's forty-one-story Singer Building (1908)—the tallest in the world when built (also the tallest to be demolished, 1967)—previously stood on the site of One Liberty Plaza. Roy O. Allen was partner in charge; Paul Weidlinger and Weiskopf & Pickworth were joint structural engineers.

Lobby open 24 hours. AR 7/73, F 4/68

CHARLES CENTER (1957–69)
Charles Street, Lombard Street, Hopkins Place, Liberty Street, and Saratoga Street
Baltimore, Maryland

Greater Baltimore Committee, Planning Council
(David A. Wallace, director), general planning
RTKL Associates, urban design of public spaces

Baltimore, like most cities in the middle of the twentieth century, was faced with the deterioration of much of its central area in the post-World War II period. By the late 1950s business, shopping, and entertainment were moving away from downtown, leaving a shuttered, blighting residue in many blocks. The city's business leaders realized they must do two things if they wanted to keep the city alive: one, reverse the drain from the central business district (CBD) by making it so attractive and convenient that no one would want to leave and, two, coordinate any potential new work for overall urban betterment. Most American cities operated in the mid-fifties as they generally operate today: strictly laissez-faire, with few if any long-range planning objectives for the CBD. But Baltimore's leaders—and it took leaders to push through their plan—sought to rejuvenate a 33-acre/13-hectare plot between the business-financial section (to the east) and the retail shopping district (to the west). Part of this acreage had several substantial skyscrapers, which had to be kept, but most of the rest was occupied by old lofts and obsolescent structures that could be readily cleared. An awkward street pattern presented a problem, but it was found that several minor avenues could be eliminated to the disadvantage of few. The grade drop of 68 feet/21 meters could be used for visual variety. The site, thus, was no bulldozed urban dream, but a tough, workaday area into which the new would have to be dovetailed.

Baltimore's businessmen and planners realized, too, that this should not be a precious enclave to which one made a pilgrimage to admire the sights, but should instead be a lively round-the-clock living, working, playing, and shopping core in the fundamental sense. In addition, they reasoned, the car must not only be separated from the pedestrian, but it should have its own house under the street. A few of the early dreams of the developers, planners, and architects have not worked out, but most have, and Charles Center is without question one of the superior CBD developments in the country, one replete with lessons.

The center is laced with plazas and elevated pedestrian walkways so that one rarely has to cross a street. The planners had hoped that these aerial sidewalks would have played a more prominent, more gracious role, but one building owner refused to cooperate fully and others were unable to market retail space at two levels instead of one, thus the scope and visual quality of the walkways, while good, has not achieved the potential that was originally hoped for. On the other hand the early-morning-to-late-at-night vitality and street cheerfulness have—in general and sometimes only seasonally—turned out satisfactorily. This animation finds its epicenter in the plaza by the theater, where by day office workers, in dulcet weather, sit in its terraced and well-planted park at lunchtime, while in the evening the theater crowd takes over. The fountain spouts cheerful gallons of water per minute, and is, at night, properly illuminated. A quiet corner of the park (east end of Federal Building) enables those seeking a retreat to find a shady refuge.

Though the general architecture of the center is basically routine, there are three exceptional buildings: One Charles Center, a twenty-four-story office block by Mies van der Rohe (1962), the spirited Morris A. Mechanic Theater by John M. Johansen (1967), which enlivens the plaza, especially at night; and the two Charles Center Apartments, by Conklin & Rossant (1969), whose twenty-seven- and thirty-story towers provide excellent in-town living. Charles Center makes a meaningful contribution to the urban problems many of our cities encounter.

AF 6/58, JAIA 3/59, AF 5/69, LA 1/60, AD 10/62, AD 1/64, AD 11/64, AR 12/64, AR 9/66, Int 1/67, AF 5/67, AR 1/69, LA 1/69, AF 5/69, JAIA 2/78

MCGREGOR MEMORIAL CONFERENCE CENTER (1958)
Wayne State University
495 West Ferry Mall
Detroit, Michigan

Minoru Yamasaki & Associates, architects

A gem set in an immaculate garden, a memorial, in the finest sense of the word, to its donors, Mr. and Mrs. Tracy W. McGregor. This center is used both by the university and by civic, cultural, and educational groups. The two-story (plus basement) building is dominated by its full-height central hall and lounge, which bisects the mass into two sections. This is topped by a translucent ceiling that, with its glass end walls, suffuses the interior with a radiant quality of natural light. Along each side of the hall on both levels is a maximum of eight conference, discussion, and/or meeting rooms arranged so that they can be combined or separated to accommodate from ten to three hundred people. A dining room and kitchen on the lowest level can feed up to five hundred.

Colors and furnishings are excellent throughout, highlighted by the white marble floor, turkey-red carpet, and black leather Barcelona chairs by Mies van der Rohe. The hall-lounge, which divides the building into halves, is alive spatially, especially from the upper level. McGregor has that elusive qual-

ity so rarely seen in today's architecture—a sense of style. At night the building glows. The understated Japanese garden and L-shaped pool with three "islands"—all designed by the architect—wrap around two sides of the building, complementing the architecture, and creating quiet retreats on a crowded urban campus.

Lobby open to the public Monday–Friday 9:00 A.M.–5:00 P.M. AF 8/58

KALITA HUMPHREYS THEATER (1958–59)
(Dallas Theater Center)
3636 Turtle Creek Boulevard at Blackburn Avenue
Dallas, Texas

Frank Lloyd Wright, architect

At the Dallas Theater Center, Frank Lloyd Wright had his first chance to design a professional theater. Wright, a consummate actor himself, had long been interested in the stage as an extension of cultural expression and intergroup relations. Taliesin in Spring Green, Wisconsin has a performance area, and one of the finest units at Taliesin West in Scottsdale, Arizona (see page 390) is a theater, but the theater at Dallas was his only one designed to be a public facility. Its site is a steeply sloping park that Wright used to maximum advantage, shoe-horning the building into the hillside so that level changes within would reflect the grade. The visual indifference that would normally result from a theater's many necessarily blank walls has been tempered by a play of curves versus straight planes and overhangs versus sheer walls, thus producing a satisfactory exterior.

On entering, the theatergoer is taken on an angled path before being delivered to the auditorium entrance. This widened corridor also serves as lobby (with critically tight circulation to lower lobby and rest rooms). The auditorium itself, radiating around an apron stage and initially accommodating 416 with only eleven to twelve rows of seats, suggests a family gathering more than a theater, with admirable intimacy between audience and actors, free from any "peep-show proscenium character" (as FLW put it). (Three rows of seats were recently added to the balcony to make a total capacity of 466.) The stage has a revolving central section (32 feet/9.7 meters in diameter) within a 40-foot/12-meter cylindrical stage house, partly cantilevered over the stage itself. This doubles as a cyclorama, with side stages on both right and left. Three 4-inch/10-centimeter steps are all that separate actors from audience. If needed, a curtain bisects the revolving section. Wright originally planned to have the scene changes lugged from the basement by hand via the ramps on either side, but, in addition to the labor problem, the curves are too tight to accommodate large flats, so an elevator was installed. Other set changes can be dropped from the fly gallery. The balcony can also be used for supplemental lights. There are faults, as suggested, at the Dallas Theater Center—and some actors do not favor it—but it has advanced the art of drama in its relation of actors to audience, the unreal to the real. George C. Izenour was theater consultant.

Open during performances. Free tours can be arranged by calling (214) 526–8210, ext. 464. AF 3/60, AR 3/60

TWA FLIGHT CENTER (1958–62)
John F. Kennedy International Airport
New York (Queens), New York

Eero Saarinen & Associates, architects

Expressionism in contemporary architecture is somewhat questionable, and we are not likely to produce again a building as boldly expressionistic as this TWA Flight Center. But as Eero Saarinen said, "I wanted to catch the excitement of the trip." (For contrast it is useful to quote Mies van der Rohe, "I am, in fact, completely opposed to the idea that a specific building should have an individual character" [quoted in Peter Carter, *Mies van der Rohe at Work*, Praeger, 1972]). The space within TWA's sprawling, crablike shell sparkles with excitement. It is, as Edgar Kaufmann, Jr., wrote in *Interiors* (July 1962), "a festival of ordered movements and exhilarating vistas."

The enclosure uses four angled carapaces for the roof, each separated by a band of skylight; these strips of light not only make the complicated structure graspable by dividing it into components, they liberate any potential oppression of being under a shell. Ribbons of sunshine dart back and forth across the interior. The four roof vaults fuse into four extraordinarily powerful Y-shaped columns without, and cantilever at the ends in an impressive act of concrete engineering. As one progresses into the terminal, the changes of level play an important visual role. Moving up a broad flight of low steps to the departure area, one formerly found a climax in the red-carpeted "conversation pit" placed in front of and just below those headed for their planes, but this seating has been removed and the floor level raised. Overhead near the center of the terminal an angled bridge connects the upper sections of the two ends (restaurants), adding another three-dimensional element to this vast room, one that ranks among the most spirited spaces of our time.

Expansion of flight facilities has proved difficult with the unexpected acceleration of air traffic, but with few exceptions the architects, engineers, and TWA have achieved a beautifully constructed terminal. It is a major adventure into an architectural direction that is always dangerous but here so exciting that it gives its client identity, and—more importantly—delights cash customers. Kevin Roche was co-designer; Ammann & Whitney were engineers. A pedestrian shelter 330 x 22 feet/101 x 6.7 meters was added to the roadway in front in 1978. This concrete and Plexiglas canopy efficiently separates and shelters arriving and departing passengers while being respectful of the terminal. Witthoefft & Rudolph were the architects. The TWA Flight Center was designated a New York City Landmark in 1994.

JFK Airport is located southeast of New York City via the Van Wyck Expressway. Open daily 24 hours. AF 1/58, AF 8/60, AF 12/60, AF 7/62, AR 7/62, AD 10/62, PA 10/62, Int 7/64, JAIA 2/78, A 5/88, PA 5/92

DULLES AIRPORT (1958–62/1979–)
Chantilly, Virginia

Eero Saarinen & Associates, architects
Hellmuth, Obata & Kassabaum and Skidmore, Owings & Merrill,
architects of the expansions

Dulles Airport is the most stupendous architectural statement on the North American land-scape. This breathtaking structure marked a new era in the analysis of passenger-to-plane logistics, that hitherto curiously forgotten facet of air travel. For at Dulles, the myriad "fingers" of conventional airport design—those endless, wearisome corridors down which thousands eternally trudge—have been eliminated. Instead, an airport bus draws up to the terminal, the passengers walk no more than 150 feet/46 meters to a check-in station on the far side, and there board a mobile lounge that attaches to the building. They are then whisked to the plane on the airstrip. No jostling passengers, no juggling or expensive taxiing of jet planes. The building acts as a brief staging point, not a dumping ground; the bus is now architecture—a beautifully analyzed concept.

448

As one nears the terminal, one encounters the first problem with which the architect, like so many other architects, had to contend: facing north, the entire entrance side stands in shade almost all day long. Nevertheless, the scale of the 65-foot-/20-meter-high entry has great power. (It does not, however, provide any weather protection or adequate covered parking.)

The structure of Dulles is based on heavily reinforced concrete piers, sixteen per side, 65 feet/20 meters high in front, 40 feet/12 meters at back, and spaced 40 feet/12 meters apart for a total length of 600 feet/183 meters. From edge beams that connect each of the two lines of piers laterally are slung steel cables 1 inch/25 millimeters in diameter, and from these are hung 1,792 precast concrete panels, each weighing 800 pounds/363 kilograms. The thirty-two piers incline outward to counteract the roof load. (The rods that connect the piers laterally and from which the hammock roof is slung, are, contrary to appearances, not on the upper face or fascia, but at that inner point on the rear faces of the piers just behind the holes where piers and roof deck first meet.)

On stepping inside the terminal, early anticipation tends to falter, for the space proclaimed by the exterior fades as the sizable central spine of ticket offices, shops, and services blocks a full grasp of the inner volume. It is a noble frame that services tend to weaken. Moreover, glimpses of the catenary of the roof visually resting on the top of this spine are uncomfortable. The spine itself is characterized by the late Eero Saarinen's admirable attention to detail. The usual clutter of newspaper stands is cleverly masked behind partitions, the shops are restrained, the stainless steel and leather bench-chairs (by Charles Eames) have become classics. In spite of the above criticism, the room is eminently graspable, bright, and sunny.

The airport thus both thrills—it is unforgettable from a distance at dusk—yet can disappoint within when its promised sweep of space does not materialize. But even with the above reservations, Dulles ranks among the great buildings of our time. Ammann & Whitney were engineers; Dan Kiley was landscape architect.

Dulles was planned before the advent of jumbo jets carrying some 350 passengers, and before the need for strict security measures. Both of these conditions have thus somewhat compromised the airport's original flow of operations. In spring 1978 plans were announced for a substantial expansion on the field side of the terminal, with Hellmuth, Obata & Kassabaum as architects. The gates where passengers originally entered the mobile lounges (for example, the lower part of the south wall) have been removed at the east half and a 50-foot-/15-meter-wide, same-level, six-bay lounge departure station has been created (1979–80). (This abuts the side of the center projecting wing that houses the restaurant and services.) Baggage handling and mechanical services are placed directly underneath this extension (and below grade), out of sight and weatherproof. In 1991 an international arrivals building just west of the main terminal was opened; Skidmore, Owings & Merrill were the architects. These two lengthy rooms were kept purposefully low so as not to impinge on the profile of the terminal's exterior. New "planemates," carrying up to one hundred passengers, supplement the earlier mobile lounges. Both can, of course, deliver and pick up passengers at the several entries of the large planes, not simply through the nose door.

Another expansion of the airport was commenced in 1994 with completion scheduled for 1996—Skidmore, Owings & Merrill, architects. The main terminal building is being extended linearly by adding a 320-foot/97-meter matching wing to each end—much as Saarinen suggested—more than doubling the original length. The new west wing will connect the main terminal to the previously freestanding international arrivals building. Permanent midfield concourses are currently being designed, to be built within the next few years.

Located off exit 12 from Beltway (I-495) to Dulles Access Road, or I-66 to Dulles Access Road about 30 miles/48 kilometers west of Washington, D.C. Open daily 24 hours. Tours for groups of 10 or more can be arranged by calling (703) 661–2710. AF 7/63, AR 7/63, PA 8/63, JAIA 7/66, JAIA 11/80, AR 7/81, PA 3/87, A 5/88, A 11/93

BETH SHOLOM SYNAGOGUE (1959)
8231 Old York Road at Foxcroft Road
Elkins Park, Pennsylvania

Frank Lloyd Wright, architect

Crowning its hill and dominating it by day like some gigantic biblical tent perched on a
Pennsylvania Sinai, shining forth at dusk through its translucent roof, Beth Sholom—House
of Peace—commands all approaches, day and night. The structure of the building is based on
an equilateral triangle with a heavy, concrete, parallelogram-shaped pier anchoring each point.
The mighty ridge beams, which rise from the three points, lean inward as they rise from their
foundations to their truncated pinnacle, producing a towering monumentality. The panels of
these roof-walls are double-thick with wired glass on the exterior and plastic within forming,
so to speak, a translucent tent, "a lighted mountain." (Frank Lloyd Wright's original sketch was
less open.) The seven crockets that uphold this fabric recall the seven-branch menorah, hence
the seven days of the creation. The "tent" rests on an angled tan concrete base with symbolic
laver at entrance. One reaches the sanctuary via either of two straight flights of steps, angled
like the facade, an arrangement carefully calculated to permit tantalizing views upward under
the magnetic canopy of the roof. This entry epitomizes Wright's concern for three-dimensional exploration, space and light having always characterized his architecture. The focus of
this journey—the sanctuary—possibly does not altogether match the brilliance of the exterior
(what could?). There is, however, a spiritual magnificence in this great translucid prism—
Wright's "Manlight." A chapel and lounges fill the lower floor. Rabbi Mortimer J. Cohen of
Beth Sholom worked closely with Wright in developing the basic concept.

Located on Old York Road (US 611) just north of Church Road, about 11 miles/18 kilometers north of downtown Philadelphia.
Saturday services held at 9:30 A.M. Free tours given Monday–Wednesday 11:00 A.M.–3:00 P.M., Sunday 9:00 A.M.–1:00 P.M. No
tours given on holidays. Tours must be scheduled in advance by calling (215) 887–1342. AF 6/59

ROOFLESS CHURCH (1959–60)
North Street at Main Street
New Harmony, Indiana

Philip Johnson, architect

Weather can be a problem, and services difficult, however there is little question but that one can commune more intimately with heaven in a roofless church than in one hammered over by man. The silent, crumbling walls of Tewksbury and the half-blitzed old St. Michael's leading to the new Coventry Cathedral both provide spiritual experiences of the highest order—and do not, likewise, the awesome pylons of Stonehenge? So it is here in New Harmony. Philip Johnson has created his open "church" wrapped within a 12-foot-/3.6-meter-high brick wall, 231.9 feet/71 meters long by 127.5 feet/39 meters wide and then punctuated it with a softly undulating yet mathematical sanctuary of impeccable inspiration. 50 feet/15 meters high and covered with cedar shingles over laminated wood arch frame, the shrine's profile is based vertically on a parabola, while its lateral undulations stem directly from a plan of six circles interlocked with a central seventh, all identical in diameter. At the intersection points of the peripheral circles are placed six ovoid limestone "piers," 4 feet/1.2 meters high, on which the arches of the sanctuary rest. The convoluted geometry—vaguely suggestive of a Buddhist stupa—hovers compassionately over the Jacques Lipchitz's bronze *Virgin* in the center, a Virgin faceless for self-effacement. Lipchitz also created the strikingly handsome, gilded ceremonial gate (1962) at the east end, with five sculptured wreaths, the topmost of which, with the Lamb of God inside, is supported by angels. (The day-to-day entrance is via a gate in the south wall.) Just inside the processional gate lies the narthex, framed by trees. A giant golden rain tree dominates one side of the nave. The balcony on the north wall, its opening "remembering" the world outside, is overly framed in semi-Classic fashion, but this small detail is soon forgotten in the aura of a profound religious shelter. The shrine was made possible by a grant from the Robert Lee Blaffer Trust.

Open daily dawn–dusk. AF 9/60

Just opposite the processional gate stands the Paul Johannes Tillich Memorial Park (1966), designed by Zion & Breen as landscape architects with James Rosati, sculptor. It should also be seen.

ANNUNCIATION GREEK ORTHODOX CHURCH (1959–61)
9400 West Congress Street at North 92nd Street
Milwaukee, Wisconsin

Frank Lloyd Wright, architect

The problem of establishing for today a valid exterior and a proper interior setting for the Greek Orthodox Church presents an architect with a difficult task. Most observers will respond favorably to the Byzantine-influenced exterior, inner iconography, and golden setting that Frank Lloyd Wright and his associates have achieved in this Milwaukee suburb. In any case, scale, color, relationships of parts to the whole, lighting, and decoration demand firsthand experience. The exterior suggests, of course, that Greek Mother Church, Hagia Sophia (A.D. 532–37) in Istanbul, Turkey—the most audacious building in the history of architecture—which the Emperor Justinian commissioned, and of which he reputedly said on entering for the first time, "I have surpassed even thee, O Solomon!" Wright had long admired the Byzantine: "I was thrilled by Mayan, Incan and Egyptian remains, loved the Byzantine" (*A Testament*, Horizon Press, 1957). The blue-tiled dome of the Milwaukee church, incidentally, is at 104 feet/32 meters in diameter just 3 feet/.9 meter smaller (but much shallower) than that topping Santa Sophia. (In 1995 a seven-foot cross covered with gold leaf was added on the exterior, atop the dome.) Its structure employs not only a dome on top but an inverted counter-dome or bowl on bottom, the two cupped together. Their roof is surrounded by a scaled series of lunettes that progress from small on the eaves edge, to medium in the band of windows, to bay-size at entry.

On the interior this interlocked circular and semicircular geometry almost erupts. This begins with the plan itself, which expands from a small inner circle containing nave and chancel to a large, upper "nave" for the majority of the congregation. This elevated ring of five banks of walnut seats with blue cushions overlooks the sanctuary, almost like a cockpit. The inner curve of the upper section is broken by the counter-curves of the stairwells down to the small, main nave. A reredos and chancel screen of uninhibited color and complexity provide the focus.

Located west from downtown on WIS 190, north on 92nd. All visits are guided and must be scheduled in advance. Tours given Tuesday–Friday 9:00 A.M.–2:30 P.M. Closed on holidays. The cost is $2. Tours available only for groups of 15 or more (individuals may join an already scheduled tour). For more information call (414) 461–9400. AF 12/61, SAHJ 3/72

ARBORETUM (1959–61)
(formerly Garden Grove Community Church)
12141 Lewis Street
Garden Grove, California

Richard J. Neutra & Associates, architects

The Garden Grove Community Church began as a worship-in-your-car church—useful for families with babies, the poor of dress, and the many disabled and indisposed of this retirement area. It blossomed with Richard Neutra's ingenious outdoor-indoor solution. The nave has pews for 1,700 while 1,400 persons in as many as 600 automobiles fan in a semicircle about the balcony so that they can see the minister and follow the service via speakers that hang from the driver's side car window—the kind used in drive-in movie theaters. (Most of the east wall of the church is also openable.) Sixteen steel bents form the frame of the nave, with natural stone making a chancel wall. The church has been expanded several times; the fifteen-story Tower of Hope for classrooms and offices was added in 1968. Dion Neutra was the project architect. Construction was begun in 1978 for the adjacent Crystal Cathedral (see page 608).

Located south of Los Angeles, immediately north of CA 22 and west of I-5. Open daily 9:00 A.M.–4:30 P.M. Closed New Year's Day, Labor Day, Thanksgiving, and Christmas. Sunday services held at 9:30 and 11:00 A.M. Tours given every 45 minutes Monday–Saturday 9:00 A.M.–3:30 P.M.; a tour is also given after the Sunday 11:00 A.M. service. Admission and tours are free although a donation is suggested. For general information call (714) 971-4000; for tour information call (714) 971-4013. A+A 7/62, JAIA 5/79

FOOTHILL COLLEGE (1959–61)
12345 El Monte Road
Los Altos Hills, California

Ernest J. Kump and Masten & Hurd, architects

The forty-four buildings of Foothill College epitomize the classic California pavilion layout. As such they have deservedly exerted enormous influence on instructional building. The architecture at times approaches the overly picturesque, yet the basic plan, the astute rationalizing of construction on modular lines, and the total ambiance are exemplary. Moreover, the college is knit together and fortified by possibly the finest campus landscaping that one will see. The brilliant planning of the 122-acre/49-hectare site can be seen in the fact that the campus proper is built on two plateaus, with 3,000–4,000 automobiles parked about the low periphery of the mesas on which the college rests. No vehicles, except for service, are allowed on the campus; they are not even visible from it. The slight undulations and configurations of the hill topography have been employed for optimum utilization with relatively little earth moving necessary.

Foothill was designed to give two years of instruction to day and evening students; in 1995 there were approximately 13,000 students altogether. In addition, its cultural facilities, particularly the 1,000-seat theater and the gymnasium (both near parking lots) are also used by the community. The buildings are grouped in clusters according to function, with teaching units at west, library near the center, then administration, theater, and campus center. The physical education plant is on a hill by itself, reached by a short bridge. Though in design they are relaxed just short of folksiness, they are based on a very hardheaded, economical yet flexible module of reinforced concrete frame and redwood walls; almost all buildings use a 60 x 68-foot/18 x 21-meter "space module" that can be subdivided at any 4-foot/1.2-meter point. A variety of sizes—from library to teaching units—are accommodated by this structural system, simplifying and speeding erection while simultaneously developing esthetic homogeneity but not monotony. In general appearance Foothill looks like a well-knit, one-story, educational village with a friendly residential scale of vaguely Japanese ancestry. The wide overhangs of all buildings serve as outdoor corridors (there are no inner ones) creating a continuity (plus some exposure during the brief rainy season). The outdoor spaces vary from the intimate courtyards adjacent to most class units to rolling vistas across the campus. The landscaping—by Sasaki, Walker & Associates—is not only superb visually, it is also functional in defining circulation routes by its artificial berms and hills. A wonderfully attractive campus.

Located immediately west of I-280. Grounds and buildings open daily (building hours vary). Closed for holidays. Free tours can be scheduled by calling the Student Activities Office at (415) 949–7282. For general information call (415) 949–7777. AF 11/59, PA 11/60, AF 2/62, PA 9/62, PA 6/73

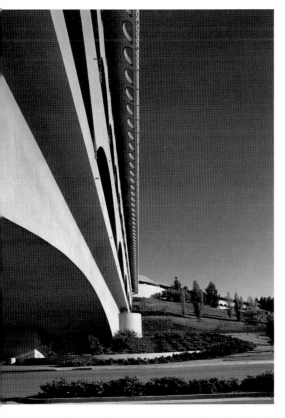

MARIN COUNTY CIVIC CENTER
(1959–62/1967–69)
Civic Center Drive
San Rafael, California

Frank Lloyd Wright and Taliesin
Associates, architects

Striding across the landscape like the Pont du Gard, the famous Roman aqueduct (19 B.C.) in the south of France, with its tiers of arches (here oblate) marching over hill and dale, the Marin County Civic Center is the most spectacular civic building in the country. (The Pont du Gard is prominently shown in Frank Lloyd Wright's last—and much recommended—book, *Architecture, Man in Possession of His Earth*, Doubleday, 1962.) Wright's noted solicitude for the landscape produced a fascinating intimacy between structure and site; the uniform-ridged building increases its depth in the valleys and cuts it on the rises to reflect the waves of topography (both natural and artificial). The straight "keels" of the roof seem to slash across the rolling hills of the backdrop. Three tunnels for automotive traffic pierce its base, adding spatial punch. The arch over these roadways is then repeated (with slightly less radius) on the first or main floor, where its curves leap in series from one end of the building to the other, shielding as they go a continuous balcony on each side. The second floor is screened by similar arches, but each a third the span of that below (and again of less radius); the top floor is marked by a continuous series of circles, two circles for each arc below, and, like the floors beneath, with balconies running along the outside. (The arch spring points form sixty-degree triangles.) The eaves are edged with open half circles; the prominently haunched blue roof rising behind is itself decorated with circular patterns around its perimeter. A 217-foot/66-meter pylon (with boiler stack inside) punctuates the midpoint of the two arms. Altogether the exterior of the Marin Civic Center is a sight of almost nacreous splendor with its shell-colored walls, blue roof, and pink and gold accents. However, as there is no structural expression in its series of metal lath and stucco, bowed and circular arcades—this would of course impinge on their rhythm—a slight impression of impermanence results; from some angles they seem thin and temporary. It should be added that the building acts somewhat as a conduit, with little invitation to enter—or even to identify the front door.

The plan of the building is based on a long, central, sky-lit corridor lined on both sides with various offices, flexibly partitioned. (The first unit was the 570-foot-/174-meter-long Administration Building; the second—by Taliesin Associates—the 800-foot-/244-meter-long Hall of Justice.) A near-continuous acrylic skylight runs most of the length of each wing, sending floods of ever-changing sunshine into the balconied corridors below. The upper passageways are narrower than the lower (reflecting their decreased traffic load); hence the open hall is wider as it rises and permits maximum sun and light to probe the floors below and to nourish its garden. The space and light of this central spine are architecturally unforgettable.

From the entrance level (a short utility floor) one takes an escalator or elevator to tax and auditing services on the second floor, or to administration and public works on the third floor; other departments are on the top floor together with the near-circular library under the central dome. All civic functions are placed in this wing while the courtrooms are in the Hall of Justice. (The drawings for the Administration Building had been completed just before Wright's death in 1959. An extensive complex for other municipal functions was built, including a community theater, an exhibit hall, meeting rooms, and a two-thousand-seat Veterans' Memorial Auditorium in 1972.)

There are Arabian Nights, dreamworld overtones in the Marin County Civic Center—influenced by the cultural center, topped by an abstraction of Aladdin's lamp, that Wright planned for Baghdad, Iraq (1957–58)—and some of the civic center's features are puzzling. But take a look: it is totally extraordinary. William Wesley Peters of Taliesin Architects was in charge of completing the first stage of the center and of designing the rest. Aaron G. Green was associate architect.

Located east off US 101 on San Pedro Road, 1.5 miles/2.4 kilometers north of San Rafael exit. Open Monday–Friday 7:00 A.M.–6:00 P.M. Closed for holidays. Guided tours given Tuesday–Friday at 10:30 A.M. at the gift shop on the second floor; the cost is $1 for adults, free for students and children. Tours can also be arranged by calling (415) 472-7470. AF 11/62, ARev 2/63, AF 12/70, JAIA 4/80, AR 11/91

ANNUNCIATION PRIORY (1959–63)
7520 University Drive
Bismarck, North Dakota

Marcel Breuer, architect

The Annunciation Priory of the Sisters of St. Benedict, plus its nearby affiliate the University of Mary, constitute one of the major and best architectural groups in the country concerned with Roman Catholic religion and education. Located near the top of a rolling site overlooking the Missouri River, the two establishments occupy opposite sides of a hill, out of sight of each other but only a few minutes' walk away. They are powerful, assertive buildings, striding over the landscape rather than emerging from it, but affiliated with their setting by their judicious incorporation of local stone.

The priory is marked by a three-dimensional, 100-foot-/30-meter-high bell banner, which recalls the one by the same architects at St. John's University Church in Collegeville, Minnesota (see page 434). It gives a needed vertical accent to the landscape and to the long, low building mass, and was designed to be seen from any angle. The basically symmetrical priory rises behind, its four main units set parallel to each other, forming a modified H shape connected across top, middle, and bottom by passages. The long three-story residence wings (the vertical legs of the H) frame and enclose the compound on the two sides, that for the nuns (at west) containing private rooms and a similar one at east providing a residence hall for women plus classrooms. In between these wings stand the tall block of the chapel, the priory's spiritual and physical center, and another unit containing dining hall, services, and a small chapel. The three courtyards between the four independent but attached buildings are paved to serve as sheltered, outdoor sitting areas. All four buildings are connected by a central transverse hall (the bar of the H plan) wide enough to contain lounges and offices, while across the front, and

connecting the ends of the two residence units, marches a covered walk whose *V* supports produce structural rhythm.

The public enters the chapel via a court between this "cloister" and the transverse hall mentioned. The chapel's interior is dominated by the strong geometry of its hyperbolic, white-painted, concrete ceiling, while its side walls toward the front are of colored *betonglass* (thick chunks of glass set in mortar) and white-painted stone (at rear). Focus is given the chancel by a gold-leaf reredos and a double-curved canopy (of plywood) cantilevered from the wall behind the reredos. The choir stalls are placed at right angles to the axis of the chapel and are divided into facing halves to facilitate the responsive chanting by the sisters. The other pews are supplemented by seats in the balcony to accommodate a total of five hundred. The community and recreation room for the sisters, projecting from the northwest corner, is particularly satisfactory.

Keen recognition of an often severe climate can be seen in the sheltered courtyards, covered walkways, and deeply recessed windows. Details, especially the use of color, are first-rate throughout. Hamilton P. Smith and Traynor & Hermanson were associated architects.

Located 7 miles/11 kilometers south of downtown via 9th Street, past airport on ND 1804. Priory open daily 9:00 A.M.–8:00 P.M. Tours can be arranged by calling (701) 255–1520. Tours of all the Breuer buildings on the University of Mary campus are given Monday–Friday 9:00 A.M.–4:30 P.M.; call (701) 255–7500 for more information. AR 4/56, AR 1/61, AR 12/63, AR 11/69

ASSEMBLY HALL (1959–63)
University of Illinois
1800 South 1st Street at Kirby and 4th streets
Champaign, Illinois

Harrison & Abramovitz, architects
Ammann & Whitney, engineers

The structure of this powerful, ingenious, multipurpose assembly hall is superbly expressed outside and in. In simplistic terms, the hall is composed of two bowls, a roof bowl over a seat bowl, each 400 feet/122 meters in diameter, the inverted, domical upper one resting on the upturned and straight-angled lower, creating an interior completely free of columns. (The lower bowl is partially set into the ground to provide midpoint access to the seats.) The assembly dome is, indeed, the mightiest in the world.

The upper dome sends out "fingers" of branching folds toward the perimeter. The folds of the roof not only provide greater strength (like folding a sheet of paper), they add greatly to the appearance, outside as well as within, where they also aid in the acoustics. The perimeter compression ring is post-tensioned by 2,467 laps of high-tension wire to contain the thrust. The roof load is then transferred via forty-eight radial buttresses to the ring footings of the foundations. The average thickness of the concrete in the dome is only 3.5 inches/89 millimeters with a further 2 inches/51 millimeters acoustic material added. Inasmuch as the upper half is supported by the inward-canted buttresses of the lower, and not by external vertical columns, the whole hall rests lightly on the horizon like some gigantic spaceship. The shell exhibits magnificent coordination between architect and engineer; nothing should be added, nothing could be taken away—it is theory defined. A glass-enclosed concourse, reached by six external ramps, provides access to the hall; this annular concourse is sufficiently wide to double as an exhibition area. All services are below.

The interior forms a dazzling, unencumbered space, 128 feet/39 meters high and, as mentioned, 400 feet/122 meters in diameter. Note the excellent scale of the ribbing of the roof. The hall accommodates ice shows, basketball games, and convocations—"any type of event that might appear on a stage." Capacity varies from 3,500 to 15,823 on permanent seats with 1,400 extra on portable chairs. Since the building of the nearby Krannert Center, the Assembly Hall is used primarily for large-scale events. The mechanics of the light ring and "grid" are complex, but overall this intriguing campus magnet is superb. Max Abramovitz was partner in charge; Abe Feder, lighting consultant; Bolt, Beranek & Newman, acoustic consultants.

Open Monday–Friday 8:00 A.M.–5:00 P.M. Also open some evenings for events. Closed for holidays; sometimes closed on days of major events. Free tours can be scheduled by calling (217) 333–2923. AF 3/63, AR 7/63, JAIA 7/64

PARADISE STEAM PLANT (1959–70)
Highway 176
Paradise, Kentucky

Tennessee Valley Authority, architects and engineers

Constructivist sculpture is now working with forms so large that much of it has to be shown out of doors. It is doubtful, however, that the work of any artist in this field can approach the esthetic impact of the Paradise Steam Plant. Three enormous hyperbolic cooling towers stand 437 feet/133 meters high with base diameter of 320 feet/98 meters and strictly mathematical profiles—their curves are straight-line generated. Together, they produce a mighty geometric interplay with three venting chimneys (the tallest is 800 feet/244 meters in height) whose tops are painted in alternate bands of red and white for airplane visibility. Against these major elements, a secondary, eerily horizontal composition of brown-painted, elevated conveyors—which feed coal to the boilers—adds an almost surrealist touch. The first two generating units were constructed in 1959–63; construction of the third unit began in 1965 and when completed in 1970, Paradise became the largest steam-generating plant in the world with a total capacity of 2,558,000 kilowatts. It is also one of the country's great architectural/engineering achievements, sculpture on perhaps an ultimate scale.

The plant was located atop extensive coal beds, the coal obtained by the stripping process. (Today the coal is supplied by a number of companies in the area.) The stripping shovels are, according to the brochure, "the largest self-propelled land vehicles in history, and can scoop up, swing, and dump a third of a million pounds [151,000 metric tons] of earth at a time."

Located 7 miles/11 kilometers southeast of Central City on US 431 to Drakesboro, then about 7 miles/11 kilometers northeast to Paradise. Some facilities open to the public Monday–Friday 7:00 A.M.–3:30 P.M. Closed for holidays. Free group tours can be arranged by calling (502) 476-3300. LA 4/72

MUNSON-WILLIAMS-PROCTOR INSTITUTE (1960)
310 Genesee Street
Utica, New York

Philip Johnson
Associates, architects

The Munson-Williams-Proctor Institute is a windowless, granite-clad box (atop a glass-lined basement), square in plan and broken externally only by its bronze-wrapped, structural exo-frame. On entering this slightly austere building, however, one is pulled forward from the low doorway into a double-height Renaissance *cortile* sparkling with sunshine that pours through its 121 coffered plastic domes by day, and that is ablaze from artificial lights by night. This unexpected spatial effervescence creates an ingratiating introduction to the art, highlighted by pieces of sculpture. Smaller galleries, basically for temporary exhibitions, open off of the main floor; one takes an elevator or the meticulously detailed double stairs to visit the main galleries above. There two lateral galleries—suspended from the structural frame—open directly onto a courtyard from opposite sides, furnishing orientation and vantage points for viewing court exhibitions and thus participating in the free volume of the museum. The major exhibition spaces—not immediately apparent—run across the front and back of the building. Windowless, they can be partitioned as desired. A 271-seat auditorium, staff offices, and services, accessible from the rear, occupy the lowest floor, which would be partially underground except for the sloping site and the fact that a dry moat encircles the building. Though at times rigid, the building is full of expertise. It has, indeed, been called "the perfect professional museum" (*Architectural Forum*, December 1960). Bice & Baird were supervising architects; Lev Zetlin structural engineer.

In 1994–95 an addition designed by Lund, McGee, Sharpe was constructed. It consists of an underground art storage area, office spaces, and an indoor walkway connecting the museum building with Fountain Elms (1850), the former home of the founders of the Munson-Williams-Proctor Institute, which is today used to display the museum's decorative arts collection.

Open Tuesday–Saturday 10:00 A.M.–5:00 P.M., Sunday 1:00–5:00 P.M. Closed for major holidays. Admission is free. Tours can be scheduled by calling (315) 797–0000. AF 12/60, ARev 3/62

CLIMATRON (1960/1990)
Missouri Botanical Garden (Shaw's Garden)
4344 Shaw Boulevard
St. Louis, Missouri

Murphy & Mackey, architects

The Climatron, a web of simple glass panes and intricate aluminum struts, provides an ideal canopy over an array of tropical plants. Buckminster Fuller's geodesic principles have been put to maximum advantage in creating this shelter, which is 175 feet/53 meters in diameter and 70 feet/21 meters high, forming a low vault that rests on five concrete piers. The components that make up the hexagonal exoskeletal framing of the Climatron are composed of aluminum tubes in two planes, approximately 30 inches/76 centimeters apart, connected by aluminum rods to make a triangulated truss. The skin of 2425 panes of heat-strengthened glass, containing an ultra-violet screening, plastic interlayer, is coated with a low-emissivity film to retain solar energy. The climate control maintains a tropical temperature from 64° to 85° F (18–29° C). There are more than 1100 different species of tropical plants inside; they include banana, cacao, coffee, orchids, and exotic, rare plants such as the double coconut. There are even several waterfalls; one is forty feet/twelve meters high.

The original Climatron (pictured here) used lightweight Plexiglas instead of glass sheathing and was climatically and vegetatively divided into four temperate zones instead of one tropical zone. (All except the aluminum exoskeletal frame were replaced during the recent renovation.) Dr. Frits W. Went, the Director of the Garden in 1960, developed the plan and the air-conditioning zoning with the architects. For the building's design, Murphy & Mackey was the first American architectural firm to receive the R. S. Reynolds Memorial Award in Architecture (1961). Synergetics, Inc. was the structural engineers. The adjacent Shoenberg Temperate House exhibits temperate-zone species; the Brookings Interpretive Center (both buildings 1990 by the Christner Partnership) contains non-living and multi-media exhibits.

Open 9:00 A.M.–8:00 P.M. in summer; 9:00 A.M.–5:00 P.M. the rest of the year. Admission is $3 for adults, $1.50 for senior citizens, free for children 12 and under. For more information call (800) 642–8842 or (314) 577–5400. PA 4/61, JAIA 5/61, A 3/89

MARINA CITY (1960–62)
300 North State Street at Chicago River
Chicago, Illinois

Bertrand Goldberg Associates, architects

The observer of these two fantastic towers will certainly be impressed by their appearance. But even more important is the architect's acute analysis of the specific problem—and even the future of the metropolis. Bertrand Goldberg writes, "We cannot burden business buildings used 35 hours a week or apartment buildings used at night and over weekends with our total tax loads. We can no longer subsidize the single shift use of our expensive city utilities. In our cities within cities we shall turn our streets up into the air, and stack the daytime and night-time uses of our land. We shall plan for two shifts within cities, where the fixed costs of operating a city can be shared by commerce, recreation, and education at the lower levels . . . and by housing above. As we spread taxes and other expenses over shared uses, we help diminish the traffic problem caused by the trip to work. Our specialists living and working in the same building complex need only vertical transportation" (*Architectural Record*, September 1963). Thus the concept and design of Marina City began with the time clock ticking off occupancy hours and the tax burden applied to multiple use, aspects that too few architects and developers consider.

Goldberg has, of course, arrived at a microcosm of the city wherein one lives and works, finds recreation and exercise, shops and dines, and parks one's car, all without leaving the premises, or even going outdoors. Whereas a few of the architectural details might be questioned, the concept is brilliant. (One wonders whether this multiple-use notion was not subliminally sparked by the Auditorium Building of Adler & Sullivan, see page 284, who in 1889 combined office building with hotel and theater.)

Placed on the edge of the Chicago River and within a few hundred yards of Lake Michigan, near the spot where the city was founded as a trading post, Marina City obviously occupies a strategic and expensive piece of real estate. Most of the important functions of the city, whether business or pleasure, are within a few minutes' walk. When one adds to this convenience the project's own attractions, the imagination of both architect and client becomes clear. (The client was the Building Maintenance Employees International Union, which conceived the idea of downtown housing and which helped finance it.) The specific site—once covered with railroad tracks—was spotted by the architect five years earlier.

The twin towers rise sixty stories and number among the highest concrete buildings in the world. The lower nineteen floors are devoted to open spiral ramps on which attendants park the automobiles belonging to the 896 apartments that sprout above for forty floors. Laundry and storage facilities are placed in the area between cars and apartments. A sixteen-story office block stands on the north side of the site; a television station, theater, exhibition hall, an extensive series of shops, service facilities, ice-skating rink, and restaurant once occupied its base, but these commercial spaces—and the marina—currently await redevelopment.

The construction of the circular towers was based on a core of reinforced concrete, about which the apartments, like petals on a daisy, fan out—"kinetic space," as the architect calls it. Each of these great utility/transportation cylinders, which are 35 feet/10.7 meters in diameter, was erected first and the ramps for cars and floors for the apartments poured later, the overall diameter being 105 feet/32 meters. The circular construction reduced wind loads, shortened utility runs, and produced an excellent ratio of floor space to exterior wall.

The building's round plan readily enables it to be divided into apartments from one-bay, or one petal, efficiencies (256 units), to one-and-one-half-bay, one-bedroom apartments (576

units), to two-and-one-half-bay, two-bedroom apartments (64 units), the latter occupying the 53rd to 60th floors. The project was planned to attract single tenants and small families. The slightly pie-shaped plan of each apartment provides a maximum of glass and light and a minimum of back wall. The semicircular balconies, approximately 20 feet/6.1 meters wide (except for half bays) and 10 feet/3 meters deep, form small open-air rooms. Besides providing a private aerie they are useful for shielding the glass from the high sun, for window washing, exterior painting, and maintenance for the unit air conditioners above each door. (Unit air conditioners are more economical for the mixed uses of the building.) The innermost space of the apartment is occupied by the kitchen and bath. Electric heat is used throughout; the heat from lighting fixtures provides a major source, particularly in the office building.

From the critical point of view, the towers are perhaps a bit close together for as much privacy as one might like, but at 70-foot/21-meter separation—the width of many streets—one could scarce ask for more space for in-town living. The whale-backed, lead-sheathed auditorium elbows its way into the plaza too forcefully, cramping an already crowded area. But if its expression is slightly uneven in spots, still Marina City stands as a brilliant, pioneering prototype for today's midcity living. Moreover it is an urban solution, not an urban problem-maker—as most gigantic buildings are. Because its lowest apartment is twenty-one floors above the street, there is far less dirt and noise than in typical apartment blocks, while conversely there are spectacular views of Lake Michigan and half the city at one's feet. Commuting time is only a short walk for most, one's car is just downstairs, and amusement, cultural fabric, shopping, and exercise facilities were intended to be a mere elevator ride away. What more can the central city provide?

Lobby open to the public. The building is included on the Chicago Architecture Foundation's river cruise tour; the cost is $15 on weekdays, $17 on weekends. For more information on CAF tours call (312) 922–3432. AR 9/63, AF 4/65, AR 10/65, AR 12/65

EZRA STILES AND MORSE COLLEGES (1960–62)
Yale University
Broadway at Tower Parkway
New Haven, Connecticut

Eero Saarinen & Associates, architects

Unlike Renaissance buildings, whose facades can be grasped from a one-point perspective, Ezra Stiles and Morse Colleges demand that the viewer move about them to realize their progression of spaces. They do not proclaim their existence, they unfurl it. This space-time aspect—Le Corbusier's "architectural promenade"—can make a stimulating venture. If the backdrop here appears medieval, this evolved because Saarinen sought to tie his group to John Russell Pope's potent Neo-Gothic Payne-Whitney Gymnasium tower (1930) at one visual terminus, with James Gamble Rogers's Neo-Gothic Hall of Graduate Studies (1930) at the other. A well-scaled conspiracy of four buildings—two old, two new—results; the passage connecting them numbers among the country's most subtle developments of open-air linear footage. As one walks through this spatial conduit, snatches of towers (old and new) appear above, while at eye level bits of strategically placed sculpture and reliefs by Costantino Nivola enliven the *passeggiata*. Throughout, angled walls of stone and concrete (walls made by dumping loose stones in grout) jump in and out of sun and shadow. This excursion does not, however, constitute the total architectural interest; it is only one of them.

Each college provides accommodations for 250 students (mostly in single rooms), a master's residence, and an excellent dining room with a single, underground, connecting kitchen. From the exterior many of the students' rooms seem to lack sufficient windows, but in actuality few do (and those mostly north-facing). The chief student complaint centers on the inadequacy of common areas and lounges. Though some observers believe that Saarinen went too far with his stage-set Neo-Medievalism, there are lessons here.

Courtyards and lobbies open to the public in the daytime during the school year. Tours of the Yale campus can be scheduled by calling Campus Tours at (203) 432–2300. AR 2/60, AF 12/62, AR 12/62

CATHOLIC PASTORAL CENTER (1960–63)
(formerly Home Federal Savings & Loan Association)
601 Grand Avenue at 6th Street
Des Moines, Iowa

Mies van der Rohe & Associates, architects

Mies, some admirers believe, was better in the singular than the plural, an exquisite exception being his identical-twin apartment houses at 860–880 Lake Shore Drive in Chicago (see page 401). Here in Des Moines he is singularly good. This three-story, prismatic building, measuring 121.9 feet/37 meters square in plan and encased in dark glass (upper floors) and dark metal, has been distilled to pure elegance. Much of its delight comes from the fact that the ground floor has been recessed on all four sides so that space is captured by the column-framed passages on each flank, allowing a penetration that reaches intensity at the corners. The building, thus, rests lightly on its setback site, fingers of three-dimensionality intertwining with the structure. The two- and three-module recess of the entry side (on Grand Avenue) also enhances the broad plaza space in front—and vice versa—where trees, grass plots, and a subtle bench enter the scene. The ground floor interior forms one well-mannered space 14.7 feet/4.5 meters high, largely walled in clear glass, and understated in its Attic propriety. Its detailing, like that throughout the building—and any of Mies's buildings—is impeccable. A community room, kitchen, and services fill the basement; the first floor is used for meetings and receptions while the second and third floors are offices. Smith-Vorhees-Jensen were associate architects.

Open Monday–Friday 8:30 A.M.–4:30 P.M. Closed for holidays. Free tours can be arranged by calling (515) 243-7653. AF 9/63, AD 1/64

GUILD HOUSE (1960–65)
711 Spring Garden Street near 7th Street
Philadelphia, Pennsylvania

Venturi & Rauch, architects

Here is no routine building; nor is its designer—Robert Venturi—a routine architect. Venturi's thesis is that "Boring is Interesting and [the] Extraordinary is Ordinary," a philosophy allied to the Pop Art approach that seeks to "reveal" the "dumb and ordinary" about us. He is, as Vincent Scully writes, "consistently anti-heroic...the essential point is that Venturi's philosophy and design are humanistic." Venturi's buildings thus tend to be architecturally Mannerist, scenographic, and rationalized, occasionally puzzlingly so. They even espouse "ornamented structure." However, do not brush off this paradoxical man, for he is incredibly learned (Phi Beta Kappa at Princeton; Prix de Rome) concerning the great historic buildings of the world and in probing and juxtaposing their essence, as can be seen in his book *Complexity and Contradiction in Architecture* (Museum of Modern Art, 1966). Venturi & Rauch's buildings, whether we are sympathetic to them or not, are among the most provocative of our time, and, it should be added, they all evolve from the spirit of their immediate environment.

Guild House for the Aged—with its "billboard" of glazed white brick blazoning the entrance, its oversized lettering, its outsized granite column, and its fanlike Neo-Palladian window at top (matching the width of the splayed entry)—sets out to provoke, intellectually, establishment architecture. The fact that the stringcourse at the fifth floor deliberately does not align with the window heads or bases is merely another design stiletto. But these seeming inconsistencies, which focus on understatement, orchestrate, if they do not harmonize, to produce a sophisticated, "naive" building that will intrigue many, vex a few, and baffle the rest. With a scale and character respecting the street and with a plan that places the maximum number of rooms on the southerly side, there is more here than meets the hasty eye. In any case the cognoscenti of the various paths of contemporary architectural development in this country will find the enigmatic flair of this building ineluctably on their list. The house provides a retirement center of ninety apartments and a reception room (behind arced window at top) for elderly men and women who lived in this neighborhood before reconstruction of the area, and who wanted to remain. It was built under the aegis of the Society of Friends. Cope & Lippincott were associate architects.

Interior not normally open to the public. Group tours can be arranged by calling (215) 923–1539. JAIA 2/80

UPJOHN COMPANY GENERAL HEADQUARTERS (1961)
7000 Portage Road
Kalamazoo, Michigan

Skidmore, Owings & Merrill, architects

The basic philosophy of this administrative Hesperides (by the Chicago office of SOM) was to make every office as tied to nature as possible. This marriage to environment begins before one enters the building, with formalized water in a large rectangular pool—complete with three landscaped islets—alongside the entrance of the building. As one enters and ascends by escalator to the main floor, one is greeted by a large (150 feet/46 meters square) planted open court off the reception area. Six smaller courts (all but one 50 feet/15 meters on a side) are placed throughout so that each work space, executive or otherwise, looks outward onto the pleasant surroundings or adjoins an intimate courtyard with pool. The progression of spaces from open nature to private garden is sequential. It is a concept that flows with inner space and easy intercommunication. Partly one story in height (at rear), but largely two (at front and midsection), the 432-foot-/132-meter-square building is covered by one flat roof with wide overhang on all four sides to give weather and sun protection. The chevron pattern of the over-hang (strongly) reflects the space-frame structure of the roof. All service functions, including cafeteria, are located on the lower floor, all offices on the upper. Bruce Graham was partner in charge of design; the landscaping was by Sasaki & Associates.

Located 2 miles/3.2 kilometers southeast of town beyond the airport. The interior is not open to the public. AR 12/61, A+A 5/62

CHURCH OF THE ABBEY OF ST. GREGORY THE GREAT (1961)
Portsmouth Abbey School
285 Cory's Lane
Portsmouth, Rhode Island

Pietro Belluschi, architect

Beginning with his pioneering efforts in Oregon, Pietro Belluschi designed notable religious buildings over a wide span of years; few, however, can match this chapel for 180 boys and 60 Benedictine brothers. Its use of wood and local stone, its sympathetic scale, its embracing liturgical plan and religiosity, and its deft provisions for monks as well as lads combine with its outstanding art to produce a marvelous religious building. The plan—an octagon and abutting rectangle—provides a focused worship room for boys and visitors with retrochoir for the monks, who sing or chant here seven times each day. Quiet side chapels for the monks, each private yet each in visual touch with the main altar, are set in the facets of the octagon on both main floor and gallery. The high altar acts as fulcrum between nave and chancel. Above the altar Richard Lippold's brilliant crucifix radiates throughout the sanctuary, its gold and silver wires interacting and supporting a small Christ in such a fashion that its minute height is communicated throughout much of the church. This is one of the finest examples of twentieth-century religious art to be seen. The upper part, or lantern, of the octagon is enclosed with strips of colored glass—largely greens and blues with accents of red—alternating with wood mullions in a design by H. L. Willet and the architect that brings subdued vitality to the nave. Much of the furniture, including altar, pews, and stalls, was designed by George Nakashima. The art work, including the front door with its incised ancient Roman lettering, was by Father Peter. Anderson, Beckwith & Haible were associated architects.

Located west off RI 114. Visits must be arranged in advance by calling (401) 683-2000. AR 12/54, AR 7/59, AR 6/61

NORTH CAROLINA STATE LEGISLATIVE BUILDING (1961–63)
16 West Jones Street at Salisbury, Wilmington, and Lane streets
Raleigh, North Carolina

Edward Durell Stone Associates, architects

The State Legislative Building—located a block from the North Carolina State Capitol (see page 182)—solves its difficult problem of combining official "monumentality" and current "democracy" by using formal terms with a welcoming scale on the exterior and good spaces within. The 340-foot-/104-meter-square building rests on a low, non-authoritarian podium that "levels" the uneven site and permits a large parking garage in half of the basement floor. A continuous colonnade of square, marble-clad columns frames the two main floors of the building on all sides. The third partial floor projects upward in the middle in a Greek-cross plan with an open-air garden at each corner. At entry level a brace of fountains set in wide bowls occupies the corners in front of the main facade.

One is surprised, however, on stepping inside the front door to confront abruptly a magisterial flight of stair in vivid red carpeting, which cheers visitors to the third floor (elevators are also available). The ground floor is taken up by individual offices that completely line the building's periphery, with a variety of committee rooms placed in the inner core. The second floor houses the circular Senate chamber and the larger, square House of Representatives, with, again, individual offices along the outer walls. A library and services take up the central area. Four interior courtyards, two stories high and capped with skylights, penetrate the building near its corners, injecting space and light into the two working floors. The third floor—the only one open to the public—is given over to the upper half of the two legislative chambers, plus an auditorium. Here one can enjoy views of both Senate and House via their upper-level galleries, gaze down upon the waters and trees of the central rotunda court that rises from the second floor, and stroll out to enjoy the rooftop gardens and the view. The strongly patterned pyramidal ceilings of the top floor are insistent, but spaces, play of light, and planting are fine. The furniture was designed by the architect; Edward D. Stone, Jr., and Richard C. Bell were the landscape architects; Holloway-Reeves were associate architects.

Open Monday–Friday 8:00 A.M.–5:00 P.M., Saturday 9:00 A.M.–5:00 P.M., Sunday 1:00–5:00 P.M. Closed Christmas and New Year's Day. Admission is free. Guided tours are available. Group visits should be scheduled in advance by calling (919) 733–4111. AF 12/63

CARPENTER CENTER FOR THE VISUAL ARTS (1961–63)
Harvard University
24 Quincy Street between
Broadway and Harvard
Cambridge, Massachusetts

Le Corbusier, architect

Space-time progression via ramps—the visual excitement of walking aloft—has characterized many of Corbusier's most provocative buildings from Poissy to Chandigarh to Ahmedabad. The use of an elevated ramp at the Carpenter Center sought to tie two parallel streets, Quincy and Prescott (and future campus expansion), to the core of the center and its upper-level studios in order to inject the student and public into the activity of the building as they moved from one thoroughfare to the next. As Carpenter is an art facility for the undergraduate body (providing studios, galleries, lecture hall, and the like), this concept of injection, of making the building and its glass-lined art showcases intimately, indeed inescapably, tied to the very path of the students, carries logic. The resulting building with its multiplicity of elements and its almost rude scale is somewhat of a *tour de force*. Moreover the building proper cannot be called a conciliatory neighbor—Corbu, incidentally, never saw it personally—but then the visual arts are not necessarily conciliatory either. Logic and rationalization aside, a stroll across the ramp and through the building, with spaces manipulated at each step, provokes a quickening reaction. Albeit not from the Swiss-French maestro's top drawer, it is a product of one of the greatest architects who ever lived, and his only building in the United States (see, also, the United Nations Secretariat Building in New York, page 398, whose skyscraper was to a large degree Le Corbusier's design). Technical realization of Carpenter Center was in charge of Sert, Jackson & Gourley.

Perhaps of equal importance with the material building is the educational concept. Carpenter seeks to sensitize the process of perception—in both intellectual and psychic terms—for students, many of whom will eventually be called upon to help commission future environments. And unless our bankers, insurance men, and developers know the arts, in addition to knowing mortgage rates, there will be little hope for a finer physical tomorrow.

Open Monday–Saturday 9:00 A.M.–5:00 P.M., Sunday 12:00 noon–5:00 P.M. Closed for holidays. For more information call (617) 495-3251. AF 12/61, AF 3/63, AR 4/63, AF 10/63, ARev 12/63, A 10/87

BEINECKE RARE BOOK AND MANUSCRIPT LIBRARY (1961–63)
Yale University
121 Wall Street
New Haven, Connecticut

Skidmore, Owings & Merrill, architects

Beinecke Rare Book and Manuscript Library is sandwiched between the Neo-Roman of the University Dining Hall and the Neo-Gothic of the Law School: its designer, not unexpectedly, simply ignored both, except for their cornice lines. The resulting building, though impeccably chilly—almost arrogant—on the outside (compare Paul Rudolph's Yale Art and Architecture Building, page 472, and Eero Saarinen's Ezra Stiles and Morse Colleges, page 464), possesses one of the most sumptuous interiors to be seen. It is actually two buildings in one, an outer shell harboring an inner core. The exterior wrapping consists of four Vierendeel trusses, whose granite-covered steel grid rests dramatically on four corner bronze "hinges." Enclosing the walls are squarish panels of 1.3-inch-/33-millimeter-thick marble, whitish on the face but chameleon-like in their translucency within. The Vermont marble panels provide a stunning veil around the building, and when the sun moves in the sky or clouds move over the sun the opalescence of the walls comes alive, then subsides. At night the building shines outward.

Arising serenely and detached in the middle of the outer box stands a six-story glass cage of rare books, their spines of varying colors creating a gigantic tapestry. This glass showcase lends preciousness to the books, although interestingly enough it was first planned to leave them unenclosed. As the ancient volumes require a temperature of 68° F/ 20° C and a humidity of 45 percent, the glass enclosure was needed to maintain this index for the books. A less humid one was required for the exhibition gallery to keep the marble shell from sweating inside in cold weather. A second-floor mezzanine surrounds the central shrine of books; com-

fortably furnished and with vitrines for special exhibits along its walls, it provides an excellent spot for witnessing this exciting interior. There are at present some 23 miles/ 37 kilometers of stacks and over 600,000 books. The library has used the area below street level for expansion. A sunken courtyard—with geometric sculpture by Isamu Noguchi—gives light to the study rooms, offices, and reading room grouped about. Gordon Bunshaft was chief of design, Paul Weidlinger consulting engineer.

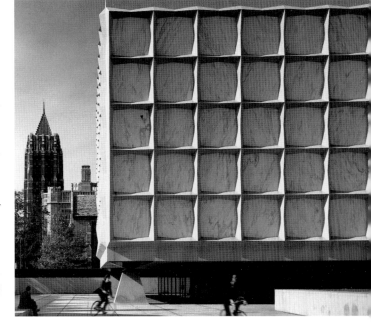

Open Monday–Friday 8:30 A.M.–5:00 P.M., Saturday 10:00 A.M.–5:00 P.M. Tours of the Yale campus can be scheduled by calling Campus Tours at (203) 432– 2300. AF 11/60, PA 12/61, AR 8/63, AR 11/63

ART AND ARCHITECTURE BUILDING (1961–63)
Yale University
180 York Street at Chapel
New Haven, Connecticut

Paul Rudolph, architect

Whirlwinds of both praise and damnation have been flung against this "furiously ambitious building" (Vincent Scully). Yet both proponents and opponents are right. It stands castle-like on its corner, its seven-story form proudly holding down its urban and campus functions. It is a good neighbor considering the architectural equivocation on several sides; and its great two-story drafting room was, until a fire heavily damaged the interior (1969), one of the inspired spaces of its time. However, this emotionally demanding building (with entrance seemingly for initiates only) solved only some of its problems: architects were dominant and painters, sculptors, and printmakers were shunted to spaces in either attic or basement. Yet the interior, until post-fire partitioning, offered almost electric three-dimensional exploration; it still has powerful moments. Since 1994 the exterior and interior have been under renovation.

Open Monday–Friday during business hours. Also open Saturday during the academic year. Closed for holidays. Tours of the Yale campus can be scheduled by calling Campus Tours at (203) 432–2300. AR 4/62, A+A 2/64, AF 2/64, AR 2/64, PA 2/64, AD 4/64, ARev 5/64, AF 6–7/67

AMON CARTER MUSEUM (1961–1964/1975)
3501 Camp Bowie Boulevard at Montgomery and West Lancaster streets
Fort Worth, Texas

Philip Johnson, architect

This pristine showcase for art was originally designed to display the Amon Carter's unequaled collection of sculpture and paintings by Frederic Remington and Charles M. Russell. It now contains a broader selection of American art, with particular focus on the "westering" of the continent. Situated near the top of a long, gentle slope, and placed at right angles to the street, the museum extends its stepped terraces to possess the countryside. The plaza dimensions (140 x 300 feet/43 x 91 meters) are defined by a low wall of the same shellstone as the building itself. Designed by the architect, these levels and their landscaping tie the museum to the city—a city that Carter partly shaped.

A classic formalism marks the five-arched facade, and one is injected into the milieu of art as soon as one steps through the front door. (The main gallery measures 24 feet/7.3 meters wide by 120 feet/36 meters long and 24 feet/7.3 meters high.) Opening off the major hall on the ground floor are five intimate galleries with additional exhibition space filling the mezzanine. The architect's noted sensitivity to detailing is quietly stated throughout: the five tapered shellstone arches (each with 3-inch/76-millimeter steel inner column) rippling across the front are themselves works of art—in design and in their hand-carving. The lighting, worked out with Richard Kelly as consultant, allows a glare-free radiance to pour over the exhibition spaces; five black-painted ceiling fixtures in the main gallery are the source of both natural and artificial illumination.

In October 1975 an annex designed by Philip Johnson and John Burgee was dedicated. With 31,800 square feet/3,344 square meters, the new wing doubles the size of the original museum and includes a 102-seat theater, vastly expanded library, services, and enlarged bookstore. Like the main building, the new is also faced with Texas shellstone.

Open Tuesday–Saturday 10:00 A.M.–5:00 P.M., Sunday 12:00 noon–5:00 P.M. Closed for holidays. Admission is free. Tours given daily at 2:00 P.M. For more information call (817) 738–1933. AF 3/61

ABBEY OF ST. MARY AND ST. LOUIS (1962)
St. Louis Priory School
500 South Mason Road
St. Louis, Missouri

Hellmuth, Obata & Kassabaum, architects

The Baptistry of Nocera, Italy (A.D. 350), was probably the first to espouse a circular plan for a Christian religious building, but San Stefano Rotundo (A.D. 470) in Rome gets credit for being the first precisely cylindrical church (210 feet/64 meters in diameter). Later architects, from the sixteenth-century Donato Bramante in Rome to the twentieth-century Otto Bartning and Gottfried Böhm in Germany, have designed circular, altar-centric churches. In general they have not been satisfying essays. And in spite of the commanding and photogenic exterior of this church near St. Louis, we encounter the weaknesses that plagued its historic prototypes: the priest has his back to a section of the congregation (here 1,000 maximum), while spatially there is little buildup, and little architectural climax or concentration of light. One inescapably faces a window. The result is that the admirably simple altar floats under the eye of the "dome" with the same parade of windows behind it as in front. On the other hand, the central position of the sanctuary does encourage liturgical intimacy—the rationale of its shape—with the faithful grouped about and the monks in the retrochoir.

The exterior is intriguing in itself and is a masterful exposition of sprayed concrete, both in design and in execution. Twenty parabolas, 21 feet/6.4 meters high, form the lower periphery, which is 138 feet/42 meters in diameter, with a second tier of arches, 12 feet/3.6 meters high, above, and a 32-foot/9.7-meter arched steeple—belfry topping all. The interior cross section reveals an organization of complex geometry, whose ribs neatly cascade from the compression ring at top and are tied by a horizontal tension ring between upper and lower tiers. The windows are of plastic laminate, black on the outside yet sufficiently translucent to admit

satisfactory illumination. The exterior at night glows from its inner light. A screen of colored glass by Emil Frei gives a quietly colorful yet largely transparent background to the celebrant's seat, and also partly conceals the monks' entry. The surrounding school was also designed by Hellmuth, Obata & Kassabaum. Gyo Obata was principal in charge of design; Paul Weidlinger was structural engineer; Pier Luigi Nervi, the famous Italian architectural engineer, was structural adviser. The church received a major renovation in 1994.

Located 18 miles/29 kilometers west of downtown on US 40, north .4 mile/.6 kilometer on Mason Road (3 miles/4.8 kilometers west of I-244). Open Monday–Friday 9:00 A.M.–5:00 P.M. Also open on weekends by appointment; call (314) 434–2557 or 434–3712. Tours can be scheduled by calling the above numbers. PA 1/58, PA 10/58, AF 11/62

FIRST UNITARIAN CHURCH (1962–63)
220 Winton Road South
Rochester, New York

Louis I. Kahn, architect

In this building Louis I. Kahn unequivocally expressed the Unitarian thesis that education must accompany intelligent worship. He nested the congregation in the center of the First Unitarian Church and surrounded it with two floors of classrooms. By top-lighting its solid-walled, unsentimental worship space in dramatic fashion he created a vigorous interior. The square assembly room (in early studies a dodecagon) is dominated by a concrete roof forming a Greek cross, as it were, with its undersides splayed upward. Setting this "cross" within a square leaves the corners open, and the nave at these four corners continues upward to receive a downpouring of light from each of the four roof monitors. From these near-invisible sources the natural light floods down, producing a corner brightness and, inevitably, a corresponding lack of emphasis on the altar; indeed the brightness of the angles distracts the eye from the sanctuary. But as Kahn wrote, "I felt that getting the light from above and down a well into the corners of the space gave expression to the form, to the shape, of the room chosen" (*Perspecta* 7). The visual dryness of the natural concrete-block inner walls and the raw concrete ceiling and upper sections is relieved—chromatically and acoustically—by the flair of sixteen banners hung on the two sides. The exterior, of red brick, clearly reflects the interior division, its hood-ed classroom windows developing a two-story, lateral, in-and-out rhythm, while four light tow-ers project upward to create a strong silhouette. Dr. August E. Komendant and the Keast & Hood Company were structural consultants.

Open Sunday–Friday 9:00 A.M.–5:00 P.M. (Memorial Day Weekend–Labor Day, open Sunday–Friday 9:00 A.M.–1:00 P.M.). Also open Saturday 9:00 A.M.–1:00 P.M. (except July and August). Other times by appointment. Sunday services held at 9:00 and 11:00 A.M. (Memorial Day Weekend–Labor Day, Sunday services held at 10:00 A.M.). Tours can be scheduled in advance. For more information call (716) 271–9070. AD 4/61, AF 9/64

CLOWES MEMORIAL HALL (1962–63)
Butler University
4600 Sunset Avenue at West 46th Street
Indianapolis, Indiana

John M. Johansen and Evans Woollen, architects

Clowes Memorial Hall was placed at the entrance to the campus of Butler University so that it could conveniently serve both college and city. This combined concert hall and theater is given architectural prominence by its clustering of tall, boxlike forms whose varying heights and projections develop a play of rhythm and shadow. However, in spite of the inviting color of the limestone facing and the engaging roof line, some formidableness is evident.

The main lobby itself is four stories high and laterally constricted as it continues, reflecting the rigorousness of the exterior. The auditorium, on the other hand, with watermelon-red curtain, red seats, and gold, acoustic, wire-hung "clouds," is an exciting space. This heart, this rationale, of the building is inviting, and its acoustics are excellent. The 2,200 seats of Clowes are arranged in gentle curves with no aisles. This seating arrangement demands exits no more than 15 feet/4.6 meters apart; the architects took this mandatory module and enclosed the sides with a series of the aforementioned staggered, boxlike wall elements that reflect the shape of the hall. Interior safety demands of the building code thus became a design key. The generous lateral lobbies pulsate between the uneven (but carefully calculated) spaces formed between auditorium and outer walls, and are arranged so that they provide alcoves for conversation, some with seats, away from the circulation flow. The large stage topped by a high stage loft can accommodate a variety of performances ranging from a symphony orchestra to Broadway shows to films. The two pits in front can be raised to orchestra level or stage height. Clowes Memorial Hall was financed in the main by a generous grant from the Clowes Foundation. Fink, Roberts & Petrie were the structural engineers; Jean Rosenthal, state consultant; Bolt, Beranek & Newman, acousticians.

September–May open Monday–Saturday 8:30 A.M.–6:00 P.M., May–August open Monday–Friday 8:30 A.M.–5:00 P.M. Closed for holidays. Also open for performances. Free tours can be scheduled by calling (317) 283-9696. AF 12/63, AD 12/64

TENNECO BUILDING (1962–63)
1010 Milam Street between Lamar and McKinney
Houston, Texas

Skidmore, Owings & Merrill, architects

There is no need to hesitate: the thirty-three-story Tenneco Building ranks high among a handful of postwar skyscrapers in the United States. Although it lacks the regal approach and the impeccable entrance of the Seagram Building in New York (see page 420), it exceeds that mentor of the high-rise world with the sterling quality of total urban three-dimensionality—which Seagram lacks on the back—for one can walk around the square Tenneco and find it richly identical on all four faces. (It measures 195.3 feet/59.5 meters on a side.) Much of the building's fascination stems from its subtly screened facades, for the walls are set back from the building frame to provide space for peripheral sun control. The extension of the floor slabs 5 feet/1.5 meters beyond the windows gives substantial horizontal sun and weather protection, which is augmented in each bay by a clever auxiliary louver, curved on the outer face, angled on the inner, and hollow within, with smart midpoint auxiliary suspension. As with other exoskeletal buildings, the slab projection also permits speedy window-washing (one sash per building side is openable for the window washer). Floor projection and louvers keep all but very low sun from the glass-walled offices; thus blinds and curtains are rarely needed within. From the outside the dark, anodized aluminum sets up an ever-changing relationship between sun and shadow.

The ground floor is inset on four sides, creating a sheltered 50-foot-/15-meter-high galleria around the building, while a two-story bank is imaginatively slung from underneath the third floor, further freeing the sidewalk and adding more spatial drama. The pink granite plaza around the building (on the ascetic side) was created by setting the building back 25 feet/7.6 meters from property lines (and thus enabling an unbroken tower). The setback also provides two truck ramps (one down, the other up) for service. The unusual elevator lobby employs a pinwheel arrangement of four arms of passenger lifts. The office floors are completely column-free, with a 55-foot/17-meter span of built-up girders between the square central service core and the aluminum-sheathed, concrete-protected columns of the steel structural frame. The Tenneco Building's quietly stated sophistication and its answer to the stinging problem of its local climate rank it with the great. It was designed by the San Francisco office of Skidmore, Owings & Merrill.

The interior is closed to the public. AF 9/63, JAIA 6/69

TYRONE GUTHRIE THEATER
(1962–63/1993)
725 Vineland Place off
Hennepin Avenue
Minneapolis, Minnesota

Ralph Rapson &
Associates, architects

Few theaters in the United States deliver such intimacy between actors and audience as the 1308-seat Tyrone Guthrie Theater. (The architect worked closely with Sir Tyrone Guthrie in developing the unusual concept.) No person sits more than 52 feet/ 16 meters from the stage; the audience becomes vicarious participants as they almost engulf the players. The theater provides a "lively and strangely satisfying" experience, as Walter Kerr put it (*Progressive Architecture*, December 1963). The projected stage derives, of course, from early Greek examples, the most impressive being the almost perfectly preserved hillside Theater at Epidaurus (c. 350 B.C.) by Polyclitus the Younger. The Rapson-Guthrie concept—one also influenced by the Elizabethan stage and the Shakespearean theater in Stratford, Ontario (on which Guthrie also worked)—is an asymmetrical variation that centers on a circular "orchestra" (the stage) with steeply banked seats fanned approximately 200 degrees about it. (Greek plays appear often in the repertory of the Guthrie, and this was a further factor—in addition to developing greater intimacy—that prompted this theater's thrust design as opposed to the more typical proscenium.) In overall plan the Guthrie tightly fills a rectangular space, with little backstage depth and only a shallow fly loft.

The orchestra seats are supplemented by an asymmetric balcony level, one third of which the architect brought down to the main floor at one end to help erase the "second-class" stigma of the balcony, a move that also loosens the entire interior. It is an effective measure. The ceiling consists of multiple and often overlapping rectangular panels or acoustic clouds hung from the roof trusses; this allows catwalks and light ports to reach any section above and surrounding the stage. The asymmetry, the liveliness of the ceiling, and the colorful upholstery of the seats all combine to create an exciting milieu. The promenading spaces are reasonably adequate, while the lobby serves both theater and the adjacent Walker Art Center with inspired friendliness. As Will said, "the play's the thing," and the interior generates one of the country's happy theatrical experiences. In 1993 the theater was renovated both inside and out: although the stage itself was not touched, the seats were repaired, the acoustics and lighting improved, and a new glass curtain wall facade erected on the north side, expanding the size of the lobby.

Open for performances. A one-hour tour of the building is given Saturday at 10:00 A.M.; the cost is $3 for adults, $1.50 for students and senior citizens. Tours can be scheduled at other times by calling (612) 377–2224. PA 12/63, AD 8/64, ARev 2/72

F. G. PEABODY TERRACE (1962–64)
Harvard University
900 Memorial Drive at Sterling Street
Cambridge, Massachusetts

Sert, Jackson & Gourley, architects

The vertical village for housing married students is now a fact of life for most urban universities, and while there are those who claim with theoretical justification that young children are better off digging up the garden outside their own kitchen windows, such an ideal will rarely be possible. This cluster, originally built for married students (it currently houses both single and married graduate students) seeks to humanize the high rise: its search has been for the most part very successful. Three-, five-, and seven-story terraced units, their height building up from the Charles River and Putnam Avenue sides to maintain a residential scale along the roads, are combined with three twenty-two-story towers to provide 499 rental apartments (efficiency to three-bedroom), a garage (off Putnam Avenue) for 352 cars, plus a small shopping center and an even smaller community room. The spatial relationship between high and low units is admirable; the lower buildings knit the tall into the overall fabric and at ground level define circulation and mold local areas.

Although the buildings vary in both height and shape, they are all based on a standardized, reinforced concrete, three-story unit, three bays wide with a central stair in each. In the towers this economy-producing module is made possible by corridor access from the north or east side on each third floor with skip-floor elevators. Such an arrangement also permits cross ventilation in almost all apartments in addition to cross-connection and joint elevator sharing by the lower buildings.

As the main views of two of the three towers are westward over the Charles River, rotatable, vertical louvers are installed to control low sun yet permit vistas. On the south side the windows are generally hooded by the balconies above. The visual play of the louvers and the juxtaposition of balconies make for intriguing facades and break up any tendency to aerial boxiness on the part of the twenty-two-story masses. Pedestrian experiences—one of Sert, Jackson & Gourley's strong points—are stimulating throughout; the scale of the courts (and their landscaping) is excellent. The individual apartments are tightly planned because they had to be competitively priced. Moreover the community rooms and facilities (such as laundries) are far too slighted. Nonetheless this is probably the finest group of its kind in the country. Sasaki Associates were the landscape architects.

Open Monday–Friday 8:00 A.M.–4:00 P.M. (June–September also open Saturday 10:00 A.M.–1:00 P.M.) Closed for holidays. PA 12/64, JAIA 7/65, AD 8/65, PA 10/79

CBS BUILDING (1962–64)
51 West 52nd Street at 6th Avenue
New York, New York

Eero Saarinen & Associates, architects

Understatement has rarely been so totally stated: the aloof, granitic solemnity of this thirty-eight-floor skyscraper—the only skyscraper that Eero Saarinen designed—stands out with forceful character amid the slick spandrels around it. Inset from the avenue and the two side streets that mark its site, with a sedately landscaped terrace providing breathing space, the tower (of reinforced concrete frame) rises unflinchingly uniform as though extruded from the mysterious depths of the earth, an impression intensified by the fact that the entrance lies five steps down from street level.

Today the "active" functions of the window in skyscraper design have been made largely obsolete by air conditioning and fluorescent lighting, and Saarinen was one of the first architects to state this in the fenestration of this building. As occasional visual relief is now the window's chief claim to attention (although operable sash will always be useful in an emergency, as brownouts prove), the CBS Building alternates window and wall, each with a 5-foot/1.5-meter module, instead of wrapping a strip of windows around the complete floor. To accommodate air-conditioning ducts and other utilities, he made these "solid" modules into structural utility triangles, with outer faces at 45 degrees, creating a saw-toothed exterior that vibrates as the pedestrian moves by, the wall calmly opening and closing as one goes. Saarinen then clad these triangles with thin slabs of dark gray granite (running into problems on the corners). On the interior, the flat (that is, office) face of these piers is flush, facilitating movement of partitions. Moreover, there are no columns between outer wall and central service-elevator core, thus divisions can be made at any 5-foot/1.5-meter interval. The spandrels between the triangles are also clad in granite with frameless panes of plate glass windows above.

The use of reinforced concrete bearing columns on 10-foot/3-meter centers—instead of wide-bay steel construction—was quite new when Saarinen tried it, with the enthusiastic collaboration of Paul Weidlinger as structural engineer. The result is a concrete bearing wall rather than a bearing frame. As the exterior walls are based on continuous (and uniform) piers from top to bottom, the module of 5 feet/1.5 meters was adopted so as to be flexible with office partitioning and also provide space for revolving doors at entry.

The pedestrian's impression of the exterior is one of sobriety; it is only when one views the building from on high from one of its neighbors that its deeply grained character stands out amid the riffraff of the skyscraper world about it. In the restaurant and bar (by Warren Platner of the Saarinen office) one can sample the elegance at first hand; it is worth every shilling. After Eero Saarinen's death (1961) the building was completed by Kevin Roche/John Dinkeloo & Associates.

Lobby open to the public Monday–Friday 9:00 A.M.–5:00 P.M. AR 4/62, AR 7/65, Int 1/66, PA 3/66, AF 4/66, AR 6/66, JAIA 7/66

DEERE & COMPANY ADMINISTRATIVE CENTER (1962–64/1977–78)
John Deere Road
Moline, Illinois

Eero Saarinen & Associates, architects of Deere Headquarters
Roche/Dinkeloo & Associates, architects of West Office Building

The Deere Center forms one of the great America's mid-century buildings; many believe that it is Eero Saarinen's most brilliant achievement. With a superb site (1,060 acres/429 hectares of wooded, rolling countryside), an enthusiastic, knowledgeable client, and a (then) pioneering material (Cor-Ten, the weathering, self-preserving steel), Eero Saarinen (1910–61) wrought one of his seminal buildings. Lamentably, he died four days after the final building contract had been signed and before ground had been broken. Saarinen always sought to express the psychology of use in his architecture (such as the excitement of air travel at the TWA Flight Center in New York, 1958–62, see page 446), plus the personality of his client's product—and this, of course, is the chief reason why his buildings vary so widely. (Compare Mies van der Rohe's antipodal philosophy: his buildings are distinctly all of a family.) For the administrative headquarters of the vast John Deere organization, one concerned basically with the rough, tough world of farm machinery, Saarinen chose a rough, tough material. Though inaugurating Cor-Ten's architectural usage, Saarinen fully understood the material's limits and concentrated on its "stick"—as oppposed to sheet—form.

 The Deere Headquarters is divided into three units: an exhibition hall for Deere products with adjacent auditorium (a 378-seat theater for special presentation of products and a variety of other Deere programs, also available to local community organizations), a detached main administrative building, and (in 1978) the West Office Building by Roche/Dinkeloo. The 210-foot-/64-meter-long exhibition hall forms a rectangle 36 feet/11 meters high abutting the hill on the entry (east) side and fully glazed along the west (toward offices). Entrance, because of grade drop-off, is at midheight; an elevated passerelle bisects the hall to form the main entry (at the fourth floor) to the main building. (The bridge also offers a survey of Deere products below.) As personnel walk across this bridge they inject elevated motion into the showroom, while exhibits constantly remind staff of the company's range of products. The highlight of the hall is an ingenious, 174-foot-/53-meter-long, three-dimensional mural of some two thousand items relating to John Deere and early farming memorabilia, brilliantly assembled and composed by Alexander Girard.

The seven-story (plus basement) main administration building (shown in photograph) stretches 330 feet/101 meters (eleven bays of 30 feet/9.1 meters) across a benign valley and faces the smoothly landscaped approach to the complex. The approach includes two artificial lakes (one of which cools the water for the air-conditioning system), and Henry Moore's *Hill Arches* on an island in an upper pool. The main building contains all amenities for a town-detached headquarters, with its own dining facilities for approximately one thousand employees. Its architecture—"an iron building" requested by the client—represents a consummate expression of the headquarters of a farm machinery manufacturer, the antithesis of a frangible glass box. An outrigging of weathering steel louvers surrounds and projects from the building, with four slightly haunched and suspended vanes shielding the offices from the sun without interfering with the view. (They provide redundant "sun protection" on the north side.) Open grille decking, also of weathering steel, projects out to provide balconies for window washing. The placement of beam on beam, and of beam fastened to column, as expressed on these balconies suggests the simplicity of the finest in Japanese wood temple joinery, but here logically expressed in welded steel. (Exposed—that is, non-fireproofed—steel could be used because the structure stood outside urban zoning limitations.) The ground floor is devoted to building services and an executive dining room, lounge, and gallery projecting almost into the lake. Directly above is the executive floor, with private offices lining the periphery, and largely open secretarial spaces down the middle. The cafeteria and executive floors are inset from the outer walls. The upper five floors of the building are given to general office space, with a maximum of employees near the windows. All floors are sheathed with solar-reflecting bronze plate glass. Ammann & Whitney were the structural engineers; Sasaki, Dawson, Demay Associates designed the landscaping. A stupendous building with an integrity not likely to be seen again soon.

In 1978 the West Office Building was opened on a site that had been selected for possible expansion by Saarinen himself. Only three stories in height—so as not to impinge on the headquarters—the newer structure is set back on the hillside and connected to the older by a glazed bridge 194 feet/59 meters long. The exterior uses the same weathering steel that was pioneered in the Saarinen buildings. The most spectacular aspect of Deere West is its interior garden court with a 315-seat cafeteria. This rises 54 feet/16 meters to a glazed roof composed of two main vaults and several minor ones, and separates the two identical but slightly offset rectangles. Numerous works of art are found throughout. The Roche/Dinkeloo addition is a sympathetic partner to the headquarters. It contains 200,000 square feet/18,580 square meters of space. Kevin Roche and John Dinkeloo were formerly members of and successors to the original Saarinen firm.

Located 3.9 miles/6.3 kilometers east of I-74 on IL 5, 7 miles/11 kilometers southeast of Moline. Lobby and display floor open to the public daily 9:00 A.M.–5:30 P.M. A film about the building can be seen on the display floor Monday–Friday at 10:30 A.M. and 1:30 P.M. For more information call Visitor Services at (309) 765-4235. AF 7/64, AR 7/64, Int 1/65, ARev 5/65, AD 8/65, PA 9/74, JAIA 8/76, JAIA 5/79

ERDMAN DORMITORIES (1962–65)
Bryn Mawr College
Merion Avenue
Bryn Mawr, Pennsylvania

Louis I. Kahn, architect

The architect has put together a sophisticated basically black and white building with an unusual geometry. Virtually all of Louis I. Kahn's work is based on interacting geometric forms—an approach that never fails to be exciting in his handseven if, at times, it becomes formal. Here he has evolved a plan of three separate "hollow" squares attached at their diagonal corners and strung across the brow of a small hillside. The understated, almost difficult-to-find main entrance is in the central square, with dining room and kitchen to left, lounges to right. The central cores, two stories high, form the major interior spaces, and are wrapped by minor ones. (Compare Kahn's First Unitarian Church in Rochester, New York, page 475.) The second floor of each square comprises bedrooms on four sides, leaving the central space open to form "a molecular structure that looks for the light" (Kahn). Because of the site gradient some bedrooms—of which there are 150—are on the lower level. The fenestration in the bedrooms— two slender windows at the extreme ends of some rooms alternating with one recessed central window in the rooms adjoining—approaches the arbitrary, as does the extension of the slate walls to form the roof parapet. However, its use of a difficult site and its use of scale make the building interesting to architects, and the surprising variety of its interior spaces makes it eagerly sought by the students for residence.

Open Monday–Friday 9:00 A.M.–5:00 P.M. during the academic year. Closed between Christmas and New Year's Day and for national holidays. Tours can be scheduled by calling (610) 526–5135. AF 11/65

PASEO DEL RIO (River Walk)
(1962–68)
San Antonio River—midtown
San Antonio, Texas

As vital as an artery of the human body, the River Walk infuses animation—and almost bucolic relief—to the asphalt midriff of San Antonio. Winding and pulsating in a horseshoe shape through the downtown area, lined with diverting shops, cafes, and restaurants, with promenades on either side and a *bateau-mouche* ferrying sightseers (with police boats making their appointed rounds), this tiny meander (about 3 miles/4.8 kilometers long) is the delight of the city. The Paseo extends non-authoritarian contact with flowing waters almost totally unencumbered by fences, barriers, or even guide rails; it is a brilliant example of responsible humans and responsive nature. At night proper illumination cheers the way. Water taxis and sight-seeing (and dinner) barges are available; fiestas are often scheduled. A few of the pedestrian bridges are bulky, and one can quarrel with other details, but the concept is glorious, the landscaping and plant variety in general excellent—at times superb—and the overall a crown for St. Anthony of Padua, for whom the city was named.

This small stream, lying some 20–25 feet/6–7.6 meters below street level—where the world above, fortunately, disappears—was sentenced to become a paved-over culvert in the 1920s (following a severe flooding). Debate ensued and a stay of execution was effected by aroused citizens. Run-off dams for flood control were erected, and during the Depression much of the groundwork of what can be seen today was commenced under the Works Progress Administration (1937–41—Robert H. Hugman, architect). Following World War II and the flight to the suburbs, a puzzling neglect set in. But in the 1960s, when the Paseo's potential as a tourist attraction—plus its very great value as a local amenity—was realized, a River Development Feasibility Study was completed and a River Walk Advisory Commission created (1962). Cyrus Wagner and O'Neil Ford, of the American Institute of Architects' local chapter, and David Strauss, of the Chamber of Commerce, were key figures in the activity that followed. The city's 1968 HemisFair hastened the work. There are now plans to extend the walk to the entire length of the river within the city limits (10 miles/16 kilometers). Much of the river bed, incidentally, is paved with concrete and—like Venice's canals—is drained and cleaned at proper intervals.

The most imaginative architectural accent along the Paseo is the River Square Project (1970) off Commerce Street, Cyrus Wagner, architect, and the marvelous hundred-year-old Stockman Building (1868/1971) remodeled by Ford, Powell & Carson—all, it should be added, without commercialism. The Paseo is one of the country's delightful urban experiences; it might even be what downtown is all about.

Open daily 24 hours. River barge tours available; call Paseo del Rio Boats at (210) 222–1701 for information. LA 4/73, PA 6/75, JAIA 7/79

GATEWAY ARCH (1962–68)
Jefferson National Expansion Memorial
Memorial Drive between Washington Avenue and Poplar Street
St. Louis, Missouri

Eero Saarinen & Associates, architects

Flaming in sun, disappearing in mists, ghostly by the light of the moon, and, above all, proclaiming that here verily is the country's gateway to the West, the Gateway Arch ranks with the signal monuments of world architecture. In an era that feels uneasy with monuments, here is a monument of an age's potential, a mighty parabola of polished steel astride the path to half the nation. This incredible monumentality and its symbolism were achieved by the slenderest of catenaries, by honed geometry—and questing minds.

The arch, which rises to 630 feet/192 meters, has a span to match its height. Its structural cross section forms an equilateral triangle 54 feet/16 meters wide at the base, with a flat side facing out and a point facing in. The sections are all double walled, the two faces separated by 3 feet/.9 meter. The outer skin is of stressed stainless steel .25 inch/6 millimeters thick, the inner face of carbon steel .37 inch/9.5 millimeters thick. It was constructed by placing one triangular section atop another by a traveling creeper derrick, which marched (simultaneously on each arch arm) slowly up its sloping flank on a special demountable track, lifting the sections in place, then filling their double walls with concrete (for stabilization) to the 300-foot/91-meter level. When the arch was closed—fantastic precision was needed so that the two arms would align—the cranes lowered themselves (and their tracking) to the ground. The lower steel triangular sections are 12 feet/3.6 meters high and, as mentioned, 54 feet/16 meters on a side; the upper ones are 8 feet/2.4 meters deep by 17 feet/5.2 meters laterally; 142 triangles were used altogether. Passengers ride to the top (highly recommended) in self-leveling "gondolas" or capsules, attached in tandems of eight, each holding five passengers. There are two of these trams, one in each leg. An emergency stair (1,076 steps) descends each side. A Museum of Westward Expansion (well worthwhile) occupies the underground Visitors Center.

The Saarinen arch is a euphoric summation of architecture, engineering, and sculpture working together; it almost seems alive. Erected with uncanny exactness—even the film of its construction is electrifying—it stands as a realization, perhaps *the* realization, of what late-twentieth-century people can do. The arch (in spite of insufficient but improving landscaping) has helped spark the renaissance of downtown St. Louis, with new buildings, a new stadium, new shops, and new apartments filled with former suburbanites. (Unfortunately too much of the character of old "levee" St. Louis was eliminated in the process.) Of all the structures in this book, the Gateway Arch, it is safe to say, will be the one most admired when the country celebrates its Tricentennial. The MacDonald Construction Company was the prime contractor, with the prefabricated steel sections made by Pittsburgh-Des Moines Steel Company. Severud-Elstad-Krueger Associates were the structural engineers.

Memorial Day–Labor Day open daily 8:00 A.M.–10:00 P.M. The rest of the year open daily 9:00 A.M.–6:00 P.M. Closed Thanksgiving, Christmas, and New Year's Day. There is a $2 per person/$4 per family fee to enter the park, as well as additional fees for the tram ride and admission to the museum. Free tours given daily; call (314) 425–6010 for more information.
AR 4/48, PA 5/48, AR 7/51, AR 5/63, AF 6/68, JAIA 11/78, JAIA 6/83

NORTH CHRISTIAN CHURCH
(1963–64)
850 Tipton Lane
Columbus, Indiana

Eero Saarinen & Associates,
architects

Conceived in symbolism and nurtured by perceptive talent, this church was among Eero Saarinen's favorite designs of all his work. It was completed by his associates after his death in 1961. Symbolism generated its plan, which is an oblate hexagon somewhat reminiscent of the Star of David, hence the Judeo-Christian tradition. The spire is raised 192 feet/59 meters toward heaven and topped with a cross of gold leaf on steel. The upward continuation of the six steel ribs that double-bend to form the spire provides one of the smoothest facets of the church's design; spire and church are organically fused. The dominating roof extends like a conical hat of steel and slate over the elongated hexagon of the concrete base. The slightly elevated nave rests in the center of this hexagon, surrounded on both narthex and lower levels by classrooms, meeting rooms, and offices. The brim of the "hat" projects as a shield over the peripheral windows—as it also emphasizes the dominance of the primacy of worship over the ancillary of services. This envelopment by the roof is intensified by a berm that surrounds the building and largely conceals the fenestration of the narthex level, while completely hiding the windows of the moated basement.

When one first enters, the nave seems small, though it seats 465 in a stepped dish in the center of the church, while 150 more can be accommodated in the upper ranks. This smallness, this drawing within, is intensified by the fact that the six ceiling planes that enclose the upper part of the worship room slant up toward a central oculus or skylight. Daylight enters from this round skylight and from a peripheral, invisible glazed band of borrowed light (somewhat insufficiently borrowed) that entirely surrounds the nave and separates it from its sloping hexagonal ceiling. (Compare Saarinen's earlier chapel with similar lighting at MIT in Cambridge, Massachusetts.) In the North Christian Church nave, one is celestially isolated; however, the nave is strongly altar-centered—the long altar rests in the middle of the hexagon—and develops an admirable liturgical intimacy. The communion dais and tables are removable, creating a versatile space that can also be used for dramatic and musical presentations. A stepped chancel and boldly silhouetted organ pipes form the only accents. A youth activities center, kitchen, auditorium, and services are found on the lower level.

Located east off Washington Street. Open Monday–Friday 8:00 A.M.–5:00 P.M., Sunday 8:00 A.M.–12:00 noon. Sunday services held at 9:45 A.M. Free tours can be requested. For more information call (812) 372–1531. The Columbus Visitors Center gives a two-hour tour Monday–Friday at 9:30 A.M. that includes the interior of the church; the cost is $9.50 for adults, $9 for senior citizens, $5 for students, $3 for children ages 6–12. For more information about the tour call (812) 378–2622. AR 9/64

UNITARIAN MEETING HOUSE (1963–64)
50 Bloomfield Avenue
Hartford, Connecticut

Victor A. Lundy, architect

A provocative church both structurally and esthetically. The structural frame of the Unitarian Meeting House, precisely expressed without and within, is based on twelve irregularly spaced reinforced concrete piers that rise from the ground to form an uneven crown. At their top these semitriangular piers are interlaced by a series of steel cables that uphold the wooden "tent" over the sanctuary. The interior centers, literally and figuratively, on the sanctuary, over which an inverted calix of wooden strips or gills hovers like an escape hatch to heaven. This centrally placed sanctuary is surrounded by church school rooms, offices, and library on the outer periphery. As the whole church is encompassed under the sweep of the one roof, and as the inner walls of all the outer rooms are topped with Plexiglas, the high central roof over the chancel—the calix—can be seen throughout. This also brings to the center of the church a halo of outer daylight, supplementing that from the clerestory and that filtering through the fantastic web of wooden slats. A 7-foot-/2.1-meter-high wood enclosure encircles the worship room, lending it preciousness while encouraging spatial flow (and creating some acoustical problems). A fellowship hall and classrooms occupy the basement.

Located off US 44 at CT 189. September–June open Monday–Friday 8:00 A.M.–4:00 P.M. July–August open Monday–Friday 9:00 A.M.–1:00 P.M. Closed for holidays. Sunday services held at 10:30 A.M. For more information call (203) 233-9897. AF 8–9/64

RESTON NEW TOWN (1963–)
Reston, Virginia

Conklin & Rossant and RTKL Associates, planners
Sasaki Associates, landscape architects

The domestic tragedy of the United States is that it has produced almost no major solutions to twentieth-century habitation. Compared to Europe, especially Sweden, Finland, and England, our record is disgraceful: we have nothing in a class with Vallingby (Stockholm), Tapiola (Helsinki), or Roehampton (London). Washington, where the power and decisions and the money to finance the so-called "new towns" lie, and where the large insurance companies and corporations operate, are equally to blame, but in a democracy one reaps what one votes.

Reston, some 18 miles/29 kilometers west-northwest of Washington, was the first large-scale (7,419 acres/3,002 hectares), new town of merit, with fully rounded living, education, recreation, and partial employment, in the United States. It is, in plan, an admirable effort, a brilliant tribute to its original developer, Robert E. Simon, Jr. (In 1967 Simon sold Reston to the Gulf Oil Corporation, and in 1978 it was resold to Reston Land Corporation, a Mobil Oil subsidiary.) As such it glows with substantial lessons, while warning us by its shortcomings, which are evident away from central areas.

Reston's main virtues are epitomized by Lake Anne Village (1963–64, see photo below)— the first section to be completed—and its pedestrian plaza of shops, town houses, and a high-rise apartment knowingly grouped around a 28-acre/11-hectare artificial lake. The first of six proposed village clusters, this section, designed by Conklin & Rossant, represents one of the distinctive achievements of American planning, for it carries a sense of belonging, of being a part of a cohesive whole, which will not be found elsewhere. Moreover it is full of surprise, efficiency, and imagination, and deploys its elements—its buildings—with spatial élan, using water to unify and highlight. The main shopping plaza steps down to welcome the lake, and towards the middle of these waters spurts a grandiose jet (40–50 feet/12–15 meters high). For a short distance on both sides of the lake, extending from the plaza, stretch town houses, those at right climaxing in the tall apartment building. This fifteen-story structure is not only strategically located to punctuate the view down the mall, it is handsomely designed. Across the lake attached town houses, designed by Chloethiel Woodard Smith, and a few individual dwellings

are grouped both. These can be reached by an underpass so that no one—child or adult—has to cross a major street to shop, go to school, or visit a friend.

Reston's Town Center Phase 1 (1986–90), designed by RTKL Associates, adds a vast expansion. The central piazza, Fountain Square, sports a playful fountain topped by the bronze figure of Mercury, designed by sculptor Saint Clair Cemin. Across the street sits the Fountain Square Pavilion, used for concerts and other events in summer and doubling as a skating rink in winter. Two eleven-story office buildings, faced in concrete, beige brick, and granite, overlook the square and incorporate retail spaces and restaurants at ground level. Off the main tree-lined thoroughfare are a 515–bed hotel, health club, library, parking garage, and multiplex cinema. The wide sidewalks and large public spaces were designed with pedestrians in mind—yet the avenues also allow for a comfortable flow of traffic. Phase 2 for Town Center, designed by Florance Eichbaum Esocoff King Architects, is currently under way. Four major buildings—largely offices and retail spaces—are planned for the area directly west of the existing town center. A one-acre urban park will adjoin.

Thus, the central parts of Reston are admirable, but the farther one moves out from its cores, the more the licensed speculative builders move in, and the less the quality. On the fringes houses indistinguishable from those in any Suburbia, USA will be found, except that the land planning and usage is far better. Moreover a self-conscious seeking of variety militates against a restful atmosphere.

Reston has had its well-publicized troubles: chief among its early difficulties was the strange lack of communication with downtown Washington and with Dulles Airport. Reputedly there were forces, both official (including a highway department and a governmental agency) and private, that conspired against a logical rapid transit system. However, in 1984 a toll road connecting Reston and Dulles was opened, and as a result the town is currently a ten-minute drive from the airport and a half-hour from downtown Washington. The road spurred development in the Reston area, making it the second-largest employment center in Virginia. Reston currently has its own local transportation system, as well as a bus link with Washington's Metrorail and a bus shuttle to Dulles Airport. (There are plans for a Metrorail station to be constructed in Reston within the next ten years.)

Reston will eventually (by the year 2000) be a city of 62,000 (by late 1993 it had approximately 57,000 citizens in some 20,000 units). As the finest effort the U.S. has made toward "new city" living and working, it has many lessons to offer, as has Columbia, Maryland (see page 525). Its land planning and usage is on as high a plane as Columbia's, while the architecture and planning of Reston's central area is considerably better. Both have seemingly settled on routine house types done by speculative builders but on preplanned and prepared (with utilities) land. Hence this major sector is disappointing. But we have much to learn from each, and each should be intently studied for what it has, and what it does not have, to offer. When this is constructively done, we can—in fact, we must—start building new towns that conceivably will match those in Europe. Happily, Reston has in recent years attracted a broad employment base (approximately 32,000 jobs), both governmental and corporate.

Located west from Washington, D.C. on Route 66, then west on Route 267 to Reston Parkway. Tours can be arranged by calling the Reston Visitors Center at (703) 471–7030. AR 7/64, AF 7–8/65, PA 5/66, Int 9/66, AD 2/73, A 12/91

RICHARD J. DALEY CENTER
(1963–66) (formerly Civic Center)
66 West Washington at Dearborn,
Clark, and Randolph streets
Chicago, Illinois

C. F. Murphy Associates,
Skidmore, Owings & Merrill, and
Loebl Schlossman Bennett & Dart,
associate architects

A fresh scale and a businesslike certitude characterize Chicago's Richard J. Daley Center. The design of the thirty-one-story center posed a number of unusual problems in that the bay size (that is, the free floor area established by four columns) had to be unusually large to accommodate the numerous, intermixed courtrooms that make up much of the building. Moreover, the ceiling height had to rise correspondingly, some courtrooms actually piercing through two floors. The resulting bay of 48.3 x 87 feet/14.7 x 26.5 meters is one of the largest yet achieved in any office building. The columns needed to frame these bays and support the building—twelve on the periphery, four within—are expressed on the exterior, the key factors in generating the center's astounding scale. Built up in cruciform plan, the columns measure 5 feet/1.5 meters across at the base (note detail of juncture of vertical and horizontal), and step back (reduce in size) thrice to 2 feet/.6 meter across at the top, lending a subtly tapered profile to the building. In addition, the architects had to contend with another factor that exerted an impact on structure: ventilation in the courtrooms. This required duct sizes up to 4.5 feet/1.4 meters in diameter, hence determined a truss pattern through which the ducts could be woven. The corresponding depth of these trusses, plus the high ceilings needed, make a floor-to-floor height of 18 feet/5.5 meters, or fifty percent greater than a routine building.

The center—which reflects the design influence of Mies van der Rohe—is clad with Cor-Ten steel, its rich, almost velvety finish complemented by bronze-colored, heat-absorbing plate glass. The near monochrome of steel and glass combine to produce majestic solemnity. However, any tendency toward visual heaviness is ameliorated by the lofty, glass-encased ground floor, which is inset from the edge of the building, and by the plaza that flows under the building and into the sunshine on its south side. Continuity is emphasized by using the same granite paving throughout.

The planning of the center's floors could not proceed as with a routine skyscraper, each floor subdivided at will into peripheral offices. In this case, the building not only had an extremely complicated elevator system to contend with (separate cabs for judges, public, prisoners, freight), it also had to accommodate a vast and varied collection of courtrooms (121 in seven different sizes—some small, some two-story and holding 150 people) and to provide public circulation plus office space, in addition to its own corridors, for judges, clerks, and related personnel. To meet these needs the architects devised first the large bay size mentioned, then grouped all the courtrooms on the interior of the building, as the courts did not need windows but definitely required sound insulation. The corridors are along the outer walls (on the court floors)—turning the building inside out, so to speak—where they provide excellent access to the elevators, the various courts, and offices (and offer wide-ranging views of the city). Across the east and west ends on most floors the offices for the judges and secretaries are placed. Inner circulation enables the justices to move in privacy to any courtroom. Except for the equivocal treatment of the ninth and tenth floors, which accommodate mechanical equipment, the building is magnificent. Jacques C. Brownson was in overall charge of design.

In the plaza (345 x 220 feet/105 x 67 meters), sun and light changes play tag with sculpture by Pablo Picasso, the low jets of the fountain sparkle, and the leaves of well-placed trees rustle. Picasso's *Untitled*, 50 feet/15 meters high and weighing in at 324,000 pounds/147,000 kilograms, was installed in 1967. It masterfully accents the square. It is constructed of the same Cor-Ten as the building, but as Sir Roland Penrose, Picasso's biographer, writes, "The materials of which it is made are primarily air and light, held together decisively by the rigid metal." Picasso himself, in an act of wonderful generosity, donated his design and its model "to the people of Chicago." Its construction was made possible by private donations and foundations.

Open Monday–Friday 6:00 A.M.–6:00 P.M., Saturday 6:00 A.M.–12:00 noon. Closed for holidays. For more information call (312) 443–7980. The building is included on the Chicago Architecture Foundation's "Modern and Beyond" tour; the cost is $10. For more information on Chicago Architecture Foundation tours call (312) 922–3432. AF 10/66, PA 10/66, AD 11/66, JAIA 1/68

BOSTON CITY HALL (1963–69)
Government Center Square
Boston, Massachusetts

Kallmann, McKinnell & Knowles, architects

The 1962 competition for the design of the Boston City Hall (which drew 256 entries) was supposedly the first major competition for a comparable civic building in the United States since that of 1909 for the San Francisco City Hall. (In much of northern Europe competitions are held by law for almost *all* public buildings.) It was won by a firm of young architects—Kallmann, McKinnell & Knowles. But more important than the means were the results, which established a powerful, tantalizing direction for American architecture. Before discussing the building, however, Boston's fathers are to be commended for the boldness with which they attacked the large-scale rehabilitation of the skid-row area where the city hall now stands. Several years before the competition (1958) the Boston Government Center Urban Renewal Project retained I. M. Pei and Associates to prepare a master plan for the 60 acres/24 hectares of moribund downtown that they wished to rejuvenate and much of which they had already cleared. Pei's subsequent plan not only stipulated such matters as traffic patterns and vehicular circulation, it established locations and heights for most buildings. Moreover it even demanded that an arcade be included in the projected skyscraper adjacent to the delightful Old State House (206 Washington Street at State Street) so that this could be tied to the new city hall. The plan also required that the decorative 1839 Sears Crescent at the southwest corner of city hall be maintained and renovated—work carried out by F. A. Stahl & Associates. Unfortunately Pei came on the scene too late to save other historic buildings in the area, and equally unfortunately no residential development was mandated, thus leaving the sector deserted (except the Quincy Market—see page 76) after five o'clock.

The city hall itself, though it was kept purposely low (six stories on the plaza side, nine on the lower Congress Street), attains a virile monumentality in concrete, a grandeur with which the exterior is invested and the interior invaded. The influence of Le Corbusier's Monastery of La Tourette (1960) is strong in its design, as reference to the "top-dominating" cantilevered floors of each will attest (and as most critics point out). The contrast of strict mathematics with

the irregular—as seen also in Corbusier's buildings in Chandigarh, India (1956–65)—is prominent in the Boston building where the modular window grid of the upper floors gyrates against irregular, sculptured, hooded projections. In all cases this remarkable three-dimensionality is vigorous.

The architects of the city hall tied the plaza in front to the very heart of the building with a continuous carpet of red brick, Boston's historic building material even before the great fire of 1872. The entrance, which because of the grade change is at the third level, leads to a staggering series of spaces and floors that terrace upward around one: some are anticipated horizontal ones,

while several spaces shoot up five floors to the roof. The lobby creates a dynamic atmosphere of tempting circulation; it is fluid, not fixed. Moreover this great chamber and its surrounding balconies double as an auditorium, serving functions that range from concerts (with excellent acoustics) to fashion shows. Exhibition galleries and access to the mayor and the city council are reached by wide flights of stairs. The top four floors, which form a rectangle around a central light well, accommodate departmental offices. The dominating regularity of their fenestration, as opposed to the variation below, states cellular offices, rather than public areas. The tax, registration, and licensing bureaus are located in a three-story semiseparate brick wing whose daily contact with the public is acknowledged and expressed on the exterior.

There are complexities and extravagances of space in the Boston City Hall that are dubious (as in the 126-foot-/38-meter-high light shafts); the circulation within is sometimes confusing; a soullessness is occasionally apparent; and the all-concrete finish could stand a few touches of color (banners, anyone?). There are, however, few civic interiors of today that carry the city hall's excitement. On the exterior, though the plaza (its basic size and location taken from the Pei plan) is most welcome (in non-snow, non-wind conditions) and is carefully detailed, a lack of spatial cohesiveness can be seen except near the fountain. But enough nit-picking: this is one of our most stimulating contemporary buildings. And like all great buildings—and herein lies an understandable "danger"—it is spawning a dismal collection of weak imitations, which is hardly the fault of its clever architects. Campbell, Aldrich & Nulty were consulting architects; LeMessurier Associates, consulting engineers.

Open Monday–Friday 9:00 A.M.–5:00 P.M. Tours can be scheduled by calling (617) 635-4000. PA 4/63, AR 3/64, AF 6/64, AF 12/67, AF 1–2/69, AR 2/69, Int 4/69, ARev 5/70, AF 6/70, AP 2/73

The Old State House, built in 1712–13, rebuilt in 1748, was plastered with billboards a hundred years ago, shrieking with the importance of the shops and offices within. Scheduled for demolition in 1881 because of the value of its land, it was saved just in time by the Bostonian Society and restored in 1882 by George A. Clough, the city architect. It now serves as a museum.

Open daily 9:30 A.M.–5:00 P.M. Admission is $3 for adults, $2 for senior citizens and students, $1.50 for children ages 6–18. For more information call (617) 720-3290.

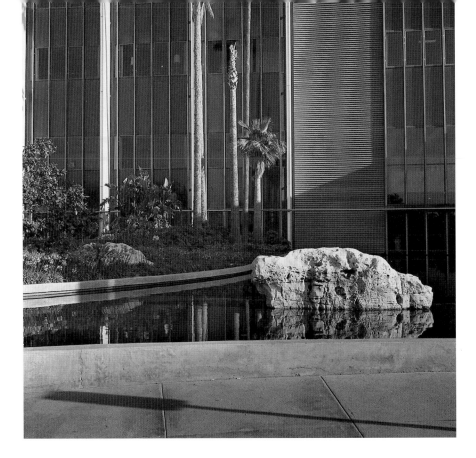

ORANGE COUNTY COURT HOUSE (1964–65)
700 Civic Center Drive at Flower Street
Santa Ana, California

Richard and Dion Neutra in collaboration with
Ramberg, Lowrey & Associates, architects

Richard Neutra (1892–1970) added immeasurably to the architectural development of the United States. The contribution of this Viennese-born maestro is seen at its apogee in his brilliant houses: Lovell (1929), von Sternberg (1936), Nesbitt (1942), Kaufmann (1946), and Tremaine (1948)—among others—stimulating a revolutionary effect on domestic designing. They number, unequivocally, among the finest houses in the country. (Unfortunately all these dwellings—except the superb von Sternberg, which was destroyed—are in private hands and are not open to the public.) Among Neutra's larger works the Orange County Court House is the most successful. The building is functionally and expressively divided into a broad, low (three-story) unit for municipal offices routinely used by the public, with a high block (eleven stories) for superior courtrooms and offices projecting at right angles and set back from the street by a particularly well-landscaped garden and pool. The building's exterior is marked by a prominent play of fins and louvers for sun protection (a Neutra trademark); the south side of the high block is almost totally screened by banks of electronically actuated vertical louvers. Would that more buildings were so shielded. The interiors are quietly efficient, with great care taken to make the courtroom atmosphere as sympathetic as possible.

Open Monday–Friday 9:00 A.M.–5:00 P.M. Closed for holidays.

ST. FRANCIS DE SALES CHURCH (1964–66)
2929 McCracken Avenue
Muskegon, Michigan

Marcel Breuer and Herbert Beckhard, architects

The trapezoidal front wall—a "banner"—of St. Francis de Sales Church splays out laterally as it rises, while at the same time leaning backward; its two side walls are double curved in parabolic sections; and its back, also a trapezoid, splays in toward the top, and leans in. Structure was the driving force of this design. As Marcel Breuer has said, "Church architecture, at its best, is always identical with the structural logic of the enclosure" (*L'Architecture d'Aujourd'hui* 108, 1963). The strength of the exterior is carried through within, where we find a walled-in, virtually windowless (except for skylight) nave of great power. The spatial effect on entering under the low balcony, then encountering the lofty nave, is significant, as is the relation of the freestanding balcony to the church.

The sanctuary is theatrically understated, with an uncluttered stone altar and pulpit resting on a low red brick podium, and with a plain concrete ciborium or canopy cantilevered from the rear wall. The altar (with bright colored *betonglass* in the ceiling of its niche) lies off-center and above and is reached dramatically by sixteen steps. The choir is asymmetrically placed at left in front of the organ. The nave, which seats 972 (with 231 in the balcony), slopes downward in theater fashion. As the prime source of all lighting, natural or artificial, comes from either the roof skylights or from ceiling fixtures placed between the beams, a stern atmosphere results, but the solidity of encircling concrete offers protection and comfort against the outside world. The narthex shelters the baptistry in the center, with a stained-glass window overhead. The parish offices stand at the rear. In 1989 a social hall and small chapel were added to the front of the church.

West from town on Sherman Boulevard or Norton Avenue. Open Monday–Friday 8:30 A.M.–12:00 noon and 1:00 –4:30 P.M. Sunday services held at 8:00, 9:30, and 11:30 A.M. Free tours can be arranged by calling (616) 755–1953. AR 3/62, AR 11/67

SALK INSTITUTE (1964–66/1993)
10010 North Torrey Pines Road
San Diego (La Jolla), California

Louis I. Kahn, architect
Anshen & Allen, architects of the addition

This vast, haunting agora, flanked by angled walls focused on the infinity of the Pacific, provides a brilliantly formal setting on a gloriously informal site. To some observers the Salk Institute's symmetry (most of Kahn's buildings are symmetrical) seems ill at ease in the free landscape of rolling hills, with the sea beyond. Kahn himself worried about this and asked Luis Barragán, the noted Mexican architect and landscape architect, for suggestions. Barragán said, "I would not put a tree or blade of grass in this space. This should be a plaza of stone, not a garden" (*L'Architecture d'Aujourd'hui* 142, March 1969). The resulting effect, when one enters the gates, is that one is immediately mesmerized by the space and by the pencil-thin channel of water bisecting the courtyard and aimed for Mother Ocean. Even the travertine paving is scored to emphasize the adventure to infinity, an impression abetted by the insistent perspective of the blank, angled walls of the studies.

The east-west-oriented court is lined with study towers—the private offices for thirty-six Fellows—arranged in two-story banks of nine per side and angled to face the sea. These retreats are separated from the two enormous blocks of laboratories, which frame the far sides, by an elaborate, semi-enclosed circulation cloister. The offices for the Fellows plug directly into the laboratories (a half flight up or down), each of which forms a structurally open rectangle 65 x 245 feet/20 x 75 meters in size and subdivisible at will. All three floors of the laboratories are topped by full-height (9 feet/2.7 meters) service floors that carry the trusses, freeing the labs beneath of the need of columns. In addition these floors provide total flexibility for the elaborate pipe- and duct-work that feed the experiments below. Projecting behind each laboratory block are five service towers containing toilet facilities, storage spaces, laboratory equipment, elevators, and stairs. Every major element is precisely stated.

Walking through the articulated circulation between the study wings and the lab blocks—to Kahn "architecture is a thoughtful making of spaces" (*Progressive Architecture*, April 1961)—one encounters passages of sunshine and shadow, freedom and enclosure. This experience is even more exciting than that of the simple Italian cloisters that Dr. Jonas Salk—who was an eager, knowledgeable client—initially had in mind. The laboratories themselves, with their divisible-at-will loft structural framing, stand in pointed contrast to Lou Kahn's famous Alfred Newton Richards Medical Building in Philadelphia (see page 438), whose genesis was the intimate, in-touch-with-neighbor approach.

Onto the west (ocean) end of the Salk blocks are tacked—without the clarity that distinguishes the major elements—four floors of offices, plus library and cafeteria on the ground floor, all overlooking the Pacific. At the opposite, or entry, end are the mechanical wings with open service floors so that future changes can be made without interrupting any research facility. Guest housing and a meeting center were also planned but never built. Dr. August E. Komendant was structural consultant. The Versailles of the virus.

Note: In 1977 a below-ground laboratory space was added under the south terrace by Naramore, Bain, Brady & Johanson in association with Deems/Lewis & Partners. In 1993 a very substantial addition, which upsets the original space unfurling, was begun to the east by Anshen + Allen Architects.

Located off Genessee exit of I-5, west on Genessee Street. Open Monday–Friday 8:30 A.M.–5:00 P.M. Free tours given at 10:00 A.M., 11:00 A.M., and 12:00 noon. Group tours can be arranged by calling (619) 453-4100 ext. 1200. AF 5/65, AF 12/67, JAIA 3/77, A 7/93, PA 10/93, A 3/96

WHITNEY MUSEUM OF AMERICAN ART (1964–66)
945 Madison Avenue at 75th Street
New York, New York

Marcel Breuer and Hamilton P. Smith, architects

As one approaches the Whitney, its upside-down, stepped pyramidal form might well conjure esthetic juggling: in actuality, the shape grew from a logic so programmatic that its form was in effect self-generating. Marcel Breuer believed museum "identity" should be expressed, but within the parameters of reason: "sculpture with rather serious functional requirements" as he put it (quoted by Cranston Jones, *Horizon*, summer 1967). The generating mandate of the Whitney's Board of Trustees insisted—wisely—that an open sculpture court be incorporated in the museum's design, with maximum gallery areas above; exposed sculpture would subconsciously "tease" people into the museum. Inasmuch as the amount of land available was severely limited, the open court was placed a full floor below street level and across the front of the lot with only a curtain of glass separating it from the exhibition and restaurant space directly behind. This "moat" is imaginatively bridged to inaugurate a stimulating parade to the museum—a "ritual," it has been called—while the sunken sculpture court issues constant invitations to the passersby to come in.

The entrance lobby, which occupies most of the front of the ground floor, contains ticket and sales counter and checkroom under a ceiling with too much visual agitation, a nervousness that fades into serenity as one enters the galleries on the three upper floors. These totally flexible, largely column-free spaces, especially the extra-high one (17.5 feet/5.3 meters) on the fourth floor, are scintillating exhibition areas, which is, after all, what a museum is about. An open egg-crate grid of precast concrete on 2-foot/.6-meter squares is suspended from the ceiling: its waffle reticulation contains continuously wired tracking, which allows complete freedom in the placement of spotlights. Partitions 4 feet/1.2 meters wide (with aluminum cores) are like the lights in that they can be affixed to the grid where needed to subdivide the spaces. As most of the Whitney shows are temporary, such flexibility is essential. Partitions and walls are painted to reflect the needs of each exhibition. In addition to the major spaces on the three floors, there is a more intimate, more "domestic" gallery on the north side of two floors, which not only provides a different kind and texture of space for difficult (and semi-permanent) exhibits, but makes for greater perceptual stimulation, because of its variety, for museum-goers. The largely concealed fifth floor houses museum offices. Below the sculpture court, lower gallery, and restaurant there is a full working basement. The vertical circulation of the museum is not altogether sufficient—more could have been made of the stairs—and its hooded windows are personal, but in its essential object-displaying function under extremely cramped conditions, the Whitney is hard to beat: its fourth floor is unequaled. Its only problem is its overwhelming success. Michael H. Irving was consulting architect.

Open Wednesday 11:00 A.M.–6:00 P.M., Thursday 1:00–8:00 P.M., Friday–Sunday 11:00 A.M.–6:00 P.M. Closed July 4, Thanksgiving, Christmas, and New Year's Day. Admission is $7 for adults, $5 for students and senior citizens, free for children under 12. Admission is free Thursday 6:00–8:00 P.M. Free tours available; group tours can be scheduled in advance. For more information call (212) 570-3676. AF 1/64, AF 9/66, Int 10/66, PA 10/66, AD 12/66, JAIA 9/78, A 8/85, AR 10/85

SEA RANCH (1965–)
Sea Ranch, California

Moore, Lyndon, Turnbull & Whitaker, architects of condominium
Joseph Esherick & Associates, architects of store/restaurant
Lawrence Halprin & Associates, planners and landscape architects

The Sea Ranch enterprise, primarily for second homes, is located a bit over 100 miles/160 kilometers north of San Francisco. The site covers a 10-mile/16-kilometer stretch of rolling, generally lovely land that rises from the rock-strewn Pacific to meadows and wooded hills. "Dynamic conservation" and careful land stewardship have characterized the philosophy, and initially the practice, of the development of its 5,000 acres/2,023 hectares. Its concern for quality of environment is benevolent (though not as pristine as early on), and the extraordinary research that went into bioclimatic needs, wind and soil studies, etc., which preceded site planning and prompted building design guidelines, is impressive. So that maximum freedom of land would result, no routine strip planning was allowed, only clusters and commons of houses grouped together to leave the ground around them open to all property owners. Moreover there are only a few houses along the oceanfront blocking the views of those behind, with most groups screened by rows of trees and shrubs from the predominant (and cool) northwest breeze. It is a remarkably well-planned residential development.

The architecture of Sea Ranch, particularly that of Condominium 1 (visible from the public center), has exerted a pervasive (when misunderstood, perversive) influence on recent American architecture. Here it represents a back-to-nature school that was logically evolved (using wind-tunnel tests, among others) and is regionally appropriate. In less capable hands this approach is plucked from the architectural magazines and degenerates into a shack cliché. Shelter, security, and scale in a wide-open landscape were of prime concern to the condominium's architects, as well as "territoriality" and a sense of coherence, followed by a hierarchy of spatial experiences from outdoors to in. The ten condominium units—redwood town houses on a sea-girt point—form an almost defensively clustered small hilltown. But whereas imagination and the intuitive played their part in design, close technical studies indicated angled or shed roofs to create tranquil lee side shelters. The result is not one of capriciousness. The approach was meticulously developed with a broad motor court containing garages, then a smaller sheltered court, and finally one's unit—with the whole stepping down the hillside as it clutches the topography.

The condominium bears, for some, a curious relation to the wild but magnificent nature about it. This stems from the fact that the outdoors is almost an enemy. Thus from the interior one observes the sea, maybe the coastline—rarely a glimpse of other units—yet one participates with the surroundings generally through plate glass. The apartment interiors are climaxed by exuberant three-dimensionality with skylights pulling vertically and south views probing the coast laterally. Each unit has a key room about which the spaces revolve. Sadly— as the architects point out in their book *The Place of Houses* (Holt, Rinehart and Winston, 1974)—the beautiful, promising beginnings are weakening. Although former design restrictions still exist, current designs do not always live up to earlier examples. However, there is still much to be gleaned from the notable successes of Sea Ranch, and if a few lessons are negative, the overall achievement is very positive.

The lodge, restaurant, and store are at their best within, where the natural-finish wood (Canadian cedar), the changes in level, and the play of angles are full of imagination. The dashing graphics are by Barbara Stauffacher. The restaurant and store were expanded (1969) by Alfred Boeke and Louis McLane to include a twenty-unit lodge.

Located on CA 1, 2.5 miles/4 kilometers north of Stewarts Point, 11 miles/18 kilometers south of Gualala. Only the lodge and restaurant are open to the public. Lodge open daily 7:30 A.M.–8:00 P.M. Restaurant (located inside the lodge) open at mealtimes. AR 11/65, PA 5/66, PA 3/70, AR 11/74, AR 3/75, A 12/84, PA 2/93

JESSE H. JONES HALL (1965–66)
615 Louisiana Street between Texas and Capitol streets
Houston, Texas

Caudill, Rowlett, Scott, architects

Well wrapped in Italian travertine, and surrounded by a stately but logical peristyle of piers, which clearly support an independent roof, the Jesse H. Jones Hall for the Performing Arts sets a seignorial scene. The exterior, though formal, is not dour, while within, the building is ingeniously planned. The great sheltering roof is upheld by eight slender piers per side with the concert hall proper expressed as a freely shaped cocoon beneath, the entry to this cocoon standing clear and inviting. Moreover the peristyle surrounding the hall is illuminated at night and, as the marble facing is carried right into the inviting lobby, one finds oneself welcomed, pulled inside before knowing it. This transfer of spaces, from out to in and back again, works easily, while the overhang of the roof on all sides facilitates arrival and departure by car in dirty weather. (There is also direct under-cover entrance via the public garage beneath the square in front.)

Inasmuch as the city block—which slopes down toward the front and which the hall completely fills—measures 250 feet/76 meters on a side, and as a three-thousand-seat theater was desired, the architects were put to it to reconcile requests with realities. They achieved this by placing the auditorium, stage, and lobbies, and the free-form curved walls that enclose them, on a diagonal under the square roof, thus gaining maximum depth. This further permitted a wide entry in one corner, with a diminishing lobby wrapped around the sides and back of the auditorium. This extra width at the front door—facilitated by the narrow stage end adjacent—has been used to make a graciously wide, tall foyer, which steps up in three terraces to the rear of the auditorium. An ambitious Richard Lippold wire sculpture arches over all.

Lateral doors on stepped platforms give access to the hall proper, each door serving three rows of seats that radiate in the aisle-less fashion, their bright red covering creating a cheery note. The inner walls of the auditorium are divided by piers wrapped with teak, creating an undulating effect that serves both acoustics and scale. The ceiling is made of 870 independent, bronze-colored, hexagonal panels that not only provide acoustic reflection but also screen the house downlights. Rows of these panels can be raised and lowered (as much as 27.5 feet/8.4 meters) to change seating capacity and acoustic reverberation demands for various types of music from an orchestra to a play to a single voice. The system works beautifully. In addition to the main floor seating 1,781, boxes accommodate 286, a mezzanine (with distracting front edge) 326, and a balcony 608, for a total of 3,001.

Jesse Jones Hall was designed primarily for the Houston Symphony; however, it is also used for opera, ballet, and theatrical events. For concert performances the acoustic hexagons that cover the auditorium can be extended over the stage, and side wings pivoted into place, making one room of stage and auditorium. For other events this stage extension of ceiling and sides can be neatly folded and stored against the rear wall, enabling the overhead fly loft to be used. George C. Izenour, the theatrical consultant and engineer, developed the imaginative theater mechanics for electronically controlled acoustic flexibility; Bolt, Beranek & Newman were acoustic consultants; Charles E. Lawrence was the design partner of CRS. Jones Hall has been termed "the most sophisticated building of its kind anywhere in the world" (*Architectural Record*, February 1967).

Open during performances. Tours can be arranged by calling (713) 227–3974. AR 2/67, JAIA 6/67

NATIONAL CENTER FOR ATMOSPHERIC RESEARCH (1965–66)
1850 Table Mesa Drive
Boulder, Colorado

I. M. Pei & Partners, architects

The National Center for Atmospheric Research's setting and the building's relation to it are highly congenial. The complex rests on a mesa south of Boulder with the Rockies as backdrop, with evergreens on all sides, and with the flat plains of eastern Colorado fanning out in front. Though chromatically tied to the mountains by pinkish concrete walls echoing the hills, the structure asserts itself and its independence by vertical abruptness and by an emphasis on what might be termed "top thrust," as opposed to any built-up evolution from the ground. At some angles the center, from a distance, appears almost toylike and untethered in this wild pageant of nature, a lonely bastion against the mountain gods.

This community of buildings—two tall units connected by a lower base—evolved from diffuse program requirements, but with a specific operating philosophy. As space needs at the planning stage could not be precisely defined, flexibility was of utmost importance. The philosophy, in turn, sought a non-dogmatic, non-slick research center where teams of experts could work together on common problems, yet each specialist could at will repair to his or her adjacent—and sacrosanct—office. The building thus evolved in clusters with offices, in general, adjacent to central work, discussion, and lab areas.

The NCAR is reached by a road that allows tantalizing vignettes as one winds up to the summit. One enters past a sculptured "gate" (of some self-importance), to be confronted by two five-story blocks, resembling castellated strongholds, hooded and mysterious. (Some critics believe that the Cliff Dwellings in Mesa Verde, Colorado—see page 23—were of influence here.) One faces the end of the office-laboratory unit, its three "heads" poking from the top like gigantic sentry posts surveying the approaches. Nearest the entry and projecting at right (and at right angles to the other) is a similar unit housing the non-lab-related offices for the center. These two precisely sliced masses—the dominant elements of the design—are both stunning and disturbing. One is transfixed by their power, yet one wonders what goes on behind those neat, narrow bands of dark windows that run up the center of the broad sides of each tower, then erupt in wide canopied glass horizontals at top. Offices and labs, one finds, lie behind, and though some sacrifice of natural illumination results, wall space, not window space, was sought, with offices focused on work inside, not views out. Visual infinity and contact with nature await in the top-floor offices and the terraces. Between the two five-story blocks is the service wing common to all. This includes lobby and display area on the ground floor, with cafeteria, kitchen, and dining terrace in the southwest corner and library above. A ramp from the second floor leads directly to the west mesa. A ground-level terrace also offers relief from office confinement. The other five-story block is connected on the second level (as well as first floor and basement) with the common facilities.

One of the stimuli of the center is its total three-dimensionality. One can walk completely around it and view fresh juxtapositions and intergroup relations. Though verging toward the dogmatic in its arsenal character, it is nonetheless exciting, and is, one understands, much liked by the four hundred to five hundred scientists and support staff who work there. Dr. Walter Orr Roberts, the first head of NCAR, had an active hand in planning the center. James P. Morris and Robert Lym were associates in charge. Dan Kiley was landscape architect.

Located 2.5 miles/4 kilometers southwest off Broadway (COL 93). Open Monday–Friday 8:00 A.M.–5:00 P.M., Saturday–Sunday and holidays 9:00 A.M.–3:00 P.M. Labor Day–mid-June tours given Wednesday at 12:00 noon; mid-June–September tours given Monday–Saturday at 12:00 noon. For more information call (303) 497–8602. AF 1/64, AF 10/67, AR 10/67, PA 10/67

MAUNA KEA BEACH HOTEL (1965–68)
62–100 Mauna Kea Beach Drive
Kamuela, Hawaii, Hawaii

Skidmore, Owings & Merrill, architects

It is not just the stepped terraces of rooms overlooking the views that make this hotel distinctive: André Lurçat did this at Ajaccio in 1931. And it is not just the deft planting outside and in—at times it is difficult to tell outside from in—that gives it so much élan. Such "landscaping" is found in much sensitive building on the Hawaiian Islands. Mauna Kea's greatest impact comes from the unfolding and interweaving of its inner spaces, both vertical and lateral; these are almost staggering in their three-dimensional sensuousness. From the longitudinal spine whose roof is open to the sun by day and the stars by night (with full-grown palms down its middle probing the sky), to the stepped-back levels that form the inner gallery/corridors and overlook the garden courts, the unexpected awaits at every step. Such architectural experiences (by the San Francisco office of SOM) do not come readily.

The spaces commence their happy task at the entry, a subtly innocuous, indeed almost invisible opening with a small bridge escorting one to the reception hall where the Pacific lures one forward. All is open. One looks down to the lower level, out to the ocean, up to the sky, and sideways to the garden court, with a bouquet of restless palms towering directly in front. There is no glass there, only space. No architectural flabbiness is to be seen, no ersatz vernacular, simply an exquisite understanding of what architecture, not stage-setting, is all about.

The entry level is given over to administration, with the lower floors, notched into the hillside, occupied by shops, a two-story colonnade, and bar and buffet, the latter overlooking beach and sea. A 220-seat auditorium is set in the hillside. The rectangular, wood-framed dining pavilion lies separate but attached on the ocean side, with a broad terrace onto the Pacific. The main building, with small lateral angling to minimize bulk, contains three levels of hotel rooms, half facing the water, half the mountains, each level stepping back as it rises to create tiers of privately screened balconies on both sides. As mentioned, these tiers do not meet at the top, thus the center is open to the sky, while the inner overhangs resulting from the stepped profile provide weatherproof corridors for room access. Cross-bridges at intervals excite the spaces. The natural ventilation, incidentally, is so good most of the year that bedroom air-conditioning is rarely needed. The bedroom furnishings reflect the quiet luxury of a fine home. The extensive artwork, drawn from a wide range of Polynesian culture, is often of museum caliber. It was selected by the architects who also designed the elegant interiors.

The main structure is of reinforced concrete (of excellent formwork scaled with a V profile) and painted white, with local woods used for many walls. The hotel is named for the Mauna Kea volcano ("White Mountain"—it is often topped with snow, being 13,796 feet/4,205 meters high)—that lies 25 miles (40 kilometers) to the southeast. The hotel was built with 154 rooms; 102 more were added three years after opening in a separate building designed by Wimberly, Whisenand, Allison & Tong. A clubhouse with full sports facilities and snack bar is set back on the land side. The landscaping, with considerable cover brought in from other islands because of difficult local lava growing conditions, has been very imaginatively handled, outside and in, by Eckbo, Dean, Austin & Williams. Superb, and, at last, a contemporary building that fully reflects the architectural potentialities of the Islands.

Located on the coast, south of HI 26. AR 10/64, Int 3/66, AF 5/66, JAIA 3/82

HAWAII STATE CAPITOL (1965–69)
235 South Beretania Street
between Richards and Punchbowl
Honolulu, Oahu, Hawaii

John Carl Warnecke & Associates and
Belt, Lemmon & Lo, architects

Architectural symbolism, being elusive, finds rare use today. However in this capitol we find a bowed roof profile with a voluptuous void in the center that hints of the island's volcanic origin, a moat recalling the seas around it, and a towering (65 feet/20 meters high) peristyle of twenty-four columns reminiscent of the palms that line its shores. The large walk-through central court develops strong architectural forces with its contrast of lateral versus vertical spaces and its sharp chiaroscuro. This courtyard also imaginatively serves as a viewing platform for the Senate and House of Representatives chambers—both ovoid—that occupy lower levels on opposite sides. Their end walls are of glass, enabling the public to watch proceedings even when outside the building. (There are, of course, interior spectator galleries.) Senate offices (second floor) and House offices (third) are tucked under and shaded by the larger fourth level, which is devoted to departmental offices and is immediately identifiable by its frieze of vertical louvers. The square "well" in the center diminishes slightly above the third floor. The setback executive level occupies the top (fifth) floor and is surrounded by a deck. Parking for 234 official cars is in the basement. Construction is of earthquake-resistant concrete. John Carl Warnecke was architect in charge of design; Cyril W. Lemmon architect in charge of project development. The master plan for the area is now fully developed and the capitol's grounds flow into those surrounding the nearby 'Iolani Palace (see page 265).

Open daily 7:45 A.M.–4:30 P.M. Closed for holidays. Free tours given daily. Tours can also be scheduled by calling (808) 586–0178. AR 5/69, AF 6/61, AR 6/61, PA 1/62

UNIVERSITY OF MASSACHUSETTS AT DARTMOUTH (1965–72)
North Dartmouth, Massachusetts

Paul Rudolph and Desmond & Lord, architects

Architecturally imaginative in many facets, the university was planned, designed, and detailed primarily by Paul Rudolph. It was originally intended to be the state's technical college. However, after the completion of many of the class units the curriculum was changed to embrace a fully rounded university, with five undergraduate colleges and a graduate program. Basic to the overall site planning was the decision to confine all vehicular circulation, including trucks, to the outer periphery of the academic area with small service roads direct to the buildings. Dormitories, service structures, and athletic facilities are located outside the peripheral drive. As most of the staff and students arrive by car, parking was a major concern; it has been smartly handled by a series of parking lots placed around the university but covered by berms and trees so that they are almost invisible.

The academic complex fronts on an undisturbed grass mall lined by classroom buildings at the upper end, with communal and administrative units loosely but carefully composed beyond. As the approach is from the north one initially comes upon the buildings from the sunless side—an unfortunate introduction, but one whose cheerlessness is soon dissipated on encountering the vigorous play of sun and shadow, light and shade, and intermeshing building forms of the two class rows that define the mall. Relatively close together at the north end, these three-story instruction units splay outward and step back as they proceed southward down the slight grade; their horizontal sweep is punctuated at the end by a 180-foot/55-meter television tower (by Grattan Gill). The space between the two rows escapes westward in a surprise right-angle vista that pivots around tower and library and carries the eye to a distant lake. This vista is framed by an amphitheater to the north and a fine arts building to the south. (The fine arts building, library, auditorium, and administration building were designed by Desmond & Lord.)

The classroom rows are composed of six-bay clusters that step back in three stages to total eighteen units. All are of reinforced concrete frame with walls of ribbed concrete block. Lecture and general-purpose classrooms are located on the ground floor and are inset to provide a covered, open-air circulation arcade along the edges of the mall. Other classrooms, including some specialized laboratories and studios, are found on the second floor, with offices on the top. These office units are placed at right angles to their access corridors and to the axis of the class block, and from the outside can be immediately recognized by their prominent cantilevered projections. At each nodal point between the three clusters there is a spacious hall that not only serves vertical circulation, but doubles as a spot for spontaneous gatherings and study nooks. These spaces range in size from small stages to intimate corners and are most popular. An elaborate system of hollow piers sets the structural module; they are sufficiently large to accommodate all utilities. Rigidity can be seen in the locked-in divisions of the three-story class blocks, their eternal concrete surfaces are not continually sympathetic, few of the windows can be opened, and an agitated complexity can be seen at times. But in overall plan UMass Dartmouth is conceptually excellent, its spatial experiences from covered conversation pits to outdoor arenas to building relations are stimulating, while strong design continuity ties all together.

Located between Fall River and New Bedford, off Old Westport Road, 1.4 miles/2.3 kilometers south of US 6 and just south of I-195. Grounds open daily. Closed for holidays. 90-minute tours are available Monday–Saturday and can be scheduled by calling (508) 999–8782. AR 10/66, AR 1/75

INTERMOUNTAIN GAS COMPANY (1966)
555 Cole Road at McMullen
Boise, Idaho

Kenneth W. Brooks, architect

"Care, imagination and skill have made what might have been a prosaic utilitarian structure into a fine architectural achievement" (American Institute of Architects upon giving the building a national Award of Merit). Four separate but carefully related units comprise this facility on a bluff on the western edge of the city: the headquarters office block, a service center to west, conference center at east, and—greeting one at entry and on axis with the office—a power house of putty-gray brick. The power house, a truncated cone in shape, was assigned its strategic position to emphasize natural gas as a source of energy. Its location was determined by architect and landscape architect working together. Its interior presents an array of color-coded machinery that makes a stimulating functional palette. The building once used solely natural gas but now uses outside electrical power to supply electricity, heat, and air conditioning for all units. The service building and conference center are of muted, glazed blue brick, which plays an active role in reflecting the sun and clouds. On a beautifully landscaped low podium on the north side sits the trim story-and-a-half administration building, both of whose levels overlook the Boise Valley; its all-glass upper walls are protected by a wide arcade. The interior of the open main floor is broken by two solid blocks that house workrooms and conference rooms and that are sheathed in the warm gray brick also used outside. The conference center is used for lectures, dining, meetings—both company and community—and cooking demonstrations, using its two completely equipped gas kitchens. The landscaping, by Lawrence Halprin & Associates, pulls the four buildings together in commendable fashion, and, in the process, carefully hides the eighty-four sheltered parking spaces behind rows of trees.

Open Monday–Friday during business hours. Closed for holidays. Tours can be scheduled by calling (208) 377–6000. JAIA 7/67

MCMATH-PIERCE SOLAR TELESCOPE (1966)
National Solar Observatory
AZ 386
Kitt Peak, Arizona

Skidmore, Owings & Merrill, architects and engineers

Most industrial and technical architecture takes a prosaic turn; here it has been lifted to imaginative heights using the simplest of shapes and the most mundane of materials. The McMath-Pierce Solar Telescope —the largest solar telescope in the world—is a fixed instrument 500 feet/152 meters long, 300 feet/91 meters of which are underground, and is angled at thirty-two degrees into its mountain base. On its top (110 feet/33 meters high) an 80-inch/203-centimeter in diameter heliostat, driven with incredible precision, follows the arc of the sun. This then reflects the solar image down the long optical tunnel (oriented along a north polar axis) to a 60-inch/152-centimeter mirror at bottom, which returns it to another mirror (48 inches/122 centimeters in diameter) near the spot where the casing enters the earth. This last shoots the sun's image into the observation room with its vacuum spectrographs for analysis. To prevent temperature and lateral (from wind) fluctuations, which would upset extremely delicate calculations, the whole shaft is encased by a water-cooled wind shield whose outer skin is the sun-reflective, white-painted copper sheathing that we see. By placing the square solar tunnel and its square vertical support on diagonals relative to each other, a functional shape resulted—the relation minimizing wind pressure and facilitating rain and snow removal. In addition, a geometric interaction that is extremely potent esthetically, both at a distance and close up, has been created.

A section of the telescope's interior at ground level is open to the public. Here one can observe some of its workings and hear a taped recording on its functioning. From the area's base height (6,760 feet/2,060 meters) one also enjoys far-stretching panoramas. Note the mosque-like domes of the stellar telescopes that pepper the mountain (these are not open to the public). The Kitt Peak site was selected, after a long search, for sky clarity, lack of turbulence, and convenience to a city relatively free of light pollution. It occupies land leased from the Tohono O'odham tribe, on whose reservation it sits. Magnificent. The National Solar Observatory, which is supported by a number of noted universities, was designed by the Chicago office of SOM, with Myron Goldsmith chief designer and William E. Dunlap partner in charge. It was named for Dr. Robert R. McMath and Dr. A. Keith Pierce, who proposed it.

Located 39 miles/63 kilometers west of Tucson on AZ 86, then 13 miles/21 kilometers south on AZ 386 at the end of the road. Open daily 9:00 A.M.–3:45 P.M. Closed Christmas Eve, Christmas, and New Year's Day. One-hour guided tours given at 11:00 A.M., 1:00 P.M., and 2:30 P.M.; a $2-per-person donation is suggested. For more information call (520) 318–8200. AF 10/67, A 3/84

FORD FOUNDATION BUILDING (1966–67)
320 East 43rd Street
New York, New York

Roche/Dinkeloo & Associates, architects; Dan Kiley, landscape architect

Humanity's initial experience in a garden got off to a shaky start, but the rewards of embracing nature are obviously tempting. Eden was momentous while Babylon was imperishably hailed as one of the Seven Wonders. However, it is doubtful that any designer has achieved so much in so little space as in this dramatic garden in a stronghold of philanthropy. As one enters the building from the shadowy main (43rd Street) entrance—it can be approached from 42nd Street—the unexpected confrontation with a sun-dappled forest ensorcells. Municipal zoning laws require that a certain proportion of a site (the proportion depending on the building's height) be kept open; when Roche & Dinkeloo proposed an enclosed garden instead of an open-to-the-street court to meet this code requirement, the firm was logically granted a variance to permit the building to be so designed. The structure is almost precisely square in plan, with its working area concentrated in an *L* shape that enfolds the garden on the north and west sides. Except for the offices facing 43rd Street, most of the remaining ones open (literally) onto the enclosed court for their full ten-story height. The eleventh floor, containing the chairman's office, conference rooms, and the executives' and employees' dining rooms, completely frames the court on four sides, but allows the space of the courtyard to burst through in the center to vanish in the skylight that caps its ceiling 160 feet/49 meters above. From the ground floor to the tenth, the east and south sides enclosing the garden are largely of glass, through which the sun pours by day, and thus lights the offices on the court side; by dusk the court is internally spot-lit and thus delights the passersby. The three granite-faced parallelograms poking from the east and south sides (angled to provide a better view of the East River) contain fire stairs (the two near the office wings) and air-conditioning discharge pylon (on the corner).

The garden court is conditioned to keep a year-round temperature of a low of 50° F/10° C in winter to a high of 85° F/29° C in summer. Heating coils along the window-walls keep the glass-conducted cold of winter in control. The garden is, of course, interconnected with the air-conditioning system of the entire building. Comprising a mere third of an acre (.13 hectare), the garden deploys an intriguing series of levels (it steps down 13 feet/4 meters from 43rd to 42nd streets), so that its exploration produces new and unexpected vistas at almost every turn: it is not a two-dimensional layout, but a bountiful bit of landscaped witchcraft. The earth-tone colors of the Cor-Ten weathering steel and the granite give the greenery a sympathetic background. Among the plants are a magnolia, eucalyptus, and Japanese cedar, plus a vast assortment of shrubs, vines, and flowers. There are numerous planting zones, each automatically watered and nourished with liquid fertilizer by underground piping. Some of the planting has not lived up to expectation, and bugs are a problem at times (there being no birds), but this patch of greenery still refreshes all who see it. In addition to providing a visual focus, the garden acts as a cohesive agent for the foundation staff in that it makes a "family" of the glass-walled offices, including those of the president. All are working for the common goal—to dispense monies wisely; thus most of the staff enjoy offices that partake of a mutual—and stunning—collective space. The garden court ties human to fellow human and both to nature. From the imagination of concept, to the boldness of realization, to impeccable detailing, the building is superb. The Ford Foundation has never made a more wonderful, or more lasting, bequest to the city—and indeed to all of us.

Garden is open to the public Monday–Friday 9:00 A.M.–10 :00 P.M. Closed for holidays. AR 2/68, PA 2/68, Int 3/68, AD 7/68

RIVERPLACE TOWER (1966–67)
(formerly Gulf Life Center)
1301 Riverplace Boulevard
Jacksonville, Florida

Welton Becket Associates, architects

Riverplace Tower brings a fresh look at skyscraper construction, with an exoskeletal, precast, post-tensioned concrete frame. The result not only produces an economical structure but a measure of sun control and effective modulation and play of light and shade. The twenty-seven-story building (plus concourse and mechanical floors) forms the pivotal unit of a complex that includes an adjacent hotel and shopping mall. The center helped spark Jacksonville's urban redevelopment. The entire San Marco peninsula, across the St. Johns River from the city's downtown core, had been a run-down area, crowded with depressed buildings. Gulf Life acquired a large section (12 acres/4.8 hectares) of this land, which is strategically adjacent to the Main Street Bridge and across the river from the new Civic Auditorium and other riverfront improvements, and rejuvenated much of the area. This imaginative skyscraper and the adjacent Jacksonville Hilton (also designed by Welton Becket Associates, it is now closed) were only the first units of this redevelopment. In 1978 construction began on an adjoining 16-acre/6.5-hectare site called St. Johns Place. This includes the 322-room Marina Hotel, a shopping center, an extensive boardwalk along the river, and a small office block (1981). Saxelbye, Powell, Roberts & Ponder are the architects. Jacksonville is among the few riverfront cities that has been farsighted enough to rediscover and utilize its water location for other than industrial use. Most river cities in the United States either ignore the visual possibilities of their sites or erect a barrier reef of highways around their periphery.

Riverplace Tower itself is a muscular building measuring 430 feet/131 meters high (above podium) and 144 feet/44 meters square. Its floors are supported by eight massive external concrete columns, two per side (near the third points), and the poured-in-place central service core. There are no interior columns. The prominent T-shaped beams are each made of fourteen prefabricated segments strung on 12.5-inch/32-centimeter, high-strength cables or "tendons" and post-tensioned in the method pioneered by the late Eugene Freyssinet. The beams taper horizontally to their ends and bulge outward from the building—reflecting their loads—and produce a mercurial sculptured effect as the sun moves about them. Strips of plate glass windows are set just behind the beams, their gray tint lending contrast to the white concrete frame. The tower rests on a podium and from this spring the eight supporting columns, which are freestanding (49.5 feet/15 meters high) to the top of the mezzanine and which make a dramatically scaled entry. Slung under the building and set back from the edge is the Sun Bank of Jacksonville, reached by escalators from the glass-enclosed lobby. Richard R. Bradshaw, Inc. were structural engineers; Kemp, Bunch & Jackson, associate architects.

Located east of the Main Street Bridge (US 1 and 90). Stores open to the public during business hours. Riverplace Tower lobby open to the public Monday–Friday 8:00 A.M.–5:00 P.M. PA 4/66, AR 11/66, AR 3/68

HYATT REGENCY ATLANTA HOTEL (1966–67/1969)
265 Peachtree Street Northeast
Atlanta, Georgia

John Portman & Associates, architects

The Hyatt Regency Atlanta Hotel strikes a rich vein via brilliant architectural imagination and know-how. Its open, soaring, twenty-one-story lobby restores the festive to that once-moribund species, the downtown hotel. Moreover, it demonstrates that ideas still have a place in this world. One of the key notions here was three-dimensional exhilaration. Down with tight lobbies, narrow, dingy corridors, and insipid rooms. Down with determining financial success by amount of rentable square footage instead of the quality of that footage. "The whole idea of Hyatt Regency is openness," said the architect, and the results changed the world of hotels.

The concept of a central open core for a skyscraper hotel with balconies from each floor opening onto it is not new. The grand court of the Palace Hotel in San Francisco (1875) had a marvelous, top-lit, six-story atrium; while the famous Brown Palace Hotel in Denver (see page 293), finished in 1892 (and still going strong), boasts a tamer version. Then, too, Frank Lloyd Wright's Guggenheim Museum in New York (see page 431)—which John Portman admired—offers potent lessons wherein "negative" is positive. But Portman has updated the three-dimensional vacuum, transforming nothingness into everything: turning elevators into exposed mobile sculptures (they vanish through the roof to a revolving restaurant), placing a 40-foot/12-meter domed skylight on top of the courtyard to catch sunbeams, and rendering the scale agreeable by balconies and trellises dripping with vines. The bowered trellises prevent a "penitentiary" effect, serving in addition to counter acrophobia. Thus visitors feel like spatially involved spectators/actors, comforted by the fact that they always know where they are, and generally where they are going. This central area is exciting if restless, and at times details approach the overelaborate, but flair springs from this multi-tiered delight, and flair is no ordinary product in today's building world.

A 200-room wing built in 1971 and a wing consisting of rooms and meeting spaces built in 1980 were also designed by Portman. In 1994–95 a ballroom and exhibit hall addition designed by the office of Thompson, Ventulett, Stainback, and Associates was constructed.

Lobby open 24 hours. The top-floor restaurant is open after 4:00 P.M. Int 7/67, PA 7/67, AD 2/68

PORTLAND CENTER PROJECT (1966–68)
200 Southwest Harrison Street at 1st Avenue
Portland, Oregon

Skidmore, Owings & Merrill, architects

Urban renewal has been attempted in many cities of the United States, too often with depressing results. However, Portland's three rental residence towers, plus adjacent shopping mall, garage, and related functions, provide a generic model of what should be possible for all our cities. Located within easy walking distance of Portland's central business district, only a block or so from the civic auditorium, and replacing substandard structures, this residential-commercial development makes a sirenic stand in luring tax-paying residents back from the suburbs. The quality of its planning, architecture, and landscaping—not a little reminiscent of Le Corbusier's famous La Ville Radieuse of 1923—attains such urban civility that the three apartment blocks are almost always full. Skidmore, Owings & Merrill's Portland office had been retained in 1960 to develop a comprehensive plan for the 83.5 acres/34 hectares (the site had been acquired by the city's Urban Renewal Agency with its citizens' approval in 1958). Superblocks and a green grid of parks evolved from their studies, with a mixture of functions to generate day and some night activity. In 1965 the land was sold, as prescribed, to the privately held Portland Center Development Company as the highest bidder; they in turn retained SOM as architects for the first stage (29 acres/12 hectares) of the plan. The layout called for three concrete apartment towers of twenty-three to twenty-six floors each (comprising 528 units altogether), plus twenty-four two-story garden apartments, a restaurant, a broker's office, a shopping center with offices above, and several (too small) garages. The apartments, all with balconies and generally eight per floor, come in one-, two-, and three-bedroom models.

The lobbies are open to the public Monday–Friday 9:00 A.M.–6:00 P.M., Saturday–Sunday 10:00 A.M.–4:00 P.M. Tours of model apartments can be arranged by calling (503) 224-3050. AF 7–8/66, JAIA 9/68

JOHN HANCOCK CENTER (1966–70)
875 North Michigan Avenue
Chicago, Illinois

Skidmore, Owings & Merrill, architects and engineers

The John Hancock Center is Chicago's bold and gutsy—and inescapable—landmark. Exoskeletal skyscrapers have been tried before and tapered buildings constructed, but none has sprung from the structural demands or delivers the startling visual impact of John Hancock—"Big John." It dominates much of the city, and no one can avoid seeing it—and there must be only a few who would so want. Do not miss the observation floor and/or cocktail and dining lounge at dusk if the weather cooperates (it might well be cloudy down below but sunny above).

Bruce Graham, the architect who was in charge of the building's design, is technically minded, "interested in that part of architecture that is related to structural engineering," and

this sometimes-ignored approach is evident here. Graham likes to explore the many possibilities, the new options of working with today's tools, including the computers extensively employed on this job. Compare, for instance, this excursion with the even taller Sears Tower, also in Chicago (see page 581), which he also designed. For the Hancock Tower, Graham and his cohorts, principally chief structural engineer Dr. Fazlur Khan, arrived at the straight tapered form as a strictly structural, basically wall-bearing, trussed-box response to heavy winds and great height. (The building takes almost the full blast from nearby Lake Michigan.) Structurally, the floors of Hancock contribute only a minor stiffening element to the frame. The prominent exterior diagonals form the least expensive way of bracing (in transferring lateral wind forces to the entire structure) because they use less steel. Moreover they are also effective in establishing scale, thus the exoskeleton.

John Hancock is not just a building, it is indeed a "center," with shops, offices, and apartments stacked like a vertical town (and probably inspired in this regard by the pioneering, not distant, Marina City, see page 462). Retail stores occupy the lower levels; mechanical services on floor 3; parking for 750 cars (reached by strident exterior ramp) on floors 4–12; offices and more mechanical services on 13–17; commercial office space 18–41; mechanical 42–43; with the sky lobby 44–45, where all apartment dwellers and visitors change elevators—and, on these floors, swim in their own pool, shop in their own shops, or dine in their own restaurant. Above this, 703 condominium apartments (efficiencies to four-bedroom) occupy the 46th–92nd floors, with observation deck (94), restaurant (95–96)—by IDS Incorporated—and television and mechanical (100) above. The total height, without masts, is 1,107 feet/337 meters. Amusingly the apartments with diagonal cross-breaking on their windows were the first rented: the occupants wanted to identify with the structure.

An assessment of a building of such dominating size and with so many occupants obviously should take into account the milieu in which it rises. But as Bruce Graham put it, "People say that it is on the wrong site, but of all areas in Chicago that are changing, it is this portion of town—and not because of John Hancock." (The building, incidentally, occupies a bit less than half of its ground.) Moreover if this were solely an office building disgorging almost one hundred floors of workers every afternoon at 5:03, the building in this largely upper-bracket apartment and shopping section of the city would be intolerable. But, as indicated, there are only twenty-seven floors of offices and forty-six of apartments, certainly not menacing numbers. Each group follows its staggered hours and keeps the area alive throughout the day and much of the night. A number of residents also work in the building.

The exterior finish is dark aluminum and bronze-tinted glass except for the light travertine on the ground floor. The sharp eye will note from the street that the office floors have higher ceilings than the apartments above, and it will also readily pick out the garage decks, sky lobby, and restaurant, but there are no other—there really could be no other—expressions of occupational function. John Hancock is brutal, but breathtaking.

In 1993–94 a large-scale redevelopment program designed by Hiltscher Shapiro Associates was undertaken. A number of these changes have taken place on the Michigan Avenue side of the building: an open-air plaza with plantings, a seating area, and a waterfall have been created, leading to a new lobby intended specifically for use by shoppers and visitors to the observatory. The retail area off Michigan Avenue has been expanded and renovated. A dedicated office entrance and lobby has also been added on the south side of the building, and the elevators now descend to this lobby area.

Located on Michigan Avenue between Delaware Street and Chestnut Street. The lobbies and retail areas are open to the public during business hours. The observatory on the 94th floor is open 9:00 A.M.–12:00 midnight; admission is $5.75 for adults, $4.50 for senior citizens, and $3.25 for children ages 5–17. For more information call (312) 751-3680. AD 10/68, AF 7–8/70, ARev 4/72

WORLD TRADE CENTER (1966–80)
1 World Trade Center
bordered by Church, Liberty, Vesey, and West streets
New York, New York

Minoru Yamasaki & Associates and
Emery Roth & Sons, architects

Unflinchingly stalwart, this pair of foursquare, sheer towers has changed—probably forever—the madcap profile of lower Manhattan. At 110 stories in height (1,350 feet/411 meters) the twins surpass the Empire State Building's long-held record of the world's tallest building by 100 feet/30 meters (but were in turn outstretched by Chicago's Sears Tower, see page 581, in June 1973). The World Trade Center's fourteen-block site was chosen because it contained virtually no buildings of architectural merit, while three subway lines and the PATH (Port Authority Trans Hudson to New Jersey) train could be incorporated within the structure on the concourse level, with a fourth subway only a block away. (There are some forty-five to fifty thousand workers a day who pour in and out of these great towers at appointed hours.)

To arrive at the size of the projected building, the Port Authority calculated the number of square feet of office space that they thought would be required by the various firms and organizations concerned with world trade, plus offices requested by New York State (almost one quarter of the total), and a new U.S. Custom House. This worked out to be approximately 9 million square feet/836,000 square meters. To house this economically and efficiently the architects proposed two identical towers measuring 209 feet/63.7 meters on a side. Opting for two towers instead of a single mammoth one was brilliant, and the overall concept was further advanced when a plaza in front of the towers was suggested with eight-story buildings giving edge definition and scale transfer. As Minoru Yamasaki wrote, "The real opportunity at the Trade Center was to open up one area of our largest urban concentration and provide a great outdoor space, shielded from vehicular traffic, easily accessible to pedestrians and which could bring pleasure to the occupants, visitors, and people who work in and around the Trade Center site." He adds, this is a place "to give [man] a soaring feeling, imparting pride and a sense of nobility in his environment."

The next problem was the specific design of the (then) tallest buildings in the world on a totally exposed site, partially landfilled, where winds of 140 miles/225 kilometers per hour occur. The "squared tube" concept that evolved was advanced by the architects and its details worked out jointly with the engineers, Skilling, Helle, Christiansen, Robertson. Though there might be disagreement concerning the esthetics of the World Trade Center (primarily—to some—the lack of exterior scale and the treatment of the public spaces), there has been only praise for its superbly engineered structure.

The process of excavating and laying foundations was incredibly difficult because almost half the site was, as mentioned, filled land while an underground railroad and a subway tube both had to be accommodated without interrupting service. A "slurry trench" foundation, first perfected by Italian engineers, was used (and the engineers imported for the job). This was carried out by using a clamshell bucket to dig a connecting series of trenches 3 feet/.9 meter wide and 22 feet/6.7 meters long around the periphery of the site, and filling the trenches with slurry (bentonite clay and water) as the earth was removed. Each trench extended to bedrock and was notched into it; steel reinforcing cages were then lowered and anchored, and the concrete poured, displacing the slurry, which was drained off. This system permitted erecting the 65–100-foot-/20–30-meter-deep foundation walls without excavating on either side—and with the Hudson River next door. When the entire peripheral foundation was complete the inner

section was excavated—probably the largest hole in the ground Manhattan has ever seen—and cleared for construction. The excavated earth and rock were used to create landfill for the nearby site of Battery Park City.

Routine skyscrapers consist of a cage of steel or concrete bays with the exterior in effect hung from the framing structure; loads (weight and wind) are carried throughout the building primarily by a series of columns and braces. In the World Trade Center each of the four sides of the towers is built up of closely spaced columns welded to substantial spandrels to become an enormous load-bearing and wind-resisting wall for the full height of the building, a construction system known as a Vierendeel truss after the Belgian engineer who invented it in 1896. As Henry Wright, a distinguished architect and editor, put it, "The WTC wall is not only structurally unique; there are reasons for considering it the first truly rational skyscraper envelope" (*Architecture Plus*, January–February 1974). The only interior columns are those framing the elevator/service core. With the towers formed as an uninterrupted squared tube—on a scale never previously approached—the enclosing fabric was composed of built-up steel wall columns (for the most part 14 inches/36 centimeters square). These were insulated for fireproofing and to minimize temperature differential, then wrapped in a special alloy aluminum (outside width 18.75 inches/47.6 centimeters) and set 40 inches/102 centimeters on center (which permits great flexibility in office partitioning). These columns alternate with window openings, typically 21.3 inches/54 centimeters wide, with glass measuring 19.3 inches/49 centimeters, thus in cross section solid and void are almost precisely equal. (Compare Eero Saarinen's CBS Building, page 480, with concrete bearing walls and identical window/wall width of 5 feet/1.5 meters and SOM's adjacent One Liberty Plaza, page 440, where window and structural spandrel are equal but horizontal.) The wall sections of the WTC were prefabricated in two- and three-story-high panels framed horizontally by 52-inch-/1.3-meter-deep steel spandrel plates. The vertical alternation of narrow solid and glass—as seen also in the new west buildings of Rockefeller Center, page 374—produces an unusual scale on the exterior, while on the inside it totally transforms the routine horizontal sweep of large-pane fenestration. There are, however, advantages in this, among them (as Yamasaki has often pointed out) being a freedom from the acrophobia that for some attends vistas from most high buildings. Moreover the slender glass panes are recessed from the framing edge 11.5 inches/29.2 centimeters, effecting a reduction of sun load, thus saving energy and cutting glare. (Glass comprises about thirty percent of the outside skin.) The appearance within the offices, with windows almost flush with floor and ceiling, is extraordinarily bright and airy. There are, incidentally, 43,600 standard windows in the towers, all of which are washed by unmanned automatic machinery that runs on built-in stainless steel tracks.

Spans between the outside bearing walls and the interior service core are of steel truss construction 30 inches/76 centimeters deep. The elevators are divided into three zones each served by its own "skylobby." These are located on the concourse (one floor below plaza level at the subway-PATH convergence) and at the 44th and 78th floors, with high-speed express cars, capacity fifty-five persons, providing direct service to each skylobby and also non-stop to the 107th floor restaurant atop WTC 1 and the observation platforms atop WTC 2. Local floors are served by local elevators from the skylobbies and thus have to take care of only one third of the buildings' height; in effect three local elevators operate within a single shaft.

Perhaps the chief architectural criticism that has been leveled at the World Trade Center is the fact that the two mid-building service floors—the 44th and 78th levels mentioned—are camouflaged on the exterior to a large degree, thus vitiating scale. It is only under an oblique light that these floors become semiprominent, and it is then that the towers have more assertiveness. (Compare the "banded" United Nations Secretariat Building, page 398, in this regard.) In addition their almost Venetian-Gothic meeting with the plaza is not to everyone's taste. It should be added, in defense, that there is a welcome "transparency" at the towers' base, while the melding of a triad of upper columns to produce one wide bay at ground level was necessary to create sufficient intercolumniation for entries, not to mention the desirability of stating and lighting the tall lobbies.

The 5-acre/2-hectare plaza in front of the towers is bounded with sensitive irregularity by the eight-story Custom House, the two plaza buildings, and (in 1981) the 829-room, 22-story hotel (WTC 3) designed by Skidmore Owings & Merrill. It acts "to set off the buildings facing it and to create an environment totally for pedestrians, away from automobiles—an oasis, a paved garden where people can spend a few moments to relieve the tensions or monotonies of the usual working day" (Yamasaki). However, as matters now stand, the paving of this vast plaza is unrelieved, except by sculpture and fountain accents. The sculpture consists of a potent black granite pyramidal grouping by Masayuki Nagare (34 feet/10 meters long) holding down the entry, Fritz Koenig's spherical, bronze sculpture and fountain shining in the sun at center, and James Rosati's *Ideogram* at left background. At the west entrance to WTC 1 is a fine red stabile by Alexander Calder.

The six levels below the plaza provide parking for almost two thousand automobiles, plus PATH and subway lines, some fifty shops, and a wide variety of dining facilities. At the other end—the top—there are two spectacular observation platforms in the south tower, one enclosed and one open, while the Windows on the World Restaurant in the north tower is superb: Warren Platner & Associates were the interior architects. Controversial or not, the World Trade Center is an extraordinary document on the New York skyline and a brilliant chapter in high-rise engineering.

As a result of the bombing of the WTC in February 1993, portions of the building have been reconstructed (notably the parking garage, now closed to the public), and there have been a number of security and safety enhancements. However, none of these has altered the overall design of the structure.

The lobbies are open daily 24 hours; offices are closed to the public. The mall and plaza on the mezzanine level are open during business hours. The observation deck is open daily 9:30 A.M.–11:30 P.M. Admission is $6 for adults, $3.50 for senior citizens, $3 for children ages 6–12, free for children under 6. For more information call (212) 435–7397. For information and reservations at Windows on the World call (212) 938–1100. AR 2/64, AF 3/64, ARev 7/72, AF 4/73, AP 1–2/74, Int 2/74, Int 2/77, AR 9/77, ARev 3/78, AR 5/88

COLUMBIA NEW TOWN (1966–)
US 29
Columbia, Maryland

Howard Research & Development Corporation, developer
Morton Hoppenfeld, chief planner

No city in the United States has been planned with more conscientious expertise or with more determination to make the city work as a social organism than Columbia, Maryland. Located off a major highway between Baltimore and Washington, but nearer the former, and occupying 22 square miles/57 square kilometers (an area larger than Manhattan) of former farmland, this "new town" was planned as a coalescence of "villages." These will eventually reach a total of nine, with an overall population of 100,000. (In 1995 its eight existing villages housed approximately 81,000.) Columbia's actual planning is of overwhelming importance, but much of the thinking behind it is even more meaningful for the future of America's urban development. For Columbia's "planning" did not begin with a "plan" at all, but with a search for objectives that aimed at a pragmatic urban utopia within the framework of private enterprise. A lengthy series of conferences and consultations with experts far removed from land usage conceived Columbia's goals. Sociologists, administration and government specialists, economic researchers, human relations professors, ministers, recreational commissioners, women's sociologists, transportation experts, behavioral scientists, city managers, doctors and public health professionals, psychologists, educators, and even a historian were among those in the preplanning think tank. They sought an approach that would "lift community life to a new level of dignity and inspiration" and make Columbia, to quote James W. Rouse, the city's messianic brains, progenitor, and father, "a garden where people grow."

The ideas that evolved suggested an interlocking series of villages, each approximately 1 mile/1.6 kilometers in diameter and accommodating ten to fifteen thousand people. These

would all have the full facilities of a small town. The fully integrated villages would be broken down into relaxed, non-grid "neighborhoods," three to five per village, with three hundred to five hundred families in each. The focus of the neighborhood unit would be the communal buildings/assembly hall, elementary school, day-care facilities, swimming pool, and shops—virtually all of which could be reached by walking. A major town center, surrounded by a greenbelt, would provide the nexus for the whole development, with office buildings and a large shopping center, including a department store, a hotel, theaters, and all the necessities and amenities of a medium-sized city. A band of clean industry, well isolated on the periphery, would establish a base for employment. (At present some 57,000 jobs are provided by about 2,500 businesses.) Nature would be protected everywhere and would interpenetrate neighborhoods and villages, offering direct contact to outdoor recreation and intergroup activities for all. Dammed-up streams would create several lakes, while golf courses, riding trails, and even a wildlife refuge would be part of the picture. As regards personal health, comprehensive services would provide a master health insurance plan that would cover all contingencies for those who subscribed to it. These, then, were the objectives. What is the reality?

Wonderfully enough, reality—at least in land usage—mirrors theory. Columbia's location (between two of the East's most important cities, and straddling one of its major highway linkages, with an interstate on one border) establishes a viable location with excellent communications. Its respect for the rolling terrain is admirable, probably the finest in the country, while its own road network is sensitive to every opportunity of its uneven topography. No bulldozer transgressed, no slaughter of the trees was permitted. Moreover, lot pattern and disposition were not cranked out of a musty duplicating machine, but reflect and fit the terrain and its natural features so that few houses face onto a thoroughfare and most open at the rear onto an unspoiled park setting. As a consequence, children can play unmenaced by cars, and can in many cases walk to school without crossing a road. All of this constitutes a planning paradigm almost unique (with Reston, Virginia—see page 490) in the United States, though often seen in much of Scandinavia and some of the British new towns. The manifold lessons of land usage, almost land worship, at Columbia should be on the desk of every real-estate developer in the country. Columbia is so rich with lessons on its use of the ground, let us hope that its subsequent architecture will be more of consequence on top of it.

Located 17 miles/27 kilometers southwest of Baltimore, 20 miles/32 kilometers northeast of Washington, D.C. Public welcome at all times. The Columbia Welcome Center offers orientation on the planning of the town. Open Monday–Friday 8:30 A.M.–5:00 P.M. and Saturday 11:00 A.M.–4:00 P.M. Closed on major holidays including weekend after Thanksgiving and Christmas Eve and New Year's Eve. For more information call (410) 715-3103. AF 8–9/64, AF 11/67, AR 3/72, AR 12/75, PA 2/76, JAIA 9/76

PALEY PARK (1967)
3 East 53rd Street (just east of 5th Avenue)
New York, New York

Zion & Breen Associates, landscape architects

Niagara's is higher, Victoria's wider, but for urban impact nothing equals this minipark's waterfall, a mere 20 feet/6 meters high and 42 feet/13 meters across, cascading into a pool 6 feet/1.8 meters wide. The rush of waters over its pebbled wall provides visual fascination as it sparkles and fades in the sun, while equally importantly its white sound muffles the rudeness of the street. Here is a retreat for the neighborhood, the passerby, and the visitor—even in winter when delicate snow limns its ghostlike chairs and the then spindly trees. Twelve honey locusts, planted at 12-foot/3.6-meter intervals in alternate rows of two and three, roof this minuscule area (42.9 x 100.3 feet/13 x 30 meters), while walls of simple gray brick, flourishing with ivy, delineate the two sides. Movable pots of flowers, on a floor of pink granite blocks, serve as accents. Five additional trees frame the entry and cleverly extend the park onto the sidewalk while heralding its approach. Simple refreshments are available from April to November. The park was presented to the city by William S. Paley as a memorial to his father Samuel Paley, 1875–1963.

New York has on the same street and within a block of each other two notable, twentieth-century, tiny parks. Paley Park is introspective, and its comfortable retreat cossets one from the outside world. At the Museum of Modern Art's Abby Aldrich Rockefeller Sculpture Garden by Philip Johnson (see page 387), the museum itself supplies the rewards and the pleasures reside largely in what one finds. Both are marvelous, but Paley's functional use of a few square feet provides an empyrean urban retreat: pure poetry. Albert Preston Moore was consulting architect.

Open daily 8:00 A.M.–8:00 P.M. Closed 1 January to mid-February. Closed for major holidays. JAIA 3/66, AR 8/67, A 12/85

BLOSSOM MUSIC CENTER
(1967–68)
1145 West Steels Corners Road
Cuyahoga Falls, Ohio

Schafer, Flynn & Van Dijk,
architects

The Blossom Music Center's structure is based on a stupendous, obliquely angled, steel arch with a 400-foot/122-meter span and a 200-foot/61-meter rise. Its outspread legs are buttressed underground by enormous concrete footings, and its sharply inclined frame is upheld by ten exposed steel columns (inclined to meet the arch at ninety degrees). From the upper section of this arch and its supports a series of trusses are hung; these horizontal members extend to rest on columns and to uphold a low conical roof. Under this great umbrella, which is partially open on the two sides and fully so across the open end, are 4,642 seats, an orchestra pit for 110 musicians, and a broad stage that accommodates a 110-person orchestra, 200-person choir, and a children's choir. The hall was designed with extra-wide peripheral aisles so that rain would be no problem. The stage proper has variable wings so that its size and acoustic reflection can be geared to the renowned Cleveland Orchestra—which uses Blossom as its summer home—down to a small jazz group or soloist. Offices, green room, dressing rooms, and services are located behind and below the stage. The center's 800-acre/324-hectare site was carefully chosen so that the auditorium could "expand" outward and upward on the hillside in a dished fan shape that provides 10,000–12,000 additional seats under the stars—a delightful spot, incidentally, for a pre-concert picnic. In keeping with the center's bucolic setting, the control gates and ticket offices are placed out of sight, along with the extensive parking lots.

The steel trusswork of the roof has twenty-one small pipe trusses instead of the eleven larger ones that the architects would have preferred, but economics prohibited this expensive simplicity. (The longest truss spans 175 feet/53 meters.) Economic constraints also leave their mark on the weathering steel of the great arch and its supporting columns, which should have been sandblasted to a uniform color. These, however, are small details of a great concept. The architecture and engineering are of a superior order, the shell is totally at home in its unspoiled setting, acoustics (amplification is almost never needed) and sight lines are superb (even on the hillside): hall and hill are one. Peter van Dijk was chief of design; Pietro Belluschi served as consultant to the client; Christopher Jaffee was principal acoustician, aided by Heinrick Keilholz. The center was named for the Blossom family of Cleveland, who generously supported the Cleveland Orchestra and this brilliant shell. R. M. Gensert Associates were the structural engineers.

From Cleveland (30 miles/48 kilometers): 5 miles/8 kilometers south of exit 12 of Ohio Turnpike (I-80) on OH 8, then 2 miles/3.2 kilometers west on West Steels Corners Road. From Akron (8 miles/13 kilometers): north on OH 8, then 2 miles/3.2 kilometers west on West Steels Corners Road. Open May–September, Friday–Sunday 1:00–5:00 P.M. and for performances. For more information call (216) 566-8184. AR 6/69, JAIA 8/69, AF 12/73, AR 3/74

LAKE POINT TOWER (1967–68)
505 North Lake Shore Drive, off Grand Avenue
Chicago, Illinois

G. D. Schipporeit and John C. Heinrich, architects

Dominating the Navy Pier promontory of Chicago in isolated splendor, this "visual instrument responding to the sky and light" (AIA Honor Award description) enjoys one of the enviable sites in the country. Lake Michigan laps its edge, while a dazzling panorama of the city unfolds on the other side. Though admittedly influenced by Mies van der Rohe—its architects worked for some years in Mies' office—this seventy-story building housing nine hundred luxury apartments possesses a boldness and imagination all its own. The trefoil tower rests on a rectangular base containing a four-level garage for seven hundred cars and two floors of commercial and retail facilities; the base is topped by a 2.5-acre/1-hectare "park," complete with pond and waterfall, swimming pool, and children's play area. Atop the building, a restaurant is housed in a rotunda penthouse. Some of Chicago's finest shopping is only a few blocks away.

An equilateral triangle forms the structural core of the building, housing elevators, stairs, and utilities in its spine and framing its circulation lobby. Three short arms from this central hall give access to the apartments. Apartment partitions are arranged so that there is freedom to alter available sizes. Living rooms with dining alcove and kitchen occupy the end of each rounded arm; the "soft" form of this totally glazed shape is surprisingly agreeable. Ingenious, low components containing individual air conditioners and direct fresh-air vents line the peripheral walls.

Lake Point Tower is obviously a retreat, a private roost not impinged upon by others, but there is room, and need, in this world for such a building. The concrete frame—when built it was the highest concrete structure in the world—is sheathed in bronze-toned aluminum of excellent detail (note ventilators), with tinted glass providing most of the skin: very fresh, very handsome. Graham, Anderson, Probst & White were associate architects.

Only the lobby and grounds are open to the public. The building is included on the Chicago Architecture Foundation's "Navy Pier" tour; the cost is $5. It is also included on the CAF's river cruise tour; the cost is $15 on weekdays, $17 on weekends. For more information on CAF tours call (312) 922–3432. AR 10/69, JAIA 6/70

ALLEY THEATRE (1967–68)
615 Texas Avenue,
between Smith and Louisiana streets
Houston, Texas

Ulrich Franzen & Associates, architects

The Alley Theatre shelters two separate units, the larger seating 824, the smaller 296, with an internal driveway separating the two while providing covered access. It also brings a distinct exterior to the scene—"It is at once Southwestern and medieval, a fortress and a temple of art," says the official brochure. (Its nine "turrets" house stairs and elevators.) The main theater provides seventeen rows of well-raked seats radiating one hundred degrees about its semithrust stage. No member of the audience is more than 75 feet/23 meters from the center of action, and, as there is no proscenium or curtain, a fine relationship is established between actors and audience. Lateral extensions, or calipers, project from the stage to envelop the auditorium. The side walls are matte black and thus disappear when the house lights are dimmed. The ceiling follows the curves of the seats in seven boldly stated bands: these are vertical on the rear, but variously angled facing the stage—their angle depending on the acoustic-reflective index—and covered with natural wood strips. Though strong to the eye, they are gentle to the ear: the acoustics are excellent. The stage itself is highly flexible, with numerous and effective multi-level actors' entries. A large lift for scenery is augmented by lateral "preset areas." The smaller theater—recalling the arena-style configuration at the Alley's previous address—is square in plan, with six ranks of seats framing its four-sided central stage, and is reached from the main lobby by an almost secret passage. Its 296 seats enjoy a cockpit intimacy. Nina Vance, who founded the Alley Theatre in a dance studio at the end of an alley in 1947, worked closely with the architect on its design. Theatrical designer Paul Owen helped Vance in defining the functional needs of the building. MacKie & Kamrath were associate architects; George C. Izenour, lighting and theater consultant; Bolt, Beranek & Newman, acoustic consultants.

Tours given on Mondays by appointment only; to schedule a tour call (713) 228–9341. Open for performances. For information on upcoming events call (713) 228–8421. AF 3/69, JAIA 5/72

OAKLAND MUSEUM (1967–69)
1000 Oak Street between 10th and 12th streets
Oakland, California

Roche/Dinkeloo & Associates, architects

The *Oakland Tribune* in the early part of this century predicted that Oakland would be "the Athens of the West," far outstripping its neighbor across the bay, otherwise known as San Francisco. Although this rosy notion did not materialize, Oakland has matured with determination and foresight in the past few decades, and today offers much to both visitor and citizen. Among its most outstanding newer buildings, and one of the most imaginative in the country, is the Oakland Museum—actually composed of three interconnected museums. Occupying four square city blocks, the building comprises four levels of landscaped and terraced museum wings, lawns, and gardens, stepped down the grade with a flair that would appeal to Nebuchadnezzar. The architects had to provide exhibition spaces for California art, history, and natural sciences, and the chief problem facing them was to sort out these various functions, provide identity and circulation for each, yet tie them together in a manageable whole that the public could readily grasp. The designers spent much time analyzing the cultural background and cultural needs of not only the city but the region, producing thus "a total museum related to the California scene." "Otherwise you are building shells for a function that may not exist," said Roche, "and you are building a monument, not a living thing" (quoted in Paul Heyer, *Architects on Architecture*, Walker and Company, 1966).

This "impossible" program has been solved with exterior brilliance on the court side with its series of tempting planted terraces, and with reasonable success on the interior, though complexity arises. The west entry (at the third level on Oak Street) provides a partly open, partly roofed introduction that gives onto the main art gallery with the permanent collection at the left, the gallery for circulating exhibitions to the right, with a panorama of spaces and views out in front. (The need for greater security has compromised some indoor-outdoor interaction.) The entrance to the art gallery is not prominent, and one (at least if right-handed) tends to turn to the door of the circulating exhibit space—called the great hall—at the right. Tentacles of circulation lead from the great hall to the central courtyard, to the other exhibition spaces, and occasionally to outdoor terraces as they step down the grade. Space for California history (along with some parking) shares the second level with the great hall. On the first level, and slid partly beneath the history wing, rests the natural sciences museum, plus more parking (for an overall total of two hundred cars). The natural sciences wing opens onto a large landscaped court, approximately 200 feet/61 meters on a side. It is framed by wings on two sides (the museum and a three-hundred-seat theater/auditorium

placed at right angles), and by pergolas and property line wall on the other two. This courtyard, a public park, doubles for festivals and concerts.

As indicated, fully landscaped terraces—some with works of art—top all major and most minor changes of level, so that all outdoor promenades are marked by luxuriant planting, plus spatial and level changes that make exploration dramatic. Dan Kiley was landscape architect. Within, one can feel at times enmeshed by the labyrinthine circulation and by the lack of a dominant space, other than the temporary exhibits gallery, but the tension and release of spaces, interior and exterior, and the delights of the landscaped terraces make this building exciting.

Open Wednesday–Saturday 10:00 A.M.–5:00 P.M. Sunday 12:00 noon–7:00 P.M. Closed July 4, Thanksgiving, Christmas, and New Year's Day. Admission is $5 for adults, $3 for students and senior citizens, free for children six and under. Tours of the collection are given daily. Tours can be scheduled by calling (510) 238-3514. For general information call (510) 238-3401. AR 5/68, PA 12/69, AR 4/70, JAIA 6/77

PEPSICO WORLD HEADQUARTERS (1967–70)
700 Anderson Hill Road
Purchase, New York

Edward Durell Stone Associates, architects

A posh corporate headquarters sympathetically tied to its carefully preserved 112-acre/45-hectare site (an ex-polo field). The complex is divided into seven square and equal-size units that connect only at corner towers and that frame three well-landscaped, slightly sunken courts. Each of the upper floors of the three-story structure overhangs the one below to prevent sky glare and to reduce sun load on the uninterrupted strips of windows. A slight patterning in the precast concrete panels enlivens these exterior wall overhangs. Continuous planting boxes are placed outside the windows, and the free growth of their ivy keeps the buildings from being rigid in this shepherd's setting. The landscaping, which included the planting of some three thousand trees of thirty-eight varieties, is not only excellent (and beautifully maintained), but the grounds boast over forty top-flight pieces of sculpture (including that by Henry

Moore, Seymour Lipton, Alexander Calder, Jacques Lipchitz, and David Smith). A fountain in the central court welcomes and a *jet d'eau* in the 4.5-acre/1.8-hectare lake—whose waters are seasonally preempted by several hundred Canadian geese—gives an outdoor accent. Be sure to take the road around the edge of the site. Edward Durell Stone, Jr. & Associates were the original landscape architects, succeeded by Russell Page (1980–85) and François Goffinet (1985–).

Located off exit 28 of the Hutchinson River Parkway; north 1 mile/1.6 kilometers on Lincoln Avenue, then east on Anderson Hill Road. Grounds open to the public daily during daylight hours. The interior is closed to the public. AR 2/72

MOUNT ANGEL ABBEY LIBRARY
(1967–70)
Abbey Hill
St. Benedict, Oregon

Alvar Aalto, architect

An amicable building, almost timid on the exterior, this library is only the second structure in the United States by the great Finnish architect Alvar Aalto (1898–1976), a man who early—and continuously—injected humanism into the development of modern architecture. (Aalto's other building on these shores is his Baker House for MIT in Cambridge, Massachusetts—see page 396) One of Aalto's earliest designs to electrify the international scene was his library for Viipuri (1930–35), a town ceded to the Soviet Union by Finland in 1944. Badly damaged in the war, the building is now properly restored. In this Oregon grandson of that still unexcelled masterpiece some of the maestro's compassionate handling of scale, interior space, light, and detail can be seen. The Mount Angel Abbey Library, which is used by the Benedictine Abbey monks and seminary students, faces south onto the central mall of the monastery, forming a low-keyed, brick closure between its Romanesque-derived neighbors. One story high at the entry level, it takes advantage of its hillside site to develop three floors, dramatically dropped below on the north side.

The building forms a long, basically rectangular block stretched out on the edge of the hill with a fan-shaped block of stacks and reading rooms attached at the rear. As one enters, a one-hundred-seat conference and rare-book room stands to the right (note its ceiling), with staff and technical rooms to the left. One then steps forward from the low lobby to survey, indeed command, the curved asymmetric sweep of the two levels of stacks pulsating with space before and below one. It is in this all-white interior that Aalto's mastery of three dimensions, and his talent for manipulating light via skylights, roof monitors, conventional windows, and, of course, artificial lights (which emanate from the same areas), are most evident. The illumination concept and detailing are potent contributions from this late northern giant. (Note the radiating slat fixture over the control desk.) Aalto was preoccupied (perhaps overly preoccupied) with the fan-shaped plan since his German experiments with the famous apartment house in Bremen (1962) and the Cultural Center for Wolfsburg (1963), but here at Mount Angel it works with spatial come-on and unobtrusive logic, the angles of all stacks, for instance, radiating from the control desk for complete surveillance. There is open stack space for 350,000 volumes, with expansion allowance for 100,000 more. Study carrels line the perimeter of the four-angled faces of the fan; those on the middle level are lockable. Fortunately, the furnishings, including important hardware and lighting fixtures, are also of Aalto's design. Erik T. Vartiainen, a young American architect, worked with Aalto on the project; Demars & Wells were associate architects. Architectural humanism is not dead.

Mount Angel Abbey is located 20 miles/32 kilometers northeast of Salem, on a hill east of Mount Angel, Oregon. Open Monday–Thursday 8:30 A.M.–5:00 P.M. and 6:30–9:30 P.M., Friday 8:30 A.M.–5:00 P.M., Saturday 10:30 A.M.–4:30 P.M., Sunday 10:30 A.M.–4:30 P.M. and 6:30–9:30 P.M. During vacations (December 15–January 15, Thanksgiving weekend, May 1–September 1) open 10:30 A.M.–4:30 P.M. Closed for holidays. Free tours can be scheduled by calling (503) 845-3317. AF 6/67, AR 5/71, ARev 6/72, JAIA 9/80

BRADFIELD HALL (1968)
New York State College of Agriculture at Cornell
Tower Road
Ithaca, New York

Ulrich Franzen & Associates, architects

Punctuating the skyline above Cayuga's famous waters, Bradfield Hall (see photograph on facing page) might well be called a sanctum for agronomic research. The thirteen-story, virtually
windowless tower is completely filled with laboratories and attached offices, plus a library and
a large classroom on the top floor. Adjacent to this tower stands a low block with central entry
for staff offices, with a four-story separate classroom and lab building (Emerson Hall) adjoining this. In plan the tower forms a near-square 90 by 100 feet/27 by 30 meters with a corridor down the middle and offices opening on either side. A line of laboratories are attached
behind the offices, and, with service corridors, line the outer (east and west) walls. Though the
three parallel circulation divisions that run the length of each floor—the two outside service
corridors or galleries and the central hall—are fixed, the lab-office rows that are sandwiched
between them are longitudinally flexible.

Fresh air is pumped up from near the ground via the quarter-round towers at the north and
south ends; noxious air is dissipated above the roof through the four prominently projecting
"snorkels" with hoods on the east and west sides. The building's reinforced concrete floor
structure, based on parallel T beams 18 inches/46 centimeters deep, permits flexibility in utility layout, air ducting, lab service modules, and lighting, alternating as needed between the
flanges. A windowless solution was purposefully sought so that freedom from contamination,
plus precise light, temperature, and humidity, could be attained over plant growing experiments. It is a plant-generated plan, and if visual relief is desired there are small (too small)
lounges at the south ends of the main corridors. The exterior, sheathed in rust-colored brick,
carries well its strong silhouette on the
horizon, yet maintains an impressive
sense of scale—a difficult feat for a
windowless bulk.

Open Monday–Friday during business hours. Closed
for holidays. AR 4/65, AF 7–8/68, AR 7/71, AP 5–6/74

Ulrich Franzen's Research Laboratory
(1973—see photograph at right) for the
College of Veterinary Medicine, at the
east end of Tower Road, will be of interest to the architect. (Lobby open Monday–Friday during business hours.) Its
north wall is largely of dark-tinted glass;
the south wall, where the labs are concentrated, is of windowless brick. This
powerful facade, topped by hooded ventilators, proclaims a striking, if at times
formal, statement of the dramatic possibilities of one of the oldest building
materials.

VAN WEZEL PERFORMING ARTS HALL (1968–69)
777 North Tamiami Trail (US 41) at 10th Street
Sarasota, Florida

Taliesin Associated Architects

Perched on a point of land overlooking Sarasota Bay, its two-tone purple colors shining in the sun, the Lewis and Eugenia Van Wezel concert hall/theater/auditorium suggests a geometric heliotrope. (Its color scheme was selected by Mrs. Frank Lloyd Wright.) Van Wezel Hall is the key and only unit in a civic center that Taliesin Associated had planned for the city. Originally this was to include a community hall, an arena, and several miscellaneous smaller structures, all situated between 6th and 10th streets on Sarasota Bay; plans to build these additional facilities have been canceled. Van Wezel was designed primarily as a concert hall and auditorium, secondarily as a theater to be used mainly by traveling companies that truck in their own scenery. There are thus purposely few backstage facilities such as would be found in a repertory or experimental theater.

The auditorium's stepped rows of continental seating accommodate 1,761 in 28 double-angled rows. Three additional rows, holding 54 seats, can be placed on the forestage lift wagon. This number can be reduced to 1,200 or 900 by two drop curtains at rear, which provide visual enclosure. Acoustic demands shaped the hall's plan and section, with "tuning" to fit most types of performances made possible by the variable use of acoustic curtains invisibly hidden behind the range of grilles on each side. For each three rows of seats a side exit is provided, and these feed directly into the lounges overlooking the bay (or the front lobby). The grand foyer on the lower level opens onto the garden terrace with a panorama of Longboat and St. Armand's Key across the bay. William Wesley Peters was partner in charge; George C. Izenour was consultant for the theater; Vern O. Knudson guided the acoustics.

Open during performances. November–April free tours are given Monday–Friday 10:00 A.M.–12:00 noon and 2:00–4:00 P.M. For more information call (813) 955–7676.

TUSKEGEE CHAPEL (1968–69)
Tuskegee University
Tuskegee, Alabama

Fry & Welch, architects; Paul Rudolph, associated architect

This exhilarating chapel bears little kinship to other churches, yet it is one whose 1,100-seat nave states dramatically that the word of the Lord is spoken here. The most striking feature of the inner design—which looks almost exactly like Paul Rudolph's original drawing published in 1960—is the extraordinary flow, really ebb and flow, of spaces. This is accentuated by the daylight that floods the side walls and that comes from horizontal, glazed peripheral bands in the ceiling. Their supporting beams shield the direct light source so that glare does not result. The enclosing walls are thus made visually independent, while the solid central part of the ceiling, which carries the carefully balanced artificial lights, floats as a canopy above the congregation. All sense of confinement vanishes, while a seeming continuum of horizontal space escapes around the corner of the right-hand side.

The chancel is distinguished by its arrangement for the famous Tuskegee University Choir—whose space is almost embraced by three sheer angled walls—and by the projected brick pulpit with its declaratory sounding board above. Though there is a passage to the left of the pulpit leading to the meditation chapel, this, surprisingly, does not distract or become a disturbing vacuum. Near the floor level along the sides note the incorporation of the ventilation units with the walls, their light-struck geometry stepping down the slightly canted floor. The walls of the chapel, both inside and out, are of reddish-salmon brick—the material used for the older buildings on the campus—laid with red mortar. (The first design for the church was in reinforced concrete; brick proved less expensive—and better.) There is an extravagance of planes and even a disjointedness about the exterior, with its porch projecting in front, while windows push unnecessarily out the back, but the interior is spectacular, one of the most extraordinary religious rooms in the country. The lower level—there is a drop-off in grade—is used by the Tuskegee School of Music.

Campus located west of town on AL 126. Open Monday–Friday 8:00 A.M.–4:30 P.M., Sunday 8:00 A.M.–12:00 noon. Sunday services held at 9:30 A.M. Closed for school holidays. Free tours of the campus, which include the chapel, can be scheduled by calling University Escorts at (205) 724-4403. AF 9/60, A+A 12/60, AR 11/69

KNIGHTS OF COLUMBUS HEADQUARTERS (1968–70)
1 Columbus Plaza
Church Street between George Street and North Frontage Road
New Haven, Connecticut

Roche/Dinkeloo & Associates, architects

Until the Knights of Columbus Headquarters, the skyscraper consisted of a skeletal cage of steel or concrete or both. The bones could be on the inside or the outside but they almost invariably necessitated a grid system with a geometric network of columns wrapped by repetitive bays of windows. The twenty-three-story K of C Building boldly broke away, in most respects, from this relatively small-scaled, thickly patterned skeleton. Instead of utilizing a steel cage for its structure, it employs four mighty concrete cylinders, 30 feet/9.1 meters in diameter, set in a square and well spaced from each other. These four independent structures are then connected to a concrete elevator core in the center to form floors; 36-inch-/.9-meter-deep steel spandrel beams bridge the 72-foot/22-meter space between towers, with secondary floor beams framing into these outside beams and the central core. The cage is gone: there are only five vertical solids per floor—the round towers and the square internal elevator block. This allows the windows on each floor (above the third) to consist of continuous end-butted ribbons of glass sealed with mastic.

The function of steel in the Knights of Columbus Headquarters is readily grasped from the exterior, for its steel—like Gothic buttresses—provides structure inseparable from esthetics. The yard-deep main beams that connect the midpoints of the towers stand 5 feet/1.5 meters in front of the glazed walls so that the steel could be completely exposed yet not constitute a fire hazard, a pioneering and ingenious engineering technique. (In virtually all other skyscrapers the steel must be protected against fire by concrete or other casing even though this might also be wrapped in a metal jacket.) It should be added that the piercing of the tile towers by the steel beams at K of C is visually discomforting. The floor beams that frame the center rest their outer ends directly on the large spandrel beams, as can be seen. A horizontal steel sun-screen fills the space between spandrel and outer frame, forming also a platform for window washing. All of this steel is of the weathering variety, taking on a brown velvety color that oxidizes to blackness. With the purplish color of the silo tile that revets the concrete towers, and with the dark bands of window glass, an overall somberness results, but it is an intentional—and effective—one.

The towers, which are tangential to the enclosed volume and barely nip the corners of floor area, contain the services: toilets and air conditioning on one diagonal, with fire stair, storage, and mechanical equipment on the other. Inasmuch as this is a one-organization building, many of the floors are open work spaces without room divisions or high partitions. The resulting sense of space and freedom, both within the office area and looking outward from the offices, creates spatial exhilaration.

The "para-military" (Vincent Scully) statement of the building as a gateway on the cityscape has been criticized as being on the strong side, but the Knights of Columbus Headquarters is full of the traditionally non-traditional ideas that one expects from Roche/Dinkeloo.

The interior is not open to the public. PA 9/70, ARev 4/73, AR 8/90

MASSACHUSETTS STATE GOVERNMENT SERVICE CENTER

(1968–70)
Charles F. Hurley
Employment Security
Building,
19 Staniford Street
Erich Lindemann Mental
Health Building,
25 Staniford Street
Boston, Massachusetts

Paul Rudolph, coordinating architect, with M. A. Dyer, Desmond & Lord, and Shepley, Bulfinch, Richardson & Abbott

This intricate complex made up of the Charles F. Hurley Employment Security Building (Shepley, Bulfinch, Richardson & Abbott) and the Erich Lindemann Mental Health Building (Desmond & Lord) shelters a miscellany of state functions and services. A twenty-three-story tower for Health, Education, and Welfare, originally designed by Paul Rudolph and M. A. Dyer and later redesigned to double its floor area by Shepley, Bullfinch, Richardson & Abbot, was unfortunately never built, nor were the swirls of terraced levels on the plaza between the buildings, designed by Rudolph—both key symbolic and visual elements in the overall plan. However, that the various firms of architects involved were able to produce an articulated group for diverse needs speaks well of their cooperation, and for Rudolph's overall planning and design contribution. The two connected buildings are located next to a large pedestrian plaza, which sits atop a parking area made feasible by changing grade conditions. Thus the staff can go directly from car to office under cover. Monumentality abounds, often under control, at times with complexity. As the *Architectural Record* (July 1973) put it, this center "is a hymn to enclosure: the freedom of protection, the sweeping spaces of a defined openness, and the reassurance of massive pylons."

Grounds and lobbies open Monday-Friday 8:30 A.M.-5:00 P.M. Closed for holidays. AD 1/71, AR 7/73

In 1994 the government of Massachusetts designated the empty lot at the corner of Merrimac and New Chardon streets, once intended for the Health, Education, and Welfare tower described above, as the site for a new courthouse building. The Suffolk County Courthouse, designed by the office of Kallmann McKinnell & Wood Architects, is currently under construction and is scheduled to be completed in 1998. Triangular in shape with an atrium in the center, this six-story structure will have an exterior of limestone and granite. A rotunda space just inside the entrance will welcome the public. In front of the building will be a plaza, and behind, facing the Hurley-Lindemann buildings, will be a landscaped park. A parking garage is to sit directly underground. The courthouse will be a welcome addition to this long-neglected site, and to the Government Center area as a whole.

ORANGE COUNTY GOVERNMENT CENTER (1968–70)
124 Main Street between Erie Street and Scotchtown Avenue
Goshen, New York

Paul Rudolph, architect

The Orange County Government Center shatters the prim box concept inside and out with a building of unique plasticity. One does not stroll quietly into this public facility, one progresses into its vigorous combinations of forms, a process that does not cease until one gets one's driver's license or takes one's jury seat. Few large planes of unbroken exterior walls exist: walls are pushed in and out to proclaim a design approach that veers toward the sophistic but operates (mainly) in the context of function. These carefully composed, multiple planes moreover present completely blank facades on both east and west sides: windows dominate only on north and south. The scale buildup of the exterior of the county center is thus both provocative and substantial, while, within, the central halls are filled with power, an effect that was achieved by space and light, not luxury of materials, which are economical, at times austere spaces. (The top light floods in from north-south-aligned clerestories.)

The center is divided into three buildings grouped around a terraced entrance court: note the spatial role played by the canopy extending as a partial frame to the courtyard. County and supreme court stand at right (north); the family courts behind; and the county executive, legislative, clerks', and other municipal offices are in the unit at left (south). Each building is complete within itself but structurally interconnected by passages on the first and third floors and by an outdoor passage across the court. Public access and public areas face the plaza side of each building, with administrative areas to the rear. As the eight courtrooms—from supreme (125 seats) down to family (24 seats)—required windowless walls, Rudolph placed these near the center of the buildings and wrapped the ancillary chambers about them. Though little or no flexibility was permitted for the standardized courtrooms, their mutual relation and the formation of halls and circulation areas could be developed freely. Breaks, changes of levels, and shafts of sunlight have all been fused.

The smooth reinforced concrete of the structural frame is clearly stated, while the walls are finished with sand-colored, ribbed concrete blocks, their warm color abetted within by appro-

priate orange carpeting. A prickliness appears in the smaller areas of the interior with so much unrelieved ridged surface, but the effect in the major spaces is rugged, the natural lighting dramatic. Though complexity and some inflexibility appear—a monumental variety of rooms had to be synchronized—the structural system is basically simple and modular, with column spacing regular. Beams are 4.8 feet/1.5 meters by 2 feet/.6 meter, spaced 18 feet/5.5 meters apart, and span up to 50 feet/15 meters. Peter P. Barbone was associate architect; Lev Zetlin Associates were the structural engineers.

Open Monday–Friday 9:00 A.M.–5:00 P.M. Closed for holidays. AR 6/66, AR 8/71

MCCORMICK PLACE (1968–71/1986/1993–97)
East Building, 2301 South Lake Shore Drive
North Building, 450 East 23rd Street
Chicago, Illinois

C. F. Murphy Associates, architects and engineers
Skidmore, Owings & Merrill and Thompson, Ventulett, Stainback,
architects of additions

Since the publication of the famous Burnham Plan of 1909, Chicago has been the most progressive city in the country in reclaiming and extending a lakeside site. It has built up a nearly continuous strip of waterside parks—almost 17 miles/27 kilometers of them—by landfill. Recreation and unimpeded motor traffic resulted. Carl Condit has called this "the greatest civic project ever undertaken by an American city" (*American Building Art, 20th Century,* Oxford University Press, 1960). It should be added also that the "inland" landscaping of Frederick Law Olmsted and Jens Jensen was another and equally important facet of the city's realization of the need for comprehensive, far-seeing planning and planting. And even today Chicago's architecture is, as it almost always has been, the most exploratory in the United States. (The skyscraper, after all, was invented here and taken to many of its greatest heights.)

The McCormick Place exhibition hall, perched on filled land, sits boldly next to the city's historic contributions. The first of the complex to be constructed is now known as the East Building (shown here). Originally opened in 1960, it was destroyed by fire in 1967 and was completely redesigned and rebuilt in 1968–71. Even at a distance the enormous overhangs of its cantilevered roof give one pause while close up its black triangulations visually enmesh one in the structural geometrics of its 15-foot-/4.6-meter-deep, two-way trusses. The great projection (75 feet/23 meters) was calculated so that trucks could load and unload exhibition material (which has a rapid turnover) under cover on both east (lake) and west sides, and on upper and secondary levels. The structure is surrounded by a terrace, with Lake Michigan (enlivened by sailboats) and Meigs Field (busy with its planes and helicopters) forming the backdrop. By quietly hugging its hillock, and being sandwiched tightly between lake and expressway, the building makes a minimum intrusion on the landscape, and a maximum expression of controlled architectural strength. Gene Summers was chief of design with Sherwin Asrow structural engineer. Traffic approaches the East Building via a tunnel on the lower level, parallel to the long side of the building. Both outdoor and covered parking are adjacent.

The building is divided into two separate sections on its glass-wrapped main floor. A highly flexible exhibition area of 375,000 square feet/34,770 square meters occupies the north part; its roof is upheld by reinforced concrete columns 150 feet/46 meters on center and 50 feet/15 meters high. A 4,451-seat theater (filling two levels, and entered from the lower) takes up the south section, along with three 345-seat auditoriums, various meeting rooms, a restaurant for 2,000, and service facilities. There is also a large exhibition area on the second level. Below are mostly services, including the kitchen.

The interior of the cavernous exhibition arena can be exciting or confusing, depending completely on what is going on inside. When lined with precise rows of chairs (or when empty), it delivers structural punch; when cluttered with exhibition stands, each outshouting the other, one is not tempted to tarry. The theater, on the other hand, is a good-looking typical auditorium essential for conventions. Much of the interior was renovated in 1993–94.

Skidmore Owings & Merrill's design for the North Building addition (1986) is smartly engineered. Though separated from the earlier structure by heavy lanes of city traffic, the new is connected to the older by both above-grade bridging and an underground tunnel. The addi-

tion is in imaginative contrast to the East Building; it uses a pylon- and cable-suspended roof and a bright silver-gray exterior color instead of somber black. The building's twelve concrete pylons incorporate ventilating ducts that dispense stale air 60 feet/18.2 meters above the roof.

The South Building, commenced in 1993 and scheduled for completion in 1997, was designed by Thompson, Ventulett, Stainback & Associates, and adds over one million square feet of exhibition and meeting room space to the complex. A glass-enclosed grand concourse connects all three buildings. New roadways have also been constructed to improve access. As a result of this expansion, McCormick Place will be the largest exhibition and convention center in North America.

Open for events. For more information call (312) 791–7000. The complex is included on the Chicago Architecture Foundation's bus tour; the cost is $25. For more information on CAF tours call (312) 922–3432. AR 5/71, AF 11/71, ARev 4/72

DALLAS/FORT WORTH
INTERNATIONAL AIRPORT (1968–74)
Dallas/Fort Worth, Texas

Hellmuth, Obata & Kassabaum, architects

Dallas/Fort Worth International Airport is not as innovative as is Dulles (Chantilly, Virginia—see page 448) with its mobile lounges—considered here but rejected as not being large enough for jumbo jets (plus being subject to drivers' strikes); nor is it as convenient to use as Tampa International (see page 546) with its rooftop parking—initially proposed here but bypassed, some think unfortunately, for lateral garages. The DFW is, however, an altogether staggering achievement. It is close in basic layout to its contemporary, the smaller Kansas City International Airport. Like the latter, DFW uses four gigantic arced-in-plan terminal buildings, here horseshoe shaped, off of whose outer faces the airplanes can berth. These extended half-circles, 2,625 feet/800 meters in inner diameter, are deployed in a symmetrical plan on either side of a 4-mile/6.4-kilometer north-south, multilaned, vehicular spine. Most of the open inner area described by each arc of buildings is given over to three zones of outdoor parking (beyond the attached covered garages), framed by a concentration of planting toward the center. This automobile and bus axis can be entered from either end where it taps onto existing highways; rapid transit facilities to and from Dallas and Fort Worth were not part of the original plan and are only now being developed.

Passenger flow is, of course, one of the key elements in airport design, and it has been meticulously studied here. Pleasures begin when one drives one's car to the airport and swings off the central roadway to the appropriate terminal and airline. One's luggage is checked at curbside—and is whisked immediately to the flight loading platform—and one parks the car in the covered garage directly opposite (if there is room), on its deck below if it is filled, or in the open-air (and cheaper) grade-level lot just beyond, which holds up to twelve hundred automobiles. Long-term, open-air, "remote" parking is accommodated at either end of the spine. Having taken care of the car, one then ascends by escalator to the lobby security check and departure lounge, a distance of about 75 feet/23 meters from curbside or an average of 250 feet/76 meters from parking facilities: a simple, smooth process. The deplaning passengers move directly from plane and across the lobby to the baggage claim area and public transportation, all on one easy floor. (One's automobile might also be on this level on top of the three-decked garage.) Departure and arrival lounges are generally separate, the latter, of course, being smaller. Restaurants, rest rooms, and shops are conveniently spaced in between.

If one is transferring to another airline (the greatest weakness of the airport), to long-term parking, rental cars, or the on-site, six-hundred-room hotel, one takes the Airtrans, the automated trains that run directly below each terminal, thus obviating walking. This 13-mile-/21-kilometer-long rail facility is, of course, a key to the entire airport design. Though it may take some time (up to twenty-four minutes) to reach one's objective, its forty-passenger cars move along with reasonable speed and comfort. It also requires some sophistication to use without mix-up on its several lines. The cross section of a building shows the central placement of Airtrans and reveals the excellent organization of a terminal's flow lines and activities, including an under-cover service road on the outer periphery directly adjacent to baggage handling and operations.

Architecturally the buildings and details at DFW are obviously capable from the design point of view. They are in effect straightforward, semi-industrial structures, well massed and scaled. There is, however, a tendency toward linear anonymity without a rallying accent to enliven these long-stretched masses. Close up the expression of their beige-colored concrete framework is superb, particularly the placement of beam on bracketed column. This explicit statement of structure, both outside and in, was aided and speeded by off-site prefabrication and by post-tensioning. Though the terminals form a semicircle, they are made up of straight-line components with wedge elements (often services) creating an organized planning module every 90 feet/27 meters. The development of interiors was left to the individual airlines with varying results, but in all of them one can enjoy that almost-forgotten pastime of being able to watch the planes land and take off, for each station overlooks the field. At times the surfeit of "desert" colors intrudes, but it is at least peaceful. All glass is bronze-colored.

The extraordinary Dallas/Fort Worth International Airport, which covers 17,707 acres/ 7,166 hectares, might well be "the bigger than Manhattan, the Year 2001 Air Terminal": it definitely has lessons—mostly positive—for all subsequent international air facilities. As the *AIA Journal* wrote (March 1978): "It must be understood the DFW's purposes were as much political as they were rational, and as much symbolic as they were functional. If it is an operational inconvenience, it is also a cultural landmark of the first order."

Among the more than score of major consultants were: Gyo Obata of HOK, principal in charge of design; Brodsky, Hopf & Adler, associate architects; Tippetts-Abbett-McCarthy-Stratton, airport planner, engineer, general consultant; Richard Adler of BHA, principal in charge of administration; Preston M. Geren, Jr., and Harrell & Hamilton, associate architects; LeMessurier Associates, Terry-Rosenlund & Company, structural engineers; Richard B. Myrick & Associates, landscape architects.

The Dallas/Fort Worth Airport is located directly between these two cities and is open 24 hours, 365 days per year. From downtown Dallas, 21 miles/34 kilometers west via TX 114 or 183; from downtown Fort Worth, 25 miles/40 kilometers east via TX 121 or 183. AR 8/70, PA 12/73, AD 6/74, Int 1/77

TAMPA INTERNATIONAL AIRPORT (1968–93)
Tampa, Florida

Reynolds, Smith & Hill, architects

The basic concept—and most of the reality—of the Tampa Airport is brilliant. First of all it is based on a "landside/airside" plan (by Leigh Fisher) that divorces all ground-generated functions (that is, passenger needs) from air-related ones, providing widely separated (1,000 feet/305 meters) shelter for each. The landside main building is connected with six airside units (four of which are original; the fifth was added in 1987, the sixth in 1993) by high-speed, horizontal but elevated, automatic shuttles. The sixteen shuttle cars are admirable. Trimly designed by architect Eliot Noyes and built by Westinghouse, they are non-attended, automatic, horizontal people-movers accommodating approximately one hundred standees for a forty-second fun ride, and operating on a seventy-second or so headway. They are double-tracked to operate both outbound and inbound at once—on quiet rubber tires atop concrete trackways. (If only they went all the way to Tampa.)

Second, its design is directly concerned with the automobile—that of passengers driving their own cars—instead of conjuring up a terminal as an end in itself and tolerating the private automobile as a nuisance. (An airport serves only as a ground-to-air transfer system: it is not a goal.) To this end the top half of the landside building is a garage.

Third, the landside building was developed as a sandwich of nine floors, each classified for various passenger processing functions and services. The ground floor is devoted to deplaning passengers and baggage claim, and—there being no planes around—is surrounded by access roads. The second level—reached directly by car, taxi, or limousine via elevated ramps on each side—is given over to enplaning passengers and ticketing. It provides a spacious, quiet retreat, with good furniture, warm colors, and sculpture (by Roy Butler). The third floor comprises the shuttle level and main concourse with concessions, restaurant, and cocktail lounge. It was originally less satisfactory, its central area being crowded with concessions, but it has subsequently been completely reconfigured. On top of these three working floors are five floors and one open roof-deck for short-term parking. The self-driven, ticketed passenger thus drives directly to a parking spot atop the landside building, drops down by elevator to the concourse level, and is shuttled immediately to the airside terminal and plane. If one needs a ticket, one proceeds to the enplaning-ticketing floor and then by escalator to the third floor and by shuttle to the proper airside satellite. Total maximum walking distance from car seat to plane seat was limited in the original design process to 700 feet/213 meters, but generally it is a good deal less than half that. A long-term parking garage for 4,800 vehicles is connected to the interior of the transfer level by its own monorail system.

The garden-surrounded exterior of the landside building, which measures roughly 350 x 420 feet/107 x 128 meters, bristles with elevated straight ramps or helixes for automotive access both to the terminal and to the short-term garaging above. The only "facade" it shows is that at the top, around the two semienclosed parking decks. The open but undercover deplaning driveways at ground level are particularly impressive, with three-story-high piers upholding the lateral overhang of the parking decks. Incidentally, both deplaning and enplaning passengers can—for a welcome change—proceed under cover to the rental car annex directly adjacent. First-rate landscaping and fountains add to the spatial pleasures here. One million dollars was spent on the landscaping so that "the passengers would *know* they were in Florida the minute they arrived."

J. E. Greiner & Company were engineers and coordinators; Leigh Fisher Associates, airport consultants. Joseph A. Maxwell & Associates designed the terminal interiors, the graphics were by Architectural Graphics Associates, and the landscaping by Stresau, Smith & Steward. The Hillsborough County Aviation Authority played no small hand in the overall project, leading the design team and insisting from the beginning that the solution be passenger, not airline, oriented. The original airside terminals are leased to the airlines and were designed by them, hence vary in architectural quality. A three-hundred-room hotel was added to the airside structures in 1974. One of the best airports in the United States.

Located off I-4/75 via FL 60 or Kennedy Boulevard. Open daily 24 hours. AR 8/70, F 10/71, AR 10/72, Int 10/73, JAIA 10/82

STAGE CENTER (1969–70)
(formerly Oklahoma Theater Center)
400 West Sheridan, between Hudson and Walker Avenues
Oklahoma City, Oklahoma

John M. Johansen, architect

Stage Center (now owned by the Arts Council of Oklahoma City) is one of the most intriguing buildings in the country. It is not, nor was it intended to be, "a thing of beauty," and it might well puzzle more than it endears. Startlingly different on the exterior and without formal facades, its logic and its peculiar delight grow upon one. As the architect John M. Johansen, somewhat esoterically, put it, in likening its design process to the field of electronics, there are "three 'components' with 'subcomponents' attached, plugged into one 'chassis' or 'gate,' and then connected by four 'circuiting systems,' superimposed at separate levels to avoid cross-circuiting. . . . And these components are connected by interlaced circuiting systems—ramps, stairs, bridges, and ductwork. It matters little, once the organizing idea is determined, what the actual number, or forms, of these elements may be" (*Architectural Forum*, May 1968). He thus takes the thrust-stage theater, the arena theater, and the administrative block with children's theater and rehearsal space on top, and gives each component its freedom and ability to assume its optimum shape, lacing them all together by mutually needed services.

Moreover, most buildings in these days of comfort devote some forty percent of their space and expense to circulation and to mechanical systems (air conditioning, electricity, elevators). Johansen, instead of absorbing these "non-productive" elements within the fabric of the structure to produce a pristine cover-up, has dramatically flung the mechanical and circulatory functions into and onto the spaces atop each of the three units, producing perhaps an "anti-building," but one logically generated and enormously stimulating to use. Color (only on the steel) adds no little to this milieu. Blue is used for the three "gangplanks" from the street, red for the outside stairs and "people tubes," ocher for the lobby projections around each unit, white for the cooling towers and air-conditioning machinery (where detached placement minimizes motor noises), black for the corrugated supply ducts from them, and natural concrete for all structures. A Fernand Léger-like impression results.

The 592-seat main theater is circular in plan with a thrust stage that pokes its angles into the audience. It seemingly disappears *under* the audience, for the seats that surround the acting arena are gigantic balconies in form, cantilevered lightly over the stage, hovering in space with actors appearing and disappearing in any of a dozen vomitoria. A certain "bear pit" relationship between actors and audience might be noted, but the place is alive with action. The intimate 240-seat arena theater, ovoid in plan, has a simple arrangement of four rectangular ranks of seats that frame and rise from stage level; entrances for all are at the open corners. Ticket booths and administrative offices occupy the street level of the smallest unit, with a children's theater and rehearsal hall combined above. The central space between the three buildings doubles as a fair-weather intermission piazzetta. There is even a pool (of dubious need). Interior finish throughout is at times minimal, but so was the cost. Altogether a fantastic complex. As the Honors Jury of the American Institute of Architects wrote, "it is an extraordinarily fresh and provocative work of architecture—rational, but wonderfully witty; mechanistic but joyfully humane" (*AIA Journal*, May 1972). Charles A. Ahlstrom was associate in charge; David Hays was stage designer; Seminoff-Bowman-Bode were the supervising architects. Having experienced growing pains, the center was thoroughly renovated in 1992 by Elliott + Associates Architects.

Lobby open Monday–Friday 9:00 A.M.–5:00 P.M. Also open during performances. Tours can be scheduled by calling (405) 270–4800. AR 4/68, F 5/68, AF 3/71, JAIA 5/72, JAIA 8/81, A 11/92

CRATE AND BARREL SHOP (1969–70)
(formerly Design Research Shop)
46 Brattle Street
Cambridge, Massachusetts

Benjamin Thompson & Associates, architects

A minimum of building with a maximum of effect: honed slabs of concrete wrapped in the thinnest of glass walls. An entirely new technique of glass detailing had to be evolved, for these exterior walls are totally of glass, no metal mullions upholding or enframing or interrupting their diaphanous skin. The tempered-glass plates (.39 inch/1 centimeter thick by 5 x 7 feet/1.5 x 2.1 meters in standard size) are end-butted, fastened in place by tiny stainless steel clips, and braced by internal steel arms. The effect, especially at dusk, is seductive as one observes the activities on different levels, the colors of the displays, and the movement of people in this total show window. But dusk or day or night; it is very stimulating. Note that the building is not a simple prism, hence a simple answer, but one with breaks and angles to give *divertimento* to its nearly invisible form, and especially to create greater transparency via a series of open corners and to emphasize the horizontal interaction of floor levels.

Open Monday–Friday 10:00 A.M.–7:00 P.M. (Thursday until 9:00 P.M.), Saturday 10:00 A.M.–6:00 P.M., Sunday 12:00 noon–6:00 P.M. AF 3/70, AR 5/70, Int 5/70, ARev 1/72

WEYERHAEUSER HEADQUARTERS (1969–71)
33663 Weyerhaeuser Way South
Federal Way, Washington

Skidmore, Owings & Merrill, architects

Built in stepped layers as it fills a small valley, and clutched by trees at each end, this extraordinary headquarters building by the San Francisco office of SOM constitutes a brilliant corporate structure. Its fascinatingly stretched-out low mass—oriented east and west—worships the earth with its horizontality, stepping outward longitudinally to mesh with the valley's contours as the building's floors increase, then retiring modestly at the top (fifth floor) over its brood of offices. It also steps back in lateral (that is, cross) section as it rises, so that the widest (and shortest) floor is that on the ground, the four above each being narrower, with the top scarce more than one third the breadth of the bottom. In short, the building waxes in length and wanes in breadth as its floors increase. It resembles a low-slung, stepped pyramid enamored of its valley and forest setting. (To increase the horizontal emphasis, observe that the vertical columns on each floor alternate in line.)

The narrowing of the cross section as the height rises is taken up on the exterior by wide, uninterrupted, full-length, planting boxes, slightly triangular in section. (The longest measure almost 1,300 feet/396 meters.) With flowers and plants—over two dozen varieties—thus outside each row of windows, and a sizable, 10-acre/4-hectare artificial lake lying northward, contact with the outside world from inside offices is never lacking. (The lake was made by damming an existing stream with the building itself and carrying the southbound overflow underground.) Even the parking lots, carefully right-angled on opposite sides of opposite ends of the building to hold 1,300 cars, are terraced and landscaped. A substantial menhir, sensitively installed by Gordon Newell (and chemically treated to encourage lichen and moss), dominates the main (west) entrance with appropriate symbolism, fulfilling the encompassing Mother Earth syndrome.

The inset fifth floor, which is covered by a copper-clad, low gambrel roof, is devoted to top management, plus small executive dining area (most executives prefer to eat in the cafeteria), and an enclosed briefing room. The fourth floor, which serves as the entry level, contains a reception area at each end, with a lounge, a 350-seat cafeteria, and a kitchen in the center. The three lower floors are filled with various research and specialized group facilities. An unusual feature of the interior—and the genesis of the design of the building—is that all office floors, except for small special rooms, are completely open and without partitions. Individual divisions are made by 5-foot-/1.5-meter-high movable standard components (of red and white oak and mohair). This "office landscape," or *Bürolandschaft*, permits maximum flexibility and a sense of openness and facilitates personal communication, yet in most cases maintains a sufficient degree of privacy. The decision to use it here, one reached after lengthy space-planning studies by Sydney Rodgers Associates, made possible the very wide lower floors: rows of partitioned offices would have been intolerable. The building thus materialized from its initial philosophy of office disposition. It was probably the first totally open landscape commitment for a major building in the United States.

The interiors were impeccably designed by the architects. The north and south walls of all floors are glazed from end to end. Their glass is end-butted, hence without mullions: "a landscape in a landscape" as *Interiors* (March 1972) put it. Sasaki, Walker Associates were the landscape architects, and it is important to note that they were on the scene with the architects from the very beginning—before a spe-
cific building was
even conceived. They
helped with site selec-
tion and develop-
ment, then tied the
building to the site—
and vice versa, the ter-
races of planting box-
es playing no small
part in this. Alto-
gether superb.

From Tacoma: (8 miles/13
kilometers) north on I-5, exit
142B, east on WA 18, first road
north. From Seattle: (22
miles/35 kilometers) south
on I-5, exit South 320th
Street, south on WA 99, right
on South 348th Street (WA
18). Interiors not open to the
public. AF 3/72, Int 3/72, JAIA
7/77, A 5/85

PHILLIPS EXETER ACADEMY LIBRARY
(1969–71)
Front Street
between Elm Street and Tan Lane
Exeter, New Hampshire

Louis I. Kahn, architect

Quiet without, the Exeter Library erupts within. In plan it forms a simple square 108 feet/33 meters on a side. Its corners are carefully lopped, left "open," and its planar facades project to emphasize the separation of outer brick from inner concrete frame. A ground-level enclosed arcade surrounds the building, masking, it should be mentioned, the main entrance on the north side (should not a library be the most inviting to enter of any building on campus?). The exterior walls are of locally made traditional Exeter brick and untraditional teak spandrels. Note the subtle widening of the flat arched windows as the building rises to its open terrace at top; this progression not only lightens the mass visually but relieves any tendency toward rigidity. (The small windows in the spandrels of the second and third levels open onto study carrels.)

It is on the inside, however, that the building springs to life. As one winds up an arm of the twin-curved stair past mighty concrete beams, one encounters the startling climax of the second-level great hall. Here Louis I. Kahn's famous play of geometry and equally celebrated play of light—"light, the giver of all presences"—create stunning sequences, along with a monumentality reminiscent of his work in Dacca, Bangladesh and Ahmedabad, India. The geometrics begin with the square plan of this central concrete-framed hall, which flings its open core up six floors to the prodigious X bracing at top. High on all four sides, a circular opening 29 feet/8.8 meters in diameter liberates lateral enclosure and enables one to realize the books behind. Above the X bracing a peripheral skylight pours light into the great hall. It is no casual experience. The concrete inner frame also supports the stacks, which embrace the core on all sides; they have a capacity of 250,000 volumes. An outer wrapping of brick surrounds the concrete book area, providing on the second and third levels the study carrels mentioned earlier (220 in all). Thus the student can retreat from the monumentality of the hall to the intimacy of a shielded desk, and can view either the world of nature (by opening a wood panel) or the private world of books. The roof terrace (in effect the ninth floor) offers an open-air reading spot. The interiors were furnished with distinction by Benjamin J. Baldwin. The difficult structural problem of combining a concrete frame with a brick bearing wall structure was solved by Kahn's consultants, the Keast and Hood Company.

Open Monday–Friday 8:00 A.M.–9:00 P.M., Saturday 8:00 A.M.–4:00 P.M., Sunday 2:00.–9:00 P.M. Tours can be arranged by calling (603) 772–4311. AF 7–8/72, AF 10/73, A 2/85

CHRISTIAN SCIENCE CENTER (1969–72)
175 Huntington Avenue at Massachusetts Avenue
Boston, Massachusetts

I. M. Pei & Partners, architects

One of the main problems the architects faced in designing this center was to make it an urban pleasure for the public after answering the practical demands of the private. To achieve this a vertical Church Administration Building, a horizontal Colonnade Building (now called the Christian Science Broadcasting Center), and a separate Sunday School Building were summoned together about a long and broad reflecting pool, landscaped on the avenue side, the whole producing a tranquil retreat on this southwest edge of downtown. It provides a place, as intended, to stroll or sit, to read, mull, or pray. The twenty-eight-story Church Administration Building acts as a vertical accent for the motorist and pedestrian on Huntington Avenue, while the five-story horizontal block for clerical staff and cafeteria closes the space opposite and leads, via a vigorous colonnade, directly to the Christian Science Mother Church. The quarter-circular Sunday School Building of muscular bent (containing classrooms, offices, and an auditorium seating 1,100) stands detached at the far end of the pool, which measures 686 feet/209 meters long by 88 feet/27 meters wide and 2 feet/.61 meter deep. Note its edge detail. A 550-car garage lies underneath. The architecture, smartly cast in reinforced concrete, is overly monumental for some but it sets the stage for the Romanesque Mother Church of 1894 and the large Neo-Roman addition of 1904. The expansive pool, the garden with benches, and the triple rows of 121 linden trees make definite contributions to the city: altogether a careful orchestration of buildings old and new, one that exerted a salutary upgrading of an entire urban area. Cossutta & Ponte were associate architects; Sasaki, Dawson, DeMay Associates were landscape architects.

The church is open Tuesday–Friday 10:00 A.M.–4:00 P.M., Sunday 11:15 A.M.–2:00 P.M. Services held on Wednesday at 7:30 P.M. and Sunday at 10:00 A.M. and 7:00 P.M. (no 7:00 P.M. service in July–August). The Church Administration Building lobby is open Monday–Friday 8:00 A.M.–6:00 P.M. The Broadcasting Center is closed to the public, with the exception of the Bible exhibit in the north end, which is open Wednesday–Saturday 10:00 A.M.–4:00 P.M., Sunday 11:15 A.M.–4:00 P.M. The Sunday School Building is closed to the public. All buildings closed for holidays. Free tours are available. For more information call (617) 450–3790. AF 9/73

GEORGE GUND HALL (1969–72)
Harvard University
48 Quincy Street between Cambridge and Kirkland streets
Cambridge, Massachusetts

John Andrews/Anderson/Baldwin, architects

Harvard's Graduate School of Design syncretizes under one roof its hitherto scattered Departments of Architecture, Landscape Architecture, and Planning and Urban Design, plus the Frances Loeb Library, the Computer Resources Department, and related facilities. The philosophy of its evolution, one fiercely debated by faculty and students alike, was that space design today is so complex that it must be interdisciplinary. To bring these curricula together where the students of each could—hopefully—stimulate one another, the architects of George Gund Hall evolved a series of four slightly overlapping and stepped terraces or "trays" extending the width of the building. The almost fantastic teaching agora that results, rising upward and backward in platformed splendor under one gigantic, steeply slanting roof, corrals all concerned with the design process into visual proximity, if not into the embrace of intellectual camaraderie. It is a startling space. Overhead (a bit close overhead) seven magnificent, sharply canted tube-trusses 134 feet/41 meters long and 11 feet/3.4 meters deep span the column-free area, with heating and ventilating conduits paralleling the trusswork. (There have been student complaints about both ventilation and noise level.) As the roof rises, long narrow bands of windows fit vertically between the angled trusses—from direct rear elevation one sees almost all glass—and from these skylights pours a flood of daylight. The four major instructional levels are flexibly divided longitudinally, depending on enrollments, with the broadest terrace on the second floor, the three others narrowing as they rise.

Gund Hall represents a startling architectural concept of intense dedication to an idea; but the resulting floating yet visually related platforms are perhaps more persuasive in theory (and model form) than in use, where their identities are blurred by furniture, tracing paper, and coats. Moreover, this prodigious canopied chamber, while exciting to some, can lead others toward a hankering for privacy in their search for personal identity. However, whether the individual exults as a participator or suffers as a cog from the building's overriding philosophy, Gund Hall is an audacious and highly provocative addition to our architectural thinking.

Staff offices wrap in an *L* shape around the front and the north side. The main floor contains the two-level Frances Loeb Library at left and the W. T. Piper Auditorium at right. In the basement are the second level of the library (cleverly visible from the outside), audiovisual rooms, and services. The exterior has a few awkward moments (as with some angles along

Cambridge Street), but circumnavigation, particularly when the building glows at dusk, produces exciting contrasts. Edward R. Baldwin was partner in charge; LeMessurier Associates were the structural engineers. Unfortunately only the lobby is open to the public except on tours.

Open daily 9:00 A.M.–5:00 P.M. For more information call (617) 495–4731. AR 2/70, AR 11/72, F 12/72, JAIA 1/79

KIMBELL ART MUSEUM
(1969–72)
3333 Camp Bowie Boulevard
Fort Worth, Texas

Louis I. Kahn, architect

The Kimbell Art Museum's drive-in entrance is anonymous and its plan highly symmetrical (and oriented precisely north-south), but the potential formality evaporates on the interior in a radiation of waves of space to create one of the country's greatest museum interiors. It is, to quote the architect, "a friendly home," a home of welcoming scale where the evanescent, non-rigid moods of natural light (with artificial backup when necessary) bathe the works of art with subtle nuances and variations throughout the day. It should be mentioned immediately that although the Texas sun furnishes by far the greater part of the illumination, no direct rays strike the paintings on the walls: all lighting is indirect. This is achieved by running continuous—and for a few viewers prominent—Plexiglas skylights (2.5 feet/.76 meter wide) down the center of thirteen of the sixteen cycloidal vaults that form the building's distinctive roof. Finely pierced metal screens, suspended directly underneath the skylights, reflect and spread the light over the soffit of the vaults thence onto the works of art. Architecture, in Louis Kahn's words, is "a harmony of spaces in light"; and light and life are fused throughout the museum.

The overall building is 318 feet/97 meters in length and resembles a Tunisian *ghorfa* with its barrel-vaulted profile. Each of its post-tensioned vaults, of which three form entry porches, measures 104 feet/32 meters long, 23 feet/7 meters wide, and 4 inches/10 centimeters thick. Note that at their ends the vaults are separated from the vertical walls by thin lunettes of light to emphasize the independence of structure from non-structure. Note, too, the subtle difference of the two curves of the lunettes. The vaults, which rest on supports only at their ends, are separated laterally by 7-foot-/2.1-meter-wide concrete channels that contain air-conditioning outlets and electrical conduits.

An openness and flexibility grow under the amicable and domestic spaces of these inspired roof ripples; they encourage gallery identity yet induce a questing spirit to probe the museum's artistic riches. Exhibition space is flexible because there are few supporting columns, while all partitions are readily movable. A 180-seat auditorium and a buffet restaurant lie adjacent to the north court. All services and the parking entry for visitors are in the lower level. Two courts, the larger used for outdoor sculpture, extend the display possibilities and give accents to the exterior. Note the pools and terraces in front. Workmanship throughout is notable, particularly in the exposed concrete vaulting, while detailing, whether in concrete, stainless steel, oak, or travertine, is impeccable. The museum was made possible by the will and collection of the late Kay Kimbell, who left his entire and considerable fortune to the Kimbell Art Foundation. The project architect was Marshall D. Meyers; Preston M. Geren, Jr., was associate architect. Dr. August E. Komendant was the structural consultant, Richard Kelly and Edson Price the lighting consultants, and George Patton landscape architect.

Located between Will Rogers Road West and West Lancaster Avenue (visitor parking and entrance also off Arch Adams Road). Open Tuesday–Thursday 10:00 A.M.–5:00 P.M., Friday 12:00 noon–8:00 P.M., Saturday 10:00 A.M.–5:00 P.M., Sunday 12:00 noon–5:00 P.M. Closed July 4, Thanksgiving, Christmas, and New Year's Day. Admission to the permanent collection is free; admission prices vary for shows. Free tours can be scheduled by calling (817) 332–8451. AF 7–8/72, Int 3/73, JAIA 5/75, JAIA 8/82, A 10/89

A block west up Lancaster Avenue stands the Amon Carter Museum (see page 473), while across the street is the Modern Art Museum of Fort Worth, all three collaborating to give the city an enviable art museum center, with the Museum of Science and History conveniently nearby.

IDS CENTER AND CRYSTAL COURT (1969–72)
Nicollet Mall, 7th Street, Marquette Avenue and 8th Street
Minneapolis, Minnesota

Johnson/Burgee, architects

Though the Investors Diversified Services tower in no way resembles the Campanile in the Piazza San Marco, in function this elegantly sheathed fifty-seven-story skyscraper polarizes the city much as the Venetian fulcrum does. It forms a beacon, figuratively and literally, on the city's profile, while close up its Crystal Court acts as a spontaneous magnet for much of the activity of downtown Minneapolis—as, of course, does the Piazza for Venice. Thus vertically and horizontally the impact of each quickens the city and the citizen. Moreover this block-square complex also contains a 281-room hotel (the nineteen-story Marquette Hotel, at the corner of Marquette and 7th), an eight-story office block (on Marquette) with an underground garage for 640 cars, and along Nicollet and 7th Street—a key shopping corner—a two-story building containing a variety of retail shops. The chief generating factor in developing the plan was to have these four units embrace and define the central Crystal Court and do so not just on one level but two, the second one tying into and expanding the city's extraordinary network of elevated pedestrian skyways, a series of air-conditioned bridges that interconnect forty downtown blocks. Thus after leaving one's car in an underground garage, one can work, lodge, shop, wine, dine, and play throughout the city's center without once having to face the chill blasts of winter or summer's downpours.

The IDS skyscraper at 775 feet/236 meters remains the tallest structure in the city, despite a flurry of new developments, and this profile "responsibility" was not lost on the architects. To keep its bulk from urban abruptness, even intrusiveness, they stepped in each of the four corners with seven uniform vertical setbacks—"zogs" Philip Johnson calls them—so that the two ends of the building are precisely half as wide as the midsection. By this means the greenish-blue mirror glass that encases the building is not one "boring" mass but a series of faceted facades that catch and enjoy the sun. In addition further exterior interest is created by the spacing of the muntins, hence window width, which are approximately twice as close as normal, being 30 inches/76 centimeters on center: "more the aspect of a birdcage than a glass box" (Johnson).

The Crystal Court forms one of the most spirited mid-city crossroads that one will see. Vaguely pentagonal in plan, it is an irregular cube in three dimensions topped by a startling roof—almost constructivist sculpture—that rises in deeply coffered tiers (note structure) to a maximum height of 121 feet/37 meters. Through the pyramids of plastic and glass that roof this animated concourse streams the sun—and below streams the populace. Its marked lack of horizontal and vertical rigidity is emphasized by the second-level balconies—reached by escalators—that wrap around almost three-quarters of the *cortile* and afford festive viewing platforms for observing the flow of people. A tempting variety of shops on both levels, a 24-foot/7.3-meter kinetic sculpture by Jonathan Borofsky, and an overall atmosphere of pleasure, even glamour, have been skillfully created. Four skyways, carefully unaligned, lead from the upper level to tie the Crystal Court to the city's department stores and office buildings, and also to afford access to the hotel. The street-level entrances to the court are directly underneath the mid-block skyways.

On the exterior of the IDS Center there are some awkward junctures between tower and hotel, and the facades of the latter are not overwhelming, but altogether this is a brilliant contribution to urban design, one that carefully embraces downtown Minneapolis and stitches its space into the very fabric of the city instead of walling it off. As a result it has become an urban umbilicus, the delight of shoppers winter or summer—and long after 5:00 P.M. It is in this new dimension of civic integration and welcome that its prime significance lies. Edward F. Baker was associated architect.

Open daily 8:00 A.M.–8:00 P.M. Closed for holidays. AF 1–2/73, F 11/73, JAIA 5/75, JAIA 8/78, JAIA 6/79

FEDERAL RESERVE BANK OF MINNEAPOLIS (1969–73)
250 Marquette Avenue (Plaza off Nicollet Mall)
Minneapolis, Minnesota

Gunnar Birkerts & Associates, architects

The Federal Reserve Bank, whose structure veers near the obstreperous, is at once both improbable and stunning. The rationale for its structural swoop (that is, the catenary expressed in its facades) was the need to create column-free floors underground—where all the bullion is stored—because a grid of vertical supports would compromise the movements of armored cars and complicate related storage problems. Moreover, routine offices and high-security areas were to be separated. The architect therefore concentrated the loads at two points 275 feet/84 meters apart, ran two great piers up eleven floors above a plaza, connected and braced them with a 28-foot-/8.5-meter-deep roof truss plus rigid frame facades, slung cables from the tower tops, then tied his floors onto these cable supports. It is the same simple notion as multidecking a suspension bridge. A not inconsiderable additional advantage is that the suspended office floors thus are columnless. (Floor access is via a central semi-detached elevator tower; emergency exits and toilets are at each end of the building.) To underscore vividly the drama of the catenary, the architect detailed the tawny reflective glass that sheathes the building in two planes, putting all glass below the curve flush with the outside edge and all above the catenary a few inches inset to reveal the vertical mullions.

A broad sloping terrace rises from Nicollet Mall, flows beneath the building, and terminates 20 feet/6.1 meters above Marquette Avenue, thus giving further importance to this urban spine. It is carefully landscaped, fitted with numerous clever benches (note their concealed lights), and accented with several excellent pieces of sculpture and a fountain. The personnel entrance—and a quiet entrance it is—is off Marquette with two truck ramps, closed except when in use, along this same street. Underground employee parking uses the two side streets. The bank is planned so that a fifty percent addition in office space can be realized by adding six floors at the top, floors that in this case would be suspended from an arch on either side, the reverse, thus, of the catenary. Skilling, Helle, Christiansen, Robertson were structural engineers. Though rationalized, this is one of the most imaginative buildings one will see.

Lobby open to the public Monday–Friday 8:00 A.M.–5:00 P.M. AF 1–2/69, AF 6/71, AR 10/71, AF 11/73

JOHN F. KENNEDY MEMORIAL (1970)
Main, Market, Commerce, and Record streets
Dallas, Texas

Philip Johnson, architect

Understated to the point of starkness, the John F. Kennedy Memorial suggests the elusive, inexorable turns of fate in contemporary terms. With a curiously unsettling embrace, its entry cantilevers suggest the tenuous forces of nature—and the balance of life. Construction is of seventy-two simple precast concrete slabs, eight of them longer than the others to form legs that elevate its palisade lightly above the ground. Post-tensioning binds these slabs together (note the circular metal cover plates). The design forms an enclosure of two *U* shapes—"like a pair of magnets about to clamp together," says the architect.

It measures 50 feet/15 meters square and 30 feet/9 meters high. One of the weaknesses of the American ethos is that we almost never produce a distinguished memorial to an individual (compare the Gateway Arch in St. Louis, page 486), but this monument to the late president—who was gunned down a few hundred yards from this spot—partially succeeds in evoking the disturbing concept of life, death, and even aspiration. Moreover, it must be seen if only to jolt our conscience and shatter our complacency.

Open daily 24 hours. AF 1–2/66

Just west of the memorial stands a 16-foot-/4.9-meter-square cedar log cabin said to be erected in 1843 by John Neely Bryan—"the original speculator of North Texas" (*Dallasights*, AIA, 1978). In spite of its minute size it once served both as post office and temporary courthouse (1848–50). In 1935 it was moved to its present site and restored. Directly behind rises the Dallas County Courthouse (1891–92), a fine Romanesque number that until 1919 sprouted a 205-foot-/62-meter-high central tower. Orlopp and Kusener were the architects. In 1966 the entire building was remodeled into offices by architect Moffatt D. Adams. It is currently vacant, and the future use of the structure is as yet undetermined.

USX TOWER (1970)
(formerly U.S. Steel Building)
600 Grant Street
Pittsburgh, Pennsylvania

Harrison & Abramovitz & Abbe,
architects

Building codes for fire protection have always dictated that the steel frame of multistory buildings must be encased in concrete, masonry, or asbestos to prevent the steel from buckling in a conflagration. The steel frame of this startling sixty-four-story skyscraper, however, is fully exposed, achieving its necessary fireproofing by having its exoskeletal hollow-box columns filled with water—and antifreeze. Exposed steel is both structure and finish. This ingenious technique has, of course, opened structural and visual possibilities in high-rise design, and the architects have taken bold advantage of it in this showcase for the U.S. Steel Corporation. It should be added, however, that the idea for the exoskeleton came before that for the water-filled columns: by having the structure on the outside a column-free interior, subdivisible at will, would result. The columns—six per side—are set with 39-foot/11.8-meter spacing and frame three-story-high sections, the largest that the fabricator, American Bridge, recommended. They were made as sizable as feasible for esthetic reasons and to accommodate the water, which is used both for fireproofing and, by circulation, to minimize temperature changes on opposite sides of the building. The resulting exterior framework produces a new and dramatic scale. The two intermediate floors of the building's three-floor module do not frame into the exterior steel columns, but are supported internally by two-story columns that are upheld by each "primary" floor. The skin of the building is set back 3 feet/.9 meter from and completely independent of the exoskeleton; thus the air space contributes to the fireproofing. Both framing and walls are made of Cor-Ten, a weathering, self-protecting steel that needs no upkeep—and was developed by U.S. Steel.

Not only is the building innovative in its structural concept, but its plan, which was determined only after considerable analysis, forms an unusual equilateral triangle notched at the corners. Though this might prove awkward in a smaller building, it works readily here, providing three contiguous column-free rectangles of office area each 221 x 45 feet/67 x 4 meters, quickly divisible at will, with all services and vertical circulation in an inner triangular core. This imaginative and handsome building epitomizes steel construction, as three blocks down Grant Street, H. H. Richardson's Allegheny County Court House and Jail (see page 272) heralded the zenith—and the swan song—of masonry. Skilling, Helle, Christiansen, Robertson were structural engineers.

Lobby open to the public Monday–Friday 7:00 A.M.–7:00 P.M. The 62nd-floor Top-of-the-Triangle restaurant is also open to the public. AR 4/67, JAIA 12/67, AF 12/71, Int 12/71

AUDITORIUM FORECOURT FOUNTAIN (1970)
Southwest 3rd and 4th avenues, between Clay and Market streets
Portland, Oregon

Lawrence Halprin & Associates, designers

Lawrence Halprin & Associates' Lovejoy Fountain seen in the nearby Portland Center Project (see page 519) was merely a warm-up for this masterpiece created four years later in front of the city's auditorium. As at Lovejoy, this is no isolated jet that merely tinkles, splashes, and sprays for our auditory and visual pleasure, but a block-square summoning of waters that creates spontaneous involvement and gladness, a fountain for participators as well as observers, a fountain that is total theater with lines erased between audience and actors. Alive with grateful young people in varying degrees of dampness, it also serves older people. The multiform potentialities of water are brightly evident in its terraces and platforms, its cascades and still pools, its flat decks and secret caverns. While exhilaration leaps from its cataracts, peace can be found in its secluded corners. It is, in short, a work of genius, the finest display of urban waters that one will see anywhere.

The fountain rises (via recirculated water) from the grassed and placid upper reaches of its sloping site. It then gathers momentum to build up a taunted torrent searching for outlets as it dashes almost angrily between its 80-foot-/24-meter-wide series of concrete embrasures and spillways, until with freedom it leaps over the cunningly irregular waterfall's edges (18–20 feet/5.5–6 meters high) to surcease in the deep pools at its base. At this lower level a series of largely square concrete platforms, with slightly different heights and overlaps—to establish territoriality and bases for grouping and exploration—transfer the vertical drop of the waters to the horizontality of the urban milieu. A backup of small trees and planting provides a frame. Designed for and built of reinforced concrete, the fountain when dry acts as urban sculpture,

its canted and striated walls producing strength by themselves. The waters start to flow in mid-morning, pushed by a 200-horsepower vertical-flow pump, and the sight of 13,000 gallons (49,000 liters) per minute searching their destinies over the wide waterfall make it one of the attractions of Portland. It is illuminated at night by spotlights—largely for the crowd in the auditorium it faces (a current restoration will light the fountain as it was originally designed). Only on a rare winter day does the temperature force it to close down. It is probably the finest urban glory since Francesco de Sanctis's stairs at the Piazza di Spagna (1721–25) in Rome. Satoru Nishita was partner in charge; Byron McCulley project director; and Angela Danadjieva Tzvetin project designer. Beamer/Wilkinson Associates were mechanical and electrical engineers.

PA 5/68, ARev 11/68, AF 10/70

ARCOSANTI (1970–)
Cordes Junction, Arizona

Paolo Soleri, architect

The philosophy behind the planning and buildings of Arcosanti, a community that will eventually accommodate 5,000–7,000 inhabitants, seeks an intimate, indeed revelatory, relationship between man and nature, a unity of those forces that shape—and that too often have misshaped—the world. Arcosanti's physical manifestation heralds "arcology"—architecture and ecology—and, according to Paolo Soleri, "is seen also as a societal framework that can give a higher quality to humankind's physical, psychological and aesthetic well-being." This "alternative urban environment" will preserve most of its site for agriculture and recreation, using only 13 acres/5.3 hectares of its 860-acre/348-hectare property for buildings. It will eliminate sprawl by sheltering all life functions—housing, work, education, recreation, shopping, religion, and culture—within a series of three fantastic complexes. Revering "the theology of the sun," it will depend upon it for most of its energy needs via a vast (5-acre/2-hectare) south-facing greenhouse and solar-heat-collecting unit stepped down the mesa in front. Waste and pollution will be almost nonexistent, as will the need for the automobile.

Construction of the "first generation" units of Arcosanti began in 1970 and by the late seventies several substantial structures, all amateur-built, were out of the ground. The first that the visitor meets is the Crafts III Building (1977), an exploded-box reception and restaurant center nearest the parking lot. This energetic design is characterized by rectangular concrete panels, both poured and prefabricated, many of them pierced with large circular openings somewhat reminiscent of Louis I. Kahn's work in Bangladesh. Behind this rise two apses (both 1974), the nearer housing the foundry with the ceramics workshop where Soleri's famous bells are made. A short distance to the east spring twin in-line barrel vaults of prefabricated concrete sections forming a splendid open work space for the wood and metal shops (1972). Separated from each other by 6 feet/1.8 meters, they measure 63.3 feet/19.3 meters wide and 32.8 feet/10 meters deep. Work on the East Crescent, just east of the vaults, is expected to be completed in the year 2000. Residential but flexible in character, it will house sixty to seventy people. In time this can be used for studio and work space, functioning as a playground, meeting and performance place, and market. Other housing will progress when funding becomes available.

The existing structures and the East Crescent will be part of a larger group of structures known as the Critical Mass. The Critical Mass will be comprised of guest and residential spaces, mixed-use buildings, a conference center, art and craft studios, and five acres of solar greenhouse. The final phase of construction will include two twenty-five story mixed-use megastructures. Chimeric, cosmic, mystic, and almost beyond belief in imagination and complexity, this microcity in the desert may well develop new insights for the metropolis of the future. Any major effort to harmonize humanity and nature and minimize the need for non-renewable sources of energy will bear some of the fruit that the world sorely needs. This alternative to present-day urban chaos "will demonstrate that we can rearrange the structure of our cities and towns in a very different way" (Soleri).

Located 2.5 miles/4 kilometers northeast of Cordes Junction exit of I-17 (70 miles/113 kilometers north of Phoenix). Open daily 9:00 A.M.–5:00 P.M. Closed Thanksgiving and Christmas. One-hour tours given daily every hour on the hour; a $5 donation per person is suggested. For more information call (602) 632–7135. AF 3/61, PA 4/73, JAIA 5/82

ROTHKO CHAPEL (1970–71)
1409 Sul Ross Street at Yupon and Branard streets
Houston, Texas

Howard Barnstone and Eugene Aubry, architects
Philip Johnson, collaborating architect

Mark Rothko and Barnett Newman were two of the great American artists of our time, and both have found a sympathetic architectural setting in this nondenominational chapel and center for meditation. One arrives at Newman's superb 26-foot-/8-meter-high, weathering-steel *Broken Obelisk*, a memorial to Dr. Martin Luther King, Jr., pointing its shattered finger—the chapel's "steeple"—poignantly heavenward in the small reflecting pool. One then approaches the chapel, whose modified octagonal shape of salmon-colored brick is relieved only by the black metal fascia over the front entrance. A darkened narthex leads via two separate doors into the inner octagon where three enormous Rothko triptychs and five single canvases, varying in size from 9–11 feet/2.7–3.3 meters wide and 11–15 feet/3.3–4.6 meters tall, virtually fill every wall. For many observers peace and transcendence are evoked from these fourteen paintings—one gets from them

more than one brings. For others these enormous purple, blackish, almost solid-color canvases—the colors of blood and wine—tend to weaken each other collectively. There is mystery but little relief because the canvases are so similar. A sizable, centrally placed octagonal skylight, recalling—at Rothko's request—studio light floods the chapel/gallery with natural illumination. The room itself—with its grayish concrete walls, speckled gray asphalt paving-block floor, and elemental benches—sets a stern stage for the art. But see this chapel: it is puzzlingly provocative.

Open daily 10:00 A.M.–6:00 P.M. Admission is free. For more information call (713) 524-9839. JAIA 4/72, F 7–8/73

ART CENTER (1970–71)
Columbia Basin College
2600 North Chase Street
Pasco, Washington

Brooks Hensley Creager, architects

An architectural arcanum whose startlingly plain, boxlike walls brilliantly serve two services: as enclosures and as heroic screens for after-dusk films and slides. Works of art, announcements, and casual delights are projected from machines in the eight turrets built into the berms surrounding the building. As a two-year community college with a substantial evening attendance, it would be difficult to imagine a more tempting come-on. The three-level complex combines art studios, a multiform theater for drama, music studios, speech classrooms, and administrative offices.

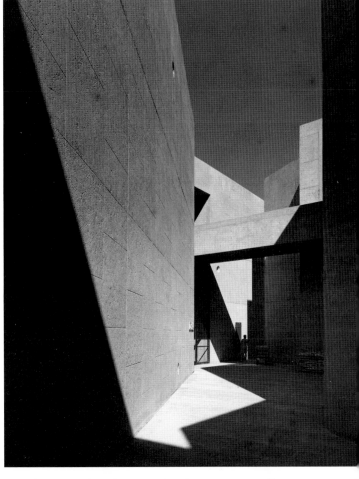

The narrow slotted entrances of the simple square exterior, which measures 135 feet/41 meters on a side, unexpectedly open onto a tantalizing inner labyrinth of "streets" and small courts. These separate and demarcate the four divisions, each discipline taking the form most suited to its functions. These inner spaces —suggestive of Middle Eastern urban patterns—are cool and shaded in the desert-like climate of this part of Washington. Their heavy concrete walls reflect the changing geometry of sunshine and shadow, while overhead several bridges add spatial accents to this cultural casbah. At night invisible-source theater spotlights maintain the drama and cast people-shadows. Although it might seem that this compact composition is more suited to an urban campus than one with almost endless plains surrounding it, the reverse is true: it offers inner focus and life in a flat, featureless landscape.

Located immediately north of US 12. Open Monday–Friday 7:30 A.M.–4:30 P.M. Tuesday and Thursday also open 7:40 P.M.–10:00 P.M. Admission is free. Tours can be scheduled by calling (509) 547–0511, extension 331. JAIA 5/78

BURROUGHS WELLCOME HEADQUARTERS (1970–72)
3030 Cornwallis Road
Research Triangle Park, North Carolina

Paul Rudolph, architect

The Burroughs Wellcome Headquarters is one of the most original administrative complexes in the country. Standing firmly astride the top of the most prominent ridge in Research Triangle Park, it forms a "manmade extension" and marches down the slope with a series of splayed-wall, articulated units. Faint recollections of Zoser's Stepped Pyramid at Saqqara (c. 2800 B.C.) come fleetingly to mind, but this is no exercise in historicism. Burroughs Wellcome is a hardheaded attempt to establish a major research institute with flair and flexibility within a realistic budget.

Two of Paul Rudolph's chief concerns in architecture involved the psychology of space and movement through buildings and the play of natural light within them. In both of these he was—as what perceptive architect is not?—influenced by the work of Frank Lloyd Wright and Le Corbusier. Rudolph was also concerned with multiples, that is, similar forms put together in such rhythmic fashion that the banality of the base unit vanishes in the orchestration of the whole. All of the above are present here. Spatial excursions will be seen even in the smaller dimensions of the laboratories, where, as elsewhere in the building, rigidity evaporates in canted planes and in the absence of the right angle. Three-dimensional enclosure and dramatic lighting reach a climax of progression in the towering lobby. The flood of natural light in the outer offices and laboratories is controlled by a clerestory and "outrigging" of baffles so that the effect illuminates the room, but the source (direct sun) is little evident. Inward-slanting bands of windows provide a direct view outward for the occupants. Artificial light is equally well handled. Rudolph's employment of similar units or modules multiplied to create a building finds imaginative exposition at Burroughs Wellcome. The lozenge-shaped elements interact up and down the slope, coalescing to form the total fabric of the building as it grows from the hill. There is expressionism here, and in spots suggestions of the arbitrary, but the results are very spirited.

Interior not open to the public. Grounds open Monday–Friday during business hours. AR 11/70, AR 4/72, AR 6/72

ART MUSEUM OF SOUTH TEXAS (1970–72)
1902 North Shoreline Drive
Corpus Christi, Texas

Johnson/Burgee, architects

Seemingly sliced out of reinforced concrete (chosen so as to be hurricane proof), this smartly angled and curved, dazzlingly white, almost Greek-island exterior suggests few of the spatial pleasures that await within. The architects perched the museum on an embankment directly on Corpus Christi Bay with an approach from a main road; thus development of the three-dimensional form—plus strong identity—was of particular importance.

As soon as one enters the lofty great hall (all white like the exterior), the spatial tricks begin. The most immediate is a large, square window—"a picture"—on the far wall opposite the entry framing the bay as it pulls one forward. A 60-foot/18-meter passerelle, with an access stair purposefully near the front door, cuts across the left side of the hall with visual snatches of galleries on both floors behind. Beyond this a small, squarish gallery opens with walled outdoor sculpture garden on top.

In the center of the hall, which is used for the display of large works, a freestanding elevator housing punctuates the space. To the right near the entry is the 231-seat auditorium with library, small gallery, and services beyond. In plan these elements form a loose composition, almost like a village square, to define the central hall. After exploring the main floor, walk, don't ride, to the upper galleries, a spatial excursion that is rewarding no matter what works of art are on display. (The privately built but willed-to-the-city museum has a small permanent collection and an active program of loans and circulating shows.) Carefully calculated natural light, alive and changing, floods the major exhibit areas via skylights, supplemented by artificial sources when needed. Offices, shipping rooms, storage units, and classrooms—art education is a major emphasis—occupy the first level.

Open Tuesday–Saturday 10:00 A.M.–5:00 P.M., Sunday 1:00–5:00 P.M. Closed July 4, Thanksgiving, Christmas, and New Year's Day. Admission is $3 for adults, $2 for senior citizens and students, $1 for children ages 2–12. Tours can be scheduled by calling (512) 884–3844. AF 1–2/73, ARev 7/73

RIVERSIDE PLAZA (1970–72)
(formerly Cedar Square West)
Cedar Avenue between South 4th and South 6th streets
Minneapolis, Minnesota

Ralph Rapson & Associates, architects

The Cedar Riverside project—the country's first New-Town-in-Town—was an imaginatively ambitious plan to build a high-density living environment for 30,000 within the central city. Unfortunately, only one phase—Riverside Plaza—was ever constructed, as the project underwent financial collapse before it could be completed. It occupies a once-depressed area a dozen blocks from downtown Minneapolis and almost adjacent to the West Campus of the University of Minnesota. Its land usage and architecture are full of expertise and sympathetic social concern, and the project could have been a bellwether for much urban redevelopment if its full program had been carried to completion. There are those who claim that the basic high-rise, high-density design is socially destructive. But to build on expensive land obviously demands a high-rise response. As Ralph Rapson has said, "I don't advocate high-rise housing for everybody and every situation. But to house so many people in this area with its pressing need for shelter, what is the alternative?"

Riverside Plaza is probably the finest large-scale housing in the United States. The complex, initially called Cedar Square West, changed its name in 1988 when it was purchased by a limited partnership, who renovated it in 1989–90. Its great variety of heights combines—without perceptual identification—upper bracket rental apartments with subsidized low-income units in a complex group, yet there are no indications of municipal "do-goodness," few vistas without rewards, and less than a hint of architectural ennui. This paragon of midcity shelter for some 3,000, occupying 8 acres/3.2 hectares not far from the Mississippi River (and Interstate 94), is made up of interconnected buildings clustered about a central plaza and containing a total of 1,303 apartments in buildings ranging in height from two to thirty-nine stories. Individual units range from studio to four-bedroom sizes. An 860-car garage lies under the plaza or is attached; automotive access uses different levels from pedestrians. Most living rooms have floor-to-ceiling glass doors that visually expand the smallish quarters while opening onto narrow balconies. By judiciously contrasting the various building heights, by using vividly colored panels (red, yellow, blue), and by creating a provocative interaction of spaces and scale build-up, lively interest results. The complex is, of economic necessity, tightly compacted, and the lack of shopping and related facilities—which were intended to be a part of the community centrum that was never built—is unfortunate.

Barton-Aschman Associates were the technical coordinators for site planning, traffic, and engineering; Sasaki, Walker & Associates, environmental design; and Gingold-Pink, associate architects. Heikki von Hertzen—the Finnish backer of Helsinki's famous Tapiola—was consultant on community development.

Grounds and lobbies open daily 24 hours.
AR 12/73, JAIA 12/74, JAIA 5/75, JAIA 11/77

OMNI, CNN CENTER, CONGRESS CENTER, GEORGIA DOME COMPLEX (1970–92)
Atlanta, Georgia

Thompson, Ventulett, Stainback, & Associates architects

The Omni, CNN Center, Congress Center, Georgia Dome Complex, one of the most comprehensive sports, convention, office, hotel, resort, entertainment, shopping, eating, and exhibition complexes in the United States, abuts the south edge of downtown Atlanta. Together with the Decks, its 1,950-car parking structure, this coordinated group of mixed-use facilities (measuring over 100 acres/40.5 hectares) has helped make Atlanta one of the most popular convention cities in the country. Almost all of it, it is pertinent to note, was built over railroad tracks via air rights (23 feet/7 meters clearance), and all structures were designed by the same firm of architects. Located adjacent to downtown and all mass transportation, the Omni Complex forms an important element in making the central business district alive for 200–240 nights a year. The buildings, in order of completion, are:

Omni Coliseum (1970–72), 100 Techwood Drive Northwest. The gutsy, weathering-steel frame of Omni is matched within by a mind-boggling columnless space. It exudes power outside by day as well as by night when pools of artificial light shine from its glazed corners. The unusual structural expression of this 362-foot-/110-meter-square coliseum springs from four gigantic trusses 100 feet/30 meters high that rise from the centers of its four sides, cantilever to the corners, and are joined and topped by a patented "ortho-quad" roof truss. (One of the key reasons for this four-point concentrated frame arose from the fact that the building is stilted over railroad tracks, as mentioned.) A broad, landscaped, concourse level—useful at intermission in clement weather—surrounds most of the building and provides entries at the midpoint of the seating ranks. Inner peripheral circulation opens at the corners into lofty, bannered lobbies (under the cantilevers) to form colorful interior gathering spots. The arena within, which has a ceiling height of 130 feet/40 meters, is placed on the diagonal to obtain the maximum number of premium seats. It is roofed by sixteen 50-foot-/15-meter-square pyramids or pods, which alternate in checkerboard fashion with flat ceiling panels of the same dimension. The open, lightweight pods aid acoustics and lend interest to the ceiling, while their pyramidal projection on the roof produces a distinctive exterior profile. The overall effect of the interior is strong, but a few awkward corners appear when the area's angled placement meets the squared frame. Moreover the random intermixture of warm colors on the seats lacks zest plus the seat-finding ease of color coding. The lower service level is completely separate from that of the spectators. The outer concourse leads directly to a 1,950-car garage with over twice this automobile capacity at grade. Omni's multivalent uses range widely, as its name implies, accommodating sports such as hockey and basketball, plus circuses, concerts, and other events. It is owned by the City of Atlanta and the Fulton County Recreation Authority.

Open for events.

CNN Center (formerly Omni International) (1971–75), Marietta Street at Techwood Drive. The CNN Center megastructure stands adjacent to the slightly earlier Omni Coliseum (though without covered connection), and provides a 470-room hotel, two eleven-story office blocks, three floors of shops, cafes, and restaurants, and television studios. Though the exterior almost inevitably lacks coordination, these varied facilities are wrapped, with a purposefully irregular series of angles, around a sparkling, airy, twelve-story-high covered atrium—the great space

(shown in photograph). (Though expensive to roof, substantial savings were effected on the non-weatherproof interior facings of all units.) An ice-skating rink originally occupied the floor and focus of this arena; the space now contains shops, gardens, and a television interview set for CNN. The hotel, many rooms of which overlook these activities, is revetted in the same limestone employed for the other buildings. White paint is used extensively, even on the Warren trusses of the roof (one truss spans 180 feet/55 meters). Two cascades of sculptured forms, ingeniously conjured from open-ended cubic boxes strung on the diagonal, give vertical accent to the ends of the court. A peripheral skylight surrounds the top level and admits slashes of sun, while glass encloses the west end. Seven hundred prisms were fixed on the skylights by Rockne Krebs to split and manipulate beams of colored light—"sun sculpture"—throughout. At night multicolored laser beams dart around the atrium. Sun and games, visitors and office workers admix in a brilliant, non-rigid, three-dimensional pleasance.

Atrium open daily 7:30 A.M.–11:00 P.M. Hotel open daily 24 hours. A 35-minute tour of the CNN studios is given daily 9:00 A.M.–6:00 P.M.; the cost is $7 for adults, $5 for senior citizens, $4.50 for children ages 12 and under. Reservations are suggested; for reservations or more information call (404) 827–2300.

Georgia World Congress Center (1974–93), 285 International Boulevard Northwest. The first phase of the Congress Center—adjacent to Omni—provides three mammoth interconnectable exhibit halls of 350,000 square feet/32,516 square meters of total space, a 1,952-seat auditorium, 32 meeting rooms, and all necessary backup facilities. With a ceiling height of 30 feet/9.1 meters it can accommodate an almost limitless range of exhibitions. There have been two subsequent expansions, each more than doubling the original facility. Phase two included a conference center and a 35,000-square-foot ballroom, and the completed Congress Center includes approximately 1,000,000 square feet of exhibition space.

Some areas open daily 8:30 A.M.–5:00 P.M.; some areas open for events only.

Georgia Dome (1989–92), One Georgia Dome Drive Northwest. The Georgia Dome, whose floor measures 102,000 square feet, functions as a football/basketball stadium but can double as an exhibition and reception hall. Its roof structure—which spans 790 feet—is a membrane of Teflon-coated glass cloth stretched over ridge cables.

Open for events. AR 8/74, PA 5/76

INNER HARBOR REDEVELOPMENT (1970–)
West end of Baltimore Harbor
Baltimore, Maryland

Wallace, Roberts & Todd, planners and landscape architects

Baltimore has undertaken one of the most extensive—and one of the most brilliant—of down-town urban renewal projects in the United States. The Charles Center development (see page 442), which arose largely in the 1960s, created a nucleus for the city and proclaimed with almost magnetic force that the central business district was here to stay. Moreover, it gave this CBD breadth and depth with the presence of middle- to upper-income apartments that enrich the center, and a fine theater to make it more viable at night. This splendid work has now been extended as the Inner Harbor project by the same capable and imaginative business, civic, and government interests that, with the planners and architects, created Charles Center. This team is working on the long-range development of a once run-down site of 240 acres/97 hectares within a few blocks of the center and hugging three sides of Baltimore's historic harbor. With its wonderful openness, its views over the water, and access by automobile, bus, subway, and light rail, the Inner Harbor has enormous urban possibilities. It is important to add that the Charles Center/Inner Harbor program was approved sixteen times by voters when bond issues were raised; citizen interest and endorsement, plus private enterprise, have been vital to Baltimore's success.

Because of its enormous scope, the program is being constructed in several stages, the first concerned with the physical transformation of the south, west, and north sides of the harbor basin, along Key Highway and Light and Pratt streets. Many buildings have been completed along the north and western sides of this *C* shape. The green swath, parks, and promenades around the water's edge have blossomed into a folk park, highlighted by numerous festivities with multitudes of ethnic celebrations reflecting the city's multinational and multiracial back-ground. The U.S. frigate Constellation, the first ship commissioned for the United States Navy (launched in 1797)—and the oldest ship in the world continuously afloat—is tied up at Constellation Dock, lending a proper nautical touch to the country's fourth busiest port. (The ship is closed indefinitely for repairs.)

The anchor and focus of the development are the two buildings—Harborplace—that frame and give coherence to the west (main) end of the harbor. Designed in 1980 by Benjamin Thompson & Associates for the Rouse Company, these low, inviting pavilions provide attrac-tive stores, restaurants, and high-level shops (some 130 in all) and create a spirited frame for the harbor. Their promenades in front add dawn-to-dusk life.

Other notable structures and facilities (beginning at the southeast corner of the Inner Harbor) are thus far complete:

Rash Field (1976), Key Highway—RTKL Associates, architects. This waterside park provides game and recreational facilities and acts as a coordinated spatial transfer from historic Federal Hill, directly behind, to the harbor's edge.

Maryland Science Center (1976), 601 Light Street at Key Highway—Edward Durell Stone, architect. The center holds down the southwest corner of the harbor rehabilitation. Its angled brick exterior develops a positive, not pompous, scale and its terraces extend politely out to greet the view. The exhibitions within are superior. Nes, Campbell & Partners were associate architects. Two additions (1986 and 1987) include a theater and an entrance oriented to the harbor as well as expanded exhibit space and improved visitor circulation.

Open Monday–Friday 10:00 A.M.–5:00 P.M., Saturday–Sunday 10:00 A.M.–6:00 P.M. Closed Thanksgiving and Christmas. Admission is $8.50 for adults, $6.50 for senior citizens and children ages 4–17. For more information call [410] 685–5225.

Christ Church Harbor Apartments (1972), 600 Light Street directly across from the Science Center—Don M. Hisaka & Associates, architects. Elevated in the Le Corbusier fashion—thus creating spatial lightness and revealing the far garden side from the street—this nine-story block provides 288 units of housing for the elderly (32 efficiencies, 256 single bedrooms). Each apartment has a balcony, those on the east facing the Maryland Science Center and harbor (and street), those to the west the quieter but less spectacular small plaza and garden. Every floor has a lounge with large reception room at entry level. The apartments were built by and are affiliated with the nearby Christ Lutheran Church (built 1935, extended 1956). Grounds are open daily.

Deaton Specialty Hospital and Home (1972), 611 South Charles Street (directly behind the apartments)—Cochran, Stephenson & Donkervoet, architects. Like the housing, the Deaton Specialty Hospital was conceived, developed, and is supported by Christ Lutheran Church. The five-level building stands adjacent to the old; thus, to be a good neighbor, it is discreet in design and of brick similar to that on the church. Polite outside, it is efficient within. The congregation of Christ Lutheran Church should be proud of the results of their social and architectural involvement with and support of both the Hospital and Home and Harbor Apartments. In 1989 a 120-bed addition designed by Fred Peltier of H2L2 was completed; the hospital now accommodates 360 patients in private and semiprivate rooms.

(Open to the public daily 8:00 A.M.–4:30 P.M.)

The Baltimore Convention Center (1977–79), 1 West Pratt Street at Charles Street—Naramore, Bain, Brady & Johanson and Cochran, Stephenson & Donkervoet, architects. The most compelling building of the Inner Harbor Redevelopment, this crystal and spacious structure gives the city prime exhibition and assembly facilities. In addition to meeting rooms accommodating fifty to two thousand people, there are four main exhibit halls measuring 140 x 180 feet/43 x 55 meters, each of which can be used with total flexibility. Skilling, Helle, Christiansen & Robertson were the structural engineers for the unusual post-tensioned pyramidal domes of bridgelike form. An expansion designed by the same architects to double the present size of the facility is under way; the existing building will then be completely renovated on the interior to match the new structure. All work is scheduled to be completed in 1997.

United States Fidelity & Guaranty Company (1971–74), 100 Light Street—Vlastimil Koubek, architect. Besides being a handsome forty-story skyscraper—Baltimore's tallest—USF&G acts as an urban pivot for Inner Harbor, its height and podium position turning the corner from Light Street to Pratt where the redevelopment continues. In addition it acts as a liaison with the nearby Charles Center. The building's slip-form elevator and utility core are of concrete, while its piers and framing are of steel. Enis Y. Baskam was the structural engineer.

World Trade Center (1976–77), Pratt Street on Pier 2—I. M. Pei & Partners, architects. This thirty-story, pentagonal building's beaconlike form turns its back on no one; its position is of the sea as well as the land. The building is also of structural interest in that five, massive, claw-like piers of reinforced concrete uphold the corners, with a pentagonal concrete inner core for elevators and services—no intermediate columns are necessary. Henry N. Cobb was design partner; Richter, Cornbrooks, Matthai, Hopkins, associate architects; Weiskopf & Pickworth, structural engineers.

Ground floor open during business hours. Top of the World observation deck on the 27th floor open Monday–Saturday 10:00 A.M.–5:30 P.M., Sunday 11:00 A.M.–5:30 P.M.; in summer open Friday–Sunday until 7:00 P.M. Closed Thanksgiving and Christmas. Admission is $2 for adults, $1 for senior citizens and children ages 5–15.

National Aquarium in Baltimore (1979–81), Pratt Street on Pier 3—Cambridge Seven, architects. The Aquarium's boldly fractured geometry of concrete is topped by a lively glass pyramid containing a complete tropical rain forest. Circulation around its great ocean tanks is one-way. Four levels of galleries supplement the tanks. LeMessurier/SCI were the structural engineers. In 1990 a marine mammal pavilion designed by Grieves and Associates opened on Pier 4; it is connected to the main building by a walkway.

November–February open Saturday–Thursday 10:00 A.M.–5:00 P.M., Friday 10:00 A.M.–8:00 P.M. March–June and September–October open Saturday–Thursday 9:00 A.M.–5:00 P.M., Friday 9:00 A.M.–8:00 P.M. July–August open Sunday–Thursday 9:00 A.M.–6:00 P.M., Friday–Saturday 9:00 A.M.–8:00 P.M. Closed Thanksgiving and Christmas. Admission is $11.50 for adults, $9.50 for senior citizens, $7.50 for children ages 3–11. For more information call [410] 576–3800.

The Non-profit Baltimore Development Corporation is primarily responsible for all land negotiations and for supervising "the design and construction of public facilities and coordinating the activities of the various city agencies and private developers. The corporation serves as liaison between the City and private business interests to expedite completion of the projects." Their work has been admirable thus far—full of lessons for all United States cities. Let it also be noted that a brilliant, overall plan was prepared before any ground was broken. From its site clearing beginning in 1968 to 1996, when the Museum of Dentistry is scheduled to open, there are potent lessons here.

For more information call the Inner Harbor Visitors Center at (410) 837–4636. Int 9/80, AR 10/80, JAIA 6/81, JAIA mid 5/82, AR 5/82, A 6/85, A 9/92, A 11/92, A 1/95

SCOPE CULTURAL AND
CONVENTION CENTER (1971–72)
bordered by Charlotte Street, Monticello Avenue,
East Brambleton Avenue, and St. Paul's Boulevard
Norfolk, Virginia

Williams & Tazewell Partnership, architects
Pier Luigi Nervi, dome engineer

The two buildings of Norfolk's SCOPE, the larger a striking circular multipurpose hall, the smaller a rectangular theater, provide the city with outstanding cultural, assembly, and sports facilities. Occupying 14 acres/5.7 hectares on the eastern edge of downtown, SCOPE provides for a full range of public events and entertainment. The complex is raised slightly above street level because of the water table and also to offer under-cover parking for 640 automobiles (with additional parking nearby). An exhibit hall of 65,000 square feet/6,039 square meters is also located under the podium.

  SCOPE Arena and Exhibit Hall (1971), 201 East Brambleton Avenue. The elegant structure of the SCOPE Arena and Exhibit Hall (shown in photographs) immediately asserts itself as one approaches the group, with the incomparable Pier Luigi Nervi's sculpted buttresses support-ing the smooth reinforced concrete cap of the roof. The array of these twenty-four V-shaped buttresses gives verve to the plaza. They are structurally reminiscent of the Gothic cathedrals of the twelfth to fourteenth centuries and more directly of Nervi's Palazzetto dello Sport for Rome's 1960 Olympics. Note the manner in which the flying buttresses form broadly flat-tened rectangles at top, the better to receive the weight of the roof, and then rotate ninety degrees to transmit this thrust into the bases. The building exhibits exquisite engineering and extremely competent workmanship.

The interior is dominated by the underside of the dome with its mathematical diagram of the stresses and strains that its 336-foot/102-meter span (inner diameter) sustains. Its nervation is composed of 2,500 beautifully precast concrete triangles—contained by a peripheral tension ring—with a thin roof of poured concrete on top. From the dome a slender circular light-bridge 100 feet/30 meters in diameter, also of precast concrete, is hung. Unlike many lighting/audio systems, this is not intrusive. Arrayed below are 8,300 permanent seats with 3,700 portable ones readily available. For concerts and conventions the hall can accommodate 11,800-12,000; for sports, 9,500 for ice hockey, and up to 12,000 for boxing. There are also meeting rooms and banquet facilities for 5,000.

Chrysler Hall (1972), 215 St. Paul's Boulevard. Chrysler Hall is a key element of SCOPE, with 2,500 seats, arranged in continental fashion, in the theater/concert hall proper, and a 350-seat little theater adjacent. The orchestra lift can accommodate 90 musicians. Altogether a complex of which Norfolk can be very proud. Fraioli-Blum-Yesselman Associates were the structural engineers.

Lobby is open to the public Monday–Friday 9:00 A.M.–5:30 P.M. Also open for events.

WORLD OF BIRDS (1971–72)
Bronx Zoo
Pelham and Bronx River parkways at
Fordham Road
New York (Bronx), New York

Morris Ketchum, Jr., & Associates, architects

Rejecting the caged prison for birds, the architect, in consultation with the Bronx Zoo staff, has created instead an unfettered, natural environment that sets an exciting milestone in ornithology. It is quite likely that the birds enjoy it as much as the humans. One approaches the Lila Acheson Wallace World of Birds to find a provocative collection of strange ellipses and cylinders crowning a rocky hillock. These varyingly sized, rounded forms cluster together to provide an intriguing introduction as they state clearly that the whole is made up of a series of separate but coordinated exhibits. A central approach leads to the entry, while on each side ramps swoop down, that on the right rising again and jutting back. Circulation within the building is also largely ramp- and bridge-controlled, at times whisking one from the ground to the very treetops of a rain forest. The resulting one-way flow pattern moves the visitors—at their own paces—through twenty-five bird habitats, ranging from desert to tropical forest. Each setting recreates with impressive fidelity the microculture of the birds that fly merrily about within their diorama world (which the rounded forms facilitate), complete with living plants. A natural environment—not a jail—was sought for each of the two hundred species and over five hundred birds. Five of the aviaries are completely open: in two of the largest the uncaged public walks through the habitat with birds flying freely overhead. In the rain-forest section there are some one hundred birds flying about, made quite at home by occasional artificial rain, lightning, and thunder, plus, of course, proper temperature and humidity control. Small screens with continuous projections explain such themes as courtship, mating procedures, nest construction, and ecology. Banks of separately controllable artificial lights outside and above each cylinder deliver the proper amount of illumination to each habitat, with excellent quality of light within. Developed closely with the staff of the Wildlife Conservation Society (a private organization), the World of Birds opened an exciting era for ornithological education and pleasure.

World of Darkness (1969), at the southerly end of the Bronx Zoo, was also designed by Morris Ketchum, Jr., & Associates. This exhibit reverses day and night so that visitors can see in "our" daylight hours some of the activities of that sixty percent of the animal world that moves mostly after dark. The exhibits inside invert the life cycle of the animals by using strong artificial light during exterior darkness, and red light, which is invisible to most nocturnal animals, during our daylight. Thus they and their lifestyle can be observed. The exterior of this building expresses the mysterious dusk within by means of its blackish, angular, pebble-concrete panels (note the varying heights) that enclose its three-quarter doughnut shape. The sunken central court exposes the original glacial rock surface. Morris Ketchum, Jr., was partner in charge of both buildings.

Located west of the Bronxdale parking field or south of the Rainey Gate entrance. April–October open Monday–Friday 10:00 A.M.–5:00 P.M., Saturday–Sunday and holidays 10:00 A.M.–5:30 P.M. November–March open daily 10:00 A.M.–4:30 P.M. April–October admission is $6.75 for adults, $3 for senior citizens and children ages 2–12. November–March admission is $2.50 for adults, $1 for senior citizens and children ages 2–12. Admission is free on Wednesdays. Parking is $5. For general information call (718) 367-1010. Free one-hour tours can be arranged by calling (718) 220–5141. A 6/68, F 6/69

PYRAMIDS AT COLLEGE PARK (1971–72)
(formerly College Life Insurance Company of America Building)
3500 DePauw Boulevard
Indianapolis, Indiana

Roche/Dinkeloo & Associates, architects

Architecture as a prismatic sculptural expression was first, and most substantially, made evident by that vibrating collection of pyramids at Gizeh, Egypt, where the interaction of profiled angle on profiled angle practically shakes the Sahara. Today, the back-to-the-pyramids, mathematical approach toward the sculptured aspect of architecture has probably reached a climax in this group of three startling forms northwest of Indianapolis. They represent an unusual but by no means frivolous approach to sheltering businesses. One may or may not be sympathetic to these truncated, strangely scaled, quarter-pyramidal forms with vertical (but splayed) walls of solid concrete forming two sides, and sloping, walls of mirror glass forming the other three. However, one will certainly not forget the reflections of their mirrors inching across those mighty walls of concrete. The interiors, all interconnected by bridging, provide highly satisfactory work spaces.

In 1991 the building and grounds underwent major renovations: the landscaping was completely redesigned by Simmons and Associates, and the lobbies were redone and mechanical systems updated by Kassler and Associates.

Located just southeast of the intersection of I-465 and US 421 (10 miles/16 kilometers north-northwest of downtown via Northwestern Avenue and US 421). Lobby and grounds open to the public Monday–Friday 8:00 A.M.–5:00 P.M. AF 3/74

TOUGALOO COLLEGE DORMITORIES AND LIBRARY (1971–73)
500 West County Line Road
Tougaloo, Mississippi

Gunnar Birkerts & Associates, architects

Though the early plans for a total rebuilding of Tougaloo College never materialized, the first stage of two dormitories and an adjacent library was completed. Birkerts initially had proposed a spectacular three-level scheme on the sloping site, with roads and parking on the first level, groups of varied-length classrooms oriented north and south on the second, and fingers of dormitories airily propped in space at right angles to the academic grouping on the third.

Much of this intended aerial effect can be seen in these two dormitories, one for men, the other for women, both propped on stilts to absorb the grade fall-off and to counter the weak subsoil conditions of unstable clay. To prevent any feeling of lateral enclosure, Birkerts boldly cantilevered the dormitories in space. This benefited ground (and transportation) freedom, while enhancing the sense of privacy and liberation in the bedrooms. The result almost suggests a train of Pullman cars on a trestle, but the space games are stimulating.

The reinforced bell-bottom concrete supporting piers are paired 12.2 feet/3.7 meters apart and 30 feet/9.1 meters on center. Modules of two and three bays make up the groups of dormitory rooms for a total length of 210 feet/64 meters. Access to each is by means of an open passageway suspended under the two floors of rooms, with three sets of stairs, one at the center, two near the ends, leading to clusters of double bedrooms and lounges. (On the interior, emergency doors connect the full building length in case of fire.) At the uphill entry only a few steps lead to each underslung passerelle but at the far end the stairs are several platforms high. The rooms cantilever approximately 9 feet/2.7 meters on either side of the supporting piers, lending an untethered freedom to the dormitories. The abrupt cutoff of their far ends, however, tends to leave them momentarily poised in space. Their walls are of prefabricated, natural color, concrete panels, striated in texture with unusual but effective square windows surrounded by a circular frame painted to indicate lounges versus bedrooms.

The L. Zenobia Coleman Library, centered between the two dormitories and close to the old administration building on the crest of the rise, had a lateral space problem inasmuch as its entrance (near top) was at a major walkway. To keep the library from bifurcating the campus, the uphill corners were left open so that the building forms an inviting horizontal pedestrian pivot, while its vertical setbacks create two-story pavilions with play of spaces and dramatic structural expression. The construction employs the same deep, belled foundation piers used in the dormitories. On these were erected an ingenious series of prefabricated piers, prestressed beams, and panels that permit flexibility, with speed of erection and economy. The library bay size, like that in the dormitories, is 30 feet/9.1 meters square. Efficiency and inner spaces are excellent.

Tougaloo, a small, historically African-American college stressing a liberal arts curriculum, made an impressive start with these three buildings; it is unfortunate that the rest of the plan was never followed through.

Located west off Tougaloo exit of I-55, about 9 miles/14 kilometers north of Jackson. The library is open Monday–Friday 8:00 A.M.–10:00 P.M., Saturday–Sunday 8:00 A.M.–1:00 A.M. The dormitories are open daily during business hours (closed in August). Both closed for holidays. AF 4/66, PA 4/68, AR 10/68, AR 11/73

EDWIN J. THOMAS PERFORMING ARTS HALL
(1971–73)
198 Hill Street at
University Avenue
Akron, Ohio

Dalton, Van Dijk, Johnson
& Partners and Caudill,
Rowlett, Scott, architects

The Edwin J. Thomas Per-
forming Arts Hall—the first
phase of an ambitious cultural
complex for both the Uni-
versity of Akron and the city—
faces onto University Avenue
and lies just across an important bridge from downtown.
The architects realized that the hall would gain by day as well as by night (when, of course,
most performances are held) if it could tap into the business community using this thoroughfare. Thus by day one passes a multiterraced, richly landscaped introduction to a provoca-
tively angled concrete building, while by night floods of warm light pour out from its great
glass front, revealing the structure within. The latter is an almost irresistible attraction, particularly when animated by crowds during intermission. (This glass, incidentally, is thick
plate, end-butted to eliminate mullions.)

The program for the Thomas Hall called for facilities that could accommodate a wide variety of events, and instead of building several separate units it was decided that it would be better and less expensive to produce one that was highly flexible. The result is an auditorium that
can be almost immediately adjusted in seating capacity from 900 to 3,000. The computer-controlled means of effecting these changes lie in the extraordinary ceiling, made up of 3,600
acoustically dampened steel plates in seven random shapes suspended in catenary "loops"
over both audience and stage. Sections of the ceiling can be raised or lowered to meet the size
desired, while the counterweights, in the form of twenty-seven lead-filled chromed steel cylinders, are cabled to the lobby to double as excellent abstract sculpture.

The main floor of the auditorium is divided by a change in level into orchestra and grand
tier with a "floating" balcony above. Acoustical dynamics—in metal instead of traditional concert hall wood—and seating geometry have been combined with architectural shape (eleven-
degree sidewall splay) for sophisticated theater design; technically brilliant and acoustically
excellent. There is, however, a visual "presence" of the tentlike ceiling with its prominent
joints. The treatment of the sidewalls and the merger of auditorium with stage are very good,
as is the lighting. The lobbies are enjoyably capacious, the front part embellished, as mentioned, with the tension "sculpture" of the chromed counterweights. Covered automobile
access and underground garage are commendable.

Charles E. Lawrence was chief of design. George C. Izenour, the theater consultant, and
Dr. Vern O. Knudsen, the acoustician, have been working together for many years. They and
the architects have produced here one of the most advanced theater/concert halls to be seen.

Open for performances. Free tours can be scheduled by calling (216) 972–7595. AF 12/73, F 12/73, AR 3/74

SEARS TOWER (1971–74)
233 South Wacker Drive at Franklin, Adams, and Jackson streets
Chicago, Illinois

Skidmore, Owings & Merrill, architects and engineers

The Sears Tower, at 110 floors (1,454 feet/443 meters) once the tallest building in the world, is technically ingenious. Its designers have likened it to a clutch of squared cigarettes of varying lengths bundled together, a structural simplification of nine statically independent units, each 75 feet/23 meters on a side, strapped together, so to speak, as one. Five 15-foot/4.6-meter bays comprise a unit's side. At the fiftieth, sixty-sixth, and ninetieth floors two of these square "tubes"—on opposite corners—terminate, producing the notched profile on the exterior and marking sky lobbies for elevator changes within. The remaining two, structurally bound like the others by belt trusses and internal diaphragms, rise to the limit set by the Federal Aviation Administration. The steel frame is clad with black aluminum and 16,000 bronze-tinted windows. But the building's relation to the horizontal, where it meets the street, is not amiable—"an un-Chicagoan brutishness" (*Architectural Review*, May 1977)—particularly on the Adams and Jackson sides. Moreover, the most frequently used entry (on Franklin) lacks the bravura one might expect. In addition, the building raises urbanistic questions of whether so many office workers should be housed in any single high building, pouring in and out, more or less en masse, and with limited transportation options. (The not-distant John Hancock Center, see page 520, by the same architects, rivals Sears in height at one hundred floors, but approximately half is devoted to apartment occupancy.) Though a technical triumph—and obviously an impressive sight—the Sears Tower raises questions for future building limits in all major cities. Bruce Graham of the Chicago office of SOM was partner in charge of design, Fazlur Khan chief structural engineer. The lobby and bank interiors were by SOM, the Sears interiors by Saphier, Lerner, Schindler.

In 1985 a pavilion entranceway (familiarly known as the "lunchbox atrium" because of its shape) designed by SOM was added on the Wacker Drive side of the building. Then in 1993 a new entrance with an outdoor patio in front was built on Jackson, for use strictly by tourists going up to the Skydeck; the lobbies were also remodeled. DeStefano & Partners were the architects.

The lobby is open to the public daily during business hours. The 103rd-floor Skydeck is open March–September daily 9:00 A.M.–11:00 P.M.; open October–February daily 9:00 A.M.–10:00 P.M. Admission is $6.50 for adults, $4.75 for senior citizens, $3.25 for children ages 5–12. For more information call (312) 875-9696. The building is included on the Chicago Architecture Foundation's "Modern and Beyond" tour; the cost is $10. The building is also included on the CAF's river cruise tour; the cost is $15 on weekdays, $17 on weekends. For more information on CAF tours call (312) 922-3432. AP 8/73, PA 5/86

CITICORP CENTER (1971–77)
153 East 53rd Street at Lexington Avenue
New York, New York

Hugh Stubbins & Associates, architects

Citicorp Center represents a brilliant extension of the commercial possibilities of very expensive midtown real estate beyond nine-to-five office usage. (At the time, it was the most costly block acquisition in New York history.) Thus in addition to providing 1,300,000 square feet/120,694 square meters of office space (some, of course, occupied by Citibank itself) the center contains a marvelous three-story shopping arena, featuring a series of intriguing restaurants and shops deployed around a skylit central court (currently closed and undergoing renovation by Gwathmey Siegel and Associates, to be reopened in late 1996), with four stories of

office space above, plus a freestanding church in one corner. St. Peter's Lutheran Church was, indeed, the begetter of the elevated office tower, for its previous home was an eclectic Gothic building (1905) on this site, and it would only sell if its dedicated parish could rebuild on the same spot.

With the church's provocative requirement in the contract, the architects and engineers elevated the great bulk of the office tower on 120-foot-/36.5-meter-high piers, left the northwest corner of the site free for the new church, and created a small sunken plaza, a busy galleria, and the broad array of restaurants and shops mentioned. It should be pointed out that the covered pedestrian ways and the bright central agora represent "incentive" zoning trade-offs with the city whereby greater building area was allowed if public amenities and circulation were incorporated in the overall design.

The most striking statement of the center is, of course, its extraordinary skyscraper—one of the world's highest at 914 feet/278 meters—a silver, soaring object. In simplified terms the lower structure upholding this dazzling high rise is based on four legs (25 feet/7.6 meters square), which envelop stairs and services, placed at the midpoint of the 152-foot/46-meter square building. (Note that these legs have a slight chamfer that plays an active role in reflecting the sun when low.) Together with a concrete inner core, they uphold a 26.8-foot-/8-meter-deep trussed platform. On this thirteen-story-high elevated platform rises the sleek-skinned, superbly fabricated, unbroken shaft of the office tower. Its forty-eight floors are divided into six structurally independent tiers of eight floors each triangulated by internal framing. Primarily because of the expense, this chevron triangulation was enclosed by an aluminum skin; it can be traced through the fenestration. This resourceful framing is integrated with horizontally triangulated floor bracing, almost eliminating the need for internal columns. Four 5-foot-/1.5-meter-wide mast columns, one per side, provide the chief vertical supports for the tower, forming extensions of the legs below. On top a 400-ton/363-metric-ton "tuned mass damper" of reinforced concrete can be actuated to minimize building sway in a high wind. The forty-five-degree angled roof was designed from the beginning to give a distinctive profile to the center (compare the Pennzoil Place in Houston, page 590). LeMessurier Associates/SCI and James Rudermanwre the structural engineers

St. Peter's Church, which traces its founding back to 1861 and twenty-three German immigrants, was also designed by Hugh Stubbins & Associates, and achieves polygonal personality in spite of its towering neighbor. Its handsome sanctuary, one level down, is temptingly visible from the street. The interior is unusual yet provides a reverent background for worship, highlighted by a 2,150-pipe boxed organ made by Klais Orgelbau of Bonn, Germany, and by a spider web of a circular stair in one corner. Vignelli Associates were responsible for the colorful and flexible furnishings except in the Erol Beker Chapel, which was decorated by Louise Nevelson (and is on the agitated side). Emery Roth & Sons were consulting architects; Sasaki Associates, landscape architects. Today it sits comfortably accessible, perhaps a unique proclaimer of today's religion under the benevolent arm of capitalism.

Hugh Stubbins wrote the bank in 1970 saying that "We must use the resources of big business, reinforced by moral and social ideas, to develop a new generation of office buildings planned for the community and expressive of the humanity of the individuals who use them. By revitalizing urban development with an emphasis on people, we could produce a more enjoyable place in which to live and work" (quoted in *Architectural Record*, June 1978). As a consequence of this thinking, Citicorp Center is an exhilarating urban experience.

Lobby and public atrium of Citicorp Center open Monday–Friday 7:00 a.m.–12:00 midnight, Saturday–Sunday 10:00 a.m.–12:00 midnight. St. Peter's Church open daily 7:00 a.m.–9:00 p.m.; Sunday services held at 8:45 a.m., 11:00 a.m., and 5:00 p.m. AR mid-8/76, AR 6/78, PA 12/78, Int 9/79

NATIONAL GALLERY OF ART EAST BUILDING (1971–78)
Constitution Avenue at 4th Street
Washington, D.C.

I. M. Pei & Partners, architects

The requirements for the East Building of the National Gallery were formidable: extensive galleries, research center, library, staff offices, auditorium, cafeteria, underground connecting link with West Building, and services, the whole shaped, it should be stressed, by a difficult trapezoidal site bounded by Pennsylvania Avenue and Madison Drive on the Mall. Moreover, the new building obviously had to be a good neighbor to its highly respected parent—and to the Capitol down the street—while not exceeding a cornice limit of 111 feet/34 meters along the avenue. To solve this the architects evolved a plan of two opposingly faced but conjoined triangles, with secondary parallelograms at the corners, all proportionally related. The larger isosceles triangle shelters most of the public area, while alongside an attenuated right triangle contains offices, library, and the Center for Advanced Studies in the Visual Arts. The major triangle provides entries to both sections across its base; this side also opens onto a plaza, which it partially frames with the West Building opposite. A granite-paved fountain "court" (of some irresolution) joins them. The point of the secondary triangle that houses staff and research touches this plaza, and its acutely angled (nineteen-degree) marble edge forms a daring and superbly constructed detail. The base of this triangle is parallel to the plaza side but faces east (toward the Capitol), and its main facade overlooks the Mall.

The elevations resulting from this dynamic combination of geometry and function vary as they reflect internal needs. The entry off the plaza on 4th Street welcomes one with a vast expanse of glass and a glistening, Henry Moore bronze, *Knife Edge Mirror Two Piece* (1978), commissioned for this spot and a gift of the Morris and Gwendolyn Carritz Foundation. The adjacent staff and research entry discreetly proclaims private versus public. The 405-foot/123-meter Pennsylvania Avenue side with one long low window seems scaleless, even dry, from a distance, but it is given a sidewalk accent by the sculpture (at present *Adam*, 1970—by Alexander Liberman). Adjacent, behind a low parapet, stretches a 143-foot-/44-meter-long Japanese rock garden. The east elevation is a straightforward, largely glass statement of six floors of offices with an inset seventh floor marking the president's, director's, and deputy director's rooms. The long facade on the Mall is comprised of a series of interlocked, complex geometric forms mostly containing offices; because of its fracturing and because it faces the southerly sun, it is the most alive. The same carefully graded pinkish Tennessee marble used in the old building was used in the new (here 3 inches/76 millimeters thick); it was even selected by the same expert.

Entering the East Building one finds a skylit interior brilliant with an eruption of light and shade and spaces. This provides the most exhilarating introduction to the visual arts that one will encounter. Its explosive quality—beginning with low entry to lofty release—the dartings of sun and shadow, and even the accent of full-grown trees inside constitute art in themselves. This great central atrium almost vibrates, intensified by the multilevel choreography of visitors, particularly those on the high passerelle that bisects the midriff. The triangular steel and aluminum space-frame skylight is made up of twenty-five tetrahedrons, each measuring 30 x 45 feet/9.1 x 13.7 meters, with an overall dimension of 225 feet/69 meters on two legs and 150 feet/46 meters across the base. Sunscreens are placed below and injurious-ray filters are placed between its double glazing. Several large-scale specially ordered works of art complement this glass-roofed agora, particularly a magnificent 86-foot/26-meter Alexander Calder mobile (1977—completed just before the artist's death).

Some ambiguity arises as to where the major collections are located, for they are not immediately apparent, and herein, perhaps, lies a weakness. However, the visitor soon discovers the building's fascinatingly varied series of galleries. Some of these are almost closetlike, others capable of displaying large works, but virtually all establish intimacy between observer and art. One is never overwhelmed by walls of paintings, and thus a domestic atmosphere results (which recalls the Frick Museum in New York). The 20,000 square feet/1,858 square meters of galleries on the upper level—there are four exhibition floors altogether—establish a continuum via their off-center junctures; their spatial flow is intensified by the fact that almost no rooms are rectangular. The experience of going from gallery to atrium to gallery is quickening. The top level also provides an inside terrace for very large works and a cafe overlooking the Mall. Like New York's Guggenheim Museum (see page 431) and to a certain extent Berkeley's University Museum, the East Building's basic concept groups the collections around a self-orienting open core. And perhaps also like Frank Lloyd Wright's Guggenheim, the East Building is so exciting that people swarm to see it—and stay for the art.

Artificial light is used as the primary source of illumination but the three top galleries are (or can be) skylit. This flood of daylight is particularly effective in the tiered northwest upper room, where David Smith's *Voltri XVII* (1962) are stunningly installed. The entire museum is highly flexible, with many areas—especially the two medium-sized galleries at ground level and the 18,000-square-foot/1,672-square-meter space below ground—often used for changing exhibitions. Besides workshops and services, the concourse level also includes a 492-seat auditorium, a 90-seat lecture hall, with a moving walkway connecting East and West buildings and a 700-seat cafeteria/coffee bar in between. A 37.5-foot-/11.4-meter-long waterfall entertains diners. Altogether there are 627,500 square feet/58,200 square meters of exhibit and service space.

The West Building of the National Gallery of Art (1938–41), John Russell Pope and Eggers & Higgins, architects, forms an instructive contrast to the new. One might summarize this as elegant rigidity versus explosive informality, the volumetric versus the kinetic. The main entry to the old is circuitous, up the stairs, and almost arcane; that to the new is immediate, welcoming, and at ground level. The rotunda of the old is of subduing impressiveness; the atrium of the new bursts with sunny vitality and excitement. In the impeccably detailed, always rectangular galleries of the Pope building there is an architectural "insistence" in many galleries with an emphasis on wainscoting and elaborately framed doors and paneling—the walls would look almost as handsome without the paintings; in the Pei wing the plain angled walls exist for the art alone. But see them both, for each epitomizes a period—it might be said from elitist to populist—and each building is a tribute to the extraordinary generosity of one great American family. Andrew W. Mellon gave the West Building (and with incredible foresight reserved the plot to the east for future expansion), and his son, Paul, and late daughter, Ailsa Mellon Bruce, together with the Andrew W. Mellon Foundation, provided construction funds for the new. Almost four hundred donors—including, of course, Andrew Mellon, who gave 126 paintings—have contributed works of art and collections to the nation's magnificent National Gallery. It should be mentioned that only maintenance and administration are paid by the federal government.

I. M. Pei was design partner in charge for the East Building; Leonard Jacobson project architect; Weiskopf & Pickworth were the structural engineers; Kiley, Tyndall, Walker, the landscape architects.

The National Gallery (East and West Buildings) is open Monday–Saturday 10:00 A.M.–5:00 P.M., Sunday 11:00 A.M.–6:00 P.M. Closed Christmas and New Year's Day. Admission is free. Guided tours given daily. For more information call (202) 737-4215.
PA 5/78, AR 8/75, AR 8/78, PA 10/78, ARev 1/79, JAIA 5/79, JAIA 5/81, PA 8/83, A 10/84, AR 9/86

KRESGE COLLEGE
(1972–74)
University of
California at
Santa Cruz
Santa Cruz,
California

MLTW/Turnbull
Associates and
Charles W. Moore
Associates,
architects

A madrassah, architecturally hinting of North Africa, full of excitement, and spatial surprises. One enters Kresge College via a gate—in the approved Moorish fashion—and penetrates the college's spinal street. This is approximately 1,000 feet/305 meters long, rises 45 feet/14 meters as it proceeds, and is angled sharply. Heightened responses greet each new three-dimensional revelation. In many respects the whole suggests a gigantic stage set in the redwoods (with some proscenium thinness); but it is a stage set where each of the 284 resident students feels an important member of the cast. The resulting sense of belonging—it conjures up almost a secret society—may make Kresge the most sought-after college in this extraordinary university. In addition to its challenging unfurling of spaces, the extensive use of color adds further flair. The backsides of the buildings tend to earth colors, while their street facades are basically off-white but with bold color accents along the way (although a significant number of these "accents" have been repainted white in recent years).

The facilities around the entry comprise offices, provost's house, and some general-activity buildings. Leading from these are the first apartment groups, whose buildings are identical inside and out, and all two stories high. (Construction is of wood frame and stucco.) Taking a sharp left-hand turn, one encounters the centrally located classroom and local library nexus (major university facilities are in the academic core). Further along stretches another lane of additional apartments (all with individual kitchens) in which students are housed in flats for four, suites for seven, and quartet (that is, community) accommodations. The excursion terminates with a large, roughly octagonal assembly hall, dining room, and cafe. (There has been fairly extensive remodeling of many of the interiors.) Rigidity has no place in the layout; no building aligns with its neighbor, natural grade meanders throughout, formality is unknown. Charles W. Moore, William Turnbull, Jr., and Robert Simpson were the principals in charge of this very stimulating small campus.

Kresge College is located off Heller Drive on the west edge of campus. Grounds open daily throughout the year. Tours can be arranged by calling (408) 459–4558. AR 11/65, PA 5/66, PA 3/70, AR 11/74, AR 3/75, A 12/84

YALE CENTER FOR BRITISH ART (1972–77)
1080 Chapel Street at High Street
New Haven, Connecticut

Louis I. Kahn, architect

The architect of the Yale Center for British Art had to solve a difficult site problem. He had to incorporate lines of shops on the ground floor so that the museum, as an extension of Yale University, would not preempt a section of two of New Haven's important shopping streets. The handsomely scaled—but for Kahn curiously boxlike—exterior of pewter-finished stainless

steel and poured concrete is thus on the quiet side; its 200-foot-/61-meter-long inset of dignified shops (which eases the juncture with Chapel Street) adds a note of restrained activity. On entering the Yale Center via the low corner portico, one is greeted by an austere but almost breathtaking four-story-high lobby, skylit and lined with superb white oak panels, with some openings allowing a glimpse of the paintings above. But one is then shunted—under a 40-foot-/12-meter-long beam—into a one-story hall containing information desk and elevators, with lecture hall and stairs almost hidden behind. This progression into the building is not elating; moreover the location of the art is only vaguely sensed.

The building is organized on a grid of 20 feet/6.1 meters (expanded in the shops and courts) with gallery divisions flexibly based on this. Two courts open up the interior vertically and provide internal foci, the four-bay entry square and the six-bay library court. The latter, also skylit, rises three floors on top of the lecture hall. The library court displays a fine series of large-scale paintings, as opposed to the purposefully clean-walled entry, but it is marred by an intrusive concrete stair tower. (The architects wanted glass here but were overruled by the fire marshal.)

The most satisfactory method of approaching the art is to take an elevator to the top floor (as in Frank Lloyd Wright's Guggenheim Museum in New York—see page 431) and walk down. All of the galleries are freely adjustable within their square grid division. The fourth-floor exhibition space is top-lit via ingenious truncated pyramids containing square, double acrylic skylights with internal baffles angled against direct sun and furnished with ultraviolet filters. The joy of light was one of Louis Kahn's credos, but here, while it has its rewards, for some viewers the geometric cadence of deep pyramids, each topped with bright oculus and each heavily structured, can distract the eye from the art. (It is useful to compare this treatment with Kahn's less insistent daylighting in his beautiful Kimbell Art Museum in Fort Worth—see page 555) The use of natural light at Yale, including of course some windows, has the additional advantage of imitating the light in the English mansions where the pictures originally hung. This analogy of provenance is carried further in the entertaining, informal study gallery along the south wall of the top floor; here the paintings are crowded together in the fashion of the eighteenth–nineteenth centuries.

An unexpected pleasure of the galleries on all three floors can be seen in what might be called the variety of spatial options. One can observe the art at comfortable, almost domestic, range, then find visual relief through the rectangular openings between many gallery and gallery-courtyard divisions, and finally enjoy occasional views out. Detailing throughout is impeccable. Benjamin J. Baldwin was primarily responsible for interior design; Richard Kelly was consultant for lighting—particularly the skylights; Pellecchia & Meyers completed the building after Kahn's death (17 March 1974); David P. Wisdom was project manager. The building, its collection of 1,200 paintings, 50,000 drawings and prints, 30 pieces of sculpture, and some 20,000 rare books were a gift to the university from Paul Mellon, Yale Class of 1929.

Open Tuesday–Saturday 10:00 A.M.–5:00 P.M., Sunday 12:00 noon–5:00 P.M. Closed July 4, Thanksgiving, Christmas Eve, Christmas Day, New Year's Eve, and New Year's Day. Admission is free. One-hour tours can be arranged by calling (203) 432–2858. For general information call (203) 432–2850. AR 8/74, AR 6/77, ARev 7/77, JAIA 5/78, PA 5/78, A 1/80

Upon leaving, cross Chapel Street to Kahn's older Yale Art Gallery (1951–53—see page 410)— his first major work and facing his last. Here the dark, reticulated ceiling tends to disappear (particularly in the loftier ground floor), as its spotlights explode onto canvases hung on white walls. The paintings here leap forward, whereas in the Yale Center—as perhaps befits their more domestic nature—they are more "possessed" of the wall. The Yale Center for British Art, it should be explained, is as much a research institution as a general museum. See them both.

PENNZOIL PLACE (1973–75)
711 Louisiana Street
Houston, Texas

Johnson/Burgee, architects

In the increasingly exploratory world of skyscraper design, these twin thirty-six-story towers established a new and vibratory profile for downtown Houston. In plan they form two opposing trapezoids, their "opposing" ends angled at forty-five degrees. The point of each trapezoid aligns with the rectangular base of the other to define a square block. In space, these wedge-shaped towers set up an exquisite tension at the point of their near meeting. This geometric interplay is accented by the forty-five-degree-angled roof atop each, providing constantly changing silhouettes as one moves around the city. (The angled roof was a suggestion of J. Hugh Liedtke, the Chairman of the Board of the Pennzoil Company. He wanted the towers "to soar, to reach, and a flat-top doesn't reach.") Abstract mathematics continue at ground level where slanting roofs that connect the bases of the towers to form covered entries meet the sidewalks (not altogether smoothly). Their angled triangular forms, again at forty-five degrees, change as they interact with the street-level viewer that changes in motion. Wind-tunnel testing was conducted with models to be certain that turbulence would not be created by the towers' shapes, in particular by the 10-foot/3-meter slot between them.

The Pennzoil towers are sheathed in dark glass for both windows and spandrels (the latter backed by concrete block)—a questionable decision for a latitude parallel with Cairo—but this native somberness is heartened by its sharp geometry. On the interior the eight-story high, glass-roofed entries are flooded with light, trees, and people, providing a cheerful introduction. Note the white-painted space frame of its roof in contrast with the dark walls. On the first basement level there is a shopping mall and below this three levels of garage with space for five hundred automobiles. An underground pedestrian way connects Pennzoil Place with a network of weatherproof communications—Houston's downtown tunnel system. This extends nine blocks from Pennzoil and will eventually interlace most of the central business (and hotel) district. The building was awarded the R. S. Reynolds Memorial Award for distinguished use of aluminum in 1978. S. I. Morris was associate architect; Ellisor Engineers were structural consultants.

Located at Louisiana, Capitol, Milam, and Rusk streets. Lobby open to the public Monday–Friday 8:00 A.M.–5:00 P.M. The building is included on the Houston American Institute of Architects walking tour, offered the third Sunday of every month; the cost is $3 per person. For more information call the AIA at (713) 622–2081. AR 11/76, PA 8/77, JAIA 5/78, JAIA 6/82

WATER GARDEN (1974)
1300 Houston Street at 12th, Commerce, and Lancaster streets
Fort Worth, Texas

Johnson/Burgee, architects

Rising—descending is a more appropriate word—immediately across 12th Street from the Tarrant County Convention Center, this four-block, sunken oasis brings an artful retreat to the midtown hurly-burly about it. A series of irregular geometric steps and stepped gardens and pools cascade like a topographical model to create a three-dimensional stimulus for the city. This profusion of stepped-down levels offers a marvelous variety of options—some active, some quiescent; some planted, some sittable; some wet, some dry. One area cannily focuses— almost like a theater—on the active pool while containing its spray from baptizing the innocent. Nearby, yet with its own identity, is an aerating pool whose forty jets deliver a cloud of dew, while beyond a quiet pool, some 16 feet/4.9 meters below street level, thoughtfully banishes for its users all contact with the city around it. A central plaza and a parterre area (off Lancaster) complete this solution to a tough problem. This is a brilliantly refreshing addition to the dry, dry city about it, and one of Philip Johnson's best works. The Water Garden was a gift of the Amon G. Carter Foundation.

Open daily 7:00 A.M.-11:30 P.M. Fountains operate daily 10:00 A.M.-10:00 P.M.

KEMPER ARENA (1974–75)
1800 Genessee at 17th Street (via 12th Street Viaduct)
Kansas City, Missouri

C. F. Murphy Associates, architects and engineers

The white metal exterior of the Kemper Arena is dominated by eight steel tube space frames that embrace the sides and uphold the roof. Walking under its trusses almost suggests Le Corbusier's book *When the Cathedrals Were White*, so powerful is this outrigging of "flying" buttress trusswork. In plan the upper half of the building forms a rectangle with tightly rounded corners: the lower (entry) half is, however, amply rounded to reflect the ovoid seating pattern within. As the entrances are at the four corners, the overhang of the top gives some shelter below. The interior, partly below grade to facilitate seating, is visually passive after the structural dynamism and bright "purity" of the exterior—but then any room would be. The arena accommodates the full panoply of events including basketball, circuses, rodeos, ice hockey, and rock concerts. It seats up to 17,600 for concerts, while the lowest ranks of seats can telescope under the upper ones to make a larger floor area.

Kemper is located in what was once largely a stockyard and industrial section of the city and its shining whiteness is purposefully attention-drawing in its plebeian neighborhood. It is also a catalyst for upgrading many of its warehouse neighbors, some of which are sturdy examples of their period and well worth notice.

Open for events. Free tours can be arranged by calling (816) 274–1900. AR 3/76, ARev 7/76, PA 11/79

LAS VEGAS STRIP (late 20th century)
Las Vegas Boulevard South (US 91 and 466)
Las Vegas, Nevada

The "vulgarity" of several areas of the United States is so preposterous as to assume a valid index of twentieth-century folk culture. New York's Broadway once reveled in a make-believe of improbability and delight, but Broadway has fallen on sordid days and more sordid nights. Vegas's Strip—a word that adroitly defines it—now reigns as queen, a bawdy queen brandishing aerial signs that engage from dusk to dawn in uninhibited battle to lure all comers to the dens that line this boulevard. The resulting neon Armageddon, as one drives the gauntlet between flashing phalanxes (including plaster warriors), lays siege to the senses. One finds oneself with defenses down, willingly trapped, engagingly shilled, so electric are the forces and so imaginative the means. And the structures behind these aerial fireworks—which, of course, constitute their goal—are almost invisible, so subdued are they in scale. One casino is dwarfed by a sign over 200 feet/61 meters high; when is a building a sign and when is it a symbol? This is one of the world's most successful "playgrounds for adults."

In 1968 the thought-provoking Robert Venturi took fifteen of his Yale School of Architecture students to examine the Strip, an excursion that led to the book *Learning from Las Vegas* (MIT Press, 1972) that he wrote with his wife, Denise Scott Brown and with Steven Izenour. It is a challenging book and one that can perhaps be encapsulated in his statement, "Architects who can accept the lessons of primitive vernacular architecture, so easy to take in an exhibit like 'Architecture Without Architects' [by Bernard Rudofsky], and of industrial, vernacular architecture, so easy to adapt to an electronic and space vernacular as elaborate Neo-Brutalist or Neo-Constructivist megastructures, do not easily acknowledge the validity of the commercial vernacular" (*Forum*, March 1968). Perhaps we should look again at the Strip.

AF 3/68, A 10/90

ART CENTER COLLEGE OF DESIGN
(1974–75/1992)
1700 Lida Street
Pasadena, California

Craig Ellwood Associates, architects
James Tyler, architect of addition

Craig Ellwood, who has been called "a poet in steel," was one of the most ardent disciples of Mies van der Rohe, and for the energetic Art Center College of Design he produced his most spectacular—and most Miesian—building. On the almost wild slopes of the San Rafael Hills a bit northwest of and overlooking the famous Rose Bowl, he bridged a small canyon with an impeccable building 672 feet/205 meters long by 144 feet/44 meters wide. With its ends anchored on the ridges, the central part of the building, made of multiple king-post trusses, leaps across the chasm with a free span of 192 feet/58 meters. The access road dashes underneath so that both on approaching and leaving the college there is an almost breathtaking levitation of mass and flow of tethered spaces. The freestanding triangulation of the "bridge" trusses is fully expressed and gives visual relief to what otherwise would be a tedious length. The end sections are both two stories high with the lower floor set two thirds into the grade. The central area is occupied by administrative offices and library, with reception, offices, and exhibition space in the south wing.

Corridors line the outer periphery of most of the building, thus classrooms are inset with light coming only from high transoms. The decision to place classrooms inside was determined by the school board and the architect in early studies (1970). This has a positive value because of the sun-shading that the outside corridors give the east and west sides, while they themselves are not important thermally. The interiors are structurally expressive with ceiling and framework painted black and the walls white, with widely displayed student work providing

colorful accents. The College of Design—one of the most noted in the United States—has architectural antecedents in Mies's never-built House in the Alps (1934) and in Craig Ellwood's small Weekend House (1968) in San Luis Obispo, California. A south wing, designed by James Tyler (who worked with Ellwood on the original building), was added in 1992; it includes additional classrooms as well as computer labs. Some rigidity is evident in this one-building "campus" for a thousand students, and its remote residential location raises questions, but the result is a potent affirmation of two of the century's most characteristic materials—steel and plate glass.

Located west off Linda Vista Avenue, 1 mile/1.6 kilometers west on Lida Street. Open daily 8:30 A.M.–5:00 P.M. Closed for holidays. Also closed July 4 weekend, Thanksgiving weekend, and the week between Christmas and New Year's Day. Guided tours are available by appointment Monday–Thursday at 2:00 P.M. and Friday at 10:30 A.M.; to make an appointment call the admissions office at (818) 396–2373. PA 1/76, PA 8/77, ARev 8/78

POLICE MEMORIAL BUILDING (1974–77)
501 East Bay Street between Liberty and Catherine
Jacksonville, Florida

William Morgan, architect

Terraces as a major architectural statement probably originated at Queen Hatshepsut's Temple at Dêr el-Bahari, Thebes (1520 B.C.). In our own time Le Corbusier's Unité d'habitation at Marseilles (1952) demonstrated that a roof—as terrace—and its engagement of levels and forms can not only shield a building but also constitute its chief delight, while utilizing the entire site. William Morgan, always open to the lessons both of past and present an excursion in itself, not only made the roof of his Police Building with its multiple terraces and surprises, he also added the kinetics of Rome's Piazza di Spagna, and embellished all with luxurious planting, a pool, and a fountain. Moreover, the underlying philosophy of the building is perhaps of even greater significance than its physical rewards: the architect sought to transform a routine, often formidable (if not hostile) municipal function into a public park that welcomes, day and night, the citizen, the visitor, and the lunchtime picnicker. The Police Memorial Building extends rapport and public accessibility to all in a celebration of the city and the people who make it up.

The design of this low-profiled neighborhood garden spot and official headquarters— named for the Jacksonville police killed in the line of duty—was won in 1971 through a limited geographical competition. (The building's program was subsequently changed when the state reorganized its judicial system and the design altered accordingly.) Its plan, which fills a site measuring 700 feet/213 meters long, divides public access on Bay Street from official use on the other side. Its two business floors are elevated above ground-level parking (for 244 cars and some services), taking advantage of the 15-foot/4.6-meter falloff in grade.

The public is drawn to the building by a wide cascade of stairs flanked with planters, and it enters via an anti-monumental door into a towering central hall. Four freestanding columns uphold its roof while a peripheral clerestory pours down a flood of indirect light. A comfortably scaled reception desk fills the far side, with ready access to the records section adjacent. A generous, well-lit hall, lined with staff offices and highlighted by banners painted by local schoolchildren, leads to a second skylit hall, primarily for official use, which is open for the full height of the building and topped by a heliport. The building's concrete structure is dramatically stated here.

The expansive roof, as intimated, rejoices in an astounding parade of levels, tiers of steps, and almost secret nooks, while a fountain gushes water in front of the glass-walled cafeteria, which welcomes the public. The trees on several terraces furnish generous shade: their planting boxes—note their stepped shape—are placed directly over structural columns. The chief cohesive element of the facades is the horizontal banding of smooth structural concrete that ties all together and lends sophisticated scale to the vertically striated walls. Virtually no windows were used because of security needs; skylights provide most illumination.

In summary, the building flexibly integrates structural, mechanical, electrical, acoustical, illuminating, communicating, and partitioning systems through an economical, cast-in-place, structural tree system designed with the help of William J. LeMessurier. William M. C. Lam was lighting consultant. Thomas A. McCrary was associate in charge. Altogether a marvelous municipal concept.

Terraces open daily 24 hours. Building open Monday–Friday 8:00 A.M.–5:00 P.M. Free group tours can be scheduled by calling (904) 630–2160. AR 9/72, AR 1/78

FEDERAL RESERVE BUILDING (1974–78)
600 Atlantic Avenue between Summer and Congress streets
Boston, Massachusetts

Hugh Stubbins & Associates, architects

The dominant structure on Boston's waterfront is the Federal Reserve Building, its power deriving in part from its location but far more importantly from its geometry of smooth verticals versus ribbed horizontals. In developing the Federal Reserve the architects emphasized the separation of general office space from money handling spaces, using an elevated tower for the former sphere and a spread-out, four-story unit for high-security areas, with two additional levels below ground. (Compare Gunnar Birkerts's Federal Reserve Bank of Minneapolis, page 558.) The void under the tower underscores this dichotomy of function and also proclaims the structural independence of the tower while moderating ground-level wind disturbances on an exposed site. Utilities, such as vertical circulation and toilets, are placed at the ends of each floor in the towers (windowless for fire protection and efficient wind bracing), with 143 feet/44 meters of flexible, open office space between. The floors are supported by two rows of four columns each inset from the slab edge; they are carried below by monumental trusses, at 36 feet/11 meters deep among the largest ever fabricated. From the exterior the horizontality of the floors is emphasized by their spandrels, which are angled outward to help screen the hot, high summer sun yet welcome its warmth in winter. Bright aluminum is used for both towers and spandrels. Two mechanical floors, one at bottom (and which receives the trusses) and one at top, give horizontal framing to the tower.

In addition to the thirty-two floors in the high rise, there is, as mentioned, a four-story unit branching behind the double-height lobby. This contains a gallery and a four-hundred-seat auditorium (often open to the public—inquire) on the front part of the ground floor, with some bank operations behind and above, and employees' cafeteria on top overlooking a roof garden. A small plaza gives welcome at entry. Hugh Stubbins was principal in charge and designed the two lobby murals; LeMessurier Associates/SCI were the structural consultants. (Note, in passing, Shepley, Rutan & Coolidge's South Station of 1896–99 across Summer Street.)

Open Monday–Friday 9:00 A.M.–5:00 P.M. Gallery open Monday–Friday 10:00 A.M.–4:00 P.M. Closed for holidays. For gallery information call (617) 973-3454. Tours can be scheduled by calling (617) 973-3371. PA 8/77, AR 9/78, Int 12/78

IBM SANTA TERESA LABORATORY (1975–77)
555 Bailey Avenue
Santa Teresa, California

MBT Associates, architects

IBM has a policy of limiting the size of its installations so that they will not burden a community with too much personnel (with need for housing, schools, shopping) or demands for municipal services (water, sewage systems, power, police). Thus this West Coast programming development center was located on the site of a former orchard well removed from the more extensive complex that the company had earlier built on the south edge of San Jose. It is IBM's first installation designed specifically for programming activities and this determined its highly specialized design.

One of the basic problems was the reconciliation of providing private, individual offices, where approximately one third of a programmer's time is spent, with areas for accommodating several team members in activities that take up about half of a programmer's time, with common terminal rooms, conference rooms, and the main computer center, plus, of course, the usual services (library, cafeteria). Flexibility had to be built in, with easy interior circulation throughout. "Outside awareness" and a mind-relaxing environment when away from work were also sought. And although some two thousand employees would be on the scene, a noninstitutional ambiance was important.

The above demands were met by grouping eight identical four-story office blocks, each cruciform in plan, around a one-story, ground-level computer center. A two-story food service unit

abuts at rear. Reflecting the uneven site, the lowest floor, which serves as the common link, is partially in the hillside while an enormous terrace—the roof of the computer center—serves as a garden quadrangle onto which all office blocks (here three stories) open. This elevated agora forms the visual focus and outdoor circulation area for the complex.

The design of the eight blocks began with a meticulous study of the space demands of an office for a single individual. An office module 10 x 10 feet/3 x 3 meters—thoroughly tested with mock-ups—was eventually standardized. Though uniform in size, each work unit has numerous layout options. Every detail of the furniture was studied to mesh with the work space. After exploring various dispositions of multiples of the basic office—from linear to clustered—a squared U plan was adopted, with four offices on each of the two sides of the U, five across the end, and six inside. The inner ones are variably used as offices or conference centers. The resulting almost square bays of offices, approximately 45 x 50 feet/13.7 x 15.2 meters in size, were then grouped around and plugged into the four sides of a large central service core to establish the cruciform plan mentioned. All buildings connect at ground level while many are also bridged above.

Though natural aluminum predominates the exterior, color coding, at times vibrant in its positiveness, gives identity to each of the similarly shaped office blocks. This attains striking heights in the semihidden courtyards framed by arms of adjacent buildings. Construction is of steel capable of withstanding severe earthquakes. The sleek enclosure of reflective glass flush with bright aluminum makes a highly sophisticated set of buildings. There is a slight "citadel" aspect to the overall complex on the approach but on its private plaza the campus quality, excellent scale, and color touches have both individual and collective rewards. Gerald M. McCue was design principal assisted by David C. Boone and Alan R. Williams; the SWA Group were the landscape architects.

Located 6 miles/9.6 kilometers south of freeway on US 101, west 1 mile/1.6 kilometers on Bailey Avenue. The interior is closed to the public. AR 8/77, JAIA 5/78, ARev 5/81, AR 2/86

DALLAS CITY HALL (1975–78)
1500 Marilla Street
Dallas, Texas

I. M. Pei & Partners

Productive urbanism and startling geometry are the chief characteristics of the Dallas City Hall. The urban contribution—in a city where downtown graciousness is almost unknown—resides in the 425-foot-/130-meter-wide plaza that stretches northward from the building toward the nearby ramparts of the central business district. This welcome disjunction is planted with local trees, highlighted by a circular pool 180 feet/55 meters in diameter, and completed by Henry Moore's *The Dallas Piece*, a superb work in three parts. Steps on the two edges of the northwest corner mediate the modest grade changes while three ovoid flagpoles recall (massively) the three rounded towers projecting from the building's facade. A garage lies under the entire plaza and accommodates 1,325 automobiles.

The building itself combines an outward-angled front (fifty-six degrees to the plaza) with three round-ended vertical utility/circulation cores asymmetrically disposed, defining bay divisions. The result is a seven-story facade 560 feet/171 meters long of no small monumentality. (The city hall bears some similarity in facade angle, pier, and orientation to Eero Saarinen's

Dulles Airport in Chantilly, Virginia—see page 448.) The meeting of the ground floor with the plaza is closed—there is no liaison—except at the glazed entry. The two ends are basically triangular, which, with their horizontal cutbacks marking floors, produces a complexity of form that for some observers weakens the geometric probity of the overall. The windows on the long sunny side are inset for solar protection.

A three-story-high lobby with entrances on both sides forms a bright introduction to the interior. Moving stairs then take one up a single level to the dramatic great court, the inner focus of city hall. This 100-foot-/30-meter-high core is cheerfully top-lit by quarter-round vaulted clerestories, and each floor is surrounded by balconies lined by plants (compare this top lighting and step-backed use of balconies with Frank Lloyd Wright's Marin County Civic Center in San Rafael, California—see page 455). The two lower floors of this space are occupied by those municipal functions most used by the public, while the upper are more specialized.

In understanding the structure of the Dallas City Hall, it is useful to realize that the first and second floors of the building establish its basic width, which is 122 feet/37 meters. The northerly (plaza) side of the court level rises vertically within, but each upper floor projects beyond the one below to produce the angled front. The southern half of the great court, however, steps back 9 feet/2.7 meters on each successive floor, thus admitting a maximum of light to the core and developing a nonrigid space. Each internal step-back equals the projection forward reflected in the angled front of the building, thus the combined widths of the front and back sections of each floor—the two being divided by the court—equal that of the second (and first) level(s), even though they vary individually as the floors rise. The space and ambiance of the great court make an adventure of what could be a prosaic or even unpleasant task (such as taxes) for the citizen. It is one of a few exciting public interiors.

Located off Young Street between Akard and Ervay. Open Monday–Friday 8:30 A.M.–5:00 P.M. Closed for holidays. The 250-seat, theaterlike council chamber with entry on the sixth floor holds meetings open to the public each Wednesday. Harper & Kemp were associated architects. JAIA 5/78, AR 2/79, PA 5/79

UNITED STATES COURT HOUSE AND FEDERAL BUILDING (1975–79)
299 East Broward Boulevard at Northeast 3rd Avenue
Fort Lauderdale, Florida

William Morgan, architect

A provocative government building. It is best approached going northward on Broward Boulevard; one then appreciates its urban assurance, the parasol of its hovering roof, its cascades of water, and its tiers of planting. It is safe to say that few federal buildings and, in particular, fewer courthouses are as ingratiating. Whether one's business is routine or a major courtroom ordeal, the architecture does its best to comfort the passage. Though there are architectural extravagances here, it is important to note that the project came in substantially under budget.

The complex contains seven federal courts—civil, criminal, and bankruptcy—with full security and supportive functions, 150,000 square feet/13,936 square meters of office space for federal agencies, and in-house parking for 230 automobiles. The structural system is based on reinforced concrete "trees" 30 feet/9.1 meters on center, cast-in-place concrete floor slabs, and concrete masonry infilling. The parasol roof provides sun protection (and spatial venturesomeness). All windows are shielded by broad overhangs, while extensive shaded walkways are used where feasible in place of interior corridors. The watercourses amuse the eye, dampen street noises, and, with the ramps, provide an agreeable linkage between the entry and the four-story-high atrium. Note the lateral offsets of the ramps. Extensive planting reflects the semitropical climate of Fort Lauderdale.

As the architect put it, "The underlying principle of design is that this facility must be an exceptionally delightful place for the citizen to visit at any time." H. J. Ross Associates were the engineers; Stresau, Smith & Stresau the landscape architects; Vida Stirby Brown the interior designer.

Lobbies open to the public Monday–Friday 8:00 A.M.–4:30 P.M. Closed for holidays. AR 12/78, AR 10/79, JAIA 5/80

RAINBOW CENTER MALL AND WINTER GARDEN (1976–77)
302 Rainbow Boulevard North
Niagara Falls, New York

Gruen Associates, architects

A fanciful castle in botanical garden guise well designed to add noncommercial delight—there are no concession stands within—to downtown Niagara Falls. This glass and steel, jauntily angled pleasure dome terminates the city's East Mall, with the Johnson/Burgee Niagara Falls Convention and Civic Center at the other end of the 1,500-foot/457-meter landscaped promenade. An all-weather arcade parallels the mall with a hotel at midpoint. The gesture of the city and its Niagara Falls Urban Renewal Agency in commissioning the Rainbow Center Mall and Winter Garden was intrepid; the results by the architects brilliant. The garden magnetizes by day with its intriguingly airy structure, and radiates light and welcome by night when it is aglow. Filled with an exotic collection of trees, bushes, pools, and an indoor observation tower, it graciously offers itself as urban refreshment. Though measuring only 175 x 155 feet/53 x 47 meters, it contains almost secret retreats within. Picnics are encouraged, even weddings have taken place here. A shopping center connected to the Winter Garden on the north side acts as an urban conflux (the shops are attached at either side to form a second mall at right angles to the existing one), while at the same time the building doubles as gateway to nearby Prospect Point and the famous Niagara Falls.

The structural problems in designing this glass palazzo—which might be described as a cross between London's Crystal Palace (long gone) and Milan's Galleria—were considerable. This fragile-surfaced building 107 feet/33 meters high must contend with heavy snow and wind loads and a temperature range that easily encompasses 100° F/38°C. To create a dynamic elevational profile and to establish tension with the symmetrically arced convention center down the mall, the architects evolved the notched and angled frame we see. The structural sys-

tem employs four rows of cylindrical concrete columns, twenty in all, with horizontal and angled steel lattice trusses resting on top. Glass, vertically clear and generally tempered (shatterproof) otherwise, encases the roof and side walls. Heating was originally by electricity but is now by gas. Cesar Pelli was in charge of design; M. Paul Friedberg & Partners were landscape consultants; DeSireone & Chaplin, structural engineers; Cosentini Associates, mechanical/electrical engineers; and Herbert Levine, lighting consultant. A transparent delight night and day.

Open daily 9:00 A.M.–11:00 P.M. PA 8/78,
JAIA 5/79, ARev 3/81

HYATT REGENCY AND REUNION TOWER
(1976–78)
300 Reunion Boulevard at
Stemmons Freeway
Dallas, Texas

Welton Becket Associates,
architects and engineers

The world's oldest glass is thought to be Egyptian from around 2000 B.C., and though glass was industrialized early in the nineteenth century, it only fluoresced as a building skin in the 1960s and 1970s. Glass then became available with insulating factors, with a variety of tints, and with reflective and mirror attributes, providing sheets of a material with tantalizing possibilities. Architects have not been slow to seize—at times over-seize—these new means of sheathing a building, but it is doubtful if any new structure can equal the glass exuberance of this hotel. Mercurial by day, this compound of shapes clad in silvered reflective glass can evaporate against the sky; at sunset, when the low sun emblazons its fantasia of forms, it approaches the spectacular; while at twilight the hotel glows with mystery. This act, it should be added, is fully visible from the nearby interstate highway. There are those with reservations about so much glass at latitude 33, but *sui generis* this is one of the nation's dazzling exteriors. The interior focuses on an almost square atrium, 200 feet/61 meters high, which lacks the brio of the exterior. In addition to extensive public accommodations, including a ballroom, there are 939 well-designed guest rooms. It should be added that the hotel's structure is very innovative in using steel plate shear walls for wind resistance.

Hotel lobby open daily 24 hours.

Alongside the hotel rises the 564-foot-/172-meter-high Reunion Tower, with a geodesic sphere 118 feet/36 meters in diameter, held aloft by four concrete piers. This contains a revolving cocktail lounge, restaurant, and observation deck with a geometric net of some 260 long-life exterior lights forming a web around it.

Tower open Sunday–Thursday 10:00 A.M.–10:00 P.M., Friday 10:00 A.M.–midnight, Saturday 9:00 A.M.–midnight. Admission is $2 for adults, $1 for senior citizens and children ages 11 and under. Free tours can be scheduled by calling (214) 651–1234. AR 8/78, AR 10/78

The area surrounding the hotel is under development both by the city and private enterprise. The nearby Union Terminal railroad station (1916—Jarvis Hunt, architect) has been rehabilitated and is directly connected to the hotel and to Reunion Tower by an underground walkway, and in 1980 the city opened a Special Events Center—Reunion Arena in an adjacent large park. Designed by Harwood K. Smith & Partners, with Paul Gughotta consulting engineer, the arena is a 420-foot-/128-meter-square building covered by a 4-acre/1.6-hectare steel space-frame roof. Seating 17,200, it accommodates professional basketball and hockey, rodeos, concerts, and a variety of other events.

DENVER PERFORMING ARTS COMPLEX (1976–92)
14th and Curtis streets
Denver, Colorado

The four-block Denver Performing Arts Complex is one of the most enterprising—and successful—in the United States. Led by the 2,200-seat Auditorium Theatre, designed by Robert Willison in 1908 for the Democratic National Convention, it has invigorated the cultural life of the city. Its architecture probes new directions, while its 76 feet/23 meters high glazed galleria adds a welcome note to downtown, lacing the units together while providing attractive shelter along the way.

Open during performances. Tours can be scheduled by calling (303) 893–4000. A 8/92

BOETTCHER CONCERT HALL (1976–78)
Hardy Holzman Pfeiffer, architects

The Boettcher is housed in an almost square box of pronounced angularity on the exterior but exhibits an explosive play of circles and spaces within. Its seats, arranged in swooping arcs, completely surround the orchestra. (The 360-degree "surround" layout for an orchestral hall was pioneered by the late Hans Scharoun in his Berlin Philarmonie of 1963.) The fourteen tiers and terraces of seats—which hold 2,750—project in irregular clusters of four to nine rows each, the majority facing the front of the off-center stage. No person is more than 85 feet/26 meters from the stage; most are less. The result is an auditorium of refreshing intimacy. Seats

are of natural wood finish and cheerful red cloth, the backs high for sound reflection. The Boettcher stage is split and hydraulically adjustable, holding as many as 120 musicians. Overhead disks of acrylic plastic lighting fixtures lend reflected geometry and form an acoustic canopy as they largely fill the ceiling. They can be adjusted in height to meet varying needs. The immediate center of the ceiling is filled with a circular light bridge. The lobby, which brandishes some of the building's mechanics, is overly restricted in size (budget), but when one enters the auditorium one gasps at its excitement.

AR 1/78, AR 3/79

HELEN G. BONFILS THEATRE COMPLEX (1979–80)
Roche/Dinkeloo & Associates, architects

The entry side of the Bonfils Theatre projects a tawny concrete exterior—it has been called "robust"—forming a quarter-circle, its shape generated by the curve of the lobby. With the Boettcher Concert Hall opposite, it frames the entrance to the airy galleria that bisects the complex, a prominent curved stair between them. The Bonfils comprises four main theaters: the 750-seat Stage—the focal unit—with thrust platform and eleven rows of semicircular stepped seats around it; the 450-seat Space, a pentagonal theater on axis with the Stage; the straightforward 195-seat Ricketson, below, with separate entrance; and the 150-seat Source, with an experimental thrust format. The spacious lobby is outstanding as it embraces the stage, highlighted by four ingenious, semi-enclosed, angled entrances to the auditorium. The center point for the radii that describe the curve of both lobby (exterior) wall and the seating plan is, of course, the same.

JAIA 5/90

TEMPLE HOYNE BUELL THEATRE (1990–92)
Beyer Blinder Belle/van Dijk, Pace, Westlake, architects

The Buell, with its 2,830 seats, adds a general-purpose auditorium to the Performing Arts Complex. From the beginning it was designed to be "populist," and the spaces, colors, and graphics (by Sussman Preja) restively carry out this purpose. The theater's facade opens directly onto the galleria via a wall of glass that parades both patrons and passersby. The 60-foot/ 18-meter-high lobby behind is thus an alive space. The auditorium is relatively standard in shape, with gently sloping arcs of seats, mezzanine above, and prominent projecting boxes on the two sides. The lateral walls are of buff-colored Colorado sandstone panels. Small panels near the rear are angled for acoustic diffusion.

Also part of the complex is the Galleria Theatre (1986), which was designed by Dominick & Associates and which seats 208. An adjacent eight-level garage (1977—Muchow Associates) conveniently handles the pesky problem of parking. Initial overall planning studies for the Center were carried out by Kevin Roche (1973).

There are shortcomings in the center, primarily its compromised site squeezed between the 1908 Auditorium Theater and the eight-level garage. Moreover there is no hint of festivity at entrance, no theatrical beckoning. Indeed there is no adequate automobile access (except by garage), just a curb without canopy. However on entering the galleria, which is composed of three slightly offset towering sections, an almost casbah-like atmosphere takes over: sparks fly. The center is one of the delights of Denver—as it would be of any city.

LOCKHEED MARTIN ASTRONAUTICS BUILDING (1977)
(formerly Johns-Manville World Headquarters)
12999 Deer Creek Canyon Road
Littleton, Colorado

The Architects Collaborative, architects

The Colorado topography is the most abruptly dramatic in the United States. After hundreds of miles of eastward plains and prairies, the western fortress of the Rocky Mountains rears suddenly from flatness with Denver clustered at its base. The most impressive man-made addition to the city's rumpled backdrop is this building for Lockheed Martin. (See also the Air Force Academy in Colorado Springs, page 436.) Though of shining aluminum and 1,100 feet/335 meters long, the rests contrapuntally at peace with its mountain setting, notching into the hillside with a minimum of cut-and-fill. The nearest (southeast) end rests on two-story-high columns that inject a slight vertical note into the basic horizontality. However, the road then leads between the two long office blocks that make up the building and one is soon surrounded by the grandeur of its structure. This structural potency is emphasized by the fact that the left unit (facing the mountains) is elevated on pilotis to mesh with the space. Two parallel wings, bridged at the second level, were used instead of one massive building to maintain a sympathetic scale yet not cower before the mountains. The reception area is on the ground floor of the east building and on entering one enjoys a stunning panorama of a reddish rock outcropping with plains beyond seemingly stretching to infinity. A triangular pool and terrace below entry level ease the transition between the enclosed and the wild. The slope-roofed cafeteria conveniently adjoins.

Located 23 miles/37 kilometers southwest of Denver via I-70 West to State Highway C-470 South to Ken Caryl Road West. Lobby open to the public Monday–Friday 8:00 A.M.–4:00 P.M. AR 9/77, JAIA 5/78, JAIA 5/79

THANKS-GIVING SQUARE (1977)
Pacific Street at Ervay
Dallas, Texas

Johnson/Burgee, architects

Philip Johnson has designed two monuments in Dallas; there is a hint of the Renaissance in one, the John F. Kennedy Memorial (see page 559) and the Baroque in the other, Thanks-Giving Square, a half mile/.8 kilometer to the north. The latter was built as a center of world thanksgiving to celebrate humanity's gratitude to God. One can enter the triangular square under an open belfry that forms the major gateway (there are three other entries). One then winds through a small but surprisingly tempting and rewarding garden accented by waters. Channels of water run along some paths; a sparkling pool awaits at the top. The garden's climax is at far end—a chapel wrapped in a form taken directly from the minaret of the Great Mosque of al-Mutawakkil in Samarra, Iraq (847–52). Its cylindrical, spiraling geometry produces a day-long interaction with the sun, and gives a visual focus to a difficult street intersection. A small bridge leads to the nondenominational chapel within; its nautilus interior reflects the outside. Upward swirling bands in the ceiling, highlighted by decreasing circles of stained-glass panels, establish a quietly colorful and reposeful place of contemplation. The juncture of ramp and chapel might not be totally dexterous, but the sculptural form and its brilliant sun-consciousness, the pleasures of its garden in mid-city clutch, and the retreat offered by the chapel make a compelling whole. The square was built by and is supported by the Thanks-Giving Foundation.

Open Monday–Friday 9:00 A.M.–5:00 P.M., Saturday, Sunday, and holidays 1:00–5:00 P.M. Group tours can be arranged for a fee by calling (214) 969–1977.

CRYSTAL CATHEDRAL (1977–80)
12141 Lewis Street
Garden Grove, California

Johnson/Burgee, architects

Appropriately called the Crystal Cathedral, this building is probably the ultimate technical extension of Joseph Paxton's 1851 Crystal Palace in London. The church's roof and walls—like its English prototype—are totally wrapped in glass, here reflective glass held in white-painted steel. With an all glass mandate from its charismatic minister, Dr. Robert Schuler, who had been excited by Lloyd Wright's Wayfarers' Chapel of 1949–51 (see page 404)—a mere half-hour away—Philip Johnson has created a religious space frame whose lithic limits were reached some 700 years ago with the stone-roofed greenhouse of Ste. Chapelle in Paris.

The church's sleek, flush-sided, star-shaped form—a mirrored tabernacle—might suggest a secular hall more than a house of God. However its strangely euphoric, even worshipful interior, especially when filled with people, seemingly opens to heaven above and nature about—precisely as Schuler wanted. Moreover it also encourages a congregational sense of belonging even when one is seated in one of the semi-balconies—really elevated extensions of the nave. It forms a setting, one might add, for the religiously convinced, its fundamentalist architecture reflecting the congregation's creed, one shunning the mystery that characterizes Gothic cathedrals and many churches.

The church's star plan measures 415 x 207 feet/126 x 63 meters, with a height of 127 feet/39 meters. The main floor is augmented by three triangular balconies—a Trinity?—all focused on the chancel; they rest on independent concrete foundations for earthquake protection. Capacity is thus adaptable to fluctuating congregations; total seating is 2,890. The construction of roof and walls is of space-frame trusses formed by slotted-end pipe members welded to gusset plates, which give visual accent to the tubular framework. So complicated was the framing that some connections involve eleven pipes. Pipe size averages 3 inches/76 millimeters. The reflective glass skin is silver coated to transmit only a small percentage of light. The roof is of tempered glass as are the 550 moveable sash, while the fixed wall panels are of annealed glass. The 10,661 panels/measure 2 x 5 feet/.6 x 1.5 meters and 2 x 6 feet/.6 x 1.8 meters—only a bit larger than those Paxton employed. Operating sash are placed on all sides to provide cross-ventilation, effectively eliminating the need for air-conditioning. In spite of the heat load the church is reputedly rarely uncomfortable. To keep the skin from being too acoustically uniform, one-half of the glass is .25 inch/6.3 millimeters in thickness and the other half .125 inch/3.2 millimeters, both randomly laid.

The Crystal Cathedral has been criticized by some as being more theater than church, more didactic than questing. Indeed one can quarrel with some of the details, the organ (not by the architects) for one. However most worshippers—the church is usually packed on Sunday—find it religiously welcoming and technically brilliant. For the casual visitor this high-tech glass tent is staggering. Be certain to see the cathedral's adjacent antecedent, the Arboretum (1959–61, see page 453) by Richard Neutra.

Located south of Los Angeles immediately north of CA 22 and west of I-5. Open daily 9:00 A.M.–4:30 P.M. Closed New Year's Day, Labor Day, Thanksgiving, and Christmas. Sunday services held at 9:30 and 11:00 A.M. Tours given every 45 minutes Monday–Saturday 9:00 A.M.–3:30 P.M.; a tour is also given after the Sunday 11:00 A.M. service. Admission and tours are free although a donation is suggested. For general information call (714) 971–4000; for tour information call (714) 971–4013. AR 11/80, Int 12/80, PA 12/80, ARev 1/81, JAIA mid-5/81

ATHENEUM (1978–79)
North Arthur Street
New Harmony, Indiana

Richard Meier, architect

New Harmony is an early landmark in American history. It was initially settled in 1814–24 by religious dissenters from Germany whose agricultural and manufacturing expertise soon so surpassed local market opportunities they moved to a location on the Ohio River west of Pittsburgh. However their land and their distinctive buildings in Indiana were almost immediately (1825) bought by Robert Owen and William Maclure to establish a community of "Universal Happiness through Universal Education." Though dissolved by the early 1830s, this utopian group introduced one of this country's first kindergartens, free public schools, and trade schools. Moreover architecture "was given a role as the agent of social change." This emphasis on education and architecture has been given testament by Richard Meier's Atheneum, the gateway to New Harmony's heritage.

Prominently capping a small rise in a verdant field just outside the village, the Atheneum is one of a number of structures that make up the Museum of the New Harmony Experience. Dazzling in the sun with its bright square porcelain panels, this somewhat lonely white knight seems puzzlingly large and complicated for a building that houses only a 180-seat auditorium, exhibition spaces, and offices. While the zigzag outrigging of the stairs on the outside is potent in anchoring the left end of the building, it is within that Meier's imagination explodes. Here lateral switchbacks of ramps probe horizontally while above assorted whirlwinds of space open and close, framing the blue sky beyond. (Le Corbusier's Villa Savoye of 1931 comes to mind.) If this intense complexity—to say nothing of its blinding whiteness in a bucolic setting—seems immoderate, it has established a landmark for New Harmony, extending a lively welcome to all.

April–October open daily 9:00 A.M.–5:00 P.M. November–March generally open daily 10:00 A.M.–4:00 P.M. (hours may vary). Closed Thanksgiving, Christmas Eve, Christmas Day, New Year's Eve, and New Year's Day. Admission is $3 per person, free for children under 7. Various tours available. For more information call (812) 682–4488. PA 1/79, PA 2/80, JAIA 5/80, A 5/85

SONY PLAZA (1978–84/1993)
(formerly AT&T Building)
550 Madison Avenue, between 55th and 56th streets
New York, New York

Johnson/Burgee, architects

There are not many buildings of which a simple sketch could create a furor on the front page of the *New York Times* (16 April 1978), but then rarely has iconoclasm been so divertingly flaunted. Philip Johnson was the early torchbearer for Modern architecture, an apostle of the new; thus the thirty-four-floor Sony Plaza is for some an apostasy. But there is more here than meets the casual eye.

As an office structure originally owned and occupied solely by AT&T, there were design options that gave the architects imaginative freedom, the most tangible being the almost total-ly open street floor. In return for this covered plaza the building was allowed extra height. This sheltered *Pausenplatz* was intended to serve the public as a refuge from shopping and a place for lunchtime chats, but wind exposure and competition from the air-conditioned Bamboo Court of 590 Madison Avenue (see page 620) directly across the street lessened its use.

The building itself is one of the most superbly detailed and constructed that one will see. Rising 657 feet/200 meters without setback, it is divided into base, shaft, and pedimented cor-nice impeccably clad in granite. The famous wall-to-wall "Chippendale" pediment on top is, of course, idiosyncratic, but thank you Johnson/Burgee for enlivening the high-rise spectrum.

In 1990 the building was sold to the Sony Corporation and renamed Sony Plaza. In 1993 the open ground floor was converted into shops. Gwathmey Siegel & Associates were the ren-ovation architects; Edwin Schlossberg designed the interiors.

Lobby open daily 7:00 A.M.–11:00 P.M. PA 6/78, PA 2/84, ARev 8/84, A 2/85, PA 7/94

THORNCROWN CHAPEL (1979–80/1989)
Highway 62 West
Eureka Springs, Arkansas

E. Fay Jones, architect

Almost hidden in the woody uplands of northwest Arkansas and, indeed, resembling a geometric forest itself, Thorncrown Chapel is at one with nature. There is a Genesis atmosphere here, a conspiracy of man and nature with a return to simple and, one might say, unadorned truths that long ago fled architecture. And although the chapel might be called a vernacular in wood, it was honed with mathematics.

So concerned with environmental preservation was the architect and his patron that construction was limited to pine two-by-fours and two-by-sixes easily portaged through the narrow approach path. The church, thus, is almost invisible in the woods. The self-effacing path leading to it gradually parts to reveal the enormous parasol of a roof lightly upheld by a cadence of supports. The interior revels in a cross-hatched web of truss geometry all assembled on site. The sides are of glass, the slender daylight filtering through the woods augmented by a ridge clerestory. Low lighting fixtures are attached near the bottom of the built-up supporting columns but there are no other fixtures or ornamentation. There are eleven rows of pews with

three steps up to the chancel with its pulpit and lectern. Instead of a centric altar there is simply a large window framing a view of nature beyond. Flooring is of local flagstone. The plan measures 24 x 60 feet/73 x 18 meters with the nave rising to 48 feet/114.6 meters. A small worship chapel also designed by E. Fay Jones was added in 1989.

The chapel has proved to be so popular that it has understandably become a regular tourist stop for those at the Ozark Mountains summer resorts. Worshipful simplicity.

April–November open daily 9:00 A.M.–6:00 P.M. March and December open daily 11:00 A.M.–4:00 P.M. Closed Thanksgiving and Christmas. Sunday services held April–October at 9:00 and 11:00 A.M., November–December at 11:00 A.M., June–October at 7:30 A.M. 15-minute tours given daily. For more information call (501) 253-7401. AR 3/81, JAIA 5/81, Int 5/81, ARev 7/81

PORTLAND PUBLIC SERVICES BUILDING (1980–82)
1120 Southwest Fifth Avenue
between Main and Madison
Portland, Oregon

Michael Graves, architect

Architecture is a mirror of the roofs and walls of civilization, reflecting the foibles and delights of the ages. For years after the completion of New York's famous Seagram Building (see page 420), skyscrapers around the country emulated this 1951 masterpiece by Mies van der Rohe and Philip Johnson. Hard, dark, rectangular, wrapped in a flat-topped bronze shell, they peppered with businesslike precision many downtowns. And in time they spurred a counter-reformation, with the Portland Building amongst the most singular.

This boldly polychromed and bedecked 15-story skyscraper for municipal employees, it is important to note, was not only a competition winner but one where strict economy played a key role. The Portland Building comprises a two-story square base with setbacks from which rises an eleven-story concrete office shaft topped by one inset upper floor. The low base, which fills the block, serves as a scale transfer to its elderly neighbors, while its blue color enlivens the street. The ground floor is surrounded by inset shopping arcades on most of three sides. The facades of the startling, cream-colored office shaft are punctured by the punch-card staccato of dark square windows (4 x 4 feet/1.2 x 1.2 meters) that frame a seven-story decorative panel on each side. These panels are comprised of clusters of reddish pilasters alternating with mirrored glass, and on two sides of the structure are topped by bolted-on concrete swags. The panel on the other two sides, facing Chapman Square on the east and the transit mall on the west, is capped by two projecting "capitals," while a gigantic red tile "keystone"—half the width of the building—crowns all, with a squared belvedere puncturing the middle. Just above the entry projects a 35-foot/10-meter copper statue of Portlandia by Raymond Kaskey. All of this embellishment, it should be added, was even more vigorous in the competition drawings but had to be reduced for economy: the early sketches show a roof sporting tiny classic temples, while bands of stainless steel enliven the sides. Although the architect states that "we weren't merely decorating a box" (*Progressive Architecture*, February 1983), obviously an effort was made to elevate a routine, inexpensive government building into a cheerful downtown landmark.

Lobby open Monday–Friday 6:00 A.M.–6:00 P.M. Closed for holidays. Tours can be arranged by calling the General Services Department at (503) 823-4000. PA 5/80, AR 8/80, JAIA 1/81, AR 11/81, ARev 11/82, AR 11/82, PA 2/83, JAIA 5/83, A 12/85

333 WACKER DRIVE
(1981–83)
Chicago, Illinois

Kohn Pedersen Fox,
architects

This thirty-five-story green convex mirror reflects a slice of edge-of-downtown Chicago and perks up the neighborhood with its games of light. Evolving from its diagonal location where the Chicago River makes a right-angle turn, and fronting Wacker Drive, 333 is another of the city's skyscrapers that explores a provocative direction. And as it entirely fills its triangular lot, it rises unencumbered by neighbors. (The river, incidentally, once emptied *into* nearby Lake Michigan, the city's source of drinking water. In 1900 engineers reversed its flow by building a 28 miles/45 kilometers Drainage Canal to the Desplaines River downstream: Chicago, "the city that works.")

The dramatic green glass facades are divided horizontally into 6 feet/1.8 meters high bands: note the prominent band at two-thirds height and the notched top. At ground level, the curved river facade is countered at each end by a straight flank (at right angles to each other to fit the street pattern); with the main facade it produces a crossbow in plan. Recessed arcades line the three flat sides. The building, which is framed in steel, is prominently decorated on its lower seven floors by various-width horizontal stripes of gray granite and green marble. On the curved Wacker Drive side the symmetrical striping lends prominence to the facade, which tends to become complicated around the two-story main entrance. Perkins & Will were associate architects.

Lobby open to the public daily 7:00 A.M.–7:00 P.M. The building is included on the Chicago Architecture Foundation's river cruise tour; the cost is $15 on weekdays, $17 on weekends. The building is also included on the CAF's west loop tour. For more information on CAF tours call (312) 922-3432. PA 10/83, A 5/84

HIGH MUSEUM OF ART (1981–83)
1280 Peachtree Street NE
at 16th Street
Atlanta, Georgia

Richard Meier, architect

A white castle brightly crowning its hillock with a buildup of unusual geometry. Strategically located between downtown and the edge of the residential district, and directly adjacent to an earlier arts complex, the High Museum of Art presents a shining front. In plan the building is divided into two rectangles abutting a square; this forms a ninety-degree, equal-arm "frame" enclosed by the quarter-arc of the main facade. A semi-detached auditorium stands at left.

The drum of the entry is approached via a long, semi-elevated processional way (a slender invitation) that delivers one, after a sharp turn to the right, to the entrance. One proceeds into the museum via a low control area to burst into the brilliant four-story atrium. This low entry leading to an explosion of space of course recalls Frank Lloyd Wright's Guggenheim Museum in New York (see page 431), which Richard Meier has long admired. (However the High's switchback ramp occupies only half of the atrium.) Two straight walls appear opposite and contain the corridors that provide access to the galleries behind; their right-angle meeting serves as a counterpoint for the arc of the ramp (and the exterior elevation). They are semi-enclosed by large square panels on which the sun often projects shadows through the clerestory on top; their inner walls serve for display. There is some geometric agitation in the atrium plus a hesitation regarding the location of the art, but it forms a lively museum introduction and often serves as the city's social forum. A mural by Sol LeWitt entitled *Irregular Bands of Light* was painted in the atrium in 1994.

To visit the three upper floors of galleries one ascends the ramp—à la Guggenheim—or takes the elevator. The top (fourth) floor is basically devoted to twentieth-century art and to exhibitions on loan—it can handle enormous circulating shows—with American and European painting and sculpture on the third level, and decorative and non-Western art on the second. All galleries, it should be noted, have a comfortable relation to the atrium core and the green world outside. Each, of course, can be flexibly divided and illuminated. Total display area is 46,000 square feet/4,273 square meters. The building's structural grid is 21 feet/6.4 meters. The ground floor is devoted to administration, a small conference room, and an education gallery.

The museum has been so successful that it has become a shining talisman for Atlanta and expansion has already been discussed.

Open Tuesday–Saturday 10:00 A.M.–5:00 P.M., Sunday 12:00 noon–5:00 P.M. Closed for holidays. Admission is $6 for adults, $4 for students and senior citizens, $2 for children ages 6–17. Admission is free on Thursday 1:00–5:00 P.M. Tours given Tuesday–Thursday at 11:00 A.M. and 1:30 P.M., Friday at 11:00 A.M., Saturday–Sunday at 1:00 and 3:00 P.M. For more information call (404) 733–4444. AR 8/81, AR 1/84, ARev 2/84, A 5/84, AR 11/86, A 12/89

JAMES R. THOMPSON CENTER (1981–85)
(formerly State of Illinois Center)
La Salle, Randolph and Clark streets
Chicago, Illinois

Murphy/Jahn, architects

Somewhat resembling a defrocked spaceship, this tapered glass menhir injects a futuristic note into midtown Chicago. It galvanizes the street. As former Illinois Governor James R. Thompson put it, "We are a brave people, undaunted by new and innovative ideas."

The building in plan is stabilized by its two, right-angled, seventeen-story, vertical sides, not quite equal in length, which establish the pivotal southeast street corner. The dramatically curved and sloping main facade that connects these vertical walls is generated by a radius from their corner point. It sweeps around the front and half the third side in three startlingly angled and set-back bands, each layer representing nine floors. Alternating vertical stripes of blue and reflective glass enclose this truncated cone, the whole resting on a slightly gaudy colonnaded entry level.

Within, the rotunda/atrium (160 feet/49 meters in diameter) soars as a dramatic cone straight through the top, where it is sliced off at a jaunty angle. Its inside perimeter is broken only by the slight projection of the bank of elevators. All of the building's seventeen floors open onto the balconies that encircle three-quarters of the interior, providing access to the offices behind. Upper-echelon offices occupy the outer (straight) walls, with routine offices, conference rooms, and services between. The two lower floors are commercially rented. Not only is this great cylindrical space impressive, it extends a democratic welcome to the public, which most government buildings do not. Though perhaps spectacle-generated, the center adds a rousing note to urban architecture. Helmut Jahn was designing architect, Lester B. Knight associate/ interior designers.

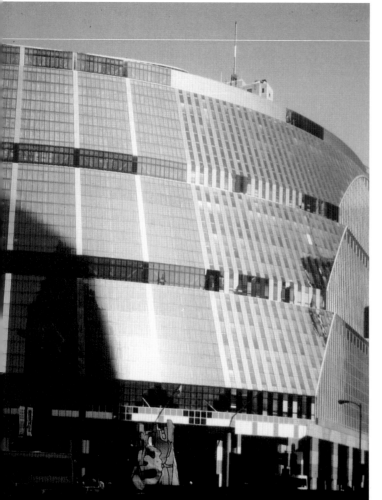

Open Monday–Friday 8:00 A.M.–6:00 P.M. Closed for holidays. Free tours can be arranged by calling (312) 814-6660. The building is included on the Chicago Architecture Foundation's "Modern and Beyond" tour; the cost is $10. For more information on CAF tours call (312) 922-3432. ARev 12/80, PA 2/81, AR 4/81, A 11/85, PA 12/85

PORTLAND MUSEUM OF ART
(1982–83)
7 Congress Square
Portland, Maine

I. M. Pei & Partners, architects

A museum that employs a complexity of means to arrive at some splendid exhibition spaces. Its red brick facade, topped by an unusual cornice, holds down Congress Square with a "billboard" statement (as it has been termed) that stretches 122 feet/37 meters wide by 67 feet/20 meters high. Behind this two-dimensionality is a pyramidal buildup of giant cubic modules, twenty-six in all, each of which measures 20 x 20 x 11.5 feet/6 x 6 x 3.5 meters, and is separated by 7.5-foot/2.3-meter interstices. The ten modules of the main floor diminish to four on the fourth, producing a stepped building profile as the number of space-cubes diminishes from facade to rear. This complexity, it should be added, stemmed from the architect's desire—perhaps an overreach—to create a comfortably scaled new building, the back of which would not overpower the adjoining 1911 old museum (now the L. D. M. Sweat Memorial Galleries) and the 1801 McLellan-Sweat House to which the new is attached.

Inside the front door rewards begin. The entry extends an airy welcome with its open ambiance, a glimpse of an overlook above, and the prominent stairs down to the lower level in one corner. A 187-seat auditorium and small gallery space occupy the lower ground floor. However, the stairs to and between entry and the main gallery floors above are puzzling, being semi-hidden in a corner on all levels.

It is within its lofty galleries that the museum shines, reaching a climax in the double-height top floor. The overall grid of the units permits combinations of exhibition sizes from one to four modules with right-angle partitions. Light and lateral vitality play roles throughout, vistas from all points reach out to a tantalizing space beyond, while an open core creates vertical contact. One detail seems puzzling: this is a narrow passage that separates the galleries from the arched windows on the street side, opening up the facade, but creating a spatial problem within.

The most striking features of the exhibition spaces—the building's core—are the skylights, which change in shape from squares into deep octagons and flood the exhibitions with illumination. On the double-height top floor four skylights in a row help to create a magnificent museum space. Henry N. Cobb, the designing architect of the museum, says that the inspiration for these well-recessed skylights came from the Dulwich Art Gallery in London—the city's first museum—designed by the great Sir John Soane in 1811–14. The outside vanes of the Portland's light sources—prominent on the exterior—are precisely fixed for optimum daylight without requiring adjustment. Supplementary artificial track lighting is, of course, laid on and forms the basic gallery illumination.

The intriguing flow of gallery spaces with unexpected vistas, the welcoming scale, and the quality of light make the Portland a splendid contributor to museum architecture—and to this pleasant Maine city.

Open Tuesday–Saturday 10:00 A.M.–5:00 P.M. (Thursday until 9:00 P.M.), Sunday 12:00 noon–5:00 P.M. July 1–Columbus Day also open Monday. Closed for holidays. Admission is $6 for adults, $5 for senior citizens and students, $1 for children ages 6–12. Admission is free Thursday 5:00 P.M.–9:00 P.M. and the first Saturday of the month 10:00 A.M.–12:00 noon. Tours of the collection given daily at 2:00 P.M. and Thursday at 5:30 P.M. Tours can also be scheduled by calling (207) 775–6148. PA 8/83, AR 11/83, A 5/84, AR 6/84

VIETNAM MEMORIAL (1982–84)
off Constitution Avenue near 21st Street
Washington, D.C.

Maya Ying Lin, architect

Most memorials aspire heavenward to celebrate distant victories or heroic deaths or even native pride. This extraordinary black granite slash in the earth shuns historicism to produce the most soul-wrenching memorial one will encounter. The competition for its design—there were 1,425 entries—was won by Maya Ying Lin, a young architecture student at Yale, who wrote, "The names would become the memorial. There was no need to embellish." An open *V*-shaped wall eased gradually into the ground and inscribed with the dead resulted. Virtually invisible in its park setting—its top is almost even with the lawn—the memorial's path slopes downward until the visitor becomes wondrously detached from the world above. Moreover the polished black Indian granite wall reflects the ghostly figure of the onlooker, tying dead and living in an unsettling embrace. The observer is a participant.

The 58,191 American dead and missing, listed chronologically as they fell, are inscribed on contiguous panels that measure 40 inches/1 meter wide. The top of the memorial stands 12 inches/30 centimeters above ground at the two ends, angling down to 10.1 feet/3.1 meters at base. It rests on 140 deep pilings. The Cooper-Lecky partnership is the architect of record.

Located near the Lincoln Memorial. Open daily 24 hours. AJ 8/81, PA 3/83, AJ 5/83, A 5/88

DALLAS MUSEUM OF ART (1982–84/1993)
1717 North Harwood Street
Dallas, Texas

Edward Larrabee Barnes, architect

There is a relaxed atmosphere about the Dallas Museum of Art that makes it very congenial in a busy city; beckoning at the edge of the skyscraper district, it helps civilize downtown. The museum is also the key unit in Dallas's Arts District, an ambitious, ongoing urban outreach with focus on the arts—visual, auditory, and performing. Anchored by the museum, this twenty-block plan (1977) has as its spine a tree-lined, landscaped avenue (Flora Street) whose development is given impressive uplift by the Morton H. Meyerson Symphony Center (Pei Cobb Freed & Partners, 1989). It is hoped that a theater will eventually terminate the avenue. Throughout the summer months it hosts a variety of street festivals.

The museum's vaulted, somewhat scaleless hall has a square gallery in each of its four corners. Its 12,000 square feet/1,1114 square meters of space are basically devoted to contemporary art. One then mounts a few steps—there are, of course, elevators—to begin the pleasures of the major galleries. The most important comprise two large, slightly offset, rectangular spaces (100 x 150 feet/30 x 46 meters), each with inner court. The spatial relationship of these two galleries to each other, the invitation of their terraced change in level, plus the bright open patio in each create a tempting series of spaces. The galleries are divided by fixed right-angle partitions into basic art periods. Their illumination by linear skylights can be supplemented by ceiling fixtures. The building is finished with limestone walls, including the roof of the vault—which is highly visible to its lofty neighbors. Interior floors and most walls are also of limestone. Detailing is exemplary.

In September 1993 a three-story addition—the Hamon Building, also designed by Edward Larrabee Barnes—was opened to the public. The new is not only intimately a part of the old, it serves as the entry for both. On the interior this link results in a block-long "concourse" leading to the lofty vaulted hall that initially formed the museum's introduction and is still what might be called the starting point for the collections. (There is an arboreal approach via the adjacent sculpture garden.) This new section houses exhibition spaces, offices, a library, and the museum store. Its collections trace developments in the Western Hemisphere from pre-

history to 1940 in a variety of well-installed galleries. This addition has a basic emphasis on educational and participatory activities—more than half of the visitors are children—and the Education Resource Center in the Hamon is a key unit in this admirable museum.

Take the St. Paul Street exit off the Woodall Rodgers Freeway. Open Tuesday, Wednesday, and Friday 11:00 A.M.–4:00 P.M., Thursday 11:00 A.M.–9:00 P.M., Saturday–Sunday 11:00 A.M.–5:00 P.M. Closed Thanksgiving, Christmas, and New Year's Day. Admission is free. Tours of the collection given Monday–Friday at 12:00 noon, Saturday–Sunday at 2:00 P.M. For more information call (214) 922–1200. A 4/84, PA 4/84, A 2/90

590 MADISON AVENUE (1982–84)
(formerly IBM Building)
590 Madison Avenue at 57th Street
New York, New York

Edward Larrabee Barnes, architect

The substantial rewards of this forty-three-story skyscraper lie not so much in its ingenious angled shape and impeccable granite-and-glass skin as in the visionary development of its site. The New York City Planning Commission long ago established an equation of building height versus land coverage, a formula that allows extra floors of offices or apartments if public space (setbacks, parks, or similar amenities) are provided at street level. 590 Madison Avenue's use

of its very expensive lot evolved, to the benefit of all, with its tower covering only forty percent of the site and the remainder occupied by a veritable forest of bamboo trees under a glass canopy. This 68-foot-/21-meter-high oasis, lightly captured by a spider web of hollow-pipe trusses (one is 113 feet/34 meters long), forms one of the city's tranquil delights. A food and drink kiosk provides snacks, tables and benches are abundant, and brown-baggers, weary tourists, and shoppers are cordially welcome. The New York Botanical Garden has an information center in one corner, while concerts and recitals frequently take place on a small stage. Moreover there is direct connection with some of the city's most exclusive shops.

The building's bulk may bully its prominent corner site and some details will puzzle, but 590 Madison Avenue is a building far beyond the commerce of available square feet. There is an urban outreach here—and New York City is richer for it. Zion & Breen were the landscape architects.

Atrium open daily 8:00 A.M.–10:00 P.M.
AR 5/84, LA 9/89

JACOB K. JAVITS CONVENTION CENTER (1982–86)
655 West 34th Street at 11th Avenue
New York, New York

I. M. Pei & Partners, architects

Stretching the length of four city blocks, this geometric spider web of glass celebrates—like Philip Johnson's Crystal Cathedral (see page 608)—a new horizon in architecture with, en route, a proper nod to Joseph Paxton's heroic Crystal Palace of 1851 in London. The building is a 1,000-foot/305-meter long, two-level rectangle made up of 90 feet/27 meters square structural bays, eleven across the front by seven deep. Its function is the display of goods, rapidly and effectively, for the non-stop series of trade shows held throughout the year. The logistics of turnover are of great importance—each show is brief—and to this end the entire west side is lined with truck loading docks. Administration and services occupy most of the southwest corner.

Though the building's purpose is display, its delight is the dazzling 90-foot/27-meter wide glass-walled, glass-roofed promenade that lines the entire front of the building, efficiently providing access to the display areas behind via escalators while enveloping one in a sparkling embrace. This four-block-long lobby reaches a climax near the south end with its own "crystal palace," an elevated cross-axis where one is almost intimately enveloped in gossamer tracery; shadows add their own games. Rising to a height of 150 feet/46 meters, this galleria and viewing platform—New York's skyline is in the distance—makes the Jacob K. Javits Convention Center a pleasure for participants and visitors alike. The center is not just an efficient series of exhibit spaces; it is an experience.

The space frame that supports this metal tracery is of tubular design based on a 10-foot/3-meter module; its diamond trusses are at times of extraordinary complexity. The building is sheathed in semi-reflective tawny glass with clear glass only across the pedestrian level. Note the elegance of the beveled edges. The double-level, concrete-framed exhibition spaces are of only routine interest. James Ingo Freed was partner in charge of design; Weidlinger Associates were the structural engineers.

Open Monday–Friday 9:00 A.M.–5:00 PM. Closed for holidays. Only certain areas are open to the public. Group tours are available at a cost of $150 and up per group; tours must be arranged in advance. For more information call (212) 216-2000. AR 8/80, AR 9/86, A 3/87

CONOCO HEADQUARTERS (1984–86)
600 North Dairy Road
Houston, Texas

Roche/Dinkeloo & Associates, architects

In the last few decades there has been a distinct movement on the part of corporations in the United States to develop headquarters outside the city proper. Downtown has become so expensive in rent and taxes, and so mired in traffic, that an escape to a country setting with inexpensive land, easy parking, and generally available nearby employee housing offers many advantages. Among the most imaginative of suburban headquarters anywhere is this group of interconnected three-story buildings interwoven with a 9 acre/3.6 hectare man-made lake. There could scarce be a more refreshing answer to a hot climate. The sixteen units, which vary in metered size to reflect different corporate divisions, are joined at the second level by elevated walkways, thus almost totally eliminating the need for elevators. They total more than 1.5 miles/2.4 kilometers in length and are protected by awnings of fiber panels in aluminum frames. These reduce the air-conditioning load substantially in addition to creating a harmonic grouping, one which Kevin Roche describes as "a campus . . . very Southern, and very traditional." Water sparkles all around while wide overhangs keep the blazing sun and heavy rain off walls and walkways. Parking areas for 2,100 cars (1,280 covered spaces) stand adjacent. They were placed on opposite sides of the complex to keep a reasonable scale, their connecting walkway forming an access spine through the entire layout. An outdoor running track and an indoor fitness facility are available to all, as is the 900-seat cafeteria. The standard width of the various buildings is 62 feet/19 meters with a double corridor in the middle. This allows the maximum of private offices—1,977 altogether—along the outside walls with services and work sections in the center. Basic office size is 12 x 15 feet/3.6 x 4.6 meters, which is doubled for top executives. Overall construction is of reinforced precast concrete frame with precast concrete panels. A brilliant building answering demanding conditions.

Located off of I-10 West, 17 miles/27 kilometers west of downtown Houston. The interior is closed to the public. The building can be seen from the road, and visitors are free to walk around the grounds. A 12/86

MENIL COLLECTION (1985–87)
1515 Sul Ross Road at Branard and Mandell streets
Houston, Texas

Piano & Fitzgerald, architects

A trim small museum housing a choice family art collection. Set in a modest Houston neighborhood, it maintains a considerate scale with its neighbors, down to its local cypress clapboards. This "village" museum forms a one-story rectangle 402 feet/122 meters in length by 142 feet/43 meters in width, with a full-length penthouse stretched across the top. Oriented east-west, the building is nearly symmetrical in plan, with its entrance near its midpoint. It is divided within by a spinal corridor that separates the entry (back) side, with its stretch of professional offices and studios, from the bank of galleries that fills the north side. There are three major divisible gallery blocks—the two at west end measuring 80 feet/24 meters square, the third measuring 80 feet/24 meters by 60 feet/18 meters—and each independent from the other, accessible only from the corridor. That one must leave a gallery to visit another provides unusual selective viewing. Several delightful small galleries adjoin.

This simple block of a building is shielded from the sun—Houston is on the same parallel as Cairo, Egypt—by a startling outrigging of fixed louvers. Moreover its high-tech "roof canopy" of ferrocemento leaves is extended around and beyond the entire structure to make a protected walk. The design of the louvers was finalized only after extensive mock-ups of sun angles and material compatibility, the end result is S-shaped louvers made of lightweight ferrocemento forming the lower component of an elaborate ductile iron truss-work. The louvers were of course designed to protect the works of art in the skylit galleries from the direct sun. Further protection is given by the use of ultraviolet glass. The overall suffusion of sunlight throughout the day, with its accents of passing clouds, brings life throughout. There is, however, a problem with the louvers in that their size was determined for scale compatibility with the large exhibition halls; in the small galleries their uniform size can be distracting. The narrow top floor, elevated 6 feet/1.8 meters above the main body, is termed "The Treasure House" for the 10,000 works of art it holds under conditions of precise temperature and humidity; it is available to scholars and students by appointment.

In February 1995 the Cy Twombly Gallery, also designed by Renzo Piano with Twombly's help, opened to the public. Designed to house approximately 35 major works by the artist, the structure—which sits opposite the Menil Collection building—has concrete block walls and a roof composed of a lightweight system of planes to allow daylight to filter into the gallery spaces.

Open Wednesday–Sunday 11:00 A.M.–7:00 P.M. Closed for holidays. Admission is free. For more information call (713) 525–9400.
A 5/87, PA 5/87, AR 9/87, AR 5/95

FOUNTAIN PLACE (1986)
(formerly First Interstate Bank Tower)
1445 Ross Avenue at Field Street
Dallas, Texas

I. M. Pei & Partners, architects

The skyscraper from its 1870s birth in Chicago has clung to rigid rectangular cage construction while undergoing largely cosmetic changes through the years. Early on, temples sprouted atop aspiring frames; in the latter days of our own minimalist period (1950s and '60s), it was thought proper to slice off the top cleanly when floors ran out; in the waning era of Postmodernism (1970s and '80s), narcissism took over and the roof was curiously decorated. In almost all cases, however, the structural frame was a rectangular grid, generally of steel. Recently, when computer developments opened previously unknown technical possibilities, architects (and their clients) began to leave "the box" and to produce startling new shapes. Among the most dazzling of this new generation is Fountain Place in Dallas by Henry Cobb of I. M. Pei & Partners with Harry Weese associated. It is a structural apotheosis sheathed in light green glass—sculpture at the ultimate scale.

Located on the uncluttered edge of the business district—where its sliced geometry can be widely appreciated, particularly from the freeway—the sixty-story building rises aloofly from Fountain Place plaza, with a forested water garden at its feet. The frame of the 720-foot-/219-meter-high tower is based, according to the architect, on "the diagonal of a double square maintaining an exact 2:1 ratio of rise to slope." A ten-faceted prismatic form results, measuring 192 feet/59 meters square for the twelve lower floors, then tapering, its sides sloping in with knife-edge precision. A triangular prism of sixteen floors tops all, the whole seamlessly knit together. A few space inefficiencies occur under the slanted roof planes and a touch of science fiction can be seen in its almost spaceship profile, but architectural and urban horizons have been significantly extended by Fountain Place.

The building, however, does not stand alone: it welcomes the public at its base with an oasis of 220 Texas cypress trees set in cascading terraces of water. Spaced in circular tubs 15 feet/4.6 meters apart, the trees establish a rhythmic forest with 172 pools of active water and bubbling fountains adding to make-believe in a hot, dusty city. The central fountain has computer-controlled jets (some 400 of them) giving focus to the plaza, seventy percent of which is covered with water. Dan Kiley was the landscape architect. It is a much-loved urban asset. Cobb and Kiley have been brilliantly imaginative.

Plaza open daily 24 hours. Lobby open Monday–Friday 7:00 A.M.–7:00 P.M., Saturday 8:00 A.M.–2:00 P.M. Closed Sundays and holidays. Tours can be scheduled by calling (214) 855–7766. A 12/86, ARev 8/88

MUSEUM OF CONTEMPORARY ART (1986)
250 South Grand Avenue
Los Angeles, California

Arata Isozaki, architect

The architect of the Museum of Contemporary Art had a difficult task in establishing a street presence for the building, since most of it is underground. Its site crowns a hill with the museum inside it, and the entry to the galleries is via a terrace and down an outdoor stair. On approaching, one might indeed ask, "Where is the museum?" The query will be rewardingly answered, but the terrace platform should be seen first. On it at left (north) the four-story administrative wing with elevated library—note its paraboloid roof—rises commandingly along the street side (with shop and offices behind). The right side of the roof terrace is closed by the projecting top of the underground galleries, with a rich red sandstone from India revetting its walls and a glazed pyramid puncturing its roof. A narrow sculpture garden lines the back of the terrace, while a platoon of high-rise buildings behind dwarfs all.

The basically underground museum is reached by wide right-angled stairs leading down to the inset entrance court. Court and galleries form a precise rectangle with reception in the center, the two major galleries at the ends, and five smaller ones in between. The square J. Paul Getty Trust Gallery adjoins the reception hall, its towering height (58 feet/17 meters) lit by the glazed pyramid mentioned earlier. The 18-foot/5.4-meter high Brawerman/Firks Foundation Gallery adjoins and leads to the South Gallery. This is the museum's most impressive single space, not only because of its size but also its highly flexible, almost distractingly complex ceiling illumination. Eleven skylights with controllable vanes admit daylight as desired. (Approximately two-thirds of the galleries' lighting is natural.) The other galleries form a sequential layout with the divisible North Gallery at end. A 162-seat auditorium and services are below.

A feeling of space (at times emptiness) pervades the museum with its high ceilings, large white walls throughout, natural maple floors, and few pictures per wall. Whereas much of the display area is relatively routine, the care given to materials and textures is outstanding. From inquisitive and extensive uses of metal (some novel), to translucent onyx panels, to lighting fixtures and details, care and thoroughness are evident throughout. Gruen Associates were associate architects.

Open Tuesday–Sunday 11:00 A.M.–5:00 P.M., Thursday until 8:00 P.M. Closed Thanksgiving, Christmas, and New Year's Day. Admission is $6 for adults, $4 for students and senior citizens, free for children under 12. Admission is free on Thursday 5:00–8:00 P.M. Free half-hour tours of the collection given Tuesday–Sunday at 12:00 noon, 1:00 P.M., and 2:00 P.M., and on Thursday at 6:00 P.M. For more information call (213) 626–6222. AR 5/87, AR 1/88

ALICE BUSCH OPERA THEATER (1987)
Route 80
Cooperstown, New York

Hardy Holzman Pfeiffer, architects

A summer opera house in a bucolic setting, its architecture quietly reflecting the area's farm vernacular. (Cooperstown's famous Farmer's Museum is just seven miles down the road.) The building is set well back from the highway on a tree-girt site, with a reflecting pool in front. The scale buildup is first-rate, with a high saddle roof anchoring the 96 x 48-foot/29 x 15-meter stagehouse. The block of the auditorium, with its own saddle roof, abuts this at a right angle and is surrounded by a low roof over the aisles. Three small ventilators atop the auditorium perk up the profile while recalling nearby dairy farms. The facade is strategically punctuated by an amusing "serenading balcony" (used for fanfares and announcements) while the strongly stated horizontal of entry pulls matters together. The sharp white planes of the roofs play geometric games with the warm tan of the corrugated steel panel walls throughout.

The squarish auditorium and balcony, together seating 900, are laid out in the standard U-shaped opera plan with orchestra pit accommodating 80 musicians. Acoustics are excellent, and the details of the auditorium are good, though the ceiling patterning seems agitated. Taking advantage of its summer-only use and its country setting, the architects imaginatively used retractable sliding panel steel walls to enclose both sides of the theater, providing "air-conditioning" and intermission views out. An outdoor bar and services are adjacent: workshops are in the rear. Hugh Hardy was architect in charge and Sir Peter Shepheard the landscape architect.

Located 8 miles/13 kilometers north of Cooperstown on Route 80. Open during performances. In July and August tours are given Saturday at 10:00 A.M.; the cost is $5 per person. Tours can also be arranged by calling (607) 547–5704. AR 8/88

WEXNER CENTER FOR THE ARTS (1989)
Ohio State University
North High Street at 15th Avenue
Columbus, Ohio

Eisenman/Trott, architects

The Wexner Center's enemy was banality, provocation its goal. Peter Eisenman and Richard Trott (who died in 1990) were the winners of the five-team competition for its design. For some visitors the center is more rewarding as a rite of passage beneath its whirlwind of outrigging than as an arts complex. This extended space frame stitches together—almost literally—two back-to-back earlier cultural structures: the large Mershon Auditorium (1957) and Weigel Hall (1979). The sewing process has been spectacularly achieved by what the architects call a "scaffolding" of square, white-painted, steel pipes whose open frame formation is a "metaphoric microcosm of the urban grid." However this is no rigid cage but an experience of elusive perspectives and angles that make a routine narrow passage a walking experience. This busy pathway debouches at its south end—at the understated entry to the center—and is given unexpected testament by the red brick "ruins" that deliver visual counterpart, scale transfer, and anchoring to the whole. These sharply carved brick forms are an elegy to the 1898 Armory that burned on this site in 1958. As the architects wrote, "it postulates the continuous transformation of memory in the inventions of art and architecture."

Works of art are, of course, the building's rationale, and here questions arise. A (too) small upper lobby receives one and directs most visitors to the busy floor below, where a sizable

bookstore, a cafe, and a comfortable gallery are located. From this core there extends, gradually upward, a ramped corridor, roughly parallel to the outdoor "caged" approach to the museum mentioned above, which terminates the galleries. At 480 feet in length—and narrow in width—this passage does not beckon. The galleries themselves are, however, flexible in housing the experimental art the center emphasizes. A theater and music facilities with blank rear walls to the campus are behind. The fine art library and art storage facilities are underground at right.

Open Tuesday–Sunday 10:00 A.M.–6:00 P.M. (open Wednesday until 9:00 P.M.). Closed for holidays. Admission is generally free; there may be a charge for certain performances and exhibitions. Tours of the building and the exhibitions are available. For more information call (614) 292–0330. PA 10/89, ARev 6/90, A/93

OCEANSIDE CIVIC CENTER (1989–90)
300 North Coast Highway
Oceanside, California

Charles W. Moore/Urban Innovations Group, architects

Irving Gill (1870–1936) was one of the great pioneers in the development of the Proto-Modern architecture of early twentieth-century California, marked by flat roofs, shaved blocks of white stucco, and sharply incised openings. (See his La Jolla Woman's Club, page 337.) Not only are there reminiscences of Gill in the design of the Oceanside Civic Center, two of his 1920s buildings—due to Charles Moore's respect—are carefully incorporated in its overall concept.

The center, the winner of a limited competition, opens up the rather lonesome business street of the town, extending a cheerful invitation via a grove of palm trees, a water garden splashing on all sides, and colored bands of mosaic enlivening the pavement. Civic pride at its best. The public library anchors the complex on the left (northwest) corner of the site, giving an urban presence to the whole. Stepping back and slightly up is the city hall, carefully divided into two major (and one minor) interconnected buildings, thus maintaining a receptive scale as it covers the slight rise. The two units are fancifully bridged at the top, with bands of colored tiles and a freestanding "crown" in the middle. The interiors are very competent, highlighted by the cheerful council chambers. Landscaping throughout, including the hiding of parked cars, is excellent—and growing. Altogether a prideful urban uplift. Danielson Design Group were associate architects.

Open Monday–Friday 8:00 A.M.–4:30 P.M. Closed for holidays. Self-guided tours available. Group tours can be arranged by calling (619) 966–4410. AR 11/90

SOUTHERN PROGRESS BUILDING (1990/1994)
2100 Lakeshore Drive
Birmingham, Alabama

Jova/Daniels/Busby,
architects

An admirable suburban office building that embraces its 27 acre/ 11 hectare forest setting with affection; not a tree was cut unnecessarily, no bulldozer smoothed its sloping hillside site. Architecture and nature have rarely been so sensitively conjoined. Working with a thickly wooded suburban lot, complete with a 35-foot-/11-meter-deep ravine, the architects have designed a 142,000-square-foot/13,936-square-meter office block that is almost invisible from the highway while providing a sylvan setting for its staff. The ravine's small stream is reinforced every working day at 8:00 A.M. by recycled air-conditioning water.

The Southern Progress Corporation is the largest regional publisher of magazines and books in the country; its century-old philosophy has been "responsible and enlightened use of the land." Thus from the terraced parking lot to the building's winter garden reception room, which bridges the ravine, nature is respected. Even the exterior walls were erected from the inside to spare the trees, while the site was cleared by hand for the same reason. The entry/reception level of this respectful box is notched into the irregular hillside with three rectangular office floors above. The second floor contains the photography department as well as over twenty test kitchens, with tightly packed editorial and administrative offices on the third, fourth, and fifth floors. The building's frame is of poured-in-place concrete; bronze reflective glass encloses it. Landscape architect Robert E. Marvin was intimately involved—from site selection to planting detail. Kidd/Plosser/Sprague were associate architects. An extension was added in 1994. Memorable.

Interior not generally open to the public. Free tours are given Tuesday–Thursday at 10:00 A.M.; they must be scheduled by calling (205) 877–6121. A 10/90, ARev 6/91

SEATTLE ART MUSEUM (1991)
100 University Street
at 1st and 2nd avenues
Seattle, Washington

Venturi, Scott Brown & Associates, architects

Working with land that is 15 feet/ 4.6 meters higher at rear than at main entrance, the architects have designed a museum that not only solves the demanding problems of site and slope, but one that does so with outward sprightliness and interior efficiency. Occupying a lot between the edge of the business district and the increasingly up-scale waterfront area, the museum also fills an active role in the life of the city. Its setback position was a site restriction skillfully used by the architects to tie museum to city. The five-story building is composed of entry, shop, auditorium, lecture hall, and art studio on ground floor, three floors of galleries, and a top level for administration. It creates a formidable block whose virtually windowless bulk is relaxed by a rhythm (two-three-two) of vertical lines incised in its tawny limestone walls, by a parade of arched-angled-arched terra cotta and red granite framed windows at base, and by the 10-foot/ 3-meter-high letters at top proclaiming the museum.

The main entrance of the museum is at the curved and counter-curved corner of the building at University Street and 1st Avenue. The curve of the facade opens the view toward Puget Sound. The lobby is not scintillating, nor is the corridor from it that leads to the distant elevators, but the grand stair off the lobby at right is a sparkling asset. Lined with the band of windows noted earlier and 14 feet/4.3 meters wide, this majestic stair ties the museum's two-level entrances on 1st and 2nd avenues together with a flourish. Several strategically placed pieces of fifteenth-century Chinese sculpture give vertical accents under a series of colorful, cusped ceiling arches. The museum cafe is at midpoint. The stairs are directly repeated outside, binding building and sidewalk together.

The three floors of galleries are windowless, thus artificially illuminated. The second floor—which also opens onto the 2nd Avenue entrance to the museum—is a completely undivided space to be adaptable for circulating and special exhibitions. Slightly curved corridors divide both the third and fourth floors into small, intimate exhibition spaces on the south side, with large, flexible galleries opposite. (More might have been made of inter-floor camaraderie.) The third floor art is devoted to the museum's outstanding collection of Asian, African, and Native American (Pacific Basin) works, while the fourth floor concentrates on the art of Europe and the United States. Olson Sundberg Architects were associates.

Open Tuesday–Sunday 10:00 A.M.–5:00 P.M., Thursday until 9:00 P.M. Admission is $6 for adults, $4 for students and senior citizens, free for members and children under 12. Open until 7:00 P.M. on the first Tuesday of each month; admission on this day is free. PA 5/90, A 8/92

AMERICAN HERITAGE CENTER AND
UNIVERSITY ART MUSEUM (1992)
University of Wyoming
2111 Willett Drive
Laramie, Wyoming

Antoine Predock, architect

In the high (7,180-foot/2,189-meter) tumbled landscape of southeastern Wyoming, with the Rocky Mountains as backdrop, this mysterious truncated cone seemingly pushes upward from the earth. Its copper carapace echoes the setting as it thoughtfully pays homage to the tepee. Moreover it also belongs to a new freedom in architecture, a growing liberation that uses today's computers and tools in our sometimes perilous quest for fresh horizons. The University of Wyoming, seeking to celebrate its role in the fabled history of art and the cowboy/Indian saga, and also to make available to scholars its outstanding historic archive, held a competition for this new building, won by Antoine Predock, a distinguished architect from New Mexico well familiar with the West. The American Heritage Center is basically devoted to research on American and western history.

The center's conic profile commands attention. From this branches the east-west-oriented museum wing with a sharply geometric series of small galleries extending from the main exhibition room. An outdoor sculpture court adjoins. Inside, a special room is devoted to the fascinating stages of the building's design development. A stovepipe chimney, framed in natural-finish wood, penetrates the cone, and forms a vertical focus for the research rooms around it. The five diminishing floors terminate in an observation deck. As might be expected, there are problems in a few of the work areas within a Euclidean shape; we are, however, richer for it.

Mid-May–August open Monday–Friday 7:30 A.M.–4:30 P.M., Saturday 11:00 A.M.–5:00 P.M. September–mid-May open Monday–Friday 8:00 A.M.–5:00 P.M., Saturday 11:00 A.M.–5:00 P.M. The art museum is also open Sunday 10:00 A.M.–3:00 P.M. Closed for holidays. Admission to the American Heritage Center is free. Admission to the University Art Museum is $3.50 for adults, $1.50 for senior citizens, children ages 6–17, and students. Guided tours can be scheduled by calling the center at (307) 766–4114 or the museum at (307) 766–6622. A 12/93, PA 3/94

FREDERICK R. WEISMAN ART MUSEUM (1993)
University of Minnesota, East Bank Campus
333 East River Road
Minneapolis, Minnesota

Frank O. Gehry, architect

A small university museum with an exterior exploding in acrobatics of stainless steel panels and orange brick. Obstreperous, certainly, but would lesser joys entice the several thousand students who pass its front door every day? Perched on the edge of a steep site overlooking the Mississippi River, the building's single gallery floor opens directly onto the campus. (There are two lower work floors with uninspired entry plus garage.) Extra-large windows in the facade act as sidewalk showcases for outsize paintings. The five major gallery spaces are lofty (16–25 feet/4.8–7.6 meters) to accommodate large canvases and are capped by deep skylights. This results in spatial games that create lively interiors but hinder the need for occasional intimacy: smaller works can look lonely. The collection, incidentally, is outstanding in works by American artists from the first half of the twentieth century. A small auditorium and seminar rooms are incorporated to encourage interdisciplinary study in the arts. Meyer, Scherer & Rockcastle, were associate architects.

Open Tuesday, Wednesday, and Friday 10:00 A.M.–5:00 P.M., Thursday 10:00 A.M.–8:00 P.M., Saturday and Sunday 11:00 A.M.–5:00 P.M. Closed for holidays. Admission is free. Free 40-minute tours offered daily. For more information call (612) 625-9494. A 1/94, PA 2/94, A 6/94, PA 3/95

HOLOCAUST MEMORIAL MUSEUM (1993)
100 Raoul Wallenberg Place SW at 14th Street
Washington, D.C.

Pei Cobb Freed & Partners, architect

The Holocaust Memorial Museum's task—to document one of the most heinous crimes in history—was no routine architectural challenge. Emotions in three dimensions are elusive. Whereas the two facades (the main on 14th Street, the second on Raoul Wallenberg Place SW) are irresolute, being compromised by neighbors, the great entrance hall within stuns—as do the displays throughout. The central skylit Hall of Witness—a demonic space of brick and steel—sets the stage of deadly efficiency that is echoed in the four floors of exhibits. The unrelenting use of exposed steel trusswork and details is a masterful reminder of death chambers. The lower level contains theater, auditorium, special exhibition space, and education center (with labyrinthine circulation). From the main floor one climbs an intriguingly ominous angled stair to the second floor, which is highlighted by the calm hexagonal Hall of Remembrance and the Wexner learning center. The third and fourth levels are filled with displays of the unspeakable. The top floor exhibits are in a blacked-out space with back-lit photographs: shattering.

There is a lack of inter-floor communication in the museum, and the impact of the exhibition can be overwhelming, but the experience leaves one aghast at the brutality of man. James Ingo Freed was partner in charge. Notter Finegold & Alexander were associate architects. Jeshajahu Weinberg, museum director, supervised museum directors Martin Smith and Ray Farr, with Ralph Appelbaum exhibition designer.

Open daily 10:00 A.M.–5:30 P.M. Closed Christmas and Yom Kippur. Admission is free. Tickets should be reserved in advance by calling (800) 551–7328. For more information call (202) 488–0455. PA 2/93, AR 5/93, A 7/93, AR 7/93, ARev 2/94, PA 10/95

CENTER FOR THE ARTS—YERBA BUENA GARDENS (1993–94)
Third Street at Mission, Howard, and Folsom streets
San Francisco, California

Yerba Buena Gardens is San Francisco's ambitious celebration of the arts, both performing and visual. Tracing its development to the late 1960s—Kenzo Tange designed a high-rise project for it in 1969—it was not until 1985 that the final architects were chosen and not until 1995 that the center was completed. The main buildings are the Center for the Arts Theater by Polshek & Partners and the San Francisco Museum of Modern Art by Mario Botta, both described below. Adjacent to the theater are Fumihiko Maki's (with Robinson, Mills & Williams) quietly sensitive Galleries and Forum, with Romaldo Giurgola and MGA Partners' ovoid Esplanade behind. Facing the Theater across Howard Street is the cheerfully efficient Moscone Convention Center (1981) by Hellmuth, Obata & Kassabaum with the architects' 1993 extension—dedicated to Martin Luther King, Jr.—opposite. There are plans to include a shopping block on Fourth Street, plus child-care center and even an ice skating rink. Convenient to downtown—and replacing low-income housing—Yerba Buena presents a collection of individually superior, if unfocused, buildings that purposefully emphasize the Bay Area's multi-cultural arts community.

Galleries and Forum open Tuesday–Sunday 11:00 A.M.–6:00 P.M., open until 8:00 P.M. on the first Thursday of every month. Admission is $5 for adults, $2.50 for senior citizens and children ages 16 and under.

CENTER FOR THE ARTS THEATER (1993)
James Stewart Polshek & Partners, architect
701 Mission Street

The Center for the Arts Theater, a commanding exercise in cubic geometry, is dominated by a 90-foot-/27-meter-high stage house, smartly angled and revetted in white aluminum panels. Behind this is a square "black box" auditorium with proscenium inset to mark the juncture with stage house. The main entrance, on Howard Street facing the convention center, tends to be jumpy next to the two peaceful forms behind, but the invitation to enter is appealing. A secondary lobby on the north side faces Maki's buildings and sports an enormous screen on which slides and films can be projected. On the west side there is a balcony for outdoor performances facing the adjacent garden.

The pristine exterior is a conspiratorial preparation for the auditorium: it is bold, black, and altogether marvelous. Square in form, its interior is dominated by sides of gray steel panels, some lining the walls, others projected for acoustic reasons. Narrow vertical panels of yellow, with ranks of exposed spotlights, flank the stage. Acoustics are reportedly superior. A spirited new era of theater architecture results.

Open for events only. Tours can be scheduled by calling (415) 978–2700. For general information call (415) 978–2787. A 2/94, AR 3/94, ARev 8/94, A 5/95

SAN FRANCISCO MUSEUM OF MODERN ART (1994)
Mario Botta, architect
401 Van Ness Avenue

Mario Botta's San Francisco Museum of Modern Art, pictured here, states its presence against a backdrop of skyscrapers via a seemingly windowless pillbox of striped red brick capped by a

gigantic, circular, forty-five-degree angled skylight (unfortunately barely visible from the street). This westerly angled paean to the sun—recalling the eighteenth-century gnomons of Jaipur, India—brings daylight into the center of the museum. Though the museum's exterior is not ingratiating to the sidewalk or to the Center for the Arts Theater across Third Street, it firmly establishes the presence of art downtown. The ground floor erupts with space, dominated by a five-story shaft of skylight that pierces the building and houses a stair turned into dramatic sculpture. The entry level is occupied by a large public lobby, rooms for public events, a museum shop, a café, and a 299-seat theater. The galleries, almost all with skylights, are of several ceiling heights, climaxed by the large, top-lit main exhibition space.

Open Tuesday–Sunday 11:00 A.M.–6:00 P.M.; Thursday until 9:00 P.M. Closed holidays. Admission is $7 for adults, $3.50 for students and senior citizens, free for children under 13. Tours given daily. For more information call (415) 357–4000. ARev 2/94, AR 11/94, A 12/94, PA 2/95

DENVER INTERNATIONAL AIRPORT TERMINAL BUILDING (1995)
via I-70 to Peña Boulevard
Denver, Colorado

C. W. Fentress, J. H. Bradburn & Associates, architects

The Denver International Airport projects the most invigorated profile of any complex in the United States. It is a mathematically aligned "tent city" whose strictly clustered white pinnacles assert geometry on the plains as they echo the snow-topped Rockies behind.

The mammoth terminal building—its great hall measures 900 feet/274 meters long by 240 feet/73 meters wide—is roofed with a double layer of Teflon-coated fiberglass slung from steel masts placed 150 feet/46 meters apart and braced by cables. Its thin double roof transmits only ten percent of daylight; its end walls are glazed. Rain and snow drain immediately. On the interior the quality of light, the spatial games—plus the view of the mountains at south end—create a space-age welcome. (When visited the terminal was fully enclosed, but the interior was not altogether finished, hence no full description can be given here. However, as seen, and with presentation perspectives at hand, the prospects are very promising.)

The terminal building is twin-sided with two levels of parallel facilities on each side of the hall, and five levels of parking. Conveniently under the center of the hall is the double-tracked Automated Ground Transportation System, which whisks passengers to and from the three (eventually four) field concourse buildings. The landside/airside communication net is highly efficient, a particular concern in Denver where passenger transfer to other flights (hubbing) can constitute half the turnover. C. W. Fentress was chief of design.

Open daily 24 hours. A 8/94, AR 11/94

THE LITERATURE OF AMERICAN ARCHITECTURE:
A General Introduction

Kazys Varnelis

With literature on American architecture growing exponentially, writing an up-to-date survey of it must seem like a thankless task, perhaps explaining why no useful one has appeared since the 1970s. Vincent Scully, *American Architecture and Urbanism* (New York: Henry Holt and Company, 1988) is an updated edition of a book originally published in 1969, approaching the history of architecture from a formal viewpoint. Also taking a formal approach, though more in depth, is Marcus Whiffen and Frederick Koeper's *American Architecture Since 1780: A Guide to the Styles* (Cambridge: MIT Press, 1981). Perhaps the most readable survey is Leland M. Roth, *A Concise History of American Architecture* (New York: Harper & Row, 1979). Roth's volume has the virtue of being accompanied by a selection of essential primary sources in Leland Roth, ed., *America Builds: Source Documents in American Architecture and Planning* (New York: Harper & Row, 1983). Another selection of primary sources that might interest the reader is Lewis Mumford, ed., *Roots of Contemporary American Architecture: 37 Essays from the Mid-nineteenth Century to the Present* (New York: Dover, 1972). For setting American architecture in its social and cultural contexts, turn to John Burchard and Albert Bush-Brown, *The Architecture of America: A Social and Cultural History* (Boston: Little, Brown and Company, 1961). Readers more interested in a visual rather than textual account might turn to G. E. Kidder Smith, *Architecture in America: A Pictorial History* (New York: American Heritage, 1976).

The series *American Buildings and their Architects* gives up overall coherence in favor of comprehensive studies of key moments in the history of American architecture and should be the starting point for the seriously interested reader. The individual volumes are: William H. Pierson, *The Colonial and Neoclassical Styles* (Garden City, New York: Doubleday, 1970); William H. Pierson, *Technology and the Picturesque: The Corporate and the Early Gothic Styles* (Garden City, New York: Doubleday, 1978); William H. Jordy, *Progressive and Academic Ideals at the Turn of the Twentieth Century* (Garden City, New York: Doubleday, 1972); and William H. Jordy, *The Impact of European Modernism in the Mid-Twentieth Century* (Garden City, New York: Doubleday, 1972).

For a history of American building in terms of its structural development, see Carl Condit, *American Building Art: The Nineteenth Century* (New York: Oxford University Press, 1960) and *American Building Art: The Twentieth Century* (New York: Oxford University Press, 1961).

On the American city, the best source is John W. Reps, *The Making of Urban America: A History of City Planning in the United States* (Princeton: Princeton University Press, 1965). Interesting contrasts, more limited in scope, can be found in Giorgio Ciucci, *The American City* (Cambridge, Massachusetts: MIT Press, 1979); M. Christine Boyer, *Dreaming the Rational City: The Myth of American City Planning* (Cambridge, Massachusetts: MIT Press, 1983); and Morton Gabriel White, *The Intellectual Versus the City* (New York: New American Library, 1964).

Regrettably, a survey of American architecture must also include monuments that have been destroyed: see Constance M. Greiff, ed., *Lost America From the Atlantic to the Mississippi* (Princeton: Pyne Press, 1971) and *Lost America From the Mississippi to the Pacific* (Princeton: Pyne Press, 1972).

The Preservation Press's *Building Watchers Series* is another good introduction to American architecture. John C. Poppeliers, S. Allen Chambers, and Nancy B. Schwartz, *What Style is It? A Guide to American Architecture* (Washington, D. C.: Preservation Press, 1983) is a basic primer on styles. For a brief introduction to more than 100 significant architects and builders, see Diane Maddex, ed., *Master Builders. A Guide to Famous American Architects* (Washington,

D. C.: Preservation Press, 1985), consisting of capsule essays by many of the leading scholars in the field. A more intriguing way to look at architecture is presented in Dell Upton, ed., *America's Architectural Roots: Ethnic Groups that Built America* (Washington, D. C.: Preservation Press, 1986). Avoiding an Eurocentric bias, this guidebook is extremely useful as a means of understanding where the architecture in the "Melting Pot" came from and how ethnic groups maintained their identity through their buildings.

The first two Preservation Press series books have counterparts. Another introduction to styles, with more detail—although more obsessed with the process of classification—is Marcus Whiffen, *American Architecture Since 1780: A Guide to the Styles* (Cambridge, Massachusetts: MIT Press). More detailed biographies, but of fewer architects, can be found in Joseph J. Thorndike, Jr., *Three Centuries of Notable American Architects* (New York: American Heritage, 1981).

Two books accompany recent PBS mini-series on architecture: Robert A. M. Stern, *Pride of Place: Building the American Dream* (Boston: Houghton Mifflin, 1986) and Spiro Kostof, *America by Design* (New York: Oxford University Press, 1987). Both are organized by topic—such as academic villages, dream houses, the street, or suburbs—rather than by chronology, architect, or style and are highly opinionated but generally readable introductions to the field. Kostof attempts to address the entire built environment.

A number of guidebooks and histories of specific areas of the country exist to deepen the quest for architecture begun in this book. For pre-Civil War architecture of the South, Mills Lane's series *Architecture of the Old South* is the amply illustrated comprehensive guide. Lane addresses buildings in a chronological order and sets them in their cultural background. Individual volumes have been published on Virginia, Maryland, South Carolina, North Carolina, Mississippi-Alabama, Louisiana, and Kentucky-Tennessee. Lane provides a one volume overview in *Architecture of the Old South* (New York: Abbeville Press, 1993).

Catherine W. Bishir, *North Carolina Architecture* (Chapel Hill: University of North Carolina Press, 1990) outdoes the Mills Lane volume for that state, extending her investigation into the twentieth century. It should, however, be read along with an important article on the interactions between the Colonial Revival and white supremacy by the same author: Catherine W. Bishir, "Landmarks of Power: Building a Southern Past, 1885–1915," in the inaugural issue of the journal *Southern Cultures*, published by the Duke University Press in 1993.

On the architecture of Florida see Hap Hatton, *Tropical Splendor: An Architectural History of Florida* (New York: Alfred A. Knopf, 1987). For California, see Harold Kirker, *Old Forms on a New Land: California Architecture in Perspective* (Niwot, Colorado: Roberts Rinehart, 1993).

Buildings of the United States is an ambitious series planned by the Society of Architectural Historians. While intending to cover all fifty states, thus far only four volumes have appeared: Alison K. Hoagland, *Buildings of Alaska*; Pamela Scott, *Buildings of the District of Columbia*; Kathryn Bishop Eckert, *Buildings of Michigan*; and David Gebhard and Gerald Mansheim, *Buildings of Iowa*—all four books New York: Oxford University Press, 1993. Each volume consists of a historical introduction briefly describing the growth of architecture in each state and is followed by a lengthy county-by-count guide to the architecture. Maps are included.

The American Institute of Architects has published a number of guides to individual cities and regions including Atlanta, Boston, Chicago, Nassau and Suffolk Counties, New York City, San Diego, Syracuse, and Washington D. C.

There are a number of current guides to the city of New York besides the useful *AIA Guide*: Gerard R. Wolfe, *New York: A Guide to the Metropolis, Walking Tours of Architecture and History* (McGraw-Hill, 1994); Francis Morrone, *The Architectural Guidebook to New York City* (Salt Lake City: Gibbs-Smith, 1994); and Donald Martin Reynolds, *The Architecture of New York City* (New York: John Wiley & Sons, 1994). See also Margot Gayle, *Cast-Iron Architecture In New York: A*

Photographic Survey (New York: Dover, 1974) and M. Christine Boyer, *Manhattan Manners: Architecture and Style 1850–1900* (New York: Rizzoli, 1985). Rem Koolhaas, *Delirious New York: A Retroactive Manifesto for Manhattan* (New York: Oxford University Press, 1978) is a wonderful book on the city, but the new Monacelli Press edition mistakenly edits some of the drawings of Koolhaas's collaborations with Elia Zenghelis, in spite of their importance to the book. A counterpoint to all these, more in the realm of social history than architectural, but essential nonetheless is Luc Sante, *Lures and Snares of Old New York* (New York: Farrar Straus Giroux, 1991). For New York in the twentieth century, turn to this exhaustive series: Robert A.M. Stern, Gregory Gilmartin, John Montague Massengale, *New York 1900: Metropolitan Architecture and Urbanism 1890–1915* (New York: Rizzoli, 1984); Robert A.M. Stern, Gregory Gilmartin, Thomas Mellins, *New York 1930: Architecture and Urbanism Between the Two World Wars* (New York: Rizzoli, 1987); and Robert A.M. Stern, Thomas Mellins, and David Fishman, *New York 1960: Architecture and Urbanism between the Second World War and the Bicentennial* (New York: Monacelli Press, 1995).

For Washington, D. C. refer to the *AIA Guide* and to John W. Reps, *Monumental Washington: The Planning and Development of the Capital Center* (Princeton: Princeton University Press, 1967).

For Miami, turn to *Miami: Architecture of the Tropics* (New York: Princeton Architectural Press, 1993) and Nicholas N. Patricios, *Building Marvelous Miami* (Gainesville, Florida: University Press of Florida, 1994).

Buffalo's architecture is covered in Reyner Banham, *Buffalo Architecture* (Cambridge, Massachusetts: MIT Press, 1981). Pittsburgh is amply surveyed by Franklin Toker, *Pittsburgh: An Urban Portrait* (University Park, Pennsylvania: Pennsylvania State University Press, 1986). Philadelphia's history is recounted in George B. Tatum, *Penn's Great Town: 250 years of Philadelphia Architecture* (Philadelphia: University of Pennsylvania Press, 1961). On Boston, turn to Douglass Shand Tucci, *Built in Boston: City and Suburb 1800–1950* (Boston: New York Graphic Society, 1978).

For guides to Chicago architecture see Franz Schulze and Kevin Harrington, *Chicago's Famous Buildings: A Photographic Guide to the City's Architectural Landmarks and Other Notable Buildings* (Chicago: University of Chicago Press, 1993) as well as Ira J. Bach and Susan Wolfson, *Chicago on Foot* (Chicago: Chicago Review Press, 1994). Another excellent introduction featuring color photography by Hedrich-Blessing is George A. Larson and Jay Pridmore, *Chicago Architecture and Design* (New York: Harry N. Abrams). Carl W. Condit, *The Chicago School of Architecture: A History of Commercial and Public Building in the Chicago Area, 1875–1925* (New York, Oxford University Press, 1961) addresses the technological and economic developments that made the Chicago school possible. For the development of Chicago as a whole see William Cronin, *Nature's Metropolis: Chicago and the Great West* (New York: W. W. Norton, 1991). Two exhibition catalogs, John Zukowsky, ed., *Chicago Architecture, 1872–1922: Birth of A Metropolis* (Munich: Prestel-Verlag, 1987) and John Zukowsky, ed., *Chicago Architecture and Design 1923–1993: Reconfiguration of an American Metropolis* (Munich: Prestel-Verlag, 1993) contain some of the best writing to date on the city. On Richard Nickel's attempt to save the architecture of the Chicago school and on the growth of the historic preservation movement in America in general see Richard Cahan's *They All Fall Down: Richard Nickel's Struggle to Save American Architecture* (Washington, D. C., Preservation Press, 1994).

For San Francisco see David Gebhard, Eric Sandweiss, and Robert Winter, *Architecture in San Francisco and Northern California* (Salt Lake City: Peregrine Smith Books, 1985) and Sally B. Woodbridge and John M. Woodbridge, *San Francisco Architecture: The Illustrated Guide to Over 1,000 of the Best Buildings, Parks, and Public Artworks in the Bay Area* (San Francisco: Chronicle Books, 1992). The best guides to Los Angeles are Charles W. Moore, Peter Becker, and Regula Campbell, *The City Observed: Los Angeles* (New York: Random Mouse, 1984) and

David Gebhard and Robert Winter, *Architecture in Los Angeles* (Layton, Utah: Peregrine Smith Books, 1985). Reyner Banham, *Los Angeles: The Architecture of Four Ecologies* (New York: Harper & Row, 1971) and Mike Davis, *City of Quartz: Excavating the Future in Los Angeles* (New York: Random House, 1990) are the key histories of the city.

The specialized studies on individual periods in American architecture offer a wealth of information to the reader. Indigenous building traditions on the continent are covered by Peter Nabokov and Robert Easton, *Native American Architecture* (New York: Oxford University Press, 1989), an excellent, amply illustrated introduction to an understudied field. See also William M. Morgan, *Ancient Architecture of the Southwest* (Austin, Texas: University of Texas Press, 1994) and for good photography, Jeffrey Cook, *Anasazi Places: The Photographic Vision of William Current* (Austin, Texas: University of Texas Press, 1994). On the adobe architecture of the Southwest, the classic texts are the reprint of the 1942 George Kubler, *The Religious Architecture of New Mexico in the Colonial Period and Since the American Occupation* (Albuquerque: University of New Mexico, 1972) as well as George Kubler and Martin Soria, *Art and Architecture in Spain and Portugal and Their American Dominions, 1500–1800* (New York: Penguin Books, 1959). More recently, Marc Treib, *Sanctuaries of Spanish New Mexico* (Berkeley: University of California Press, 1993) examines the churches against the environmental, social, and political history of New Mexico.

William Pierson's *The Colonial and Neoclassical Styles*, the first volume of the *American Buildings and their Architects* series mentioned above is a starting point for those periods although Hugh Morrison, *Early American Architecture: From the First Colonial Settlements to the National Period* (New York: Oxford University Press, 1952) is still useful. Turn also to George B. Tatum's section in Louis B. Wright, *The Arts in America: The Colonial Period* (New York: Charles Scribner's Sons, 1966). Marian Card Donnelly, *The New England Meeting Houses of the Seventeenth Century* (Middletown, Connecticut: Wesleyan University Press, 1968) explores the blending of parish church and market hall in that unique building type as well as its origins in medieval English village building.

Although originally published in 1944, Talbot Hamlin, *Greek Revival Architecture in America* (New York: Dover, 1969) is still an essential introduction to the period. Roger G. Kennedy, *Greek Revival America* (New York: Stewart Tabori & Chang, 1989) is a massive, heavily illustrated, and often provocative survey of the architecture in its cultural context. A survey of the taste for the Gothic in American architecture since the seventeenth century can be found in Calder Roth and Julius Trousdale Salder, Jr., *The Only Proper Style* (Boston: New York Graphic Society, 1976). A study with a much narrower and consequently more detailed focus on the Gothic revival movement that began in the mid-nineteenth century and its relations to the religious movements of the time is Pheobe B. Stanton, *The Gothic Revival and American Church Architecture: An Episode in Taste, 1840–1856* (Baltimore: Johns Hopkins University Press, 1968).

The religious sects that proliferated in the nineteenth century often left their mark on the built environment. See for example Charles Mark Hamilton, *Nineteenth Century Mormon Architecture* (New York: Oxford University Press, 1995) and Dolores Hayden, *Seven American Utopias: The Architecture of Communitarian Socialism, 1790–1975* (Cambridge, Massachusetts: MIT Press, 1976). Paul Rocheleau and June Sprigg, *Shaker Built: The Form and Function of Shaker Architecture* (New York: Monacelli Press, 1994) is notable for its color photography.

Originally published in 1952 and later in a revised edition, Vincent J. Scully, *The Shingle Style and the Stick Style: Architectural Theory and Design from Richardson to the Origins of Wright* (New Haven, Connecticut: Yale University Press, 1971) brought home the importance of those styles in the development of Modern architecture. Scully's book would have a significant impact on architects rethinking Modern architecture in the 1960s and 1970s, notably Robert

Venturi and Robert A. M. Stern. Scully wrote a follow-up volume on this movement entitled *The Shingle Style Today or The Historian's Revenge* (New York: George Braziller, 1974) and subsequently summed up and expanded the original volume in *The Architecture of the American Summer: The Flowering of the Shingle Style* (New York: Rizzoli, 1989). The Shingle Style is also covered in a chapter of Mark Girouard, *Sweetness and Light: The Queen Anne Movement, 1860–1900* (New York: Oxford University Press, 1977). While Girouard's book is on the development of the Queen Anne movement in Britain, he admirably explores the transactions between British and American architecture at the end of the nineteenth century.

For a broad overview of the cultural aspirations of the country as it became a world power, including essays on architecture, decorative art, and painting and sculpture, see Richard Guy Wilson, ed., *The American Renaissance: 1876–1917* (New York: Pantheon, 1979). The eclectic period from 1870 to 1930 is surveyed in Walter C. Kidney, *The Architecture of Choice: Eclecticism in America 1880–1930* (New York: Braziller, 1974). The architecture of the large country house of the time is covered in Mark Alan Hewitt, *The Architect and the American Country House, 1890–1940* (New York: Yale University Press, 1990).

On the architecture of the skyscraper, see Cervin Robinson and Rosemarie Haag Bletter, *Skyscraper Style: Art Deco New York* (New York: Oxford University Press, 1975) and Paul Goldberger, *The Skyscraper* (New York: Knopf, 1981). One can also turn to the elliptical but often more interesting views of Thomas A. P. van Leewen, *The Skyward Trend of Thought: The Metaphysics of the American Skyscraper* (Cambridge, Massachusetts: MIT Press, 1988).

It appears to be too early for decent histories of the postwar era to exist. The initial surveys are dated. John Jacobus, *Twentieth-Century Architecture: The Middle Years 1940–65* (New York: Frederick A. Praeger Publishers, 1966) could serve as an introduction as could Robert A. M. Stern, *New Directions in American Architecture* (New York: Braziller, 1977). One could contrast the works pictured in those books with an anthology of architectural writing not restricted to America: Joan Ockman, ed., *Architecture Culture 1943–1968: A Documentary Anthology* (New York: Columbia Books on Architecture/Rizzoli, 1993) to sense the need for a new survey. Architects of the postwar era discuss their work in Paul Heyer, *Architects on Architecture: New Directions in America* (New York: Van Nostrand Reinhold, 1993) and in John Peter, *Oral History of Modern Architecture: Interviews with the Greatest Architects of the Twentieth Century* (New York: Abrams, 1994). Turn to Barbara Goldstein, ed., *Arts & Architecture: The Entenza Years* (Cambridge, Massachusetts: MIT Press, 1990) for the story of one of the more interesting periodicals of the period.

For the institutional architecture of the 1980s, see *American Architecture of the 1980s* (Washington, D. C.: AIA Press, 1990). A promotional account of more self-consciously avant-garde architecture since the 1970s can be found in Aaron Betsky, *Violated Perfection: Fragmentation in Modern Architecture* (New York: Rizzoli, 1990), while a number of reflections on recent American architecture can be found in K. Michael Hays and Carol Burns, ed., *Thinking the Present: Recent American Architecture* (New York: Princeton Architectural Press, 1990).

Too many good studies exist on individual architects to list them all here. Regrettably, the best sources on Thomas Jefferson, Benjamin Henry Latrobe, and Richard Upjohn are quite old at this point: see Fiske Kimball, *Thomas Jefferson: Architect* (New York: Da Capo Press, 1968); Talbot Hamlin, *Benjamin Henry Latrobe* (New York: Oxford University Press, 1955); and Everard Miller, *Richard Upjohn: Architect and Churchman* (New York: Da Capo Press, 1968). For Charles Bulfinch's life and career as an architect see Harold and James Kirker, *Bulfinch's Boston: 1787–1817* (New York: Oxford University Press, 1964); for his architecture see Harold Kirker, *The Architecture of Charles Bulfinch* (Cambridge, Massachusetts: Harvard University Press, 1968)

On Richard Morris Hunt, the standard text is Paul R. Baker, *Richard Morris Hunt* (Cambridge, Massachusetts: MIT Press, 1980). For H. H. Richardson, the standard texts are Henry-Russell Hitchcock, *The Architecture of H. H. Richardson and His Times* (Cambridge, Massachusetts: MIT Press, 1975) and James F. O'Gorman, *H. H. Richardson: Architectural Forms for an American Society* (Chicago: University of Chicago Press, 1987) although Mariana Griswold van Rensselaer's *Henry Hobson Richardson and His Works* (New York: Dover, 1969), originally published in 1888, is both still serviceable and an interesting historical document in its own right, written by one of the most important architectural critics of the late nineteenth century. James F. O'Gorman, *Three American Architects: Richardson, Sullivan, and Wright* (Chicago: University of Chicago Press, 1991) is useful for all three.

One of the earliest works on Louis Sullivan, Hugh Morrison, *Louis Sullivan: Prophet of Modern Architecture* (New York: W. W. Norton, 1962) is still important, but see also Sullivan's own writings, *Autobiography of an Idea* (New York: Dover, 1956) and *Kindergarten Chats and Other Writings* (New York: Dover, 1979). The most reliable guide is Robert Twombly's *Louis Sullivan: His Life and Work* (New York: Viking, 1985).

James F. O'Gorman and George E. Thomas, *The Architecture of Frank Furness* (Philadelphia: Philadelphia Museum of Art, 1973) has now been complemented by George E. Thomas, Michael J. Lewis, and Jeffrey A. Cohen, *Frank Furness: The Complete Works* (New York: Princeton Architectural Press, 1991). In addition to illustrations of Furness's work and a number of historical essays, the latter also contains texts by Furness, and Louis Sullivan's reminiscences about the architect.

Richard Guy Wilson, *McKim, Mead & White, Architects* (New York: Rizzoli, 1985) and Leland Roth, *McKim, Mead & White, Architects* (New York: Harper & Row, 1983) are good starting points for investigating the New York architects of the American Renaissance.

On Daniel H. Burnham, turn to Thomas S. Hines, *Burnham of Chicago: Architect and Planner* (New York: Oxford University Press, 1974) and the reprint of Burnham's *Plan of Chicago* (New York: Princeton Architectural Press, 1993). Burnham's partner Root is covered in Donald Hoffmann, *The Architecture of John Wellborn Root* (Baltimore: Johns Hopkins University Press, 1973).

The literature on Frank Lloyd Wright is copious and too often promotional. Some decent works are: Henry-Russell Hitchcock, *In the Nature of Materials, 1887–1941: The Buildings of Frank Lloyd Wright* (New York: Da Capo Press, 1973); Grant Manson, *Frank Lloyd Wright to 1910: The First Golden Age* (New York: Van Nostrand Reinhold, 1979); Robert Twombly, *Frank Lloyd Wright: His Life and Architecture* (New York: John Wiley, 1978); and William Allin Storrer, *The Frank Lloyd Wright Companion* (Chicago: University of Chicago Press, 1993). For a biographical treatment see Brendan Gill's *Many Masks: A Life of Frank Lloyd Wright* (New York: Putnam, 1987). There are plenty of collections of writings by Wright. The most economical is Edgar Kaufmann and Ben Raeburn, eds., *Frank Lloyd Wright: Writings and Buildings* (Cleveland and New York: Meridian, 1960).

On the work of the Tennessee Valley Authority, see Walter L. Creese, *TVA's Public Planning: The Vision, The Reality* (Knoxville, Tennessee: University of Tennessee Press, 1990).

There are a number of books on twentieth-century architects in California, including Sara Holmes Boutelle's authoritative and well-illustrated *Julia Morgan: Architect* (New York: Abbeville Press, 1988). Esther McCoy, *Five California Architects* (New York, Reinhold, 1960) is a classic survey of modern architecture in California. For more detail, see Thomas S. Hines, *Richard Neutra and the Search for a Modern Architecture* (New York: Oxford University Press, 1982); August Sarnitz, *R. M. Schindler, Architect 1887–1953: A Pupil of Otto Wagner Between International Style and Space Architecture* (New York: Rizzoli, 1988); Bruce A. Kamerling, *Irving J. Gill, Architect* (San Diego: San Diego Historical Society, 1993); Randell L. Makinson, *Greene and Greene: Architecture as Fine Art* (Salt Lake City: Peregrine Smith, 1979); Sally Byrne Woodbridge, *Bernard Maybeck: Visionary Architect* (New York: Abbeville Press, 1992), and Pat Kirkham, *Charles and Ray Eames: Designers of the Twentieth Century* (Cambridge, Massachusetts: MIT Press, 1995).

Two popular architects of the postwar era are covered in Carol Herselle Krinsky, *Gordon Bunshaft of Skidmore, Owings, & Merrill* (Cambridge, Massachusetts: MIT Press, 1989) and Victoria Newhouse, *Wallace K. Harrison, Architect* (New York: Rizzoli, 1989).

For Walter Gropius see Reginald Isaacs, *Gropius: An Illustrated Biography of the Creator of the Bauhaus* (Boston: Little, Brown, and Company, 1991). On Ludwig Mies van der Rohe, the standard introduction is Franz Schulze, *Mies van der Rohe: A Critical Biography* (Chicago: University of Chicago Press, 1985). But look also to Jordy's volume mentioned above, *The Impact of European Modernism in the Twentieth Century*. More theoretical essays on Mies's later work can be found in Detlef Mertins, ed., *The Presence of Mies* (New York: Princeton Architectural Press, 1994). Schulze is also responsible for the important introduction to the complicated life of Philip Johnson: Franz Schulze, *Philip Johnson: Life and Work* (New York: Albert A. Knopf, 1994).

One of the most remarkable architects in twentieth century America or elsewhere is Bruce Goff: see David G. DeLong, *Bruce Goff: Toward Absolute Architecture* (Cambridge, Massachusetts: MIT Press, 1988).

Better books on Louis I. Kahn include Romaldo Giurgola and Jaimini Mehta, *Louis I. Kahn* (Boulder, Colorado: Westview Press, 1975); David B. Brownlee and David G. DeLong, *Louis I. Kahn: In the Realm of Architecture* (New York: Rizzoli, 1991); Alexandra Tyng, *Beginnings: Louis I. Kahn's Philosophy of Architecture* (New York: Wiley, 1984); and for his own writings Alessandra Latour, ed., *Louis I. Kahn: Writings, Letters, Interviews* (New York: Rizzoli, 1991).

For a biography of Charles Moore, see David Littlejohn, *Architect: The Life and Work of Charles W. Moore* (New York: Holt, Reinhard and Winston, 1984). For his buildings see Eugene J. Johnson, ed., *Charles Moore: Buildings and Projects 1949–1986* (New York: Rizzoli, 1986). The most complete source on Venturi, Rauch, and Scott Brown is Stanislaus von Moos, *Venturi, Rauch, and Scott Brown: Buildings and Projects* (New York: Rizzoli, 1987).

GLOSSARY

A

abacus	The topmost, blocklike element of a capital, that on which the architrave (beam) rests
acropolis	Literally a city on a hill, the most famous example being in Athens
acroterion	A small pedestal at ends and/or on top of a pediment to hold a statue (as on Greek or Roman temples); the term often includes the figure(s); also commonly an eave ornament
Adamesque	Influenced by Scot Robert Adam (1728–92) and his brother James (1732–94), the most important British architects of their time
adobe	Sun-dried brick generally mixed with straw binder
aggregate	Gravel or crushed stone mixed with cement and water to form concrete
agora	An open square or marketplace in ancient Greece generally surrounded by a peristyle
allée	An avenue of trees
anthemion	Pattern of foliated leaf clusters in Greek and Roman friezes
architrave	The bottom part of an entablature—that which rests on the columns
archivolt	The outside molding of an arch; also the ornamental molding on the face of an arch
Art Deco	The "jazzed," zigzag design approach popular in the late 1920s and the '30s. Its name stems from L'Exposition Internationale des Arts Décoratifs et Industriels Modernes of 1925 in Paris, also known as Moderne
ashlar masonry	Stone cut in blocks; it can be smooth or rough-faced, aligned or random
atrium	In a Roman house an open inner courtyard generally surrounded by a colonnade

B

baldacchino	The canopy supported over an altar; also called a ciborium
balloon frame	Framing of precut light wood studs, generally 2 x 4's, often two stories long and spaced less than 2 feet/.6 meter apart
baluster	The upright supports of a railing
balustrade	The railing around the head of stairs or atop some buildings
band course	*See* stringcourse
barge board	A decorative, often scroll-cut board at gable ends
batten	A narrow board nailed to cover the joint of two vertical boards
bay	A vertical wall module (as between structural columns in a skyscraper)
belt course	*See* stringcourse
bema	In a synagogue, a raised platform from which religious services are conducted
berm	A man-made low earth "boundary"
betonglass	Thick faceted glass (generally 1 inch/2.5 centimeters)
blind arcade	An "arcade" indicated by pilasters applied to a wall surface
blind arch	A relieving arch built into a wall to distribute overhead weight
bolection mold	The prominent roll mold that covers the juncture of door panel and frame
box girder	A rectangular, hollow girder usually of steel
brackets	Angled supports, often elaborate, to uphold an overhang
brise-soleil	Exterior louvers, fixed or movable, to control the sun load on a building

C

cartouche	A shield or coat of arms used as a decorative panel on a wall
cavetto cornice	An outward-curved, usually quarter-round, cornice used in Egyptian Revival buildings
cella	The inner room(s) primarily the sanctuary of a Classical temple
chamfer	A beveled edge at the meeting of two planes
chancel	The (east) end of the church, the part reserved for the clergy
Chicago window	A large fixed central pane of plate glass flanked by sash windows
ciborium	*See* baldacchino
clapboard	A covering board that is thin on inner (upper) edge and thicker at butt; the boards are overlapped horizontally for weather protection. Sometimes called "weatherboards"
clerestory	The topmost windows of a church nave, those above the aisle roof, thus any high band of windows
console	An elaborate, often scroll-shaped, bracket
coquina	A soft limestone of marine origin found in Florida; it hardens on exposure to air
corbel	A (series of) cantilevered short projection(s) supporting an overhang
Corinthian order	The richest of the Greek and Roman orders whose capital represents stylized acanthus leaves; at ten diameters its column is the most slender of all the orders
cornice	Technically the top and most projected element of an entablature; in contemporary buildings it refers to the entire projecting eave
cortile	A small courtyard
crockets	Ornamental decorations, usually vegetation-derived, on Gothic members
cupola	A domed accent on a roof with either round or polygonal base
curtain wall	An enclosing wall or wall panel independently attached to the frame of a building

D

dendrochronology	Dating of a wooden building by counting annual tree rings in a beam cross section or core; the method was developed by Professor A. E. Douglass of the University of Arizona
dentils	A continuous line of small blocks in a Classical molding just under the fascia
dependencies	Smaller buildings symmetrically placed on either side of a major one; rankers
distyle in antis	Two Classical columns set between end walls
dogtrot	A breezeway separating two sections of a (log) house, early popular in Southern vernacular
Doric order	The oldest and simplest of the Classical orders. The Greek Doric column is fluted and has no base
drum	The (circular) base and support of a dome

E

Eastlake Style	Style named for the English architect C. L. Eastlake and popular toward the end of the nineteenth century; it helped popularize the Stick Style
ell	An addition to a house making an L shape
English bond	A brick pattern with alternating rows of headers (brick ends) and stretchers (brick sides)
entablature	The horizontal element that tops Classical columns. The lowest part—that resting on the columns—is the architrave, the middle (often decorated) the frieze, and the top the cornice
entasis	The slight swelling profile curve of a Greek or Roman column as it diminishes upward (an optical correction)
exedra	A semicircular (or rectangular) niche, often half-vaulted and with seats
extrados	The outside face or edge of an arch

F

facade	The face of a building, usually the main elevation
fanlight	A window over an entry, either semicircular or semielliptical
fascia	The flat band(s) of an entablature; also the flat top edge of a building
Federal Style	The planar, tightly restrained yet elegant style that budded in the United States following the Revolution; found largely in the Northeast, it lasted until the 1830s
fenestration	The disposition of the windows of a building
flankers	Flanking wings or dependencies usually symmetrically disposed about the main building
Flemish bond	Alternate brick headers and stretchers in the same row
frieze	The mid-member of the three-part entablature (architrave, frieze, cornice), often with decorative panels
furring	Inner blocking of an exterior wall to create air space with an inside wall

G

gable	The (triangular) upper wall established by the roof planes
galleria	A roofed, usually glass-enclosed passageway
gambrel roof	A roof with two slopes on each side, the lower sharply pitched; it stems from the Mansard roof
Georgian	The architectural period from the reign of George I (1714–27) to the Revolution; symmetry and Classically derived details are characteristic
ghorfa	A long, mud-brick paraboloid "warehouse" (piled horizontally like cigarettes) found in south Tunisia
girder	A major horizontal supporting beam
girt	A heavy beam at the ends (and often flanking the chimney) of a Colonial house to receive upper floor joists and sometimes the summer beam
Greek cross	A (church) plan with all four arms of equal length
Greek Revival	A style based on Greek architectural prototypes or details, popular in the first half of the nineteenth century

H

hall	The name given to the living room of a seventeenth-century New England house
hammer beam	A short cantilevered beam or bracket supporting a timber roof arch
hatchment	An escutcheon with armorial insignia
headers	Bricks laid with their ends facing out
hexastyle	Having six columns at one end
hip roof	A roof with four sloping planes, at times meeting in a flat roof-deck
hogan	The traditional semirounded, earth-covered log dwelling of the Navajo
Howe truss	A (bridge) truss made up of a series of X frames; similar to a Long truss but with vertical wrought-iron or steel tie rods
hyphen	In Georgian architecture, a connecting link between the main house and the flanking dependencies

I

impost	The springing point or block of an arch
in antis	The end of a (Classical) building with columns between the side walls
International Style	The first organized architectural movement against Academicism, dating largely from the 1920s and '30s
intrados	The under surface or soffit of an arch
Ionic order	One of the major Classical orders; its capitals are identified by their volutes or scrolls

J

jalousies	Slatted exterior blinds, often adjustable to control light and air
jerkin-head	The small triangular nipping off of the gable end of a roof
joist	The parallel secondary beams upholding a floor

L

lantern	A small geometric structure atop a roof, most frequently glazed and usually for appearance only
lights	The panes of glass of a window
lintel	A beam over an opening, or over two or more vertical members (post-and-lintel)
Long truss	A bridge truss composed of continuous boxed X panels
lunette	A small round or half-round window generally in a gable

M

Mansard roof	Like the gambrel roof, a roof with two sloping planes per side, the lower much more sharply pitched; named for François Mansart (1598–1666)
mastaba	A flat-roofed, slope-sided tomb from Egypt's Old Kingdom
metope	The plain or sculptured panel between the triglyphs of a Doric frieze
Moderne	See Art Deco
modillions	Small scroll brackets, larger and wider than dentils
mortise	In a beam or member, a cut-out hole that receives a tenon
mullion	The vertical division between windows (and windows and doors)
muntin	The pane divider within a window frame

O

oculus	A circular opening in the crown of a dome
oriel window	A bay window projecting on brackets or corbels

P

Palladian	Architecture influenced by the Italian architect Andrea Palladio (1508–80); characterized by majestic symmetry often with flanking dependencies.
Palladian window	Window having a broad arched central section with lower flat-headed side portions
passerelle	A footbridge
pavilion	A projecting center section—for prominence—of a (usually) symmetrical building
pediment	The triangular space of the gable end of a building; also space used over doors and windows—triangular, segmental (curved), and broken pediments
pendentive	A triangular spheroid section used to effect the transition from a square or polygonal base to a dome above
pent roof	A small "attached" roof used over first-floor windows
peripteral	Having columns completely surrounding a temple (or building)
peristyle	A colonnade surrounding a building on the outside or a court inside
piano nobile	The main floor of a house, generally elevated a floor above grade
pilaster	In effect a column reduced to a thin rectangle to establish wall divisions; an engaged pier
pilotis	Columns that uphold the upper floor(s) of a building leaving the ground level largely open
plate	The top horizontal member of a wood-framed wall; the rafters spring from the plate
platted	Surveyed and laid out, as of a town
plinth	The square block under a column; also the base for a statue
portal(es)	The covered porch or veranda fronting a Spanish building
portico	A columned shelter at entry; a porch
post-and-lintel	Construction by vertical uprights supporting horizontal beams
prestressed concrete	Reinforced concrete whose end-threaded steel bars or cables are prestretched to develop extra strength
purlin	Secondary horizontal beam supporting roof rafters

Q

quadriga	A representation of a four-horse Roman chariot used as a decorative feature
Queen Anne Style	A late-nineteenth-century, almost frantic melange of styles, often with prominent triangular gable
quoins	Prominently beveled stones (or wood in imitation of stone) used to give emphasis to corners; from French coins (corners)

R

rafters	The (generally) angled framing members that directly support a roof
raised basement	A "basement" partly or totally above grade
random ashlar	Miscellaneously sized, non-aligning, rectangular stones
reredos	An ornamental screen placed on the wall behind an altar
retable (retablo)	The niches and shelves behind a Spanish altar; in Gothic architecture, often an encased shrine
return	The carrying of a molding partly around a corner, often on gabled ends
reveal	The depth of inset from the wall face of a window or door
ridgepole	The topmost horizontal roof member receiving upper ends of rafters

rinceau	A low-relief, vine-like, running ornament
riser	The vertical measure between stair treads
roundel	A small circular opening or window
rustication	Exaggeration of joints and/or surface of stone or wood imitating stone

S

saltbox	A New England cottage with rear addition and asymmetrically extended roof
segmental arch	A partial arch over a window
shaft	The part of a column between base and capital
shakes	Hand-split shingles, generally large and thick
sheathing	Boards or panels enclosing a structural frame
shed roof	A one-slope roof
Shingle Style	A late-nineteenth-century domestic style using (unpainted) shingles on walls as well as for the roof (a term made popular by Professor Vincent Scully)
sill	A wood (or metal) member atop and fastened to foundation walls to which the upright framing is attached
single-loaded	Rooms on one side only of a corridor
soffit	The underside of an arch or overhead beam
spandrel	In high-rise construction the enclosing panels between window head below and windowsill above; the solid bands between rows of windows
spire	The tapered section of a steeple
steeple	A church tower and its spire
stepped gable	A gable whose slope or rake is stepped rather than straight (or curved); also called crow-foot and Dutch gable
stereotomy	The art of stone cutting and placing
Stick Style	A middle- to late-nineteenth-century style of complex projections, roof, and wood outrigging
stile	The vertical framing member of a door or window
stretchers	The long sides of bricks laid facing out
stringcourse	A generally flat band of minute projection horizontally stretching across a brick facade; also called a belt course or band course
studs	The (secondary) upright members of a wood-framed wall, often 2 x 4's
stylobate	The usually stepped base for a columned building or colonnade
summer beam	A heavy intermediate beam that carries floor joists and is itself supported by chimney and end girts; mainly used in seventeenth-century New England

T

tache	Literally a spot, used here as a wall accent
temenos	A sacred confine
tenon	A projection on a wooden beam designed to fit the mortise in another beam to effect juncture—the two are fastened with a dowel
tholos	A round building, especially Greek
tie beam	A horizontal beam connecting the ends of rafters to make a truss
Town truss	A lattice panel truss with alternate closely spaced diagonals
trabeated	Post-and-lintel construction
tread	The step of a stair
triglyphs	The rectangular blocks in a Doric frieze with two vertical channels and half channels on its edges
truss	A generally triangulated combination of wood, concrete, or metal members to span a space and provide structure for supporting a roof
Tuscan order	A Roman adaptation of the Greek Doric order without fluting but with a base; the frieze is plain
tympanum	The framed (triangular) inner area of a pediment; also the framed semicircular panel above door

V

vermiculated	Grooved stone imitations of worm tracks
vigas	The projecting roof beams in Indian pueblo and Spanish Colonial architecture
volutes	Spiral ornament as on an Ionic capital
voussoirs	The wedge-shaped stones or bricks that make up an arch

W

wainscot	The paneled protective wall lining of a domestic interior, usually not to the ceiling
weatherboard	Lapped horizontal wood siding using boards often of parallel faces—as opposed to the radial-cut clapboards that they resemble

MID-ATLANTIC

1 | 100 miles

MIDWEST

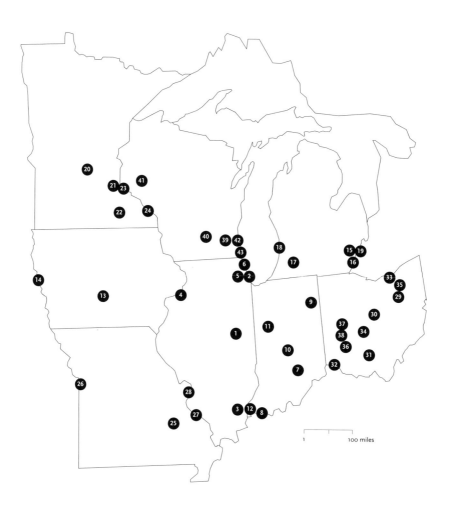

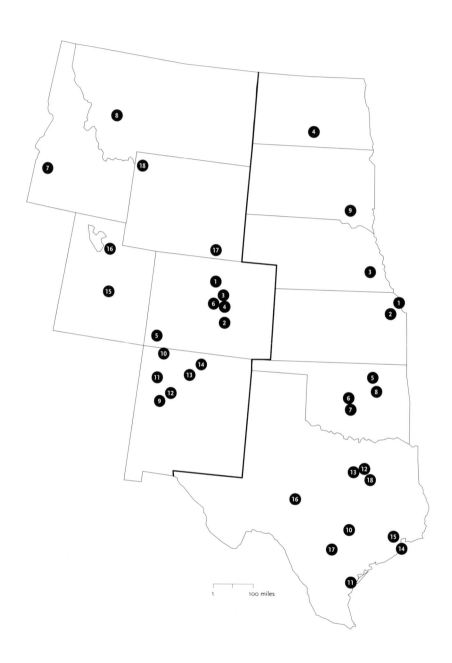

ROCKIES

PLAINS

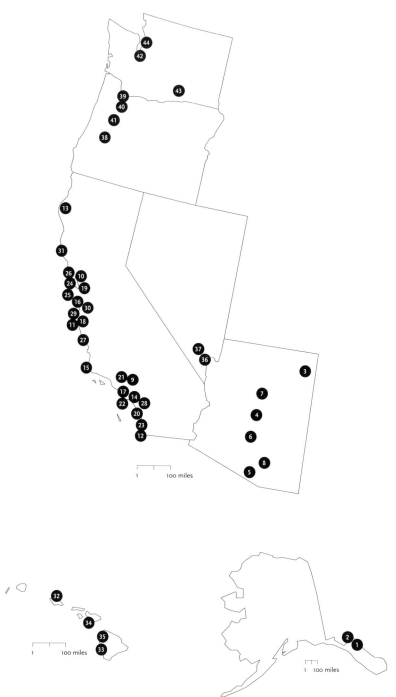

LIST OF BUILDINGS

ARCHITECTS AND DESIGNERS

BUILDING TYPES

Academic Buildings

Academical Village, University of Virginia, Charlottesville, VA, 163

Air Force Academy, Colorado Springs, CO, 436

Alfred Newton Richards Medical Research Building, University of Pennsylvania, Philadelphia, PA, 438

American Heritage Center and University Art Museum, University of Wyoming, Laramie, WY, 631

Art and Architecture Building, Yale University, New Haven, CT, 472

Art Center, Columbia Basin College, Pasco, WA, 565

Art Center College of Design, Pasadena, CA, 594

Assembly Hall, University of Illinois, Champaign, IL, 458

Baker House, Massachusetts Institute of Technology, Cambridge, MA, 396

Beinecke Rare Book and Manuscript Library, Yale University, New Haven, CT, 471

Billings Student Center, Burlington, VT, 270

Blair Hall, Princeton University, Princeton, NJ, 311

Bradfield Hall, New York State College of Agriculture at Cornell, Ithaca, NY, 534

Carl Schurz High School, Chicago, IL, 330

Carpenter Center for the Visual Arts, Harvard University, Cambridge, MA, 470

Chapel, Massachusetts Institute of Technology, Cambridge, MA, 415

Chapel, University of Georgia, Athens, GA, 176

Clowes Memorial Hall, Butler University, Indianapolis, IN, 476

Concordia Theological Seminary, Fort Wayne, IN, 426

Cranbrook Educational Community, Bloomfield Hills, MI, 357

Crow Island School, Winnetka, IL, 392

D. S. Ingalls Hockey Rink, Yale University, New Haven, CT, 430

Egyptian Building, Medical College of Virginia, Richmond, VA, 208

Erdman Dormitories, Bryn Mawr College, Bryn Mawr, PA, 484

Ezra Stiles and Morse Colleges, Yale University, New Haven, CT, 464

F. G. Peabody Terrace, Harvard University, Cambridge, MA, 479

Flagler College (formerly Hotel Ponce de León), St. Augustine, FL, 278

Florida Southern College, Lakeland, FL, 389

Foothill College, Los Altos Hills, CA, 454

Founder's Hall, Girard College, Philadelphia, PA, 184

Frederick R. Weisman Art Museum, University of Minnesota, East Bank Campus, Minneapolis, MN, 632

George Gund Hall, Harvard University, Cambridge, MA, 554

Goddard Biology Laboratory, University of Pennsylvania, Philadelphia, PA, 438

Harvard University Graduate Center, Cambridge, MA, 402

Hillsdale High School, San Mateo, CA, 424

Kresge College, University of California at Santa Cruz, Santa Cruz, CA, 587

McGregor Memorial Conference Center, Wayne State University, Detroit, MI, 444

Mount Angel Abbey Library, St. Benedict, OR, 533

Nassau Hall, Princeton University, Princeton, NJ, 91

Old Albany Academy, Albany, NY, 155

Pennsylvania Academy of the Fine Arts, Philadelphia, PA, 252

Phillips Exeter Academy Library, Exeter, NH, 552

St. John's University Church, Collegeville, MN, 434

S. R. Crown Hall, Illinois Institute of Technology, Chicago, IL, 422

Tougaloo College Dormitories and Library, Tougaloo, MS, 578

Tuskegee Chapel, Tuskegee University, Tuskegee, AL, 537

University of Massachusetts at Dartmouth, North Dartmouth, MA, 510

Wexner Center for the Arts, Ohio State University, Columbus, OH, 627

Yale Center for British Art, New Haven, CT, 588

Yale University Art Gallery, New Haven, CT, 410

Agricultural Buildings

Farmers' Museum and Village Crossroads, Cooperstown, NY, 136

Grain Elevators, Topeka, KS, 419

Round Barn, Pittsfield, MA, 171

Banks

Chemical Bank (formerly Manufacturers Trust Company), New York, NY, 414

Federal Reserve Bank of Minneapolis, Minneapolis, MN, 558

First Alabama Bank, Huntsville, AL, 188

Home Federal Savings and Loan (now Catholic Pastoral Center), Des Moines, IA, 465

Ladd & Bush Bank, Salem, OR, 244

Merchants National Bank, Winona, MN, 335

Norwest Bank Owatonna (formerly National Farmers' Bank), Owatonna, MN, 328

Old Bank of Louisville (now Actor's Theater), Louisville, KY, 189

Peoples Federal Savings and Loan Association, Sidney, OH, 345

People's National Bank, McLeansboro, IL, 266

Second Bank of the United States, Philadelphia, PA, 166

Civic Buildings

Corn Palace, Mitchell, SD, 300

First Religious Society Meeting House, Newburyport, MA, 141

Georgia Dome, Atlanta, GA, 569

Georgia World Congress Center, Atlanta, GA, 569

Jacob K. Javits Convention Center, New York, NY, 621

La Jolla Women's Club, San Diego (La Jolla), CA, 337

Mabel Tainter Memorial Building, Menomonie, WI, 291

McGregor Memorial Conference Center, Wayne State University, Detroit, MI, 444

Masonic Hall (now Grand Opera House), Wilmington, DE, 250

Municipal Auditorium, Kansas City, MO, 381

Oceanside Civic Center, Oceanside, CA, 628

Old Ship Meeting House, Hingham, MA, 48

Richard J. Daley Center (formerly Civic Center), Chicago, IL, 492

Rockingham Meeting House, Rockingham, VT, 123

Rocky Hill Meeting House, Amesbury, MA, 119

Scope Cultural and Convention Center, Norfolk, VA, 574

Snug Harbor Cultural Center (formerly Sailors' Snug Harbor), New York (Staten Island), NY, 179

Waioli Mission House, Hanalei, Kauai, HI, 204

Wingspread Conference Center, Racine, WI, 386

YWCA Laniakea Center, Honolulu, Oahu, HI, 358

Commercial Buildings

Arcade, Cleveland, OH, 286

Arcade, Providence, RI, 172

Brick Market, Newport, RI, 100

Carson, Pirie, Scott Store (formerly Schlesinger and Mayer Department Store), Chicago, IL, 314

Cast-Iron Architecture, SoHo, New York, NY, 225

Circle Galley (formerly V. C. Morris Shop), San Francisco, CA, 400

Crate and Barrel Shop (formerly Design Research Shop), Cambridge, MA, 549

Faneuil Hall Marketplace, Boston, MA, 76

G. E. Kidder Smith (1913–97) was born in Birmingham, Alabama, and received his A.B. and M.F.A. from Princeton University. An architect and Fellow of the American Institute of Architects, he devoted most of his professional life to documenting distinguished buildings in much of the world. He and his wife Dorothea—who played a key role in all of his work—lived in New York City.

Supported by a dozen fellowships, he wrote and illustrated nine other books on architecture: *Sweden Builds, Switzerland Builds, Italy Builds* (for which he received the ENIT Gold Medal from the Italian Government), *New Architecture of Europe, New Churches of Europe, A Pictorial History of Architecture in America,* **The Architecture of the United States,** *A Guide to New England Houses of Worship,* and *Looking at Architecture.* He and Philip L. Goodwin were decorated by the Brazilian Government for their *Brazil Builds* book and exhibition for the Museum of Modern Art, for which Smith contributed the photographs.

Smith lectured with his slides in many schools of architecture in the United States and abroad—as far as Afghanistan and Argentina, and much of Europe in between. His hour-long television program for PBS celebrated the United States Bicentennial. Smith helped save from immediate destruction both Frank Lloyd Wright's Frederick C. Robie House (which was to be replaced by a dormitory) and Le Corbusier's Villa Savoye (its site scheduled for a school) by organizing a campaign of telegrams from international organizations to the owners. According to Smith, such a writing campaign can help to save threatened architecture today.

COLOPHON

Project editing and design
Clare Jacobson

Research
Caroline Green

Research assistance
Sarah Lappin

Additional assistance
Jonathan Bell, Therese
Kelly, Heidi Liebes, David
Lewis, and Sharon Stultz

Copy editing
Claire Zimmerman

Cover design
Deb Wood

Special thanks to
Ann Alter, Amanda Atkins,
Eugenia Bell, Nicola
Bednarek, Jan Cigliano,
Jane Garvie, Beth Harrison,
Mia Ihara, Leslie Ann Kent,
Mark Lamster, Anne
Nitschke, Lottchen Shivers,
and Jennifer Thompson of
Princeton Architectural
Press —Kevin C. Lippert,
publisher

Typography
Scala (1990) and
Scala Sans (1993)
Designed by
Martin Majoor
Distributed by
FontShop

Production and Printing
Friesens Printers

Paper
Somerset Matte